Locating American Studies

EDITED BY *LUCY MADDOX*

Locating American Studies

The Evolution of a Discipline

The Johns Hopkins University Press
Baltimore and London

© 1999 The Johns Hopkins University Press
All rights reserved.
Published 1999
Printed in the United States
of America on acid-free paper
9 8 7 6 5 4 3 2

The Johns Hopkins University Press
2715 North Charles Street
Baltimore, Maryland 21218-4363

www.press.jhu.edu

Library of Congress
Cataloging-in-Publication Data
will be found at the end
of this book. A catalog
record for this book is available
from the British Library.

ISBN 0-8018-6056-3 (pbk.)

CONTENTS

PREFACE

The essays included in this volume were chosen to represent the development and growth of American studies as an academic enterprise devoted to the interdisciplinary study of American history and culture. Each of the essays first appeared in *American Quarterly,* the journal of the American Studies Association, which published its first issue in 1947. The volume, therefore, also marks the fiftieth anniversary of the journal. These essays were chosen, out of the hundreds that have been published since the appearance of that first issue, because—in the judgment of the editors of the volume—each has played an important role in either advancing the kinds of scholarly inquiries that have characterized American studies from its inception or, in many cases, marking significant shifts in the direction and scope of American studies scholarship.

In choosing to present the essays in chronological order, the editors are acknowledging the opportunity that a retrospective volume in American studies provides for considering the development of an academic field over time. Because American studies as an organized field of inquiry is comparatively new, with locatable origins, and because *American Quarterly* has over the life of the discipline been a major outlet for the publication of American studies scholarship, these representative essays, collectively, provide a useful window into the history and the evolution of the practice of American studies from its early, formational days to the present. In addition to marking some stages in a chronological development, the essays also call attention to the significant contributions of a few among the many individual scholars who have helped to define and redefine the field by the new questions they have posed, the new perspectives they have brought to the study of the cultures of the United States, and the new information they have introduced into scholarly conversations about national identity and experience. If the frequency with which an essay is cited in subsequent scholarship and assigned as required reading in academic courses may be taken as an indication of the respect it has achieved and the importance it has been granted, then many of the essays in this volume have come to be considered milestones, even classics, in the scholarly literature of American studies. Some of the more recent essays in the volume are included to represent the kinds of current scholarship that are opening up new perspectives and new directions in the work of American studies.

Because of its relatively recent appearance as a discrete field of study, American studies has from the beginning invited a critical examination, especially from its own practitioners, of its methods of inquiry, its aims, its intellectual coherence, its relationship to other disciplines and fields of study—in short, it has invited questions about its very reasons for being, even as it has continued to grow more robust. Several of the essays in this volume reflect the nature of what Gene Wise, in his 1979 essay in this volume, called the "stock-taking consciousness in the movement." The essays by Wise, Henry Nash Smith, Bruce Kuklick, R. Gordon Kelly, and Robert Berkhofer Jr. are representative of the efforts of scholars to describe an American studies practice in either its ideal or its actual form; at times these efforts are offered as models—attempts to answer the question, "What is American studies?"—and at times they are offered as critiques of the epistemological, ethical, or practical limitations of the models advanced by others.

The chronological arrangement of the essays suggests that this concern with describing and defining American studies has largely given way, as the field has matured, to a concern with expanding the areas of inquiry, as well as the methods of inquiry, that fall under the rubric of American studies. The earlier interest in marking out the boundaries of American studies, that is, has yielded to an interest in pushing those boundaries outward to include objects of study, and methods of study, that reflect more accurately and honestly the varieties of experience in the United States and that can, by their inclusion, decenter the older, monolithic narratives of national history. In his 1957 essay (included in this volume) on the possibility of establishing a distinctive American studies methodology, Henry Nash Smith—who received the first Ph.D. degree from Harvard's interdisciplinary program in the History of American Civilization in 1940—also spoke of expanding boundaries. "The best thing we can do, in my opinion," Smith wrote, "is to conceive of American Studies as a collaboration among men working from within existing academic disciplines but attempting to widen the boundaries imposed by conventional methods of inquiry." Smith's conception has in many ways become actual practice, in the sense that most American studies teaching and scholarship has been done by faculty who are institutionally identified with one of the "existing academic disciplines," other than American studies, that Smith mentions. Yet those disciplines themselves have been modified and expanded, in ways that Smith could not have foreseen, through the effects of a number of inter-related intellectual movements and influences, including poststructural-ist theory, cultural studies, ethnic studies, and, perhaps especially, femi-nism. Smith, writing in 1957, articulated a vision of American studies as a collaboration in which only men participated. Several of the essays in this collection—particularly those by Barbara Welter, Linda Kerber, Nina Baym, and Janice Radway—offer evidence of the revolutionary effects of the introduction of a feminist perspective (and concurrently, of significantly larger numbers of women) into the collaborative venture of American studies scholarship.

The essays by Alexander Saxton, Houston Baker, George Lipsitz, Ramón Gutiérrez, Kevin Mumford, and K. Scott Wong reflect the grow-ing importance of a number of perspectives and areas of study—here represented by African American studies, popular culture studies, La-tino/Latina studies, gender studies, and Asian American studies—in reformulating the critical questions that shape the study of American social, political, and cultural life. In their interdisciplinarity and in their methodological debts to earlier scholars, these essays give evidence of the kind of intellectual collaboration—the kind that succeeds in making obsolete the "boundaries imposed by conventional methods of inquiry" —that Henry Nash Smith envisioned in 1957.

Each of the essays in the volume is followed by a brief comment from a scholar whose own research and teaching position him or her well to reflect on the essay's place in a history: in the history of a par-ticular discipline or area of study, or in the history of American studies scholarship in general, or in the respondent's own intellectual history. These responses provide useful critical guides to reading the essays; they also suggest the crucial and continuing intellectual correspondences be-tween American studies and other disciplinary fields of study. Perhaps more importantly, the responses indicate the continuities as well as the shifts, the abiding concerns as well as the new kinds of discourse in which those concerns are addressed, that have characterized the life and growth of American studies over the last fifty years.

Special thanks for invaluable assistance with this project go to Ramón Gutiérrez, Daniel Horowitz, and Ellen Todd, who served as an edito-rial committee and undertook the difficult and time-consuming task of helping to choose the articles included in the volume. The selections reflect their insight, wisdom, judgment, and plain hard work. It is no exaggeration to say that this is in large part their project.

I would also like to thank the many other people who were part of this collaborative effort: the writers of the commentaries; the Board of Advisory Editors of *American Quarterly;* Teresa Murphy, Associate Editor of *American Quarterly;* Sharon O'Brien, who originally suggested the format for the volume; Linda Tripp, of the Johns Hopkins University Press; John Stephens, of the American Studies Association; and Justin Hoffman, who served as managing editor for the volume.

Locating American Studies

HENRY NASH SMITH

Can "American Studies" Develop a Method?

I MUST ask the reader to accept for the present occasion two definitions. By "American Studies" I shall mean "the study of American culture, past and present, as a whole"; and by "culture" I shall mean "the way in which subjective experience is organized."

The problem of method in American Studies arises because the investigation of American culture as a whole does not coincide with the customary field of operations of any established academic discipline. The phrase "as a whole" does not, of course, imply a global attack directed simultaneously toward all the aspects of our culture. The defining characteristic of American Studies is not the size of its problems but the effort to view any given subject of investigation from new perspectives, to take into account as many aspects of it as possible.

In order to illustrate the need for such a shift of perspective, I should like to draw upon my own experience by considering the example of Mark Twain. He was a writer and his work belongs to the traditional field of American literature. But I can think of no other man whose work so clearly needs to be placed in a social setting before it can be fully understood. No other American writer of comparable importance is so unmistakably of the people. He took his materials and his technique from American culture, and he developed in collaboration with his audience. He served his apprenticeship in newspaper offices; he perfected his style by practicing the art of oral story-telling. His work is an almost uninterrupted commentary on matters uppermost in the minds of his readers and hearers, and he had a remarkable ability to objectify the memories and dreams of his public. It would be peculiarly artificial to try to deal with his books as if they were self-contained autonomous universes.

But how can one do justice to this central phenomenon of nineteenth-century American culture? It is true that much study of Mark Twain's life and work needs to be undertaken along perfectly conventional lines: his dependence upon literary predecessors, for example, has even yet not been fully investigated. Yet the student of this remarkable career soon finds himself asking questions that lead beyond the usual limits of literary history or criticism. One question, which is probably at bottom anthropological, concerns the matter of taboos governing what may be said, what may be represented, what may be published. Since Van Wyck Brooks's *The Ordeal of Mark Twain* (and that is now thirty-five years) a great deal has been written about the supposed censorship of Mark Twain's work, either imposed by others or self-imposed. The subject is of primary importance in the study of Mark Twain; at the same time it bears very widely on the recent history of American literature, and on the development of attitudes in the culture generally. But no one knows very much about it. We are at a loss if we ask to what extent the taboos evident in Mark Twain's work are individual idiosyncrasies and to what extent they were actually (as he often maintained) imposed by the culture. It is even more difficult to determine whether these canons of propriety were enforced uniformly throughout the society, or whether they varied according to geographical regions (as Bernard De Voto assumes in his chapter on "Cryptorchism") or according to social classes (as is implied in Santayana's celebrated identification of a "genteel tradition" in America).

The literary historian approaches this problem by examining the fiction published in magazines and books during this period; the correspondence between editors and writers; and book reviews, especially those which comment adversely upon supposed violations of taboos. But the information gathered from these sources needs to be interpreted in the light of a thorough knowledge of class structure, of the stratification of taste according to levels of sophistication, and of the different audiences to which different magazines and publishing houses addressed themselves. I do not believe, for example, that the usual methods of literary history enable us to explain why Harriet Beecher Stowe's "The True Story of Lady Byron's Life," published in the *Atlantic Monthly* in 1869 under the editorship of William Dean Howells after careful revision by Oliver Wendell Holmes, should have cost the magazine fifteen thousand subscribers—more than one-fourth of its list. The incident suggests that the public which read books (and literary magazines, among which the *Atlantic* enjoyed the highest status) had an appreciably stricter sense of decorum than did Howells and Holmes. The New York *Tribune*, mouthpiece for a larger but still relatively literate segment of public opinion, asserted that *Innocents Abroad* showed "an offensive irreverence for things which other men held sacred." Yet Howells published a highly favorable review of *Innocents Abroad* in the *Atlantic*. At the other end of the spectrum of tastes, or of degrees of sophistication, *Innocents Abroad* had an enormous sale among people who seldom read anything except newspapers. Perhaps the exaggerated concern for literary propriety came neither from the extreme highbrows nor from the public at large but from a kind of upper-middlebrow audience defined by the subscription lists of the literary magazines. If there were regional differences among segments of this audience, they have not been clearly defined.

In any event, during the 1870's Mark Twain had a complex problem of adaptation to his various audiences. Howells was introducing him to the world of polite letters through the pages of the *Atlantic*. The canvassers for the American Publishing Company were selling tens of thousands of his books to quite unliterary purchasers. On the lecture platform Mark Twain himself was in direct contact with large miscellaneous audiences—in the Middle West, in the East, and (as early as 1872) in England. He was, in fact, one of the pioneers in the discovery and the formation of the mass audience which is so conspicuous in the twentieth century. In these circumstances, he could obviously not have been the free creative artist in the Romantic mode that seems to have been Brooks's ideal. The autonomy of Mark Twain's works was impaired before they were written, and by forces that were in large part internalized in the author. It does not take us very far to conclude, as Brooks did, that this is a scandal. We must recognize that the inhibitions on literary expression (that is, the demands of various special audiences and of the embryonic mass audience) were a complex trait of the culture in which Mark Twain lived. We need to understand them in order to understand Mark Twain's work. We also need to understand them in order to understand the culture.

Indeed, it may turn out that one of the distinctive fields of American Studies is precisely this ambiguous relation between works of art and the culture in which they occur. Certainly the student of Mark Twain is confronted at every turn with problems arising in this area. Let me cite another example. In his early work, especially in *Innocents Abroad* and *Roughing It,* Mark Twain uses three distinct prose styles. One of these is a vernacular style, based on the everyday speech of men with little formal education— rivermen, stagecoach drivers, prospectors. The second is patterned on the ornate, elevated rhetoric of the pulpit and of political oratory in the manner of Daniel Webster. The third is a direct, unpretentious style representing the impersonal attitude of the skilled reporter. The vernacular style is felt to be appropriate to characters of low social status and reflects various attitudes toward them—sometimes a little patronizing, more often sympathetic and admiring. The elevated style embodies an aspiration toward genteel culture, for which indeed it serves as a matrix; it is often used with perfect seriousness, yet is also often burlesqued. The direct style is apparently felt as being neutral, as being somehow outside the hierarchy of classes. The relation of these styles to one another, and Mark Twain's development (never complete) toward an integrated personal idiom, are delicate indices to his perception of distinctions among social classes, of his own place in the status system, and of the status of the audience he believes himself to be addressing.

An examination of these aspects of Mark Twain's style requires a careful discrimination between attitudes toward social status that he has taken over unconsciously from the culture, and attitudes that spring from his conscious recognition of social stratification and of his place within the status system. It is possible, for example, that his most satisfactory style might turn out to depend on his achievement of a personal autonomy—an achievement that was intermittent rather than accomplished once and for all. Furthermore, we have to recognize drastic changes in Mark Twain's relation to the status system at different periods of his career. Especially in the five or six years immediately preceding his marriage in 1870, and for a year or two after it, he shows the signs of rapid upward social mobility, and this movement along the dimension of social status is inextricably involved with his development as a writer. Thus almost concurrently he moved from California to the East coast; he ceased being a newspaper correspondent to become a platform 'lecturer,' a contributor to literary magazines (including the *Atlantic*), a writer of books, and even a dramatist; after several years of a hand-to-mouth Bohemian existence he began to make a large income from his writing; and despite the perfectly rational misgivings of the Langdon family, he married Livy. He made his celebrated efforts at reform by trying to give up liquor and profanity, and to become a Christian as that term was understood in Elmira. He built his expensive house in Hartford. In place of Steve Gillis, Joe Goodman and the members of the San Francisco Minstrel Troupe, he acquired as friends the Rev. Joseph Twichell, Charles Dudley Warner and William Dean Howells. These biographical facts point in two directions: toward American culture (or the varieties of American regional subcultures) at the end of the Civil War, and toward the literary development recorded in Mark Twain's writings. The problem is at once biographical, historical, sociological and literary.

Mark Twain's attitudes toward American society found expression not only in his style, but in the use of recurrent figures or types of character: in his early work, for example, what has been called the vernacular character (most fully illustrated in Huck Finn); in his later work, a figure that might be called the transcendent character (the best illustration being Young

Satan in *The Mysterious Stranger*). These figures occur in many different guises over a long period of time. They are persistent themes in Mark Twain's writing, and they exert a strong influence on the shaping of plots in his works of fiction, on his imagery and especially on his language (what would *Huckleberry Finn* be if the language were altered?). Both figures embody the author's attitudes toward society, or rather his reading of social situations. The vernacular character is, so to speak, outside society because he is beneath it; the transcendent character is outside society because he is above it. There are strong hints here of Mark Twain's own alienation from the society. His principal problem as a novelist was how to conceive of significant action for characters whose relation to society was so special. The problem was evidently forced upon him by the culture of late nineteenth-century America. It lies at the center of his literary development, yet it cannot be adequately dealt with by literary methods alone. What is needed is a method of analysis that is at once literary (for one must begin with an analytical reading of the texts that takes into account structure, imagery, diction, and so on) and sociological (for many of the forces at work in the fiction are clearly of social origin). Such an analysis would not only take us much farther into Mark Twain's fictive universe than criticism has gone in the past; it would also give us a new insight into American society of the late nineteenth century, for the vernacular figure and the transcendent figure are not peculiar to Mark Twain. They were widely current in American literature and thought; they are cultural, not merely private and individual, images.

The final problem I shall mention that is posed by Mark Twain's career is his relation to the established role of the Man of Letters, the Author, as that role had been defined by New England in the place accorded Emerson, Longfellow, Lowell, Holmes, and so on. This role, one of the massive features of nineteenth-century American culture, was undergoing rapid change during Mark Twain's lifetime, and by the time of his death it had, I think, all but disappeared. In our own day the figure of the Alienated Artist has to some extent taken the place of the figure of the Man of Letters. Mark Twain felt the impact of the social forces that created both the older and the newer role of the artist in America, and at the same time his unprecedented popularity gave tantalizing glimpses of yet another role for the artist—that of the darling of the mass audience, a poker-faced bard whose jokes concealed his Whitmanian function of bringing the great democracy to knowledge of itself. This last possibility was never more than a possibility, but the partial extent to which it was realized defines one dimension of the unique achievement of *Life on the Mississippi, Huckleberry Finn* and *A Connecticut Yankee*. After the 1880's the pressures of personal misfortune and even more importantly of cultural change prevented this kind of achieve-ment. *Pudd'nhead Wilson, The Mysterious Stranger* and the lesser works of Mark Twain's last two decades are written from the perspective of alienation (an alienation which, it should be pointed out, was accompanied by increasing fame and popularity). To explain the shift in the direction of his development has long been a capital problem of criticism. It is an equally important problem of cultural history, and neither can be solved without full exploration of the other. To find out what was happening to the man and to the society we have to ask questions which lead simul-taneously to literary analysis and to analysis of social change.

Yet I must confess that the inquiries I have described are largely hypo-thetical. The student who tries to explore American culture even in this limited fashion by drawing upon the techniques of literary criticism and of the social sciences soon encounters difficulties.

The difficulties are due in part to the trend of literary studies in this country during the past two or three decades, which has moved away from rather than toward the social sciences. Just recently there are signs of a major shift of direction in literary criticism which may conceivably lead to more interest in the social setting of works of art. Such a change of direction would be most welcome. The techniques of analysis that have been developed by recent literary criticism should ultimately make it possible to deal with the relation between literature and culture at a much more profound level than has been attainable in the past. But change of this sort does not occur overnight, and the dominant force in literary studies is likely for some time yet to continue to be what we are familiar with as the New Criticism. This means that in general, the guiding principle will be a concern for the autonomy of the work of art.

If the New Criticism is about to give way to an even newer criticism, there is all the more reason to acknowledge its solid accomplishments. Like all literary revolutions, the New Criticism proposed to *écraser l'infâme*: it set about purifying criticism from the contamination of everything that was not literary. Again like other revolutions, this one brought with it a remarkable élan. It improved the morale of literary studies. It gave to scholarship and criticism a new penetration and intensity, and it markedly raised the level of literary instruction in American colleges and universities.

But these results were achieved only at a certain cost. The New Criticism has made it extraordinarily difficult to relate literature to the culture within which it occurs and of which it is indisputably a part. From the beginnings of the movement in the work of Ezra Pound and T. S. Eliot, it has borne the imprint of the image of the alienated artist. The cult of pure literature has implied a strongly negative attitude toward society, which within this tradition is habitually viewed as irredeemably Philistine and depraved: in Eliot's phrase, a "panorama of futility and anarchy." Although the actual techniques were largely invented and applied by other men, the master image of the movement has been Eliot's *The Waste Land,* and the critical undertaking has been strongly influenced by Eliot's idea of literature as a timeless order of eternal objects. This order he calls tradition, but it is very different from the usual conception of tradition because it is outside time and thus unhistorical or even anti-historical.

The pioneer technician of the New Criticism, I. A. Richards, had a somewhat different set of assumptions—he was at the outset, during the 1920's when he exerted his greatest influence on literary studies, an avowed Benthamite. His effort to state the doctrine of pure literature in positivist terms seems at first glance quite remote from the ideas of Pound and Eliot. But the effect of his teaching was essentially the same. Although he has now modified his original distinction between the statements of science, capable of being verified by empirical tests, and the pseudo-statements of poetry, which seem to be verifiable propositions but actually have no referent outside themselves, it has had great influence. And it separates art from society just as drastically as does Eliot's supernaturalism or Pound's denunciations of the "old bitch gone in the teeth," the "botched civilization."

Despite the sincere desire of some of the leaders in the movement to recognize the intimate relation between a work of art and its social setting, the effect of the New Criticism in practice has been to establish an apparently impassable chasm between the facts of our existence in contemporary society and the values of art. In this respect, the philosophical position of the New Criticism seems to me to bear a striking resemblance to Edgar Allan Poe's conception that art belongs to a non-empirical realm of 'ideality' totally divorced from the sordid or commonplace facts of everyday life. The root of the matter is the belief in an extreme dualism of nature and spirit. If society is taken to be a part of the natural order, and art is assigned to the realm of spirit, it becomes impossible to relate art (except negatively) to the actual culture within which it occurs.

We are no better off if we turn to the social sciences for help in seeing the culture as a whole. We merely find society without art instead of art without society. The literary critic would cut esthetic value loose from social fact; the social scientist, despite his theoretical recognition that art is an important aspect of culture, uses techniques of research which make it difficult or impossible for him to deal with the states of consciousness embodied in serious art.

To a student of literature, the social scientists seem to proceed ordinarily as if certain tangible values inherent in society were the only values that need to be taken into account. They find their reality in observed fact, and like all other scholars they have defined facts as the data which their methods of inquiry enable them to discover and record. The extreme form of this tendency is the emphasis on quantification, on the use of data susceptible of statistical treatment. The sociological studies of literature which I have encountered characteristically involve a 'content analysis' of large numbers of works of popular fiction or drama. The assumption on which they are based is, in the words of one such study, that popular literature "can be regarded as a case of 'social fantasy'—that the psychological constellations" in such material "indicate sensitive areas in the personalities of those for whom the work has appeal; their needs, assumptions and values are expressed ('projected')" in the play or novel or short story. Popular literature is used as if it were a body of material resulting from a series of projective psychological tests. This seems to me entirely justified, although I am not sure one can accept Lyman Bryson's contention that "today's popular art did not come out of yesterday's fine art . . . [but] is something developed out of natural social habits and needs by the machine." Popular art is certainly notable for its lack of originality; it is meant to be a homogeneous product identified by brand labels that the customer can count on. Its characters and situations are indeed, as another sociological study maintains, "ubiquitous mass symbols," extremely limited in range at any given moment. The relative homogeneity of popular art lends itself to the quantitative methods of content analysis.

But is nothing of consequence about a culture to be learned from its serious art? I suppose that when we speak of a serious novel, for example, we have in mind a work whose meaning is not exhausted by the identification of stereotyped ideas and attitudes in it. It is serious precisely because it differs in some respects from the mass of popular literature with which it is contemporary and with which, to be sure, it probably has something in common. The serious work has its period flavor but it also has other qualities, and some of these other qualities may be quite unique. Yet what the serious work uniquely expresses is not on that account unreal, or on that account alone unrepresentative. A description of the culture within which this book of permanent interest was created would be incomplete if we left it out of account. Subtract the work of a few dramatists from what we know of Periclean Athens, or of Elizabethan England, and our image of the culture undergoes a drastic change, quite apart from merely esthetic considerations.

The procedures of content analysis do not seem to be adapted to the analysis of works of art differing appreciably from popular art. The content that is analyzed is too rudimentary; it is, again by definition, a factor common to large numbers of works, which means a factor that is very far from exhausting the particularity of even a simple work of art. We need a method that can give us access to meanings beyond the range of such a systematic simplification—meanings that are not, so to speak, homogenized. Lacking such a method, the sociological study of the arts will inevitably yield an image of the culture which is truncated. Contemporary American culture is no doubt frightening enough, but it is made unnecessarily appalling by studies of popular art which by implication define the culture without reference to any subtleties beyond the horizon of the mass media. There is more to us than that!

In fact, there is more than that in the sociological findings. Reading the articles in the journals, one may easily forget that after all, the same culture which has produced the soap opera has also produced the sociological journals. Yet if the mass culture is there, so also are the observers and interviewers, the statisticians and the appraisers. Only, they have hidden themselves. The man who conducts the content analysis and identified the obsessive fantasies in the movies describes a world from which freedom is entirely absent and in which consciousness itself is rudimentary. He silently assumes that he and the colleagues to whom he reports his findings monopolize freedom and consciousness. The mores of his craft (borrowed from the natural sciences) oblige him to conceal his own consciousness behind statistical tables, and he seeks to deny his own individuality by a ceremonial avoidance of the first person. A kind of automation is suggested by these devices of rhetoric: the third person and the passive voice seem to establish as the model of the society a self-contained mechanism from which consciousness has been banished. The scientific observer is outside the field of his observations. He simply makes dial-readings.

I have suggested that the rhetoric of the social sciences seems to reflect an effort to minimize the role of consciousness. This observation can be justly extended to other aspects of the attitude toward language that an outsider encounters in reading current scholarship in these fields. Content analysis of works of literature, for example, requires the investigator to leave entirely out of account the actual words of the individual texts. The content which is extracted for counting and comparison with the content of other texts is detached from its original form of expression and thereafter exists (if it exists at all) in the neutral linguistic matrix of paraphrase. Here again, a procedure which may be suitable in dealing with texts lacking distinction of style is inappropriate in dealing with a serious work of literature. For what can be paraphrased is a small part of the whole meaning of such a work. The range of possible human experiences beyond the limits of paraphrasable meaning is the province of imaginative or poetic language.

The complex modes of statement which characterize the truly imaginative use of language (and I would be understood here as referring to the different vocabularies of the several arts) are the only instruments we have for embodying and communicating the full content of consciousness.

These more complex meanings are just as real as are the stereotyped fantasies of popular art; in fact, they are more real, because they are more precisely and durably embodied in the medium. And they are part of the culture. A hundred years ago it might have been said that they make up the whole of culture. We believe differently now, and I trust I have made it clear that I have no intention of trying to reinstate a conception of the arts as existing in a separate esthetic realm which contains all values. But I believe the social sciences have reacted too strongly against Matthew Arnold's view of culture. A fully adequate science of society will recognize the existence and the importance of the experiences and attitudes with which Arnold was concerned. And this recognition is possible only for one who is aware of the almost infinite subtlety and complexity of imaginative modes of statement. To recognize no serious and accurate function of language except its use as an instrument of precise denotation is to reduce the scope of consciousness and to deny the significance of whole universes of human experience. The result is a mutilated image of man and of culture.

I have described a situation in which, as it seems to me, the characteristic methods of literary criticism and the social sciences exhibit, each in its own way, serious shortcomings from the standpoint of the enterprise of understanding American culture as a whole. The social sciences seem to me to assume too hastily that all value is implicit in social experience, in group behavior, in institutions, in man as an average member of society. Current literary criticism assumes, also too hastily, that value lies outside society, in works of art which exist on a plane remote from the Waste Land of our actual experience. I have sincere respect for the accomplishments of American scholarship in all these areas, and I recognize that these accomplishments have been made possible only by the rigorous narrowing of fields of inquiry, by the specialization of interests that has been so marked a feature of scholarship in this country during the past half-century. On the other hand, I also believe that the desire to study American culture as a whole, which underlies the nascent movement toward American Studies, has valid motives behind it, and that without disturbing sociologists or literary critics in their important undertakings we can properly ask whether a method can not be found for investigating the whole of the culture.

The concept 'culture' seems, in the abstract at least, to embrace the concepts 'society' and 'art.' Why may we not say quite simply that the problem of method in American Studies can be solved by presupposing a value implicit in culture which includes and reconciles the apparently disparate values assumed in the disciplines of, say, literature and sociology? From this point of view, the problem of method in American Studies might seem to find its answer in the already existing field of cultural anthropology. But is this formula more than a verbal solution to the dilemma? The central question is whether cultural anthropology can take account of the full range of meanings available to us in the arts of complex modern societies like our own. From a sketchy acquaintance with some of the scholarship in this field, I gain the impression that when it undertakes the study of complex societies, it tends to resemble sociology, with perhaps a stronger inclination to invoke comparisons between advanced and preliterate cultures. Moreover, cultural anthropology does not seem to differ appreciably from sociology in its assumptions about the relation of fact and value.

I conclude, in short, that no ready-made method for American Studies is in sight. We shall have to develop one for ourselves, and I am afraid that at present we shall have to be content with a very modest program. The best thing we can do, in my opinion, is to conceive of American Studies as a collaboration among men working from within existing academic disciplines but attempting to widen the boundaries imposed by conventional methods of inquiry. This implies a sustained effort of the student of literature to take account of sociological, historical and anthropological data and methods, and of the sociologist or the historian to take account of the data and methods of scholarship in the fields of the arts. I am optimistic enough to believe that inquiries which have their starting-points in various academic departments can converge as they are brought to bear upon a single topic, namely, American culture past and present.

Method in scholarship grows out of practice, or rather out of repeated criticism of practice intended to remedy observed shortcomings. In the inadequacies of answers we have found to our questions we discover clues to the reformulation of the questions, and the reformulated questions in turn suggest new ways of finding answers. If I insist that the development of a method for American Studies is bound up with an effort to resolve the dilemma posed by the dualism which separates social facts from esthetic values, I do not imagine that a new method can be deduced from philosophical premises. A new method will have to come piecemeal, through a kind of principled opportunism, in the course of daily struggles with our various tasks. No one man will be able to redesign the whole enterprise. What will count is the image in our minds of the structure we believe we are helping to build. Such an image will influence a long series of particular decisions, will determine a tendency over a period of time rather than give us a new apparatus all at once.

From the standpoint of the social sciences the lines of investigation I have mentioned probably seem of limited value because they point to the analysis of specific, individual cases. This is an inevitable consequence of the nature of literary and historical inquiry. But I venture to suggest that individual instances embody whatever uniformities may exist in a culture, and that a really exhaustive knowledge of the concrete case—a work of art, a specific situation, a career—might well lead to the recognition of aspects of the culture which have previously escaped attention. At the very least one might hope for suggestions capable of being formulated as hypotheses and then tested against more extensive evidence. Why is it not conceivable that the masterpiece of literature, or the exceptionally productive career, might turn out to be an expression of the culture in ways beyond the scope of stereotyped examples of popular art or merely average life-patterns?

Lawrence Buell

The question posed by Smith's title is anything but rhetorical. His essay focuses especially on the obstacle to interdisciplinary work posed by methodological centripetalism in both literary studies and the social sciences. The effect of "the New Criticism in practice has been to establish an apparently impassable chasm between the facts of our existence in contemporary society and the values of art," while social science "uses techniques of research which make it difficult or impossible for [one] to deal with the states of consciousness embodied in serious art." Smith is forced to conclude "that no ready-made method for American Studies is in sight," that "we shall have to be content with a very modest program" of working as collaboratively as possible across different disciplinary boundaries.

Forty years later, this pronouncement looks both strangely timorous and strikingly prophetic.

To one approaching the essay in the 1990s for the first time, Smith's cautiousness may seem exceedingly peculiar given that his era is today generally presumed to have been the one epoch in the history of the American studies movement that *did* manage to generate something like a method: the so-called "myth-symbol" approach of isolating a putatively defining image of American culture and exploring it by recourse to an interweave of literary and cultural analysis. Indeed, Smith is justly considered at least as responsible as any other single person for developing that method. Smith was after all the first person to receive a Ph.D. in the field (Harvard, 1940), on the strength of the dissertation that later became *Virgin Land: The American West as Symbol and Myth* (Cambridge: Harvard University Press, 1950). *Virgin Land* was the method's first monument; its subtitle supplied the canonical rubric. By the time of Smith's *American Quarterly* article it had already been followed by R. W. B. Lewis's *The American Adam: Innocence, Tragedy, and Tradition in the Nineteenth Century* (Chicago: University of Chicago Press,

Henry Nash Smith, "Can 'American Studies' Develop a Method?," originally appeared in *American Quarterly* 9, no. 2, pt. 2 (summer 1957), Copyright, 1957, University of Pennsylvania.

1955) and John William Ward's *Andrew Jackson: Symbol for an Age* (New York: Oxford University Press, 1955); within a decade were also to appear Leo Marx's *The Machine in the Garden: Technology and the Pastoral Ideal in America* (New York: Oxford University Press, 1964), Alan Trachtenberg's *Brooklyn Bridge: Fact and Symbol* (New York: Oxford University Press, 1965), Edwin Fussell's *Frontier: American Literature and the American West* (Princeton: Princeton University Press, 1965), and David W. Noble's *The Eternal Adam and the New World Garden* (New York: Braziller, 1968).

Since 1970, the myth-symbol approach has been taken to task both for methodological naiveté and for its consensualist ideology, its attempt to contain cultural diversity and conflict within a unitary formation. Among the critics has been Smith himself, in an exceptionally thoughtful, gracious retrospect of 1986, "Symbol and Idea in *Virgin Land*" (in Sacvan Bercovitch and Myra Jehlen, ed., *Ideology and Classic American Literature* [Cambridge: Cambridge University Press, 1986]). In particular, the post-Vietnam "hermeneutics of suspicion" ushered in by such revisionary interpretations of the frontier as Richard Slotkin's *Regeneration through Violence* (Middletown: Wesleyan University Press, 1973) have made it impossible for most scholars to conceive of American myth except in terms of its ideological character—so impossible, indeed, that one is tempted to suspect that myth scholarship will make a comeback some day. But what has remained pretty much uncontested all the while is the vision of an age of relative consensus within the history of the American studies movement: if not a Golden Age, precisely, then at least an age of greater intercommunication and mutual understanding for which it is easy sometimes to long, even if one does not wish to replicate it.

A professor of English at Berkeley striving in the mid-1950s to carry the torch for interdisciplinarity within a department of literature scholars would not have seen matters quite that way, however. Indeed, Smith would have found some things to envy about this present age of Americanist dissensus. American studies would have seemed to him at the time he wrote his essay a far more struggling, precarious affair than it is now. To be sure, Smith might not have approved of the specific ways American studies has developed since 1970, becoming a combination of home base, contact zone, and debating ground for an increasingly complex, politicized, and centrifugal array of revisionisms—gender and sexuality studies, race and ethnicity studies, and (trans)national theory in particular. Yet he could not have failed to be impressed by the much greater flow of intellectual energy into "Americanist" forms of interdisciplinarity than was the case in the 1950s, when the "new criticism" more or less dominated English departments in the United States, and neither they nor departments of history and social science had been much influenced by the percolations of literary and cultural theory that would begin flowing into the American academy from Europe and create a destabilization of traditional boundary lines during the last quarter of the twentieth century that would arrest and reverse the specializing tendencies created by such movements as formalism in literary studies and quantification in historiography. In 1957, American studies was a very small niche indeed. As yet only one journal was devoted to it, and even in it, as Smith's title shows, it was necessary to speak about the movement with considerable self-consciousness. "American studies" had to be put in quotation marks, because even though Smith's method might be almost on the verge of becoming a short-lived orthodoxy, the whole enterprise was still very much in its pioneer stage.

Although the historical situation has greatly changed, so that Smith's specific concerns are no longer relevant, both the question itself and the presumption of doubt behind it are more pertinent and appropriate than when he posed it. Smith could expect a degree of intimacy, mutuality, and consent on the part of his audience that no longer prevails today. Smith could stipulate without fear of contradiction that a scholar was a "he"; he could assume that the fomenters of the new movement were more or less personally and professionally acquainted; he could assume that they all faced more or less similar uphill battles against disciplinary hegemony; he could assume that the literary figures to which they were likely to want to give primary emphasis were the major canonical figures like Mark Twain (his essay's primary *exemplum* of the need for interdisciplinary studies); and he could assume that "cultural history" meant the history of major ideational themes, sociological trends, and political events. Today the membership of the American Studies Association is so far-flung, the institutional epicenters so many, the semi-competing/semi-overlapping scholarly discourses so numerous that one cannot help feeling certain that it is far more unlikely now than in Smith's day that American studies can in fact develop *a* method. Or should. Surely today's paradigm, if there is one, has got to be cultural contestation—the border, the ecotone, hybridization, the queering of heteronormativity. This abbreviated roster of equivalent concepts from different contributing communities of inquiry suggests both the pervasiveness and the contestedness. In such a climate, however, what at first sight may strike contemporary readers as a slightly disingenuous or deadpan innocence on Smith's part may on second thought also seem very wise. His essay ends, or nearly ends, with a call "to widen the boundaries imposed by conventional methods of inquiry." That's what we're still trying to do. The present scene in American studies could hardly be encapsulated better.

WARREN I. SUSMAN

History and the American
Intellectual: Uses of a Usable Past

WRITING DURING WHAT MUST NOW APPEAR TO MANY AS HALCYON DAYS OF faith in the possibilities of social studies, Charles and Mary Beard could declare that "The history of a civilization, if intelligently conceived, may be an instrument of civilization." [1] Buried within what was clearly for the Beards a significant normative proposition—the call for a special kind of history—there rests a fundamental truth even more important for the student of a civilization. The idea of history itself, special kinds of historical studies and various attitudes toward history always play— whether intelligently conceived or not—a major role within a culture. That strange collection of assumptions, attitudes and ideas we have come to call a "world view" always contains a more or less specific view of the nature of history. Attitudes toward the past frequently become facts of profound consequence for the culture itself. Many students of historiography, of course, have expended much worthwhile energy in attempting to unearth the cultural causes of various approaches to the study of the past. This paper, however, suggests, with a series of broad hypotheses, the possibilities involved in a full-scale examination of the cultural consequences of special attitudes toward the past and the uses of history within a culture. In order to do so, I first would like to suggest in the most general sense how two kinds of treatments of the past, designated "mythic" and "historical" for purposes of the discussion, are related to each other and to culture. The rest of the essay proposes a basic outline of the history of some of these key relationships throughout American history.[2]

The idea of "history" itself belongs to a special kind of social and cultural organization. In status or community societies there is no written

---

1 This is the first sentence of their introduction to *The Rise of American Civilization* (New York, 1927), p. vii.

2 An earlier version of this paper was read to a joint American Studies Association— American Historical Association luncheon held in New York, December 28, 1960.

"history" (although there may be epics or chronicles).[3] Myth predominates in the prevailing world view: a special class—most generally a priesthood—exists in whose hands the monopoly of the interpretation of the myths of the society resides. Few question the nature or kind of social order. The institutional and normative pattern remains relatively static. The myths are sufficient to unify the whole, to answer the largely emotional needs of the members of the community and to provide, when necessary, the collective dreams of the society about the past, the present and the future in the same instant. The myths "explain" all. The function of myth is largely utopian: it provides a vision of the future without providing in and of itself any essential dynamic element which might produce the means for bringing about any changes in the present order of things. Ritual is generally enough to assure the fulfillment of the promise of the myth.

History, however, comes into existence in contract or associational societies. Here the social order is changing in ways which contrast dramatically with the more static nature of a status society. New institutions and values arise; associations become increasingly defended not because they exist but because they fulfill a function which can be more clearly seen and understood. The social order itself must be rationalized; reasoned explanations are called for. It is history which can more reasonably explain the origin, the nature and the function of various institutions and their interaction. Further, history seems able to point the direction in which a dynamic society is moving. It brings order out of the disordered array that is the consequence of change itself. As a result history is often used as the basis for a political philosophy which while explaining the past offers also a way to change the future. History thus operates ideologically. But by the very nature of its enterprise and the very kind of society which calls it into existence, historical interpretation cannot be effectively monopolized for long by any special class or group.[4] Its study is open to all who can reason and to all who participate in the various contractual or associational aspects of the society.

3 This distinction, so important in modern historiographical discussion, is made effectively in Benedetto Croce, *History: Its Theory and Practice* (London, 1920).

4 History arose in an effort to analyze new problems in a changing social order, problems now believed possible of such analysis by rational inquiry. Scientific inquiry had its origins in similar circumstances with the realization that the nature of the physical world was likewise amenable to such analysis. In both instances, of course, a special kind of professionalism developed. But again, in both instances, the existence of a special class of trained inquirers failed to give these men a real monopoly over their fields: others could use the results of such inquiries for their own purposes. This continues to be especially true in the study of history where special technical difficulties such as exist in today's scientific inquiry have really never developed. I am of course aware that there is in fact a kind of sociology of historians; not everyone was interested

Obviously what I have presented in excessively brief form is a contrast of two models of social organization and one significant element in the world view an investigator might be expected to discover in each. In status societies the prevailing attitude toward the past is mythic and its function utopian; in a contract society the past is viewed historically with consequent ideological uses. Probably no such ideal types ever existed. Certainly, for example, a contract society does not surrender its mythic elements; the psychological and social need for myth seems to persist in the most dynamic and rationalized social organizations. For it is in the realm of myth, in my usage, to provide much of the vision, the hopes and the dreams of any group. Myth, therefore, continues as what I call the utopian element in any world view, although I would like to suggest that in a complex contract society the number and kinds of myths are multiplied and frequently conflict more dramatically than they would in an ideal status society.[5]

What is significant, then, about an historical approach to the past in the newer social order is not that it replaces a mythic approach or even that history sometimes finds itself in conflict with myth. I am not proposing only a battle between mythos and logos (although surely this too does exist) but a special interaction between myth and history, utopianism and ideology, which has significant cultural consequences for any society. History is frequently called upon to play a new role in relationship to the older mythic views. Perhaps a metaphor will explain what I have in mind. Myth traditionally provides the central drama of any social order—witness the sacred drama of the Christian myth. But history offers something vastly different in its ideal form. Since it is concerned with change,

in history in every period. In the classical world history was generally written by and for members of the governing classes, for example. My point is simply that history *could* in fact be available to all who could read. It presented no special mysteries. Also, in the discussion that follows I am interested only in professional historians when they have an impact on the more general intellectual community. Obviously, after 1885 the professional historian is an important cultural fact, but I am more interested in the cultural consequences of the uses of history by intellectuals who may indeed not be professional historians.

5 I realize that my social categories are "ideal types" that are not perhaps acceptable for more sophisticated social analysis but I believe that they can still be useful in a more general way, a rough background for my analysis. I am sorry, too, to insist on my own usage for the words "myth," "ideology," "history" and "utopia." I am well aware that others use these terms differently and, since precise definition would take more space than I may have, I hope that my meanings are clear from the context. I have been influenced in part by Kenneth Burke, "Ideology and Myth," *Accent*, VII (Summer 1947), 195-205. Mr. Burke sees myth as a way of stating a culture's "essence" in narrative terms. Two very important recent discussions of myth and ideology have been published by Ben Halpern: "The Dynamic Elements of Culture," *Ethics*, LXV (July 1955), 235-49; "'Myth' and 'Ideology' in Modern Usage," *History and Theory*, I (1961), 129-49.

movement, the on-going course of action and ideas, since it is more clearly related to the dynamic aspects of social life, it provides what I have called an ideology as distinguished from a utopian vision. But the two frequently work hand in hand; myth provides the drama and history puts the show on the road. Myths often propose fundamental goals; history often defines and illuminates basic processes involved in achieving goals.

Philosophies of history—attitudes toward history as process—frequently influence the *kind* of action (or retreat to inaction) men adopt as a result of belief in a fundamental myth. If one needed further proof about this important relationship between myth and history, a brief examination of millennialist interpretations of history would prove most illuminating. All Christians believe in the central myth (and therefore promise) of their faith; but this belief clearly has different consequences culturally when coupled with different theories of history. Millennialism, as a special theory of history, is itself of crucial cultural importance. But those who hold a premillennialist view are going to act far differently in the world than those who hold a postmillennialist position, as any student of eighteenth- or nineteenth-century American intellectual and social history can attest, in spite of their fundamentally shared view of the truth of the Christian myth.[6]

In the complex relationship between myth and history within a culture it is clear that there are conditions which frequently lead to the attempt to use each cultural force—myth and history—in ways which emulate the natural function of the other. We are perhaps most clearly aware of the consequences that result from an attempt to make history into myth (or at least make history *perform* mythically). W. Lloyd Warner's extended discussion of the particular uses of American history in his latest Yankee City volume provides a most graphic instance. Here history has in fact become myth, complete with ritual, pageant and even a kind of priesthood. A relatively complex contract society is unified, the existing social order justified, basic values reinforced and community goals sanctified— all by resort to major incidents in Yankee City's history treated in mythic ways in which all citizens of the town are invited or perhaps socially compelled to share. In the process, however, something significantly different is made from history—and even the history of Yankee City and the U.S.A.—than as we usually think of it.[7]

---

6 While this point is obvious it unfortunately escapes too many writers. Stow Persons is consistently excellent in indicating these differences and their significance in his *American Minds* (New York, 1958).

7 *The Living and the Dead* (New Haven, 1959), pp. 101-225.

But there is also a drive to make the myth something historically real; that is, to turn the utopian promise into a specific kind of ideology. The nineteenth century began its detailed search for an historical Christ, for example, undoubtedly to provide a rational basis for a belief in the Christian myth. But that very process of putting Christ *in* history has enormous cultural consequences for society and for the nature of Christianity itself. For once the chief mythic character of the Christian religion, the man-god who died and was reborn, became a figure within the limits of rational historical inquiry, he became subject to special interpretations and uses. Jesus became a great "representative man"—an idea which in its very nature was a threat to the mysteries of the Christian myth— who was a great moral teacher and prophet. By the end of the century the American people could be told that if they would truly walk "in His steps" they ought to become Christian socialists. They were presented with a set of immediate social consequences if He came to Chicago. Within a few decades He would become Comrade Christ, the social revolutionary.[8] Ideological consequences of a striking kind result from the effort to make a mythic vision of the past function as history. But, if only to emphasize the problem, that very act of making history out of myth, the act of treating Jesus as an historical figure shaped by historical conditions and circumstances and shaping in turn his society and world as any great man might, opens the way to a variety of ideological uses, not just one. History is seldom the monopoly of the few as the interpretation of the mystery of myth may indeed be in some cultures. And as a result, it is this same historical Christ who could become in 1925 "The Man Nobody Knows," the eminently successful salesman-businessman of Bruce Barton.

I have selected two extreme examples of history becoming myth and myth becoming history to establish my basic hypothesis. Yet somewhere in between there is a special meeting ground between history and myth that frequently provides a key to the central tensions within a culture. It is in this area of the tensions between established myths and developing ideologies, between the efforts of converting history to mythic ends and of using history in its more traditionally ideological way, where much of the story will have to be told. This conflict is often quite clearly recognized by many intellectuals within the culture. Artists, especially, are able to see and use this important intellectual and cultural fact. Two novels will perhaps indicate the existence of this awareness. In Mel-

8 For examples of this transformation see Upton Sinclair's extraordinary anthology of the literature of social protest, *The Cry for Justice* (Philadelphia, 1915). Book VII, 345-82, is called "Jesus" and in it appear many examples of the use of the historical Jesus as a figure of social protest.

ville's *Billy Budd* many commentators have seen the significant use of both the myth of Christ and the myth of Adam. But too few have seen that these mythic representations are put into a very special and carefully defined historical context. For Melville goes to great lengths to set his scene within history—precisely and in some detail, with dates, events and all the trappings of historical reality. We see the mythic enactments against the backdrop of meticulously established historical detail, a particular time and place, a particular series of historically true events. It is the tension between the historical demands (ideology) and the mythic ones (utopia) that gives the novel its tragic pertinence. Sixty years later William Faulkner was to use the same kind of central tension in *A Fable*. The enactment of the Christ myth is again presented against a most specific and realistic historical background. Not only does Faulkner place his tale during the First World War as Melville did his during the aftermath of the French Revolution, but he also uses an amazing number of details that come from the actual history of that war. Thus it is this very tension between the mythic beliefs of a people— their visions, their hopes, their dreams—and the on-going, dynamic demands of their social life recorded by the students of the real past and the actual present (with perhaps an often implied future) which provides many artists with their theme, a theme reflecting a basic conflict within the culture itself. This is in fact one of the basic tensions which helps define the nature and kind of culture that exists.

American civilization begins with a unique set of cultural circumstances. On the shores of New England a group of able intellectuals—some ministers, others reflecting their important university training—established a kind of social order that was clearly, by definition, a contract society. It was organized on the theoretical base composed of a series of major compacts; it was prepared to carry out an on-going mission within history, the task no less than the reformation of the whole world. It was also, however, a social order committed with grave earnestness to a belief in the Christian myth. But intellectually, for its particular kind of organization to survive and its mission to be fulfilled, the myth alone, no matter how interpreted, would not suffice. It is always important to remember that this was a society dominated largely by those we would today call intellectuals. The nineteenth-century image of the alienated intellectual would surely seem strange to these Puritans, even to the Hutchinsons and Williamses and Taylors who were driven from the colony or forced to keep their private thoughts very private indeed. And these intellectuals who functioned as leaders from the very beginnings of the enterprise carried with them a special view of history;

they made the study of history and its interpretation a vital part of the cultural development of the colony. The view of history which the settlers and those who followed brought was one which clearly explained, defined and justified the specific kind of contractual society they proposed to establish and develop. The writing of history, the keeping of journals at least in part for historical purposes, the discussions of history in various sermons and addresses makes clear the central role—second only I would argue to the expounding of the Christian myth itself and its meanings—of historical inquiry to the colonizing efforts. For it is history which provides the ideology, the dynamic view that makes possible the onward movement of the society to its historically appointed task. The tension between the promise of the Christian myth and its obligations upon man and the promise of their special view of history and its demands forms a central theme in any analysis of the culture they built.

By the end of the seventeenth century that brilliant series of covenants and compromises, that essential tension between myth and ideology directed by America's first intellectual elite, had broken down forever. In an almost final gesture, Cotton Mather characteristically resorted again to history in an effort to restore the old order socially and intellectually. But the age was over, the tensions too great; nothing—not even Mather's monumental and most significant history—could save it. Two important groups, both denied an effective place within the old order, were now ready to face each other in a major struggle reflecting again a basic tension in the eighteenth century. Each had its own view of the nature of the process of history, derived in some measure from the original Puritan synthesis but each stressing its special aspects as ideology for its own kind and class.

The revivalists of the Great Awakening took the millennialist and providential elements of the old synthesis as their own. In their frankly supernatural view of history they saw in the revival movement itself the hope of the coming millennium. In their enthusiastic and optimistic view they were committed, then, to a theory of history which might provide an effective threat to the social order and stability in the name of the currently disinherited. On the other hand, the new leaders of the American social order who had taken over after the older Puritan leadership had faltered found it necessary to fight back with a philosophy of history and a view of American development that could be used to defend the newly-arrived-at contractual order in which they were now the elite, intellectually and socially. Stow Persons has shown with acute awareness how these men developed a cyclical theory of history without significant reference to the Christian myth and yet without attempting to deny this mythic vision directly. Rather, they stressed the law and order which ruled the universe in terms of clearly discernible moral qualities, qualities reflected most effectively in the accumulation of property and position, in the special moral character exemplified by their own group in society. Thus their theory of history justified the new social order and their place in it and sought to counter the "dangerous" theories of the enthusiasts and millennialists of the revival movement.[9]

The intellectual tensions of the century—and in some sense the real social tensions as well—were reflected in a basic conflict of historical theories, one in which the Christian myth was about to be actualized in time and thus posed a radical threat to the stability of the social order, and the other in which the Christian myth itself had become some sort of regularized goal at the end of history, a goal which might be best achieved through the orderly and moral progress of men under the leadership of those of good character and sound social position. The conservative philosophy of history of the Enlightenment in America largely dominated public policy and the newer intellectuals who espoused it continued to maintain effective control in society as had an earlier elite in Puritan New England.

By the second and third decades of the nineteenth century several important new factors could be witnessed on the American cultural scene. First, the intellectuals in the society could no longer easily assume that through the professions of the ministry or the law social power would be assured to them within the American community. The problem of vocation for the intellectual in America became for the first time a serious issue: for this reason Emerson's soul-searching struggle to find a proper vocation becomes a key symbolic instance for the student of the role of the intellectual in America. Secondly, the emergence of the idea of progress in its variant forms provided an easy view of the nature of history for every man and an all too easy rationalism that engulfed all before it. So much had history taken hold in American society that the very mystical and intuitive nature of fundamental myths seemed to lose place and meaning for many. So easily did the notion of progress adapt all events past and present to its use that the whole social order became too readily (for some) justified—any change, any development, any direction.

9 "The Cyclical Theory of History in Eighteenth Century America," *American Quarterly,* VI (Summer 1954), 147-63. This seems to me one of the most important articles on the Enlightenment in America and yet it is not sufficiently well known or used by those who continue to talk about the period in traditional ways, be they the ways of a Becker or a Boorstin.

For those who felt these dislocations there were several courses open. They might reject history in its currently accepted sense and seek beyond it or apart from it some sense of the importance and meaning of life. This, of course, was the path of Emerson and Thoreau who refused to allow rational historical analysis to take away from them the transcendental vision of the basic myths they still wished to and needed to believe in. If history did have a value, it was not the history as on-going process but rather the study of what might be abstracted from the past as a standard in the present—exactly those transcendent virtues and ideas that were unaffected by the relativities of the historical process itself.

This particular use of the past was of course not new nor was it uniquely the property of Emerson and his followers. The eighteenth-century elite had drawn on its studies of the classical world for models of behavior and conduct; the nineteenth century frequently found ideal patterns for society and morals (as well as art and architecture) in a special and static vision of the Middle Ages, Gothic and Romanesque; the later nineteenth century and early twentieth century looked especially to the glories of the Renaissance for standards of taste, virtue and judgment; and in the early twentieth century the American Humanists (following what they believed to be the lead of the Renaissance Humanists) again proposed a vision of the classical world as ideal. But such a use of history—abstract, outside of time and circumstances, detached from the whole process of development—was largely a device to overcome, to halt, to stem the tide of the on-going process itself. It was almost always the tool of a small elite and its effect was seldom widely felt. It was, in my terms, essentially an anti-historical use of history. Its function was mythic in purpose, but it failed too often to elicit a proper mythic response from the mass of society—no matter how monumental and overpowering its architectural representations all over the American landscape.

Perhaps more effective but still limited in appeal was the resort to myths of a purer kind in which more of the community might easily share. R.W.B. Lewis has sketched for us the story of *The American Adam* which deals with a major aspect of that effort. And if Emerson and the transcendentalists generally failed to reaffirm the vital mystery of their particular vision of the Godhead to large numbers of Americans, the continuing revivalist tradition did keep alive a more readily emotional and social response to the Christian myth, although in this case once again usually related to a millennialist historical view whose considerable consequence I have previously suggested. The transcendentalist and revivalist attempts to reassert the value and function of myth in American society are, after all, parts of a single process and in some very real sense transcendentalism can well be considered a kind of revivalism among the intellectuals.

But there were intellectuals in this period who did not turn away from the study of history itself. One of the most significant aspects of the intellectual history of the mid-nineteenth century is the special effort made by American intellectuals to recapture control over the study of history itself as a vehicle of intellectual and social influence and power. Most of these intellectuals had been trained, initially, for either the law or the ministry, the previous career patterns available to those intellectuals who sought power in American society.[10] These intellectuals trained themselves in the best of the methods provided by the newer "scientific" historical scholarship then thriving in Germany. They were, moreover, much admired and much read by a goodly segment of the American community. In an age when a special kind of historical imagination flourished, these intellectuals discovered that through the writing of history itself they might achieve some of the ends their more a-historical fellows were unable to achieve.

But in capturing, in some meaningful sense at least, part of the intellectual leadership through their study of history, what ends were the Bancrofts and the Sparkses, the Prescotts and the Parkmans actually seeking? David Levin ably has shown how they conceived of history as a "romantic art" and how clearly they used the major devices of that art in their works of scholarship.[11] They wrote colorful narrative history; they made characters and events come alive. But such history—and it is again being called for in our own age—with all its serious and studied scholarship yields itself to fulfilling the very kind of mythic function (albeit much more popularly received) in a way that the more self-conscious non-historical mythic efforts of the period seemingly failed to do. Almost always narrative history attempts a mythic function and the more carefully analytical history (most characteristic in the monographs and studies in the period from 1890 to 1940) lends itself to ideological uses. In the unstable world of the nineteenth century, filled with change, teeming with developments bent on upsetting the fundamental nature of the social order itself—developments which were to include a civil war— these great historians of the middle of the century produced American epics. They provided, perhaps, a way of understanding what was happening through an almost mystical notion of the divine law of progress,

10 I have often wondered whether there is any significance in the fact that most of those who were originally headed for a career in law generally selected European history as their field of inquiry while those prepared for the ministry, like Sparks and Bancroft, devoted themselves to the American story.

11 *History as a Romantic Art*, (Stanford, Cal., 1959).

as in the case of Bancroft. Here is history offering hope without program, faith without a searching investigation of basic issues and problems. In the words of R. W. B. Lewis, Bancroft's kind of history was a demonstration "in historical terms of the validity of the hopeful legend, the legend of the second chance." [12] In the case of Parkman, on the other hand, history became a kind of tragedy, the unfulfilled promise of both savagery and civilization. But whether optimistic or pessimistic, the histories of the period provided certain fundamental values, a certain commitment to moral law, certain reinforcement through examples of exemplary social and political behavior. In spite of all their scholarship and science, then, these epic accounts are mythic in consequence in maintaining older social arrangements and values, utopian in essence and objective. These historians try to speak out as high priests in charge of interpreting a newer and more scientifically composed mythology. It is perhaps not surprising that a scholar like R. W. B. Lewis should discover mythic elements in their work similar to that in the work of some of those who rejected traditional historical analysis.

Mid-nineteenth-century American intellectuals adopted an approach to the study of the past that led to a fundamentally utopian outlook; the method of analysis was primarily mythic—no matter what the more formal trappings. This attitude toward history and toward the world itself reached a most dramatic climax in the 1880s—the decade in which more Americans sought to outline in print their utopian visions than perhaps any other decade in our history.[13] Significantly, however, most of these attempts to devise a utopia were presented without any ideological basis which might indicate how the existing social order could propel itself toward the achievement of such a new and ideal ordering of society.

The intellectual historian fond of dramatic contrasts might delight in comparing the essential utopian outlook of much thought of the 1880s with the fundamental return to the historical vision of the 1890s. Such a contrast might easily, it is true, be overdrawn. But nevertheless, here, amidst a series of basic problems too harsh to be overlooked, too significantly earnest and demanding of immediate attention to be judged on the basis of a mythic view of some distant future, history emerged again as a vehicle for the intellectual with a new and special set of functions significantly in line with the ideological usefulness of certain attitudes toward history.

Many defenders of Frederick Jackson Turner and many critics have tried to sum up his greatness. Many have pointed to a considerable group

---

12 *The American Adam* (Chicago, 1955), p. 161.

13 V. L. Parrington Jr., *American Dreams* (Providence, 1947) is an account of utopian works with a good checklist of titles.

of forerunners or precursors who held views similar to his. But the genius of Turner was essentially a simple and yet vital one culturally. He took a major American myth and made from it effective history. He took a utopian set of attitudes and beliefs and made them ideologically effective for his own times. First, he compiled no great narrative, used almost none of the current literary conventions. His was an effort in analysis. His starting point was not some vague feeling of instability but a set of specific problems in the American scene which were of significant moment in his own era—labor unrest, the farmers' revolt, the consequences of a vast new immigration, the rise of urban problems, a world-wide depression in the face of a world-wide transportation and communications revolution. He wanted to account for these problems; he wanted to suggest why they had not arisen previously in our history. He made, therefore, the frontier thesis, a long-established myth as many authorities agree, a major tool for social analysis. What is more, since he could reveal *why* America had developed the way she had, since he knew the key ingredient in producing the kind and quality of social institutions and character types that made America unique, his analysis might more easily provide some clues about what must be done to preserve that order. Thus his analysis might make it possible for one to act—not resign oneself to the myth of a second chance with some inevitable progress under God's benign direction nor surrender to the essential tragedy of the human condition nor carry on precisely as one had in the past under the leadership of one's betters.[14]

I hope this analysis will not be taken as approval of the kind of approach Turner and his followers undertook, or the kind of ideology that emerged in part because of that approach. Rather, I am suggesting that what followed from this kind of history was precisely that—an ideology and moreover one which was in striking ways to become in part the official American ideology since at least 1893. If from 1893 to 1963 Americans find themselves committed to a search for new frontiers to replace the one Turner announced was no more, they do so in large part because the study of history pointed the way ideologically. It is precisely because this did become a major ideological force, adapted to many ends in the America of the twentieth century, that there has been such a wide-scale

[14] It is important at this juncture to recall Turner's extraordinary essay on "The Significance of History" which antedates his more famous paper of 1893 and which is really one of the earliest statements in the "New History" position that Beard and Robinson were to espouse. This essay is reprinted in *The Varieties of History,* ed. Fritz Stern (New York, 1956), pp. 197-208. For the setting out of which the Turner thesis itself came see Lee Benson, "The Historical Background of Turner's Frontier Essay," *Agricultural History,* XXV (April 1951), 59-82.

public debate on the validity of the so-called Turner thesis and that important groups of American intellectuals found it necessary to discuss the values which followed from a frontier America, values which some were trying to preserve in our century while others equally vigorously were trying to disavow them.[15]

Out of the historical awareness that dawned in the 1890s in America came still another example of the importance of history as ideology. This involves another pattern of historical inquiry. If Turner turned a myth into history, others in the period, again for ideological purposes, attempted to take the mythic out of what had previously passed for history. All through the nineteenth century there had been a rumbling of dissatisfaction with the inheritance from seventeenth-century Puritan theology and social organization and values. One can point to many landmarks along the way which reveal the challenge to the Puritan tradition that had become so important a part of official American mythology. But the real explosion occurred in the 1890s—an explosion that was to continue to reverberate throughout American intellectual life until the 1940s.

For any student of culture one question must seem apparent at the outset. Why should anyone bother to attack the life and ideas of men long dead or a social order no longer in existence? Why, after all, in any culture should anyone, save perhaps those professionally involved with the study of the past, care about what the seventeenth century was *really* like? Yet in that great era of historical awareness beginning roughly in the 1890s, American intellectuals *did* care. They cared because they realized the vital ideological importance in a society like ours of history and the "proper" attitudes toward it. They cared because they realized that views held about the past generally had consequences for the present. It was not simply that the past "determined" the present in some rather simple casual order of things, but that the way one viewed the past had significant consequences on the way one acted in the present. It was precisely because in our kind of social order history becomes a key to ideology, a key to the world view that shapes programs and actions in the present and future. At least this was a fundametal view of the majority of American intellectuals in the period between 1890 and 1940. Since current ideology is based on a particular view of the nature of the past, since present problems are frequently solved by reference to the way past experience dealt with similar problems, the control over the

15 I have discussed this point in my article "The Useless Past: American Intellectuals and the Frontier Thesis, 1910-1930," *Bucknell Review*, XI (March 1963), 1-20. For ideological consequences of the kind I mean, see, for example, William Appleman Williams, "The Frontier Thesis and American Foreign Policy," *The Pacific Coast Historical Review*, XXIV (November 1955), 379-95.

interpretation of the nature of that past becomes a burning cultural issue. This is, in effect, the driving force behind the movement James Harvey Robinson called the "New History" in 1913; it colors the achievements of other professional historians like Charles Beard and Carl Becker.[16] And it is not beside the point that these historians, like Turner, played significant roles in the general culture of their era that went way beyond their purely professional responsibilities. These attitudes in fact came generally to be held by a generation or more of intellectuals who were in no sense professional historians.

There is, of course, still a further assumption behind this historic struggle within history itself. Not only is it important that we have the "right" view of the past, the proper attitudes toward history, if we are to operate effectively in the world today and tomorrow, but also the right view, the proper attitudes *can* help us to solve our problems and change the course of the stream of history itself. This is why Van Wyck Brooks' call in 1918 for a "usable past" made sense to American intellectuals all through the period under discussion, no matter how they might agree or disagree about which view of the past was most especially useful. There was a basic agreement that an intelligent reading of the past might make possible man's intelligent direction over the future course of history.

The preoccupation of the brothers Adams with special phases of the American past is well known by students of our civilization. Further, there has been extensive discussion of these remarkable men against the background of the very special problems they faced as intellectuals in a society in which they seemed to have, in the current social order of their day, little place or function. They fit rather easily into the image of the alienated intellectual, that image which began to emerge significantly on the American scene in the nineteenth century. But the special relationship between this seeming lack of function and their interest in the study of the past has not been sufficiently explored. For as "aliens" seeking positions of intellectual authority and power, they did not follow the path of the transcendentalists in turning against the past or the tradition of the historians of the earlier days of the century who would become high priests for society by turning history into a special mythic form, an epic art. Rather, they turned to the study of the past in an effort to find a new ideological position that they could offer in refutation of accepted contemporary ideologies, ideologies justified by a view of the past currently in vogue and for them significantly untrue and dangerous.

---

[16] See Morton White, *Social Thought in America* (New York, 1949) and Cushing Strout, *The Pragmatic Revolt in American History* (New Haven, 1958).

If they told the story of the Antinomian controversy, for example, they did so not simply to set the record straight. (How few historians, professional or otherwise, really seem interested in the pastness of the past!) They did so because they believed that the defense of Puritan America, which had become part of the official creed, perpetuated values and social attitudes intolerable to them, impossible for the America they would see develop. If Brooks Adams, more forcefully than any figure before him and in advance of the more sophisticated analysis of the same relation made slightly later by Max Weber, undertook to relate the development of modern capitalism and the Reformation, he did so because he found Puritan values reinforcing capitalist values and the resultant social and economic organization destructive of the kind of culture he wished to see flourish in America. If as a result of the new economic man who emerged as a major social type from the fusion of capitalism and protestantism it was, as he believed, impossible to have a decent art, architecture and literature, and it was unlikely that an effective civilization could endure in the United States, obviously something must be done to modify if not overthrow the ruling ideology that perpetuated this social type. *The Law of Civilization and Decay* was in effect a kind of "new history." The philosophies of history advanced by Brooks and Henry Adams were not simply statements of pessimistic surrender to the world as it was, but a new reading of how the world got that way: an effective, critical beginning of a search for a new ideology that might produce a culture more agreeable. It would not be easy to achieve this reorganization, but the place to begin was clearly with a re-examination of the past and the effort to discover from such study the possible new laws that might provide a new dynamic approach to the world's problems. At the same time, of course, it might provide a new role for the intellectual as agent of discovery, critic of the old history, the old social order and the old ideology, and liaison to the new men of power bringing them a new history, a new ideology, new insights for the development of programs of action. If the older view of the Puritan past sanctified the purging of individualist dissent or the more vicious values and consequences of capitalism, it must give way to a new view, a true view of what the Puritans *really* were.

This form of intellectual activity became common in the period after 1890. The whole of American history and its official version came under the scrutiny of American intellectuals in a way unique in our development. The frontier past and its consequences for culture, the Puritan tradition and its results were but two areas of growing concern on the part of those who sought from a newer version of the American past some new orientation for American civilization itself.[17] It became especially the function of the intellectual to find a useful past, a version of American history and of the nature of history itself that would propel America on to the road to a desirable culture or at least provide the critical tools with which to overthrow the official view—the view Van Wyck Brooks suggested put a "talmudic seal" on institutions, values and policies repellent to these intellectuals. Brooks and Lewis Mumford, for example, felt they must rewrite our literary history, if only to provide some new basis for literature in their own time and some worthwhile relationship between the artist, the intellectual, and his society. Other intellectuals joined suit; their useful pasts frequently differed and they quarreled about this among themselves. Southern agrarians, for whom the nature of the southern past became a matter of vital concern, an obsession that led literary men to write history and biography, found their view of the past directly challenged, for example, by the views of a growing number of Marxist intellectuals. Some were concerned only with "debunking" the past—a new and rather common pastime, introducing a new word into the language itself; others developed more profound philosophies of history. But the fundamental point remains: during this era in our intellectual development attitudes toward history played a key role in many debates and all seemed to agree that some special view of the past was necessary, some view of history which challenged the assumed truths about the past and the ideological positions based on such "truths."

The extraordinary importance placed on the control of the past was reflected in all fields of activity. The Social Gospel movement depended upon its special version of history and its special view of Christ's mission in history. Certain factions of the so-called Progressive movement made the "New History" a key ally. It is ironic to think that a book as dry, painfully detailed and scholarly as Beard's *An Economic Interpretation of the Constitution* could become a work of political significance—but it did for some Progressives. The New Criticism in literature (and the new literature itself), while frequently believed to be antagonistic to historical study, was in fact simply antagonistic to special versions of history. Many literary figures found themselves in their battles with the entrenched literary standards of the day forced to rewrite the whole of literary history to support their own critical and creative activities. T. S. Eliot is but one outstanding example of a "New Critic" who gave us, in rough outlines at least, a brand new version of European literary history. The most advanced movements in the arts frequently were based in large part on

---

17 This present paper barely suggests one of the major attacks on the Puritan past. I am at work on a fuller analysis of the whole question. But see esp. Frederick J. Hoffman, "Philistine and Puritan in the 1920's," *American Quarterly*, I (Fall 1949), 247-63.

a profound restudy of the past, be it in painting, in architecture or in music, in an effort to support the newer visions.

It is striking to examine from this perspective some of the major literary figures and their most important works. Here again the artist believed that somehow it was his special function (a function that would afford him special status, a way out of alienation) to make history his own, to offer in his art a vision of that history that would be more meaningful for culture. Ezra Pound became deeply involved in the study of America's past—as well as the past of Europe and China. *The Cantos* represent a major effort to come to grips with historical materials and to use them in a special mythic way. To many students of our civilization it must seem strange indeed to discover in the body of this complex and difficult work not simply allusions to John Adams and Martin Van Buren (two of Pound's special American heroes whom he believes American official history has ignored) but long passages from the writings of these men and other historical figures. For Pound was trying to "make it new" in this as in other areas, to provide for his audience some newer insight into what he believed was the true nature of the American tradition and therefore the special promise of American life. Hart Crane's *The Bridge* likewise insists on a special historical vision. And the career of William Carlos Williams can be assessed in terms of a persistent effort—from his earliest work to the end of his brilliant career—to make meaningful his nation's history in a special mythopoetic way. Williams is especially clear about his objective; he wished to make the past alive and important in the present. Official or "scientific history" was for Williams a lie. It was the kind of history that "portrays us in generic patterns, like effigies or the carving on sarcophagi, which say nothing save, of such and such a man, that he is dead." It is the pastness of the past which is dangerous for a culture. We need history, for when we regret the past, not realizing that "what we are has its origins in what *the nation* in the past has been," we lose immeasurably because of our ignorance. The past, as brought to new and meaningful light by the artist's imagination which makes it present to us all, is "our greatest well of inspiration, our greatest hope of freedom (since the future is totally blank, if not black.)" [18]

Thus the culture of America in the period between 1890 and 1940 was based in large measure on a view of the importance of history in solving human problems on every level and on a firm commitment to the special role that the intellectual might develop for himself in a world in which he felt alien as critic of the official ideology and champion of the truer meanings of the nation. Toward the end of this period, it is clear, what

---

[18] *In the American Grain* (New York, 1925), pp. 188, 109, 189. Italics in the original.

Richard Chase has called *The Quest for Myth* again became a major occupational and imaginative concern for many artists and intellectuals. The need for myth began to reassert itself—be it the Christian myth or any number of mythic visions out of history. As depression and world war engulfed the world, the stabilizing and utopian function of myth again seemed important. But throughout the major portion of the period, leading figures dealt directly with the tensions created between history as myth and history as ideology in a brilliant effort to make a new civilization and to make it move in directions established by a newer historical view. It is this fact which gives special tone to the period and can in part be held responsible for the very special kind of cultural consequences that developed.[19]

The last two decades in America have been marked by a singularly anti-historical spirit among the leading figures of our intellectual life. This trend, of course, had existed as a sharp undercurrent during the previous era as part of the ever-present tension between myth and ideology. I have already indicated the beginnings of what were to be a ground swell of interest in and search for (even conscious creation, if that is possible) myth. T. S. Eliot's career can be seen, from one perspective, as a continual lyric battle raging within the poet himself between the mythic and the ideological, between the utopian vision and the historical. The "cunning passages, contrived corridors" of history that Eliot speaks of always presented for him dangerous traps from which man finally must escape. In *Four Quartets* it becomes clear to the poet that "right action is freedom from past and future also," a vision of man in relation to history that stands in effective contrast to the views of his contemporary, William Carlos Williams, cited previously.

In the realm of religion the historically-oriented Social Gospel no longer commands the allegiance of the major Protestant intellectual leaders. The existential eye sees no historic Christ and no Christian mission that can be accomplished within time. The ideology of the Social Gospel depended upon a specific role of Christ in history and a view of the nature of history that made possible the achievement within history of a Christian society. The existential temper sees in the mythic Christ a "concrete absolute" which provided the model for those who would have the "Courage to Be" but who realize that within the relativities of history it is not really possible for man to solve any important problem facing him.

19 It might be well to recall at this point that the two novels I discussed in the first section of this paper in effect mark the beginning and end of the period under discusion, Melville's novella at the start of the era and Faulkner's novel marking in some real sense the end of an era.

Many of our newer literary vogues—some of them brilliantly evocative of major moral dilemmas of our time to be sure—are deliberately wedded to the present moment alone. For the Beat Generation the past—and even the future—is an enemy, threatening man with a vicious traditionalism (sometimes called conformity) or a series of problems to which there is no solution except individual action. They return to an almost Thoreau-like ritual burning of the past, preferring the immediate sensation, the experience of the moment or the escape into timelessness offered by some oriental philosophies (or their versions of them) which are strictly a-historical. Our leading movements in painting, especially abstract expressionism and "pop" art, offer the most immediate kind of experience, more clearly divorced from any sense of history than any other movement in painting since the Renaissance.

The study of history as a discipline has again become major literature, frequently superbly written and compiled, but often based on an underlying assumption clearly taken from American existential theology and stated most effectively by one of our leading intellectuals who is himself the writer of much admired history:

> History is not a redeemer, promising to solve all human problems in time; nor is man capable of transcending the limitation of his being. Man generally is entangled in insoluble problems; history is a constant tragedy in which we are all involved, whose keynote is anxiety and frustration, not progress and fulfillment.[20]

It is a history, then, which escapes from ideology (in my sense) by returning to the mythic and dramatic. It specifically attacks the ideologies and the theories of history from which they came in the previous era. In its hostility to a Beard or a Turner it offers no new system of analysis, no new theory of the operation of the historical process. Rather, it disapproves of such theories and such ideologies. Once again, as in the middle of the nineteenth century, we return characteristically to the multivolume narrative historical work. In Arthur Schlesinger Jr. we discover our new Bancroft, ironically a pessimistic Bancroft. In Allan Nevins we find our own Parkman, albeit a surprisingly optimistic Parkman. And in Admiral Morison's brilliant and many-volume history of the Navy during the Second World War we have perhaps the greatest literary achievement by any historian in our century. But in these works we look in vain for

---

20 This is of course from Arthur Schlesinger Jr.'s famous *Partisan Review* essay "The Causes of the American Civil War: A Note on Historical Sentimentalism," written in 1949. The essay is most conveniently found in *The Causes of the American Civil War*, ed. E. C. Rozwenc (Boston, 1961). The passage I have quoted appears on pp. 189-90 in that text.

a vision of the past which will enable us to remake the present and the future. Here ideology is specifically rejected. Here we find a history which offers a reinforcement of current moral values and no effective challenge to the decision makers within the social order who *do* most frequently operate in terms of some view of history, some ideology. It is characteristic, in fact, of many American intellectuals these days to talk about how Americans have traditionally solved the problems that faced them—when they were in fact able to solve them at all—pragmatically and without reference to ideology. But the fact remains that there are many ways to solve a given problem and the choice of specific solution is frequently determined by a set of attitudes toward history which may be unarticulated but are within the consciousness. And if this paper has any validity at all, it should be clear that a retreat from ideology to the mythic use of the past has its special cultural consequences as well. Thus our own age retreats from history or derives intense excitement from what is often called "history" in its most brilliant mythic or theological forms (witness the enthusiastic response to the works of Toynbee and Niebuhr). The escape from history leads us to the world of myth. And yet, surprisingly, in terms of my definition of myth, the new mythic vision seems almost anything but utopian, seems to offer no happy goals for man or culture. We are left with a mythic past, an anxious present and an anti-utopian, Orwellian future.

What I have briefly attempted to sketch in roughest and most general terms were five major periods reflecting the relationships between history and myth as they were developed by American intellectuals responding to the circumstances of their own eras. In the first social order, intellectuals led the way in attempting to stabilize the tension between myth and history to protect the very special contract society they had organized and to enable it to fulfill its mission within history. In the eighteenth century, in the wake of the failure of the first position, the newer intellectual and social elite continued to dominate with its own special conservative philosophy of history, highly rationalized and secularized, removed from the power of the Christian myth. This myth, however, supported by a millennialist philosophy of history, continued to galvanize the sons of the Great Awakening who found themselves in intellectual and social battle with the sons of the Enlightenment. With the special conditions and problems of the early nineteenth century came an entirely new approach to the problem and American intellectuals became, through the use of history but with the repudiation of its rational powers, essentially the mythologists of America, the creators and revitalizers of a series of major myths which dominated the culture and determined its significantly utopian intellectual quality. In the last decade of the century a new intellectual order was born on the heels of a new social order created in part by the communications revolution, an order in which a special kind of historical awareness contributed a dynamic element and where once again the intellectuals, removed from seats of social or political power but frequently anxious to achieve such power or contribute to its effective use, brought to life for their own present a special new tension between the mythic and the historic, stressing the ideological significance of their work. Finally, in our own day history has become once again the enemy, useful only if it points up the mythic tragedy of our inability to solve our problems in any meaningful sense.

Of course there are still those conscious of history, although ironically it would seem that these days to have some view of the past which has clear-cut ideological consequences for the present and future is generally thought of as a special function of what is left of a radical tradition. But it is not unfair to see in the major intellectual trends of the years since World War II a fundamentally anti-historical view of the world. It is in fact a view which has been praised as marking the end of innocence or the end of ideology. But the cultural consequences of this triumph, so-called, over ideology, so-called, have yet to be assessed. In a world where leading intellectuals become committed to a view that human problems cannot really be solved, where the public ideology therefore too often goes unchallenged in our incredibly bipartisan age, where history flourishes most brilliantly in epic or mythic or theological forms, and yet where enormous problems do continue to confront us, there are grave dangers to the culture itself. But the fundamental tensions between the mythic and the ideological still remain, even though the balance may be tipped more to one side at the moment. Perhaps we are simply re-enacting the plot of our story as it was played out in the middle decades of the nineteenth century where once again great and frightening changes seemed too often more than man could handle. Perhaps there will yet be a reawakening, as there was in the 1890s, to the other real need and function of history in our kind of society. Perhaps there will even be another kind of social order.

Michael Frisch

There are relatively few journal articles that can be counted as lastingly significant thirty years and more after initial publication. And of these, surely even fewer seem still fresh and engaging, whatever their importance. Warren Susman's "History and the American Intellectual" is one of the rare ones. It is strikingly provocative read in the context of contemporary concerns and debates. These debates, it is true, have migrated a considerable distance from the terrain of intellectual history Susman surveyed with a simple but powerfully deployed conceptual apparatus. But his equipment was designed with portability in mind, and he seems to have anticipated some of the places to which it would need to be moved.

The first part of Susman's title suggests his scholarly focus—examining the notions of history embedded in the work of intellectuals over the course of American history. The second part suggests a far broader issue in culture and society to which the first is applied—the matter of how history, conceived as something usable, has been actually engaged and mobilized, and to what ends.

The first focus helped make Susman's article a staple of American studies and intellectual history syllabi since its first appearance in *American Quarterly,* and especially since its republication as the lead essay in the collection that is Susman's major legacy, *Culture as History* (New York: Pantheon Books, 1984).

But it is the second title phrase that accounts for the essay's power today. It seems to address recently hyperbolic debates about the problematic relation of historical scholarship to broader representations of history in American culture, and contentious claims on historical memory itself—which is to say, debates about uses and usability, among diverse users, of American history. These are hardly restricted to the realm of formal intellectual engagement Susman traced in his essay. As he noted himself in the 1984 collection's introduction to his republished

Warren I. Susman, "History and the American Intellectual: Uses of a Usable Past," originally appeared in *American Quarterly* 16, no. 2, pt. 2 (summer 1964), Copyright 1964, Trustees of the University of Pennsylvania.

essay, "History . . . is not just something to be left to the historians. In fact, in recent years the interest in history has grown while professional historians have felt increasingly left out. Some understanding of the role of history in American culture would help them to understand why." Because this paradox has only become more pronounced since 1984, and because explaining its "why" continues to prove vexatious, to put it mildly, a revisiting and recasting of Susman's question for the present may prove, in one of his favorite words, useful.

Modern students encountering this text through some online search engines could quickly produce a "hit" parade of the thinkers it examines, names that include and are largely limited to such figures as Anne Hutchinson, Roger Williams, Cotton Mather, Emerson, Thoreau, Bancroft, Prescott, Parkman, Turner, Beard, Becker, Henry and Brooks Adams, Eliot, Pound, Crane, William Carlos Williams, Toynbee, Niebuhr, Morison, Schlesinsger Jr., and Nevins. Given this pantheon, such students would have few initial reasons for not regarding the article as an American Studies chestnut from the classic era. That it is much more requires a brief review of the argument these intellectuals inhabit and illustrate without quite encompassing.

Susman begins with an ideal typology drawn from an historical anthropology itself as dated as the name list: he imagines two kinds of societies in world history, the traditional "status or community" societies on the one hand and more modern "contract" or associational societies on the other. The former, he posits, see the past in terms of myth, with myth understood as essentially utopian in function in that it explains the present and imagines a future without seeing any process connecting the two. In contract societies, however, explaining the past involves rationalizing the social order in terms of the processes that produce it and that project it towards the future. This is what Susman calls historical, and he calls the function of history, in contrast to myth, ideological in the somewhat special sense that it imagines a connection between past, present, and future, and seeks to make understanding the past a means for effecting particular visions of the future.

Susman hastens to specify that in reality both types are intertwined in modern life. Indeed, he is most interested in their real-life conflict, combination, and unstable relationship, especially under conditions of change "that frequently lead to the attempt to use each cultural force—myth and history—in ways that emulate the natural function of the other." Such combinations for Susman illustrate how the past comes to matter at different points and in different, contested ways, suggesting "a special interaction between myth and history, utopianism and ideology, that has significant cultural consequences for any society."

The body of Susman's essay maps this interaction through American intellectual history, presenting a capsulized atlas with five broad plates each illustrated by thinkers drawn from the list noted above: Puritan New England, harnessing utopianism to the instrumental historical mission of a self-conscious contract society; an eighteenth-century social order defended by secular rationalism and challenged by a millennial Great Awakening; the mid-nineteenth century when romantic narrative turned mythic and utopian; the new intellectual order of the 1890s that linked analytic history, ideology, and social change; and the postwar period in which history turned from ideology to myths anything but utopian in spirit—leaving us, at the time he wrote in the early 1960s, with "a mythic past, an anxious present, and an anti-utopian, Orwellian future." He closes his essay with a stark choice drawn from his historical examples: American intellectuals could retreat further from engaging intimidating changes, as he feels they had in the mid-nineteenth century, or, perhaps, "there will yet be a reawakening, as there was in the 1890s, to the other real need and function of history in our kind of society. Perhaps there will even be another kind of social order."

If not the latter, the 1960s certainly produced the former. Among the tests impressively passed by this framework is the test of how well it gauged historical forces at work in the world around it, which is to say how useful it proves for describing the history that those forces inscribed over the next several decades. This is manifestly true for historiography in the narrow sense, including the steady rise, the more recent plateau, and the contemporary retreat of an analytic new social history that never shrank from claiming to be ideological in the broad, catholic sense Susman gives the term. There is, of late, a similar lack of hesitation in the embrace of mythic function by those so critical of multiculturalism and social history. And more broadly based calls for a revival of narrative and synthesis in modern historical writing are also usefully illuminated by Susman's reminder that "almost always narrative history attempts a mythic function, and the more carefully analytical history . . . lends itself to ideological uses."

To the considerable extent these debates have moved dramatically beyond historiography and the work of intellectuals, becoming struggles over the appropriate meaning and representation of history in cultural life, they underscore Susman's central observation that "there is a special meeting ground between history and myth that frequently provides a key to the central tensions within a culture."

This key has a capacity to open up these tensions to view, ventilating constricted debates that have, in contemporary discourse, grown increasingly shrill, stale, and predictably one-dimensional with each new attack on a museum, each new textbook controversy, each jeremiad about political correctness, multiculturalism, or the easy-target excesses of narrow specialization and obscure theorizing in academic practice.

Susman's terms help us see these conflicts as something other than Manichean struggles between various enshrinements of historical integrity and what are imagined to be its antihistorical opposites. That these are postures adopted by both sides in any of these debates is a pretty good indication of the degree to which they mirror each other, sharing the assumption that the historical mode of thinking has a particular, fixed essence and purpose, however differently defined.

A revealing example of how unhelpful such assumptions can be is David Lowenthal's book, *Possessed by the Past: The Heritage Crusade and the Spoils of History* (New York: Free Press, 1996), which I happen to have been reviewing while rereading Susman's essay and preparing this comment. Lowenthal's contempt for what he calls heritage—the title manages to imply lunacy, religious fanaticism, and rape, quite an accomplishment in ten words—presumes its opposite, a pillaged, victimized historical vocation standing somewhere outside culture. This is history as a search for truth based on the goal, if not the achieved reality, of objectivity, history in inevitable tension with a host of appropriations, mostly crude and vulgar, that seek to make it an instrument for contemporary use.

Susman's approach couldn't be more different and more useful for avoiding the blind alley into which arguments such as this inevitably lead. By embracing tensions and contradictions, by reminding us of the inevitable implication of these tendencies to myth and history, utopianism and ideology, in the very nature of perceiving history in the present and in imagining the nature and possibilities of change, he places history and historians back where they belong—as part of a broad history-making continuum linking intellectuals and ordinary citizens in the struggle to make sense of their lives, communities, and the world around them. This is a continuum on which one way or the other, to think about the past is to think about the present and future, and vice versa. The choice is not whether to do this, but rather how, and to what ends. In these terms, Susman's challenge is as pertinent and profound now as it was in 1964, and probably more so.

The Cult of True Womanhood:
1820–1860

THE NINETEENTH-CENTURY AMERICAN MAN WAS A BUSY BUILDER OF BRIDGES and railroads, at work long hours in a materialistic society. The religious values of his forebears were neglected in practice if not in intent, and he occasionally felt some guilt that he had turned this new land, this temple of the chosen people, into one vast countinghouse. But he could salve his conscience by reflecting that he had left behind a hostage, not only to fortune, but to all the values which he held so dear and treated so lightly. Woman, in the cult of True Womanhood[1] presented by the women's magazines, gift annuals and religious literature of the nineteenth century, was the hostage in the home.[2] In a society where values changed fre-

---

[1] Authors who addressed themselves to the subject of women in the mid-nineteenth century used this phrase as frequently as writers on religion mentioned God. Neither group felt it necessary to define their favorite terms; they simply assumed—with some justification—that readers would intuitively understand exactly what they meant. Frequently what people of one era take for granted is most striking and revealing to the student from another. In a sense this analysis of the ideal woman of the mid-nineteenth century is an examination of what writers of that period actually meant when they used so confidently the vague phrase True Womanhood.

[2] The conclusions reached in this article are based on a survey of almost all of the women's magazines published for more than three years during the period 1820-60 and a sampling of those published for less than three years; all the gift books cited in Ralph Thompson, *American Literary Annuals and Gift Books, 1825-1865* (New York, 1936) deposited in the Library of Congress, the New York Public Library, the New-York Historical Society, Columbia University Special Collections, Library of the City College of the University of New York, Pennsylvania Historical Society, Massachusetts Historical Society, Boston Public Library, Fruitlands Museum Library, the Smithsonian Institution and the Wisconsin Historical Society; hundreds of religious tracts and sermons in the American Unitarian Society and the Galatea Collection of the Boston Public Library; and the large collection of nineteenth-century cookbooks in the New York Public Library and the Academy of Medicine of New York. Corroborative evidence not cited in this article was found in women's diaries, memoirs, autobiographies and personal papers, as well as in all the novels by women which sold over 75,000 copies during this period, as cited in Frank Luther Mott, *Golden Multitudes: The Story of Best Sellers in the United States* (New York, 1947) and H. R. Brown, *The Sentimental Novel in America, 1789-1860* (Durham, N. C., 1940). This latter information also indicated the effect of the cult of True Womanhood on those most directly concerned.

quently, where fortunes rose and fell with frightening rapidity, where social and economic mobility provided instability as well as hope, one thing at least remained the same—a true woman was a true woman, wherever she was found. If anyone, male or female, dared to tamper with the complex of virtues which made up True Womanhood, he was damned immediately as an enemy of God, of civilization and of the Republic. It was a fearful obligation, a solemn responsibility, which the nineteenth-century American woman had—to uphold the pillars of the temple with her frail white hand.

The attributes of True Womanhood, by which a woman judged herself and was judged by her husband, her neighbors and society could be divided into four cardinal virtues—piety, purity, submissiveness and domesticity. Put them all together and they spelled mother, daughter, sister, wife—woman. Without them, no matter whether there was fame, achievement or wealth, all was ashes. With them she was promised happiness and power.

Religion or piety was the core of woman's virtue, the source of her strength. Young men looking for a mate were cautioned to search first for piety, for if that were there, all else would follow.[3] Religion belonged to woman by divine right, a gift of God and nature. This "peculiar susceptibility" to religion was given her for a reason: "the vestal flame of piety, lighted up by Heaven in the breast of woman" would throw its beams into the naughty world of men.[4] So far would its candle power reach that the "Universe might be Enlightened, Improved, and Harmonized by WOMAN!!"[5] She would be another, better Eve, working in cooperation with the Redeemer, bringing the world back "from its revolt and sin."[6] The world would be reclaimed for God through her suffering, for "God increased the cares and sorrows of woman, that she might be sooner constrained to accept the terms of salvation."[7] A popular poem by Mrs. Frances Osgood, "The Triumph of the Spiritual Over the Sensual" ex-

[3] As in "The Bachelor's Dream," in *The Lady's Gift: Souvenir for All Seasons* (Nashua, N. H., 1849), p. 37.

[4] *The Young Ladies' Class Book: A Selection of Lessons for Reading in Prose and Verse*, ed. Ebenezer Bailey, Principal of Young Ladies' High School, Boston (Boston, 1831), p. 168.

[5] A Lady of Philadelphia, *The World Enlightened, Improved, and Harmonized by WOMAN! ! !* A lecture, delivered in the City of New York, before the Young Ladies' Society for Mutual Improvement, on the following question, proposed by the society, with the offer of $100 for the best lecture that should be read before them on the subject proposed;—What is the power and influence of woman in moulding the manners, morals and habits of civil society? (Philadelphia, 1840), p. 1.

[6] *The Young Lady's Book: A Manual of Elegant Recreations, Exercises, and Pursuits* (Boston, 1830), p. 29.

[7] *Woman As She Was, Is, and Should Be* (New York, 1849), p. 206.

pressed just this sentiment, woman's purifying passionless love bringing an erring man back to Christ.[8]

Dr. Charles Meigs, explaining to a graduating class of medical students why women were naturally religious, said that "hers is a pious mind. Her confiding nature leads her more readily than men to accept the proffered grace of the Gospel." [9] Caleb Atwater, Esq., writing in *The Ladies' Repository,* saw the hand of the Lord in female piety: "Religion is exactly what a woman needs, for it gives her that dignity that best suits her dependence."[10] And Mrs. John Sandford, who had no very high opinion of her sex, agreed thoroughly: "Religion is just what woman needs. Without it she is ever restless or unhappy. . . ."[11] Mrs. Sandford and the others did not speak only of that restlessness of the human heart, which St. Augustine notes, that can only find its peace in God. They spoke rather of religion as a kind of tranquilizer for the many undefined longings which swept even the most pious young girl, and about which it was better to pray than to think.

One reason religion was valued was that it did not take a woman away from her "proper sphere," her home. Unlike participation in other societies or movements, church work would not make her less domestic or submissive, less a True Woman. In religious vineyards, said the *Young Ladies' Literary and Missionary Report,* "you may labor without the apprehension of detracting from the charms of feminine delicacy." Mrs. S. L. Dagg, writing from her chapter of the Society in Tuscaloosa, Alabama, was equally reassuring: "As no sensible woman will suffer her intellectual pursuits to clash with her domestic duties" she should concentrate on religious work "which promotes these very duties."[12]

The women's seminaries aimed at aiding women to be religious, as well as accomplished. Mt. Holyoke's catalogue promised to make female education "a handmaid to the Gospel and an efficient auxiliary in the great task of renovating the world."[13] The Young Ladies' Seminary at Bordentown, New Jersey, declared its most important function to be "the form-

---

8 "The Triumph of the Spiritual Over the Sensual: An Allegory," in *Ladies' Companion: A Monthly Magazine Embracing Every Department of Literature, Embellished With Original Engravings and Music,* XVII (New York) (1842), 67.

9 *Lecture on Some of the Distinctive Characteristics of the Female,* delivered before the class of the Jefferson Medical College, Jan. 1847 (Philadelphia, 1847), p. 13.

10 "Female Education," *Ladies' Repository and Gatherings of the West: A Monthly Periodical Devoted to Literature and Religion,* I (Cincinnati), 12.

11 *Woman, in Her Social and Domestic Character* (Boston, 1842), pp. 41-42.

12 *Second Annual Report of the Young Ladies' Literary and Missionary Association of the Philadelphia Collegiate Institution* (Philadelphia, 1840), pp. 20, 26.

13 *Mt. Holyoke Female Seminary: Female Education. Tendencies of the Principles Embraced, and the System Adopted in the Mt. Holyoke Female Seminary* (Boston, 1839), p. 3.

ing of a sound and virtuous character."[14] In Keene, New Hampshire, the Seminary tried to instill a "consistent and useful character" in its students, to enable them in this life to be "a good friend, wife and mother" but more important, to qualify them for "the enjoyment of Celestial Happiness in the life to come."[15] And Joseph M' D. Mathews, Principal of Oakland Female Seminary in Hillsborough, Ohio, believed that "female education should be preeminently religious."[16]

If religion was so vital to a woman, irreligion was almost too awful to contemplate. Women were warned not to let their literary or intellectual pursuits take them away from God. Sarah Josepha Hale spoke darkly of those who, like Margaret Fuller, threw away the "One True Book" for others, open to error. Mrs. Hale used the unfortunate Miss Fuller as fateful proof that "the greater the intellectual force, the greater and more fatal the errors into which women fall who wander from the Rock of Salvation, Christ the Saviour. . . ."[17]

One gentleman, writing on "Female Irreligion" reminded his readers that "Man may make himself a brute, and does so very often, but can woman brutify herself to his level—the lowest level of human nature— without exerting special wonder?" Fanny Wright, because she was godless, "was no woman, mother though she be." A few years ago, he recalls, such women would have been whipped. In any case, "woman never looks lovelier than in her reverence for religion" and, conversely, "female irreligion is the most revolting feature in human character."[18]

Purity was as essential as piety to a young woman, its absence as unnatural and unfeminine. Without it she was, in fact, no woman at all, but a member of some lower order. A "fallen woman" was a "fallen angel," unworthy of the celestial company of her sex. To contemplate the loss of purity brought tears; to be guilty of such a crime, in the women's magazines at least, brought madness or death. Even the language of the flowers had bitter words for it: a dried white rose symbolized "Death Preferable to Loss of Innocence."[19] The marriage night was the single great event of a woman's life, when she bestowed her greatest treasure upon her hus-

[14] *Prospectus of the Young Ladies' Seminary at Bordentown, New Jersey* (Bordentown, 1836), p. 7.

[15] *Catalogue of the Young Ladies' Seminary in Keene, New Hampshire* (n.p., 1832), p. 20.

[16] "Report to the College of Teachers, Cincinnati, October, 1840" in *Ladies' Repository*, I (1841), 50.

[17] *Woman's Record: or Sketches of All Distinguished Women from 'The Beginning' Till A. D. 1850* (New York, 1853), pp. 665, 669.

[18] "Female Irreligion," *Ladies' Companion*, XIII (May-Oct. 1840), 111.

[19] *The Lady's Book of Flowers and Poetry*, ed. Lucy Hooper (New York, 1842), has a "Floral Dictionary" giving the symbolic meaning of floral tributes.

band, and from that time on was completely dependent upon him, an empty vessel,[20] without legal or emotional existence of her own.[21]

Therefore all True Women were urged, in the strongest possible terms, to maintain their virtue, although men, being by nature more sensual than they, would try to assault it. Thomas Branagan admitted in *The Excellency of the Female Character Vindicated* that his sex would sin and sin again, they could not help it, but woman, stronger and purer, must not give in and let man "take liberties incompatible with her delicacy." "If you do," Branagan addressed his gentle reader, "You will be left in silent sadness to bewail your credulity, imbecility, duplicity, and premature prostitution."[22]

Mrs. Eliza Farrar, in *The Young Lady's Friend*, gave practical logistics to avoid trouble: "Sit not with another in a place that is too narrow; read not out of the same book; let not your eagerness to see anything induce you to place your head close to another person's."[23]

If such good advice was ignored the consequences were terrible and inexorable. In *Girlhood and Womanhood: Or Sketches of My Schoolmates*, by Mrs. A. J. Graves (a kind of mid-nineteenth-century *The Group*), the bad ends of a boarding school class of girls are scrupulously recorded. The worst end of all is reserved for "Amelia Dorrington: The Lost One." Amelia died in the almshouse "the wretched victim of depravity and intemperance" and all because her mother had let her be "high-spirited not prudent." These girlish high spirits had been misinterpreted by a young man, with disastrous results. Amelia's "thoughtless levity" was "followed by a total loss of virtuous principle" and Mrs. Graves editorializes that "the coldest reserve is more admirable in a woman a man wishes to make his wife, than the least approach to undue familiarity."[24]

A popular and often-reprinted story by Fanny Forester told the sad tale of "Lucy Dutton." Lucy "with the seal of innocence upon her heart, and a rose-leaf on her cheek" came out of her vine-covered cottage and ran

20 See, for example, Nathaniel Hawthorne, *The Blithedale Romance* (Boston, 1852), p. 71, in which Zenobia says: "How can she be happy, after discovering that fate has assigned her but one single event, which she must contrive to make the substance of her whole life? A man has his choice of innumerable events."

21 Mary R. Beard, *Woman As Force in History* (New York, 1946) makes this point at some length. According to common law, a woman had no legal existence once she was married and therefore could not manage property, sue in court, etc. In the 1840s and 1850s laws were passed in several states to remedy this condition.

22 *Excellency of the Female Character Vindicated: Being an Investigation Relative to the Cause and Effects on the Encroachments of Men Upon the Rights of Women, and the Too Frequent Degradation and Consequent Misfortunes of The Fair Sex* (New York, 1807), pp. 277, 278.

23 By a Lady (Eliza Ware Rotch Farrar), *The Young Lady's Friend* (Boston, 1837), p. 293.

24 *Girlhood and Womanhood: or, Sketches of My Schoolmates* (Boston, 1844), p. 140.

into a city slicker. "And Lucy was beautiful and trusting, and thoughtless: and he was gay, selfish and profligate. Needs the story to be told? . . . Nay, censor, Lucy was a child—consider how young, how very untaught—oh! her innocence was no match for the sophistry of a gay, city youth! Spring came and shame was stamped upon the cottage at the foot of the hill." The baby died; Lucy went mad at the funeral and finally died herself. "Poor, poor Lucy Dutton! The grave is a blessed couch and pillow to the wretched. Rest thee there, poor Lucy!"[25] The frequency with which derangement follows loss of virtue suggests the exquisite sensibility of woman, and the possibility that, in the women's magazines at least, her intellect was geared to her hymen, not her brain.

If, however, a woman managed to withstand man's assaults on her virtue, she demonstrated her superiority and her power over him. Eliza Farnham, trying to prove this female superiority, concluded smugly that "the purity of women is the everlasting barrier against which the tides of man's sensual nature surge."[26]

A story in *The Lady's Amaranth* illustrates this dominance. It is set, improbably, in Sicily, where two lovers, Bianca and Tebaldo, have been separated because her family insisted she marry a rich old man. By some strange circumstance the two are in a shipwreck and cast on a desert island, the only survivors. Even here, however, the rigid standards of True Womanhood prevail. Tebaldo unfortunately forgets himself slightly, so that Bianca must warn him: "We may not indeed gratify our fondness by caresses, but it is still something to bestow our kindest language, and looks and prayers, and all lawful and honest attentions on each other." Something, perhaps, but not enough, and Bianca must further remonstrate: "It is true that another man is my husband, but you are my guardian angel." When even that does not work she says in a voice of sweet reason, passive and proper to the end, that she wishes he wouldn't but "still, if you insist, I will become what you wish; but I beseech you to consider, ere that decision, that debasement which I must suffer in your esteem." This appeal to his own double standards holds the beast in him at bay. They are rescued, discover that the old husband is dead, and after "mourning a decent season" Bianca finally gives in, legally.[27]

Men could be counted on to be grateful when women thus saved them from themselves. William Alcott, guiding young men in their relations with the opposite sex, told them that "Nothing is better calculated to

---

[25] Emily Chubbuck, *Alderbrook* (Boston, 1847), 2nd. ed., II, 121, 127.
[26] *Woman and Her Era* (New York, 1864), p. 95.
[27] "The Two Lovers of Sicily," *The Lady's Amaranth: A Journal of Tales, Essays, Excerpts—Historical and Biographical Sketches, Poetry and Literature in General* (Philadelphia), II (Jan. 1839), 17.

preserve a young man from contamination of low pleasures and pursuits than frequent intercourse with the more refined and virtuous of the other sex." And he added, one assumes in equal innocence, that youths should "observe and learn to admire, that purity and ignorance of evil which is the characteristic of well-educated young ladies, and which, when we are near them, raises us above those sordid and sensual considerations which hold such sway over men in their intercourse with each other."[28]

The Rev. Jonathan F. Stearns was also impressed by female chastity in the face of male passion, and warned woman never to compromise the source of her power: "Let her lay aside delicacy, and her influence over our sex is gone."[29]

Women themselves accepted, with pride but suitable modesty, this priceless virtue. *The Ladies' Wreath,* in "Woman the Creature of God and the Manufacturer of Society" saw purity as her greatest gift and chief means of discharging her duty to save the world: "Purity is the highest beauty—the true pole-star which is to guide humanity aright in its long, varied, and perilous voyage."[30]

Sometimes, however, a woman did not see the dangers to her treasure. In that case, they must be pointed out to her, usually by a male. In the nineteenth century any form of social change was tantamount to an attack on woman's virtue, if only it was correctly understood. For example, dress reform seemed innocuous enough and the bloomers worn by the lady of that name and her followers were certainly modest attire. Such was the reasoning only of the ignorant. In another issue of *The Ladies' Wreath* a young lady is represented in dialogue with her "Professor." The girl expresses admiration for the bloomer costume—it gives freedom of motion, is healthful and attractive. The "Professor" sets her straight. Trousers, he explains, are "only one of the many manifestations of that wild spirit of socialism and agrarian radicalism which is at present so rife in our land." The young lady recants immediately: "If this dress has any connexion with Fourierism or Socialism, or fanaticism in any shape whatever, I have no disposition to wear it at all . . . no true woman would so far compromise her delicacy as to espouse, however unwittingly, such a cause."[31]

America could boast that her daughters were particularly innocent. In a poem on "The American Girl" the author wrote proudly:

28 *The Young Man's Guide* (Boston, 1833), pp. 229, 231.

29 *Female Influence: and the True Christian Mode of Its Exercise; a Discourse Delivered in the First Presbyterian Church in Newburyport, July 30, 1837* (Newburyport, 1837), p. 18.

30 W. Tolles, "Woman The Creature of God and the Manufacturer of Society," *Ladies' Wreath* (New York), III (1852), 205.

31 Prof. William M. Heim, "The Bloomer Dress," *Ladies' Wreath,* III (1852), 247.

Her eye of light is the diamond bright,
Her innocence the pearl,
And these are ever the bridal gems
That are worn by the American girl.[32]

Lydia Maria Child, giving advice to mothers, aimed at preserving that spirit of innocence. She regretted that "want of confidence between mothers and daughters on delicate subjects" and suggested a woman tell her daughter a few facts when she reached the age of twelve to "set her mind at rest." Then Mrs. Child confidently hoped that a young lady's "instinctive modesty" would "prevent her from dwelling on the information until she was called upon to use it."[33] In the same vein, a book of advice to the newly-married was titled *Whisper to a Bride*.[34] As far as intimate information was concerned, there was no need to whisper, since the book contained none at all.

A masculine summary of this virtue was expressed in a poem "Female Charms":

I would have her as pure as the snow on the mount—
    As true as the smile that to infamy's given—
As pure as the wave of the crystalline fount,
    Yet as warm in the heart as the sunlight of heaven.
With a mind cultivated, not boastingly wise,
    I could gaze on such beauty, with exquisite bliss;
With her heart on her lips and her soul in her eyes—
    What more could I wish in dear woman than this.[35]

Man might, in fact, ask no more than this in woman, but she was beginning to ask more of herself, and in the asking was threatening the third powerful and necessary virtue, submission. Purity, considered as a moral imperative, set up a dilemma which was hard to resolve. Woman must preserve her virtue until marriage and marriage was necessary for her happiness. Yet marriage was, literally, an end to innocence. She was told not to question this dilemma, but simply to accept it.

Submission was perhaps the most feminine virtue expected of women. Men were supposed to be religious, although they rarely had time for it,

[32] *The Young Lady's Offering: or Gems of Prose and Poetry* (Boston, 1853), p. 283. The American girl, whose innocence was often connected with ignorance, was the spiritual ancestress of the Henry James heroine. Daisy Miller, like Lucy Dutton, saw innocence lead to tragedy.

[33] *The Mother's Book* (Boston, 1831), pp. 151, 152.

[34] Mrs. L. H. Sigourney, *Whisper to a Bride* (Hartford, 1851), in which Mrs. Sigourney's approach is summed up in this quotation: "Home! Blessed bride, thou art about to enter this sanctuary, and to become a priestess at its altar!," p. 44.

[35] S. R. R., "Female Charms," *Godey's Magazine and Lady's Book* (Philadelphia), XXXIII (1846), 52.

and supposed to be pure, although it came awfully hard to them, but men were the movers, the doers, the actors. Women were the passive, submissive responders. The order of dialogue was, of course, fixed in Heaven. Man was "woman's superior by God's appointment, if not in intellectual dowry, at least by official decree." Therefore, as Charles Elliott argued in *The Ladies' Repository*, she should submit to him "for the sake of good order at least."[36] In *The Ladies Companion* a young wife was quoted approvingly as saying that she did not think woman should "feel and act for herself" because "When, next to God, her husband is not the tribunal to which her heart and intellect appeals—the golden bowl of affection is broken."[37] Women were warned that if they tampered with this quality they tampered with the order of the Universe.

The Young Lady's Book summarized the necessity of the passive virtues in its readers' lives: "It is, however, certain, that in whatever situation of life a woman is placed from her cradle to her grave, a spirit of obedience and submission, pliability of temper, and humility of mind, are required from her."[38]

Woman understood her position if she was the right kind of woman, a true woman. "She feels herself weak and timid. She needs a protector," declared George Burnap, in his lectures on *The Sphere and Duties of Woman*. "She is in a measure dependent. She asks for wisdom, constancy, firmness, perseverance, and she is willing to repay it all by the surrender of the full treasure of her affections. Woman despises in man every thing like herself except a tender heart. It is enough that she is effeminate and weak; she does not want another like herself."[39] Or put even more strongly by Mrs. Sandford: "A really sensible woman feels her dependence. She does what she can, but she is conscious of inferiority, and therefore grateful for support."[40]

Mrs. Sigourney, however, assured young ladies that although they were separate, they were equal. This difference of the sexes did not imply inferiority, for it was part of that same order of Nature established by Him "who bids the oak brave the fury of the tempest, and the alpine flower lean its cheek on the bosom of eternal snows."[41] Dr. Meigs had a different analogy to make the same point, contrasting the anatomy of the Apollo of the Belvedere (illustrating the male principle) with the Venus de Medici (illustrating the female principle). "Woman," said the physician,

36 Charles Elliott, "Arguing With Females," *Ladies' Repository*, I (1841), 25.
37 *Ladies' Companion*, VIII (Jan. 1838), 147.
38 *The Young Lady's Book* (New York, 1830), American edition, p. 28. (This is a different book than the one of the same title and date of publication cited in note 6.)
39 *Sphere and Duties of Woman* (5th ed., Baltimore, 1854), p. 47.
40 *Woman*, p. 15.
41 *Letters to Young Ladies* (Hartford, 1835), p. 179.

with a kind of clinical gallantry, "has a head almost too small for intellect but just big enough for love."[42]

This love itself was to be passive and responsive. "Love, in the heart of a woman," wrote Mrs. Farrar, "should partake largely of the nature of gratitude. She should love, because she is already loved by one deserving her regard."[43]

Woman was to work in silence, unseen, like Wordsworth's Lucy. Yet, "working like nature, in secret" her love goes forth to the world "to regulate its pulsation, and send forth from its heart, in pure and temperate flow, the life-giving current."[44] She was to work only for pure affection, without thought of money or ambition. A poem, "Woman and Fame," by Felicia Hemans, widely quoted in many of the gift books, concludes with a spirited renunciation of the gift of fame:

> Away! to me, a woman, bring
> Sweet flowers from affection's spring.[45]

"True feminine genius," said Grace Greenwood (Sara Jane Clarke) "is ever timid, doubtful, and clingingly dependent; a perpetual childhood." And she advised literary ladies in an essay on "The Intellectual Woman" —"Don't trample on the flowers while longing for the stars."[46] A wife who submerged her own talents to work for her husband was extolled as an example of a true woman. In *Women of Worth: A Book for Girls,* Mrs. Ann Flaxman, an artist of promise herself, was praised because she "devoted herself to sustain her husband's genius and aid him in his arduous career."[47]

Caroline Gilman's advice to the bride aimed at establishing this proper order from the beginning of a marriage: "Oh, young and lovely bride, watch well the first moments when your will conflicts with his to whom God and society have given the control. Reverence his *wishes* even when you do not his *opinions*."[48]

Mrs. Gilman's perfect wife in *Recollections of a Southern Matron* realizes that "the three golden threads with which domestic happiness is

---

[42] *Lecture,* p. 17.

[43] *The Young Lady's Friend,* p. 313.

[44] Maria J. McIntosh, *Woman in America: Her Work and Her Reward* (New York, 1850), p. 25.

[45] *Poems and a Memoir of the Life of Mrs. Felicia Hemans* (London, 1860), p. 16.

[46] Letter "To an Unrecognized Poetess, June, 1846" (Sara Jane Clarke), *Greenwood Leaves* (2nd ed.; Boston, 1850), p. 311.

[47] "The Sculptor's Assistant: Ann Flaxman," in *Women of Worth: A Book for Girls* (New York, 1860), p. 263.

[48] Mrs. Clarissa Packard (Mrs. Caroline Howard Gilman), *Recollections of a Housekeeper* (New York, 1834), p. 122.

woven" are "to repress a harsh answer, to confess a fault, and to stop (right or wrong) in the midst of self-defense, in gentle submission." Woman could do this, hard though it was, because in her heart she knew she was right and so could afford to be forgiving, even a trifle condescending. "Men are not unreasonable," averred Mrs. Gilman. "Their difficulties lie in not understanding the moral and physical nature of our sex. They often wound through ignorance, and are surprised at having offended." Wives were advised to do their best to reform men, but if they couldn't, to give up gracefully. "If any habit of his annoyed me, I spoke of it once or twice, calmly, then bore it quietly."[49]

A wife should occupy herself "only with domestic affairs—wait till your husband confides to you those of a high importance—and do not give your advice until he asks for it," advised the *Lady's Token*. At all times she should behave in a manner becoming a woman, who had "no arms other than gentleness." Thus "if he is abusive, never retort."[50] *A Young Lady's Guide to the Harmonious Development of a Christian Character* suggested that females should "become as little children" and "avoid a controversial spirit."[51] *The Mother's Assistant and Young Lady's Friend* listed "Always Conciliate" as its first commandment in "Rules for Conjugal and Domestic Happiness." Small wonder that these same rules ended with the succinct maxim: "Do not expect too much."[52]

As mother, as well as wife, woman was required to submit to fortune. In *Letters to Mothers* Mrs. Sigourney sighed: "To bear the evils and sorrows which may be appointed us, with a patient mind, should be the continual effort of our sex. . . . It seems, indeed, to be expected of us; since the passive and enduring virtues are more immediately within our province." Of these trials "the hardest was to bear the loss of children with submission" but the indomitable Mrs. Sigourney found strength to murmur to the bereaved mother: "The Lord loveth a cheerful giver."[53] *The Ladies' Parlor Companion* agreed thoroughly in "A Submissive Mother," in which a mother who had already buried two children and was nursing a dying baby saw her sole remaining child "probably scalded to death. Handing over the infant to die in the arms of a friend,

49 *Recollections of a Southern Matron* (New York, 1838), pp. 256, 257.

50 *The Lady's Token: or Gift of Friendship*, ed. Colesworth Pinckney (Nashua, N. H., 1848), p. 119.

51 Harvey Newcomb, *Young Lady's Guide to the Harmonious Development of Christian Character* (Boston, 1846), p. 10.

52 "Rules for Conjugal and Domestic Happiness," *Mother's Assistant and Young Lady's Friend*, III (Boston), (April 1843), 115.

53 *Letters to Mothers* (Hartford, 1838), p. 199. In the diaries and letters of women who lived during this period the death of a child seemed consistently to be the hardest thing for them to bear and to occasion more anguish and rebellion, as well as eventual submission, than any other event in their lives.

she bowed in sweet submission to the double stroke." But the child "through the goodness of God survived, and the mother learned to say 'Thy will be done.' " [54]

Woman then, in all her roles, accepted submission as her lot. It was a lot she had not chosen or deserved. As *Godey's* said, "the lesson of submission is forced upon woman." Without comment or criticism the writer affirms that "To suffer and to be silent under suffering seems the great command she has to obey." [55] George Burnap referred to a woman's life as "a series of suppressed emotions." [56] She was, as Emerson said, "more vulnerable, more infirm, more mortal than man." [57] The death of a beautiful woman, cherished in fiction, represented woman as the innocent victim, suffering without sin, too pure and good for this world but too weak and passive to resist its evil forces. [58] The best refuge for such a delicate creature was the warmth and safety of her home.

The true woman's place was unquestionably by her own fireside—as daughter, sister, but most of all as wife and mother. Therefore domesticity was among the virtues most prized by the women's magazines. "As society is constituted," wrote Mrs. S. E. Farley, on the "Domestic and Social Claims on Woman," "the true dignity and beauty of the female character seem to consist in a right understanding and faithful and cheerful performance of social and family duties." [59] Sacred Scripture re-enforced social pressure: "St. Paul knew what was best for women when he advised them to be domestic," said Mrs. Sandford. "There is composure at home; there is something sedative in the duties which home involves. It affords security not only from the world, but from delusions and errors of every kind." [60]

From her home woman performed her great task of bringing men back to God. *The Young Ladies' Class Book* was sure that "the domestic fireside is the great guardian of society against the excesses of human passions." [61] *The Lady at Home* expressed its convictions in its very title and concluded that "even if we cannot reform the world in a moment,

---

[54] "A Submissive Mother," *The Ladies' Parlor Companion: A Collection of Scattered Fragments and Literary Gems* (New York, 1852), p. 358.

[55] "Woman," *Godey's Lady's Book*, II (Aug. 1831), 110.

[56] *Sphere and Duties of Woman*, p. 172.

[57] Ralph Waldo Emerson, "Woman," *Complete Writings of Ralph Waldo Emerson* (New York, 1875), p. 1180.

[58] As in Donald Fraser, *The Mental Flower Garden* (New York, 1857). Perhaps the most famous exponent of this theory is Edgar Allan Poe who affirms in "The Philosophy of Composition" that "the death of a beautiful woman is unquestionably the most poetical topic in the world. . . ."

[59] "Domestic and Social Claims on Woman," *Mother's Magazine*, VI (1846), 21.

[60] *Woman*, p. 173.

[61] *The Young Ladies' Class Book*, p. 166.

we can begin the work by reforming ourselves and our households—It is woman's mission. Let her not look away from her own little family circle for the means of producing moral and social reforms, but begin at home." [62]

Home was supposed to be a cheerful place, so that brothers, husbands and sons would not go elsewhere in search of a good time. Woman was expected to dispense comfort and cheer. In writing the biography of Margaret Mercer (every inch a true woman) her biographer (male) notes: "She never forgot that it is the peculiar province of woman to minister to the comfort, and promote the happiness, first, of those most nearly allied to her, and then of those, who by the Providence of God are placed in a state of dependence upon her." [63] Many other essays in the women's journals showed woman as comforter: "Woman, Man's Best Friend," "Woman, the Greatest Social Benefit," "Woman, A Being to Come Home To," "The Wife: Source of Comfort and the Spring of Joy." [64]

One of the most important functions of woman as comforter was her role as nurse. Her own health was probably, although regrettably, delicate.[65] Many homes had "little sufferers," those pale children who wasted away to saintly deaths. And there were enough other illnesses of youth and age, major and minor, to give the nineteenth-century American woman nursing experience. The sickroom called for the exercise of her higher qualities of patience, mercy and gentleness as well as for her housewifely arts. She could thus fulfill her dual feminine function— beauty and usefulness.

The cookbooks of the period offer formulas for gout cordials, ointment for sore nipples, hiccough and cough remedies, opening pills and re-

[62] T. S. Arthur, *The Lady at Home: or, Leaves from the Every-Day Book of an American Woman* (Philadelphia, 1847), pp. 177, 178.

[63] Caspar Morris, *Margaret Mercer* (Boston, 1840), quoted in *Woman's Record*, p. 425.

[64] These particular titles come from: *The Young Ladies' Oasis: or Gems of Prose and Poetry*, ed. N. L. Ferguson (Lowell, 1851), pp. 14, 16; *The Genteel School Reader* (Philadelphia, 1849), p. 271; and *Magnolia*, I (1842), 4. A popular poem in book form, published in England, expressed very fully this concept of woman as comforter: Coventry Patmore, *The Angel in the Home* (Boston, 1856 and 1857). Patmore expressed his devotion to True Womanhood in such lines as:
> The gentle wife, who decks his board
> And makes his day to have no night,
> Whose wishes wait upon her Lord,
> Who finds her own in his delight. (p. 94)

[65] The women's magazines carried on a crusade against tight lacing and regretted, rather than encouraged, the prevalent ill health of the American woman. See, for example, *An American Mother, Hints and Sketches* (New York, 1839), pp. 28 ff. for an essay on the need for a healthy mind in a healthy body in order to better be a good example for children.

freshing drinks for fever, along with recipes for pound cake, jumbles, stewed calves head and currant wine.[66] *The Ladies' New Book of Cookery* believed that "food prepared by the kind hand of a wife, mother, sister, friend" tasted better and had a "restorative power which money cannot purchase." [67]

A chapter of *The Young Lady's Friend* was devoted to woman's privilege as "ministering spirit at the couch of the sick." Mrs. Farrar advised a soft voice, gentle and clean hands, and a cheerful smile. She also cautioned against an excess of female delicacy. That was all right for a young lady in the parlor, but not for bedside manners. Leeches, for example, were to be regarded as "a curious piece of mechanism . . . their ornamental stripes should recommend them even to the eye, and their valuable services to our feelings." And she went on calmly to discuss their use. Nor were women to shrink from medical terminology, since "If you cultivate right views of the wonderful structure of the body, you will be as willing to speak to a physician of the bowels as the brains of your patient." [68]

Nursing the sick, particularly sick males, not only made a woman feel useful and accomplished, but increased her influence. In a piece of heavy-handed humor in *Godey's* a man confessed that some women were only happy when their husbands were ailing that they might have the joy of nursing him to recovery "thus gratifying their medical vanity and their love of power by making him more dependent upon them." [69] In a similar vein a husband sometimes suspected his wife "almost wishes me dead —for the pleasure of being utterly inconsolable." [70]

In the home women were not only the highest adornment of civilization, but they were supposed to keep busy at morally uplifting tasks. Fortunately most of housework, if looked at in true womanly fashion, could be regarded as uplifting. Mrs. Sigourney extolled its virtues: "The science of housekeeping affords exercise for the judgment and energy, ready recollection, and patient self-possession, that are the characteristics

[66] The best single collection of nineteenth-century cookbooks is in the Academy of Medicine of New York Library, although some of the most interesting cures were in hand-written cookbooks found among the papers of women who lived during the period.

[67] Sarah Josepha Hale, *The Ladies' New Book of Cookery: A Practical System for Private Families in Town and Country* (5th ed.; New York, 1852), p. 409. Similar evidence on the importance of nursing skills to every female is found in such books of advice as William A. Alcott, *The Young Housekeeper* (Boston, 1838), in which, along with a plea for apples and cold baths, Alcott says "Every female should be trained to the angelic art of managing properly the sick," p. 47.

[68] *The Young Lady's Friend*, pp. 75-77, 79.

[69] "A Tender Wife," *Godey's*, II (July 1831), 28.

[70] "MY WIFE! A Whisper," *Godey's*, II (Oct. 1831), 231.

of a superior mind." [71] According to Mrs. Farrar, making beds was good exercise, the repetitiveness of routine tasks inculcated patience and perseverance, and proper management of the home was a surprisingly complex art: "There is more to be learned about pouring out tea and coffee, than most young ladies are willing to believe."[72] Godey's went so far as to suggest coyly, in "Learning vs. Housewifery" that the two were complementary, not opposed: chemistry could be utilized in cooking, geometry in dividing cloth, and phrenology in discovering talent in children.[73]

Women were to master every variety of needlework, for, as Mrs. Sigourney pointed out, "Needle-work, in all its forms of use, elegance, and ornament, has ever been the appropriate occupation of woman." [74] Embroidery improved taste; knitting promoted serenity and economy.[75] Other forms of artsy-craftsy activity for her leisure moments included painting on glass or velvet, Poonah work, tussy-mussy frames for her own needlepoint or water colors, stands for hyacinths, hair bracelets or baskets of feathers.[76]

She was expected to have a special affinity for flowers. To the editors of *The Lady's Token* "A Woman never appears more truly in her sphere, than when she divides her time between her domestic avocations and the culture of flowers." [77] She could write letters, an activity particularly feminine since it had to do with the outpourings of the heart,[78] or practice her drawingroom skills of singing and playing an instrument. She might even read.

Here she faced a bewildering array of advice. The female was dangerously addicted to novels, according to the literature of the period. She should avoid them, since they interfered with "serious piety." If she simply couldn't help herself and read them anyway, she should choose edifying ones from lists of morally acceptable authors.[79] She should study

[71] *Letters to Young Ladies*, p. 27. The greatest exponent of the mental and moral joys of housekeeping was the *Lady's Annual Register and Housewife's Memorandum Book* (Boston, 1838), which gave practical advice on ironing, hair curling, budgeting and marketing, and turning cuffs—all activities which contributed to the "beauty of usefulness" and "joy of accomplishment" which a woman desired (I, 23).

[72] *The Young Lady's Friend*, p. 230.

[73] "Learning vs. Housewifery," *Godey's*, X (Aug. 1839), 95.

[74] *Letters to Young Ladies*, p. 25. W. Thayer, *Life at the Fireside* (Boston, 1857), has an idyllic picture of the woman of the house mending her children's garments, the grandmother knitting and the little girl taking her first stitches, all in the light of the domestic hearth.

[75] "The Mirror's Advice," *Young Maiden's Mirror* (Boston, 1858), p. 263.

[76] Mrs. L. Maria Child, *The Girl's Own Book* (New York, 1833).

[77] P. 44.

[78] T. S. Arthur, *Advice to Young Ladies* (Boston, 1850), p. 45.

history since it "showed the depravity of the human heart and the evil nature of sin." On the whole, "religious biography was best." [79]

The women's magazines themselves could be read without any loss of concern for the home. *Godey's* promised the husband that he would find his wife "no less assiduous for his reception, or less sincere in welcoming his return" as a result of reading their magazine.[80] *The Lily of the Valley* won its right to be admitted to the boudoir by confessing that it was "like its namesake humble and unostentatious, but it is yet pure, and, we trust, free from moral imperfections." [81]

No matter what later authorities claimed, the nineteenth century knew that girls *could* be ruined by a book. The seduction stories regard "exciting and dangerous books" as contributory causes of disaster. The man without honorable intentions always provides the innocent maiden with such books as a prelude to his assault on her virtue.[82] Books which attacked or seemed to attack woman's accepted place in society were regarded as equally dangerous. A reviewer of Harriet Martineau's *Society in America* wanted it kept out of the hands of American women. They were so susceptible to persuasion, with their "gentle yielding natures" that they might listen to "the bold ravings of the hard-featured of their own sex." The frightening result: "such reading will unsettle them for their true station and pursuits, and they will throw the world back again into confusion." [83]

The debate over women's education posed the question of whether a "finished" education detracted from the practice of housewifely arts. Again it proved to be a case of semantics, for a true woman's education was never "finished" until she was instructed in the gentle science of homemaking.[84] Helen Irving, writing on "Literary Women," made it very clear that if women invoked the muse, it was as a genie of the household lamp. "If the necessities of her position require these duties at her hands, she will perform them nonetheless cheerfully, that she knows herself capable of higher things." The literary woman must conform to the same standards as any other woman: "That her home shall be made a loving place of rest and joy and comfort for those who are dear to her, will be

[79] R. C. Waterston, *Thoughts on Moral and Spiritual Culture* (Boston, 1842), p. 101. Newcomb's *Young Lady's Guide* also advised religious biography as the best reading for women (p. 111).

[80] *Godey's*, I (1828), 1. (Repeated often in *Godey's* editorials.)

[81] *The Lily of the Valley*, n. v. (1851), p. 2.

[82] For example, "The Fatalist," *Godey's*, IV (Jan. 1834), 10, in which Somers Dudley has Catherine reading these dangerous books until life becomes "a bewildered dream. . . . O passion, what a shocking perverter of reason thou art!"

[83] Review of *Society in America* (New York, 1837) in *American Quarterly Review* (Philadelphia), XXII (Sept. 1837), 38.

[84] "A Finished Education," *Ladies' Museum* (Providence), I (1825), 42.

the first wish of every true woman's heart." [85] Mrs. Ann Stephens told women who wrote to make sure they did not sacrifice one domestic duty. "As for genius, make it a domestic plant. Let its roots strike deep in your house. . . ." [86]

The fear of "blue stockings" (the eighteenth-century male's term of derision for educated or literary women) need not persist for nineteenth-century American men. The magazines presented spurious dialogues in which bachelors were convinced of their fallacy in fearing educated wives. One such dialogue took place between a young man and his female cousin. Ernest deprecates learned ladies ("A *Woman* is far more lovable than a *philosopher*") but Alice refutes him with the beautiful example of their Aunt Barbara who "although she *has* perpetrated the heinous crime of writing some half dozen folios" is still a model of "the spirit of feminine gentleness." His memory prodded, Ernest concedes that, by George, there was a woman: "When I last had a cold she not only made me a bottle of cough syrup, but when I complained of nothing new to read, set to work and wrote some twenty stanzas on consumption." [87]

The magazines were filled with domestic tragedies in which spoiled young girls learned that when there was a hungry man to feed French and china painting were not helpful. According to these stories many a marriage is jeopardized because the wife has not learned to keep house. Harriet Beecher Stowe wrote a sprightly piece of personal experience for *Godey's,* ridiculing her own bad housekeeping as a bride. She used the same theme in a story "The Only Daughter," in which the pampered beauty learns the facts of domestic life from a rather difficult source, her mother-in-law. Mrs. Hamilton tells Caroline in the sweetest way possible to shape up in the kitchen, reserving her rebuke for her son: "You are her husband—her guide—her protector—now see what you can do," she admonishes him. "Give her credit for every effort: treat her faults with tenderness; encourage and praise whenever you can, and depend upon it, you will see another woman in her." He is properly masterful, she properly domestic and in a few months Caroline is making lumpless gravy and keeping up with the darning. Domestic tranquillity has been restored and the young wife moralizes: "Bring up a girl to feel that she has a responsible part to bear in promoting the happiness of the family, and you make a reflecting being of her at once, and remove that lightness and frivolity of character which makes her shrink from graver studies." [88] These stories end with the heroine drying her hands on her apron and

[85] Helen Irving, "Literary Women," *Ladies' Wreath,* III (1850), 93.
[86] "Women of Genius," *Ladies' Companion,* XI (1839), 89.
[87] "Intellect vs. Affection in Woman," *Godey's,* XVI (1846), 86.
[88] "The Only Daughter," *Godey's,* X (Mar. 1839), 122.

vowing that *her* daughter will be properly educated, in piecrust as well as Poonah work.

The female seminaries were quick to defend themselves against any suspicion of interfering with the role which nature's God had assigned to women. They hoped to enlarge and deepen that role, but not to change its setting. At the Young Ladies' Seminary and Collegiate Institute in Monroe City, Michigan, the catalogue admitted few of its graduates would be likely "to fill the learned professions." Still, they were called to "other scenes of usefulness and honor." The average woman is to be "the presiding genius of love" in the home, where she is to "give a correct and elevated literary taste to her children, and to assume that influential station that she ought to possess as the companion of an educated man." [89]

At Miss Pierce's famous school in Litchfield, the students were taught that they had "attained the perfection of their characters when they could combine their elegant accomplishments with a turn for solid domestic virtues." [90] Mt. Holyoke paid pious tribute to domestic skills: "Let a young lady despise this branch of the duties of woman, and she despises the appointments of her existence." God, nature and the Bible "enjoin these duties on the sex, and she cannot violate them with impunity." Thus warned, the young lady would have to seek knowledge of these duties elsewhere, since it was not in the curriculum at Mt. Holyoke. "We would not take this privilege from the mother." [91]

One reason for knowing her way around a kitchen was that America was "a land of precarious fortunes," as Lydia Maria Child pointed out in her book *The Frugal Housewife: Dedicated to Those Who Are Not Ashamed of Economy.* Mrs. Child's chapter "How To Endure Poverty" prescribed a combination of piety and knowledge—the kind of knowledge found in a true woman's education, "a thorough religious *useful* education." [92] The woman who had servants today, might tomorrow, because of a depression or panic, be forced to do her own work. If that happened she knew how to act, for she was to be the same cheerful consoler of her husband in their cottage as in their mansion.

An essay by Washington Irving, much quoted in the gift annuals, discussed the value of a wife in case of business reverses: "I have observed that a married man falling into misfortune is more apt to achieve his

[89] *The Annual Catalogue of the Officers and Pupils of the Young Ladies' Seminary and Collegiate Institute* (Monroe City, 1855), pp. 18, 19.

[90] *Chronicles of a Pioneer School* from 1792 to 1833: Being the History of Miss Sarah Pierce and Her Litchfield School, Compiled by Emily Noyes Vanderpoel; ed. Elizabeth C. Barney Buel (Cambridge, 1903), p. 74.

[91] *Mt. Holyoke Female Seminary*, p. 13.

[92] *The American Frugal Housewife* (New York, 1838), p. 111.

situation in the world than a single one . . . it is beautifully ordained by Providence that woman, who is the ornament of man in his happier hours, should be his stay and solace when smitten with sudden calamity."[93]

A story titled simply but eloquently "The Wife" dealt with the quiet heroism of Ellen Graham during her husband's plunge from fortune to poverty. Ned Graham said of her: "Words are too poor to tell you what I owe to that noble woman. In our darkest seasons of adversity, she has been an angel of consolation—utterly forgetful of self and anxious only to comfort and sustain me." Of course she had a little help from "faithful Dinah who absolutely refused to leave her beloved mistress," but even so Ellen did no more than would be expected of any true woman.[94]

Most of this advice was directed to woman as wife. Marriage was the proper state for the exercise of the domestic virtues. "True Love and a Happy Home," an essay in *The Young Ladies' Oasis,* might have been carved on every girl's hope chest.[95] But although marriage was best, it was not absolutely necessary. The women's magazines tried to remove the stigma from being an "Old Maid." They advised no marriage at all rather than an unhappy one contracted out of selfish motives.[96] Their stories showed maiden ladies as unselfish ministers to the sick, teachers of the young, or moral preceptors with their pens, beloved of the entire village. Usually the life of single blessedness resulted from the premature death of a fiancé, or was chosen through fidelity to some high mission. For example, in "Two Sisters," Mary devotes herself to Ellen and her abandoned children, giving up her own chance for marriage. "Her devotion to her sister's happiness has met its reward in the consciousness of having fulfilled a sacred duty." [97] Very rarely, a "woman of genius" was

[93] "Female Influence," in *The Ladies' Pearl and Literary Gleaner: A Collection of Tales, Sketches, Essays, Anecdotes, and Historical Incidents* (Lowell), I (1841), 10.

[94] Mrs. S. T. Martyn, "The Wife," *Ladies' Wreath,* II (1848-49), 171.

[95] *The Young Ladies' Oasis,* p. 26.

[96] "On Marriage," *Ladies' Repository,* I (1841), 133; "Old Maids," *Ladies' Literary Cabinet* (Newburyport), II (1822) (Microfilm), 141; "Matrimony," *Godey's,* II (Sept. 1831), 174; and "Married or Single," *Peterson's Magazine* (Philadelphia) IX (1859), 36, all express the belief that while marriage is desirable for a woman it is not essential. This attempt to reclaim the status of the unmarried woman is an example of the kind of mild crusade which the women's magazines sometimes carried on. Other examples were their strictures against an overly-genteel education and against the affectation and aggravation of ill health. In this sense the magazines were truly conservative, for they did not oppose all change but only that which did violence to some cherished tradition. The reforms they advocated would, if put into effect, make woman even more the perfect female, and enhance the ideal of True Womanhood.

[97] *Girlhood and Womanhood,* p. 100. Mrs. Graves tells the stories in the book in the person of an "Old Maid" and her conclusions are that "single life has its happiness too" for the single woman "can enjoy all the pleasures of maternity without its pains and trials" (p. 140). In another one of her books, *Woman in America* (New York, 1843),

absolved from the necessity of marriage, being so extraordinary that she did not need the security or status of being a wife.[98] Most often, however, if girls proved "difficult," marriage and a family were regarded as a cure.[99] The "sedative quality" of a home could be counted on to subdue even the most restless spirits.

George Burnap saw marriage as "that sphere for which woman was originally intended, and to which she is so exactly fitted to adorn and bless, as the wife, the mistress of a home, the solace, the aid, and the counsellor of that ONE, for whose sake alone the world is of any consequence to her."[100] Samuel Miller preached a sermon on women: "How interesting and important are the duties devolved on females as WIVES . . . the counsellor and friend of the husband; who makes it her daily study to lighten his cares, to soothe his sorrows, and to augment his joys; who, like a guardian angel, watches over his interests, warns him against dangers, comforts him under trials; and by her pious, assiduous, and attractive deportment, constantly endeavors to render him more virtuous, more useful, more honourable, and more happy."[101] A woman's whole interest should be focused on her husband, paying him "those numberless attentions to which the French give the title of *petits soins* and which the woman who loves knows so well how to pay . . . she should consider nothing as trivial which could win a smile of approbation from him."[102]

Marriage was seen not only in terms of service but as an increase in

---

Mrs. Graves speaks out even more strongly in favor of "single blessedness" rather than "a loveless or unhappy marriage" (p. 130).

[98] A very unusual story is Lela Linwood, "A Chapter in the History of a Free Heart," *Ladies' Wreath*, III (1853), 349. The heroine, Grace Arland, is "sublime" and dwells "in perfect light while we others struggle yet with the shadows." She refuses marriage and her friends regret this but are told her heart "is rejoicing in its *freedom*." The story ends with the plaintive refrain:

> But is it not a happy thing,
> All fetterless and free,
> Like any wild bird, on the wing,
> To carol merrily?

But even in this tale the unusual, almost unearthly rarity of Grace's genius is stressed; she is not offered as an example to more mortal beings.

[99] Horace Greeley even went so far as to apply this remedy to the "dissatisfactions" of Margaret Fuller. In his autobiography, *Recollections of a Busy Life* (New York, 1868) he says that "noble and great as she was, a good husband and two or three bouncing babies would have emancipated her from a deal of cant and nonsense" (p. 178).

[100] *Sphere and Duties of Woman*, p. 64.

[101] *A Sermon: Preached March 13, 1808, for the Benefit of the Society Instituted in the City of New-York, For the Relief of Poor Widows with Small Children* (New York, 1808), pp. 13, 14.

[102] *Lady's Magazine and Museum: A Family Journal* (London) IV (Jan. 1831), 6. This magazine is included partly because its editorials proclaimed it "of interest to the English speaking lady at home and abroad" and partly because it shows that the preoccupation with True Womanhood was by no means confined to the United States.

authority for woman. Burnap concluded that marriage improves the female character "not only because it puts her under the best possible tuition, that of the affections, and affords scope to her active energies, but because it gives her higher aims, and a more dignified position."[103] *The Lady's Amaranth* saw it as a balance of power: "The man bears rule over his wife's person and conduct. She bears rule over his inclinations: he governs by law; she by persuasion. . . . The empire of the woman is an empire of softness . . . her commands are caresses, her menaces are tears."[104]

Woman should marry, but not for money. She should choose only the high road of true love and not truckle to the values of a materialistic society. A story "Marrying for Money" (subtlety was not the strong point of the ladies' magazines) depicts Gertrude, the heroine, rueing the day she made her crass choice: "It is a terrible thing to live without love. . . . A woman who dares marry for aught but the purest affection, calls down the just judgments of heaven upon her head." [105]

The corollary to marriage, with or without true love, was motherhood, which added another dimension to her usefulness and her prestige. It also anchored her even more firmly to the home. "My Friend," wrote Mrs. Sigourney, "If in becoming a mother, you have reached the climax of your happiness, you have also taken a higher place in the scale of being . . . you have gained an increase of power."[106] The Rev. J. N. Danforth pleaded in *The Ladies' Casket*, "Oh, mother, acquit thyself well in thy humble sphere, for thou mayest affect the world."[107] A true woman naturally loved her children; to suggest otherwise was monstrous.[108]

America depended upon her mothers to raise up a whole generation of Christian statesmen who could say "all that I am I owe to my angel mother."[109] The mothers must do the inculcating of virtue since the

103 *Sphere and Duties of Woman*, p. 102.

104 "Matrimony," *Lady's Amaranth*, II (Dec. 1839), 271.

105 Elizabeth Doten, "Marrying for Money," *The Lily of the Valley*, n. v. (1857), p. 112.

106 *Letters to Mothers*, p. 9.

107 "Maternal Relation," *Ladies' Casket* (New York, 1850?), p. 85. The importance of the mother's role was emphasized abroad as well as in America. *Godey's* recommended the book by the French author Aimeé-Martin on the education of mothers to "be read five times," in the original if possible (XIII, Dec. 1842, 201). In this book the highest ideals of True Womanhood are upheld. For example: "Jeunes filles, jeunes épouses, tendres mères, c'est dans votre âme bien plus que dans les lois du législateur que reposent aujourd'hui l'avenir de l'Europe et les destinées du genre humain," L. Aimeé-Martin, *De l'Education des Meres de famille ou De la civilisation du genre humain par les femmes* (Bruxelles, 1857), II, 527.

108 *Maternal Association of the Amity Baptist Church*: Annual Report (New York, 1847), p. 2: "Suffer the little children to come unto me and forbid them not, is and must ever be a sacred commandment to the Christian woman."

109 For example, Daniel Webster, "The Influence of Woman," in *The Young Ladies' Reader* (Philadelphia, 1851), p. 310.

fathers, alas, were too busy chasing the dollar. Or as *The Ladies' Companion* put it more effusively, the father "weary with the heat and burden of life's summer day, or trampling with unwilling foot the decaying leaves of life's autumn, has forgotten the sympathies of life's joyous springtime. . . . The acquisition of wealth, the advancement of his children in worldly honor—these are his self-imposed tasks." It was his wife who formed "the infant mind as yet untainted by contact with evil . . . like wax beneath the plastic hand of the mother."[110]

The Ladies' Wreath offered a fifty-dollar prize to the woman who submitted the most convincing essay on "How May An American Woman Best Show Her Patriotism." The winner was Miss Elizabeth Wetherell who provided herself with a husband in her answer. The wife in the essay of course asked her husband's opinion. He tried a few jokes first—"Call her eldest son George Washington," "Don't speak French, speak American"—but then got down to telling her in sober prize-winning truth what women could do for their country. Voting was no asset, since that would result only in "a vast increase of confusion and expense without in the smallest degree affecting the result." Besides, continued this oracle, "looking down at their child," if "we were to go a step further and let the children vote, their first act would be to vote their mothers at home." There is no comment on this devastating male logic and he continues: "Most women would follow the lead of their fathers and husbands," and the few who would "fly off on a tangent from the circle of home influence would cancel each other out."

The wife responds dutifully: "I see all that. I never understood so well before." Encouraged by her quick womanly perception, the master of the house resolves the question—an American woman best shows her patriotism by staying at home, where she brings her influence to bear "upon the right side for the country's weal." That woman will instinctively choose the side of right he has no doubt. Besides her "natural refinement and closeness to God" she has the "blessed advantage of a quiet life" while man is exposed to conflict and evil. She stays home with "her Bible and a well-balanced mind" and raises her sons to be good Americans. The judges rejoiced in this conclusion and paid the prize money cheerfully, remarking "they deemed it cheap at the price."[111]

If any woman asked for greater scope for her gifts the magazines were sharply critical. Such women were tampering with society, undermining

---

[110] Mrs. Emma C. Embury, "Female Education," *Ladies' Companion*, VIII (Jan. 1838), 18. Mrs. Embury stressed the fact that the American woman was not the "mere plaything of passion" but was in strict training to be "the mother of statesmen."

[111] "How May An American Woman Best Show Her Patriotism?" *Ladies' Wreath*, III (1851), 313. Elizabeth Wetherell was the pen name of Susan Warner, author of *The Wide Wide World* and *Queechy*.

civilization. Mary Wollstonecraft, Frances Wright and Harriet Martineau were condemned in the strongest possible language—they were read out of the sex. "They are only semi-women, mental hermaphrodites." The Rev. Harrington knew the women of America could not possibly approve of such perversions and went to some wives and mothers to ask if they did want a "wider sphere of interest" as these nonwomen claimed. The answer was reassuring. " 'NO!' they cried simultaneously, 'Let the men take care of politics, *we will take care of the children!*' " Again female discontent resulted only from a lack of understanding: women were not subservient, they were rather "chosen vessels." Looked at in this light the conclusion was inescapable: "Noble, sublime is the task of the American mother."[112]

"Women's Rights" meant one thing to reformers, but quite another to the True Woman. She knew her rights,

> The right to love whom others scorn,
> The right to comfort and to mourn,
> The right to shed new joy on earth,
> The right to feel the soul's high worth . . .
> Such women's rights, and God will bless
> And crown their champions with success.[113]

The American woman had her choice—she could define her rights in the way of the women's magazines and insure them by the practice of the requisite virtues, or she could go outside the home, seeking other rewards than love. It was a decision on which, she was told, everything in her world depended. "Yours it is to determine," the Rev. Mr. Stearns solemnly warned from the pulpit, "whether the beautiful order of society . . . shall continue as it has been" or whether "society shall break up and become a chaos of disjointed and unsightly elements."[114] If she chose to listen to other voices than those of her proper mentors, sought other rooms than those of her home, she lost both her happiness and her power —"that almost magic power, which, in her proper sphere, she now wields over the destinies of the world."[115]

But even while the women's magazines and related literature encouraged this ideal of the perfect woman, forces were at work in the nineteenth century which impelled woman herself to change, to play a more

112 Henry F. Harrington, "Female Education," *Ladies' Companion*, IX (1838), 293, and "Influence of Woman—Past and Present," *Ladies' Companion*, XIII (1840), 245.

113 Mrs. E. Little, "What Are the Rights of Women?" *Ladies' Wreath*, II (1848-49), 133.

114 *Female Influence*, p. 18.

115 *Ibid.*, p. 23.

creative role in society. The movements for social reform, westward migration, missionary activity, utopian communities, industrialism, the Civil War—all called forth responses from woman which differed from those she was trained to believe were hers by nature and divine decree. The very perfection of True Womanhood, moreover, carried within itself the seeds of its own destruction. For if woman was so very little less than the angels, she should surely take a more active part in running the world, especially since men were making such a hash of things.

Real women often felt they did not live up to the ideal of True Womanhood: some of them blamed themselves, some challenged the standard, some tried to keep the virtues and enlarge the scope of womanhood.[116] Somehow through this mixture of challenge and acceptance, of change and continuity, the True Woman evolved into the New Woman—a transformation as startling in its way as the abolition of slavery or the coming of the machine age. And yet the stereotype, the "mystique" if you will, of what woman was and ought to be persisted, bringing guilt and confusion in the midst of opportunity.[117]

The women's magazines and related literature had feared this very dislocation of values and blurring of roles. By careful manipulation and interpretation they sought to convince woman that she had the best of both worlds—power and virtue—and that a stable order of society depended upon her maintaining her traditional place in it. To that end she was identified with everything that was beautiful and holy.

"Who Can Find a Valiant Woman?" was asked frequently from the pulpit and the editorial pages. There was only one place to look for her —at home. Clearly and confidently these authorities proclaimed the True Woman of the nineteenth century to be the Valiant Woman of the Bible, in whom the heart of her husband rejoiced and whose price was above rubies.

---

116 Even the women reformers were prone to use domestic images, i.e. "sweep Uncle Sam's kitchen clean," and "tidy up our country's house."

117 The "Animus and Anima" of Jung amounts almost to a catalogue of the nineteenth-century masculine and female traits, and the female hysterics whom Freud saw had much of the same training as the nineteenth-century American woman. Betty Friedan, *The Feminine Mystique* (New York, 1963), challenges the whole concept of True Womanhood as it hampers the "fulfillment" of the twentieth-century woman.

COMMENTARY

Mary Kelley

In the spring of 1973 I embarked upon the rite that all who pursue a Ph.D. experience—searching for a dissertation topic. The subject would be women, the century the nineteenth, that I already knew. It did not take me long to decide that I would focus upon literary women. It took even less time to decide that Barbara Welter's "The Cult of True Womanhood: 1820–1860" would provide my point of departure. And well it might have. Published in the *American Quarterly* in the summer of 1966, Welter's article on nineteenth-century America's ideology of womanhood had already had an enormous impact on the scholarship in American studies and also in the two closely affiliated fields of women's literature and women's history.

Having read widely in gift annuals, fiction, women's magazines, cookbooks, and religious literature, Welter concluded that antebellum women had been held hostage to four behavioral attributes—"piety, purity, submissiveness, and domesticity." The evidence seemed so incontrovertible I concluded that I would devote my dissertation to an elaboration of Welter's womanhood in the popular novels, tales, and sketches written by women between 1820 and 1880. During the course of my research on ten of these writers, I did come to differ with Welter. I became skeptical about the accuracy of Welter's submissiveness which denied women any power and decided that deference, which inscribed her True Woman with a measure of agency, was closer to the mark. Where Welter's womanhood was a seamless ideology with transparent directives, the fiction I was reading was shot through with ambivalence, tension, and contradiction. And where she had found docile compliance with the ideology's prescriptions, I detected acts of subversion. In the end, I substituted and rejected as much as I elaborated of Welter's womanhood. But her influence was manifest throughout—Welter had provided the initial paradigm that allowed me to go forward.

Many other scholars could tell a similar tale. Barbara Welter's "Cult

of True Womanhood, 1820–1860" seemed to be everywhere. The subject of a special session at the American Studies Association meeting in
1977, the article was also reprinted in a host of collections. "The Cult of
True Womanhood" appeared in Ronald Hogeland's widely read *Women
and Womanhood in America* (Lexington, Mass.: D.C. Heath, 1973). Welter herself reprinted it in *Dimity Convictions: The American Woman in the
Nineteenth Century* (Athens: Ohio University Press, 1976), the collection
of her essays she published a decade after the article had appeared in
the *American Quarterly*. Mary Beth Norton included it in *Major Problems
in American Women's History* (Lexington, Mass.: D.C. Heath, 1989), a collection of essays and documents that has been used in classrooms across
the nation since its publication. More recently, John R. M. Wilson made
"The Cult of True Womanhood" central to *Forging American Character*
(Englewood Cliffs, N.J.: Prentice-Hall, 1991), the interdisciplinary collection he edited.

Barbara Welter's "Cult of True Womanhood, 1820–1860" was also
widely cited in the historical and literary scholarship on nineteenth-
century women, white and black. During the 1970s, Welter's paradigm
served as a point of departure for Kathryn Kish Sklar and Nancy Cott,
both of whom influenced much of the subsequent scholarship in American women's history. Sklar's pathbreaking *Catharine Beecher: A Study
in American Domesticity* (New Haven: Yale University Press, 1973) highlighted the compromise that Beecher told white women to strike with
their male counterparts: if they agreed to restrict their participation
in the larger society, they could have control of the domestic sphere.
Welter's womanhood "demonstrated the widespread popularity of this
bargain by the 1840s," Sklar told readers. It confirmed "the image identifying women with domestic virtue" (296 n. 27). Nancy Cott's *The Bonds
of Womanhood: "Woman's Sphere" in New England, 1780–1835* (New Haven:
Yale University Press, 1977) opened with an acknowledgment to Welter.
When she began to pursue her research on New England women, Cott
told readers that she had wanted to understand how Welter's womanhood "related to women's actual circumstances, experiences, and consciousness" (1). She had turned to women's letters, diaries, and journals
and looked to the decades before 1830 "to find out what had happened
that might clarify the reception of or the need for a 'cult'" (2). Fifteen
years after the publication of *The Bonds of Womanhood* in 1977, Jo Anne
Preston embarked on a similar project in an article that she published
in the *New England Quarterly*. Preston had wanted to understand the im-

pact of Welter's womanhood on New England women's entry into the profession of teaching.

Literary critics, perhaps most notably those who focused on the narratives of black women, also used "The Cult of True Womanhood" as a point of reference. In *Reconstructing Womanhood: The Emergence of the Afro-American Woman Novelist* (New York: Oxford University Press, 1987), Hazel Carby asked readers to acknowledge True Womanhood's signal impact on black women: "It was dominant, in the sense of being the most subscribed to convention governing female behavior, but it was also clearly recognizable as a dominating image, describing the parameters within which women were measured and declared to be, or not to be, women" (23). Measured by the behavioral attributes of True Womanhood, black women were declared not to be women at all. Exclusion from this dominant and dominating paradigm had profound consequences—whether slave or free, black women were rendered all the more vulnerable to physical and psychological violation. Frances Smith Foster, Jean Fagan Yellin, Henry Louis Gates, and Beth Doriana, all of whom agreed with Carby, also noted that black women, no matter how much they resisted the ideology of True Womanhood, had to address its implications in their narratives.

Perhaps the most striking testimony to Welter's influence comes from historians and literary critics who have investigated the multiple uses of "piety, purity, submissiveness, and domesticity." In *Women and the Work of Benevolence: Morality, Politics, and Class in the Nineteenth-Century United States* (New Haven: Yale University Press, 1990), Lori D. Ginzberg showed that white women used their gendered "piety" to legitimate the powerful role they played in the charitable and reform causes of antebellum America. Barbara Leslie Epstein did the same in *The Politics of Domesticity* (Middletown: Wesleyan University Press, 1981), which linked women, evangelism, and temperance in nineteenth-century America. No passive piety here, as both Ginzberg and Epstein demonstrated. Carroll Smith-Rosenberg and Nancy Cott highlighted the similar purposes "purity" served for antebellum women. Originally published in the *American Quarterly* in 1971, Smith-Rosenberg's widely reprinted "Beauty, the Beast, and the Militant Woman: A Case Study of Sex Roles and Social Stress in Jacksonian America" charted white women's translation of feminine "purity" into a weapon of righteousness which they used to confront male sexual license and the double standard. Antebellum women translated the same feminine "purity" into female "passionlessness" and deployed the latter to secure social and familial power, as Nancy Cott showed in "Passionlessness: An Interpretation of Victorian Sexual Ideology, 1790–1850." Then there was the matter of "domesticity," which simultaneously glorified the wife and mother and consigned her to the home. From Jeanne Boydston's *Home and Work: Housework, Wages, and the Ideology of Labor in the Early Republic* (New York: Oxford University Press, 1990), we learned that a toll had also been exacted by Welter's womanhood. Women's unpaid domestic labor contributed substantially to the survival and prosperity of their households. Nonetheless, housewives themselves doubted the economic value of their labors, as Boydston's illuminating analysis showed. Capitalism had taught antebellum women that wages were the measure of an individual's worth. And yet Welter's womanhood had glorified their unpaid labor. Little wonder that they were deeply ambivalent about their status as representatives of True Womanhood.

In revisiting Barbara Welter's influential paradigm thirty years after its publication, we learn that True Womanhood's impact, which was presumed to have been uniform and transparent, was instead as diverse and complicated as the lives of those for whom the ideology had been designed—antebellum women, white and black. Although Welter provided the impetus for these many interpretations, little if any of "The Cult of True Womanhood" remains intact today. It now appears that the ideology did not have the constraining impact on the behavior of white women that historians and literary critics initially presumed. Instead of limiting impulses of self-determination, white women revised its tenets to serve expansive purposes. Its impact on black women was more complicated. Enslaved in the South and subjected to discrimination in the North, black women encountered an ideology that whites, female and male, exploited for relentlessly racist ends. However, a Nancy Prince, a Harriet Wilson, and a Harriet Jacobs, all of whom used the ideology more as a point of departure than as a determining end, managed to re-represent True Womanhood and to employ its tenets to forward their projects of emancipation.

BRUCE KUKLICK

Myth and Symbol in
American Studies

THE PUBLICATION OF HENRY NASH SMITH'S *VIRGIN LAND* IN 1950 HAS PROVED IN
retrospect a major intellectual event. The work inspired a series of books
that adopted its approach and attempted to relate consciousness to society
in the United States. Receiving its most sophisticated recent expression in
the publications of Leo Marx, this perspective has come for many to define
American Studies; the authors—Marx calls them humanists—are at least
a major movement within American Studies. But Smith and his followers
have written little about their methodological premises. As Alan Trachtenberg has stated of *Virgin Land:* "Its informing theory nowhere gets a theoretical exposition: the book prefers to exemplify rather than theorize." [1]
Indeed, one has only to listen to the persistent and recurring angst voiced
by graduates in American Studies to realize that this scholarly genre has
not adequately defined what it is about. The aim of this article is twofold: it
makes a stab at explicating the premises that guide humanist writing; and
it tries to assess the plausibility of these premises *and* of the substantive
conclusions that the humanists have reached.[2]

Most of us are familiar with the terminology which Smith and Marx borrowed from literary criticism. Smith's brief statement in *Virgin Land* urges

[1] "Myth, History and Literature in *Virgin Land,*" p. 2, read at a meeting of the American
Studies Association of Northern California, Stanford University, Aug. 30, 1967. The author
kindly lent me a copy of this paper.

[2] Although the patterns of explanation are widespread, I have been mainly concerned with
Smith's *Virgin Land* (Cambridge: Harvard Univ. Press, 1950) (all citations with the exception
of the one in footnote 20 are taken from that edition), and Marx's *Machine in the Garden* (New
York: Oxford Univ. Press, 1964), the most important publications of the school. But I have
also cited with some regularity R. W. B. Lewis, *The American Adam* (Chicago: Univ. of Chicago
Press, 1955); Charles L. Sanford, *The Quest for Paradise* (Urbana, Ill.: Univ. of Ill. Press, 1961);
Alan Trachtenberg, *Brooklyn Bridge* (New York: Oxford Univ. Press, 1965); and John William

that symbols and myths designate larger or smaller units of the same kind of thing: an intellectual construction that fuses concept and emotion into an image.[3] Marx writes that an image refers to a verbal recording of a simple sense perception,[4] but also implies elsewhere that this formulation may be misleading.[5] Although these notions are vague, I think the following illustration clarifies them. Suppose I see a man on the corner, and come home and write a story about him. The "mental picture" I have in mind when I write about him is an image when I merely wish to designate or refer to the man. I name this image with the phrase "the man on the corner." If I want to speak of the symbol or myth of the man on the corner, I am making the image "carry a burden of implication (value, association, feeling, or, in a word, meaning) beyond that which is required for mere reference."[6] We invest the image with much more than a denotational quality; we enable it to connote moral, intellectual and emotional qualities of wider and wider range.

There are two reasons for believing that the American Studies movement is committed to this view of an image as a mental entity. In the first place, symbols and myths are images for Smith, and for Marx they are, at least, the same sorts of things as images. But symbols and myths at best *reflect* empirical fact, and so are never themselves factual; they are "products of the imagination," "complex mental construct[s]."[7] So if images are of the order of symbols and myths, and the latter are not factual but "mental constructs," then images are also mental constructs, states of mind, however accurately they may refer to the factual. In the second place, the American Studies humanists make a strict dichotomy between consciousness and the world. Smith writes that symbols and myths exist "in a different plane" from empirical fact;[8] in *Brooklyn Bridge* Trachtenberg urges that facts and symbols have two separate modes of existence—facts have a specific spatio-temporal location; symbols have a place in the mind.[9] Marx—like Smith and Trachtenberg—writes that the chief concern is "the landscape of the

---

Ward, *Andrew Jackson: Symbol for an Age* (New York: Oxford Univ. Press, 1953). Aside from general considerations, I would note the authority of Marx himself for treating these men as a "movement"; see "American Studies—A Defense of an Unscientific Method," *New Literary History,* 1 (1969), 75–76.

[3] Smith, p. v; Marx, "American Studies," p. 86. See also Ward's "Looking Backward: *Andrew Jackson: Symbol for an Age,*" in *The Historian's Workshop* (New York: Oxford Univ. Press, 1970), pp. 214 ff.

[4] Marx, "American Studies," pp. 83–84.

[5] Marx, *Machine,* pp. 190, 193.

[6] *Ibid.,* p. 4; "American Studies," p. 86.

[7] Smith, p. v; Marx, "American Studies," p. 86.

[8] Smith, p. v.

[9] Trachtenberg, *Brooklyn Bridge,* p. vii.

psyche," "the inner, not the outer world"; actual objects and events are secondary.[10] The location of an image is not "out there" "but in consciousness. It is a product of imaginative perception, of the analogy-perceiving, metaphor-making, mytho-poetic power of the human mind."[11] In terms of this bifurcation between mind and the physical world images belong to the mental realm.

This explication helps explain why the humanists effectively resort to the analysis of painting in their work:[12] the painting is a striking physical example of the image or symbol in the artist's mind. As Marx writes, the symbolic landscape existed on many planes of consciousness, on the canvas, in books and in the minds of those familiar with art and literature.[13]

It would be a mistake, however, to regard images as pictorial only. For example, Marx notes that Hawthorne makes use of auditory images.[14] Sitting in my study, I can imagine the man on the corner telling a story; or recall the aroma of his shaving lotion. In short, images and symbols are often visual in quality, but are not necessarily so. More important, because we use "physical object" language to analyze images, we must emphasize their internal status. Although they are very like the kinds of things we see, hear and smell when we see a man on the corner, hear him talking or smell his shaving lotion, images are really mental entities, different in kind from what in fact exists. Finally, we ought to note that as used by humanists, images and symbols are not uniquely occurring entities. They have the capacity to appear in many minds; as I shall argue later they have what I would call a platonic status. Smith writes that they are "collective representations rather than the work of a single mind."[15] Marx and Trachtenberg also write of a "collective image" and the existence of symbols in America's "collective imagination."[16] Indeed, one of the primary purposes of the American Studies movement is to demonstrate the way in which these "collective" images and symbols can be used to explain the behavior of people in the United States.

Although there is much that is obscure in this position, I hope to have explicated it as plainly as possible. I must conclude that the humanists suppose what I shall call a crude Cartesian view of mind. There are two kinds of existents for them; the one with which they primarily deal consists of some-

---

[10] Marx, *Machine*, p. 28. Here Marx is speaking only of Hawthorne.

[11] *Ibid.*, p. 264. Here Marx is describing Thoreau's position although the implication is that Marx subscribes to it.

[12] See esp. *Brooklyn Bridge, Andrew Jackson: Symbol for an Age, Virgin Land* and *The Machine in the Garden.*

[13] Marx, *Machine*, p. 142.

[14] *Ibid.*, p. 28.

[15] Smith, p. v.

[16] Marx, *Machine*, p. 164; Trachtenberg, *Brooklyn Bridge*, p. vii.

thing very like pictures (and their aural and olfactory equivalents) which exist *in* the mind and which may or may not refer to what is "out there" in another sphere. Moreover, these ideas are platonic: they exist independently of the people who think them. Smith writes that the Lewis and Clark expedition "established the image of a highway across the continent . . . in the minds of Americans"; the image of the West was "so powerful and vivid" to Americans that it seemed "a representation of America."[17] Marx argues that Elizabethan ideas of America were "visual images" containing "the picture of America as a paradise regained"; but for Marx images of the landscape need not picture the *actual* topography—the Elizabethan images were not "representational images"; nonetheless, people "actually saw themselves creating a society in the image of a garden."[18]

It is impossible, I think, to "prove" the inadequacy of a theoretical position. But we can indicate that some versions of some positions are implausible and that they lead to dubious results. Gilbert Ryle's now classic *The Concept of Mind* (London: Hutchinson, 1949) does this by exposing the inadequacies of one kind of Cartesianism—what is essentially the humanist view of images and symbols.[19] But let us initially make a traditional counterargument.

A crude Cartesian has two options. First, he can maintain his dualism but then must give up any talk about the external world. How can he know that any image refers to the external world? Once he stipulates that they are in different planes, it is impossible to bring them into any meaningful relation; in fact, it is not even clear what a relationship could conceivably be like. Descartes resorted to the pineal gland as the source and agent of mind-body interaction, but this does not appear to be an out for the humanists. Second, the Cartesian can assimilate what we normally take to be facts about the external world—for example, my seeing the man on the corner—to entities like images, symbols and myths. (When Leo Marx calls an image a verbal recording of a simple sense impression, he may be making this move.) Facts and images both become states of consciousness. If the Cartesian does this, he is committed to a form of idealism. Of course, this maneuver will never be open to (Karl) Marxists, but it also presents problems for the humanists: they have no immediate way of determining which states of consciousness are "imaginative" or "fantastic" or "distorted" or even "value laden" for there is no standard to which the varying states of consciousness may be referred. On either of these two options some resort

[17] Smith, pp. 18, 139.

[18] Marx, *Machine,* pp. 36, 43, 143. See also p. 159.

[19] Some have complained that the "Cartesian" views Ryle condemns may never have been held by Descartes. But the views Ryle does castigate are essentially similar to those the humanists hold—"crude Cartesianist" views.

to platonism is not strange. A world of suprapersonal ideas which we all share and which we may use to order our experiences is a reasonable supposition under the circumstances. But this position, although by no means absurd, is not one to which we wish to be driven if we are setting out a straightforward theory to explain past American behavior.

In the new preface to the Twentieth Anniversary Reissue of *Virgin Land* Smith confronts these issues directly. He admits that his former dualism of mind and environment was too strict. Adopting what I have called above the second Cartesian option, Smith writes that his old view "encouraged an unduly rigid distinction between symbols and myths on the one hand, and on the other a supposed extramental historical reality discoverable by means of conventional scholarly procedures." "Our perceptions of objects and events," he adds, "are no less a part of consciousness than are our fantasies." Yet Smith wants to have it both ways. On this view, we can never reach an external standard to judge the truth value of our conscious states; but this is exactly what Smith attempts to do. The relation of images to "historical events" is always changing; images impose coherence on "the data of experience"; and most important, "images are never, of course, exact reproductions of the physical and social environment." The obvious question is, what is this "environment"?[20] If it is external to consciousness, how can we know about it on Smith's view? If it is not, how do we—again on Smith's view—distinguish it from our images?

These ruminations do not clarify the confusions in American Studies Cartesianism, and the point of Ryle's *The Concept of Mind* is not to conduct an "argument" with the doctrine as I have done. Rather, Ryle urges that this view of consciousness—the realm of images and symbols—is logically misconceived. Ideas for Ryle are not entities existing in the head; they are not occurrences, episodes or events. The Cartesian position wrongly contends that mind and body are two different sorts of *things,* and that although the mind is not a thing existing in space, it is enough like such a thing that we can fruitfully talk of mind-body relations, as we would talk of the relations between two different physical objects. Suppose a spectator were to watch a successful college football team; he says that he knows the functions of the coach, the waterboy, the doctor and of each of the offensive and defensive players. He then says "But there is no one left on the field to contribute the element of *esprit de corps* for which the team is so famous. I don't see who exercises team spirit." It would have to be explained to him that he didn't know what to look for. Team spirit is not a task supplementary to all the others which someone must perform. It is, roughly, the keenness with which each of the special tasks is performed, and performing a task keenly

---

[20] Cambridge: Harvard Univ. Press, 1970, pp. vii–x.

is not performing two tasks. Our spectator does not know how to use the concept of team spirit; it cannot be understood as a specific thing. Similarly, for Ryle, mental concepts cannot be understood as things which exist in our heads. This kind of analysis gets the connection between the physical and the mental radically incorrect. For example, if a person has a good idea, he will not write, talk and argue *and* have a peculiar entity in his head; he will simply write, talk and argue in a convincing and intelligent manner. Having a mind is for an organism to be disposed to behave in a certain way, to possess certain propensities to action. The realm of the mental is not a realm of inner things, but a realm of observable activities and processes. As Ryle puts it, to speak of a person's mind is to speak of certain ways in which some of the incidents of his life are ordered; to talk of his abilities, liabilities and inclinations to do and undergo certain sorts of things, and of the doing and undergoing of these things in the ordinary world.[21]

Using something like a Rylean analysis of mind, we can easily reinterpret the Cartesian aspect of American Studies scholarship. How can we make its ideas clear? Suppose we define an idea not as some entity existing "in the mind" but as a disposition to behave in a certain way under appropriate circumstances. Similarly, to say that an author has a particular image of the man on the corner (or uses the man on the corner as a symbol) is to say that in appropriate parts of his work, he writes of a man on the corner in a certain way. When he simply writes of the man to refer to him, let's say, as the chap wearing the blue coat, we can speak of the image of the man, although the use of "image" seems to obfuscate matters. If the man is glorified in poem and song as Lincolnesque, we might speak of the author as using the man as a symbol, and here the word "symbol" seems entirely appropriate. For images and symbols to become collective is simply for certain kinds of writing (or painting) to occur with relative frequency in the work of many authors. Even this simplified dispositional analysis of the meaning of mental constructs at once avoids many of the obscurities into which we have fallen. Indeed, the use of a sometimes oracular language of literary criticism hides a powerful explanatory pattern: we have postulated the existence of mental constructs to explain certain (written) behavior; we analyze the meaning of these constructs in terms of the existence of this

---

[21] *The Concept of Mind*, esp. chap. 1, and pp. 167, 199. No one, of course, wishes to deny that some of us may at some times have what we have learned to describe as visual pictures in our heads. What Ryle denies is that such images function as a paradigm of what it is to have ideas. Moreover, I by no means want to imply that Ryle has said the last word or that my simple "behaviorist" account is adequate; the point is rather that the humanist theory is very confused, but that much of its thrust can be easily reconstructed. Interested readers might consult *Ryle*, ed. Oscar Wood and George Pitcher (New York: Doubleday, 1970) and *The Philosophy of Mind*, ed. Stuart Hampshire (New York: Harper and Row, 1966).

behavior as we simultaneously confirm our theoretical structure in the discovery of further behavior patterns of this sort.

Although this procedure meets some difficulties, what I have called the platonic strain in humanist scholarship is apparent in the intellectual history that it has produced, and in this area their theoretical approach has reinforced suspect substantive conclusions.

Presentism is notorious among the errors that historians can make — interpreting the past in concepts applicable only to the present. Historians are liable to read their interest back into the past, and misconstrue an individual's thought so that it is relevant for the present; the result will be that historians extract from an author what is significant for us, but lose the author's intentions. Whatever the final justifiability of a platonic view of ideas, it is not difficult to see that such a view could reinforce a presentist position. For platonists there is a set of eternal ideas existing independently of the individuals thinking about them, and intellectual history, in particular, becomes the history of enduring but competing concepts, of the posing of timeless questions and answers. It is, therefore, easy for a platonist historian to formalize his present concerns (which may or may not be among the enduring ideas) in a series of conflicting options; and then read these conceptions into the past. The worth of each past writer is measured by what he had to say on each preordained topic. Consequently, praise or blame is allocated by virtue of a writer's ability to comment on problems of interest to the platonist historian.

The accusation of presentism is difficult to sustain. It depends on the assumption that we know the correct interpretation of the past and that someone else is misinterpreting it. But the correct interpretation of the past is usually just what is being questioned, and so to argue that an historian is a presentist easily begs the question. Nonetheless, presentist traps would be easy for myth-symbol school platonism to fall into; moreover, the logical character of its substantive analyses of past thinkers constitutes evidence that it has not been interested in the authors' intentions but in the authors' relevance to the humanists.

It is clear that the humanists adopt a platonic approach to intellectual history. They use phrases like "archetypal form,"[22] which commit them to something like a platonistic view. Marx asserts that a full telling of his story would require him "to begin at the moment the idea of America entered the mind of Europe and come down to the present. . . ."[23] Smith writes that the success of the Lewis and Clark expedition "reactivated the oldest of all

[22] See, for example, Marx, *Machine*, p. 228.
[23] *Ibid.*, p. 4.

ideas associated with America—that of a passage to India" and begins his account of the "activation" of the idea with Columbus.[24] Sanford speculates that the "myth of Eden" may be important for all human experience and argues that it is indeed the central myth in all American experience.[25] Ward has the Jacksonians "extending in time an idea that had been cherished in this country since the Puritans. . . ."[26] Lewis writes that "propositions" like the natural goodness of man were not novel in 19th century America but "made their appearance with the birth of Christianity."[27]

In humanist scholarship, this view prevents an understanding of the peculiar intentions of a given thinker. For example, we find that earlier men are always "anticipating" later ones: in *The American Adam* Holmes follows the psychic pattern later proposed by Jung, and *Nick of the Woods* is "a faint and fitful anticipation" of Moby Dick;[28] Smith finds the myth of the garden present "in embryo" in an early writer;[29] Marx has various people "prefiguring" others;[30] and if this language is ambiguous, he also urges that *The Tempest* anticipates the moral geography of the American imagination, that Robert Beverly's early history anticipates "the coming fashion in thought and feeling," and that Carlyle anticipates "the post-Freudian version of alienation";[31] and *The Quest for Paradise* has Dante anticipating "the future course of history."[32]

We don't lack other examples, but the point is plain. Whatever value these discussions have for determining the significance *to us* of certain texts, it does not tell us what the authors meant, what they intended to say about the world. Consider this form of historical explanation: we must suppose, for example, that Carlyle sat down at his desk and thought "in this piece of writing I want to anticipate a post-Freudian version of alienation." We credit an author with a meaning he could not possibly have meant to convey since that meaning was not available to him; if we are concerned with the author's intention, it is logically inappropriate to suppose he could have meant to contribute to a debate whose terms were unavailable to him and whose point would have been lost on him.

There is another problem closely related to this one. Lewis writes that the Adamic image was "slow to work its way to the surface of American ex-

---

[24] Smith, p. 20; see also p. 235.

[25] Sanford, pp. vi, 34–35.

[26] Ward, p. 107; see also p. 168.

[27] Lewis, p. 32; see also p. 60.

[28] *Ibid.*, pp. 39, 92; see also p. 98.

[29] Smith, p. 139.

[30] Marx, *Machine,* pp. 32, 69, 72.

[31] *Ibid.*, pp. 72, 82, 178; see also pp. 186, 280n.

[32] Sanford, p. 38.

pression."[33] Ward argues that Melville's contemporaries did not read *Moby-Dick* but "in more obscure fashion" grappled with the same problems.[34] Marx has a "fully articulate" pastoral ideal "emerging" only at the end of the 18th century.[35] The danger here is that of too readily "reading in" a doctrine which a given writer could in principle have meant to state, but in fact had no intention to convey. If a gifted writer *meant* to articulate the doctrine with which he is being credited, why is it that he so often signally failed to do so?

Of course it is possible to purge humanist scholarship of these modes of expression: for a start we could give the enduring ideas names that, at least to us, had no peculiar relation to any one temporal period (for example, we could speak of an author as struggling to elaborate a notion of the unconscious rather than as anticipating Freud). Such a program, however, could easily become ahistoric. The descriptions to be used would necessarily be so broad and general that the ideas might take on a life of their own and do battle with one another in such a way that their "history" would become irrelevant. In any event, this sort of undertaking would require a radical recasting of myth-symbol scholarship: *its* analyses of ideas proceed *via* descriptions that are closely tied to the concerns of mid-20th century intellectuals; indeed, this is what makes this scholarship so suspect. The point is not that we can demonstrate a presentist orientation; rather, we maintain that it is wildly implausible for past thinkers to have intended to speak to our very specific contemporary problems.[36]

Whatever their difficulties as intellectual historians, humanist scholars, as Marx claims, have not merely attempted to write books about books.[37] They have also tried to relate intellectual currents to the culture's zeitgeist and to argue that some symbols and myths dominated all America. The road to this claim is a difficult one, and I want to examine three of its turnings: the way in which the notion of popular culture is constructed; the connection of this culture to ordinary life; and the sort of explanation involved in the use of this culture concept.

The humanist technique in identifying the "popular consciousness" is

---

[33] Lewis, p. 6; see also pp. 40, 85.

[34] Ward, p. 202.

[35] Marx, *Machine*, p. 73; see also p. 88.

[36] The preceding discussion owes much to the work of Quentin Skinner. See "Meaning and Understanding in the History of Ideas," *History and Theory*, 9 (1969), 3–53. This article and his more recent "On Performing and Explaining Linguistic Actions," *Philosophical Quarterly*, 21 (1971), 1–21, provide bibliographic references to his other papers. Pages 14–16 of the latter article clarify the confusions of those who have complained of the "intentional fallacy."

[37] Marx, *Machine*, p. 385.

first to examine popular writing—editorials, "best seller" and pulp fiction, political speeches. We cannot assume in these instances that the writers' intentions were to tell the truth about the world; on the contrary, what we are interested in is that the writers are very likely attempting to persuade the reader or listener of something; or to express what he already feels. The language writers choose will be designed to have these effects. Humanist works are perceptively aware of this problem and use it to argue their case; because popular writers or speakers are aware of their audience in the way they are, we can extrapolate from their work what was "in the mind" of the audience. The popularity of Robert Frost, Marx writes, "would seem to argue the universal appeal" of the way he conceives of the world.[38] Smith argues: "The individual [popular] writer abandons his own personality and identifies himself with the reveries of his readers. It is the presumably close fidelity of the . . . stories to the dream life of a vast inarticulate public that renders them valuable to the social historian and the historian of ideas."[39] Ward asserts that popular speeches of the early 19th century reflect "attitudes [which] express the need of the American people" to believe Jacksonian doctrines.[40] Commenting on public oratory, Trachtenberg states that "surely the conventions of language themselves suggest predispositions among Americans to react in certain ways at certain times."[41]

The central idea is that the popularity of a book or the success of a politician indicates that writers or speechifiers express the belief of the plain man or persuade him to adopt the belief they express. Now it may in some instances be true that speeches express people's beliefs or persuade them of these beliefs, or that popular fiction functions in these ways. But it is fallacious to infer from the popularity of politicians and pulp fiction that the contents of speeches or books are accurate indicators of a people's beliefs: this is a nice instance of the *post hoc ergo propter hoc* fallacy. Suppose we know that an author wishes to sell many copies of a book and that he feels he can do so by writing of murder and mayhem since he feels they in some way reflect his audience's "needs"; he writes his book and it indeed sells very well. To assume now that his murder and mayhem expressed the "needs" of the people is an unwarranted inference. The causal linkage may be true, but we simply don't *know* why many people read mysteries, science fiction or sensational best sellers. Similarly, suppose a Gilded Age politician waves the bloody shirt in a speech, hoping that this device expresses voters' beliefs or will convince them of his own, and elect him to office. And, voila,

[38] Marx, "Pastoral Ideals and City Troubles," *Journal of General Education*, 20 (1968–69), 260; see also 266–67.

[39] Smith, p. 101.

[40] Ward, p. 113.

[41] *Brooklyn Bridge*, p. 117.

he is elected. The vote for him may then be taken to legitimate the claim that his speech reflected what the people wanted to hear or that he persuaded them of what he believed himself. Here again, although the causal connection may be true we cannot justify the inference.[42]

Even if we overcome these problems, we are left with a second large question—the relation of "popular culture" to ordinary life. The "literate public" that reads popular books is much larger in number than the intellectuals whose behavior we initially wanted to explain. Nonetheless, this public is by no means everyone, and without hesitation American Studies scholarship has jumped from the "literate public" to everyone. Smith makes a representative statement along these lines; he writes that "most Americans would have said during the 1880's that the Homestead Act had triumphantly borne out the predictions of the 1860's [concerning the growth in numbers of yeoman farmers]."[43] If opinion polls today are any indication of people's knowledge, it is much more likely that most Americans of the 1880s would not have heard of the Homestead Act or predictions about it. Ultimately, however, my supposition is as unsupported as the one from *Virgin Land.* The simple point is that the imputation of collective beliefs is an extraordinarily complex empirical procedure which ought not to be undertaken lightly. Yet the humanists are persistently eager to speak of "the anonymous popular mind," "the widespread desire of Americans," "the imagination of the American people," "the majority of the people," "the popular conception of American life," "the American view of life" or "the average American."[44]

Trachtenberg, the most astute humanist critic, has pointed out this dilemma in commenting on recent critiques of "conservative" "consensus" history. The critiques appear applicable to the American Studies school which would certainly disavow these labels, and Trachtenberg writes:

> Was American society ever so unified, even in its values? And American popular culture, hasn't it been based, especially since the Civil War, on normative ideas of "national character" which actually *exclude* many people and modes of life? When we speak of "our culture," don't we mean "majority culture," or what seems to be majority culture, for how can one tell, if evidence of this "public mind" is mostly written material, written by elites for a "public at large," or popular literature fed to its readers? Without really concrete historical studies regarding who believed what when, and why, how much confidence can we have in what passes for "the general and pervasive meanings?"[45]

[42]See Ward's comment in "Looking Backward," p. 218.
[43]Smith, p. 220.
[44]*Ibid.,* p. 57; Ward, pp. 16, 24, 45; *Brooklyn Bridge,* p. 118; Marx, *Machine,* p. 3; Sanford, p. 254. Lewis' *American Adam* is exempt from this criticism.
[45]Trachtenberg, Review of Ward, *Red, White, and Blue, Carleton Miscellany,* 1970, p. 108.

We need not be caught up in the consensus-conflict debate to view American Studies generalizations with suspicion; we need only remember that many people live in a country and that attribution of motives to all of them requires extensive evidence.[46]

The third observation on popular culture concerns its explanatory role. The myth-symbol group offers a schema—in terms of some concept of culture—which is to explain the behavior of Americans throughout our history.[47] To focus on one example, consider the application to diplomatic history. Smith writes that inferences from the myth of the garden "will be recognized as the core of what we call isolationism,"[48] and 25 pages of Sanford's *Quest for Paradise* argue that "a world mission of regeneration" associated with the "Edenic myth" is "the great underlying postulate of American foreign policy."[49]

Now consider Gar Alperovitz's *Atomic Diplomacy*.[50] The book attempts to set out the viewpoint of the U.S. diplomatic elite in the immediate post-war period and maintains that the decision to drop the atomic bomb was primarily based on the belief that the use of the weapon would make the Russians more tractable. Of all the "revisionists" Alperovitz has been the most criticized. His opponents have mounted attack after attack concerning his use of evidence and his ability to substantiate the claim he makes. I have no desire to add to this controversy. What I wish to point out is that historians make severe demands on their peers concerning the adequacy of explanation. Alperovitz' work is nearly 300 pages long, and deals with a four-month period in American history and the motivations of perhaps fifteen men. Nonetheless, his critics have not regarded as satisfactory the empirical data he has brought to bear on the questions he tries to answer.

If we turn to humanist scholarship we face, of course, a much larger explanatory schema which is not designed to explain behavior in the way that Alperovitz does. But the humanists suppose that their myths and symbols form a hierarchical structure which has a consistent and verifiable relation to those more specific beliefs with which Alperovitz, for example, is trying

[46] On this question one ought to consider Marx's notion of an "informal random sample," "American Studies," pp. 84–85; see also *Machine*, pp. 193 ff.

[47] One serious problem in the humanist movement concerns the use of the word "culture." Although writers imply that they are using the word as an anthropologist would, they do not take up, for example, the ways Americans perceive sex and kinship relations or patterns of deference and authority—traditional concerns of the cultural anthropologist. Rather, many writings in American Studies apparently combine the anthropological meaning of "culture" with its meaning as it occurs in "he's very cultured" or "he's low-culture"; "culture" here means a style of social and artistic expression peculiar to a society or class. The two senses of the word are related, but the assimilation of the two, or failure to define a third can lead only to trouble.

[48] Smith, p. 218.

[49] Sanford, p. 229.

[50] New York: Vintage, 1965.

to understand behavior. I am not at all clear what this series of relations amounts to. But before we can accept this sort of explanatory pattern at all, we must be able to specify how confirmation or disconfirmation of a lower-level explanation is connected to an American Studies symbol or myth at a higher level; in other words we must have some idea of how we can decide on the truth or falsity of humanist claims. We must know how the truth or falsity of Alperovitz' assertions supports the argument that the United States is conducting "diplomacy in Eden"; or legitimates the position that isolationism and the myth of the garden are connected. If myth-symbol generalizations have any substance, they must be subject to falsification by the conclusion of "lower-level" historical research. If we do not know how to establish links between the two levels, the humanists will not have achieved viable explanations of any behavior; what we would have instead are a series of ruminations with little empirical content, and not history.

The three criticisms concerning extrapolations from popular literature to history are serious but in some measure obvious and pedestrian. Far more important from a theoretical viewpoint is the humanist analysis of the relation between the great work of art and the culture in which it is written. Here we must explore a treacherous area involving the deepest commitments and basic assumptions of the myth-symbol school. Whatever its emphasis on popular literature, the school has evinced an immense respect for the significant works of American fiction and their position as cultural documents. Marx has explored this problem explicitly, and although I shall be concerned with his formulations, the arguments he puts forward are, I suspect, crucial for everyone who views great books as keys to the study of the cultures of which they are a part. Marx's earlier writings seem to imply that the work of art "reflects" or "expresses" historical truths about the period in question: it is a source of knowledge about some body of extra-literary experience, and a proper understanding of this art is a shortcut around masses of historical data.[51] To those not already committed to the magical qualities of the novel, this position has little, if any, merit. The question we must always ask is what grounds we have for asserting the truths the novel is supposed to express. *Ex hypothesi* the work offers its own grounds, i.e., the fact that it is great art warrants our belief in what it is said to reflect. Why we should accept this notion is unclear, and whatever his earlier perspective Marx deprecates the idea in a recent theoretical article.[52]

The argument he puts forward in its stead is powerful but, I believe, mis-

[51] Bernard Bowron, Leo Marx and Arnold Rose, "Literature and Covert Culture," *American Quarterly*, 9 (1957), 380–81; Marx, *Machine*, pp. 10–11.

[52] Marx, "American Studies." Marx sets up his discussion by posing a dichotomy between the humanist and the social science-content analyst. I do not think this dichotomy exhaustive; see also Trachtenberg, *Brooklyn Bridge*, pp. 136–37.

taken. He begins by defining the essential quality of an enduring literary achievement as the "inherent capacity of a work to generate the emotional and intellectual responses of its readers." We measure the extent to which a work has this quality by placing our faith "in the impersonal process of critical scholarly consensus. . . . trusting that in the long run it will correct or eliminate invalid observations. . . ." It is perhaps unfair to offer comment at this point, but in light of the issues Marx raises it becomes imperative. There is no objection to basing our literary appraisal of *Moby-Dick*—Marx's example—on "the process of critical scholarship."[53] But this is inconsistent with his idea that the novel has an *inherent* capacity to generate satisfactory emotional and intellectual responses. If a work has this inherent capacity, then its aesthetic merit should be clear to everyone; *Moby-Dick*, for example, would have been acclaimed as a masterpiece upon publication, and there would be no question of achieving critical consensus, or of relying on the judgment of literary critics. My feeling is that Marx's use of "inherent" cannot really be upheld, and that he would rather wish to argue that the literary power of *Moby-Dick* is demonstrated by the scholarly consensus about its merit: *Moby-Dick* is a great work of art because it continues to be emotionally and intellectually satisfying to successive generations of those who are trained in the techniques of literary criticism. This makes Marx consistent and yields a justifiable definition—for who should define literary merit but those who spend their lives considering such questions?

I am doubtful, however, if the use of "inherent" is a slip. Marx goes on to say that books like *Moby-Dick* are major sources for the humanist "in his continuing effort to recover the usable past."[54] If the work of art has an inherent capacity to generate satisfactory emotional and intellectual responses, then in recovering a usable past the humanist is merely using material whose acceptability is plain to everyone. He simply speaks for us all. But as Marx states, it is the community of humanists who define the greatness of a work of art, whatever inherent qualities it has notwithstanding. The humanists, and they alone, are determining the material out of which they are to reconstruct the usable past. In bringing together literature and history in this fashion, Marx has defined a mandarin caste—the humanists, literary critics with an interest in history—whose task it is, by definition, to determine the relation of the past to the present. But before we can understand this notion fully, we must spell out the way in which *Moby-Dick* helps us to recover "the usable past."

Marx is not concerned here with the past; he says that the best books need not tell us about past actuality: "If our purpose is to represent the

[53] Marx, "American Studies," p. 81.
[54] *Ibid.*, p. 80.

common life then we should not turn to the masterpieces we continue to read and enjoy. Probably it would be best, for that purpose, to put literature aside altogether." Rather, Marx says that books of the stature of *Moby-Dick* comprise a larger and larger portion of the consciousness of 19th century America that remains effectively alive in the present; so far as the present is concerned, *Moby-Dick becomes* the culture which produced it.[55] Since this view comprises "the crux of the method" Marx defends, American Studies does not appear to be an historical enterprise, and should we accept it, we have no business to masquerade as historians at all. More significantly, we must face up to the implications of the function of Marx's humanists: they define what has literary merit, and their interpretation of this literature frames the proper understanding of the past.

However we feel about this allocation of responsibility, there are two more substantive problems involved in Marx's analysis. First, it is not at all clear that *in fact* great novels come to comprise a larger and larger portion of past consciousness effectively alive in the present. This is true for literary critics, perhaps true for some members of the educated public; but we cannot extrapolate from generalizations about these groups to speculation about the entire culture. A much more appropriate candidate than *Moby-Dick* in this instance would be elements of Lincoln's character. But here we are dealing with a complex empirical question—what aspects of the past are alive in the present—and if we are to answer it, we cannot do so by a supposition about the significance of the literary elite.

The second substantive problem concerns what in the past *ought* to be alive in the present. As scholars I don't think we have any options: what ought to be alive are the most significant aspects of past actuality. I do not think Marx would deny this. Indeed, I think he affirms it. At one point he urges that the essential quality of great literature—its capacity to generate satisfactory emotional and intellectual responses—is identical "in a word" to "its compelling truth value"; *Moby-Dick* has "cognitive value."[56] Marx is not simply arguing that *Moby-Dick* is that part of the past most alive today, but apparently when properly understood *Moby-Dick* tells us something true and important about 19th century America. In short, I believe that when Marx stresses the novel's importance for obtaining a usable past, he is not abandoning historical scholarship. He also believes that the usable past determined by American Studies techniques corresponds to the most significant aspects of past actuality. But if this is so, we have come in a circle: *Moby-Dick* "expresses" or "reflects" essential truths about American culture, and those of us in American Studies are elected to determine these truths.

[55] *Ibid.,* p. 89.
[56] *Ibid.*

As I have previously noted, Marx rejects the expressive position, but his reasoning leads us nowhere else. Before the American Studies humanists can make a case for their approach, or before we can solve the difficult problems involved in the study of past cultures, we must have clearer thinking than this.

I should end this discussion with an apology and a defense. My conclusions are mainly negative: that humanist scholarship in American Studies illustrates a set of classic errors. But I realize that philosophical criticism is much easier to do than constructive empirical research. Nonetheless, it seems worthwhile to ascertain whether some frameworks of analysis are perhaps more likely to lead us astray than to help us deal coherently with the past. This is the modest sort of investigation I have attempted.[57]

[57]Although none should be associated with any of the positions I have taken above, the following people commented helpfully on an earlier version of this paper: Henry Abelove, Sydney Ahlstrom, Dorothy Dunn, Daniel Walker Howe, Leo Ribuffo, Alan Trachtenberg and Michael Zuckerman. I also profited from an informal discussion of some of these issues at colloquia at Amherst College and Wesleyan University.

Howard P. Segal

Bruce Kuklick's "Myth and Symbol in American Studies" is a landmark critique of the pioneering works of Henry Nash Smith, Leo Marx, John William Ward, and other giants in the field. Kuklick's straightforward but tough-minded commentary on books that largely shaped American studies in its formative period is devastating. He reveals classic philosophical errors and basic methodological failings in the efforts to identify, through myths and symbols, a distinctive and uniform American culture and experience. More specifically, he objects to the paucity of discussion of methodological premises, the use of fragmentary evidence to make questionable generalizations about what Kuklick sees as a multiplicity of American culture and experience, and the substitution of platonic forms for material realities. Calling for more "constructive empirical research," Kuklick argues that future generations of scholars will readily accept his criticisms of the pioneers' avowedly "unscientific" approach, an approach Marx had outlined in his "American Studies—A Defense of an Unscientific Method" (1969).

Rather than detail Kuklick's criticisms, I will use my own empirical research to show how right he was—and still is. I will focus on Marx's work partly because Kuklick focuses on him more than on any other pioneer and partly because my own struggles with Marx's work in the course of my research led me to see the wisdom of Kuklick's critique. When I first read Kuklick's article upon its appearance in 1972, I was a graduate student in American history at Princeton University, which unfortunately has never had a graduate program in American studies. I was working on a doctoral dissertation on American technological utopianism, or the faith that unadulterated technological progress would eventually lead to perfection. After reading Marx's *The Machine in the Garden* (New York: Oxford University Press, 1964) and related books, I had come to believe that, in modern America at least, nature and technology were invariably antagonistic; that nature in whatever form was almost always technology's

Bruce Kuklick, "Myth and Symbol in American Studies," originally appeared in *American Quarterly* 24, no. 4 (October 1972), Copyright 1972, Trustees of the University of Pennsylvania.

enemy and, usually, the victim before technology's unrelenting advance. Yet my empirical research on technological utopianism from the Civil War on increasingly suggested to me that this polarity was inaccurate and should no longer be perpetuated. If, as I discovered, even the American technological utopians, the supreme believers in technology's right to progress anywhere and everywhere, reconciled nature and technology in various ways, which Americans did not? And if comparatively few Americans actually viewed nature and technology as wholesale antagonists, how were the two reconciled?

Despite my complete agreement with Kuklick's critique of Marx's work, in pursuing these questions I eventually found the greatest assistance in, of all places, *The Machine in the Garden*—in Marx's concept of a "middle landscape" that mediates between the polarities of wilderness and civilization, rural and urban, pre-industrial and advanced industrial. It differed from the traditional pastoral not in fusing nature and civilization but in fusing them in new ways and in response to a new condition: widespread industrialism. Yet I ultimately rejected as inaccurate Marx's conclusion that nature and technology, once reconciled from roughly 1770 to the Civil War, were thereafter permanently split. After 1860, Marx contends, rampant industrialization, immigration, and finally urbanization—to recite the worn litany—overran and spoiled the real landscape. Marx reads all major American (white male) writers from Hawthorne to Fitzgerald as successively predicting, observing, and bemoaning this fact. After 1860, Marx claims, the machine and the pastoral were incompatible. The middle landscape was no longer a realistic social and cultural ideal but a cheap rhetorical device masking a painfully different reality.

Yet this bold position, initially so convincing, finally seemed at odds with what had been written by any number of other scholars, especially historians, who used more conventional, less literary evidence and whose empirical research implicitly contradicted Marx's. In case after case I discovered that the "middle landscape" ideal and experience had certainly changed but, contrary to Marx, had never disappeared, at least not among ordinary Americans as opposed to great writers. As far as I could determine, in the absence of opinion surveys, most Americans still wanted some version of the proverbial "best of both worlds." Marx's insightful readings of those great writers did not, alas, constitute "*The* American Experience" for nearly everyone else. As I steadily dissented from American studies gospel, Kuklick's article repeatedly provided much-needed intellectual reassurance.

Kuklick's article also assisted me as I analyzed Marx's metaphysical claims about the pastoral ideal itself. Marx's grandest claim is that the pastoral ideal embodies the meaning of America. Kuklick's connection of such myths and symbols to ahistorical platonic forms bearing no necessary resemblance to changing material realities made me realize that Marx's claim is simply unprovable, no matter how much additional empirical research I might do. I could now return to the middle landscape, which my empirical research had already shown to be a fact as well as a concept, and trace its evolution over time.

Eventually I came up with three new versions of the middle landscape: urban, suburban, and regional. The urban version came first. It arose after 1830 and as a "movement" lasted until about 1900. Where the original version—Marx's exclusive version—meant a fusion of nature and civilization, or garden and machine, the urban version meant, instead, their juxtaposition. Where, however, civilization in the original version did not include cities, in the urban version it did; the virtual inseparability of large-scale industrialization from urbanization was now conceded. The aim of the urban middle landscape was not to escape from the cities but to balance them against the country. Manifestations of this new middle landscape included "rural" cemeteries, "rural" walkways, and city parks. New York City's Central Park exemplifies the scrupulous planning that went into the urban middle landscape.

The suburban middle landscape developed after 1880, with the comprehensive planning of suburbs. Earlier suburbs were only retreats from cities and not, as Frederick Law Olmsted and others wished, means of revitalizing them. As I studied further I found that comprehensively planned suburbs themselves divide into three varieties: the commuter suburb (Shaker Heights, Ohio; the Country Club District of Kansas City, Missouri); the industrial suburb (Pullman, Illinois); and the "garden cities" inspired by the English reformer Ebenezer Howard (Forest Hills Gardens, Long Island; Radburn, New Jersey; Greenbelt, Maryland). In all three cases the country is accessible to the city precisely through technology—through railroads and, later, cars.

The regional middle landscape came about the same time as the suburban, but on a much larger scale. Pioneering late nineteenth- and early twentieth-century conservationists were not romantic nature lovers, as traditionally portrayed, but hard-nosed scientists and technicians determined to apply scientific techniques to their ends. They and later advocates of the regional middle landscape, such as the Regional Planning Association of

America (1923–1933), envisioned vast well-planned landscapes integrating cities, suburbs, towns, and farms. Examples of the regional middle landscape include the Tennessee Valley Authority and the "megalopolis," a massive urban-suburban tract with, to be sure, often negative connotations.

Clearly the middle landscape concept is applicable beyond Marx's restricted use of it, and his contention in 1964 that the middle landscape had passed from the American scene a century earlier was unduly gloomy. In later writings Marx has acknowledged, however reluctantly, the persistence until now of some Americans' quest for a middle landscape amidst various political, environmental, and technological upheavals. Yet his basic position remains unchanged: the pastoral ideal still defines the meaning of America. It remains a platonic form impervious to the multiplicity of American culture and experience.

I can certainly understand Marx's bitterness, as indicated in the introduction to his 1988 collection of previously published essays, *The Pilot and the Passenger* (New York: Oxford University Press, 1988), at being subjected to Kuklick's criticism of his work. But his characterization of Kuklick as having excessive "social scientific and positivistic inclinations" (p. ix) does not exactly refute Kuklick's fundamental charges; it only reconfirms Kuklick's criticism of insufficient methodological discussion in pioneering American studies works. Marx's defense is to compare himself, Smith, Ward, and others to symbolic anthropologists like Victor Turner and Clifford Geertz. The latter, however, have surely done extensive fieldwork before reaching their conclusions.

Nevertheless, American studies is ultimately stronger for having these basic methodological issues raised. And Kuklick—along with Marx—deserves praise for forcing us to raise them.

R. GORDON KELLY

Literature and
the Historian

MY PURPOSE IN THIS ESSAY IS TWOFOLD. IT IS FIRST TO RECONSIDER ASPECTS of the problem of using imaginative literature as historical evidence and to propose a solution which appears consistent with convergent tendencies in other disciplines although it is at variance with much previous work in American Studies, particularly that of the so-called myth-symbol school of interpretation. Second, I propose to illustrate the position worked out in the first part of this essay with references to a body of late 19th century American fiction for children. Any document which survives the vicissitudes of time and finds its way to the historian's desk is likely to be pressed into service in his efforts to reconstruct patterns of past behavior and belief. If nothing else, the relative accessibility of imaginative literature would tempt the historian to use it. Owing to publication, widespread distribution and our customs of preserving literary material, literature is less vulnerable than many other types of documents to the circumstances, both of accident and policy, that tend to winnow the historical record. But literary works are sometimes commended to the historian's attention not simply, or even primarily, because such documents tend to survive and be accessible. Literary works, and especially those regarded as most significant in aesthetic terms, are often said to be deeply, even uniquely expressive of the society, or the "culture," in which they were produced.[1]

---

*Portions of this essay were read at a session of the ASA convention in San Francisco, October 1973. I should like to acknowledge those who commented on the paper—Kay Mussell and Chadwick Hausen—as well as Melvyn Hammarberg and Michael Zuckerman whose criticisms of an earlier draft contributed to the improvement of this one.

[1]Significant recent efforts to accommodate both historical (or sociological) interests and critical interests include: Wesley Morris, *Towards a New Historicism* (Princeton: Princeton Univ. Press, 1972); Geoffrey Hartman, *Beyond Formalism: Literary Essays 1958–1970* (New Haven: Yale Univ. Press, 1970); Richard Hoggart, *Contemporary Cultural Studies* (Birmingham, England: Centre for Contemporary Cultural Studies, 1969); and Diana Laurenson and Alan Swingewood, *The Sociology of Literature* (New York: Schocken, 1972). William

We need not rehearse the history of this argument to appreciate its appeal for a field like American Studies. Lacking, even now, a body of theory, method and data sufficiently differentiated to distinguish it as a discipline in its own right, American Studies has been dependent in large measure on assumptions carried over from the disciplines of history and literature out of which it has been fashioned both intellectually and institutionally. The argument for the evidential superiority of great literature has had an important place in the development of the field since it preserves intact the traditional emphasis of literary scholarship and criticism on a relatively small group of classic works.[2] Nevertheless, the marriage of literary criticism and history seems not to have been made in heaven. The strain is readily apparent in the unsatisfactory efforts made to date to resolve increasingly divergent emphases in the two disciplines. The practice of literary criticism in the last thirty years has amply demonstrated that the interpretation of literary documents can be pursued in a fashion quite consciously and deliberately ahistorical and without very much attention being paid to the problem of adjudicating among conflicting interpretations of the same text.

Even when literary study has been thoroughly historicist in orientation, however, literary scholars have generally acknowledged the legitimacy, indeed the necessity, for aesthetic evaluation. They have typically concentrated their attention on the relatively small canon of superior artistic achievements considered to have present relevance and meaning largely independent of the circumstances of the works' creation. Condemned to serve the jealous demands both of history and criticism, literary historians seek a delicate balance—to avoid identifying the meaning and value of a work too closely with its cultural origins, on the one hand, or too closely with the critic's subjectivity on the other. The former, the more reprehensible apparently, invites the charge of reductionism, the latter of solipsism and "presentism." Supported by corollary assumptions about the perspicacity of great artists and the autonomy of great works, the argument that those works which are most valued on their aesthetic merits are also superior sources of historical knowledge has a considerable measure of appeal and plausibility for those who have come into American Studies from training in literature. Insofar as American Studies has been, in fact and theory, an effort to blend

---

Charvat's work remains a model for the effective blending of historical scholarship and literary interpretation; see esp. his essays on Longfellow, Melville, and literary economics in *The Profession of Authorship in America, 1800–1870*, ed. Matthew J. Bruccoli (Columbus: Ohio State Univ. Press, 1968).

[2]See, for example, *American Studies: Essays on Theory and Method*, ed. Robert Merideth (Columbus, Ohio: Merrill, 1968); Alexander C. Kern, "American Studies and American Literature: Approaches to a Study of Thoreau," *College English*, 27 (1966), 480–86; Seymour Katz, " 'Culture' and Literature in American Studies," *American Quarterly*, 20 (Summer Supp. 1968), 318–29.

literary and historical studies, its central problem is identical with that of literary historicism in general, a problem that can be traced at least as far back as the French literary historian Hippolyte Taine.

The most recent effort, within the context of American Studies, to make the argument for the evidential significance of great works of literature is Leo Marx's "American Studies: Defense of an Unscientific Method."[3] In this essay, Professor Marx justifies a traditional humanistic commitment to great literature and describes the assumptions and methods underlying his influential study of responses to industrialization in the antebellum period, *The Machine in the Garden.* In what appears to be a departure from his earlier position, Marx now defines the significance of literary documents in terms of a central tenet of formalist literary theory, namely the concept of literary power, which "refers to the inherent capacity of a work to generate the emotional and intellectual response of its readers" (p. 80 n.). An acknowledged artistic achievement like *Moby Dick,* Marx concludes, "is useful [to the cultural historian] for its satisfying power, its capacity to provide a coherent organization of thought and feeling, or in a word, for its compelling truth value" (p. 80). Moreover, "the high value attached to Melville's novel rests upon its continuing—one might say, growing—capacity, as compared with an editorial of 1851, to provide us with satisfaction, and to shape our experience of past and present" (p. 89).

If I understand Marx's argument, several comments seem appropriate. First, despite his references to cultural history, it is far from clear how his argument squares with the traditional aim of historians which he invokes early in the essay: the historian's task, Marx acknowledges, is "the effort to describe and understand the state of mind of a group (or groups) of people at some moment in the past" (p. 76). Given this purpose, however, the evidential significance of literature would seem to be a function of the group for whom the work is demonstrably the expression; and Marx himself admits that a work like *Moby Dick* may have only peripheral significance in these terms. Moreover, to establish that a work is expressive of a group's state of mind (regardless of how that phrase is construed) requires moving outside the text to considerations of audience characteristics and response. The doctrine of literary power, as sketched by Marx, provides no clear principle for specifying the character or boundaries of a work's "social domain," since the extent to which a work embodies widely shared social meanings cannot be reconstructed solely from an analysis of textual elements. Finally, when Marx concludes that "the importance we attach to [*Moby Dick*] arises, in the last analysis, from the fact that today it is read, studied, and incorporated in our sense of ourselves and of our world, past and present" (p. 89), he appears to have abandoned altogether the study of the past, at least in the only terms in

[3] In *New Literary History,* 1 (1969), 75–90.

which he defines the historian's task. *Moby Dick* is read today because it is important—and it is important to us, finally, because we read it. Marx's allegiance is to the critical evaluation of literature. The consequence of this allegiance is to construe historical knowledge as a function of documents selected on the basis of ahistorical criteria.[4]

It should also be noted that the argument from literary power contains an implicit judgment that books like *Moby Dick* have shaped our sense of antebellum America. The extent of Melville's influence is properly a problem in specifying the social distribution of knowledge and is amenable to empirical investigation.[5] But even if it is demonstrated, as it doubtless can be, that Melville's novel has substantially shaped the understanding of the past held by a subset of American intellectuals, we may properly question whether invoking the doctrine of inherent power is either necessary or sufficient to explain this phenomenon. The process "which brings the subject matter of the humanities into existence" remains imperfectly understood, as Marx himself admits (p. 76). Until that process is better understood, until we know better the social processes which legitimate art, for instance—presumably by examining the institutionalization of literature, and its ideology—we have little warrant for explaining the characteristic preoccupations of humanists by reference primarily to postulated textual qualities.

Finally, it may be asked: What is gained by reifying literature, by imputing to it a considerable measure of autonomy? The answer seems clear enough. By defining literature in terms of an inherent power to compel responses, we reduce the need to examine the social factors which might otherwise be presumed to shape both the creation and the effect of literature. Like any rudimentary theory, the doctrine of inherent power focuses attention on a range of phenomena, in this case the elements of aesthetic form of a few cherished texts, and implies an appropriate method—close textual analysis. The theory also implies an explanation for the survival of these few texts: their continued relevance is a function of inherent power, and is thus largely independent of social process. This presumed autonomy of literary works has the added advantage of making the study of literature appear to be free from political and ideological influences and of permitting the claim that aesthetic judgments are largely independent of the critic's cultural context.

If we seek to understand the factors which historically have shaped the production and consumption of literature in American society—as a necessary first step in specifying the evidential significance of literary texts—

---

[4]Ibid. Marx, it should be acknowledged, does attempt to anticipate this particular criticism, but not very satisfactorily: "Although the concept of literary power would seem at first glance to be ahistorical, it provides a more reliable and useful measure of historical significance than the older, relatively superficial test of representational value" (p. 80 n.). Why this should be so remains unclear.

[5]Cf. Bruce Kuklick, "Myth and Symbol in American Studies," *American Quarterly,* 24 (Oct. 1972), 435–50.

we can hardly avoid employing more inclusive concepts of culture and more complex social models than are implicit in the doctrine of literary power. The assumptions frequently carried over into American Studies from the study of literature—namely that great literature constitutes a qualitatively superior kind of cultural evidence, that it is autonomous, and that inferences from such works can be readily generalized to society as a whole and to a wide range of behavior—must be severely qualified, if not abandoned completely; for these assumptions appear now to hold only for the simplest model of culture and have little predictive or explanatory power for American society, past or present. Secondly, these assumptions seem especially ill-suited to understanding past behavior "in terms of the systems of thought and action of which they were a part."[6]

The saliency of the culture concept for American Studies is not a new idea, although it has received little more than cursory attention from those associated with the myth-symbol mode of interpretation, an approach which benefits from making as little distinction as possible between culture in the sense of artistic expression and achievement and culture in the more analytical and descriptive sense used by anthropologists. Ten years ago, in his well-known article "American Studies and the Concept of Culture," Richard Sykes sought to ground a definition of American Studies on the concept of culture formulated by Clyde Kluckhohn and Alfred Kroeber and to explore, particularly, the implications of that formulation for the use of literature as cultural evidence.[7] Unfortunately Sykes' argument and his examination of an episode from *Winesburg, Ohio* proved disappointing: Sykes "says nothing about the relationship to reality fiction does have. Nor does he discuss the function of fiction," one commentator remarked.[8] Significantly, the article seems to have failed to stimulate further work, by Sykes or others, using the approach he outlined.

In an effort to remedy the weaknesses of Sykes' formulations, Seymour Katz subsequently drew upon the work of Leslie White for a concept of culture that promised to restore to literature a crucial cultural function and to enhance its evidential significance. According to Katz, literature (particularly the "imagistic" genres of narrative, drama and lyric) constitutes a "cognitive model of experience, a hypothetical construction by means of which we may come to know more about experience than experience alone can show." Literary works are implicated in the "larger cultural process of forming new concepts, or extending, criticizing or reconstructing already existing concepts" (p. 323). The characters of *The Scarlet Letter,* Katz suggests, may be

[6]Murray G. Murphey, *Our Knowledge of the Historical Past* (Indianapolis: Bobbs-Merrill, 1973), p. 120.
[7]"American Studies and the Concept of Culture: A Theory and Method," *American Quarterly,* 15 (Summer Supp. 1963), 253–70.
[8]Katz, " 'Culture' and Literature," p. 320.

regarded as "Hawthorne's premises, and the action of the romance is his projection, in terms of the options available to each person, and the probabilities of each person's nature and character, of what they would choose and what they would suffer because of those choices. . . . in making those projections Hawthorne remained scrupulously within the framework of probabilities set by the natures and characters he had premised. He thereby has provided us with a cognitive model in which he shows us how persons of certain types, involved in a particular situation, 'will on occasion speak or act, according to the law of probability or necessity'" (pp. 324–25).

There is much that is useful and substantial in Katz's formulations. He cites corroborative evidence to suggest that Hawthorne was, in fact, interested in the meaning of character in the abstract at the time he was working on *The Scarlet Letter*. There is evidence, also, to suggest that some readers responded to the novel as "a cognitive model of human nature and character" (p. 327). For whom it served as a critique of existing ideas, and with what effect is not clear, however. "The determination of whether Hawthorne's romance was a significant contribution to the history of the concept of character will have to await the writing of that history," Katz concludes (p. 327). Although his choice of Hawthorne's novel is based ostensibly on a practical criterion—the relative familiarity of the novel for the purpose of illustrating his argument—Katz's choice of a theory of culture seems predicated primarily on a desire to recover a crucial cultural role for literature like *The Scarlet Letter*. He is content finally to hypothesize that Hawthorne's novel functioned as a cognitive model. This decision may be seen as legitimating the study of Hawthorne in a cultural context, perhaps, but leaves unresolved both the issue of confirming the hypothesis and the problem of specifying the range of meanings which may be appropriately attributed to a given text.

It seems a better tactic to begin with a concept of culture, one that promises to contribute to the historian's task as previously defined, rather than to begin with a commitment to great literature, and then to explore the implications of the concept for the use of literary documents as historical evidence. The definition of culture outlined below undermines any easy assumption that great literature, as it is usually defined, necessarily constitutes a superior source of historical knowledge; but the concept provides a framework in which to begin a systematic examination of the social function of literature within the various groups comprising American society.

The term "culture" has a long and complicated history. Although no single definition of culture prevails absolutely among anthropologists, there appears to be wide agreement on a number of points.[9] It seems clear, for example,

---

[9]*Man in Adaptation: The Cultural Present*, ed. Yehudi Cohen (Chicago: Aldine, 1968), pp. 7–12.

that an essential aspect of a given way of life is the "cultural knowledge" that orders, informs and gives meaning to behavior; what Clifford Geertz has called the "set of control mechanisms—plans, recipes, rules, instructions—for the governing of behavior."[10] This cultural knowledge is specific to a particular group of persons, and functions to define an environment and to relate individuals to that environment and to their fellow men. Since it is the perceptual/conceptual system of a group which defines the meaning of its members' actions, human behavior is intelligible in terms of that system.[11] The creation, publication and selective preservation of literary texts constitute kinds of behavior, after all. If we are to understand these forms of behavior, we would do well to begin with a concept of context that directs attention to the rules and definitions which order and govern the creation and consumption of literature rather than to begin with an ethnocentric commitment to a particular type of literary product. Nevertheless, Geertz is essentially correct, when, to illustrate his position, he says of the cathedral at Chartres: "To understand what it means, to perceive it for what it is, you need to know rather more than the generic properties of stone and glass and rather more than what is common to all cathedrals. You need to understand also—and, in my opinion, most critically—the specific concepts of the relations between God, man and architecture that, having governed its creation, it consequently embodies."[12] This does not comprehend all that might be designated as the "meaning" of Chartres, of course, but it begins to distinguish *historical* meaning—meaning in terms of the society which created Chartres—from whatever significance Chartres has had (and for whom) in more recent centuries.

The emphasis on cultural knowledge advocated here directs attention, then, to what passes for knowledge, to what has significance and value—and in what terms—for particular groups of people living in different times and places. It acknowledges the probability that these characteristic structures of meaning will vary greatly from one group to another. Knowledge—in the sense of the certainty that phenomena are real and possess specific characteristics—is differentially distributed in any society or group. Knowledge inheres in social roles, is expressed and sustained or altered in the course of social interaction, and these roles are specific to a particular society. Even in relatively simple societies, no person has access to the totality of knowledge and the rules for behavior that are known by all members collec-

---

[10]"The Impact of the Concept of Culture on the Concept of Man," in Cohen, *Man in Adaptation,* p. 24. Cf. Peter Berger and Thomas Luckmann, *The Social Construction of Reality* (Garden City, N.Y.: Doubleday, 1966), p. 65.

[11]See Murphey, *Our Knowledge of the Historical Past,* pp. 67–98.

[12]Geertz, "The Impact of the Concept of Culture on the Concept of Man," p. 27. Cf. Otto von Simson, *The Gothic Cathedral* (New York: Pantheon, 1956).

tively. Anthony Wallace argues, in fact, that "it would be difficult to find *any* single cognitive structure that is uniformly shared by all members of any community. . . ." All societies are plural societies.[13]

No single informant, we conclude, can be expected to comprehend even a simple culture, in the sense defined here, in anything approaching its entirety. Since no two persons perceive and internalize identical experiences, the widest possible sample of informants is desirable, if we seek to describe and account for patterns of past behavior and belief. Given the complexity and diversity of cultural knowledge in American society, it seems equally unwarranted to conceive of America as a unitary culture for the purposes of historical analysis or to define a handful of literary figures as qualitatively superior cultural informants.[14] Given the bases for aesthetic evaluation, it would be coincidental that a work's aesthetic value would be a measure of the author's significance as a cultural informant. The best intellectual historians have recognized the diversity and social distribution of cultural knowledge, and their generalizations hold for specific groups—17th century Massachusetts Puritans (rather than all colonial settlers); the 19th century gentry class (rather than all middle-class Americans); or the American school of anthropology.[15]

Crucial objections to the postulated autonomy of art ought to be clear also in light of the argument proposed here. Anthropologists have long emphasized that culture is learned. The values, attitudes, expectations and rules for behavior that characterize the members of a particular group are not genetically prescribed but are taught by procedures that are themselves specific to groups and are subject to change over time. The assumption that great works of art have some inherent capacity to persist over time and to evoke relatively uniform kinds of aesthetic responses is surely in need of severe qualification. Unless literature is an exception among classes of cultural artifacts, its social significance is maintained because specialized institutions selectively conserve certain books, provide access to them, and more or less successfully justify and defend the social significance ascribed to

---

[13]Anthony F. C. Wallace, *Culture and Personality,* 2nd ed. (New York: Random House, 1970), pp. 109–10. Elsewhere Wallace has argued that "an effective and viable sociocultural system can evolve which is categorically beyond the capacity of any of its members to incorporate in a single plan, and (ii) that the maximum size of a sociocultural system is associated with a minimal level of cognitive sharing." "Culture and Cognition," in Spradley, *Culture and Cognition,* p. 125.

[14]Although Marx acknowledges the importance of better models of social structure, he continues to use the term "national culture." "American Studies," p. 84.

[15]Perry Miller, *The New England Mind* (Cambridge: Harvard Univ. Press, 1939); Stow Persons, *The Decline of American Gentility* (New York: Columbia Univ. Press, 1973); and William Stanton, *The Leopard's Spots: Scientific Attitudes Toward Race in America, 1815–1859* (Chicago: Univ. of Chicago Press, 1960).

cherished texts.[16] In our recent history, the value of imaginative literature in general, and of the literary canon in particular, has been continuously explained and justified by functional elites who have had access to the mass media and to the public schools since the early 19th century. Assumptions about the autonomy of art or its inherent power deflect attention from the process of "literary socialization"—the procedures, that is, by which successive groups of Americans have come to accept certain definitions of literary merit and to act on those definitions.[17]

The evidential significance of literature, then, appears to depend on specifying the factors which shape its production and consumption. To specify the factors affecting the "generation" of, and response to, literary texts is to understand crucial parameters which constrain the inferences that may legitimately be made from a given document, considered as historical evidence. These factors will vary from group to group. In one social context, a novel may have a range of meanings, consistent with a particular world view, that it does not have for a group defined by a different perceptual/conceptual system. Literary works as a class of cultural artifacts must be understood historically (as opposed to critically) in the context of the groups which produced them and responded to them.

The question of meaning and of specifying the appropriate constraints on the process of inference are central to the problem of defining the evidential significance of works of imaginative literature. It is beyond the scope of this essay to explore these complicated issues, but a principal difference between the approach advocated here and the approach of myth-symbolists like Leo Marx lies in the way "meaning" is construed. For Marx, "a large part of the meaning [of a work] . . . resides in the inherent emotional power of the work."[18] Marx leaves unresolved the question of where the rest of the work's meaning may be said to be, but he clearly intends to define meaning primarily as a function of the formal literary devices employed by an author. The great work derives both its effect and its tendency to persist because it has the power to compel the reader to experience its meaning. This inference appears to be consistent with the faith Marx expresses in the "impersonal process of critical scholarship" to "correct or eliminate invalid observations,"[19] a

[16]For an interesting effort to describe social factors affecting the cultural transmission of certain texts, see Darryl McCall, "Some Factors Affecting the Literary Canon," Diss. University of Florida 1958. See also Levin Schucking's brilliant but neglected essay *The Sociology of Literary Taste*, 3rd ed., trans. Brian Battershaw (Chicago: Univ. of Chicago Press, 1966).

[17]In *The Theory of American Literature*, Howard Mumford Jones noted the lack of a history of "literary sensibility in America—that is, the patient study of what Americans have responded to in art and why they have responded to one expression rather than another. . . ." (Ithaca, N.Y.: Cornell Univ. Press, 1948), p. 180. Twenty-five years later, we still do not have such a history.

[18]Marx, "American Studies," p. 81.

[19]Ibid.

remarkably strong faith, it should be noted, in light of the disconcerting pro-
liferation of interpretations fostered by the very New Critical procedures
Marx adopts. Indeed, one of the increasingly problematic legacies of the New
Criticism is the body of diverse interpretation generated by literary scholars.
Beyond a certain point, variations in interpretation among investigators pur-
porting to explain the same data becomes itself a focus for study and concern.
This has happened in historical study, and some literary scholars, uneasy in
the face of manifold and occasionally mutually exclusive readings of the
same text, have begun to speculate about criteria for defining valid interpretations and to ask whether rules can be formulated for generating valid interpretations.[20]

Although no brief account of the complicated issue of meaning in literature
can do justice to the complexities of the problem, the issue is central to the
study of literature conceived in historical terms, as the vigorous debate now
going on concerning hermeneutics and the writing of literary history reveals.
For the purposes of this discussion, I should like to distinguish initially
between meaning in terms of the audience for a work and authorial meaning.
Secondly, I should like to make, or rather to accept, a sharp distinction
between historical meaning and "anachronistic" meaning. This distinction is
intended to discriminate between meanings imputed to a work that are
consistent with an author's world view, for example, and meanings which,
however retrospectively plausible, are not consistent with the belief system of
the author or his historical audience.

If we accept a behavioral definition of meaning common in communications research, namely meaning as "response" or change in "image," the
meaning of a literary work may be defined partly in terms of the responses it
evokes from those who read it.[21] This definition, it should be noted, is not so
alien to traditional literary studies as it might at first seem. It is consistent,
for example, with the concept of meaning presented by Robert Scholes in his
Elements of Fiction: "Discovering themes or meanings in a work," he writes,
"involves us in making connections between the work and the world outside
it. These connections *are* the meaning."[22]

Now, in theory, the audience for any given work of literature is finite,

---

[20]See, for example, E. D. Hirsch, "Three Dimensions of Hermeneutics," *New Literary History*, 3 (1971), 245–62; and D. W. Robertson Jr., "Some Observations on Method in Literary
Studies," *New Literary History*, 1 (1969), 21–33.

[21]See, for example, Wilbur Schramm, "The Nature of Communication between Humans," in
The Process and Effects of Mass Communications, rev. ed., eds. Wilbur Schramm and Donald
Roberts (Champaign: Univ. of Illinois Press, 1971) and Kenneth Boulding, *The Image* (Ann
Arbor: Univ. of Michigan Press, 1956).

[22]*Elements of Fiction* (New York: Oxford Univ. Press, 1968), p. 21.

constituting a set of individuals distributed geographically and temporally as well as socially. Whatever else may be true about the set, however, it cannot be considered a random sample of the population for the purposes of generalizing from content to society. It is one thing, however, to posit theoretically an audience of determinable size and character for a particular work—an audience presumably sharing with an author at least some components of his belief system. It is quite another for the historian to reconstruct the meaning of a work on the basis of responses. A moment's reflection suggests why this is so. If a response to a work is to become the object of the historian's study, two conditions must be met. The response must be articulated—that is, it must be translated into some conventional system of symbols. Secondly it must be preserved and eventually become accessible to the historian. Responses, in short, become the basis for reconstructing a work's meaning only to the extent that they are accessible to the historian.

It should be evident, however, that much of the response generated by a given work will be lost because the conditions described above are not, in fact, generally met. Unlike the act of buying a car or a house, getting married or going off to war, the act of reading in our society does not typically generate systematic written records that are likely to persist and that may be available for the use of future historians. Even when reading does generate a written response, it is not clear that the response is necessarily representative of the audience for the work at any given time. Potentially, the most durable and accessible responses are those made by reviewers and other commentators who have access to publication, but the relationship of these persons to the rest of the audience is not always easily specified. Thus the meaning of a literary document in terms of audience response is difficult to reconstruct.

The meaning of a work is not comprehended solely in audience response, however. Meaning may also be specified in terms of the author. The work, unlike the responses of its readers, is usually accessible to the historian, owing to its publication and wide geographical distribution—and to our customs of preserving books generally. The works of a given author constitute a response, in their own right, to features of his (or her) milieu. Since these features cannot generally be reconstructed solely from the text, there is some heuristic value in suggesting that a given literary text is analogous to a response to an interview schedule for which the questions have been lost. The text embodies the response in a complex form, and the meaning of the work may be specified, in part, by reconstructing the "questions" to which the author was responding. But the terms of the questions (and the degree to which the work formulates "answers" acceptable to other Americans) is often a matter for painstaking historical research. (In contrast to the conventions governing the creation of narrative fiction, for example, the conventions governing historical writing make reasonably clear what it is that the historian is responding to.)

Meaning in this second sense, then, will be a function of the author's belief system and of the group to which he belongs: *historical* meaning, whether in the sense of authorial meaning or in the sense of audience response, is circumscribed within specific, and hence necessarily limited, conceptual frameworks. This is simply to say that historical meaning is culture bound.

If we seek to specify a text's historical meaning, then, we seek to relate that text to the system of thought and action characteristic of particular groups— to understand, in other words, the creation and function of literary texts. If we ask, for example, about the meaning of Horatio Alger in the late 19th century, we discover a small body of articulate condemnation of Alger's work, a set of aggregate sales figures indicating enormous popularity, and over one hundred novels—variations on the theme of luck and pluck. Alger's meaning for the cultural elite who directly competed with him for readers is relatively easy to describe. Alger's popularity, on the other hand, has been variously interpreted, generally by inferring values from the fiction and describing the functionality of these values, given varying assumptions about Alger's audience. Unfortunately crucial characteristics of that audience are not known—even its size is disputed—and the fiction is sufficiently ambiguous to support several plausible interpretations.[23]

Although many students of literature prefer to keep their discipline uncontaminated by social theory, no very satisfactory historical understanding of literature is likely to come without relying heavily on analytical concepts derived from those whose primary task is to study society. If the function of theory is to direct research, the view of culture outlined above provides a very general conceptual framework in which to undertake an historical examination of literary documents. Consistent with that definition of culture is the argument advanced in a recent theoretical essay in the sociology of knowledge, *The Social Construction of Reality* by Peter Berger and Thomas Luckmann. The sociology of knowledge, which seeks to specify the social determinants of thought, is an attractive basis on which to ground a cultural study of literature, and Berger and Luckmann's emphasis on the conveyance and maintenance of systems of cultural knowledge provides an especially useful framework within which to examine literature in general and the

---

[23]For some of the anti-Alger literature, see the essays collected in the September issue of the *Library Journal*, 4 (1879). For descriptions and explanations of Alger's popularity, see: R. Richard Wohl, "The 'Rags to Riches Story': An Episode of Secular Idealism," in *Class, Status and Power*, eds. Seymour M. Lipset and Reinhard Bendix (Glencoe, Ill.: Free Press, 1953), pp. 388–95; John Cawelti, "From Rags to Respectability: Horatio Alger," in his *Apostles of the Self-Made Man* (Chicago: Univ. of Chicago Press, 1965), pp. 101–24; and Michael Zuckerman, "The Nursery Tales of Horatio Alger," *American Quarterly*, 24 (May 1972), 191–209.

children's literature, specifically, which is discussed in the final section of this essay.[24]

Briefly the authors argue that reality is socially constructed. By this they mean that the worlds inhabited by men may be conceptualized as structured systems of shared meaning, specific to a certain place and time, and consensually maintained. These worlds or symbolic universes are created, maintained and transmitted by means of symbol systems, of which language is the most important, and they are arbitrary and precarious owing to man's "world-openness". Man's "relationship to the surrounding environment," they argue, "is everywhere very imperfectly structured by his own biological constitution" (p. 47). A given social world, in this view, bears minimal relationship to some underlying stable reality either biological or environmental. Since the biological basis for human culture permits extraordinary variation in customary behavior, socialization—the process by which one becomes a functioning member of a particular group—is productive both of individual identity and social continuity. The process of socialization is a potential source of tension and concern in any society, since a measure of success in the process is a necessary (though hardly sufficient) condition for maintaining a system of belief and the distinctive way of life in which it is expressed.

In the 19th century, conditions of rapid social change and the availability of alternative systems of belief often combined to make the process of socialization in America seem extremely difficult and precarious. The family, and particularly the mother, was expected to prepare Young America for the better future promised by the doctrine of progress; but it was not always clear, either to parents, or, we may guess, to children, precisely how useful or necessary parental values would be in the altered, if better, conditions of the bright tomorrow. Standards and modes of behavior which, in the view of adults, seemed plausible, natural and inevitable, had to be carefully, explicitly justified and given persuasive form if they were to be communicated to the next generation with their meanings intact. Those who in the course of time were to inherit responsibility for sustaining in their day-to-day activity a distinctive world view had first to become convinced of its absolute legitimacy and inevitability—and then remain convinced.

Children's books—books, that is, expressly created for children—are among the several agencies which may contribute to the process of socialization or enculturation. Books, like cultural knowledge, are socially distributed in ways that are difficult to trace systematically. Hence the influence exerted by children's literature admits of no easy measure. It is interesting that Theodore Roosevelt read *Our Young Folks* as a child, and significant that he chose to testify to its influence and to record that testimony in his

[24]Cf. Alexander C. Kern, "The Sociology of Knowledge in the Study of Literature," *Sewanee Review*, 50 (1942), 505–14.

private papers. But we do not go to *Our Young Folks,* or to its popular and well-remembered successor, *St. Nicholas,* to assess effect and influence. Nevertheless the process of socialization within the family in our society typically generates no systematic written record, and children's books are one of the few elements of the process that remain accessible to historians long after the intended functions of entertainment and instruction have ceased. Even in those rare circumstances where relatively abundant evidence of the socialization process remains, the relationship of child-rearing behavior to adult personality, for example, is notoriously difficult to reconstruct with any degree of confidence. Although literature for children does not constitute satisfactory evidence for the behavior of real children, it does constitute a kind of linguistic behavior addressed to children by adults.

If systems of belief are not to die with those who hold them, the beliefs must be taught and they must be learned. Cultural continuity requires not simply that a group's beliefs be explained to the young or to novitiates, but that the validity and importance of the beliefs be successfully justified to, and internalized by, those who will eventually be responsible themselves for maintaining the belief system. Because culture is learned, the processes and terms in which it is conveyed are particularly revealing to the historian interested in reconstructing a group's world view: "The richest settings for discovering the rules of a society are those where novices of one sort or another are being instructed in appropriate behavior."[25] Children's literature may be used to examine the ways in which a group defines and symbolizes the principles of order thought to structure and sustain a given way of life. Children's stories may also define, often quite directly, the limits of permissible behavior in certain circumstances and suggest typical and acceptable modes of reward and punishment. Stories, biographies, even fantasy, may all designate those attributes of character which are held to contribute most directly to a rewarding life, however that illusive ideal may be defined by a given group.

In addition, some children's literature, certainly much late 19th century American children's literature, may be regarded, first, as efforts to make a particular way of life attractive to those considered to lie outside the boundaries of a group, whether defined in religious or secular terms—to persuade children to acknowledge, and finally to act on, particular definitions of self and society, for example. Secondly, stories for children may be regarded as carefully fashioned strategies—structures of meaning—presumed capable of confirming and reinforcing the allegiance of those children already persuaded of the truths intended in the fiction. Children's books may therefore be examined for the strategies of reassurance and

[25] James Spradley, ed., *Culture and Cognition* (San Francisco: Chandler, 1972), p. 21.

persuasion typically employed by a group as well as for clues to the group's assumptions about the nature of the reading experience, about the imputed characteristics of children's minds, and about the ways in which changes in personality, belief or styles of behavior may be effected. We may properly regard a group's children's literature, then, as constituting a series of reaffirmations over time of that body of knowledge and belief regarded as essential to the continued existence of the group. As Berger and Luckmann point out, not only must children be convinced of the validity of the truths being presented to them "but so must be their teachers."[26] Repetition may be as important to the teacher as to the learner.

These assertions have methodological as well as substantive implications. They direct attention to certain elements of the fiction—the qualities of character which prove most effective in action, for example—and, given a particular group with known characteristics, suggest some of the specific cognitive and normative elements that ought to emerge from a study of a chosen body of literature. Despite the logic of examining children's literature in the context of specific social groups, few attempts have been made to study the social factors shaping American children's fiction. The distinction between religious—really denominational—and secular literature for children has generally sufficed to define the social origins of juvenile literature. In the Durkheimian sense of religion as providing an overarching framework of meaning, a great deal of so-called secular children's literature is, in fact, "religious"—concerned, that is, with representing truly the meaning of behavior and events.

Although most secular children's books have been considered expressive of a diffuse middle-class belief system, a considerable body of late 19th century children's fiction, exemplified by such popular and long-lived periodicals as *St. Nicholas* and *The Youth's Companion,* is more properly regarded as issuing from an American gentry class, distinguishable on the basis of its members' adherence to a distinctive concept of the roles and attributes of the lady and the gentleman in a democratic society.[27] An examination of children's fiction produced by that group might be expected to reveal the following tendencies: 1) the presence, in the stories, of ladies and gentlemen as distinct social types worthy of emulation; 2) antagonism toward groups defined by different belief systems, especially those groups espousing different (and hence competitive) definitions of gentility; 3) definitions of self and society emphasizing individual discipline and service.

These expectations, which do not, of course, exhaust the range of appro-

---

[26] *The Social Construction of Reality,* p. 31.
[27] For an examination of the American gentry in the 19th century, see Stow Persons, *The Decline of American Gentility.*

priate hypotheses, are born out by a study of the fiction.[28] The key social roles are those of the gentleman and the lady, particularly the latter. These are the definitions of selfhood which structure the social world of the fiction; these are the recognizable social types which, by virtue of their attributes, are held up as being especially worthy of youthful emulation. The stories may be said to explain the function of the gentry (and hence to define the true promise of American life as they saw it) in terms of a paradigm which integrates the natural world, the social world and the individual's own experience of a private inner flow of feeling and thought and a public life of purposive activity. The paradigm organized, explained and justified those central beliefs considered essential to the perpetuation of gentry culture. As the embodiment of those beliefs, the social type of the gentleman or lady constituted an ideal of psychological integration, a standard of public service appropriate to a democratic republic, and a principle of social order in a society dedicated to personal freedom and individual achievement and characterized by intense social and economic competition.

Two stories illustrate with clarity and economy the ways in which the paradigm informed the gentry literature for children. The gentleman's role in the maintenance of social order in a democratic society, organized around concepts of personal property, individual competition and the private exploitation of natural resources, is amply demonstrated in Rebecca Harding Davis' tale "Naylor o' the Bowl," which appeared in the first issue of *St. Nicholas* magazine (1873). Mrs. Davis' characters are a motley group of rough young men, most of them former mill hands, who have been drawn to western Virginia about 1859 in hope of making a rich strike on the petroleum lands being developed there. They soon discover, however, that their capacity for cooperation deteriorates steadily amid the frustration born of their unsuccessful drilling. As mill hands, according to the author, these unlettered irreligious young men lacked the experiences of shared fun, friendships and courtesies that would have provided a more stable basis for community for a group of college students in similar circumstances. Moreover, because none of the men are married or even related to each other, the only grounds for their uneasy and brittle alliance are dependence and greed. Given these factors, violence is almost inevitable.

Conditions begin to improve, however, when Naylor, a grandfather of one of the men, arrives unexpectedly to live with his grandson. Although the old man had lost his legs and is confined to a kind of makeshift wheelchair, he has accepted the impairment with grace and dignity. Naylor is carefully identified as a gentleman; and as his quiet strength of character gradually invigorates

[28]Portions of this essay have been adapted from the text of the author's forthcoming book, *Mother Was a Lady: Self and Society in Selected Children's Periodicals 1865–1890*, courtesy of Greenwood Press, Westport, Conn.

and purifies the camp's morale, a true community begins to emerge where none existed before. We are to understand, it seems clear, that Naylor's moral strength and courage are sufficient to compel in his rough companions a particular response—namely the saving recognition that character is the only basis for an orderly society of freely competing individuals. It is no accident that soon after Naylor arrives, his grandson begins to think about the existence of God for the first time in years: the basis for character, in turn, is seen to be an understanding of the universal principles of order. When Naylor dies peacefully after a short illness, the men's memories of the old man's moral force cement the group in friendship and cooperation, for their mutual recognition of Naylor's character establishes an essential basis for social order—the shared recognition and acceptance of a compelling ideal.

Thus, the terms of Mrs. Davis' justification of the gentry ideal are readily apparent: because his moral authority derives from universal law, the gentleman is capable of bringing order into the rawest kind of economic competition, that which characterizes the scramble to exploit the nation's natural resources. The code of the gentleman softens the rigors of such competition (but does not destroy it) and fosters a sense of community without impairing either initiative or self-reliance. After Naylor's death, the drilling goes on, but it goes on efficiently, cooperatively and harmoniously, or so Mrs. Davis would have her young readers believe.

Possibly more dangerous to the gentry world view than the violence threatened by unrestrained economic competition was the insidious appeal of "fashionable" society. Claiming also to be ladies and gentlemen, the fashionable elites of the large Eastern cities offered an all too attractive alternative definition of what gentility could be. Thoroughly condemned in the gentry children's magazines, fashionable society was presented as incapable of ordering aright individual lives or American society. Its manners were affected, artificial and ostentatious. As a group, the fashionable were made to appear exclusive, snobbish and undemocratic. Theirs was a life peculiarly without higher purpose and hence antithetical to the ideal of gentry service and social responsibility. Finally, by substituting money for character in assessing individual achievement, fashionable society denied the basis for the gentry's vision of democracy perfected—a nation ably led by an elite of cultivation and merit.

In "A Summer of Leslie Goldthwaite's Life," *Our Young Folks* (1866), Adeline D. T. Whitney explored the essential distinctions between the gentry and fashionable society, demonstrating for her young readers—when she was not engaged in telling them outright—that the spirit of fashion alienated individuals from nature, aggravated social distinctions and produced shallow, aimless, unhappy people. At the beginning of the tale, a troubled Leslie Goldthwaite, recently arrived at the difficult age of 15, is trying rather unsuccessfully to discover a larger purpose in her life than displaying her wardrobe at a series of teas and parties. How much personal display is right? and How does one know? she wonders, as she recalls the biblical warning about fig trees that run to leaves and produce no fruit. A trip to a simple inn in the New Hampshire mountains (carefully distinguished from the fashionable resorts at Saratoga Springs and Newport) provides the appropriate setting in which Leslie eventually discovers her larger purpose.

Early in the story Leslie concludes that fashion makes a mockery of worship and that simple, even old-fashioned clothing is an unreliable index to the character of the person wearing it. A little later on the journey, while her fashionable companions gossip, oblivious to the splendid scenery through which they are passing, Leslie is overwhelmed by its expressiveness and, in response to the mountains, begins to feel herself emerge from a narrow preoccupation with her own problems. This diminished self-centeredness, she comes to recognize, is a necessary prelude to discovering the gentry ideal of self-effacing service which informs the story. For rightly understood, gentility promises personal fulfillment in service to others as well as social harmony in the recognition and acceptance of a natural aristocracy of character. On the other hand, spurious gentility—the spirit of fashion—leads only to isolation and selfishness, to an aristocracy of money, and to snobbishness, envy and vulgarity.

The code of the gentleman, as presented in this body of juvenile fiction, of which the foregoing examples are representative, provided a basis for social order and for individual development and fulfillment. It systematically related inner being to outward expression; universal moral law to the world of everyday experience; and man to the natural world. In these stories, fictional children learned, as the gentry undoubtedly hoped their own children would learn, that only in the gentleman and lady did behavior express the disciplined integration of feeling and intellect upon which republican institutions absolutely and finally depended. In these social types, outward manner was a perfect correlative to motives, feelings and intention. In short, the lady and the gentleman could be wholly trusted on the basis of their appearance—no light matter in a fluid mobile society.

If the principles of order underlying a given way of life must be explained and justified to children, so too must intrusions and anomalies in the world of everyday experience be explained and justified. The child's plaintive "Why me?" uttered in the wake of seeming misfortune or unmerited suffering, must be answered. The gentry, like other cultures, had interpretive schemas which could be invoked to reassure children in these critical situations. Properly interpreted, events revealed immutable law or design underlying the apparent reality of ceaseless mutability or the occasional instances of frustrated desire or unrewarded virtue. Misfortunes are divided into two categories in the gentry children's fiction—those that can be avoided through foresight and self-discipline and those that can't. "Our actions are in our own hands, but the consequences of them are not. Remember that . . . and think twice before you do anything," Louisa May Alcott reminds the readers of "Jack and Jill."[29] Experience taught that unavoidable misfortunes were best regarded as tests of character; and true gentility was defined, in part, as possessing that quality of moral vision which recognized a beneficent purpose in the day-to-day texture of events, however threatening or seemingly undeserved. This quality of vision was developed, disciplined and sustained in contact with the natural landscape. To the young, nature taught necessary lessons of self-reliance, courage and independence, the solid foundations of character on which might be erected later the refined sensibilities of the gentry ideal. For gentry adults, nature was inspiration, reassurance and symbol.

As presented in juvenile fiction, the gentry ideal functions to define and to reconcile values and beliefs that both determined their vision of democratic society and, if not carefully balanced, might jeopardize the fragile achievement of viable community. By definition and tradition the gentleman was a free, self-reliant individual. Tempered by self-discipline, integrity and social responsibility, his free nature could be trusted not to seek self-expression, at the cost of social order, in a ruthless struggle for achievement defined solely in terms of money or power. Thus the potentially antagonistic values of individual freedom, competition and opportunity found a precarious equilibrium in the image of a disciplined individual who accepted a measure of social responsibility as the price of personal freedom.

[29]In *St. Nicholas,* 7 (1879), 387.

Sharon O'Brien

R. Gordon Kelly's article "Literature and the Historian" marked an important moment in the development of American studies as an interdisciplinary field of inquiry, foreshadowing later work in readership, popular culture, and cultural studies. Here Kelly poses a question much debated in the 1970s: how can the cultural or literary historian responsibly use literature to do cultural analysis and to understand social processes? Kelly asked this question at the time of a major paradigm shift in American studies. In the early 1970s the humanist assumptions of an older American studies, grounded in literature and history, were being challenged by young scholars who—influenced by anthropology and sociology—argued that American studies needed to redefine its concept of culture. To do so meant replacing an elitist vision of "high" culture, drawn from the founding disciplines of literature and history, with the anthropological definition of culture as the beliefs, practices, and rituals of a people.

Kelly's innovation was to link the anthropological definition of culture with the appropriate work of the literary historian, arguing that one cannot make cultural generalizations on the basis of a few canonical literary texts; in order to fashion useful generalizations, he argues, the historian must have a broader and more democratic notion of culture. Kelly sets forth his theoretical defense of this move in his bold and modest "Literature and the Historian"—bold in its claims for a more populist definition of culture, modest (and stringent) in its concern with method and appropriate use of sources. American studies was self-consciously concerned with methodology in the late 1960s and 1970s, and Kelly's work should be seen in the context of this historical moment.

Kelly sets out to topple the literary and cultural assumptions held by the "myth-symbol" school in American studies, represented here by Leo Marx. If we take into account *The Machine in the Garden* (New York: Oxford University Press, 1964), we might see Marx's work moving in

R. Gordon Kelly, "Literature and the Historian," originally appeared in *American Quarterly* 26, no. 2 (May 1974), Copyright © 1974 Trustees of the University of Pennsylvania.

the direction of cultural studies instead of leading back to formalist textual criticism, but Kelly wants to concentrate on Marx's essay "American Studies: Defense of an Unscientific Method" because the literary views put forth there contrast so sharply with the argument he wants to make. Kelly pounces on Marx's definition of literary power as "the inherent capacity of a work to generate the emotional and intellectual response of its readers," contending that the tell-tale word "inherent" reveals that Marx is assuming that the literary text possesses autonomous power to shape the responses of readers—a vision of communication that does not grant readers the power to make meanings from, or with, the text.

Kelly finds the assumption that an "acknowledged artistic achievement" like *Moby-Dick* gives us special access to cultural meaning both elitist and wrong. Elitist, because the critic is relying upon a text elevated to cultural authority by professional literary critics; wrong, because we do not know that *Moby-Dick* expressed social meaning for any nineteenth-century American besides Melville. Chiding Marx not so much for his reading practices as for his assumption that he can make cultural generalizations on the basis of them, Kelly offers a polite but telling rebuke: "The extent to which a work embodies widely shared social meanings cannot be reconstructed solely from an analysis of textual elements." The key phrase here is *widely shared*. Kelly, as the cultural historian, wants to use literature to discover the cultural beliefs held by groups of people, and he is rightly suspicious of the ways in which critics can fudge the gap between text and social meaning by assuming their own individual reading must be "widely shared" because they are trained critics, as Marx does with his easy use of the plural (*Moby-Dick* provides "us" with readerly satisfaction). Such a view, based on a belief in the "autonomous power" of literary texts to move all readers in the same way, allows the critic to make cultural generalizations without exploring the "social factors which might otherwise be presumed to shape both the creation and the effect of literature."

Kelly also takes aim at the ways in which allegiance to the literary canon of classic American works restricted American studies scholarship by erasing different social groups and creating a monolithic (and top-down) concept of culture. By basing cultural generalizations on a text like *Moby-Dick,* the experience of many Americans would be silenced, just as the differences of women and African Americans were often erased in generalizations about the "American character" that stressed self-reliance and individualism. "Given the complexity and diversity of cultural knowledge in American society," Kelly observes, "it seems . . . unwarranted to conceive of America as a unitary culture," a comment that doubtless seems like an understatement in our multicultural 1990s, but needed to be said in 1974. Summing up his objections to the assumptions and methods "carried over into American Studies from the study of literature," Kelly asks his readers to severely qualify or even abandon notions that "great literature constitutes a qualitatively superior kind of cultural evidence, that it is autonomous, and that inferences from such works can be readily generalized to society as a whole and to a wide range of behavior."

And so what to do? If formalist and literary assumptions make a shaky and even specious bridge between literature and culture, where can an American studies scholar turn for a theory and a method? To anthropology, a discipline chock full of insights for a new American studies. By employing an anthropological definition of culture as the "perceptual/conceptual system of a group which defines the meaning of its members' actions," Kelly broadens the definition of "literature" to include popular literature, advice books, and other noncanonical texts that are now standard sources of data and analysis within American studies, but in the 1970s were often thought unworthy of serious scholarly attention. And to understand the cultural significance of such literature, he contends, we need to understand how literature is culturally produced, understood, and preserved by social actors: "The evidential significance of literature, then, appears to depend on specifying the factors which shape its production and consumption."

This statement, which may seem normative now, was highly controversial in 1974. Literary works are not autonomous, free-floating emanations of culture, Kelly argues, but are historically produced and read. Anticipating such later anthropological work with readers as Janice Radway's *Reading the Romance* (Chapel Hill: University of North Carolina Press, 1984), Kelly wants cultural analysis to examine the production and consumption of literary texts. We cannot fully understand the social meanings of literature, he contends, unless we know what use actual readers made of the books they read.

When Kelly turns to his own data—Victorian children's literature— he is careful to say that reader response is difficult, if not impossible, to reconstruct historically: ordinary readers do not leave the kinds of written records upon which historians rely. Unable to find historical records of reading and unwilling to assume that his own reading of the texts can stand in for the nineteenth-century reader, Kelly restricts himself to analyzing the values the producers of Victorian children's literature sought to convey to their readers.

This restriction becomes a strength for Kelly as he draws again on an anthropological framework, reminding us that "culture is learned" and quoting from James Spradley's *Culture and Cognition* (San Francisco: Chandler, 1972) to define cultural transmission: "The richest settings for discovering the rules of a society are those where novices of one sort or another are being instructed in appropriate behavior." Arguing that children's literature is a site where key cultural values are represented, Kelly can then use his sources to explore the values of the gentry class, faced in the late nineteenth century with disturbing social changes and seeking to pass on middle-class values of gentility, service, and discipline through the medium of children's literature. He cannot and does not make inferences about readers, and it remained for later scholars to explore what "consumption" of popular culture might mean.

Kelly's article, articulating as it did a methodological turning point in the development of American studies, anticipated so many important critical directions—readership studies, the serious, complex study of popular culture, and the historian's use of literature as primary data—that I have often wondered why it hasn't been cited more often by subsequent scholars. Graduate programs in American studies acknowledge the significance of "Literature and the Historian" by assigning it in theory and method classes, but it never attained the almost totemic stature of an article like Barbara Welter's "The Cult of True Womanhood." Perhaps this is because the genre Kelly chose to explore—children's literature—is of less interest to American studies scholars than women's writing; perhaps it is because he so fully anticipated the direction in which American studies was moving that within a few years his insights seemed to be ideas that we had always known. But we had *not* always possessed these perspectives on literature, history, and method. Rereading "Literature and the Historian," I am impressed by the clarity and precision with which R. Gordon Kelly—almost twenty-five years ago—presented critical and cultural issues that still engage us.

ALEXANDER SAXTON

Blackface Minstrelsy and
Jacksonian Ideology

BLACKFACE MINSTRELSY, ACCORDING TO THE PREFACE TO ONE OF E. P. Christy's countless "plantation songsters," marked the advent of a national American music. "After our countrymen had . . . confuted the stale cant of our European detractors that nothing original could emanate from Americans—the next cry was, that we had no NATIVE MUSIC; . . . until our countrymen found a triumphant vindicating APOLLO in the genius of E. P. Christy, who . . . was the first to catch our *native airs* as they floated wildly, or hummed in the balmy breezes of the sunny south." The verbs *floated* and *hummed* referred of course to the fact that the original "native airs" had been appropriated from music and dance of African slaves by white professional entertainers, including (among many others) E. P. Christy. A more realistic account explained later in the same preface that the minstrels had possessed skills which enabled them "to harmonize and SCORE systematically the original NEGRO SOLOS." From these somewhat discordant beginnings, the preface rose to a crescendo of national triumph. "The air of our broad, blest land, and even that of Europe, became vocal with the thousand native melodies."[1]

"If I could have the nigger show back," Mark Twain wrote in his autobiography, ". . . I should have but little further use for opera . . . I remember the first negro musical show I ever saw. It must have been in the early forties. It was a new institution. In our village of Hannibal . . . it burst upon us as a glad and stunning surprise."[2] During the decade recalled by Mark Twain, blackface minstrelsy became the most popular form of enter-

[1] Edwin P. Christy, *Christy's Plantation Melodies No. 4* (Philadelphia: Fisher, 1854). pp. v–vii.

[2] Mark Twain, *The Autobiography of Mark Twain,* ed. Charles Neider (New York. Washington Square Press, 1961), p. 64.

tainment in the United States.[3] Its spread coincided with the rise of mass political parties and mass circulation newspapers. All three manifested in part at least the urban culture of Jacksonian America. Hannibal, Missouri, for example, which in Mark Twain's childhood was a rural slaveholding community, could hardly have found fragments of African music or caricatures of black slaves particularly surprising. What made the first minstrel show a "glad surprise" was that it provided a window into the complex culture developing in the new cities. For approximately half a century after Mark Twain's experience at Hannibal, minstrel shows dominated the nation's public entertainment, and at their latter end merged through variety and vaudeville into the modern era of film.[4] Clearly blackface minstrelsy has comprised an important element of the "American experience." What follows is an exploration of the ideological significance of that element.

Underlying the choice of the adjective *ideological* are several starting assumptions which can be set forth, hypothetically, as follows: Minstrel shows expressed class identification and hostility; they conveyed ethnic satire as well as social and political commentary of wide-ranging, sometimes radical character; they often contained explicitly sexual, homosexual and pornographic messages. Taken as a whole, the genre provided a kind of underground theater where the blackface "convention" rendered permissible topics which would have been taboo on the legitimate stage or in the press. Spontaneity and ad-libbing favored a flexible approach to different audiences and regions, changing moods and times. This combination of adaptiveness and liberty of subject matter explains in part the popularity and staying power of minstrelsy as mass entertainment. It was linked from its earliest beginnings to Jacksonian democracy. The rise of the first mass party in America and the dominance of the minstrel show as mass entertainment appear to have been interrelated and mutually reinforcing sequences. Finally, the "convention" of blackface was by no means separate from minstrelsy's social content or neutral in regard to it. On the contrary it saturated that content. For a study of the ideology of minstrel shows, the interpenetration of form and content is relentlessly at the crux of the matter.

[3] T. Allston Brown, "The Origins of Minstrelsy," in Charles H. Day, *Fun in Black or Sketches of Minstrel Life* (New York: DeWitt, 1874), pp. 5–10.

[4] Hans Nathan, *Dan Emmett and the Rise of Early Minstrelsy* (Norman, Okla.: Univ. of Oklahoma Press, 1962); Nathan Huggins, *Harlem Renaissance* (New York: Oxford Univ. Press, 1971), pp. 244–301; Robert G. Toll, "Behind the Grinning Mask: Blackface Minstrelsy in Nineteenth Century America," Diss. Univ. of California, Berkeley 1971. Toll's study, soon to be published, provides a nearly definitive survey. Two older but still useful works are: Carl Wittke, *Tambo and Bones: A History of the American Minstrel Stage* (Durham, N.C.: Duke Univ. Press, 1930) and Dailey Paskman and Sigmund Spaeth, *"Gentlemen Be Seated!" A Parade of the Old Time Minstrels* (Garden City, N.Y.: Doubleday, 1928).

The discussion which follows will deal with the first three decades of minstrelsy, roughly 1845 to 1875. Its content will be treated as a matrix within which a dominant political line becomes discernible. Attention will then be concentrated upon that political line and its racial aspects. The final section will examine the ideological product which resulted from the infusion of social content into the specific form of blackface minstrelsy.

The social content of minstrelsy was shaped in part by the social experience of its founders and purveyors. Three men, Thomas Rice, Dan Emmett and E. P. Christy, are generally recognized as founders of blackface minstrelsy. To these should be added the name of Stephen Foster, the major white innovator of minstrel music. Where did these men come from and how did they happen to launch a new mode in mass entertainment? Rice, oldest of the four, was born in New York in 1808. He tried unsuccessfully to break into New York theater, then drifted west, working as stagehand and bit player through the Mississippi Valley. In 1831, imitating a shuffle he had seen performed by a black man on the Cincinnati levee, Rice for the first time "jumped Jim Crow." Jim Crow made Rice's fortune. Adapting it to various uses—including eventually a minstrel plagiarism of Uncle Tom—Rice was applauded in London and became a perennial favorite at New York's famous Bowery Theatre. The second founder, Dan Emmett, son of a village blacksmith of Mt. Vernon, Ohio, was born in 1815. He ran away to become a drummer in the army and served briefly at posts in Kentucky and Missouri. Dismissed for being under age, Emmett followed circuses and sideshows, occasionally singing comic songs in blackface. Early in 1843 he organized the first blackface quartet as a one night fill-in at New York's Chatham Theatre. Emmett devoted the rest of his long career to minstrelsy.[5]

Edwin P. Christy, also born in 1815, was the son of "respectable" Philadelphia parents who sought to launch him on a commercial career by arranging to place him in a New Orleans countinghouse. Christy rebelled and took to the road with traveling circuses. In 1843, he and several other young men were providing musical entertainment at a theater-saloon on the Buffalo waterfront. Apparently having heard of Emmett's success in New York, the Buffalo entertainers called themselves Christy's Plantation Minstrels; later, moving down to New York City, they became a permanent fixture at Mechanics' Hall on lower Broadway. It was through Christy's Minstrels that many of Stephen Foster's early songs reached the public (figure 1). Foster, eleven years younger than Christy or Emmett, was born in Pittsburgh in 1826. Like Christy, he came of parents with intimations of

[5]Nathan, pp. 98–120; Edward LeRoy Rice, *Monarchs of Minstrelsy from Daddy Rice to Date* (New York: Kenny, 1911), pp. 7–8.

Figure 1. Title page, *Christy's Ram's Horn Nigga Songster* (New York: Marsh, n.d. [1852?]). Courtesy of Special Collections, University Research Library, University of California, Los Angeles.

upward mobility who tried to provide him with a proper education, then sent him off to work as a bookkeeper for an older brother in Cincinnati. Foster meanwhile was writing songs for minstrel shows for which he received ten or fifteen dollars apiece. His "Old Folks at Home," according to the publisher, sold 130,000 copies in three years.[6]

The careers of these four men show several similarities. All were Northerners (but none was born in New England) and all except Emmett were of urban origin. At least three came of old-stock American families and were clearly of middle-class background. They all rejected the straight ways of the Protestant ethic and sought escape into the bohemianism of the entertainment world. Three had direct contact through their wanderings in the lower Mississippi Valley with the music and dance of black slaves, and we know from their own accounts that they consciously exploited this resource. None had achieved success in theatrical or any other pursuit prior to the venture into blackface minstrelsy; and in each case that venture

[6]*Christy's No. 4,* pp. v–vii; John Tasker Howard, *Stephen Foster, America's Troubadour* (New York: Crowell, 1934), pp. 65–201, 372–77.

brought spectacular success.[7] It seems likely that the pattern suggested by these summaries approximates the experiences of many professionals active during the first three decades of minstrelsy. A sampling group composed of 43 men born before 1838 who achieved prominence as blackface performers in large Northern cities or San Francisco yields the following information: five were born south of the Mason-Dixon line (including Baltimore); seven were of European birth (English five, Irish and French one each); all the rest (31) were born in the North, but of these only five were New Englanders. With respect to urban background, New York, Brooklyn, Rochester, Utica, Troy, Philadelphia, Baltimore, Providence, New Haven and Salem (Mass.) accounted for 24 of the 43 (with London and Paris probably claiming three or four more). Regionally, upstate New York matched New York City and Brooklyn with nine each; Philadelphia came next with six.[8]

Typical purveyors of minstrelsy, then, were Northern and urban; they were neither New Englanders nor Southerners (although their parents may have been); and if of rural or small-town origin, most were likely to have come from upper New York State. Eager to break into the exclusive but inhospitable precincts of big city theater, they needed new and exciting materials. These they found during their forced marches through the Mississippi Valley South in the music and dance of slaves and in the half-man, half-alligator braggadocio of the river and the frontier. The two separate lines had merged to some extent before the minstrels took them over.

> My mammy was a wolf, my daddy was a tiger,
> And I'm what you call de old Virginia nigger;
> Half fire, half smoke, a little touch of thunder,
> I'm what dey call de eighth wonder.[9]

Ambivalent especially toward the black component of their borrowings, the minstrels coveted the power and newness of the music, yet failed to recognize its Africanness, or to perceive in it segments of an idiom distinct and separate from the European idiom. They ascribed the impact of slave music to its being close to nature. It "floated wildly" or "hummed . . . in the breezes," to repeat the metaphor of E. P. Christy's preface, and its wildness could be taken simply as part of the general crudity of frontier style. In any

[7]Brown, pp. 5–10; *Christy's No. 4*, p. vii; Nathan, pp. 70–71, 116–22; Howard, pp. 202–14.

[8]The biographical data is from Rice, which is indexed. See also *Bryant's Essence of Old Virginny* (New York: DeWitt, 1857), pp. vii–viii and *Buckley's Melodies* (New York: Cozans, 1853), pp. v–vii.

[9]Charley White, *White's New Illustrated Melodeon Song Book* (New York: Long, 1848), pp. 51–52; *Christy's Ram's Horn Nigga Songster* (New York: Marsh, n.d.), pp. 99–100; "Twill Nebber Do to Gib it up so," *Old Dan Emmit's Original Banjo Melodies* (Boston: Keith, 1843), sheet music in "Dan Emmett" folder, Theater Collection, Harvard Library. See also Nathan, pp. 50–56 and Constance Rourke, *American Humor: A Study of the National Character* (New York: Harcourt, Brace, 1931), pp. 77–103.

case the work of white entertainers with such materials was to "turn them to shape," to Europeanize them sufficiently so that they would not offend refined ears. Thus the dual task of exploiting and suppressing African elements began from the first moments of minstrelsy. But these elements possessed great vitality. It was suggested earlier that a major factor in the popularity and staying power of minstrel entertainment was its freedom of subject matter; certainly another, perhaps *the* other, major factor was the persistence of African borrowings (especially in dance movement and sense of rhythm) throughout the entire half-century of blackface minstrelsy.[10]

Partial acceptance of these African musical elements was facilitated by the fact that they fitted logically into a portrayal of the Old South which took on a symbolic and powerful, although derivative, meaning for many white Americans during the 19th century. But before examining that somewhat removed aspect of minstrel content, it is necessary to turn to a set of meanings which were direct and immediate. For the minstrels, as for the new mass audience upon which they depended, the city was the focal experience of life. The city offered (or seemed to offer) new sorts of work, money, movement, excitement. It offered access to liquor and sex, to education, culture, progress. All this was ignored in the high culture of the established upper classes; Walt Whitman, almost alone among American 19th century poets, celebrated the city. The purveyors of minstrelsy shared in this celebration; but in order to do so, they had to impose some startling transformations upon materials whose primary reference was to frontier and plantation. Here is one of the early mutations:

> I'm de sole delight of yaller gals,
> De envy ob de men,
> Observe this nigger when he turns,
> And talk of dandies then.[11]

The Broadway dandy was in one respect a transplant of the swaggering Southwest frontier hero, already widely rendered in blackface. But the dandy also caricatured a new social type in the United States—the urban free black.

Possible uses of this stereotype, which expressed an enthusiasm for city life uncloyed by nostalgia or regret, were limitless.[12] Early in 1852, one of

---

[10]*Christy's No. 4*, p. v; Nathan, pp. 70–97; Toll, pp. 1–19; Jean and Marshall Stearns, *Jazz Dance* (New York: Macmillan, 1968), pp. 11–60; Marshall Stearns, *The Story of Jazz* (New York: Oxford Univ. Press, 1956), pp. 3–33, 109–22; LeRoy Jones, *Blues People* (New York: Morrow, 1963), pp. 1–59, 82–86.

[11]"The Dandy Broadway Swell," *Wood's New Plantation Melodies* (New York: Garrett, n.d.), pp. 50–51.

[12]See *Christy's Panorama Songster* (New York: Murphy, n.d. [1850?]), p. 93, for an example of ethnic satire in blackface.

New York's permanent minstrel companies began performing a number titled, "Wake Up, Mose." The hero appeared in the first verse as the already familiar urban free black. "He used to run de railroad—he was de bulgine tender"; and it was clear from the context that "bulgine tender" meant a railroad fireman. The chorus then made an abrupt switch, followed up in subsequent verses, to a fireman of a different sort, and presumably of a different race:

> Wake up, Mose! Wake up, Mose!
> Wake up, Mose! De Fire am burning;
> Round de corner de smoke am curling.
> Wake up, Mose! the engine's coming;
> Take de rope and keep a running![13]

So who was Mose?

Mose was an early hero of melodrama made famous through the United States by a New York actor named W. S. Chanfrau in a series of loosely structured scenes and spectacles gathered under titles such as *New York As It Is, Mose and Lize, Mose in California*. Probably a butcher by trade, or an apprentice carpenter or stonecutter, Mose was one of the city's famous "Bowery bhoys." After work he liked to dress up and go to the theater with an armful or two of his innumerable girl friends ("Bowery gals, will you come out tonight?").[14] Gallant volunteer fireman, avid participant in New York City politics, an invincible pugilist, Mose was the urban culture hero, derived from, yet standing against, older rural heroes like the New England Yankee or the half-man, half-alligator of the Southwest. Mose cared nothing for Yankees or alligators either; he breathed the fire of burning buildings; and when it came to warfare, he could tell even an old frontier fighter like Zachary Taylor how to run his campaigns. Mose, however, transcended regionalism. Essentially he stood for the new urban mass culture as against the "high" culture of the old elite.

But Mose in blackface is something else. There was of course a historical logic in rendering the Broadway dandy as Mose in blackface, since both had reached the city by different routes from a common ancestry in frontier folklore. But this hardly explains *why* it was done. The value of such a characterization was that it extended minstrel show content to include class satire. As minstrelsy became more formalized, it moved from separate

[13]M. Campbell, *Wood's Minstrels' Songs* (New York: Garrett, 1852), p. 25.

[14]*Christy's Plantation Melodies No. 1* (Philadelphia: Fisher, 1851), pp. 45–46. Playbills, Theater Collection, Harvard Library: Chatham Theatre (New York, 1848), Jenny Lind (San Francisco, 1851), St. Charles (New Orleans, 1857). See also David Grimsted, *Melodrama Unveiled: American Theater and Culture, 1800–1850* (Chicago: Univ. of Chicago Press, 1968), pp. 65–75; and Alvin F. Harlow, *Old Bowery Days: Chronicles of a Famous Street* (New York: Appleton, 1931), p. 264.

16   SANFORD'S PLANTATION MELODIES.

S. S. SANFORD, DIXEY, AND VONBONHORST, AS THE CONGO MIN-
STRELS, IN JOHNNY HOMIC IN DE HIGH GRASS.

Figure 2. Tambo, Bones and Interlocutor, late 1850s. *Sanford's Plantation Melodies*
(Philadelphia: Robert F. Simpson, 1860), 16. Courtesy of Special Collections,
University Research Library, University of California, Los Angeles.

song-dance numbers to routines including spoken repartee, and finally to elaborate composites of song, dance and drama. The original foursome of undifferentiated musicians expanded into a line in which customary position corresponded roughly to class identification. The end men, who always played tambourine and bones, were lower class. By costume and vernacular they were "plantation nigger," or "Broadway dandy,"—often one of each. The middleman, or interlocutor, served as bogus mouthpiece for the high culture.[15] His dress and speech were upper class, sometimes straight, more often burlesqued; and the plot was usually the putting down of the interlocutor by the end men. Even after the ad-lib repartee of the original line had evolved into more formal presentations, the class character and plot remained substantially the same. Blackface could thus serve to enhance the ridicule directed against upper-class pretensions.[16] More important, it had the effect of preserving the comic mood, since otherwise the role of Mose tended toward serious drama or even tragedy. The careers of real "Bowery bhoys" in politics, of John Morrissey, the prizefighter, or the proletarian congressman, Michael Walsh, and especially of David Broderick, were actings out of tragic conflict between the new urban culture and the cultures of older elites.[17] This was too serious to be fun. Blackface defused such meanings without denying them. It did so by placing social content in the background of a conventional proscenium which permitted instantaneous escape through shifts of scene and mood and which constantly intervened to discredit serious implications.

Part of the entertainment lay in skating on thin ice. Temperance, a topic taken very seriously by many mid-19th century Americans, was nearly always an object of ridicule in minstrel songs.

> Niggar, put down dat jug,
> Touch not a single drop,
> I hab gin him many a hug
> And dar you luff him stop.

Parodying the sentimental ballad, "Woodman Spare That Tree," this song, published about 1850, seemed to hint (especially in the third line) at more than the simple pleasures of alcohol. Subsequent verses elaborated in graphic detail:

---

[15]Mark Twain, pp. 65–66.

[16]"Mose he went to college, he said he was a poet . . ." in *Wood's Minstrels*, p. 25. Minstrel burlesques of tragedy and grand opera exemplified this usage. See Harlow, p. 265, for an account of T. D. Rice in a burlesque of *Othello*.

[17]"Michael Walsh," *Dictionary of American Biography* (New York: Scribners, 1936), 19: 390–91; Jack Kofoed, *Brandy for Heroes: a Biography of the Honorable John Morrissey, Champion Heavyweight of America and State Senator* (New York: Dutton, 1938); David A. Williams, *David C. Broderick, a Political Portrait* (San Marino, Calif.: Huntington Library, 1969).

> I kiss him two three time,
> And den I suck him dry
> Dat jug, he's none but mine
> So dar you luff him lie.[18]

The primary effect of these lines, rendered in blackface, would have been to attribute masturbation or homosexuality to black males. However, the prevailing stereotype of blacks (already well established in minstrelsy by the 1850s) was of unflagging heterosexuality. This apparent contradiction suggests that the song contained several layers of meaning and conveyed different messages to different listeners.

Minstrelsy had become mass entertainment in the decade of war against Mexico and the California gold rush. Until well after the Civil War minstrel shows were performed exclusively by males, before largely male audiences. Both in the East and West, the male population was concentrated in factories, boardinghouses, construction and mining camps. Frontier settlements had few women, and contemporary accounts tell of men dancing in saloons and hotel dining rooms dressed as women. Given this context, the song quoted above appears as a permissive reference to homosexuality and masturbation, veiled but not negated by the blackface "convention." The point here is not the prevalence of homosexuality, but the tolerance of sexuality in general, the realism and the flexibility of standards which flourished behind the false façade of blackface presentation. A more typical sort of minstrel pornography would be a duet titled, "Cuffee's Do-it," in which Cuffee was obviously typed as a Broadway dandy:

> *He.* Oh, Miss Fanny, let me in,
>   For de way I lub you is a sin . . .
> *She.* (spoken) Oh no I cannot let you in . . .
> *He.* Oh, when I set up an oyster cellar,
>   You shall wait upon de feller,
>   Sell hot corn and ginger pop,
>   You be de lady ob de shop.
> *She.* Oh, Sam, if dat's de trufe you tell . . .
>   Oh, Sam Slufheel, you may come in.
> *He.* Oh, Miss Fanny, I'se a comin' in . . .[19]

Moral permissiveness was not accidental or idiosyncratic. It was an aspect of life-style. The life-style expressed in minstrelsy could appropriately be called "urbanity" since it had developed in middle Atlantic cities, moved west with the Erie Canal and urbanization of the Mississippi and its tribu-

---

[18]*Christy's Ram's Horn*, pp. 76–77.
[19]Ibid., pp. 109–10. Many male performers built reputations playing "wench parts." Rice, pp. 71, 86–87. And see Frank C. Davidson, "The Rise, Development, Decline and Influence of the American Minstrel Show," Diss. New York Univ. 1952, pp. 130–31.

taries, and west again with the acquisition of California. It was both urban and frontier. During the last two major frontier decades, the 1850s and 1860s, even the frontier had become urbanized: its new cities were garrison towns and mine camps which sprang into existence before much in the way of rural hinterland had developed around them. When Charles De Long made the following entry in his diary for Christmas Eve, 1859—

> Spent the day in the office hunting up authorities . . . in the evening went to the gymnasium, and the sparring school, and then called on Elida . . . saw the Christmas tree and then went in and celebrated Christmas with Lide. Came downtown went to Nigger Festival [a minstrel show] and got supper and then went to the Catholic Church to high mass, and then down and got on a little burden and went to bed late, raining some. . . .

he might have been describing a day in the life of a moderately successful Bowery politician. Actually De Long was working out of Marysville, some fifty miles northeast of Sacramento. A political henchman of Stephen Douglas, De Long earned his living at the time by collecting the California foreign miners' tax from Chinese laborers. "Started with Dick Wade and Bob Moulthrop collecting," he wrote for October 23, 1855, ". . . supper at Hesse's Crossing went down the river in the night collected all the way had a great time, Chinamen tails cut off."[20] De Long attended performances of many of the same minstrel troupes he would have seen had he lived in New York, because minstrelsy was invading the towns and camps of the Pacific slope. So prominent was San Francisco as a minstrel city that for several years one of New York's leading companies styled itself the "San Francisco Minstrels."[21]

The dual relationship of city and frontier profoundly affected the social content of minstrelsy. Blackface singers (again like Walt Whitman) were protagonists of Manifest Destiny.

> Mose he went to Mexico, and dar he saw Santa Anna;
> He sent a message to de camp, telling Zack not to surrender.
> Says Santa Anna, "Who are you—you seem to be so witty?"
> Says Mose, "Go 'long—I'm one of de boys—I'm from de Empire City.[22]

Always the West and the westward movement were focal:

> Den I step on board de *Oregon*
> For de gemman say who bought her
> Dat she for sure's de fastest crab
> What lives upon de water.[23]

[20]Carl I. Wheat, ed., " 'California's Bantam Cock': The Journals of Charles E. De Long," *California Historical Society Quarterly,* 10 (June 1931), 185, and 8 (Dec. 1929), 346.
[21]Rice, pp. 27, 68–70.
[22]*Wood's Minstrels,* p. 25.
[23]*George Christy and Wood's Melodies* (Philadelphia: Peterson, 1854), pp. 39–40.

Stephen Foster's "Oh! Susanna" (of which the verse above was a topical variation) was first performed in the year of Scott's conquest of Mexico City and reached the height of its popularity during the California gold rush. A later cliché, perpetuated by Hollywood and television, has associated the song with westering pioneers from rural regions such as Kansas and Missouri. Kansas wagonmasters may certainly have sung "Oh! Susanna"; but its origin was at Pittsburgh and it was first popularized in New York City's minstrel halls.[24] Underlying the sociological congruency between city and frontier was a psychological identity between traveling to the city and traveling west. Each, for the individual who undertook such a transition, was a journey involving a traumatic break with a previous situation. In minstrelsy's complex matrix of social content, the *journey* became the central theme. It stood in contrast to the celebration of urban opportunity and permissiveness as a lament for what had been left behind and lost. This theme, I believe, entered minstrelsy at its earliest beginnings, not in any sense as a reflection of journeys made by black slaves, but as a projection by the white performers of their own experience. The projection was then magnified because it also expressed the psychic experience of urban audiences. The notion of a symbolic journey suggests the power of minstrelsy's impact upon white viewers. At the same time it helps to place in perspective one of the most puzzling aspects of minstrel repertory: the endless evocation of the Old South.

Early minstrels (as represented by the sampling group discussed above) had understood slave music not as African but as close to nature. Correspondingly they perceived slaves as *part* of nature, part of the nature of the South, and from this curiously ahistorical viewpoint undertook to "delineate" plantation culture. City dwellers by birth or adoption, they were strangers and interlopers in the plantation society. While they might observe and borrow from slave music, their social contacts were with whites, and it is scarcely surprising that their depiction of the South overlapped and duplicated the plantation myth which white Southerners were then bringing to perfection as part of their defense of slavery. That myth was also ahistorical because its germinating inspiration was to fix the black slave as an everlasting part of nature rather than as a figure in history. When the wandering minstrels carried their fragments of African music back to Northern and Western cities, they took them encased in a mythology of the South as a region fascinatingly different, closely wedded to nature, and above all, timeless. The word "timeless" defines the relationship which would develop between the image of the South and the anomie experienced by men and women of rural, Eastern background who lived in cities or who moved out west. The South became symbolically their old home: the place where simplicity, happiness, all the things we have left behind, exist outside of time.

[24] Howard, pp. 119, 136–39, 144–45.

Down by the river our log hut stands
Where father and mother once dwelt
And the old door latch that was worn by our hands
And the church where in prayer we knelt.[25]

What has been left behind collectively may be a rural past, but individually it is childhood. New cities and new frontiers, attractive to conspiring and perspiring adults, have little room for children; and the South, in the legend of blackface minstrelsy, became the antithesis to both.[26]

When E. P. Christy organized his first entertainments at Buffalo in 1842, he brought in a younger man, George Harrington, who adopted the name Christy and eventually became more famous than his mentor. The senior Christy retired in the mid-1850s; George Christy went into partnership with a New York theatrical promoter, Henry Wood. Under their joint direction Christy and Wood's became a metropolitan establishment and one of the best-known companies of the prewar era. Henry Wood belonged to a remarkable family. His brother Benjamin served three terms as a Democratic Congressman from the city and one term as state senator for almost half a century he presided over the aggressively Democratic New York *Daily News.* A second brother was Fernando Wood, Copperheadish mayor of New York, fighter for control of Tammany Hall, several times Congressman.[27]

George Christy went to San Francisco in 1857. There he performed under the sponsorship of Tom Maguire, West Coast tycoon of minstrelsy, opera and varied theatricals. Maguire had spent his younger days on New York's Bowery as a saloon keeper, hack driver, fight promoter, volunteer fireman and Tammany stalwart. When David Broderick, the New York stonecutter of background substantially similar to Maguire's, abandoned the Bowery for the Golden Gate in 1849, he lived for several years as a boarder at Maguire's house, and apparently helped Maguire to escape bankruptcy by arranging the sale of his Jenny Lind Theatre for $200,000 to an obliging (Democratic) city administration of San Francisco. Maguire was soon back in business with other theaters.[28]

Dan Emmett, after launching the nation's first minstrel quartet on the New York stage, toured England with middling success, then returned to

[25]*Christy's Plantation Melodies No. 2* (Philadelphia: Fisher, 1853), p. 35.
[26]Mark Twain repeatedly makes these connections. For example, *Autobiography,* pp. 5–6.
[27]Rice, p. 20; Samuel A. Pleasants, *Fernando Wood of New York* (New York: Columbia Univ. Press, 1948); Leonard Chalmers, "Fernando Wood and Tammany Hall: The First Phase," *New York Historical Society Quarterly,* 52 (Oct. 1968), 379–402. On Henry Wood, see Paskman and Spaeth, pp. 155–56.
[28]Rice, p. 20; "De Long Journals," *California Historical Society Quarterly,* 9 (Dec. 1930), 385; "Continuation of the Annals of San Francisco," *California Historical Society Quarterly,* 15 (June 1936), 178–80, 184; New York *Clipper,* May 23, 1868; Kofoed, pp. 69–86; Williams, pp. 29–31.

White's Minstrel Melodeon on lower Broadway. By the late 1850s, Emmett had worked out a lasting connection with Bryants' Minstrels of New York, next to Christy's the most enduring of the prewar troupes. Composer of dozens of songs and musical farces, Emmett was especially noted for his walkarounds or group finales. One of these, titled for its New York première, "Dixie's Land," became popular in the South, where it was taken by itinerant minstrels and emerged during the war as "Dixie," the *de facto* Confederate national anthem. In postwar years, the Bryants, following the trend of theater and fashion, moved uptown to East Fourteenth Street. Emmett by this time had drifted back to the Midwest, but the Bryants commissioned a special walkaround in honor of their uptown location and Emmett obliged with a piece called "The Wigwam." In May of 1868, "The Wigwam" climaxed the Bryants' opening in their new theater at Tammany Hall's recently constructed Fourteenth Street headquarters.[29]

Stephen Foster, drinking himself to death in New York during the Civil War, sometimes peddled his handwritten songs along Broadway, and at least one of the buyers was Henry Wood of Wood's Minstrels. In happier days, Foster had helped to organize the Allegheny City Buchanan-for-President Club. All ardent Democrats, the Fosters were related by marriage to President Buchanan's brother, an Episcopal minister. In 1856 Stephen Foster contributed two songs to the Buchanan Glee Club. One was a lampoon of Abolitionism; the other was a paean to the unifying spirit of the South:

> We'll not outlaw the land that holds
> The bones of Washington,
> Where Jackson fought and Marion bled
> And the battles of the brave were won.[30]

From such fragments of evidence, several "founding" minstrels as well as two or three of the nation's best-known minstrel companies can be placed in a scattered but consistent pattern of pro-Southern expression and intimate contact with Democratic Party leaders in New York and San Francisco. The pattern points to a more general typicality when considered against the background of minstrelsy's political orientation, which has already been defined—in a negative sense—by its social content. Temperance, hostility to recent European immigration and lack of enthusiasm for, or direct opposition to, territorial expansion were frequently (not always) characteristic of the Whig, Liberty, Free-Soil, Native American and Republican parties. Regardless of mutual antagonisms, these parties always opposed the

---

[29]*Clipper,* Apr. 25, May 30, 1868; Nathan, pp. 135–42, 214–75.
[30]Howard, pp. 27–28, 43–45, 256–64.

Democratic Party, which, in turn, was nearly always hostile to temperance, receptive to recent European immigration and strenuously in favor of territorial expansion. The positions of the Democratic Party on these issues were congruent to the outlook expressed by blackface minstrelsy; the positions of anti-Democratic parties generally were not. Minstrelsy, then, appears to have been oriented toward the Democratic Party. Since minstrels were generally Northern, as was most of their mass audience, it would seem reasonable to pursue an inquiry into the political line of minstrelsy by investigating its responses to major problems confronting the Northern wing of the Democratic Party.

The Democracy was probably the world's first mass political party. It seems to have been a loose amalgam of class and interest groups in which the new urban working class played a significant but not dominant role. Common goals, antipathies and aspirations which held this amalgam together found expression through an ideology then crystallizing around the "Jacksonian" concept of the individual producer in an expanding society. Emerging cadres of professional leadership became expert at formulating political principles and programs. For the Jacksonian party the three basic principles of its period of ascendancy were: expansion (nationalism), antimonopoly (egalitarianism) and white supremacy. Without venturing further into a theory of American parties and party systems, it may be assumed that Northern Democratic leaders during the 30 years under consideration were endeavoring to perpetuate, or regain, control over the Federal government. Pursuit of this goal presented different problems before, during and after the war.[31]

Before the Civil War, the Democratic Party was dominant nationally, having controlled the Federal government without major interruption since the first election of Andrew Jackson in 1828. Continuance of such control depended upon unity among the party's regional branches. But the price of unity, as set by Southern Democrats, was that the national party must defend the institution of slavery. Consequently a major task of Northern leaders was to resist criticisms of slavery from outside the party and to prevent antislavery sentiment from infiltrating party ranks. This was no

---

[31]The literature on parties and party systems during the Jacksonian period is extensive. Two recent essay collections with convenient bibliographies are Edward Pessen, ed., *New Perspectives on Jacksonian Parties and Politics* (Boston: Allyn and Bacon, 1969) and Joel H. Silbey, *Political Ideology and Voting Behavior in the Age of Jackson* (Englewood Cliffs, N.J.: Prentice-Hall, 1973). With respect to the "three basic principles" of the Democratic Party, see Thurman Williams, *Cherokee Tragedy* (New York: Macmillan, 1970); Richard H. Brown, "The Missouri Crisis, Slavery and the Politics of Jacksonianism," *South Atlantic Quarterly,* 65 (Winter 1966), 55–72; and James K. Paulding, *Slavery* (New York: Harpers, 1836). My own interpretation will be found in greater detail in Saxton, *The Indispensable Enemy: Labor and the Anti-Chinese Movement in California* (Berkeley: Univ. of California Press, 1971).

easy task as views hostile to slavery gained widening acceptance in the North and West.[32]

For blackface minstrelsy, given its Southern origins, slavery was an inescapable topic. Minstrelsy's political stance was a defense of slavery. That this should seem a statement of the obvious is in itself a revealing commentary. In a broader frame of reference, artistic endeavors aimed at "delineating" the cultural traditions of oppressed or enslaved peoples would more commonly be associated, I think, with ideologies of liberation than of oppression. Minstrelsy, however, faithfully reproduced the white slaveowners' viewpoint.

> Old Massa to us darkies am good
> Tra la la, tra la la
> For he gibs us our clothes and he gibs us our food . . . .[33]

Slaves loved the master. They dreaded freedom because, presumably, they were incapable of *self*-possession. When forced to leave the plantation they longed only to return. These themes in minstrelsy worked at several levels. On the one hand, propagating the plantation myth, they portrayed slavery as benign and desirable. On the other hand they reinforced the image of the South as symbol of the collective rural past and of individual childhood, thus acquiring an emotional impact logically unrelated to their content. At the same time, the docility attributed to slaves, commendable as this might seem to a Southern planter, was certain to strike Northern audiences imbued with Jacksonian principles of upward mobility as ridiculous and contemptible.

Was minstrelsy monolithic in its justification of slavery? Almost, but not quite. There appeared a scattering of antislavery expressions which entered in two different ways. First, the early borrowings of Afro-American music and dance carried antislavery connotations which sometimes persisted subliminally in traditional verses like this from "The Raccoon Hunt":

> My ole massa dead and gone,
> A dose of poison help him on
> De debil say he funeral song[34]

Subversive sentiments might be negated in chorus or verses, perhaps added later. This seems to have been the case with the ballad, "De Nigga Gineral," which referred to Nat Turner's rebellion, although parts of the song were

---

[32]Eric Foner, *Free Soil, Free Labor, Free Men: The Ideology of the Republican Party Before the Civil War* (New York: Oxford Univ. Press, 1970).

[33]*Christy's Panorama Songster*, p. 79; see also Toll, pp. 70–99.

[34]*Christy's Ram's Horn*, p. 102.

apparently of older origin. Here the antislavery thesis represented by a black general, "chief of the insurgents," is carefully set at rest by antithetical verses telling of his defeat, repudiation by his own followers, and execution.

> O, Johnson Ben he drove de waggon
> Ho, boys yere most done . . .
> And dey hung him and dey swung him
> Ho, boys, yere most done.[35]

A second and later means of entry of antislavery content was through the essentially white identity of romantic and nostalgic songs, European in tradition and style, which quickly became a staple of minstrel repertory (figure 3). Performed in blackface, yet dealing seriously with themes of parted lovers, lost children and so forth, these songs both invited identification with the situation of the slave and suggested that slavery might have been the cause of separation or loss. But to admit such a possibility was to contradict the myth of the benign plantation and yield ground to antislavery propagandists. Thus, even when given in "darkey" vernacular, sentimental minstrel songs seldom made direct mention of slavery. Occasional references did nonetheless break through. They were then usually softened or disguised by shifting specific griefs to the generalized sorrows of time and distance, or by emphasizing the troubles blacks were likely to encounter in the North.[36]

The two sorts of expressions described above represented the only penetration into minstrelsy of antislavery views. By contrast, a major trend through the 1850s and into the war years consisted of attacks against Abolitionists, who were portrayed as stupid, hypocritical, cowardly, subservient to England and practitioners of miscegenation. Minstrelsy not only conveyed explicit proslavery and anti-Abolitionist propaganda; it was in and of itself a defense of slavery because its main content stemmed from the myth of the benign plantation. Critics of slavery were well aware that the incompatibility between that myth and romantic concepts of love and family constituted a weak point in slavery's defense; and against this point was directed one of their main attacks—that slavery prevented marriage and broke up families. This was the central message of *Uncle Tom's Cabin;* and antislavery singers (never minstrels) like the Hutchinson Family of New Hampshire had been developing similar criticisms long before Harriet Beecher Stowe's novel. The counter to this attack, in which minstrelsy led the field, took the form of ridiculing the very notion of love, or any other

---

[35] Ibid., p. 200; *Christy's No. 2,* pp. 44–45.
[36] Mark Twain, p. 66; Howard, pp. 210–11, 246; *White's Serenaders' Song Book: No. 4* (Philadelphia: Peterson, 1851), p. 40.

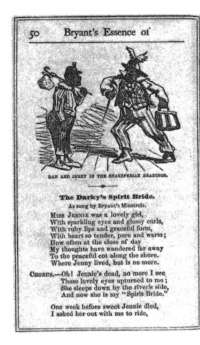

Figure 3 (above left). Shakespeare in blackface. Illustration in *Bryant's Essence of Old Virginny* (New York: Robert M. DeWitt, 1857), 50. Courtesy of Special Collections, University Research Library, University of California, Los Angeles.
Figure 4 (above right). Topsy in a minstrel show poster, about 1870. Ledger Job Printing Office, *Specimens of Show Printing* (Philadelphia, 1869 and 1872), cut no. 494. Reproduced by Cherokee Books (Los Angeles, 1972?). Courtesy of Mr. Lee Freeson.

human or humane emotion, among blacks. Within a few months after the appearance of *Uncle Tom's Cabin,* minstrels had co-opted the title and main characters, while reversing the message (figure 4). The famous T. D. Rice "jumped Jim Crow" in the role of Uncle Tom.[37] Indeed all that was needed to render a serious theme ludicrous in blackface minstrelsy was to permit its dehumanizing form to overbalance the content. In an age of romantic sentiment, minstrels sang love songs like this one:

[37] *Christy's Panorama Songster,* p. 85; *Christy's Plantation Melodies No. 3* (Philadelphia: Fisher, 1853), pp. 10–11, 40–41; *Hooley's Opera House Songster* (New York: Dick, 1864), p. 5; "Joshua" [Hutchinson], *A Brief Narrative of the Hutchinson Family: Sixteen Sons and Daughters of the "Tribe of Jesse"* (Boston: Lee and Shepard, n.d.); A. B. Hutchinson, *The Granite Songster* (Boston: Holt, 1847); George W. Clark, *The Liberty Minstrel* (New York: Saxton and Miles, 1845). On the permutations of *Uncle Tom's Cabin:* Harry Birdoff, *The World's Greatest Hit* (New York: Vanni, 1947); M. B. Leavitt, *Fifty Years of Theatrical Management* (New York: Broadway, 1912), p. 6; and Toll, pp. 104–7.

> My Susy she is handsome
> My Susy she is young . . .
> My Susy looms it bery tall
> Wid udder like a cow
> She'd give nine quarts easy
> But white gals don't know how.[38]

By 1860 the infiltration of antislavery sentiments into Northern party ranks combined with the mounting anxiety and aggressiveness of Southern Democrats had made further compromise impossible. The party split; Lincoln was elected; secession and civil war followed. Although virtually impotent at the national level, the Democracy in the North remained locally powerful in many regions. The task now facing its activists was to hold together their potentially large constituency by loyal Unionism while at the same time seeking to discredit Republican leadership. Once again slavery was at the heart of the matter. The South, Democrats argued, would fight to the bitter end, convinced that the Republicans intended to destroy slavery. But the war could be settled and the Union preserved, if, through ouster of the Republicans from control of the federal apparatus, the slavery issue were fully set at rest. This line was vigorously pushed in media of mass communication accessible to Democratic leadership; and these primarily were newspapers and blackface minstrelsy.

Minstrels re-adapted the plantation myth to wartime purposes, their message being that a struggle against slavery was neither necessary to save the Union nor desirable. Traditional blackface caricatures were politicized. The "plantation nigger" now lamented the inexplicable "white folks'" war which was causing everyone so much trouble; while up North the Broadway dandy thrived like the green bay tree. He conspired with Republican leaders, rejoiced in the war but dodged the draft; paraded in fancy uniform but took to his heels at the first whiff of gunpowder.

> Niggers dey can pick de cotton—dey'll do it very freely
> But when dey smell de bullets, how dey'll run for Horace Greely![39]

To their basic paradox of lauding the plantation system in the midst of a war against the plantation South, the minstrels added a satirical and sometimes brilliant critique of Republican war policy. They questioned the competence of particular leaders (including Lincoln). They attacked political generals, profiteers and shoddy contractors. Songs like Dan Emmett's "How Are You, Greenbacks?" provided a framework for variations upon the class and ethnic sequences worked out during the 1850s.

---

[38] *Christy's Ram's Horn*, pp. 46–47.
[39] Frank Converse, *"Old Cremona" Songster* (New York: Dick, 1863), pp. 9–10.

> We're coming, Father Abram, one hundred thousand more.
> Five hundred presses printing us from morn till night is o'er . . .
> To line the fat contractor's purse, or purchase transport craft
> Whose rotten hulks shall sink before the winds begin to waft.

The bearers of true patriotism, according to minstrel repertory, were honest workingmen who battled to save the Union. Outstanding among these were regiments raised from New York's volunteer fire companies ("For I belong to the Fire Zouaves that started from New York . . ."); and the Irish ("Meagher is leading the Irish Brigade"); and, nearly always treated comically, the lager-drinking Germans ("I'm Going to Fight Mit Sigel"). General McClellan became a symbol of the straightforward Union-loving soldier as opposed to the profiteering, Abolition-tainted Republican politician. Minstrelsy in 1864 mounted an extensive campaign for Mc-Clellan, whose platform as Democratic presidential candidate called for peace on any terms of reunion acceptable to the South.

> We're willing, Father Abram, ten hundred thousand more
> Should help our Uncle Samuel to prosecute the war;
> But then we want a chieftain true, one who can lead the van,
> George B. McClellan you all know, he is the very man . . .[40]

Thus it was loyal workingmen and soldiers who were saving the Union; but their efforts were sabotaged by profiteers and politicians, and worst of all, their lives were needlessly expended for the benefit of the "niggers."

> Abram Linkum said to me—
> Send de sojers down!
> He's gwine to make de niggers free—
> Send de sojers down!

At this level the entire spectrum of minstrelsy from the plantation myth through its urban repertory of ethnic humor and class satire was permeated by the blackface form:

> I wish I was a blinkin' [Abe Lincoln], a blinkin', a blinkin'
> I wish I was a blinkin'
> I'll tell you what I'd do . . .
>
> Oh, if I was much bigger—some bigger—great bigger,
> Oh, if I was some bigger I tell you what I'd do:
> I'd buy up all de niggers—de niggers—de colored African-American citizens,
> I'd buy up all de niggers, and—sell 'em, wouldn't you?[41]

[40] Dan Bryant, *How Are You, Greenbacks* (New York: Pond, 1863), sheet music, "Bryant's Minstrels" folder, Theater Collection, Harvard Library. *Hooley's Opera House*, pp. 16–17; *The Little Mac Songster* (New York: Dick, 1863), pp. 11–13, and 29, 42–43, 53.

[41] Converse, *"Old Cremona,"* pp. 47–48 and 44–45.

This "comic-banjo" piece, as it was described, appeared in a songster published in New York in 1863. Geographically and emotionally, it was only a block or two from a song such as this to the maiming and lynching of blacks on the sidewalks of New York during the draft riots of the same year.[42]

After the war, Democratic strategy was based upon the conviction that the old national majority could be re-created through judicious use of Jacksonian slogans adapted to fit the new situation. Moreover it was soon obvious that the party could count on a massive accession of strength when (or if) the Democratic South was restored to the Union. The three basic appeals of Jacksonianism—nationalism, egalitarianism and white supremacy—assumed the postwar form of demands for immediate readmission of the South, criticism of profiteering and monopoly, and struggle against "black" Reconstruction. The plantation myth, always central to minstrelsy, continued to serve Democratic needs since it softened wartime hostilities and tended to favor rapid restoration of the seceded states.[43] As during the war period, however, the minstrels' political line defined itself most sharply in caricatures based on the Northern, urban partner of the Tambo and Bones pair—the Broadway dandy (figure 5). "Urban" blacks were portrayed as pickpockets, crooked politicians, carpetbaggers and "colored senators"; the wartime formulae of blacks as draft dodgers and deserters were endlessly repeated. Skits and farces came increasingly into use, and the extent to which blackface "convention" permeated their content is indicated by the cast of characters in a farce published in the last year of Reconstruction: "IKEY PIKE (a gentleman of dark complexion, sometimes called an unbleached American citizen) . . . TOM (who blacks boots, still darker) . . . DINAH (the dark daughter of a dark sire . . .) . . . The rest of the characters are all so dark that they cannot be seen."[44] Ridicule continued to be the basic resource of minstrelsy's political line. Similar treatment was now extended to other minority groups which came into the focus of national hostility. As might be expected from previous orientations of minstrelsy, the extension was not to ethnic or religious minorities, but to racial minorities.

[42]James B. Fry, *New York and the Conscription Act of 1863: A Chapter in the History of the Civil War* (New York: Putnam, 1885); A Volunteer Special [William Osborn Stoddard], *The Volcano Under the City* (New York: Fords, Howard & Hulbert, 1887).

[43]For example, Franck Dumont, *Birch and Backus' Songs of the San Francisco Minstrels* (New York: DeWitt, 1881), pp. 9, 23, 53, 56, 68, 103, 105, 114, 144. And see Toll, pp. 150–51.

[44]Harry McCarthy, *Deeds of Darkness* (New York: DeWitt, 1876), p. 2. For a few other examples among hundreds, *Dick's Ethiopian Scenes, Variety Sketches and Stump Speeches* (New York: Dick & Fitzgerald, 1879), esp. pp. 151–53; Bert Richards, *Colored Senators, an Ethiopian Burlesque* (Clyde, Ohio: Ames, 1887); Charles White, *The Recruiting Office, an Ethiopian Sketch in Two Scenes* (New York: DeWitt, 1874).

Figure 5. Minstrel show poster, about 1870. Ledger Job Printing Office, *Specimens of Show Printing* (Philadelphia, 1869 and 1872), cut no. 561. Reproduced by Cherokee Books (Los Angeles, 1972?). Courtesy of Mr. Lee Freeson.

Warfare against Indians in the West intensified after Appomattox. Veterans of the Blue and Gray armies joined hands to extirpate the last independent Indian tribes from the Great Plains and Rocky Mountains. Minstrelsy supported this long-delayed opening up of the Western territories by blackface portrayals of Indians as drunken scalpers, and of those who supported the Indian cause as misguided, corrupt, effete, upper class and miscegenationist. "Oh, dear me," sighed Miss Matilda Livingston ("a young lady of society" in *The Bogus Injun*), "I never do get tired of reading about the noble braves in their forest homes of the far West." Duped by a couple of con men, one of whom impersonates a visiting Indian chief, Miss Livingston donates money to the tribal fund and arranges to have one of her friends, Miss Millefleurs, dress up as an Indian "squaw" to make the chief feel at home. "That really is a good idea," Miss Millefleurs enthusiastically agrees, "as it will allow me to be present at all events, and no doubt prove very interesting to me." The bogus Indian, stimulated by so much hospitality, draws out his tomahawk. The ladies, terrified, run away, while: "The INDIAN . . . chases PETE [Miss Livingston's black footman] around the stage once or twice, and finally catches him in the centre and scalps him while PETE is on his knees."[45]

On the Pacific Coast during these same years, Chinese immigration had been steadily increasing since the gold rush. California's Democratic Party, heavily discredited by the secessionist proclivities of its prewar leaders, focused after the war upon the Chinese menace as a means of rehabilitating the organization. Democratic platforms and oratory linked the Chinese issue directly to the party's national stance against Radical Reconstruction and black suffrage. Government of, by and for white men, on the Pacific Coast as in the South, was the gist of the party's program. San Francisco, one of the nation's leading minstrel cities since before the war, became the gateway through which stereotypes of Chinese, performed in blackface, first reached national audiences. As early as 1856 (twenty years before Bret Harte's "Heathen Chinee") "The Chinese Washerman" was performed in New York by Eph Horn, a minstrel recently returned from the Golden State. Charles Backus, who had once been Horn's partner in San Francisco, joined Billy Birch, of like background, in the 1870s to organize the San Francisco Minstrels in New York. Part of their regular repertory was "The Chinee Laundryman."

> Me workee all day in Chinee laundry
> For "Ching Chow," dat's his name;
> Me catchee all de rats in de market
> Makee pot-pie all-a-same (gong)
> All-a-same (gong) all-a-same (gong).

[45]Charles White, *The Bogus Injun: A Very Laughable Sketch in Four Scenes* (New York: DeWitt, 1875).

Me soon become a cit'zen
And votee just likee me please
By'm by me gettee a good jobbee
To workee on de police! (gong)
Police! (gong) Muchee clubbee! (gong)[46]

From the outbreak of the Mexican War to the closing years of Reconstruction, blackface minstrelsy had consistently reinforced the politics
of Jacksonian and neo-Jacksonian Democracy. Civil war, the industrial
depression of 1873 and the final phasing out of Reconstruction altered the
social and political environment in which the alliance of minstrelsy and
Democracy had originally taken shape. Elements of Jacksonian ideology
now filtered through both members of a changed party system. With
respect to the racial components of Jacksonian ideology, what this meant
may be epitomized by noting that three great Jacksonian issues—Indian re-
moval, white supremacy in the South, and Chinese exclusion—had by the
1880s become matters of bipartisan agreement. After 1877 it would no
longer be surprising to encounter a professional minstrel who was not also a
Democrat. Meanwhile minstrelsy itself was changing. This was not so much
a decline as a spreading out into other forms of mass entertainment. Minstrelsy bequeathed its cast of racial caricatures, along with the dehumanizing ridicule which had literally *informed* them, to the nation's popular
culture. As early as 1870 a melodrama celebrating the transcontinental railroad predicted uses to be made of those caricatures in ten thousand
westerns which would march across the landscape of dime novels, stage
plays, and ultimately of films, radio and television. In *Across the Continent;
or, Scenes from New York Life and the Pacific Railroad,* the minstrel roles
of Tambo and Bones were filled by a black servant, "Caesar Augustus,
called Coon because he is one," and "Very Tart, a Chinaman." The
California-bound party, barricaded in a railroad station, is expecting attack
from Indians led by the ferocious chief, Black Cloud. Very Tart, never
having seen a black man before, mistakes Caesar Augustus for the chief.
"Oh, Black Cloud—Black Cloud!" he cries in terror. But John (the hero)
reassures him, "That ain't an injun—it's only a nigger." To which Caesar
Augustus agrees: "Well, thank the Lord I'se only a nigger." The climax of
course will be the arrival of a trainload of soldiers to annihilate Black Cloud
and his horde. Just before the shooting starts, Very Tart finds a large empty

---

[46] Dumont, *Birch and Backus' Songs,* p. 57. George C. D. Odell, *Annals of the New York
Stage* (New York: Columbia Univ. Press, 1931), 6:585; Stuart W. Hyde, "The Chinese
Stereotype in American Melodrama," *California Historical Society Quarterly,* 34 (Dec. 1955),
357–65.

packing crate on the station platform, and as he crawls inside informs the audience: "Melican man like fightee. Chinaman like sleepee in a box."[47]

The ideological impact of minstrelsy was programmed by its conventional blackface form. There is no possibility of escaping this relationship because the greater the interest, talent, complexity and *humanity* embodied in its content, the more irresistible was the racist message of the form. One is tempted to borrow McLuhan's phrase: the medium was the message. Yet that would miss the point since without its content, the form would have been inconsequential. As noted earlier, the matrix of social content contained, among other elements, a style of moral permissiveness. Horizontally this style was linked to the cosmopolitanism of new urban environments and the open opportunity of the frontier. There was also a vertical linkage which went straight down under to a permissiveness to demean, ridicule and destroy all those outside the fraternity of white egalitarianism. The meaning did not reside solely in negative or ridiculous portrayals of nonwhites; it resided in the "convention" itself. Blackface performers were like puppets operated by a white puppet-master. Their physical appearance proclaimed their non-humanity; yet they could be manipulated not only to mock themselves, but also to act like human beings. They expressed human emotions such as joy and grief, love, fear, longing. The white audience then identified with the emotions, admired the skill of the puppeteer, even sympathized laughingly with the hopeless aspiration of the puppets to become human, and at the same time feasted on the assurance that they could not do so. Blackface minstrelsy's dominance of popular entertainment amounted to half a century of inurement to the uses of white supremacy.

American historians have traditionally attached a major importance to the Jacksonian era. The effects of that era have been interpreted variously in terms of nationalism, politics, social status, population movement, technological and economic growth. Each of these interpretations assumes diffusion of new ideas and attitudes through a population which, during the period under consideration, was moving from the Mississippi Valley to the Pacific Coast and increasing numerically from seventeen to fifty millions. No doubt diffusion of ideas and attitudes occurred in such old-fashioned ways as by word of mouth and written correspondence; but it occurred also by new methods including steam-powered presses and popular entertainment which brought mass audiences into the tents, town halls and theaters of new population centers. Thus gathered together, they could rejoice in what Mark Twain had described as a "glad and stunning surprise."

---

[47] James J. McCloskey, *Across the Continent: or, Scenes from New York Life and the Pacific Railroad,* in Isaac Goldberg and Hubert Heffner, eds., *Davy Crockett and Other Plays* (Princeton: Princeton Univ. Press, 1940), pp. 110–12.

At other times a vitriolic critic of American society, Mark Twain's uncritical approval of minstrelsy is testimony to the pervasiveness of its influence. He seems simply to have taken the blackface "convention" for granted and probably had no perception of the African elements in the music and dance. Minstrel songs, he wrote, "were a delight to me as long as the Negro show continued in existence. In the beginning the songs were rudely comic . . . but a little later sentimental songs were introduced, such as 'The Blue Juniata,' 'Sweet Ellen Bayne,' 'Nelly Bly,' 'A Life on the Ocean Wave,' 'The Larboard Watch,' etc."[48] Two of the five songs mentioned were Stephen Foster's. Clearly what Mark Twain preferred was the nostalgic, "white" voice of minstrelsy which had already attained full expression ten years before the Civil War.

> Way down on the Swanee ribber
> Far, far away,
> Dere's wha my heart is turning ebber . . .[49]

The "darkey" dialect is transparent. The black puppets are striving to be white, singing in white voice, while the white audience in the new city or the new West lingers through a moment of self-pity and regret for things past, before the rattle of tambourine and bones calls up the clowns again. It would be a mistake to underestimate these tearjerkers. Whatever they may or may not say to anyone in the mid-20th century, it is clear that to the author of *Huckleberry Finn* they said a great deal. For Mark Twain, as for many of his contemporaries, they touched the central chords of white consciousness—the place left behind and the endless outward journey. By setting a heroic, tragic concept of human destiny in a conventional form which denied human status to nonwhites, blackface minstrelsy acted out the most appalling aspect of Jacksonian ideology. It is useless to debate whether the minstrels created or merely reflected this ideology; mass entertainment necessarily transmits as it creates and creates in transmitting.

[48] Mark Twain, p. 66.
[49] [Stephen Foster], "Old Folks at Home," in *Christy's No. 1*, p. 7.

Eric Lott

Who better to have written this classic essay on the politics of early black-face minstrelsy than Alexander Saxton? Erstwhile labor novelist and pioneering historian, Saxton brought an immense range of experience to "Blackface Minstrelsy and Jacksonian Ideology." His novels plumbed the lives of American proletarians; his historical work, resulting first in *The Indispensable Enemy* (Berkeley: University of California Press, 1971), confronted the anti-Chinese racism so fundamental to industrializing America. Moving from there to what I think of as a great trilogy of *American Quarterly* articles, Saxton took on the ideology of the minstrel show (1975), the surprising career of journalist-entrepreneur George Wilkes (1981), and the historical trajectory of the nineteenth-century penny press (1984)—work that speaks as much to large-scale histori-cal processes as to the intricacies of the case studies at hand, and that together constitutes a remarkable advance in our understanding of the demimonde of nineteenth-century America. Some of this material was later incorporated into Saxton's magisterial *The Rise and Fall of the White Republic* (New York: Verso, 1990).

It may be, then, that Saxton's own careers influenced what I believe is one of his most distinctive contributions in the *American Quarterly* articles: a brilliant attention to the sinuous, sometimes unlikely shapes of lives and historical processes. One detects a subtle Marxist determi-nation to follow the dialectical leaps and changes afforded by the explo-sive energies of early American capitalism, but Saxton's own experiences in twentieth-century America exemplify such a pattern as well. Thus in his work he traces George Wilkes's path from antebellum penny press scandal-stirrer to American reporter of the 1871 Paris Commune. The penny press itself, witnessed through Saxton's superb documentation of its escalating economies of scale, undergoes unexpected transforma-tions all across the nineteenth century. Even in the unforgiving "Black-face Minstrelsy and Jacksonian Ideology" there is a recognition of the

Alexander Saxton, "Blackface Minstrelsy and Jacksonian Ideology," originally ap-peared in *American Quarterly* 27, no. 1 (March 1975), Copyright © 1975 Trustees of the University of Pennsylvania.

way the class realities of minstrel entertainers as well as their working-class audiences decisively inflected the racial course of blackface performance—a major intervention that has inspired much new work (not least my own) since its appearance. In the end, it is history's strange careers that occasion Saxton's most significant interest.

Saxton maps the minstrel show through the careers of four of its key artists and designers. These four, Saxton argues, were close to the center of Jacksonian political power. Saxton surveys the social origins of blackface "originator" T. D. Rice, Virginia Minstrels' leader Dan Emmet, Christy's Minstrels' E. P. Christy, and composer Stephen Foster, who, like many of minstrelsy's major innovators, were northerners of urban origin (none from New England) raised in families bent on upward mobility. Each man refused the Protestant ethic and escaped into the entertainment world. In the course of such escape they encountered the music and dance of slaves and free blacks, and were canny enough to realize that fame and money might come out of exploiting this encounter. While such "professionals" were sometimes class renegades, forgoing clerkships or better to enter the underground world of blackface theater, they nevertheless shared with their families certain political ties to the elite of the Democratic party, the party of Andrew Jackson, antimonopoly, expansionism—and white supremacy. Henry Wood of Christy and Wood's minstrels was the brother of Fernando Wood, Copperhead (that is, southern sympathizing) mayor of New York; another brother served three terms as a Democratic congressman and one term as a state senator. Stephen Foster belonged to a family of passionate Democrats related by marriage to President James Buchanan's brother, and Foster himself helped organize a local Buchanan for President club. On the basis of such evidence as well as minstrel performance itself, Saxton regards blackface minstrelsy as "half a century of inurement to the uses of white supremacy."

Though this is the most cogent study I know of the minstrel show's political containment, Saxton also casts the net wide to make observations that don't necessarily buttress his case but do demonstrate the hold minstrelsy had on its audiences. He suggests, for example, that nostalgic blackface songs spoke at once to restless migrants moving west, recently transplanted rural folk in cities, and rootless urban dwellers beginning to experience the anomie of modern metropolitan life; turning the South into a kind of timeless lost home, a safe, imaginary childhood, these songs proved supremely satisfying to a wide variety of white spectators. Saxton also notes the frequent ribaldry, extending to submerged homosexual joking, that white men enjoyed with the aid of blackface masking. And, as I have said, he is acute on the centrality of class to this most popular entertainment form; he is wonderful on the stage-fireman sources of the blackface slave Mose, a favorite of the white workers in the audience, and with the phrase "white egalitarianism" goes a long way toward unpacking the antebellum working-class contradiction of adherence to both democratic ideals and white supremacy.

Though I have in *Love and Theft: Blackface Minstrelsy and the American Working Class* (New York: Oxford University Press, 1993) presented evidence that suggests much more personal and political ambivalence in minstrelsy than Saxton finds, "Blackface Minstrelsy and Jacksonian Ideology" nonetheless offered a crucial model for my work. Not only does it call on an imaginative array of primary sources, unusual interpretive acuity, and a courageous offering of some seamy but important textual evidence. Its largest ambition is to make connections between individual careers and the motors of historical change, an ambition it admirably fulfills. Indeed, its final turn to Chinese minstrel caricature gestures to the multiracial and multiethnic burlesques minstrelsy would increasingly take on as it transmogrified into vaudeville in the early twentieth century. Not surprisingly, Saxton's essay has in turn had its own career of influence and infiltration into a great variety of articles, courses, symposia, and books; just about everyone seems acquainted with it. Together with Robert Toll's contemporaneous *Blacking Up: The Minstrel Show in Nineteenth Century America* (New York: Oxford University Press, 1974), it helped close the coffin on the sort of nostalgic indulgence of blackface that ruled American scholarship on the topic into (unbelievably) the 1960s. Not the least of all, the article pointed to matters of race, performance, and ideology whose long afterlife has generated a raft of studies in the 1990s—fitting tribute indeed to the careers of Alexander Saxton.

LINDA KERBER

The Republican Mother:
Women and the Enlightenment—
An American Perspective

THE GREAT QUESTIONS OF POLITICAL LIBERTY AND CIVIC FREEDOM, OF THE relationship between law and liberty, the subjects of so many ideological struggles in the eighteenth century, are questions which have no gender. Philosophes habitually indulged in vast generalizations about humanity: Montesquieu contemplated the nature of society, Rousseau formulated a scheme for the revitalized education of children, Lord Kames wrote four volumes on the history of mankind. The broad sweep of their generalizations has permitted the conclusion that they indeed meant to include all people in their observations; if they habitually used the generic "he" two centuries before our own generation began to be discomfited by it, then it is a matter of syntax and usage, and without historical significance.

Yet Rousseau permitted himself to wonder whether women were capable of serious reasoning. If the Enlightenment represented, as Peter Gay has remarked, "man's claim to be recognized as an adult, responsible being" who would "take the risk of discovery, exercise the right of unfettered criticism, accept the loneliness of autonomy," it may be worth asking whether it was assumed that women were also to recognize themselves as responsible beings. Is it possible, by definition, for women to be enlightened? The answers to that question have important implications for historians of political thought and for those who seek to write women's intellectual history.

We should be skeptical of the generous assumption that the Enlightenment *man* was generic. Philosophe is a male noun: it describes Kant, Adam Smith, Diderot, Lessing, Franklin, Locke, Rousseau. With the conspicuous exceptions of Catharine Macaulay and Mary Wollstonecraft, women are absent even from the second and third ranks. They hover on the fringes, creating a milieu for discussions in their salons, offering their personal and moral support to male friends and lovers, but making only minor intellectual contributions. Mme. Helvetius and Mme. Brillon, Mme. Condorcet, even Catherine of Russia, are consumers, not creators of Enlightenment ideas. Is it by accident or design that the Molly Stevensons, the Sophie Vollands, the Maria Cosways figure primarily as the address*ees* of letters by Franklin, Diderot, Jefferson?

A careful reading of the main texts of the Enlightenment in France, England and the colonies reveals that the nature of the relationship between women and the state remained largely unexamined; the use of *man* was in fact literal, not generic. Only by implication did the writers say anything of substance about the function and responsibilities of women in the monarchies they knew and the ideal communities they invented. Just as their inadvertent comments on the mob revealed the limits of their democracy, their comments on women reveal the limits of their definition of civic virtue.

Perhaps the most striking feature of Enlightenment literature is that the more abstract and theoretical his intention the more likely it is that the writer would consider the function of women in the polity. Because a standard way of reinventing natural law was to posit the first family in a state of nature and derive political relationships from its situation, philosophes were virtually forced by the form in which they had chosen to work to contemplate women's political role—even if, with Rousseau, they did so in an antifeminist mode. By contrast, the more the writer's intention was specific criticism of contemporary affairs, as it was apt to be among the Whig Opposition, the less the likelihood of serious consideration of women as political beings. But both groups shared the unspoken assumption that women acted in a political capacity only in special and unusual circumstances.

In the face of a denial that women might properly participate in the political community at all, there was invented a definition of women's relationship to the state that sought to fill the inadequacies of inherited political theory. The republican ideology that Americans developed included—hesitantly—a political role for women. It made use of the classic formulation of the Spartan Mother who raised sons prepared to sacrifice themselves to the good of the *polis*. It provided an apparent integration of domestic and political behavior, in a formula that masked political purpose by promise of domestic service. The terms provided were ambivalent and in many ways intellectually unsatisfying; the intellectual history of women is not a whiggish progression, ever onward and ever upward, toward autonomy and liberation. The tangled and complex role of the Republican Mother offered one among many structures and contexts in which women might define the civic culture and their responsibilities to the state; radical feminist political movements would develop in dialectical opposition to it. This essay seeks to describe the elements of that republican role, and the gaps in available political theory it was intended to fill.

* * *

To what extent was there room for women in the philosophe's vision of the political order? Let us begin with Locke, whose consideration of the relationship of women to public order was extensive, and who was read and generally admired by the philosophes of the eighteenth century.[1] Locke's *Two Treatises on Government* are a direct attack on Richard Filmer's *Patriarcha,* which spins a justification for absolute monarchy by divine right out of the biblical injunction to honor thy father. But the commandment, after all, is to "Honor thy father *and mother*"; Filmer's defense of absolutism in government conveniently forgot mothers; it imagined a power structure that was masculine, that was absolute, and that descended through primogeniture. To create this structure and defend it as he did, Filmer had to ignore a large network of other relationships and impose a hierarchical subordination on all those he did acknowledge. Locke needed for *his* purposes only a reader who would concede that the biblical commandment was to "Honor thy father and mother"; grant him that, and Locke could proceed to race through Filmer, restoring mothers as he went, and by that device undercutting Filmer's analogy between parental power and royal authority. If familial power is shared with women and limited by mutual responsibilities, the nature of royal authority must also be shared and limited. What Locke accomplished in the *First Treatise* was the integration of women into social theory.[2]

"The first society was between man and wife," Locke wrote in the *Second Treatise,* "which gave beginning to that between parents and children; to which, in time, that between master and servant came to be added." But these relationships are not all hierarchical: "conjugal society is made by a voluntary compact between men and women."[3] The grant of dominion made to Adam in *Genesis* is not, as Filmer would have it, over people in general and Eve in particular; it is to human beings over animals. If Adam is lord of the world, Eve is lady. The curse of Eve, Locke thought, could not justify women's permanent and universal submission to men; the curse was part of her punishment for sin, but it was a sin which Adam had shared and for which he too was punished, not rewarded. Husbands reigned over wives, wives suffered the pains of childbirth; but these were descriptions of reality and reality might be changed by human intention. Labor might be medically

---

[1] See Peter Gay, *The Enlightenment: An Interpretation—The Science of Freedom* (New York: Knopf, 1969), 189 et passim.

[2] John Locke, *Two Treatises of Government,* Peter Laslett, ed. (London: Cambridge Univ. Press, 1967); see especially *First Treatise,* §§62–65. Robert Filmer, *Patriarcha: or the Natural Power of Kings,* Thomas I. Cook, ed. (New York: Hafner Publishing Co., 1947).

[3] Locke, *Second Treatise,* §§77, 78.

eased; a woman who was queen in her own right did not become, when she married, her husband's subject.[4]

Locke came closer than most of his contemporaries and successors to defining a political role for women. He underlined the rights and powers women ought to have in their domestic capacity: mothers have a right to the respect of their children that is not dependent on the husband's will; mothers have their own responsibilities to their children; women ought to control their own property. There is not even a hint in his work that women unsex themselves when they step into the political domain.[5] But once Filmer had been disposed of, and Locke could generalize more broadly about civic powers and responsibilities, his insistence on defining the role of women in the social order diminished. He did, however, phrase his most significant generalizations in the *Second Treatise* in terms of *persons:* the legislative body is composed of persons, the supreme power is placed in them by the people, "using Force upon the People without Authority . . . is a state of War with the People."[6] Women were included, presumably, among "the people," but they had no clear mechanism for expressing their own wills.[7] Locke obviously assumed that women contributed in some way to the civic culture, but he was not very clear about what they might do were they to find themselves under a king who had forfeited their confidence. One ends by wishing he had written a *Third Treatise.*

Montesquieu also returned to first principles: "I have first of all considered mankind."[8] The principles by which governments are regulated—virtue in a republic, honor in a monarchy, fear in a despotism—are abstractions apparently devoid of gender. The virtue that buttresses the republic is transmitted by parents (not only fathers) who are responsible for raising virtuous children (not only sons).

Sensitive as he was to the implications of private manners for public style, Montesquieu argued that "The slavery of women is perfectly comformable to the genius of a despotic government, which delights in treating all with severity. . . . In a government which requires, above all things, that a particular regard be paid to its tranquillity, it is absolutely necessary to shut

[4] *First Treatise,* §§30, 47.

[5] *First Treatise,* §§61, 63; *Second Treatise,* §§52, 65, 183. In the *Second Treatise,* §§80–83, Locke argues that the primary justification for marriage is the lengthy dependence and vulnerability of the child, and he permits himself to "enquire, why this Compact, when Procreation and Education are secured, and Inheritance taken care for, may not be made determinable, either by consent, or at a certain time, or upon certain conditions, as well as any other voluntary compacts, there being no necessity in the nature of the thing, . . . that it should always be for Life. . . ."

[6] *Second Treatise,* §§124, 153, 154, 155.

[7] For women as a special case of relatively minor significance, see *Second Treatise,* §§180–83, 233.

[8] Charles Louis de Secondat, Baron de Montesquieu, *The Spirit of the Laws,* Thomas Nugent, trans. (New York: Hafner Pub. Co., 1949), lxvii–lxix.

up the women." On the other hand, "In a republic, the condition of citizens is moderate, equal, mild and agreeable . . . an empire over women cannot . . . be so well exerted."[9]

Although women did not play, for Montesquieu, a central role in shaping the civic character of the government under which they lived, the form that government ultimately took *did* have crucial implications for their private lives. By his description of the "connection between domestic and political government," Montesquieu provided strong support for the conclusion that it is in women's self-interest to live in a republic. He offered no mechanism by which a woman unfortunate enough not to be born into a republic might change her condition, but the message that it was of crucial importance for women to live under certain forms of government and not under others was there, strongly phrased, available if anyone wished to use it.

Condorcet came closest to inventing procedure for as well as justification for including women in politics. His feminist comments emerge naturally from his general vision of the social order; they appear most extensively in his essay "Sur l'admission des Femmes au Droit de Cité," and in his "Lettres d'un Bourgeois de New-Heaven" (an appealing typographical error).[10]

Condorcet argued that although it was true that women had not exercised the right of citizenship in any "constitution called free," the right to political voice in a republic is claimed by men on the grounds that they are "sensible beings, capable of reason, having moral ideas," qualities which can be equally well claimed by women. "Men have . . . interests strongly different from those of women," Condorcet said in an unusual and forceful statement (although he did not specify what those differences were), and have used their power to make laws that establish "a great inequality between the sexes." Once it were admitted that people cannot legitimately be taxed without representation, "it follows from this principle that all women are in their rights to refuse to pay parliamentary taxes." Condorcet proceeded to argue that except in matters requiring brute strength, women were obviously men's equals; the brightest women were already superior to men of

---

[9]Montesquieu, 255–56. Book VII includes a curious pair of paragraphs headed "Of Female Administration" which offer the paradox that "It is contrary to reason and nature that women should reign in families . . . but not that they should govern an empire." In families women's natural weakness "does not permit them to have the pre-eminence"; but in governments that same weakness means that they administer their governments with "more lenity and moderation." It is the classic double bind, and applies, in any event, only to women who inherit their thrones. Despite Montesquieu's defense of women's political ability, he suggests no devices which would increase the likelihood that they will use these abilities.

[10]The essay, "Sur l'admission des Femmes," originally appeared July 3, 1790, in the *Journal de la Société de 1789;* it is reprinted in *Oeuvres de Condorcet* (Paris: Firmin Didot Frères, 1847), X, 119–30. The letters were published as pages 267–71 in Vol. I of Filippo Mazzei, *Recherches Historiques et Politiques Sur les États-Unis . . . avec Quatre Lettres d'un Bourgeois de New-Heaven sur l'unité de la Législation* (Paris: A. Colle, 1788).

limited talents, and improvements in education would readily narrow what gaps there were. He concluded what was perhaps his generation's most detailed statement of the political rights and responsibilities of women:

> Perhaps you will find this discussion too long; but think that it is about the rights of half of human beings, rights forgotten by all the legislators; that it is not useless even for the liberty of men to indicate the means of destroying the single objection which could be made to republics, and to make between them and states which are not free a real difference.[11]

Condorcet is best remembered, of course, for his *Esquisse d'un tableau historique des progrès de l'esprit humain,* sometimes for the book's own sake, more often for the bravery of his authorship of a testament to the human spirit at the very moment when that same spirit was hounding him to a premature death. In the *Esquisse,* he imagined that women had been an integral part of prehistoric society and important contributors to the social order. The original society consisted of a family, "formed at first by the want that children have of their parents, and by the affection of the mother as well as that of the father." Children gradually extend the affection they naturally have for their parents to other members of their family and then to their clan. But before the first stage of primitive society has been outgrown, women have lost their central position. Condorcet suggests that the origins of governmental institutions resided in the meetings of men who planned hunting trips and wars. It seemed obvious to him that "the weakness of the females, which exempted them from the distant chase, and from war, the usual subjects of debate, excluded them alike from these consultations"; women were thus excluded at the outset from "the first political institutions" and consigned to "a sort of slavery." Their slavery is modified in the second, or pastoral epoch, and manners are "softened" and modified still more in the third epoch, which also sees the invention of alphabetical writing. "A more sedentary mode of life had introduced a greater equality between the sexes. . . . Men looked upon them as companions, . . . [but] even in countries where they were treated with most respect . . . neither reason nor justice extended so far as to an entire reciprocity as to the right of divorce. . . . The history of this class of prejudices, and of their influence on the lot of the human species . . . [evinces] how closely man's happiness is connected with the progress of reason."[12]

The more rational the government, the more improved will be the status of women. It is an important formulation, but Condorcet, oddly enough,

---

[11]*Lettres d'un Bourgeois . . .,* 281–87, translation mine.

[12]Marie Antoine Nicolas Caritat, Marquis de Condorcet, title usually translated as *Sketch for a Historical Picture of the Progress of the Human Mind* (Philadelphia: M. Carey, 1794), 24, 26, 28, 32, 43. In his list of tasks that remained unaccomplished, Condorcet specifically listed the improvement of the status of women: his words on this point have frequently been reprinted. (p. 280)

does not develop it further. In its omission of women from the fourth through ninth epochs of one of the very few histories that begins as in fact a history of mankind in the generic sense, the *Esquisse* falls into traditionalism: "he" lapses into literal usage, and the assumption that men represent the general case, women the rare and insignificant exception, is reinforced. Those who wish to find in Condorcet reiteration of the rule that the world is a man's world will find it in the *Esquisse*.[13]

Condorcet offered his comments on women in politics in direct challenge to those of Rousseau. Although much that Rousseau wrote implied sharp criticism of contemporary society and envisaged drastic change, what he said about women usually reinforced the existing order. This conservatism about women may well have served to make his radical comments about men's behavior more palatable; if the world were to be changed into a new one, characterized by a new style of men's behavior as demonstrated by Émile, governed by a General Will in accordance with a new Social Contract, it was surely reassuring to know that the women of that world, exemplified by Émile's wife Sophie, would not change—that they would remain deferential to their men, clean in their household habits, complaisant in their conversation.

The key to Rousseau's understanding of women's political function is in his discussion of the origins of government in *The Social Contract*. The General Will, after all, is a concept without gender; the freedom of the social contract comes from the paradoxical identification of the ruler with the ruled. If it is obvious that women are among the ruled, ought they not also be among the legislators?

There is a hidden paradox in this generally paradoxical essay: the women who are ruled are, at the same time, not ruled; because they are not ruled they need not participate in the General Will. They are invisible. As Rousseau explained in *Émile,* they lived in another world. Theirs is "the

[13]See Keith Michael Baker's magisterial *Condorcet: From Natural Philosophy to Social Mathematics* (Chicago: Univ. of Chicago Press, 1975). Baker does not, however, comment on Condorcet's treatment of women's role in political society or on the essay "Sur l'admission des Femmes au droit de cité" or the "Lettres d'un Bourgeois. . . ." In 1785 Condorcet's careful analysis of "the calculus of consent" was published as "Essai sur l'application de l'analyse à la probabilité des decisions rendues à la pluralité des voix"; as Baker phrases it, the essay attempts to deal with the problem of "Under what conditions will the probability that the majority decision of an assembly or tribunal is true be high enough to justify the obligation of the rest of society to accept that decision." Condorcet viewed "the process of political decision-making . . . not as a means of ascertaining the strongest among a number of opposing parties—not, that is, as a mere expression of will—but as a method for the collective discovery of truth." Like Turgot, Condorcet rejected the claim that "monarchical government" could "impose a just order in a constant war of corporate claims and counterclaims" in favor of "the doctrine of a nation of individuals united by the common, reciprocal bond of citizenship." (Baker, 228–29) This reasoning has something in common with Rousseau's General Will, in which all individuals choose to submit to the community. But even in Condorcet's formulation, women are not explicitly part of the community.

empire of softness, of address, of complacency; her commands are caresses; her menaces are tears."[14] This is not hyperbole; women have moral and physical relationships to men, but not political ones; not do they relate to any women other than their mothers. Rousseau is explicit. The shift from the generic to the literal "he" occurs before *The Social Contract* has scarcely begun: the most ancient and only natural society is the family, Rousseau remarks, but children soon outgrow their dependence on their *fathers*.[15] After that the specific terms in which the General Will is explained are masculine ones; it is only men, taken literally, whom Rousseau expects to display disinterested civic spirit. In *Émile* he takes it as self-evident that it is "the good son, the good father, the good husband, that constitute the good citizen."[16]

Émile is a book about the task of forming a citizen for an idealized society. Émile is a body at ease with its mind, a sophisticated innocent, a person as paradoxical as the society for which he is educated. But Rousseau did not rethink the terms on which women ought to be educated for his new social order. He did not posit, for Sophie, as he did for Émile, a *tabula rasa* on which a rational mentor writes only what is necessary and natural; he did not end for Sophie, as he did for Émile, with a personality radically different from the one that standard systems of education were geared to create. Sophie is as traditional a woman as it is possible to imagine, reformed only in the sense that she does not dote on fashion or read novels.

Rousseau's refusal to rethink the terms of Sophie's education was intentional. Due to his own private sexual tastes he had, after all, a substantial personal stake in the submissiveness of women. He was not loath to make the broadest generalizations: "To oblige us, to do us service, to gain our love and esteem . . . these are the duties of the sex at all times, and what they ought to learn from their infancy."[17] Relationships between men and women are always sexual, and always verge on the uncontrollable: "Woman is framed particularly for the delight and pleasure of man. . . . Her violence consists in her charms . . . [her modesty masks her] unbounded desires."[18]

Nor did Rousseau need to rethink the bases of Sophie's mental development. As men's education became more highly developed it had strayed further from the natural into bookish abstraction. Rousseau needed a revolution to arrange for Émile to grow up among things rather than books, to postpone learning to read, to postpone foreign languages until he traveled to

[14] Jean-Jacques Rousseau, *Emilius, Or, a Treatise of Education* (Edinburgh: A. Donaldson 1768), III, 10.

[15] Jean-Jacques Rousseau, *The Social Contract,* G. D. H. Cole, ed. (London: Dent, 1913), Book I, Chap. II, p. 6.

[16] *Emilius,* III, 14.

[17] Ibid., III, 74–75.

[18] Ibid., III, 5–6.

countries where they were used. But girls were already barred from books, rarely taught foreign languages, already limited to physical tasks relating to household chores. Only erase excessive attention to fashion, and women's education needed no renovation. Émile thanks his mentor for having been "restored to my liberty, by teaching me to yield to necessity." But Sophie's life is at all times largely directed by necessity; the more that women's lives were shaped by repeated cycles of pregnancy, lying-in, nursing, and child-rearing, the closer they were to nature; the less the need to reform their education.[19]

Rousseau's most substantial target was Plato, who had offered, in Book V of *The Republic,* the classic attack on assigning social roles by gender. Rousseau defended Plato against the charge of encouraging promiscuity by inventing a community of women, but he was horrified by the "civil promiscuousness" implied by the assigning of the same employments to men and women. It represented, Rousseau sneered, the conversion of women into men.[20]

The argument that women ought not be part of the political community (as they are in Plato) was reinforced by Rousseau's insistence that women who seek to do so deny their sexual identity. The woman who seeks to be a politician or philosopher does violence to her own character: "A witty [i.e. articulate] woman is a scourge to her husband, to her children, to her friends, her servants, and to all the world. Elated by the sublimity of her genius, she scorns to stoop to the duties of a woman, and is sure to commence a man. . . ." Rousseau was sure his readers would share his scorn of "a female genius, scribbling of verses in her toilette, and surrounded by pamphlets"; although if she were scribbling emotional effusions, as Julie

[19]Ibid., III, 229. In Book V of *The Wealth of Nations,* Adam Smith expresses similar admiration for the practical aspects of women's education. "There are no public institutions for the education of women, and there is accordingly nothing useless, absurd, or fantastical in the common course of their education. They are taught what their parents or guardians judge it necessary or useful for them to learn; and they are taught nothing else. Every part of their education tends evidently to some useful purpose; either to improve the natural attractions of their person, or to form their mind to reserve, to modesty, to chastity, and to economy; to render them both likely to become the mistresses of a family, and to behave properly when they have become such. In every part of her life a woman feels some conveniency or advantage from every part of her education. It seldom happens that a man, in any part of his life, derives any conveniency or advantage from some of the most laborious and troublesome parts of his education." (*The Wealth of Nations* [New York: Modern Library, 1937], Book V, ch. I, part II, article II, pp. 720, 734) When Smith comes to reform the educational system, women continue to be excluded from it. Men are to envy women the practicality of their education, and the direct relationship between women's education and their adult roles; it is harder to predict what skills boys will ultimately find most useful. That women's education can be directly related to women's adult roles precisely because these roles are so limited and so predictable does not seem to Smith to be a cause for concern.

[20]*The Republic,* H.D.P. Lee, tr. (London: Penguin, 1955), 209–10. Rousseau's comments appear in *Emilius,* III, 14.

does throughout all six books of *La Nouvelle Héloïse,* he apparently had no objection. "The art of thinking is not foreign to women," Rousseau conceded, "but they ought only to skim the surface of abstruse sciences."[21] Attacks on masculine, articulate women are one of the more common themes of English literature (both British and American) in the late eighteenth and early nineteenth centuries. The image would prove to be a formidable obstacle to feminists throughout the nineteenth and twentieth centuries; if the concept is not original with Rousseau, surely he did much to strengthen it in precisely those liberal and reformist circles where it would be logically predicted to die out.

Rousseau's impact on American thought is difficult to measure. There was no American edition of *Émile,* but it was available in translation in even more editions than Locke's *Two Treatises.* Much more widely circulated than either was Lord Kames' *Sketches of the History of Man,* which occasionally cites Rousseau and whose comments on women's place in society are in rough congruence with Rousseau's. For Lord Kames, women's history was "a capital branch of the history of man." It demonstrated a crude progress from women's debased condition among savages to "their elevated state in civilized nations." He explicitly denied that women have a direct responsibility to their nation; their relationship to their country is secondhand, experienced through husbands and sons, and they therefore have "less patriotism than men." Like Rousseau, Kames feared masculinization: "Remove a female out of her proper sphere, and it is easy to convert her into a male." He agreed that women's education ought to fit them to be sensible companions and mothers; the great danger to be guarded against was frivolity and disorderly manners. Having disposed of women in 97 pages, he was free to ignore them in the remaining 1,770 pages of his four-volume treatise; his final conclusion was merciless: "Cultivation of the female mind, is not of great importance in a republic, where men pass little of their time with women."[22]

* * *

We are left with an intellectual gap. The great treatises of the Enlightenment, which provided so changed a framework for attitudes toward the state, offered no guidance on how women might think about their own relationship to liberty or civic virtue. Even Rousseau, one of the most radical political theorists of an age famous for its ability to examine the assumptions it had inherited, failed to examine his own assumptions about women. Ought a woman dare to think? Might a woman accept "the loneliness of au-

---

[21] *Emilius,* III, 104–05, 139.

[22] Henry Home, Lord Kames, *Sketches of the History of Man* (Edinburgh: W. Strahan & T. Cadell, 1778), II, 1–2, 5, 85, 97.

tonomy"? To be alone, in fact, was to be male; women were invariably described, even by Locke, in relationship to others. Only Condorcet occasionally imagined an autonomous woman: for Locke, Montesquieu, Rousseau, Kames, women existed only in their roles as mothers and wives. If Fred Weinstein and Gerald M. Platt are right in defining the Enlightenment as the expression of "a desire to end the commitments to passivity and dependence in the area of politics," women were not a part of it.[23]

Of all branches of Enlightenment thought, Americans were most attracted to the literature of the Commonwealth and Radical Whig opposition in England. As Bernard Bailyn and Gordon Wood have shown, eighteenth-century Americans were familiar with the work of Trenchard and Gordon, Sidney, Harrington, James Burgh, Catharine Macaulay. American political theorists made much use of it. But this literature is largely concerned with specific issues of opposition to crown policy; it rarely needed a presocial family to make its argument. One result of the overwhelming influence of the Whig tradition in America was that American political theory was rooted in assumptions that never gave explicit attention to basic questions about women. It was the good fortune of male Whigs that they did not need to begin at the beginning, but that same good fortune inhibited the likelihood that they would include women in their contemplations of the good society.

As Edwin Burrows and Michael Wallace have brilliantly shown, Whigs had a major ideological concern for parent-child relationships, but their discussions faded into the specific case of sons and fathers, or the limits of the obligations of sons to mothers.[24] Other variants of familial relationships were less thoroughly explored. John Trenchard, for example, addressed himself only to the evils of marrying women for money. In all four volumes of vigorously egalitarian rhetoric which rang the changes on the theme of the relationship between the state and the individual, *Cato* always contemplates political man, narrowly defined.[25] Not even so articulate a feminist as Catharine Macaulay felt the need to discuss women in her histories and essays, though she did discuss women's education elsewhere. She attacked Rousseau, and wrote in the seven small pages of her twenty-second "Letter on Education" most of what it took Wollstonecraft hundreds of pages to

[23] *The Wish to be Free: Society, Psyche and Value Change* (Berkeley: Univ. of California Press, 1969), p. 49.

[24] Edwin G. Burrows and Michael Wallace, "The American Revolution: The Ideology and Psychology of National Liberation," in *Perspectives in American History,* VI (1972), 167–306. See especially parts II and III.

[25] John Trenchard, *Cato's Letters, or, Essays on Liberty, Civil and Religious and Other Important Subjects* (London: J. Wilkins, T. Woodward, et al., 1733), II, 201–12. There are no comments on women in Trenchard and Thomas Gordon's *The Independent Whig* (London: J. Peele, 1721).

argue in the *Vindication*. But Macaulay, who was confident enough to plunge directly into public political debate and to criticize a Hobbes or a Burke without even a passing apology for the frailties of her sex, apparently felt no need to address the responsibilities of women to political society. Perhaps she believed she had made her position clear by implication and in practice. But her direct comments speak of the private responsibilities of women—even reformed, chaste, nonfrivolous women—to individual men. In this she was more in agreement with Rousseau than she thought.[26]

American Whigs were as unlikely as their British counterparts to integrate into political theory a concept of the proper relationship between women and the body politic. It may even be that Americans ignored the problem because the British did. Any body of theory that addresses basic issues of sex role must reach back to presocial or psychological sources of human behavior. The issues are so basic that they demand probing to the deepest and most mythological layers of human experience. Americans felt little need to do this; James Otis was one of the few to try, in the opening pages of the 1764 pamphlet, *The Rights of the British Colonies Asserted and Proved:*

> The original of *government* has in all ages no less perplexed the heads of lawyers and politicians than the origin of *evil* has embarrassed divines . . . the gentlemen in favor of [the theory that government is based on] the *original compact* have often been told that *their* system is chimerical and unsupported by reason or experience. Questions like the following have been frequently asked them. . . . Who were present and parties to such compact? Who acted for infants and women, or who appointed guardians for them? Had these guardians power to bind both infants and women during life and their posterity after them? . . . What will there be to distinguish the next generation of men from their forefathers, that they should not have the same right to make original compacts as their ancestors had? If every man has such right, may there not be as many original compacts as there are men and women born or to be born? Are not women born as free as men? Would it not be infamous to assert that the ladies are all slaves by nature? If every man and woman born or to be born has and will have a right to be consulted and must accede to the original compact before they can with any kind of justice be said to be bound by it, will not the compact be ever forming and never finished?

Otis raised embarrassing questions about women's political role:

> If upon abdication all were reduced to a state of nature, had not apple women and orange girls as good a right to give their respectable suffrages for a new King as the

[26]Catharine Macaulay, *Letters on Education with Observations on Religious and Metaphysical Subjects* (London: C. Dilly, 1790); *An Address to the People of England, Ireland and Scotland, on the Present Crisis of Affairs,* 3d ed. (New York: n.p., 1775); *Observations on the Reflections of Edmund Burke* . . . (Boston: Thomas and Andrews, 1791); *Loose Remarks on Certain Positions to be Found in Mr. Hobbes* . . . (London: T. Davies, 1767).

philosopher, courtier, and politician? Were these and ten millions of other such . . . consulted?[27]

Although Otis could ask embarrassing questions and imply their answers, on this as on so many points of theory, his developing mental illness prevented him from suggesting constitutional devices for implementing them. Nor did his sister, the vigorous Mercy Otis Warren, deal with the questions he had opened. She was certainly intelligent and a fluent writer. She could viciously criticize men for their private treatment of women and counsel friends that flirting and deference were "a little game" by which one charmed male admirers into doing what one wished, but even she avoided the theoretical questions: what responsibility does the state have to women? what responsibility do women have to the state? The closest she came was to describe the political woman as observer and commentator, not participant. If the ideas were valid, she wrote, "I think it very immaterial if they flow from a female lip in the soft whispers of private friendship or are thundered in the Senate in the bolder language of the other sex."[28] But it must be said that her belief that private recognition of woman's political potential is more important than public recognition loses some of its force when held up against the fact of her own publication of her history of the Revolution, and the fact that the "soft whispers" of the sister of James Otis and the wife of James Warren were more likely than those of most women to be heard by politically influential men. Warren's comments supported the notion that the family circle is a woman's state.

* * *

It was left to postrevolutionary ideology in America to justify and popularize a political role for women, accomplishing what the English and French Enlightenment had not. Montesquieu had implied that if women had the choice they ought to choose to live in republics; Condorcet had said explicitly that republics were imperfect until they took account of the political claims of half of their people. But Americans did not move directly to the definition of women as citizens and voters. The only reference to women in *The Federalist* is to the dangers to the safety of the state posed by the private intrigues of courtesans and mistresses.[29] Instead, Americans offered an ironic compromise, one which merged Rousseau and Condorcet. It represented both an elaboration of the image of Sophie and a response to attacks like

[27] Reprinted in Bernard Bailyn, ed., *Pamphlets of the American Revolution, 1750-1776* (Cambridge: Harvard Univ. Press, 1965), I, 419–22.

[28] Mercy Otis Warren to Catharine Macaulay, 29 Dec. 1774, Mercy Otis Warren Letterbook, Massachusetts Historical Society.

[29] Edward Meade Earle, ed., *The Federalist* (New York: Modern Library, 1941), 28–29.

Rousseau's on the mental capacity of women. In this, as in so many other cases, Rousseau provided his own oxymoron.

The path *not* taken was suggested by one of the rare direct attacks on Rousseau that appeared in America, a pamphlet that contemplated the details of the integration of women into the political community. It came in 1801 from the pen of an "aged matron" from Connecticut who signed herself "The Female Advocate." She bristled at the arrogance of those who would deride "masculine women": if by

> the word "Masculine" be meant a person of reading and letters, a person of science and information, one who can properly answer a question, without fear and trembling, or one who is capable of doing business, with a suitable command over self, this I believe to be a glory to the one sex, equally with the other . . . custom, which is not infallible, has gradually introduced the habits of seeing an imaginary impropriety, that all science, all public utility, all superiority, all that is intellectually great and astonishing, should be engrossed exclusively by the male half of mankind.

The Female Advocate wished to function primarily as a citizen, only secondarily as a subject. She attacked contemporary refusals to include women in matters of church and public governance. She complained that "men engross all the emoluments, offices, honors and merits of church and state." She would grant that St. Paul had counseled women to be silent in public, and "learn from their husbands at home," but she pointed by contrast to St. Paul's own willingness to appoint women deaconesses. Women were not unsexed by taking part in community decisions:

> What if they have no husbands, or what if their husbands . . . are not of the church, or what if, as is very common, the husband knows less of the scriptures than the wife? . . . the point . . . is carried much too far, in the exclusive male prerogative to teach, to censure, to govern without the voice of women, or the least regard to the judgment or assent of the other sex. If a woman may not vote, or speak, on any occasion whatever, even tho' she have no husband, if she may not take any active part, by approbation or disapprobation, no not even in a silent vote, and that too when perhaps one of her sex is the subject of discipline or controversy, yea, when, farther, as is generally the case, the great majority of the church is female—how, pray you, is the sex to be viewed? Are they mere cyphers . . .?

The proper model for females, she thought, was the biblical Deborah, who lived actively in both the religious and the secular worlds: "Behold her wielding the sword with one hand, and the pen of wisdom with the other: her sitting at the council board, and there, by her superior talents, conducting the arduous affairs of military enterprise! Say now, shall woman be forever destined solely to the distaff and the needle, and never expand an idea beyond the walls of her house?"[30]

Other Americans had also made demands for the direct participation of women in public affairs: there is the well-known comment by Abigail Adams, which her husband jokingly turned away, that women required the right to participate in the new system of government, arguing pointedly that "all men would be tyrants if they could." All her life Abigail Adams would be a shrewd private commentator on the political scene, assuming as active an obligation to judge good and evil as though she were called on annually to vote on it. But she was known, of course, only in a circle which, though relatively large, remained private. Charles Brockden Brown sneered at the "charming system of equality and independence" that denied women a part in the choice of their governors, but the circulation of *Alcuin* was small; St. George Tucker conceded that laws neither respected nor favored females, but he made the concession in a minor aside in a three-volume work.[31] The women whom Esther de Berdt Reed and Sarah Bache led through Philadelphia collecting contributions for the American soldiers in 1780 encountered many who thought, with Anna Rawle, that "of all absurdities the ladies going about for money exceeded everything." The campaign, as we know, was a success: they collected some 300,000 paper dollars, managed to keep Washington from merging it into the general funds "contributed by the gentlemen"; and they saw to it that the soldiers knew to whom they were indebted for their new and much-needed shirts. The effort formed the model for a score of postwar women's philanthropic groups, but it did not, it has to be said, provide a model of political action except by sacrifice.[32]

Direct political participation and influence require voting and office-holding. American intellectuals who sought to create a vehicle by which women might demonstrate their political competence shrank from that solution, hesitating to join the Female Advocate in the wish that women be admitted to active participation and leadership in civic government. To do so would have required a conceptual and political leap for which they were apparently not prepared. Instead of insisting that competence has no sex, an alternate model was proposed in the 1790s. It contained many traditional elements of the woman's role, but it also had a measure of critical bite.

The theorists of this alternate position were Judith Sargent Murray, Su-

[30] *The Female Advocate* (New Haven, Conn.: T. Green, 1801), 22, 10.

[31] *Alcuin; A Dialogue* (New York: Grossman, 1971), 32–33; St. George Tucker, ed., *Blackstone's Commentaries* (Philadelphia: n.p., 1803), II, 145, 445.

[32] Anna Rawle to Rebecca Rawle Shoemaker, June 30, 1780, *Pennsylvania Magazine of History and Biography,* 35 (1911), 398; *The Sentiments of an American Woman* [broadside], Philadelphia, June 10, 1780.

sannah Rowson, and Benjamin Rush.[33] They deplored the "dependence for which women are uniformly educated"; they argued that political independence in the nation should be echoed by self-reliance on the part of women. The model republican woman was to be self-reliant (within limits); literate, untempted by the frivolities of fashion. She had a responsibility to the political scene, though not to act on it. As one fictional woman put it, "If the community flourish and enjoy health and freedom, shall we not share in the happy effect? If it be oppressed and disturbed, shall we not endure our proportion of evil? Why then should the love of our country be a masculine passion only?"[34] But her competence did not extend to the making of political decisions. Her political task was accomplished within the confines of her family. The model republican woman was a mother.

The Republican Mother's life was dedicated to the service of civic virtue; she educated her sons for it; she condemned and corrected her husband's lapses from it. If, as Montesquieu had maintained and as it was commonly assumed, the stability of the nation rested on the persistence of virtue among its citizens, then the creation of virtuous citizens was dependent on the presence of wives and mothers who were well informed, "properly methodical," and free of "invidious and rancorous passions." As one commencement speaker put it, "Liberty is never sure, 'till Virtue reigns triumphant. . . . While you [women] thus keep our country virtuous, you maintain its independence." It was perhaps more than mere coincidence that *virtù* was derived from the Latin for man, with its connotations of virility; political action seemed somehow inherently masculine. Virtue in a woman seemed to require another theater for its display. To that end the theorists created a mother who had a political purpose, and argued that her domestic behavior had a direct political function in the republic.[35]

* * *

Western political theory, even during the Enlightenment, had only occasionally contemplated the role of women in the civic culture. It had habit-

[33]See especially Judith Sargeant Murray, *The Gleaner* (Boston: I. Thomas, 1798), III, 188–224, 260–65; Benjamin Rush, "Thoughts upon Female Education, Accommodated to the Present State of Society, Manners and Government in the United States of America" (Philadelphia: Prichard and Hall, 1787), reprinted in Frederick Rudolph, ed., *Essays on Education in the Early Republic* (Cambridge: Harvard Univ. Press, 1965); Susannah Rowson, *Reuben and Rachel* (Boston: Hanning and Loring, 1798).

[34]Hannah Foster, *The Coquette* (Charlestown, Mass.: E. and S. Larkin, 1802), 62.

[35]*New York Magazine,* May 1795, pp. 301–05. I have discussed this in greater detail in "Daughters of Columbia: Educating Women for the Republic, 1787–1805," in *The Hofstadter Aegis: A Memorial,* Stanley Elkins and Eric McKitrick, eds. (New York: Knopf, 1974), 36–59. For the idealization of the Spartan mother, see Elizabeth Rowson, *The Spartan Tradition in European Thought* (Oxford: Oxford Univ. Press, 1969).

ually considered women only in domestic relationships, only as wives and mothers. It had not devised any mode by which women might have a political impact on government or fulfill their obligations to it. The Republican Mother was a device which attempted to integrate domesticity and politics.

The ideology of Republican Motherhood also represented a stage in the process of women's political socialization. In recent years, we have become accustomed to thinking of political socialization as a *process* in which an individual develops a definition of self as related to the state.[36] One of the intermediate stages in that process might be called the deferential citizen: the person who expects to influence the political system, but only to a limited extent. Deference represents not the negation of citizenship, but an approach to full participation in the civic culture. The best description of the genre is Charles Sydnor's of the voters of Jefferson's Virginia, who freely chose their social superiors to office rather than exercise a claim on office themselves.

Deference was an attitude that many women adopted and displayed at a time when it was gradually being abandoned by men; the politicization of women and men, in America as elsewhere, was out of phase. Women were still thinking of themselves as subjects while men were deferential citizens; as the restrained, deferential democracy of the republic gave way to an aggressive, egalitarian democracy of a modern sort among men, women invented a restrained, deferential but nonetheless political role. The voters of colonial Virginia did not think themselves good enough to stand for election but they chose legislators; the deferential women whom Judith Sargeant Murray prescribed for the republic did not vote, but they took pride in their ability to mold citizens who would. This hesitancy of American women to become political actors would persist. Are not the women of the postsuffrage twentieth century who had the vote but did not use it to elect people like themselves to office similar to the deferential males of Sydnor's Virginia?

There was a direct relationship between developing egalitarian democracy among men and the expectation of continued deferential behavior among women. Émile needs Sophie; the society in which he functions cannot exist without her. Just as white democracy in the antebellum South rested on the economic base of slavery, so egalitarian society similarly rested on a moral base of continuing deferential behavior among a class of people— women—who would devote their efforts to service: raising sons and disciplining husbands to be virtuous citizens of the republic. The learned woman, who

[36]See Gabriel Almond and Sidney Verba, *The Civic Culture: Political Attitudes and Democracy in Five Nations* (Princeton: Princeton Univ. Press, 1963). Almond and Verba view politicization as a gradual process by which individuals cease to think of themselves as invariably acted *on* by the state, and end by thinking of themselves as *actors*, who force governments to respond to them. There are many stages along this continuum, and there is room for internal contradictions.

might very well wish to make choices as well as influence attitudes, was a visible threat to this arrangement.[37] A political community that accepted women as political actors would have to eliminate the Rousseauean assumption that the world in which women live is separate from the empire of men. The political traditions on which American politics were built offered little assistance in defining the point at which the woman's private domain intersected with the public one. The Republican Mother seemed to offer a solution.

The notion that mothers perform a political function is not silly; it represents the recognition that political socialization takes place at an early age, and that the patterns of authority experienced in families are important factors in the general political culture. The willingness of American women to discuss politics at home is apparently more characteristic than in other western democracies; so is the rate of women's interaction in their communities, their rate of office holding in voluntary associations.[38] Americans live—and have long lived—in a political culture in which the family is a basic part of the system of political communication. This did not "just happen." It is a behavior pattern that challenges far older ones. The separation of male and female domains within a community is a very ancient practice, maintained by a wide range of often unarticulated but nevertheless very firm social restrictions.[39] There are nations today—even fairly modern democracies—in which these separate domains and premodern patterns still shape the political community: where women are much less likely than their American counterparts to discuss politics; where men are much more likely to carry on their political discussions among men, outside the home. In premodern political cultures mothers do not assume a clear political function. In this sense, Republican Motherhood was a very important—even revolutionary—invention. It altered the female domain in which most women had always lived out their lives; it justified an extension of women's absorption and participation in the civic culture.

In the years of the early republic there developed the consensus that a mother could not be a citizen but that she might serve a political purpose. Those who said that women ought to play no political role at all had to meet

---

[37] It is hard to find objective grounds for a fear of learned ladies; as Kenneth Lockridge has shown, literacy among women lagged substantially behind literacy among men in the colonial years. The subject has been insufficiently studied, but it appears that women's literacy rates do not catch up with men's until well into the nineteenth century. See Kenneth Lockridge, *Literacy in Colonial New England* (New York: Norton, 1974), 38–42; Daniel Calhoun, *The Intelligence of a People* (Princeton: Princeton Univ. Press, 1974), Appendix A.

[38] Almond and Verba, 377–401.

[39] On female spheres, see Carroll Smith-Rosenberg, "The Female World of Love and Ritual: Relations Between Women in Nineteenth-Century America," *Signs: A Journal of Women in Culture and Society,* 1 (1975), 1–30; Rayna Reiter, ed. *Toward an Anthropology of Women* (New York: Monthly Review Press, 1975).

the proposal that women might play a deferential political role through the raising of a patriotic child. The concept of Republican Motherhood began to fill the gap left by the political theorists of the Enlightenment. It would continue to be used by women well into the twentieth century; one thinks of the insistence of Progressive women reformers that the obligations of women to ensure honesty in politics, efficient urban sanitation, pure food and drug laws were extensions of their responsibilities as mothers. But the ideology of Republican Motherhood had limitations; it provided a context in which skeptics could easily maintain that women should be content to perform this limited political role permanently and ought not to wish fuller participation. For one woman, Republican Motherhood might mean an extension of vistas; for another it could be stifling. The ambivalent relationship between motherhood and citizenship would be one of the most lasting, and most paradoxical, legacies of the revolutionary generation.*

*An earlier version of this essay was read at the Annual Meeting of the Southern Historical Association in November, 1975. The author is grateful to Anne Firor Scott and Linda Grant dePauw for comments offered on that occasion.

Ruth Bloch

"Republican motherhood" is one of those rare historical concepts that has taken on a life of its own. Introduced by Linda Kerber in 1976 in an article on post-Revolutionary female education, it gained widespread currency as the final and culminating chapter, "The Republican Mother," of her widely acclaimed book *Women of the Republic: Intellect and Ideology in Revolutionary America* (Chapel Hill: University of North Carolina Press, 1980). The *American Quarterly* article reprinted here, "The Republican Mother: Women and the Enlightenment—An American Perspective," pushed the first article in a more theoretical direction and anticipated one of the main arguments of her book. In it, Kerber sharply contrasted the paucity of European Enlightenment thinking about women to the American Revolution's own creation of a new political role for mothers as the educators of citizens. For students both of the Revolution and of feminism, the term Republican Mother came to represent American women's first permanent, self-conscious step into the political arena. With the exception of "the cult of domesticity," it is hard to come up with another term within the field of American women's history that packs as much interpretive clout.

A fundamental reason for the Republican Mother's staying power has been its interdisciplinary breadth. It simultaneously reaches into American Revolutionary history, political philosophy, and feminist thought. When considered in the light of key debates within these fields, the Republican Mother appears at the crossroads of several otherwise disparate and conflicting lines of interpretation of the 1970s and 1980s. Kerber's construction cut across then-dominant understandings of the American Revolution, dissolving several key dichotomies: Enlightenment liberalism versus classical republicanism, theoretical versus practical, and conservative versus democratic. In Kerber's view, Republican motherhood owed little to any antecedent intellectual tradition, whether Enlightened or Whig republican. Her analysis juxtaposed the most high-minded civic

Linda Kerber, "The Republican Mother: Women and the Enlightenment—An American Perspective," originally appeared in *American Quarterly* 28, no. 2 (summer 1976), Copyright © 1976 Trustees of the University of Pennsylvania.

ideals to the most mundane assumptions about women's maternal roles
—suggesting that the Republican Mother's bland mix of domestic duties
and patriotic sentiments held ideological sway over grander theories
of citizenship. Her stance towards the Enlightenment political theory
similarly straddled the familiar rationalist-postmodernist fault line of
the 1980s—at once celebrating its universalist tendencies and exposing
its male biases. An early example of the intersection of women's history and political history, Kerber's work in addition pulled together two
conflicting theoretical positions of modern feminism: a commitment to
women's equal rights and an appreciation of a distinctive women's culture. Exercising citizenship through maternity, the Republican Mother
was a decidedly ambivalent construct. While underscoring its failure to
promote women's equality, Kerber at the same time refused to argue
that it was a conservative outcome.

In some ways Kerber's approach to the political thought of the period
was entirely out of date. To test the waters of eighteenth-century ideas
about women, she went straight to the most celebrated, radical thinkers of the French Enlightenment. Her detailed analyses of Rousseau
and Condorcet were grounded in the unexamined assumption that the
American Revolution was part of the same intellectual world. The relevance to American Revolutionary thought of these radical Enlightenment thinkers as well as John Locke himself, however, had already been
fundamentally challenged by the so-called "republican revisionism" of
such historians as J. G. A. Pocock, Bernard Bailyn, and Gordon Wood.
The English radical whig and civic humanist writers emphasized by these
recent works of intellectual history received comparatively shorter shrift
in Kerber's account. She noted the radical whigs only to say that they
ignored women altogether. The more abstract thinkers of the Enlightenment, by contrast, needed to consider women, however superficially, as
part of the original commonwealth of the family in the state of nature.
If Revolutionary Americans had looked abroad to any intellectuals for
instruction on the status of women, Kerber suggests, it would have been
to the political theorists of Enlightenment.

Rather than being about historical influence, however, Kerber's main
argument was about the absence of influence. The Enlightenment, she
insisted, offered Americans little in the way of guidance when it came
to theorizing women. Kerber pointed to a common intellectual vacuum
among both Enlightenment philosophers and radical whigs, minimizing the reputed differences between them. Her tactic was to show how,

even in the most radical, most universalistic thinking on citizenship, the problem of women was squarely addressed. The compromise formation of the Republican Mother, the woman glorified for her constricting domestic role, was thus not so reactionary as might appear at first glance. In this respect, Kerber was not writing history so much as feminist political theory. The Enlightenment thinkers she analyzes do not serve as historical background for her subjects so much as intellectual foils. To the degree that Enlightened writings about women failed to come to grips with the issue of female citizenship, America's invention of the Republican Mother seemed a significant intellectual achievement. By implication, Americans deserved credit for inventing a new feminine political role. With the appearance of the Republican Mother, women took a more prominent place in one of the central narratives of United States history, and, at the same time, Americans were seen to surpass the most famous figures of the European Enlightenment when it came to fashioning a political theory of women. Kerber's emphasis upon the indigenous sources of the Republican Mother portrayed the American Revolution as a unique, if limited, step forward for women.

But Kerber's crediting of America never overrides her feminist disappointment over the road not taken. If, on the one hand, she finds the European Enlightenment wanting, she also uses its value of universal equality to pose the fundamental counterfactual question, "What if?" Kerber uses the ideals of the Enlightenment to raise the specter of full female citizenship, and she queries the past about its failures to actualize this ideal. Writers like Locke, Montesquieu, and Condorcet may have lacked the resolve to elaborate on their initial assumptions of equal rights, but they deserve respect, in her view, for at least enunciating such first principles. In this, as in her argument about their philosophical shortcomings, Kerber is using history, a bit ahistorically, to make a feminist and a theoretical point. She refuses either to condemn the conservatism of the Republican Mother or to celebrate its progressive promise. The Republican Mother at once triumphs over Enlightenment thinkers who deny a practical political role for women and falls short of the more basic Enlightenment value of human equality. If the politicization of motherhood offered a way for American women to back their way later into the polity, Kerber underscores the backsidedness of this approach. Her assessment of the Republican Mother is finally an ironic one.

Like most influential critics, Kerber's concept of the Republican Mother has not gone unchallenged. I, for one, have questioned her view of motherhood as a traditionally highly valued role, suggesting that the Republican Mother was but one manifestation of a more general shift in ideas of female virtue. This shift had, I have argued, intellectual and religious roots in the period prior to the American Revolution and had subsequent repercussions in private as well as public life. Jan Lewis, concentrating like Kerber more specifically on American Revolutionary ideology, has challenged the preeminence of maternal imagery and stressed instead the salience of the more egalitarian Revolutionary symbol of the Republican Wife as political partner and conscience. Rosemarie Zagarri has still more recently reinserted the influence of Enlightenment thought into changing conceptions of women in late eighteenth-century America. In her view the assumption of female authority had less to do with American inventiveness than with the absorption of Scottish moral philosophy into American social and political thought. Kerber's formulation has thus been picked apart from several angles. Her concentration upon politics, her emphasis on the mother, and her perspective on the Enlightenment, are all now open to question. But the more fundamental achievement of Kerber's Republican Mother is more evident in the face of such criticism: the definition of woman's equality—together with its complex relationship to traditions of female domesticity—has reached the center of the American historical stage.

GENE WISE

"Paradigm Dramas" in American Studies: A Cultural and Institutional History of the Movement

[American Studies] has thus emerged not as a discipline, but as an arena for disciplinary encounter and staging ground for fresh topical pursuits. It embraces America in a Whitmanish hug, excluding nothing and always beginning.

Stanley Bailis, "The Socal Sciences in American Studies: An Integrative Conception," *AQ* (August, 1974)

If you want to understand what a science is, you should look in the first instance not at its theories or its findings, and certainly not at what its apologists say about it; you should look at what the practitioners of it do.

Clifford Geertz, *The Interpretation of Cultures*

If we have a "method," it is the approach to ideas and consequences in the round—a total approach something like the "total theatre" of Bertolt Brecht. From the communication point of view, American Studies wants more than most disciplines to include its audiences.

Jay Gurian, "American Studies and the Creative Present," *Midcontinent American Studies Journal* (Spring 1969)

FOR A MOVEMENT SO CRITICAL OF THE CULTURE AROUND IT, AMERICAN Studies recapitulates America in revealing ways. Both began as revolts against the established order—for America, the Old World, for American

Studies, the traditional disciplines. In contesting the old, both have articulated visions of a new and better order; and the insecurity of identifying with an *ought* rather than an *is* has compelled each to continue asking, "Who are we?" and "Where are we heading?" In seeking answers to these questions, neither has been particularly informed by history. Or rather, America has been informed more by fables of its past than by intimate communion with its actual past, and until lately American Studies has had little sense of its own history at all.

Almost nowhere, until recently, could anything be found in print describing how American Studies began, or seeking to explain either the evolution of consciousness and institutions within the movement, or the impact on American Studies of cultural forces outside. Like Americans, Americanists have been too busy building to pause and reflect much on their own roots. Of late, however, this trend shows signs of reversing—in the culture at large and in the movement too. Within the past decade, several articles have been published on the history of American Studies, plus one book already in print, and at least two others in the works.[1]

The present essay is part of this recent trend. It is also an effort to place that trend in a context. In the essay, I suggest that for perspective on our present situation and for guidance on our future direction in the movement, we should journey back over the history of American Studies during the course of the twentieth century. I also suggest that we try to understand our own movement as we would any other experience in America—that is, critically, in cultural and institutional context. As culture critics of American Studies, we should ask, *"What imperatives are there in the larger American culture and social structure, and in the culture and social*

---

[1] Until the early 1970s, only a handful of essays in the field had been concerned with the past of American Studies. Among these were Tremaine McDowell's *American Studies* (Minnesota, 1948), 26ff.; Robert Spiller's retrospective, "American Studies, Past, Present, and Future," in Joseph Kwiat and Mary Turpie, eds., *Studies in American Culture: Dominant Ideas and Images* (Minnesota, 1960), 207–20; Leo Marx's "American Studies: Defense of an Unscientific Method," *New Literary History*, (Fall 1969), 75–90; and Robert Sklar's two critiques, "American Studies and the Realities of America," *AQ*, 22 (Summer 1970), 597–605; and "Cultural History and American Studies: Past, Present, and Future," *American Studies: An International Newsletter*, 11 (Autumn 1971), 3–9.

Since 1972, however, several articles have critically reviewed traditions of American Studies. This trend was launched with Bruce Kuklick's influential piece, "Myth and Symbol in American Studies," *AQ*, 24, (Fall 1972), 435–50. Other works in this vein include Robert Berkhofer, "Clio and the Culture Concept: Some Impressions of a Changing Relationship in American Historiography," *Social Science Quarterly*, 53 (Sept. 1972), 297–320; Jay Mechling, Robert Merideth, and David Wilson, "American Culture Studies: The Discipline and the Curriculum," *AQ*, 25 (Oct. 1973), 363–89; Robert Spiller, "Unity and Diversity in the Study of American Culture: The American Studies Association in Perspective," *AQ*, 25 (Dec. 1973), 611–18; Gordon Kelly, "Literature and the Historian," *AQ*, 26 (May 1974), 141–59; Robert Sklar, "The Problem of an American Studies 'Philosophy': A Bibliography *structure of academe, which have made possible the quest for an integrating 'American Studies'?''* and *"How have these imperatives changed over time?"* Finally, I suggest that we view these changes through a sequence of representative acts—what I call "paradigm dramas"—which crystallize possibilities for integrated American Studies in each stage of the movement's history.

Conventionally, when handling ideas in historical context, scholars have employed a "climate of opinion" mode of explanation. In this mode, ideas are handled as surface "reflections" of underlying social forces. The social reality is seen as basic, and is thought to determine the ideas. Thus it is said that American scholarship of the 1950s was determined by consensual forces in the culture then, new left scholarship reflected the more radical climate of the 1960s, and so on.[2]

"Climate-of-opinion" history is convenient to write, since one need only catch the general tendencies of an age, then explain any particular idea simply by plugging it into the general category. There is no need here to discuss the many shortcomings in this mode of explanation.[3] For present purposes, it is enough to say that climate-of-opinion history falls short on at least two counts. First, such explanations tend to be flat and one-

---

of New Directions," *AQ,* 27 (Summer 1975), 245–62; David Marcell, "Recent Trends in American Studies in the United States," in Robert Walker, ed., *American Studies Abroad* (Greenwood, 1975), 25–33; Richard Dorson, *The Birth of American Studies* (Inaugural Address at Founding of American Studies Center at Warsaw University, Poland, October 5, 1976); Marcell, "Characteristically American: Another Perspective on American Studies," *Centennial Review,* 21 (Fall 1977), 388–400; and Luther Luedtke, "Not so Common Ground: Controversies in Contemporary American Studies," in Luedtke, ed., *The Study of American Culture: Contemporary Conflicts* (Everett Edwards, 1977), 323–67.

To date, the only book-length analysis of past American Studies scholarship is Cecil Tate's *The Search for a Method in American Studies* (Minnesota, 1973). Pershing Vartanian is currently working on a comprehensive history, based on extensive research in archives of the movement, and connecting academic American Studies to forces in the larger culture and in American higher education. Vartanian's history is to be titled *American Studies: Patterns in Academic Contra Culture.* Richard Johnson is also working on an oral history of figures in the history of the movement to be titled *American Studies: Images and Self-Images.*

For historical accounts of academic programs in American Studies, see the 1970 summer supplement of *AQ.* Especially useful are the program descriptions of Yale, Minnesota, and Pennsylvania, by Sydney Ahlstrom, Mary Turpie, and Murray Murphey, respectively. For an earlier account, see Robert Walker's comprehensive *American Studies in the United States: A Survey of College Programs* (Louisiana State, 1958).

[2] For a clear statement of this mode of explanation, see Robert Skotheim, ed., *The Historian and the Climate of Opinion* (Addison-Wesley, 1969), 1–5.

[3] I have criticized the climate-of-opinion approach to ideas, and offered a "situation-strategy" alternative, in chapter 5 of *American Historical Explanations: A Strategy for Grounded Inquiry* (Dorsey, 1973), 113–57. That alternative is adapted from the "dramatistic" approach of Kenneth Burke. For critiques of climate-of-opinion type analyses in American Studies scholarship, see Kuklick, Berkhofer, Kelly, and Tate.

dimensional. They recognize only a one-way route between the general culture and particular ideas, particular institutions, particular persons; the general climate acts, particulars simply *re*-act. This, to my mind, is too deterministic. Second, climate-of-opinion history is too monolithic. It assumes a holistic culture more thoroughly integrated, and more rigidly hierarchical, than experience of our own fragmented culture suggests to us today.

In this essay, I propose a different mode of explanation. Where the climate-of-opinion metaphor is borrowed from observation of weather, my working metaphor is drawn from the theater. It views historical ideas not as "enveloped" by their surrounding climates, but rather as a sequence of dramatic acts—acts which play on wider cultural scenes, or historical stages. The drama metaphor suggests a dynamic image of ideas, in contrast to the passive "reflector" role they play in climate-of-opinion explanations. It also gives to ideas a *trans*-actional quality. This is so because an act in the theater is always in interplay with the scene around it; an actor does not simply pass on his or her lines *to* an audience, but actor and audience (at least in a play which works) are in continual dialogue, messages traveling back and forth between one role and the other.[4]

Two additional preliminary points. In this brief retrospective, I have chosen four different acts to represent the movement for American Studies during the twentieth century. By "representative" I do not mean like a congressman or a senator—representing in the sense of holding to the middle and averaging out all extremes. By representative act, I mean something which dramatizes inherent *possibilities* in a cultural situation—an act which spotlights changing boundaries of what is possible for a person or a group at a particular time and in a particular place and in a particular milieu. Again, emphasis is on the drama of trans-actional interplay in doing cultural history; it is not on charting a succession of more or less static "climates" of intellectual opinion.

---

[4] If later in this essay I lean toward the social scientific side of culture studies, my basic metaphor—of culture as drama—is drawn from the humanities, and not by accident. I believe drama metaphors offer enormous potential for future work in American Studies, and are especially useful in bridging the long-lamented gap between humanistic and social scientific approaches to culture. For more on this, see Kenneth Burke, *The Philosophy of Literary Form: Studies in Symbolic Action* (Louisiana State, 1941; rpt. Vintage, 1957); Peter Berger, "Sociological Perspective—Society as Drama," in *Invitation to Sociology: A Humanistic Perspective* (Anchor, 1963), 122–50; and Hugh Dalziel Duncan, *Symbols in Society* (Oxford, 1968). For applications of a drama perspective to American cultural materials, see Kai Erikson's brilliant treatment of the Anne Hutchinson case in *Wayward Puritans: A Study in the Sociology of Deviance* (Wiley, 1966), 71–107.

Finally, by "paradigm act," or "paradigm drama," I employ a term heard often in scholarly circles today, too often I suspect. A careful reader once distinguished no fewer than 21 separate meanings of the word "paradigm" in Thomas Kuhn's influential study, *The Structure of Scientific Revolutions.*[5] The commonest use, at least in historical scholarship, is paradigm as a consistent pattern of beliefs held by a person, a group, or a culture. Thus we hear of the "Progressive" paradigm, or the "Einsteinian" paradigm, or the "Capitalist" paradigm.

Thomas Kuhn did of course write of paradigm in this fashion. But he also used the term in another way more relevant to this essay. In *The Structure,* Kuhn handles paradigms not only as patterns of belief but also as the characteristic acts which function to dramatize those beliefs. Hence he writes of paradigms as "exemplars"—actual examples, say, of the Newtonian style of thinking, or the Einsteinian. For Kuhn, then, a paradigm is not just the content of a thought pattern, but, more fundamentally, *an actual instance of that pattern of thinking in action.*[6]

* * *

The initial stage of American Studies' history begins before the academic movement as such. It comes to consciousness during the Progressive era early in the twentieth century. We can find there seeds of ideas which later—during the 1930s and 40s—were to supply intellectual energy for articulating the movement itself.

[5] Margaret Masterman, "The Nature of a Paradigm," in Imre Lakatos and Alan Musgrave, eds., *Criticism and the Growth of Knowledge* (Cambridge, 1970), 59–89. For Kuhn's own work, see *The Structure of Scientific Revolutions* (Chicago, 1962). For applications of Kuhn in American historical studies, see David Hollinger, "T. S. Kuhn's Theory of Science and Its Implications for History," *American Historical Review,* 78 (Apr. 1973), 370–93.

[6] For further on the idea of paradigm as "exemplar," in this case applied to Franz Boas and his influence upon the discipline of anthropology, see Anthony F. C. Wallace, "Paradigmatic Processes in Culture Change," *American Anthropologist,* 74 (June 1972), 467–69. Wallace writes, apropos of the use of "paradigm" I am adopting here,

> In the history of American anthropology . . . one can find a convenient illustration in the origin of the "fieldwork" paradigm. Whether accurately or not, one thinks of Franz Boas stepping off the boat in an Eskimo village [on Baffin Island, in 1883] with his suitcase in hand, preparing for a long stay in residence. This image *is* the paradigm: the subsequent development of field techniques, standards of ethnographic description, ethnological theory, and training requirements for the Ph.D. stem from, and are implied by, the symbol of Boas as lone fieldworker taking up prolonged residence in a small community. This symbol is opposed in a revolutionary way to a nineteenth century tradition of library scholarship and of uncritical use of the comparative method to derive models of cultural evolution. (469)

The term "paradigmatic drama" first appeared in American Studies scholarship, to my knowledge, in 1973, in Mechling, Merideth, and Wilson, 367.

Morton White has caught this stage's representative act in his phrase "the revolt against formalism."[7] From our perspective in American Studies, the figure who most fully embodies that act is Vernon Louis Parrington. No other, I believe, so clearly deserves the title "Intellectual Founder of American Studies."[8] In his work, Parrington was to construct an immensely *usable* past. Parrington's work was usable not just in the obvious sense of making the past relevant to urgencies of the present. It was usable also in offering a way to create order and direction from masses of disparate materials on the whole history of American experience. In this sense, he demonstrated in his scholarship how an integrating "American Studies" might be done.

Intellectually, Parrington's single most dramatic act was the 1927 publication of *Main Currents in American Thought*. With that act, the integrating study of American culture was to enter a new era. But the single act of *Main Currents* cannot be understood apart from what preceded it in Parrington's biography. Hence the representative act—or paradigm drama—I have selected for focus here is Parrington's entire life leading up to that event. More than any other Americanist, Vernon Louis Parrington gave life to Emerson's vision of "The American Scholar," a passionate mind encountering a dynamic world, sans the mediating forms of convention.

The general lines of Parrington's biography are well known. He was born in Aurora, Illinois in 1871; his family moved to a farm near Americus, Kansas, a small village outside Emporia, when he was six.[9] As

---

[7] *Social Thought in America: The Revolt against Formalism* (Beacon, 1949).

[8] There are others who could legitimately be called "Intellectual Founder of American Studies." Some, for example, might trace the germinating idea for the movement as far back as the second volume of Alexis de Tocqueville's *Democracy in America* (1840). Others might pick it up in more recent pre-American Studies works—e.g., Moses Coit Tyler's *A History of American Literature, 1607–1865* (1878), or Frederick Jackson Turner's "The Significance of the Frontier in American History" (1893), or Van Wyck Brook's *America's Coming of Age* (1915), or Lewis Mumford's *The Golden Day* (1925), or Norman Foerster's anthology, *The Reinterpretation of American Literature* (1928). Yet others might contend that the idea for the movement actually followed the movement itself, and that it was not until, say, F. O. Matthiessen's *American Renaissance* (1941), or, later, Henry Nash Smith's *Virgin Land* (1950) that American Studies was to achieve intellectual coherence. (A few perverse souls insist the movement never has got its act together; I'll bypass that position for now.)

Still, I stake my claim here on Parrington and *Main Currents*, and urge others to advance their counterclaims. The same holds true for my choices of the other three "paradigm dramas." I do not assume they are the only important symbolic acts in the movement's history, only that they seem most important in the context of this essay. Again, I hope others may propose other significant "moments" in the cultural history of American Studies, so we can generate more public dialogue about our movement and its past.

[9] For details of Parrington's life, I have drawn from the vivid portrait in Richard Hofstadter, *The Progressive Historians: Turner, Beard, Parrington* (Knopf, 1968), 349–434. See also Ralph Gabriel's illuminating sketch of Parrington's life in Marcus Cunliffe and Robin Winks, eds., *Pastmasters: Some Essays on American Historians* (Harper and Row, 1969), 142–66.

he later explained, he grew up a frustrated young aesthete amid the drab midwestern prairie, finally escaping east to take an undergraduate degree at Harvard. In Cambridge, Vernon Louis Parrington was the archetypal young man from the provinces: exhilarated by the freer intellectual atmosphere of the East, yet naive and hence vulnerable there to its cosmopolitanism and its social elitism.

Graduating from Harvard in 1893, Parrington returned to his prairie homeland, to teach at the College of Emporia for a princely $500 a year. Four years later—his salary having grown to but $700—he left Emporia for a better position as Instructor in English and Modern Language at the University of Oklahoma (Parrington not only served as a classroom teacher there, but preceded Bud Wilkinson by several decades as the Sooners' head football coach). In 1907, young Parrington suffered a setback; he was caught up in a faculty scandal at Oklahoma and was summarily fired. He had become identified with a cabal of young, Eastern-educated Turks who counseled subversive activities like smoking, drinking, and playing cards, and an outraged state governor, urged on by Southern Methodists, cleaned out the lot of them.

So at age 36 Vernon Louis Parrington was out of a job, with only a B.A. in hand. And here we may witness one of the more poignant acts of his life. He set down then to write the secretary of the graduate school at Harvard, requesting admission to study for a Ph.D. in English literature. But Harvard, concerned to uphold standards, rejected Parrington as too old to begin a graduate career. This decision deeply wounded him at the time, hardening him in what was to become a life-long antipathy against the East and its academic establishment.

For the American Studies story, however, Parrington's Harvard rebuff was in time to prove fortunate. For within a year, he would set his life on a course which culminated some two decades later in scholarly fame—if not quite in Parrington's own lifetime, then soon thereafter. In 1908 he accepted an offer as Professor of Literature at the University of Washington, and he soon struck up a productive companionship there with the Progressive intellectual J. Allen Smith. Inside five years he would begin work on his summa, *Main Currents in American Thought*.

Still, Vernon Parrington's career would suffer added disappointments, even if in retrospect his life would seem to have taken on pattern and direction. In Seattle, Parrington was of course freed from football coaching duties and from the prudery of Oklahoma Methodists, and he was also to flourish under the intellectual stimulus of Smith. Still, he was not to find a ready audience for his work. Publisher after publisher rejected early drafts of *Main Currents;* after almost a decade of labor, he finally despaired of the project, in fact stopping work on it. Fortunately in 1922 a draft of the first volume was seen by Van Wyck Brooks, then an editor for

Harcourt, Brace; Brooks recommended publication. Five more years were to pass, however, before *Main Currents* was finally published in 1927. In all, this was some 14 lonely years since Parrington had begun the project; by 1927, this author of his first scholarly book was a ripe 56. Doubtless in our own day, some conscientious tenure committee, committed to high standards of academic excellence, would long since have wiped him out of the profession as "lacking in scholarly promise."

Parrington is a representative figure for this pre-institutional stage of American Studies because he did it almost all *alone*. In an era when the academic disciplines of literature, economics, history, sociology, and political science all were seeking professional respectability by institutionalizing their scholarship—establishing regulations for sound academic training, creating journals of publication to give their work visibility but also to police their disciplinary borders, forming professional associations which would move the enterprise of scholarship into predictable, regulated forms of fraternal interchange, establishing reward and punishment structures to assure conformity with their norms—during all this time Vernon Louis Parrington was basically going it alone in his American intellectual journey.[10] He received no graduate training to focus and channel his interests; save for J. Allen Smith and a few others he had no sustaining companionship with fellow scholars of like interest; he never had a Guggenheim or NEH or ACLS grant; he lacked the camaraderie of professional association meetings; and he never had a Fulbright for travel or teaching abroad. Today, we would think *Main Currents in American Thought* a deprived work; it lacked all the institutional supports now felt necessary to the enterprise of scholarship. It was simply an act of human intellect reduced to the barest essentials—*a single mind grappling with materials of American experience, and driven by concentrated fury to create order from them*. And that, I would say, is *the* elemental "paradigm drama" of American Studies—elemental not only in being first, but also in embodying a characteristic urge of persons drawn to the movement from Parrington's day on to ours.

From 1927, with the publication of *Main Currents*, up through 1965, with Alan Trachtenberg's *Brooklyn Bridge*, the work of American Studies was made possible by a consensus among scholars, a loosely structured

---

[10] For a brilliant cultural and social structural analysis of this trend toward "modernization" in the academic professions, see Thomas Haskell's *The Emergence of Professional Social Science: The American Social Science Association and the Nineteenth-Century Crisis of Authority* (Illinois, 1977).

"paradigm" of sorts, on what American experience is like, and by procedural agreement on how to study it. Vernon Louis Parrington did not wholly create that paradigm. But his work is its most comprehensive expression. Later in the essay, I shall comment on this paradigm's intellectual make-up. For now, suffice it to say that those who came after *Main Currents in American Thought* had Parrington as an exemplar to move off from. They could accept his example, or they could reject it, or they could try to revise it. But whatever, the paradigm drama of *Main Currents* was there, a visible symbol, as it were, for those who followed to respond to.

Initial responses in the late 1920s and early '30s mark the halting beginnings of institutionalization in the movement. We do not yet see identification with the name "American Studies," nor all the institutional supports of the 1940s and '50s. But we do catch glimpses of dissatisfaction with old academic formalisms, and early efforts to structure new ways to study and teach about American experience. This stage of the movement is dramatized in the second of my sequence of paradigm dramas, Perry Miller's "jungle epiphany" in the heart of the Belgian Congo.

*   *   *

It is not widely known that this most intimidating of Harvard intellects was in fact a college drop-out. Bored and restless with what passed for the life of the mind at the University of Chicago in the early 1920s, Miller quit school to tour the country with a drama troupe. After a year, he quit that too to pick up on an oil tanker which eventually took him to Africa. Years later, he was to describe what happened to him then in the Congo; his preface to the 1956 publication of *Errand into the Wilderness* contains the following story:

Drawing on his background in theater, Miller began, "[I have included essays here] that seem to add up to a rank of spotlights on the massive narrative of the movement of European culture into the vacant wilderness of America." He continued,

> To the elucidation of this story I, in common with several historians of my generation, have devoted my life. . . . These papers, along with three or four books, are all I have yet been able to realize of a determination conceived three decades ago at Matadi on the banks of the Congo. I came there seeking "adventure," jealous of older contemporaries to whom that boon had been offered by the First World War. (Nobody had the prescience to teach me patience, to assure me that I too should have my War.) The adventures that Africa afforded

were tawdry enough, but it became the setting for a sudden epiphany (if the word be not too strong) of the pressing necessity for expounding my America to the 20th century.

With characteristic mock humility, Miller proceeded to a striking comparison:

> To bring into conjunction a minute event in the history of historiography with a great one; it was given to Edward Gibbon to sit disconsolate amid the ruins of the Capitol at Rome, and to have thrust upon him the "laborious work" of *The Decline and Fall* while listening to barefooted friars chanting responses in the former temple of Jupiter. It was given to me, equally disconsolate on the edge of a jungle of central Africa, to have thrust upon me the mission of expounding what I took to be the innermost propulsion of the United States, while supervising, in that barbaric tropic, the unloading of drums of case oil flowing out of the inexhaustible wilderness of America.

Miller then described how this "jungle epiphany" was to seize his imagination, setting him on a quest to consume a lifetime:

> However it came about, the vision demanded of me that I begin at the beginning, not at the beginning of a fall (wherein Gibbon had an artistic advantage, which he improved to the utmost), but at the beginning of a beginning. Once I was back in the security of a graduate school, it seemed obvious that I had to commence with the Puritan migration. (I recognize, and herein pay my tribute to, the priority of Virginia; but what I wanted was a coherence with which I could coherently begin.) One or two of my instructors warned me against throwing my career away; that field, they said, was exhausted, all the wheat had long since been winnowed, there was nothing but chaff remaining. I might have abandoned the mission, persuaded that my voices had misled me, had not Percy Holmes Boynton sustained me. He did this, I now suspect, not so much because he believed that in this area more was needed from scholarship, but simply because he held that a boy should be allowed to do what the boy genuinely, even if misguidedly, is convinced should be done.[11]

There are several things to note in this remarkable confession. First, and most notable, Miller carries here the same compulsion found in Parrington—the urge to impose form upon experience, to seize upon the American past and insist that it answer questions he is driven to ask of it. This is not the conventional academic's desire simply to make a "contribution to scholarly knowledge"; it is something deeper, more passionately existential, than that. It is the human drive—a drive occa-

---

[11] *Errand into the Wilderness* (Harper and Row, 1956; rpt. 1964), vii–ix.

sionally bordering on rage in a Miller or a Parrington—to *explain* things, to make one's own experience, and the world around that experience, comprehensible. Hence Miller's search for "a coherence with which I could coherently begin." That search would drive him back to the articulate origins of American experience, and would fixate him there for most of the 35-odd years remaining in his life.[12]

Intellectually, then, Miller's paradigm drama resembles Parrington's— the obsession to give order, *explanation,* to America's experience, and the will to break through scholarly conventions blocking that quest. But Perry Miller was born in 1905, a full generation after Parrington, and therein lies a world of difference in scholarly situation. For once Miller mounted his fury in the mid-1920s, he would then—unlike Parrington—be encouraged to return to "the security of a graduate school." Where Parrington's intellectual work was characteristically frustrated by an unresponsive world, Miller was continually nurtured by the most respected institutions of academe.

His graduate mentor at the University of Chicago, Percy Holmes Boynton, left the young Miller free to pursue his obsession with early America. Boynton, it seems, was not concerned that his student carve out an academic territory, and in time make his "contribution" to scholarly knowledge. Rather, he urged Miller to follow his own intellectual passions—his "voices," as it were. Boynton and Chicago were so flexible, indeed, that they encouraged Miller to take the bulk of his graduate courses at Harvard, where the freshest work on early America was then being done. The young graduate student was also left free to roam between the academic disciplines of history and literature, since of the two most notable colonial scholars then at Harvard, one, Samuel Eliot Morison, was a historian, and the other, Kenneth Murdock, was in literature. When Miller himself was later appointed to the Harvard faculty, his position would be in the literature department, though the bulk of his published scholarship was in history.

Where Parrington had been refused entry to Harvard, Miller was given a coveted professorship there, and soon would become one of its most distinguished scholars. It is an added insult to the Harvard-rebuffed Parrington that Miller's first scholarly article—written for Morison's graduate seminar there and published in the *New England Quarterly* when Miller was a callow 26—was an assault upon the recently-deceased Parrington and his interpretation of Thomas Hooker.[13]

---

[12] For details of Miller's life, I have drawn upon Robert Middlekauff's biographical portrait in Cunliffe and Winks, *Pastmasters,* 167–90; and upon the dedicatory essays published in the *Harvard Review* a year after Miller's death (Spring 1964). To date, no full-length biography of Miller exists, but Stanford Searle is currently working on one.

[13] "Thomas Hooker and the Democracy of Connecticut," *New England Quarterly,* 4 (Fall 1931), 663–712.

Still, it indicates something of Parrington's influence only a few years after his death that Perry Miller was obliged to attack him in order to clear ground for his own work. And when we look at broader institutional developments of the 1930s, we see that those early efforts at interdisciplinary American Studies at Harvard, and at other Eastern universities like Yale and Princeton and Pennsylvania, were energized and given direction by Parrington's monumental accomplishment in *Main Currents*. In his lifetime, then, Parrington would be refused entry to the Eastern scholarly establishment; yet after death he would in effect gain entry there by having constructed the ideas and, more fundamentally, the methods of inquiry, which many establishment scholars would go on to study themselves.

In several Eastern universities during the thirties, we can see mounting restlessness with conventional disciplinary boundaries. What gave form to this restlessness was a quest for "The American Mind" (or, in Parrington's term, for the "main currents in American thought"). No one else experienced the drama just like a Parrington or a Miller; but others could share their vision of a distinctive American culture, and could register discontent with how the conventional disciplines had obscured that vision.[14]

Discontent ran especially strong in departments of literature. For some decades prior to the thirties, momentum had been building to free the study of American literature from its role as an appendage to Anglo-Saxon literature,[15] and instead to study it "on native grounds," as it were.[16] With the renaissance in American writing during the teens and twenties, and the malaise of English and European culture following World War I, this

---

[14] Witness for example Robert Spiller:

  I am not sure just how clear the founding fathers were in their formulation of this question or in their answers to it, but I can assure you that we tackled the problem as though we knew what we were about. We said by our actions if not by our words: There is now in existence a well-formed total and autonomous American culture and it is our business to find out just what it is, how it came into being, how it functions, and how it should be studied, researched and taught.

  (Spiller, "Unity and Diversity," 612)

[15] Immediately before the founding of American Studies, classes on American literature comprised but one of every eleven undergraduate courses taught in English departments in the United States. At the graduate level, the proportion was even smaller, one in 13. Ferner Nuhn, "Teaching American Literature in American Colleges," *American Mercury*, 13 (Mar. 1928), 228–31. And as recently as 1948, Howard Mumford Jones could write, "Of the sixty-odd presidents of [the Modern Language Association], none has been distinguished for work in the American field." *The Theory of American Literature* (Cornell, 1948; rpt. 1956) 160–61.

  [16] The phrase is Alfred Kazin's. See his *On Native Grounds: An Interpretation of Modern American Prose Literature* (Harcourt, Brace, 1942). See also, for phases of this movement toward the independent study of American literature, Jones, *Theory*, 139–43, 160–87; Malcolm Cowley, *Exile's Return: A Literary Odyssey of the 1920's* (Viking, 1934; rev. 1951); Spiller, "Value and Method" and "Unity and Diversity"; and Richard Ruland, *The Rediscovery of American Literature: Premises of Critical Taste, 1900–1940* (Harvard, 1967).

movement was to gain even more momentum. It finally broke through—in a few Eastern institutions—in the late twenties and early thirties, with an added push from the Parrington exemplar in *Main Currents.*

In 1929, for example, the journal *American Literature* was founded, and that same year (the year of Parrington's death) the Modern Language Association was to sponsor its first convention session ever on American literature. Two years later, Stanley T. Williams of Yale—who at the time held one of the first chairs of American literature in the country, and who in 1926 had authored a book on *The American Spirit in Letters*—inaugurated a course on "American Thought and Civilization." Williams taught the course jointly with Ralph Henry Gabriel of Yale's history department. If the Williams-Gabriel class was not actually the first American Studies offering anywhere in the United States, it claims to be one of the first.[17] In another two years, Yale moved yet further in this interdisciplinary venture by establishing a new department of History, the Arts, and Letters; and by awarding its first Ph.D. in the American branch of this department—to A. Whitney Griswold, for a dissertation on "The American Cult of Success." Griswold's has been claimed as the first American Studies, or American Studies-like, Ph.D. ever granted.[18] Four years later, in 1937, Williams and Gabriel capped their cooperative teaching venture in "American Thought and Civilization" by editing a book for the course—significantly titled *The American Mind.* A series of documents expressive of different areas of American thought, interspersed with commentary by the editors, *The American Mind* was soon adopted in American Studies-like offerings throughout the country.

Such offerings were introduced in several American universities during the 1930s, especially in the East. In 1936 George Washington University began a program in American Studies, and the same year Harvard opened its interdisciplinary graduate program in the History of American Civilization (guided, incidentally, by the young Perry Miller and F. O. Matthiessen, among others). One year later, Pennsylvania launched its program in American Civilization, chaired dually by Roy Franklin Nichols from history and Sculley Bradley from literature. In 1938 Western Reserve started its American Studies program, headed by Lyon Richardson from the literature department. And in 1940 Harvard was to award its first Ph.D. in the History of American Civilization—to one Henry Nash Smith, for a dissertation on "American Emotional and Imaginative Attitudes Toward the Great Plains and the Rocky Mountains, 1803–1850."

[17] For more on the Williams-Gabriel class, see Gabriel, "Ideas in History," *History of Education Journal,* 11 (Summer 1951), 97–106.

[18] For Yale's claim to several "firsts" in the history of American Studies, see Sydney Ahlstrom, "Studying America and American Studies at Yale," *AQ,* 22 (Summer 1970), 503–17.

In the early 1940s, several other universities began programs in American Studies—among them Princeton, Minnesota, New York University, Texas, Brown, and Maryland. By 1947, more than 60 institutions were offering undergraduate majors in the field, with 15 going further to offer the M.A. or Ph.D.

These activities were energized and given form by a loosely organized consensus among scholars—a substantive consensus on the nature of American experience, and a methodological consensus on ways to study that experience. This might be called "the Parrington paradigm," or, more descriptively, "the intellectual history synthesis." As I have suggested, Parrington's example was widely followed in early American Studies courses and programs.[19]

Dominating Americanist scholarship of the 1930s, '40s, and '50s, the intellectual history synthesis was made up of several basic assumptions. Clustering together to form a kind of paradigm, these assumptions guided scholarship in the field and helped set boundaries within which students of American Studies were trained for well over a generation. In effect, they functioned to make the American past intellectually "usable" for those in the movement.

Reduced to essentials, these assumptions are as follows:

a) There is an "American Mind." That mind is more or less homogeneous. Though it may prove to be complex and constructed of many different layers, it is in fact a single entity.

b) What distinguishes the American Mind is its location in the "New" World. Because of this, Americans are characteristically hopeful, innocent, individualistic, pragmatic, idealistic. Theirs is uniquely a world of boundless opportunity. Europeans, in contrast, are characteristically tragic in temper, because hemmed in by all the boundaries and limitations and corruptions of the "Old" World.

c) The American Mind can theoretically be found in anyone American. But it comes to most coherent expression in the country's leading thinkers—Williams, Edwards, Franklin, Cooper, Emerson, Thoreau, Hawthorne, Melville, Whitman, Twain, Dewey, Niebuhr, et al. Hence early American Studies programs offered courses on the "Great Books"—often required—which introduced students to the field through the culture's most elevated minds.

---

[19] For Parrington's impact on the founding of American Studies, see Spiller, "Value and Method," 2–3; and Jones, *Theory,* 139–43. Howard Mumford Jones writes of Parrington:

Who can forget the tingling sense of discovery with which we first read these lucid pages, followed this confident marshaling of masses of stubborn material into position, until book, chapter, and section became as orderly as a regiment on parade! Readers in 1927 felt the same quality of excitement, I imagine, as Jeffrey experienced when in 1825 young Macaulay sent his dazzling essay on Milton to the *Edinburgh Review.* (pp. 141–142)

d) The American Mind is an enduring form in our intellectual history. Its distinctive themes—Puritanism, Individualism, Progress, Pragmatism, Transcendentalism, Liberalism—run through virtually the whole of America's past.

e) Though the study of "popular" minds—e.g., Davy Crockett, Daniel Webster, Buffalo Bill—might be academically legitimate, America is revealed most profoundly in its "high" culture. Therefore, great American literature, and the ideas therein, should hold a kind of "privileged position" in American Studies scholarship and teaching.[20]

All these assumptions were instrumental to the basic aim of scholars within the paradigm—to probe for *the fundamental meaning of America.* This search for quintessential meaning was made possible by the holistic faith of those within the paradigm. "Thought" in America is an integrated whole, they insisted; hence interdisciplinary American Studies would bring together what the conventional academic disciplines had previously split apart.[21]

Not everyone in the consensus held all these assumptions all the time, of course; total conformity is not required for a communal paradigm to function. But enough people held to enough assumptions enough of the time so that no fundamental strain was put upon its basic structure from the paradigm's first comprehensive articulation in 1927 up through the middle of the 1960s. We can find the paradigm in full form in Parrington's *Main Currents* (1927–30), in Perry Miller's *Orthodoxy in Massachusetts* (1933) and *The New England Mind: The Seventeenth Century* (1939), in F. O. Matthiessen's *American Renaissance* (1941), and in Ralph Barton Perry's *Puritanism and Democracy* (1944). And we can find strong currents of the paradigm running through H. N. Smith's *Virgin Land* (1950), Miller's *The New England Mind: From Colony to Province* (1953), David Potter's *People of Plenty* (1954), Richard Hofstadter's *The Age of Reform* (1955), Louis Hartz's *The Liberal Tradition in America* (1955), R. W. B. Lewis' *The American Adam* (1955), John William Ward's *Andrew Jackson: Symbol for an Age* (1955), Marvin Meyers' *The Jacksonian Persuasion* (1957), Charles Sanford's *The Quest for Paradise* (1961), Leo Marx's *The Machine in the Garden* (1964), on up, finally, to Alan Trachtenberg's *Brooklyn Bridge: Fact and Symbol* (1965).

These were the shaping books—the "exemplars," as it were—which set the fundamental aims of inquiry within the intellectual history paradigm, defining its outer boundaries. Because those boundaries were

---

[20] The term "privileged position" is Murray Murphey's. See his criticism of that position in "American Civilization at Pennsylvania," *AQ,* 22 (Summer 1970), 495–96.

[21] For an extended analysis of how this holistic "American Mind" syndrome has functioned within America Studies scholarship, see Tate, *Method.* See especially Tate's chapter "The Achievements and Limitations of Organic Holism," 105–26.

seldom crossed during the first three and a half decades of American Studies' history, activity and growth could flourish undisturbed inside the movement. We have already looked at this activity during the 1930s and 40s—the era of early growth and experimentation in the movement. Now let us turn to the years from 1950 to the mid-60s—an era of rapid expansion, corporate organization, and productive scholarship in the field.

*   *   *

In retrospect, the decade and a half following 1950—between *Virgin Land* at one end and *Brooklyn Bridge* at the other—has come to look like the "Golden Years" of the movement. For some time now, we have witnessed a fifties revival in the larger culture—many feeling nostalgic for an age when life seemed simpler, and Americans appeared more confident and less divided against themselves. So too for American Studies.

The retrospective simplicity is of course delusive, as the confidence at the time was deceptive. In the academic movement as in the culture at large, Americans in the fifties seemed bent on enacting David Potter's observation that "Our practice . . . has been to overleap problems—to bypass them—rather than to solve them." [22]

I have chosen as my representative act here a different sort of drama from Parrington's and Miller's. It is a seminar focused on American cultural values in the twentieth century, held at the University of Pennsylvania in 1954, and chaired jointly by Robert Spiller of the literature department and Thomas Cochran from history.

This act of the 1950s is distinguished by its *corporate* nature. It signals a basic change in the movement—where the locus of activity and power points from individuals toward groups, from offering single courses toward the establishment of programs, from articulating personal visions toward making collective contributions to scholarly knowledge. Where the earlier acts of Parrington and Miller took place outside as well as inside the academy, Penn's American Civilization 900 happened wholly inside academe.

What made the joint seminar possible was a massive foundation grant. Pennsylvania's program in American Civilization had already received two Rockefeller grants, in 1949 and 1954. This time it was to land a five-year, $150,000 grant from Carnegie Corporation, and one of its first acts was to set up the seminar.

It was a notable organizational undertaking. Money was spent not only to free Spiller and Cochran from other duties, but also to support the participation of distinguished outsiders in the seminar—among others, the

---

[22] *People of Plenty: Economic Abundance and the American Character* (Chicago Phoenix, 1954), 122.

novelist James T. Farrell, the Columbia sociologist Robert Merton, and the obligatory European scholar, this time brought in from the University of Kiel, one Hellmut Bock. With all these notables and all this money, naturally the seminar failed in its express purpose—I cite here Spiller's own confession on the matter.[23] It had too much organized activity and too much diffused prestige ever to focus down on its basic task—bringing together perspectives from history, literature, and social science to explain values in twentieth-century America.

A cultural drama should be judged not only for its manifest purpose, but for its latent functions too. The Penn seminar manifestly failed in bringing together the disparate disciplines of inquiry. But it succeeded all too well in its projective latent function for the movement: it symbolized an age in which America's bounty was made available to academic American Studies. Like David Potter's Americans of that day, American Studies too functioned as a "people of plenty."

Pennsylvania, as I have noted, was awarded three foundation grants from 1949 through 1954. In the late 1940s, Minnesota also got fellowship support from the Carnegie Corporation. And in 1950, Yale was to receive a substantial endowment from the wealthy benefactor William Robertson Coe, and that same year announced a $4.75 million drive to expand its American Studies enterprise.[24]

This theme of expansion, often backed by foundation largesse, can be found in the national movement as well. In 1949 the *American Quarterly* was established, followed two years later by the national American Studies Association. At the time, Robert Spiller persuaded the Carnegie Corporation to fund the ASA with an executive secretary, an office at Penn, and funds for regional development of the Association. Spiller's influence extended beyond academe into governmental circles too, and he was instrumental in securing for Americanists the new Fulbright fellowships for teaching and research abroad.[25]

---

[23] Spiller, "Value and Method," 6–9. See also Murphey, "Pennsylvania," 495–96.

[24] Among others who received foundation moneys to establish, maintain, or expand their American Studies activities during the fifties were Bennington (Carnegie Corporation, 1950), Barnard (Carnegie Corporation, 1952), and Stetson (Charles E. Merrill Foundation, 1955).

Charles Bassett notes that as of 1958, 20 percent of American Studies programs had received funding from outside their own institutions. By 1973, that figure had shrunk to just 5 percent. "Undergraduate and Graduate Programs in the United States: A Survey," *AQ*, 27 (Aug. 1975), 311.

[25] If Parrington ranks as the major intellectual founder of American Studies, then Robert Spiller must surely be its major institutional founder. For evidence of this, see the summer of 1967 *AQ* essays by Russel Nye, Anthony Garvan, and Louis Rubin honoring Spiller on the occasion of his retirement from Pennsylvania.

Nye wrote, for example:

In the late forties and early fifties, when American Studies needed somewhere to gather and its great centrifugal energies needed to be focused inward, Robert Spiller provided plan, precept and example

A similar pattern of corporate support can be found in the productive scholarship of this era. Where Parrington had worked 14 lonely years on *Main Currents* with virtually no help from outside, scholars in this period received substantial aid from their own institutions and from their benefactors in the society at large. Smith's *Virgin Land*, for example, was sponsored by grants from the Huntington Library, the Rockefeller Foundation, and the University of Minnesota Graduate Research Fund. For *Andrew Jackson: Symbol for an Age*, John William Ward got grant support from the American Council of Learned Societies and from the Princeton University Research Fund. For *The Jacksonian Persuasion*, Marvin Meyers received a year free from academic duties to write at the Stanford Center for the Study of the Behavioral Sciences. For *The Machine in the Garden*, Leo Marx was awarded a Guggenheim Foundation grant. And Alan Trachtenberg's *Brooklyn Bridge: Fact and Symbol* was supported by a grant from the American Council of Learned Societies.

Perhaps because people in American Studies often fancy themselves "American Adams" (and now "Eves"), perhaps because, characteristically, corporate ventures are not always seen as "corporate" by the select few on the inside, post-World War II Americanists still tended to see themselves in the image of a Parrington—that is, lone intellectual adventurers fired by a personal vision of the culture, and driven to put scholarly form on that vision. This vision is not wholly false. *Virgin Land* and *The American Adam* and *The Jacksonian Persuasion* and *The Machine in the Garden* are all passionately intense, personal books; they are not intended as simply objective "contributions" to corporate knowledge. Yet the social and economic structure of American scholarship had been fundamentally transformed since the days of Parrington, and those who still envisioned themselves isolated "American Adams" by the 1950s and 60s were largely deceived.

Leo Marx gave voice to this unwitting deception a few years back, in addressing a conference on interdisciplinary studies in Detroit. Marx opened his address with the ritual obeisance to American Studies' open and experimental character—an obligatory gesture, it seems, whenever one speaks with colleagues of the field. No one can say exactly *what* American Studies is, he insisted, because scholars in the field are free to follow their own personal visions. Then Marx went on to apologize for presuming to serve as official spokesman for what he called a "wholly

---

. . . . His knowledge of the intricate and murky mazes of Washington and New York bureaucracy has benefited ASA many times; it is said, peprhaps facetiously, that he knows more buttons to push in more bureaus than any other man in academic life.

("Robert Spiller and the ASA," *AQ*, 19 [Summer 1967], 291–92.)

For an additional perspective on the early years of the ASA, see Carl Bode's essay in this volume.

unorganized'' group of American Studies scholars—including Henry Nash Smith, Daniel Aaron, Allen Guttmann, John William Ward, Charles Sanford, R. W. B. Lewis, Alan Trachtenberg, and himself.[26]

''Wholly unorganized,'' indeed! Few political conspiracies have ever been so tightly interwoven as this one. It was no mere accident of talent that they all tended to write of America in similar ways. Beyond the corporate bonds of financial and institutional support just noted, witness the interpersonal academic ties: Smith and Marx were once colleagues on the American Studies faculty at Minnesota, where Ward, Trachtenberg, and Guttmann were graduate students. Smith, Aaron, Sanford, Lewis, and Marx all studied at Harvard within a few years of each other, and all were deeply influenced there, personally or indirectly, by Perry Miller and F. O. Matthiessen. At the time of Marx's address, he, Ward, and Guttmann were colleagues in American Studies at Amherst.

By taking only three institutions, then, Minnesota, Harvard, and Amherst, we can trace out professional and personal connections influencing the work of almost every notable symbol-myth-image scholar writing in those years. If their books were to achieve an intellectual depth which has not been seen since in American Studies, that is because they functioned amid a scholarly fraternity where basic assumptions about the culture and ways of studying it were shared and reinforced, and where powerful institutions of American society nurtured their work.[27]

By the middle of the 1960s, all that began to change. The intellectual history synthesis which had served American Studies so well for so long was shattered; and academies across the country were threatened by forces which charged them with being bastions of reaction, not a haven for free, inquiring minds. Similarly, many saw American Studies not as a vanguard movement on the frontiers of scholarship—the movement's prior

---

[26] Marx, ''American Studies,'' 75, n. 1.

[27] A glance at book acknowledgments further reveals the corporate nature of these undertakings. In *The Machine in the Garden,* Marx cites the influence of his teachers Miller and Matthiessen, and notes that Smith and Ward read the manuscript. In the 1950 edition of *Virgin Land,* Smith cites Marx and in his 1970 reissue of the book pays respect to Trachtenberg's critique of the earlier edition. In *Men of Good Hope,* Aaron cites Matthiessen and Lewis, and in *Writers on the Left* notes that Smith read portions of the manuscript. In *The Conservative Tradition in America,* Guttmann cites Marx and Ward. In *Andrew Jackson: Symbol for an Age,* Ward notes that Marx read the manuscript, and cites Smith as his teacher and *Virgin Land* as a model for his own work. In *The Quest for Paradise,* Sanford compares and contrasts his work with Smith's and Lewis'. In *The American Adam,* Lewis notes that Aaron read the manuscript, and acknowledges the influence of Matthiessen both as teacher and as author of *American Renaissance.* And in *Brooklyn Bridge,* Trachtenberg cites Marx as one of his two most influential mentors. In addition, *The Machine in the Garden, Men of Good Hope, The Conservative Tradition in America, Andrew Jackson: Symbol for an Age,* and *Brooklyn Bridge: Fact and Symbol* were all published by Oxford University Press.

image of itself—but as an overly timid and elitist white Protestant male enterprise which tended to reinforce the dominant culture rather than critically analyzing it. Borrowing from William O'Neill, I have called this the "coming apart" stage of American Studies.[28]

* * *

My choice of representative act for this stage of the movement is "Culture Therapy 202"—Robert Merideth's introductory seminar held at Miami University late in the 1960s.

Merideth had taken his graduate studies at Minnesota during the late 1950s and early '60s, under the influence there of the symbol-myth-image school. Like many of his generation, he would be jolted off that course, however, by events of the sixties—the political assassinations, the university confrontations, urban riots, escalation of the war in Vietnam, rise of the counterculture. "Culture Therapy 202" was Merideth's effort, late in the decade, to articulate a response to those events. He has described that response in a pamphlet written for the New University Conference, and published in 1969. It is entitled "Subverting Culture: The Radical as Teacher."

Merideth's act of the 1960s contrasts sharply with the three we have seen before. The acts of Parrington and Miller were dramatic personal gestures, made by individuals critical of particular institutions and values in the larger culture; but neither went on to reject the whole structure of American experience. And the Spiller-Cochran act was firmly nestled inside the culture's supporting institutions; its express purpose was to articulate that culture, not basically to criticize it.

But Robert Merideth was not satisfied merely to discover what American culture *is*. What the culture is is obvious, he felt; it is all around people, threatening to envelop them, and bent on corrupting their naturally humane impulses. Hence the teacher in American Studies must assume an adversary role against the culture. He must try to save himself from the culture's poison tentacles, and in the classroom he is obligated to help save others too, or help them save themselves. His only humane option, under the circumstances, is to serve as a cultural radical.

"The primary purpose of the radical as teacher," Merideth insisted, "is to subvert a corrupt culture as it is internalized in his students."[29] Culture *study*—academic analysis of what America is—should be subordinated to

---

[28] *Coming Apart: An Informal History of America in the 1960's* (Quadrangle, 1971).
[29] *Subverting Culture: The Radical as Teacher* (New University Conference, 1969), 1.

culture *therapy*—the larger-than-academic, radically human act of healing wounds caused by the culture's corrupting influence. Hence Robert Merideth in the late 1960s would direct people in the movement away from publishing scholarship, a distinguishing trait of American Studies the decade before, to become more involved in radical action—radical teaching, community organizing, consciousness-raising.

If the movement as a whole did not follow Merideth's lead here, a visible minority did turn in that direction, with impact well beyond their numbers. In 1972 and 1973, members of the Association's Radical Caucus (which Merideth helped found) sponsored week-long summer institutes, and these were to bear fruit at the fourth national ASA convention held in San Francisco in 1973.[30] The convention format there was restructured to include some two dozen informal workshop sessions—half the ASA's total program. Instead of a passive audience hearing a panel of formally prepared research papers, some dozen or so persons in each workshop were actively to discuss issues like: structuralism and American Studies, the uses of autobiography, the challenge to prison authority, American Studies and the community college, American Studies in the high school, Appalachia and culture studies.

These workshops expressed concern for areas of cultural experience made visible in the 1960s, areas which academic American Studies was urged to respond to. So, late in the decade, the movement would widen its boundaries to include black studies, popular culture studies, folklore studies, women's studies, ecology studies, film studies, material culture studies, ethnic studies, education studies, youth studies, Third World studies, and Native American studies, among others.[31]

---

[30] It is symbolic of this late sixties–early seventies stage of the movement that leadership for the Radical Caucus, and especially for the summer institutes, came mainly from two graduate students, Nancy Banister and Robert Scarola. The movement had come some distance from the mid-fifties Penn seminar when, as Robert Spiller had put it, "The laboratory work was done mainly by the graduate students; the direction and discussion came rather more from the senior participants." Spiller, "Value and Method," 7.

[31] See Robert Sklar, "Realities," for how this changing consciousness in the wider culture was to affect American Studies. For similar indications, see Jay Gurian, "American Studies and the Creative Present," *Midcontinent American Studies Journal,* 10 (Spring 1969), 76–84; Michael Rockland, "The Concord Complex: Some Remarks on the American Geographical Imagination," *Connections II* (Summer 1976), 28–31; my "American Civ. at Raymond: The 'Cluster' Academy as Radical Alternative," *AQ,* 22 (Summer 1970), 464–88; Doris Friedensohn, *American Studies 242: Education and Social Change* (Kirkland College Press, 1972); issues of the Radical Caucus' journals, *Connections* (1970-73) and *Connections II* (1973-); *Red Buffalo: A Radical Journal of American Studies* (University of Buffalo, 1971-); *New America: A Review* (University of New Mexico, 1974-); and *American Examiner: A Forum of Ideas* (Michigan State University, 1972-).

All these newly-academized experiences imposed massive strain on the old intellectual history synthesis. After the middle of the sixties, it was hard to assume without question that America is an integrated whole; division and conflict, not consensus, seemed to characterize the culture. It was also difficult to assume the privileged position of elite ideas as a window into the culture. Hard facts—emotionally searing events like assassinations and riots, gigantic institutions which could wreak havoc on people's lives—these held power, it appeared, to create or destroy an insubstantial idea in a flash. Students of America thus turned away from airy myths and symbols to look at earthier matters, at material artifacts like houses or bridges or buildings, at functioning social structures like the family or the city or the town or school or corporation or labor union or prison, at measurable human behavior and at people's lifestyles. These, it was felt, would penetrate to the "real" America which functions below the rationalized ideas.[32]

Hence we have seen, since the mid-sixties, a proliferation of subcultural studies focusing on one or another aspect of American life. But we have very little of wide influence in the movement attempting, like the old symbol-myth-image works, to integrate the whole culture. Intellectually, American Studies has never recovered from the earthquake-like jolts of the sixties, and the consciousness those events forced upon the culture.

*   *   *

Viewed from one perspective, American Studies has been in decline ever since. With the demise of the Parrington paradigm, the movement has lacked a larger cultural synthesis, an image of a "usable" American past to lend it purpose and direction. Where the old synthesis got intellectual mileage from setting America off against Europe—New World against Old—now we tend to see both America and Europe on one side of a cultural and economic chasm, with the poorer, often newer, nations of

---

[32] An especially virulent form of this critique was voiced in 1968 by Christopher Lasch:

> The defection of intellectuals from their true calling—critical thought—goes a long way toward explaining not only the poverty of political discussion but the intellectual bankruptcy of so much recent historical scholarship. The infatuation with consensus; the vogue of a disembodied "history of ideas" divorced from considerations of class or other determinants of social organization; the obsession with "American studies" which perpetuates a nationalistic myth of American uniqueness—these things reflect the degree to which historians have become apologists, in effect, for American national power in the holy war against communism.

"The Cultural Cold War: A Short History of the Congress for Cultural Freedom," in Barton Bernstein, ed., *Towards a New Past: Dissenting Essays in American History* (Random House, 1968; rpt. Vintage Books, 1969), 323.

the world on the other. Seen from this vantage point, America does not look as new and innocent, as idealistic, as pragmatic as it once did. Thus American Studies is deprived of its previous fascination with watching a freshly-born culture as, Adam-like, it goes about creating and naming and using new things in the world.[33]

Pursuing further this declension theme, we can say that, unquestionably, American Studies is no longer working on the frontiers of scholarship. During the fifties and early sixties, symbol-myth-image scholarship came uniquely out of an American Studies perspective, and it influenced scholars in traditional disciplines too, particularly in intellectual history and in literary history. Very little of that is happening with American Studies now.

In scholarship, we have become something of a "parasite" field—living off the creations of others but not creating much on our own, nor contributing much to any field outside ourselves. We do this in two different ways. In some cases, we draw from new work in the traditional disciplines—from the discipline of history, for example, we draw from family studies, demography, community studies, and, more generally, from social history; from literature, we draw from autobiography and structuralism; from anthropology, we draw also from structuralism, cognitive anthropology, techniques of field work, and remnants of culture-personality analysis. In other cases, American Studies has drawn from, or rather given a home to, studies which have their real base of vitality in the culture at large. This is particularly true with women's studies, perhaps the most vital and interesting new field in the movement today.[34] But it also true with black studies, Hispanic studies, American Indian studies, ecology studies, and so on.[35] The one field which we might claim

---

[33] It is no accident that the two most notable works published in the symbol-myth-image era had "Adam" and "Virgin" in their titles, nor that much American Studies scholarship of the fifties and early sixties was focused on the early nineteenth century—when the country seemed freshest and newest, and was most concerned with creating for itself a unique cultural identity.

[34] See especially Betty Chmaj's stimulating *Image, Myth, and Beyond: American Women and American Studies* (KNOW, 1972). See also Joanna Zangrando, "Women's Studies in the United States: Approaching Reality," *American Studies International*, 14 (Autumn 1975), 15–36; Annette Baxter, "Women's Studies and American Studies: The Uses of the Interdisciplinary," *AQ*, 26 (Oct. 1974), 433–39; and the new journals *SIGNS* and *Feminist Studies*.

[35] For a comprehensive bibliographical essay connecting these new fields of cultural inquiry to academic American Studies, see Sklar, "American Studies 'Philosophy.'" For the relation of black studies to American Studies, see the essays on Afro-American theatre, art, and fiction in the 1978 *AQ* Bibliography issue.

as an American Studies creation—popular culture—has broken away to form a separate movement of its own.[36]

Further, intellectual ties between American Studies and the traditional disciplines have loosened substantially of late. American literature has long since secured a territory in English departments, and has little need of American Studies now to legitimize it. The most creative work in the discipline of history is now in social, not intellectual history, a field which does not draw upon American Studies for energy and direction.[37] And since the social sciences went behaviorist some years back, they have stopped looking at American Studies (or any other humanistic enterprise for that matter) as having anything worthwhile to offer their scholarship.

American Studies has also lost some of its initiative to explain contemporary America. In fact, that initiative may be lost from academe itself (if academe ever had it). The richest works giving us intellectual bearing on our experience today are being written by journalists—e.g., David Halberstam's *The Best and the Brightest* or Frances FitzGerald's *Fire in the Lake*—or by rogue academicians turned journalists—e.g., Tom Wolfe's *Electric Kool-Aid Acid Test* or Garry Wills' *Nixon Agonistes*—or by culture

---

[36] The relationship between the popular culture movement and the American Studies movement deserves more space than I can give it here. In some ways, the two movements have been coterminous. Popular culture notables like Carl Bode, Russel Nye, and John Cawelti are notables in American Studies too—the former two having held the presidency of both national associations. Further, several American Studies classics—for example, Smith's *Virgin Land* and Ward's *Andrew Jackson: Symbol for an Age*—are richly informed by perspectives from popular culture.

Recently, however, some strain has developed between the two movements; and if many still identify with both, some have been obliged, or obliged themselves, to opt for one movement over the other. Culturally, the split developed in response to the decade of the sixties, with its anti-elitist sentiments and its affection for products of the populace. Institutionally, this split has been centered at Bowling Green State University where, under the vigorous leadership of Ray Browne, popular culture studies have become one of the more energetic forces in American academic life over the last several years. This split was dramatized in 1978, when Browne challenged the ASA and the *AQ* by founding a competing American Culture Association, with a competing journal—the *Journal of American Culture*. For more on this, see Bruce Lohof, "Popular Culture: The *Journal* and the State of the Study," *Journal of Popular Culture*, 6 (Winter 1972), 453–62; and Michael Marsden, "American Culture Studies: A Discipline in Search of Itself," *Journal of Popular Culture*, 9 (Fall 1975), 461–70.

[37] This has meant that programs founded on the old intellectual history synthesis, and functioning basically through the integration of history and literature, suffered severe setbacks after the middle 1960s. That is acutely the case with Harvard's program in the History of American Civilization, and also to a lesser extent Minnesota's. These had been the country's outstanding graduate programs during American Studies symbol-myth-image era of the 1940s and 50s. Harvard's program now survives as a shell of its former self. Minnesota's also was in the doldrums for a time; in recent years, however, the program shows signs of considerable revitalization. For more on Harvard's decline, see Dorson, *Birth*, 29–30. For the earlier years of ascendancy, see John Lydenberg, ed., *Political Activism and the Academic Conscience: The Harvard Experience, 1936–1941* (Hobart and William Smith, 1977).

critics who may or may not be academicians but clearly do not identify themselves that way—e.g., Kate Millett's *Sexual Politics,* Philip Slater's *The Pursuit of Loneliness* and *Earthwalk,* Alvin Toffler's *Future Shock,* Barry Commoner's *The Closing Circle,* Robert Heilbroner's *The Human Prospect.* In addition, we often see searching critical analysis of the culture coming from an *All in the Family,* a *Maude,* a *Lou Grant Show,* a *Selling of the Pentagon,* an *Echoes of the Guns of Autumn,* a *Scared Straight!,* a *Roots,* a *Godfather* (I and II), a *Ms. Magazine,* a *Rolling Stone* magazine, a *60 Minutes,* a *Michael Jackson Show* (KABC Talk Radio, Los Angeles). None of the cultural criticism coming today from film, television, radio, music, magazines, or newspapers owes anything at all to academic American Studies. If we borrow mightily from them in our courses and our scholarship on the contemporary, they have little reason to look at us in turn. In this sense too, we are relegated to a parasite role.

All this has happened during the last decade and a half in and around American Studies, and it makes for a depressing story. Yet it is not the whole story of our recent past, not even perhaps half of it. Indeed, a case can be made that measuring the movement through indices of growth and energy and activity, American Studies has never been stronger and healthier. That is why I am unable to choose a single symbolic act to represent this most recent stage of the movement; our direction is so clearly paradoxical that no one can say just where we are now, let alone prophesy where we may be headed.

For example, despite massive cutbacks in academe during this depression decade, the movement has continued to grow in numbers. And despite the vulnerability of interdisciplinary ventures to institutional belt-tightening, American Studies appears not to have suffered unduly. Indeed, new programs, and in several cases independent departments, have been launched throughout the seventies, and the job prospects for teachers of American Studies, though bleak, seem better than for those in traditional disciplines like literature or history.[38]

---

[38] Of 1700 four-year academic institutions in the United States by 1973, one in seven offered an American Studies degree. This was up dramatically from 1958, when the figure was but one in 20. From 1958 to 1970, American Studies undergraduate and graduate programs doubled in number; from 1970 to 1975, they almost doubled again. Doctoral programs in the field tripled from 1958 to 1973, and no institution granting a Ph.D. in 1958 had dropped it 15 years later. As of 1973, there were 32 independent departments of American Studies in the country, almost 13% of the total programs. That was up substantially from 1958, when independent departments comprised only 5 percent of the total. And recently, when local administrations sought to curtail American Studies enterprises at Washington State University and Case Western Reserve, student and faculty initiative, plus strong support from the national ASA Council, was able to save the programs. Data on American Studies activity is taken from Bassett, "Programs," and Marcell "Characteristically American" and "Recent Trends."

Activity on the national scale even more clearly indicates the movement's good health. The national American Studies Association was founded in 1951, just one year after the first major symbol-myth-image work, *Virgin Land*. Yet during all the symbol-myth-image years, in the "Golden Era" when scholarship in American Studies flourished and massive foundation moneys poured into the movement, never was enough interest generated to hold a national convention of the Association. It was not until 1967, two years after the last of the great symbol-myth-image works, that the first nationwide convention of the ASA was held, in Kansas City. Momentum has picked up since; every two years from 1967 to the present, the national ASA has mounted successful and well-attended conventions—1969 in Toledo, 1971 in Washington, D. C., 1973 in San Francisco, 1975 in San Antonio, 1977 in Boston, 1979 in Minneapolis.

In 1971 the ASA secured funds from the National Endowment for the Humanities to establish the National American Studies Faculty. Under the energetic and talented leadership of John Hague, the NASF has been a powerful catalyst in the years since. It has sponsored interchange between American Studies and the community colleges, American Studies and the high schools, museum work and American Studies, the American Studies summer institutes, and many like ventures. Further, the NASF has served as a clearinghouse for the movement, providing information on course syllabi and field bibliographies from and to American Studies programs across the country.[39]

Institutionally, if the old symbol-myth-image programs like Harvard and Minnesota have lost much of their coherence and have waned in influence, other programs have advanced to take their place. Penn and Yale are now the most respected graduate enterprises in the country—Yale because it is Yale, Penn because it has a clear sense of what it is about and for some two decades has sought to recruit faculty consistent

---

[39] David Marcell has written of the National American Studies Faculty:

Since its inception in 1971 about two-thirds of the membership of the A.S.A. . . . have become NASF volunteers. Under John Hague's extraordinary leadership, some three to four hundred of these volunteers have provided assistance of one sort or another to over three hundred educational institutions across the country. And all this has been accomplished on a budget averaging a little more than fifty thousand dollars a year.

("Necessary Angels," *Connections II* [Autumn 1975], 105)

Needless to say, such an association—based on dedicated volunteers and lacking a cumbersome bureaucratic apparatus—proved alien to the categories of government funding, so in 1975 the NASF lost its grant support from NEH. Since then it temporarily received support from the Carnegie Corporation, and now receives no outside funding at all. See also, for the NASF, Robert Walker, "The National American Studies Faculty: An Outline for Assessment," *American Studies Newsletter* (Stetson, 1976), 4–6.

with that vision.[40] Other programs have become more visible in recent years in institutions like Buffalo, Kansas, Texas, Washington State, New Mexico, Boston, Maryland, Bowling Green, George Washington, Iowa, Hawaii, Emory, Case Western Reserve, the Universities of California at Davis and Irvine, and in the California State Universities at San Francisco, San Diego, Sacramento, Los Angeles, and Fullerton. All this indicates a shift away from northeastern dominance in American Studies to a geographical distribution all across the country.

I have already noted that American Studies today lacks a single synthesis with the influence, say, of the old symbol-myth-image explanation. It also lacks any clear consensus on a "usable" American past. Hence intellectually the last decade has brought disintegration in the movement. But if in one sense dis-integration means decline, in another sense it may mean simply diversification. We have moved beyond the block assumption that there is a single holistic "American Culture," expressed in "The American Mind," to a more discriminating consciousness that contemporary cultures function on several different levels, and in several different ways. We are less inclined now to take readings from a single vantage point on *The* American Experience; instead, we look upon America from a variety of different, often competing, perspectives—popular culture, black culture, the culture of women, youth culture, the culture of the aged, Hispanic-American culture, American Indian culture, material culture, the culture of poverty, folk culture, the culture of regionalism, the culture of academe, the culture of literature, the culture of professionalism, and so on.

*   *   *

Further, the concept of culture itself, and its usage in American Studies, have come under critical review during the 1970s. Here the department of American Civilization at Pennsylvania has led the way. Indeed, the recent conflict in the movement between new and old conceptions of culture reflects, among other things, the rise to institutional power of Pennsylvania and the consequent decline of Harvard and Minnesota. Penn faculty and Penn graduates have urged the field toward a more social scientific sense of culture and culture studies. And their critiques of past humanistic positions have taken aim at Henry Nash Smith and Leo Marx, both trained as graduate students in Harvard's American Civilization program, and both for a time faculty colleagues in American Studies at Minnesota.

---

[40] For a description of the program at Pennsylvania, see Murphey, "Pennsylvania." Penn's program is influential also because it has editorial and financial control over the *AQ;* Penn, not the ASA, owns the *AQ*. In addition, many of the *Quarterly's* most notable articles of late have been written by Penn faculty or Penn graduates.

It is never easy to locate the precise beginnings of such trends. But an important early voice in the debate was Bruce Kuklick's 1972 *American Quarterly* essay—"Myth and Symbol in American Studies."[41] In this essay, Kuklick was to take on the symbol-myth-image school of explanation, particularly its habit of reading the whole culture from inside literary texts. He felt that symbol-myth-image scholars were prone to generalize through grand intellectual abstractions—"the anonymous popular mind," "the widespread desire of Americans," "the imagination of the people," "the American view of life"—but only rarely did they offer empirical grounding for their generalizations.[42]

As a student of philosophy, Bruce Kuklick laid bare the unexamined assumptions of symbol-myth-image scholars, charging that their methods of explanation broke apart under a critical eye. But, as Kuklick acknowledged, his procedure was essentially negative; he dis-assembled humanistic symbol-myth-image assumptions, but he advanced no alternative assumptions—humanistic or otherwise—to take their place.

It remained for Kuklick's colleague then at Penn, Gordon Kelly, to offer scholars in the field a new, more social scientifically oriented pattern of explanations. In a landmark essay published in the May 1974 *American Quarterly*, Kelly set American culture studies in substantially new directions. He advanced a theoretical model for the new culture studies, drawn from Peter Berger and Thomas Luckmann's *The Social Construction of Reality*, and from work of the anthropologist Cliffort Geertz. And he applied that model to a case example—American children's literature of the late nineteenth century. Kelly's 1974 essay may in time prove as

---

[41] In fact, the characteristically Pennsylvania approach to culture studies was being worked out, mostly by Anthony Garvan and Murray Murphey, as early as the late 1950s and throughout the 1960s. It appeared in print in the spring of 1967. In a neglected classic of the field, Murphey proposed that American Studies align itself more with social scientific than humanistic forms of explanation, emphasizing that "the focus [of the discipline of American Civilization] is upon the *system*, not upon the unique event." "American Civilization as a Discipline," *Emory University Quarterly* (March 1967), 48.

This emphasis forecast a powerful thrust of American culture studies in the seventies, due in no small part to Murphey himself. Through his strategic location at Penn (where colleagues in the departments of anthropology, sociology, history, and elsewhere have shared and reinforced the sense of culture studies he has been trying to establish), through the analytic brilliance of his published scholarship, through his impact in the classroom and in structuring Penn's program, and through his power over *AQ* and ASA activities as former editor of *AQ* and presently as Chairman of its Editorial Board, Murray Murphey has been perhaps the single most influential figure in American Studies during the last decade and a half. More than any other program, Penn's Department of American Civilization has come close to establishing a Kuhnian "paradigm community," or what Nicholas Mullins calls a "theory group," for contemporary American culture studies. See Kuhn, *Structure*, and Mullins, *Theories and Theory Groups in Contemporary American Sociology* (Harper and Row, 1973).

[42] Kuklick, "Myth and Symbol." 445.

influential for new American culture studies as Henry Nash Smith's classic essay of 1957, "Can 'American Studies' Develop a Method?" was for an earlier American Studies.

As his point of departure, Kelly took the most notable brief for the older humanistic position, Leo Marx's 1969 article, "American Studies—A Defense of an Unscientific Method." Marx had argued there for the unique role of imaginative literature as a key to the culture. Though other modes of inquiry—namely, social scientific methods of content analysis—might itemize the surface "public opinion" of an age, only humanistic insights, Marx felt, could penetrate to the more privileged regions of human experience, wherein lies "culture."[43]

Marx had thus defined literature and culture in transcendental language; he wrote of "the concept of literary power," "the inherent capacity of a work to generate the emotional and intellectual response of its readers," "the intrinsic power of *Moby-Dick* as a work of literature"; and he spoke of great literature as "a semi-autonomous feature of the culture."[44] Gordon Kelly, in contrast, assumed a rigorously functionalist position. He was concerned with the social "creation and function of literary texts"; and his characteristic terms contrast sharply with Marx's: the "social distribution of knowledge," "the process of 'literary socialization,'" "strategies of reassurance and persuasion," "social functions of literature," "paradigms," "principle of social order."[45]

Marx had started with particular works of great literature and then moved to the general culture. Kelly, on the other hand, started with the general culture. Or rather, he began with the social situation out of which both literature and culture are constructed. "We would do well to begin with a concept of context," he wrote, "that directs attention to the rules and definitions which order and govern the creation and consumption of literature than to begin with an ethnocentric commitment to a particular type of literary product."[46]

Kelly insisted that imaginative literature, great or not, be treated as any other human product—as a particular construction of reality coming from a particular context, created and consumed by particular types of people in response to particular experiences in their world. In contrast to Marx's sense of literature as *transcending* everyday reality, Kelly declared that literature must be deeply *grounded in* social reality before it can be understood culturally.

[43] Marx, "American Studies," 81.
[44] Ibid., 80, 89, 85.
[45] Kelly, "Literature and the Historian," 152, 144, 149, 154–55, 146, 156.
[46] Ibid., 147.

Gordon Kelly's most basic contribution to a new form of culture studies is thus his *institutional* sense, his insistence that social structures mediate between the particular work of literature and the wider culture. Such an institutional sense had been missing from previous symbol-myth-image explanations. Marx, for example, had tended to assume that the solitary individual creates and confronts the great works of literature (i.e., "culture") directly, without the mediation of other social forms. But Kelly interposed a rich array of social structures between the literature and the culture—the institutional surroundings of the author, of the publishing industry, of literary critics and changing standards for criticism, of the literary audience and its differentiated social composition, and so forth. Through this array, Gordon Kelly offered contemporary American culture studies a fresh set of questions, and a fresh body of materials, for scholarly inquiry.

Coming also from the University of Pennsylvania (though hardly restricted to that institution) is what has been variously called "the new ethnography," "ethnosemantics," "ethnoscience," or "cognitive anthropology." Its impact on American Studies in the seventies has been substantial, particularly its social scientific approach to culture. Its disciplinary base lies in anthropology, though it has roots in sociology too.

Well before the 1970s of course, American Studies had been receptive to anthropological and sociological perspectives. A substantial part of David Potter's 1954 *People of Plenty,* for example, had discussed how ideas from anthropology, sociology, and psychology might aid in understanding historic American character.[47] And in a prophetic essay of 1963, Richard Sykes had urged American Studies away from humanistic preoccupations, suggesting instead a more anthropological sense of the field.[48] Even Leo Marx—chief spokesman for the humanistic mode—had been involved in an interdisciplinary faculty research seminar at Minnesota in the mid-fifties; the resulting publication—"Literature and Covert Culture" (1957)—is steeped in ideas from social science.[49]

Still, until the last decade Americanists tended to view social scientists with some humanistic disdain, so actual borrowing from their work was slight. In perhaps the most influential essay ever published in the field, Henry Nash Smith charged in 1957 that a "mutilated image of man and culture" dominates the social sciences. Twelve years later, Leo Marx called for "commerce" between humanists and social scientists; but he then accused social science of being shallow and mechanical in its ap-

---

[47] Potter, *Plenty,* vii-xxi, 32–72, 189–208.

[48] Richard Sykes, "American Studies and the Concept of Culture," *AQ,* 15 (Summer, 1963), 253–70.

[49] Bernard Bowron, Leo Marx, and Arnold Rose, "Literature and Covert Culture," *AQ,* 9 (Winter, 1957), 377–86.

proach to culture—in contrast to the richer, more penetrating insights of the humanities.[50] Finally, as Robert Berkhofer has indicated in his 1972 article, "Clio and the Culture Concept," when Americanists did borrow from the social sciences, they took a functionalist conception of culture as holistic and as value-directed, and this conception was to run head-on into the onslaught of the 1960s.[51]

The "new ethnography" of the seventies, however, employs a less value-directed sense of the culture; and, coming as it does from observation of non-print societies, it has no special commitment to culture as written literature. It takes cultural respondents pretty much where it finds them, assuming that everyone is in effect a culture carrier. This is in contrast to the humanistic mode, which operates as if particular culture bearers—namely, great artists and thinkers—have unique access to the culture's deepest meanings, an access not available to ordinary persons.

The new ethnography was first addressed to the wider American Studies community in 1972, through John Caughey's *American Quarterly* article, "Simulating the Past: A Method for Using Ethnosemantics in Historical Research."[52] Five years later, Jay Mechling urged colleagues in the field to identify with this anthropological method: "The goal of doing American Studies is to unmask the deep-structure rules which Americans use to give meaning to their environment and which they use to generate appropriate or acceptable behavior within that environment."[53]

Though no individual wholly represents this movement within anthropology, doubtless the most influential single figure is Anthony F. C. Wallace. Wallace's influence comes both from his location at Penn, and from his ground-breaking essay of 1962, "Culture and Cognition" (later republished in his equally ground-breaking book, *Culture and Personality*).[54] Another figure of note in the new ethnography is James Spradley of Macalester College, whose works have been widely used in American Studies during the seventies.[55]

---

[50] Smith, "Can 'American Studies?'" 206; Marx, "American Studies," 75ff.

[51] Berkhofer, "Clio."

[52] Caughey, "Simulating the Past: A Method for Using Ethnosemantics in Historical Research," *AQ*, 24 (Dec. 1972), 626–42.

[53] Mechling, "In Search of an American Ethnophysics," in Luedtke, 245.

[54] "Culture and Cognition," *Science*, 135 (1962), 351–57, and *Culture and Personality* (Random House, 1961; rev. 1970).

[55] James Spradley and David McCurdy, *The Cultural Experience: Ethnography in a Complex Society* (Science Research Associates, 1972); Spradley, *You Owe Yourself a Drunk: An Ethnography of Urban Nomads* (Little, Brown, 1970); and Spradley and Brenda Mann, *The Cocktail Waitress: Woman's Work in a Man's World* (Wiley, 1972). For a fascinating portrait of Spradley and McCurdy's teaching methods at Macalester, see Evan Jenkins, "The New Ethnography: Language as Key to Culture," *Change*, 10 (Jan. 1978), 16–19.

For uses of the new ethnography in recent American Studies scholarship, see Caughey, "Ethnosemantics," and "Artificial Social Relations in Modern America," *AQ*, 30 (Spring

In the Fall 1977 *American Quarterly*, Richard Beeman of Penn's history department took the new ethnographers to task—not by rejecting anthropology as such, but by drawing upon different traditions in the field. Beeman felt the cognitive anthropologists' habit of componential analysis—that is, of itemizing a culture's codes—leads to explanations which are too static; he also charged that the categories of cognitive anthropologists are hard to get unlocked from the particular culture under study, and do not readily lend themselves to cross-cultural generalization. He proposed instead the more dynamic concepts of scene and ritual from the anthropologists Clifford Geertz and Victor Turner, and the folk-urban continuum of Robert Redfield. These, he maintained, would lead to richer, and bolder, kinds of cultural explanations.[56]

Yet another social science perspective, this time entering from sociology, has influenced American culture studies of late. In this case, a single book is chiefly responsible for its impact: Peter Berger and Thomas Luckmann's little volume, *The Social Construction of Reality* (1966).[57] There are parallels between Berger and Luckmann and the new ethnography. Both approach cultures cognitively, seeking to lay bare their underlying codes. Both look for these codes in the everyday reality of ordinary people, and both assume that every person is a culture bearer.

Berger and Luckmann, however, are concerned not only with what a culture's codes are, but, more fundamentally, with how they get constructed. Hence their book's main thrust is institutional; they seek to discover how, in the processes of everyday living, people go about building and maintaining their social universes.

This perspective has shown enormous heuristic potential for American Studies. As a teaching strategy, it addresses students not as blank tablets but as already laden with the culture; and it encourages them not simply to "learn about" their culture, but to envision their own social surround as one pattern of alternatives among a wide spectrum of human possibilities.

1978), 70–89; Mechling, "Ethnophysics"; Berkhofer, "Clio," 311ff; Richard Horwitz, "Architecture and Culture: The Meaning of the Lowell Boarding House," *AQ*, 25 (Mar. 1973), 64–82, and *Anthropology Toward History: Culture and Work in a 19th-Century Maine Town* (Wesleyan, 1978). Wallace, Caughey, Mechling, Horwitz and Beeman (see footnote following) have all been Penn faculty, or Penn graduates, or both.

[56] Beeman, "The New Social History and the Search for 'Community' in Colonial America," *AQ*, 29 (Fall 1977), 428–43. For a stimulating application of Victor Turner's ideas to American culture studies, see Roland Delattre's "The Rituals of Humanity and the Rhythms of Reality" (paper delivered at the Oct. 1977 ASA convention in Boston). For a similarly provocative application of Clifford Geertz to American culture studies, see Karen Lystra's "'Thick Description': Literature as Cultural Artifact" (paper delivered at the Dec. 1977 MLA convention in Chicago); and "Clifford Geertz, *The Interpretation of Cultures*" (paper delivered at Sept. 1979 ASA convention in Minneapolis).

[57] Berger and Luckmann, *The Social Construction of Reality: A Treatise in the Sociology of Knowledge* (Doubleday, 1966).

It also encourages them to discover what particular kinds of historical choices led Americans to construct their particular social realities in their particular ways.[58] Such a strategy has served to make cultural realities more accessible to students in the field.[59]

We have already seen some of the impact of Berger and Luckmann on recent scholarly strategies in American Studies. Their perspective was instrumental in shaping Gordon Kelly's 1974 article, "Literature and the Historian." Kelly was empowered there to pose questions which earlier had seemed unproblematic to a Leo Marx and to other symbol-myth-image scholars—Who defines what is "great" in the literature of a culture, and through what social roles? Through what institutional structures do these definitions get passed on and reinforced? What is the social composition of various literary audiences?[60] And *The Social Construction of Reality*, plus selected other Berger works, helped shape Jay Mechling's important recent statement on regionalism, "mediating structures," and American culture studies, published in the Winter 1979 issue of *Prospects*.[61]

* * *

Yet another quality of recent American Studies is a "reflexive" temper in scholarship and teaching. This temper expresses a *stock-taking consciousness* in the movement.

Obviously, that consciousness is neither unique to American Studies, nor is it limited to the past decade. Reflexiveness, rather, is widespread in

[58] For a provocative explanation of how *The Social Construction of Reality* is used in the classroom, and how pedagogical difficulties in its use may be overcome, see Jay Mechling and Merline Williams, "Teaching Up," *Chesapeake American Studies Quarterly*, 5 (Jan. 1975), 1–5.

[59] The Berger and Luckmann volume, along with the new ethnography and with broader cultural events of the last decade and a half, may have helped stimulate interest in field work and oral history in American Studies. For indications of this interest, see Howard Gillette and Jannelle Findley, "Teaching the 1930s: A Cultural Approach," *Chesapeake American Studies Quarterly*, 4 (Apr. 1974), 1–7; Richard Horwitz, "American Communities: The Coralville Strip" (course syllabus, University of Iowa, Spring 1978); Sharon Rubin, "Work in American Culture" (course syllabus, University of Maryland, Fall 1979); Ronald Grele, "A Surmisable Variety: Interdisciplinarity and Oral Testimony," *AQ*, 27 (Aug. 1975), 275–95; Jay Mechling, "If They Can Build a Square Tomato: Notes Toward a Holistic Approach to Regional Studies," *Prospects*, 4 (Burt Franklin, Winter, 1979), 59–78.

[60] Other imaginative uses of Berger and Luckmann can be found in Lonna Malmsheimer's brilliant analysis of New England funeral sermons, "Genre, Audience, and Significance: Social Contextualism and the Literature-History Dilemma" (paper presented at joint meeting of ASA Eastern chapters and British Association for American Studies, Phila., April 3, 1976); and Kay Mussell, "*The Social Construction of Reality* and American Studies: Notes Toward a Method" (unpublished paper). My own impression is that to date the Berger and Luckmann book has had even greater impact on American Studies' "oral" tradition than on its published scholarship. That is, the basic idea—of reality as socially constructed—seems to have wide currency in American Studies classrooms today, and in many other informal and unrecorded situations where ideas get communicated.

[61] Mechling, "Square Tomato."

contemporary scholarship. Doubtless, it signals a historical stage in the evolution of modern academic disciplines; after an era of heady expansionism in the late nineteenth and earlier twentieth century, a more self-critical mood now has set in among some scholars.[62]

In some ways, American Studies has always imbibed this spirit of reflexiveness. The movement got its start in the 1930s and 40s by countering the territorial imperative of conventional disciplines; and, as I noted earlier, from the beginning the identity quest of American Studies has impelled people to continue asking, "Who are we?" and "Where are we heading?"

Yet until recently Americanists seldom reflected long on their own operating assumptions; rather, their self-consciousness was expressed on the run, so to speak. In a 1970 reissue of *Virgin Land,* for example, Henry Nash Smith confessed that he had used his ordering terms "myth" and "symbol" in a naive and contradictory fashion twenty years before.[63] And an extensive methodological introduction to John William Ward's *Andrew Jackson: Symbol for an Age* had been cut out when Oxford published the dissertation as a book in 1955.[64] Further, the American Studies movement was into its fifth decade before it produced the first booklength critique of its own ideas—Cecil Tate's penetrating analysis, *The Search for a Method in American Studies* (1973).[65]

But during the last decade, a reflexive temper has become central to American culture studies teaching and scholarship. In some ways, this trend runs parallel to the other contemporary influences we have just seen—the impact of anthropological and sociological perspectives, and the institutional role of Pennsylvania. But in other ways reflexiveness is not so much the quality of a particular method or a particular place, but rather of a particular social generation in the movement. We can see this in the most articulate voice of the reflexive temper, Jay Mechling of the University of California at Davis.

---

[62] In the discipline of sociology, that mood can be found in C. Wright Mills, *The Sociological Imagination* (Grove, 1959), and, more recently, in Alvin Gouldner, *The Coming Crisis of Western Sociology* (Avon, 1970); in anthropology, in Dell Hymes, ed., *Reinventing Anthropology* (Vintage, 1972); in literature, in Richard Ohmann, *English in America: A Radical View of the Profession* (Oxford, 1976); and in history, in Bernstein, *New Past,* and Martin Duberman, *The Uncompleted Past* (Random House, 1969). I have written at more length on this "reflexive" movement, setting it against a century of territorial expansion in modern scholarship, in "Some Elementary Axioms for an American Culture Studies," *Prospects,* 4 (Burt Franklin, 1979), 517–47.

[63] Smith, *Virgin Land: The American West as Symbol and Myth* (Harvard, 1950; 2d ed. rev., 1970), vii–x.

[64] Ward's reflections were published 15 years later as "Looking Backward: *Andrew Jackson: Symbol for an Age,*" in Lewis Perry Curtis, ed., *The Historian's Workshop* (Knopf, 1970).

[65] Tate, *Method.*

It was Mechling who first wrote of "social generations" in American Studies history. In an essay published in 1977, he noted that the movement is now into its third generation of practitioners.[66] Where earlier generations had tended to align with one or another of the established disciplines—normally literature or history—many in the contemporary generation have spent their entire academic lives in American Studies, and have a distinctive intellectual and personal commitment to it.[67] Earlier, a Henry Nash Smith or a Roy Harvey Pearce might in passing lament that American Studies had not yet developed its own method, then go off to spend the rest of their careers in departments of English.[68] But many of Mechling's contemporaries either lack that option, or have chosen not to pursue it. They *live* in American Studies, hence are self-critical of it in a way prior Americanists were not.

Further, the third generation was socialized during the turbulent sixties, and imbibed a more thoroughgoing critique of the academy than previous Americanists. Mechling himself did his undergraduate and graduate work in American Studies during the sixties at Stetson and Penn, respectively. His subsequent scholarship expresses the seventies trends already noted—the new ethnography, the impact of Berger and Luckmann, the influence of Penn. But Mechling's distinctive impact comes not just from his published scholarship—brilliant and influential as it is—but also from his involvement in the program at the University of California at Davis, and from his pivotal role as Chairperson of the ASA's Standing Committee on Bibliographical Needs and Policies (now the Bibliography Subcommittee).

In 1969 the program in American Studies at Davis was established; in 1970 Robert Merideth was brought in from Miami University to chair the new program; in 1971 Jay Mechling arrived in California fresh from graduate study at Penn; and soon thereafter David Wilson moved over full-time from the English Department to American Studies at Davis. These three set out to structure a new kind of program in the field. In the fall of 1973, the *American Quarterly* published the results of their deliberations—"American Culture Studies: The Discipline and the Curriculum." The Davis essay won the *American Quarterly* Award as the finest article published in the journal that year.

---

[66] Mechling, "Ethnophysics," 242–45.

[67] It might be noted, however, that the tendency of younger scholars to identify with a distinct discipline of American Studies, and of more established scholars to take the "confederationist" approach, is not just a product of the last decade. Robert Walker noted a similar division more than two decades ago, in the Conference on Undergraduate Courses and Programs in American Studies, held at Washington, D. C. in the spring of 1957. See Walker, *American Studies in the United States,* 158.

[68] Smith, "Can 'American Studies?'"; Pearce, "American Studies as a Discipline," *College English,* 18 (Jan. 1957), 179–86.

In the years following, the Davis statement has become perhaps the most influential article in the movement since Henry Nash Smith's famous essay of 1957. Its influence differs from Smith's, however. Smith represented American Studies much as it actually existed in the 1940s and 1950s. He registered some dissatisfaction with existing approaches to American materials; but in the absence of clear scholarly consensus on an alternative, he counseled Americanists to remain with the conventional disciplines. His essay thus reinforced the "confederationist" approach; American Studies was to live in the interstices between traditional departments, not a thing unto itself but an occasional release from the regular conventions. For years, Smith's essay went almost unchallenged in the movement. Its wide acceptance, I suspect, is due to its counsel of caution; it did not basically disturb the existing order in academe.[69]

The Davis essay, on the other hand, *did* disturb the existing order. It set out to provoke, and occasionally to irritate. It opened, "There is a vast slough of genial ignorance about American Studies"; and it proceeded to condemn "tinkering," "Uncle Tomism," the "Do-it-Yourself-Synthesizer-Kit-Fallacy," the "Body-of-Knowledge Fallacy," and other assorted sins of past Americanists.[70]

The Davis essay has been influential not because it legitimized Americanists to do as they were, but because it has provoked them to question themselves. The essay made many angry, but few have been able to ignore it. Many ended up heeding the Davis counsel, not because they liked the essay, but because it raised issues which they could not avoid.

The Davis group, for example, rejected equating "American Studies" simply with "studies American"; the *mode of approach,* they contended, not the body of materials, should distinguish the field. As a consequence, they have stimulated several in the field to quit calling themselves "Americanists"; perhaps more than any other single influence, the Davis essay has established identification with "American *Culture* Studies" in the movement.

Mechling, Merideth, and Wilson have also offered the most searching critique in print of how American Studies programs have functioned (and misfunctioned) inside the academy. Because of the Davis essay, and because of other forces besetting the American academy during the sixties and seventies, many became less sanguine about the conventional de-

---

[69] One indication of such caution is the fact that the ASA waited 19 years before electing one of its own Ph.D.'s as president. In 1970–71, Robert Walker was the first American Studies doctorate to become ASA president. In the years since, the Association has elected no one but American Studies Ph.D.'s—Daniel Aaron in 1972-73, William Goetzmann in 1974-75, Leo Marx in 1976-77, and Wilcomb Washburn in 1978-79.

[70] Mechling, et al., "American Culture Studies" 363, 365, 366, 372–73.

partments than was Henry Nash Smith in the fifties. Hence the seventies has seen the creation of autonomous American Studies programs or departments on several campuses. In the forties and fifties, many Americanists seemed content to have their home base in history or in literature, and to offer a course now and then in something called "American Studies." In the seventies, however, advocates of the new culture studies have continued to draw from the traditional departments, but they have also sought a permanent home for American Studies in their institutions, in many cases successfully.[71]

Jay Mechling was one of three behind the Davis essay. He has also served the movement in his role as Chairperson of the ASA Standing Committee on Bibliographical Needs and Policies. Since 1974, that Committee has been responsible for the annual bibliographical issues of the *American Quarterly.*

More than any other single forum, the bibliographical issues have stimulated critical self-consciousness in the movement; they have also given substance and direction to that self-consciousness. In its first five issues, the Bibliography Committee has published essays on the philosophy of American Studies; various approaches to culture studies (e.g., social science approaches, quantitative approaches, film studies, American Indian studies, above-ground archaeology, folklore, women's studies, autobiography, still photography, structuralism, drama, Afro-American Studies); institutional arrangements vis-a-vis American Studies (e.g., museums, the Shawnee Indian Mission, Douglass College at Rutgers University, the 1975-76 National Humanities Institute at Yale, American

---

[71] In the mid-fifties, the chairman of Harvard's graduate program in American Civilization could write,

> We believe that the conventional departments can do most of the things that are needed in American scholarship and that our function is simply to take care of those few students who have the ability and the interest to tackle subjects which for one reason or another cannot easily be covered in one of the regular departmental programs.

(quoted in Robert Walker, *American Studies in the United States*, 44)

As recently as 1958, more than half the graduate programs in the field offered not a single course in American Studies per se! Fifteen years later, that had been reduced to a quarter—still a surprising number, but a substantial change from earlier (Bassett, "Programs," 328). Despite cutbacks during the depressed seventies, the trend in American Studies has been to establish independent programs or departments, or at least independent tenured positions in the field. Where only a handful of programs had independent status or even independent academic appointments during the forties and fifties, a large number—e.g., George Washington, Skidmore, Buffalo, Kansas, Hawaii, Heidelberg, New Mexico, Dickinson, Case Western Reserve, Bowling Green, Maryland, California State at Fullerton, Univ. of California at Davis—had such status by the seventies. And programs of long standing like Iowa and Minnesota for the first time established independent, tenured positions in the field.

For an excellent structural analysis of independent versus interdependent modes of organization in American Studies, see Pershing Vartanian, "The Voluntary American Studies Program: Strategies for Development," *AQ*, 30 (Bibliography, 1978), 410–22.

Studies and the community college, the "voluntary American Studies program"); and the Bassett Report of 1975 on the state of the national movement.[72]

The Bibliography Committee has also promoted widespread discussion about the movement and its direction, implicitly through its commissioned articles, explicitly through its open forums at recent national conventions of the ASA. This dialogue temper contrasts radically with that of the regular *AQ* establishment—which neither solicits discussion from the Association membership about its modus operandi, nor sanctions forums for dialogue within the journal.[73]

Other scholarly forums have both contributed to the reflexive temper of the seventies and offered a focus for American culture studies lacking in earlier decades. Foremost among these is the journal *Prospects*—founded in 1975 and edited by Jack Salzman of Hofstra University. As an annual, it has published only four issues to date; but it is already challenging the *American Quarterly* as the finest scholarly journal in the field. It has published not only some of the classic names in and around the field—Henry Nash Smith, Alan Trachtenberg, Daniel Aaron, Sacvan Bercovitch, Chester Eisinger, Ray Browne, Allen Guttmann, Russel Nye, Alan Gowans, John Cawelti, Cushing Strout, Robert Berkhofer, Joseph Kwiat. It has also published a remarkable number of scholars whose work points toward the future of the field—among them David Stannard, Peter Marzio, William Stott, Horace Newcomb, Henry Glassie, Gerda Lerner, Robert Corrigan, Roger Abrahams, Albert Stone, Betty Chmaj, Edward Orser, Jay Mechling, Karal Ann Marling, Lawrence Mintz, Joy Kasson, Peter Shaw, Thomas Inge, Fred Matthews.

Also of note are the special theme and period issues of the *American Quarterly;* in these issues may be found some of the richest concentrations of scholarship in the history of the movement. Five such issues have been published to date—on "Death in America" (December 1974, edited by David Stannard); "Victorian Culture in America" (December 1975, edited by Daniel Walker Howe); "An American Enlightenment" (Summer 1976, edited by Joseph Ellis); "Reassessing Twentieth Century Documents" (Winter 1977); and "Women and Religion" (Winter 1978,

---

[72] For specific references, see the 1974 through 1978 Bibliography Issues of the *Quarterly*.

[73] The reflexive temper of the Bibliography Committee may be an expression of its social makeup. It has been composed mostly of people from Mechling's "third generation," and/or those who identify basically with American Studies rather than one of the traditional disciplines. This again contrasts with the regular *AQ* establishment; its editor holds his academic appointment at Penn in the History Department, not American Civilization, and the *AQ* Editorial Board is composed almost exclusively of scholars with appointments in the traditional departments, not in American Studies.

edited by Janet Wilson James).[74] Though not specifically "reflexive," the special issues provide a point of focus for interdisciplinary scholarship, and they include some of the best examples in print of new culture studies.[75]

Other forums which have either given focus or reflexiveness to the movement of late include: the National American Studies Faculty, founded in 1971; the Radical Caucus summer institutes of 1972 and 1973; the University of Southern California American Studies Institute of 1973, eventuating in Luther Luedtke's excellent 1977 anthology, *The Study of American Culture: Contemporary Conflicts;* the ASA convention workshops begun at San Francisco in 1973 and held at every national convention since; the 1975 national ASA convention in San Antonio on "Recharting the Mainstream," the 1977 ASA convention in Boston on "Theory and Practice in Cultural Studies," and the 1979 ASA convention in Minneapolis; the radical journals *Connections* (1970-73) and *Connections II* (1973-); the Yale Humanities Institute of 1975-76[76]; recent theoretical issues of the *Journal of Popular Culture*[77]; the recently-founded *Journal of American Culture;* and the bibliographical essays published in each issue of *American Studies International.*

* * *

Thus far, we have looked at three recent characteristics of American culture studies—the concern for anthropological definitions of culture, the emphasis on social structures undergirding intellectual and artistic

---

[74] The first two special issues and a volume of collected *AQ* essays have been published as books by the University of Pennsylvania Press. See David Stannard, ed., *Death in America* (Pennsylvania, 1975); Daniel Walker Howe, ed., *Victorian America* (Pennsylvania, 1976); and Leila Zenderland, ed., *Recycling the Past: Popular Uses of American History* (Pennsylvania, 1978).

[75] Perhaps the finest article in this group is Daniel Walker Howe's "American Victorianism as a Culture," *AQ*, 27 (Dec. 1975), 507–32. In its sense of culture not as vaporous ideas but as institutionally grounded in a "communications system"; in its trans-national approach to Victorianism; in its pluralistic sense of the culture as rooted in the varied experience of different social classes, ethnic groups, and geographical regions; and in its imaginative blending of humanistic with social scientific perspectives on the past, the Howe essay is a model new culture study of the seventies.

[76] See Michael Cowan, "The National Humanities Institute: The First Year," *AQ*, 28 (Bibliography 1976), 578–86.

[77] Countering an earlier tendency to be militantly un-theoretical, the *JPC* of late has published some excellent special supplements on theoretical and methodological matters. See especially the fall 1975 issue on "Theories and Methodologies in Popular Culture" (edited by Ray Browne, Sam Grogg, and Larry Landrum); the summer 1977 issue on "History and Popular Culture" (edited by Susan Tamke and William Cohn); and the fall 1977 issue on "Sociology and Popular Culture" (edited by Gary Alan Fine).

expression, the "reflexive" temper.[78] There are of course other charac-teristics. Fortunately, Robert Sklar's splendid review of the field pub-lished in this journal four years ago ("The Problem of an American Studies 'Philosophy': A Bibliography of New Directions"), plus the com-prehensive review articles in recent Bibliography Issues of the *American Quarterly* and in *American Studies International* free the present essay from any obligation to coverage.

A brief survey turns up at least four additional characteristics—a pluralistic rather than a holistic approach to American culture; an accom-panying rediscovery of the particular; an emphasis on proportion rather than essence in cultural experience; and a cross-cultural, comparative dimension to American studies.[79]

The first trend is the most obvious and widespread. *A pluralistic ap-proach* is what most distinguishes recent American culture studies from earlier Americanist scholarship. This trend has been widely noted elsewhere, and needn't be further documented here. It comes to focus in the "new social history" of the last decade and a half; it is expressed in ethnic studies, black studies, women's studies, popular culture studies, folklore studies, family studies, and the like.

A parallel trend, actually a sub-trend of the pluralistic approach, is *a rediscovery of the particular in American culture*. This emphasis includes

---

[78] In focusing here on what is "new" in American culture studies, I should not wish to ignore what has survived largely intact from earlier years. Many of the articles published in the three major journals of the field—the *American Quarterly, American Studies*, and *Prospects*—remain untouched by new methodological forms of the last decade. This is particu-larly the case with *American Studies*, the official publication of the Midcontinent American Studies Association. The journal maintains a breezy informality in editorial tone, a refresh-ing contrast to the more sober norm in scholarly journals. And its issues of the last decades have responded to changing events, and changing perceptions in the culture (see for example its Bicentennial issue on "Change in America," Fall 1976). But the journal remains largely innocent of recent social science perspectives and of the "reflexive" temper in contempor-ary scholarship (see for example its editorial statement in the Spring 1974 issue, 103–04).

[79] Actually, there is yet a fifth characteristic, though it cannot be given a single label. If social science perspectives have been on the frontier of contemporary American culture studies, they have neither taken over nor are they alone. Older humanistic modes of inquiry still supply a great deal of the sensitivity and energy displayed in American culture studies today. They also provide a brake against the temptation of social science approaches to become overly quantitative or categorical. A healthy future for American Studies lies not in the domination of one or another approach, but in an open dialogue, indeed an open tension, between them. Especially promising humanistic perspectives have been developed of late around autobiography and structuralism. See Albert Stone, "Autobiography and American Culture," *American Studies: An International Newsletter*, 11 (Winter 1972), 22–36; Robert Sayre, "The Proper Study—Autobiographies in American Studies," *AQ*, 29 (Bibliography 1977), 241–62; and John Blassingame, "Black Autobiographies as History and Literature," *Black Scholar*, 5 (Dec. 1973–Jan. 1974), 2–9. For the latter, see Tate, *Method*, 133ff; and the articles on structuralism by John Blair and David Pace in *AQ*, 30 (Bibliography 1978), 261–97.

all the particular sub-cultures noted in the last trend, plus the particularity of things—material artifacts, the physical environment of towns and cities, geographical regions.[80] In recent years, much culture studies inquiry has stuck close to the immediate, tangible environment of people; this contrasts with many earlier studies, which tended to emphasize broad floating currents of thought in America transcending particular environments.

Another parallel trend is *the emphasis on proportion rather than on essence in cultural experience.* We have already discussed efforts of earlier symbol-myth-image scholars to locate *the* quintessential "American Mind" or "American Character," and to define the culture through its great "isms"—Puritanism, Rationalism, Transcendentalism, Liberalism, Individualism, and so on. Recent inquiries have not wholly abandoned those concerns, but they do try to particularize them. Hence they raise questions of proportion, querying, in effect, "How much in American cultural experience is shared by how many?"

Such questions are at heart quantitative, and for years were resisted by the humanist strain in American Studies thinking. In their famous essays of 1957 and 1969, for example, Henry Nash Smith and Leo Marx had caricatured social science "content analysis" and "public opinion" studies as superficial and mechanical; such approaches touched only the surface of the culture, they felt, and were no match for the depth probes of the humanities. Even in the 1970s, with greater receptivity to social science, quantification has played but a minor role within American Studies scholarship. Of the influential graduate programs in the field, only Pennsylvania's emphasizes training in quantitative techniques, and only a trickle of works by American Studies-trained scholars has relied heavily on quantification.[81]

[80] On material culture and material artifacts, see Paul Wilderson, "Archaeology and the American Historian: An Interdisciplinary Challenge," *AQ*, 27 (May 1975), 115–32; James Kavanaugh, "The Artifact in American Culture: The Development of an Undergraduate Program in American Studies," in Ian Quimby, ed., *Material Culture and the Study of American Life* (Norton, 1978), 64–75; Linna Funk Place et al., "The Object as Subject: The Role of Museums and Material Culture Collections in American Studies," *AQ*, 26 (Aug. 1974), 281–91; John Cotter, "Above Ground Archaeology," *AQ*, 26 (Aug. 1974), 266–80; Wilcomb Washburn, "American Studies at the Smithsonian," *AQ*, 22 (Summer 1970), 560–70; E. McClung Fleming, "Accent on Artist and Artisan: The Winterthur Program in Early American Culture," *AQ*, 22 (Summer 1970), 571–96; and Henry Glassie, "Meaningful Things and Appropriate Myths: The Artifact's Place in American Studies," *Prospects*, 3 (Burt Franklin, 1977), 1–49.

[81] See for example Richard Merritt, "The Emergence of American Nationalism: A Quantitative Approach," *AQ*, 17 (Summer 1965), 319–35; Robert Zemsky, *Merchants, Farmers, and River Gods: An Essay on Eighteenth Century American Politics* (Gambit, 1971); Melvyn Hammarberg, "Designing a Sample from Incomplete Historical Lists," *AQ*, 23 (Oct. 1971), 542–62; and Hammarberg, *The Indiana Voter: The Historical Dynamics of Party Allegiance During the 1870s* (Chicago, 1977).

In some ways, this under-emphasis may be healthy, as a counter to the decided over-emphasis on quantification in the social sciences, and, more recently, in the discipline of history. American historians got badly burned in the *Time on the Cross* affair of 1974; since then, the counting fad has waned, and a balance of sorts has been struck in the discipline between quantitative and non-quantitative approaches.[82]

Still, some cultural insights yield themselves up only through quantification, and others are made more refined by a detailed sense of proportion. As Richard Jensen wrote in this journal five years ago,

> By measuring error rather than merely acknowledging its existence and by specifying variables and causal linkages previously covertly assumed, quantifiers have significantly raised the sensibilities of scholars regarding the reliability and validity of historical documents and the complexities of actual events. By showing how sparse records dealing with thousands of individuals can be handled, the quantifier has opened the study of the inarticulate to scholars who once could deal only with verbose or introspective elites.[83]

Finally, several recent inquiries in the field have employed *a comparative, cross-cultural approach*. Again, such an approach is not unique to the last decade. The classic works of Parrington, Miller, Matthiessen, Marx, and Sanford et al. sought out the European backgrounds of American ideas, hence were in part cross-cultural. Still, they usually emphasized how Old World ideas took on a different coloration when transported to the New World. This was due to their sense of "American exceptionalism"—Americans had built a new culture in a new land, they believed; the task of American Studies was to explain how that had happened.

But recent experience has occasioned a different sense of the culture. Contrasted only with the "Old World" of Europe, America may seem unique; but compared with the new, post-World War II nations of Africa, the Middle East, Southeast Asia, and Latin America, America looks more like Europe and less like a "new" kind of world. Thus the polarity of New World versus Old has collapsed of late, and America is placed in a category with other modern industrialized cultures.

The concept of "modernization," originally developed in social science but increasingly applied by historians to the American past, has contrib-

---

[82] For an account of the *Time on the Cross* controversy, see Thomas Haskell, "The True and Tragical History of 'Time on the Cross,'" *The New York Review of Books* (Oct. 2, 1975), 33–39.

[83] Jensen, "Quantitative American Studies: The State of the Art," *AQ*, 26 (Aug. 1974), 226.

uted a useful tool to cross-cultural understanding.[84] Other cross-cultural perspectives can be found in recent studies of slavery; in family studies; in the December 1975 special issue of the *American Quarterly,* on "Victorian Culture in America"; and in recent social histories of colonial New England. These latter studies speak less of the culturally unique qualities of "Puritanism" in the New World, and instead look for continuities in agrarian lifestyle from Old World to New.

*   *   *

When we look back over new culture studies of the 1970s, it is evident that, like American Studies in earlier decades, they too have been shaped by forces in the wider society. In one sense, escalation of the trend toward specialization—in academe as well as in the culture at large—has made the synthesizing approach of American Studies seem more problematic of late. The forces of specialization have put interdisciplinary studies on the defensive, and have made them appear dispensable to some academies. obliged to cut back on "luxuries" in their curriculum.

But at a deeper level, recent events give an even stronger imperative to integrating culture studies. Pressures of rapid change have put enormous stress on social institutions and cultural values, laying bare their inner workings. What was once buried and taken for granted in America is now made visible for inspection, and for criticism. Those pressures have made everyone—scholar and non-scholar alike—conscious of the massive power of culture and social structure to shape people's experience. Without some such cultural consciousness, American Studies would not be possible; with it, the movement gains energy to do its essential work.

Also, recent events have dramatized inherent interconnections among experiences in contemporary culture. Doctors trained in medicine alone, for example, are powerless to understand problems of health in the inner city, the malpractice crisis, issues of birth control and of abortion, and all the other matters of modern health reaching beyond the confines of pure medical training.

Recent experience should have taught Americans that few critical problems in a culture ever get understood, let alone resolved, by attacking the problem alone. Contemporary cultural problems require understanding in their full interconnecting context. The "light at the end of the tunnel"

---

[84] For a useful review of the concept of modernization, see S. N. Eisenstadt, "Studies of Modernization and Sociological Theory," *History and Theory,* 13 (1974), 225–52. For applications of the modernization concept to America's past, see Richard Brown, "Modernization and the Modern Personality in Early America, 1600–1865: A Sketch of a Synthesis," *Journal of Interdisciplinary History,* 2 (Winter 1971), 201–28, and *Modernization: The Transformation of American Life, 1600–1865* (Hill and Wang, 1976).

metaphor erred for Vietnam not simply in its results—it proved wrong to the facts—but in its basic assumption that a "tunnel" metaphor was appropriate in the first place. A "web" metaphor would have been better. For it would have shown what was in fact the case, that America's fault in the war was not at heart technical, but cultural.

A tunnel metaphor occasions "producing" minds—minds concerned, in the time-honored tradition of American pragmatism, to get things done in the quickest and most efficient manner possible. But a web metaphor requires a different quality of mind, a "connecting" mind which can probe beyond the immediacy of the situation to search for everything which rays out beyond it. Such a connecting imagination is precisely what integrating culture studies, at their best, are structured to encourage.[85]

Finally, the quest for subcultural "roots" of the last few years has resensitized Americans to the inescapable power of the past—has emphasized that a people which presumes to outrun its history never does so in fact. Such a consciousness obliges people to get in contact with their past if they would build upon it. This message has evidently got through to Americans of late. There are indications that it may be getting through to American Studies too. Several in the movement seem more inclined now to take soundings on their own past as a means of identifying what American Studies is, and envisioning where it may be heading.

*   *   *

Hence, as we journey back over the intellectual and institutional history of American Studies, we have, I believe, encountered an ambiguous legacy. On the plus side, we find a series of creative "revolts against formalism"; we find intellectual work in American Studies offering release from the territorial imperative of conventional disciplines; we find the movement offering a place for fresh kinds of studies in the 1960s and 70s which had few other entries into academe; we find a generation of superb scholarship in the symbol-myth-image school and the promise of perhaps another generation in the "new culture studies" of the last decade; we find if not an entire movement then at least several of its programs dedicated to countering the worst sins of today's multiversity. And—I don't know how to say this without sounding sentimental—we find national conventions in American Studies which are simply more decent and more humane affairs than, say, the MLA or the AHA.

On the negative side, we in the movement have been much too ready, especially in past decades, to make peace with the dominant structures of

---

[85] In a companion piece to the present essay, I have written at more length on this "connecting mind" imperative for culture studies. See "Elementary Axioms."

the academy; we have too frequently allowed our ritual rhetoric of newness to substitute for actually thinking or doing our work creatively; we have often let intellectual flabbiness get by as "openness" or "innovation." And, most basically, we have been too faint of heart in our commitment to a distinctive American Studies venture, and all too often have retreated to our disciplinary havens when matters threaten to get precarious in the field.

Be that as it may, I believe that over the years American Studies has made itself distinctive as a movement which encourages people to be people—students as well as faculty. Given the institutional malaise of the academy, of the scholarly professions, and of the larger society these days, we might dream of, but we can hardly in fact hope for, more.[86]*

---

[86] For an evocative statement of this "small is beautiful" sense of American Studies, of how the movement seeks to embody Gemeinschaft-like qualities in a largely Gesellschaft academic social order, see Jay Mechling's essay, "If They Can Build a Square Tomato: Notes Toward a Holistic Approach to Regional Studies."

Although "modernizing" pressures, the numbers mania, and the accountability ethic have all reinforced the larger, more traditional units of the academy, it may be the smallness of American Studies which gives structure to its essential qualities, and enables it to carry out its educational mission. To my knowledge, only a single American Studies program in the country has more than 10 faculty members—the University of Hawaii's. My historian colleague Harry Stout of the University of Connecticut has suggested that because of its characteristically small units and informal academic settings, American Studies may be distinguished historically more by its "oral" than its "written" tradition. If Stout is correct, then the oral histories of key figures in the movement currently being undertaken by Richard Johnson and Linda Keller Brown could be of crucial importance.

* The present essay is a revised and expanded version of a paper first read at a session on "American Studies and the Realities of America," at the national American Studies Association Convention, San Antonio, Texas, November 8, 1975. For helpful responses to earlier versions of the essay, I wish to thank students and faculty in American Studies at the University of Minnesota, the University of Maryland, the University of Iowa, and the University of New Mexico, my students in Humanities 180 at San Diego State University, and—most basically—my graduate student colleagues in American Studies 501 at Case Western Reserve University, who first requested a course offering them historical perspective on the movement. I wish also to thank Robert Wheeler, Cecil Tate, John Caughey, Jay Mechling, Stephen Brobeck, Linda Kirby, Richard Reinitz, Karen Lystra, Robert Corrigan, Sheldon Harris, Susan Hanson, Gordon Kelly, Myron Lounsbury, Matthew Whalen, and Harry Stout for critical readings of the essay in draft. I also wish to thank Pearl Leopard for deciphering my chicken tracks in typing several versions of this essay. Mrs. Leopard deserves the heartfelt thanks of an inveterate reviser.

COMMENTARY

Jay Mechling

Gene Wise had a knack for presenting the most radical ideas in the gentlest guise. He understood from the outset the utopian impulses and possibilities in the American studies "movement," and his every act explored or tested those possibilities. Read his description (in the now-famous 1970 special issue of the *American Quarterly [AQ]* on American studies departments and programs) of the Raymond College experiment at the University of the Pacific and you will find a clear, frank analysis of those possibilities. He moved on to help revitalize the American studies programs at Case Western Reserve University (1969–77) and then at the University of Maryland (1977–83) until his untimely death. He consorted with members of the Radical Caucus (eventually renamed the Connections Collective) but also moved comfortably in the halls of university administration.

His book, *American Historical Explanations: A Strategy for Grounded Inquiry* (Homewood, Ill.: Dorsey, 1973), both unmasks the ideological underpinnings of historians' practices and proposes what we might now call a post-positivist approach to historical narrative and explanation, based on Kenneth Burke's dramatism. By 1975 he was ready to turn his culture criticism back onto the movement in which he felt simultaneously so much the insider and so much the outsider. He presented the "Paradigm Dramas" essay first at the 1975 meeting of the American Studies Association in San Antonio, then refined the piece until its appearance in 1979 as the centerpiece of the *AQ* issue featuring the Bibliography Committee's special "Thirty-Year Retrospective" on the American studies movement (for which he was guest editor). That same year his essay "Some Elementary Axioms for an American Culture Studies" appeared in *Prospects,* and both essays soon became required reading in American studies graduate courses across the country.

What is so quietly radical about this essay?

One of the most valuable of the American intellectual traditions to

Gene Wise, "'Paradigm Dramas' in American Studies: A Cultural and Institutional History of the Movement," originally appeared in *American Quarterly* 31, no. 3 (1979), come out of the turmoil of the 1960s was "the reflexive turn" in most of the culture studies disciplines. An aspect of "the linguistic turn" (as post-positivist philosophers have come to call it), the reflexive turn made the intellectual disciplines themselves—in all their personal, institutional, and cultural dimensions—the objects of analysis. Thomas Kuhn's *The Structure of Scientific Revolutions* (Chicago: University of Chicago Press, 1962) was the exemplar for much of this work. We saw anthropologists begin "studying up" (as Laura Nader put it in Dell Hymes's collection, *Reinventing Anthropology* [New York: Pantheon Books, 1972]) and, eventually, taking apart their own rhetorical practices (as in the essays in James Clifford and George Marcus's collection, *Writing Culture* [Berkeley: University of California Press, 1986]). We watched sociologists of knowledge turn their social constructionist ideas back upon themselves to write "the sociology of sociology." Literary critics began writing meta-criticism; an old American studies approach became reinvented as the "new historicism," and critics unpacked the social construction of literary "canons." Historians became even more attuned to the ways ideology enters the writing of history. The interdisciplinary project called "the rhetoric of inquiry" focused the rhetorical critic's methods on the role of narratives in the construction of "knowledge" in a variety of disciplines, including those that make claims to being scientific and, supposedly, immune to the influences of cultural ideas and narrative conventions.

If done well, the reflexive turn assaults power and hierarchy within the academic world; it unmasks privileged positions, reminding us that what we take for granted is merely contingent or, worse, planned by those who do not have our best interests at heart. Wise's "Paradigm Dramas" essay courts this danger for the good of the American studies movement. Early in the essay, Wise explains that he is writing the cultural and institutional history of American studies through close examination of four "representative acts," by which he means "something which dramatizes inherent *possibilities* in a cultural situation," and as readers we see that Wise's essay is itself another one of those representative acts ripe with possibilities. Like most utopian, radical culture critics, he believes that we are better off—freer, really—knowing as much as possible about the forms that determine our thoughts and actions. His first sentence in the essay says it simply: "American Studies recapitulates America in revealing ways." This may not be welcome news to culture critics; it resembles telling a woman "you're just like your mother" or a man "you're just like your father." These can be fighting words.

So Wise wanted the American studies community to be relentlessly reflexive, to understand its history, its present, and the trajectories of its possible futures in order to make for better culture criticism but also to make for a better society. Both of his 1979 essays, the "Paradigm Dramas" and the "Axioms" essays, invite American studies practitioners to help write the history of the movement, to articulate as best they can the assumptions and conditions governing their practices, and to be alert always to the ways we might be deceiving ourselves or, worse, harming others.

The "Paradigm Dramas" essay represents a glimpse at a larger project in the making, a project Wise did not live to complete. He was quite prescient in predicting some important trends in American studies, including "a pluralistic rather than a wholistic approach to American culture," the "rediscovery of the particular in American culture," the repudiation of exceptionalism, and the rise of a comparative, cross-cultural approach. In his view that the best culture criticism was being written by journalists and by "rogue academicians turned journalists," he anticipated the national conversation about the condition of the "public intellectual" in American life. In making this point he was opening a utopian possibility—why shouldn't the academics in American studies be writing acute culture criticism for the general audience?

I wish he had lived to see the fiftieth anniversary of the founding of the *American Quarterly,* had lived to expand his "Paradigm Dramas" essay to include several new "representative acts" since 1979. What would they be, I wonder? Certainly he would make much of the demise of the Department of American Civilization at the University of Pennsylvania, an unfortunate lesson in the ways personalities and institutions help determine the history of a discipline. He would be surprised to discover that the social sciences still have not informed American studies as much as they should. I imagine he would appreciate the utopian possibilities in the rise of virtual intellectual communities on the Internet, but he would also warn us against deceiving ourselves into thinking that the seemingly radical democracy of the Internet amounts to real power in cultural institutions, including the university. He would find some representative act to stand for the shift in university personnel practices and the ways some graduate students, tenured professors, and itinerant and other part-time teachers have turned their culture criticism upon these practices, attempting to follow C. Wright Mills's dictum that the goal of the intellectual should be to "connect private troubles with public issues."

Enough speculation. We might never see a comprehensive institutional and cultural history of American studies, though the ASA presidential addresses by Michael Cowan, Allen Davis, Linda Kerber, Alice Kessler-Harris, Paul Lauter, and others (all published subsequently in the *AQ*) provide sparkling pieces of a history that might, after all, be written collectively by the accumulation of numerous acts struggling to make some sense of our experiences (the same motive that animated Parrington and Miller, says Wise). Rereading this essay (or reading it for the first time, as will be true for some readers) even counts as one of those acts, but only if the reader takes away at least some sense of the obligation Wise urged upon us.

NINA BAYM

Melodramas of Beset Manhood:
How Theories of American Fiction
Exclude Women Authors

THIS PAPER IS ABOUT AMERICAN LITERARY CRITICISM RATHER THAN American literature. It proceeds from the assumption that we never read American literature directly or freely, but always through the perspective allowed by theories. Theories account for the inclusion and exclusion of texts in anthologies, and theories account for the way we read them. My concern is with the fact that the theories controlling our reading of American literature have led to the exclusion of women authors from the canon.

Let me use my own practice as a case in point. In 1977 there was published a collection of essays on images of women in major British and American literature, to which I contributed.[1] The American field was divided chronologically among six critics, with four essays covering literature written prior to World War II. Taking seriously the charge that we were to focus only on the major figures, the four of us—working quite independently of each other—selected altogether only four women writers. Three of these were from the earliest period, a period which predates the novel: the poet Anne Bradstreet and the two diarists Mary Rowlandson and Sarah Kemble Knight. The fourth was Emily Dickinson. For the period between 1865 and 1940 no women were cited at all. The message that we—who were taking women as our subject—conveyed was clear: there have been almost no major women writers in America; the major novelists have all been men.

Now, when we wrote our essays we were not undertaking to reread all American literature and make our own decisions as to who the major authors were. That is the point: we accepted the going canon of major authors. As late as 1977, that canon did not include any women novelists.

[1] Marlene Springer, ed., *What Manner of Woman: Essays on English and American Life and Literature* (New York: New York Univ. Press, 1977).

Yet, the critic who goes beyond what is accepted and tries to look at the totality of literary production in America quickly discovers that women authors have been active since the earliest days of settlement. Commercially and numerically they have probably dominated American literature since the middle of the nineteenth century. As long ago as 1854, Nathaniel Hawthorne complained to his publisher about the "damn'd mob of scribbling women" whose writings—he fondly imagined—were diverting the public from his own.

Names and figures help make this dominance clear. In the years between 1774 and 1799—from the calling of the First Continental Congress to the close of the eighteenth century—a total of thirty-eight original works of fiction were published in this country.[2] Nine of these, appearing pseudonymously or anonymously, have not yet been attributed to any author. The remaining twenty-nine are the work of eighteen individuals, of whom four are women. One of these women, Susannah Rowson, wrote six of them, or more than a fifth of the total. Her most popular work, *Charlotte* (also known as *Charlotte Temple*), was printed three times in the decade it was published, nineteen times between 1800 and 1810, and eighty times by the middle of the nineteenth century. A novel by a second of the four women, Hannah Foster, was called *The Coquette* and had thirty editions by mid-nineteenth century. *Uncle Tom's Cabin,* by a woman, is probably the all-time biggest seller in American history. A woman, Mrs. E.D.E.N. Southworth, was probably the most widely read novelist in the nineteenth century. How is it possible for a critic or historian of American literature to leave these books, and these authors, out of the picture?

I see three partial explanations for the critical invisibility of the many active women authors in America. The first is simple bias. The critic does not like the idea of women as writers, does not believe that women can be writers, and hence does not see them even when they are right before his eyes. His theory or his standards may well be nonsexist but his practice is not. Certainly, an *a priori* resistance to recognizing women authors as serious writers has functioned powerfully in the mindset of a number of influential critics. One can amusingly demonstrate the inconsistencies between standard and practice in such critics, show how their minds slip out of gear when they are confronted with a woman author. But this is only a partial explanation.

A second possibility is that, in fact, women have not written the kind of work that we call "excellent," for reasons that are connected with their gender although separable from it. This is a serious possibility. For exam-

[2] See Lyle Wright, *American Fiction 1774–1850* (San Marino, Calif.: Huntington Library Press, 1969).

ple, suppose we required a dense texture of classical allusion in all works that we called excellent. Then, the restriction of a formal classical education to men would have the effect of restricting authorship of excellent literature to men. Women would not have written excellent literature because social conditions hindered them. The reason, though gender-connected, would not be gender per se.

The point here is that the notion of the artist, or of excellence, has efficacy in a given time and reflects social realities. The idea of "good" literature is not only a personal preference, it is also a cultural preference. We can all think of species of women's literature that do not aim in any way to achieve literary excellence as society defines it: e.g., the "Harlequin Romances." Until recently, only a tiny proportion of literary women aspired to artistry and literary excellence in the terms defined by their own culture. There tended to be a sort of immediacy in the ambitions of literary women leading them to professionalism rather than artistry, by choice as well as by social pressure and opportunity. The gender-related restrictions were really operative, and the responsible critic cannot ignore them. But again, these restrictions are only partly explanatory.

There are, finally, I believe, gender-related restrictions that do not arise out of cultural realities contemporary with the writing woman, but out of later critical theories. These theories may follow naturally from cultural realities pertinent to their own time, but they impose their concerns anachronistically, after the fact, on an earlier period. If one accepts current theories of American literature, one accepts as a consequence—perhaps not deliberately but nevertheless inevitably—a literature that is essentially male. This is the partial explanation that I shall now develop.

Let us begin where the earliest theories of American literature begin, with the hypothesis that American literature is to be judged less by its form than its content. Traditionally, one ascertains literary excellence by comparing a writer's work with standards of performance that have been established by earlier authors, where formal mastery and innovation are paramount. But from its historical beginnings, American literary criticism has assumed that literature produced in this nation would have to be ground-breaking, equal to the challenge of the new nation, and completely original. Therefore, it could not be judged by referring it back to earlier achievements. The earliest American literary critics began to talk about the "most American" work rather than the "best" work because they knew no way to find out the best other than by comparing American to British writing. Such a criticism struck them as both unfair and unpatriotic. We had thrown off the political shackles of England; it would not do for us to be servile in our literature. Until a tradition of American literature developed its own inherent forms, the early critic looked for a standard of Americanness rather than a standard of excellence. Inevitably, perhaps, it came to seem that the quality of "Americanness," whatever it might be, *constituted* literary excellence for American authors. Beginning as a nationalistic enterprise, American literary criticism and theory has retained a nationalist orientation to this day.

Of course, the idea of Americanness is even more vulnerable to subjectivity than the idea of the best. When they speak of "most American," critics seldom mean the statistically most representative or most typical, the most read or the most sold. They have some qualitative essence in mind, and frequently their work develops as an explanation of this idea of "American" rather than a description and evaluation of selected authors. The predictable recurrence of the term "America" or "American" in works of literary criticism treating a dozen or fewer authors indicates that the critic has chosen his authors on the basis of their conformity to his idea of what is truly American. For examples: *American Renaissance, The Romance in America, Symbolism and American Literature, Form and Fable in American Fiction, The American Adam, The American Novel and its Tradition, The Place of Style in American Literature* (a subtitle), *The Poetics of American Fiction* (another subtitle). But an idea of what is American is no more than an idea, needing demonstration. The critic all too frequently ends up using his chosen authors as demonstrations of Americanness, arguing through them to his definition.

So Marius Bewley explains in *The Eccentric Design* that "for the American artist there was no social surface responsive to his touch. The scene was crude, even beyond successful satire," but later, in a concluding chapter titled "The Americanness of the American Novel," he agrees that "this 'tradition' as I have set it up here has no room for the so-called realists and naturalists."[3] F. O. Matthiessen, whose *American Renaissance* enshrines five authors, explains that "the one common denominator of my five writers, uniting even Hawthorne and Whitman, was their devotion to the possibilities of democracy."[4] The jointly written *Literary History of the United States* proclaims in its "address to the reader" that American literary history "will be a history of the books of the great and the near-great writers in a literature which is most revealing when studied as a by-product of American experience."[5] And Joel Porte announces confidently in *The Romance in America* that "students of American literature . . . have provided a solid theoretical basis for establishing that the rise and growth of fiction in this country is dominated by

---

[3] Marius Bewley, *The Eccentric Design* (New York: Columbia Univ. Press, 1963), 15, 291.
[4] F. O. Matthiessen, *American Renaissance* (New York: Oxford Univ. Press, 1941), ix.
[5] Robert E. Spiller et al., eds., *Literary History of the United States* (New York: Macmillan, 1959), xix.

our authors' conscious adherence to a tradition of non-realistic romance sharply at variance with the broadly novelistic mainstream of English writing. When there has been disagreement among recent critics as to the contours of American fiction, it has usually disputed, not the existence *per se* of a romance tradition, but rather the question of which authors, themes, and stylistic strategies *deserve* to be placed with certainty at the heart of that tradition" (emphasis added).[6]

Before he is through, the critic has had to insist that some works in America are much more American than others, and he is as busy excluding certain writers as "un-American" as he is including others. Such a proceeding in the political arena would be extremely suspect, but in criticism it has been the method of choice. Its final result goes far beyond the conclusion that only a handful of American works are very good. *That* statement is one we could agree with, since very good work is rare in any field. But it is odd indeed to argue that only a handful of American works are really American.[7]

Despite the theoretical room for an infinite number of definitions of Americanness, critics have generally agreed on it—although the shifting canon suggests that agreement may be a matter of fad rather than fixed objective qualities.[8] First, America as a nation must be the ultimate subject of the work. The author must be writing about aspects of experience and character that are American only, setting Americans off from other people and the country from other nations. The author must be writing his story specifically to display these aspects, to meditate on them, and to derive from them some generalizations and conclusions about "the" American experience. To Matthiessen the topic is the possibilities of democracy; Sacvan Bercovitch (in *The Puritan Origins of the American Self*) finds it in American identity. Such content excludes, at one extreme, stories about universals, aspects of experience common to people in a variety of times and places—mutability, mortality, love, childhood, family, betrayal, loss. Innocence versus experience is an admissable theme *only* if innocence is the essence of the American character, for example.

But at the other extreme, the call for an overview of America means that detailed, circumstantial portrayals of some aspect of American life are also, peculiarly, inappropriate: stories of wealthy New Yorkers, Yugoslavian immigrants, southern rustics. Jay B. Hubbell rather ingratiat-

---

[6] Joel Porte, *The Romance in America* (Middletown, Conn.: Wesleyan Univ. Press, 1969), ix.

[7] A good essay on this topic is William C. Spengemann's "What is American Literature?" *CentR*, 22 (1978), 119–38.

[8] See Jay B. Hubbell, *Who Are the Major American Authors?* (Durham, N. C.: Duke Univ. Press, 1972).

ingly admits as much when he writes, "in both my teaching and my research I had a special interest in literature as a reflection of American life and thought. This circumstance may explain in part why I found it difficult to appreciate the merits of the expatriates and why I was slow in doing justice to some of the New Critics. I was repelled by the sordid subject matter found in some of the novels written by Dreiser, Dos Passos, Faulkner, and some others."[9] Richard Poirier writes that "the books which in my view constitute a distinctive American tradition . . . resist within their pages forces of environment that otherwise dominate the world" and he distinguishes this kind from "the fiction of Mrs. Wharton, Dreiser, or Howells."[10] The *Literary History of the United States* explains that "historically, [Edith Wharton] is likely to survive as the memorialist of a dying aristocracy" (1211). And so on. These exclusions abound in all the works which form the stable core of American literary criticism at this time.

Along with Matthiessen, the most influential exponent of this exclusive Americanness is Lionel Trilling, and his work has particular applicability because it concentrates on the novel form. Here is a famous passage from his 1940 essay, "Reality in America," in which Trilling is criticizing Vernon Parrington's selection of authors in *Main Currents in American Thought:*

> A culture is not a flow, nor even a confluence; the form of its existence is struggle—or at least debate—it is nothing if not a dialectic. And in any culture there are likely to be certain artists who contain a large part of the dialectic within themselves, their meaning and power lying in their contradictions; they contain within themselves, it may be said, the very essence of the culture. To throw out Poe because he cannot be conveniently fitted into a theory of American culture . . . to find his gloom to be merely personal and eccentric . . . as Hawthorne's was . . . to judge Melville's response to American life to be less noble than that of Bryant or of Greeley, to speak of Henry James as an escapist . . . this is not merely to be mistaken in aesthetic judgment. Rather it is to examine without attention and from the point of view of a limited and essentially arrogant conception of reality the documents which are in some respects the most suggestive testimony to what America was and is, and of course to get no answer from them.[11]

Trilling's immediate purpose is to exclude Greeley and Bryant from the list of major authors and to include Poe, Melville, Hawthorne, and James. We probably share Trilling's aesthetic judgment. But note that he does

---

[9] Ibid., 335–36.
[10] Richard Poirier, *A World Elsewhere: The Place of Style in American Literature* (New York: Oxford Univ. Press, 1966), 5.
[11] Lionel Trilling, *The Liberal Imagination* (New York: Anchor, 1950), 7–9.

not base his judgment on aesthetic grounds; indeed, he dismisses aesthetic judgment with the word "merely." He argues that Parrington has picked the wrong artists because he doesn't understand the culture. Culture is his real concern.

But what makes Trilling's notion of culture more valid than Parrington's? Trilling really has no argument; he resorts to such value-laden rhetoric as "a limited and essentially arrogant conception of reality" precisely because he cannot objectively establish his version of culture over Parrington's. For the moment, there are two significant conclusions to draw from this quotation. First, the disagreement is over the nature of our culture. Second, there is no disagreement over the value of literature—it is valued as a set of "documents" which provide "suggestive testimony to what America was and is."

One might think that an approach like this which is subjective, circular, and in some sense nonliterary or even antiliterary would not have had much effect. But clearly Trilling was simply carrying on a longstanding tradition of searching for cultural essence, and his essays gave the search a decided and influential direction toward the notion of cultural essence as some sort of tension. Trilling succeeded in getting rid of Bryant and Greeley, and his choice of authors is still dominant. They all turn out— and not by accident—to be white, middle-class, male, of Anglo-Saxon derivation or at least from an ancestry which had settled in this country before the big waves of immigration which began around the middle of the nineteenth century. In every case, however, the decision made by these men to become professional authors pushed them slightly to one side of the group to which they belonged. This slight alienation permitted them to belong, and yet not to belong, to the so-called "mainstream." These two aspects of their situation—their membership in the dominant middle-class white Anglo-Saxon group, and their modest alienation from it—defined their boundaries, enabling them to "contain within themselves" the "contradictions" that, in Trilling's view, constitute the "very essence of the culture." I will call the literature they produced, which Trilling assesses so highly, a "consensus criticism of the consensus."

This idea plainly excludes many groups but it might not seem necessarily to exclude women. In fact, nineteenth-century women authors were overwhelmingly white, middle-class, and anglo-Saxon in origin. Something more than what is overtly stated by Trilling (and others cited below) is added to exclude them. What critics have done is to assume, for reasons shortly to be expounded, that the women writers invariably represented the consensus, rather than the criticism of it; to assume that their gender made them part of the consensus in a way that prevented them from partaking in the criticism. The presence of these women and their works is acknowledged in literary theory and history as an impediment and obstacle, that which the essential American literature had to criticize as its chief task.

So, in his lively and influential book of 1960, *Love and Death in the American Novel,* Leslie Fiedler describes women authors as creators of the "flagrantly bad best-seller" against which "our best fictionists"—all male—have had to struggle for "their integrity and their livelihoods." [12] And, in a 1978 reader's introduction to an edition of Charles Brockden Brown's *Wieland,* Sydney J. Krause and S. W. Reid write as follows:

> What it meant for Brown personally, and belles lettres in America historically, that he should have decided to write professionally is a story unto itself. Americans simply had no great appetite for serious literature in the early decades of the Republic—certainly nothing of the sort with which they devoured . . . the ubiquitous melodramas of beset womanhood, "tales of truth," like Susanna Rowson's *Charlotte Temple* and Hannah Foster's *The Coquette.* [13]

There you see what has happened to the woman writer. She has entered literary history as the enemy. The phrase "tales of truth" is put in quotes by the critics, as though to cast doubt on the very notion that a "melodrama of beset womanhood" could be either true or important. At the same time, ironically, they are proposing for our serious consideration, as a candidate for intellectually engaging literature, a highly melodramatic novel with an improbable plot, inconsistent characterizations, and excesses of style that have posed tremendous problems for all students of Charles Brockden Brown. But, by this strategy it becomes possible to begin major American fiction historically with male rather than female authors. The certainty here that stories about women could not contain the essence of American culture means that the matter of American experience is inherently male. And this makes it highly unlikely that American women would write fiction encompassing such experience. I would suggest that the theoretical model of a story which may become the vehicle of cultural essence is: "a melodrama of beset manhood." This melodrama is presented in a fiction which, as we'll later see, can be taken as representative of the author's literary experience, his struggle for integrity and livelihood against flagrantly bad best-sellers written by women. Personally beset in a way that epitomizes the tensions of our culture, the male author produces his melodramatic testimony to our culture's essence—so the theory goes.

---

[12] Leslie Fiedler, *Love and Death in the American Novel* (New York: Criterion Books, 1960), 93.

[13] Charles Brockden Brown, *Wieland,* ed. Sydney J. Krause and S. W. Reid (Kent, Ohio: Kent State Univ. Press, 1978), xii.

Remember that the search for cultural essence demands a relatively uncircumstantial kind of fiction, one which concentrates on national universals (if I may be pardoned the paradox). This search has identified a sort of nonrealistic narrative, a romance, a story free to catch an essential, idealized American character, to intensify his essence and convey his experience in a way that ignores details of an actual social milieu. This nonrealistic or antisocial aspect of American fiction is noted—as a fault—by Trilling in a 1947 essay, "Manners, Morals, and the Novel." Curiously, Trilling here attacks the same group of writers he had rescued from Parrington in "Reality in America." But, never doubting that his selection represents "the" American authors, he goes ahead with the task that really interests him—criticizing the culture through its representative authors. He writes:

> The novel in America diverges from its classic [i.e., British] intention which . . . is the investigation of the problem of reality beginning in the social field. The fact is that American writers of genius have not turned their minds to society. Poe and Melville were quite apart from it; the reality they sought was only tangential to society. Hawthorne was acute when he insisted that he did not write novels but romances—he thus expressed his awareness of the lack of social texture in his work. . . . In America in the nineteenth century, Henry James was alone in knowing that to scale the moral and aesthetic heights in the novel one had to use the ladder of social observation.[14]

Within a few years after publication of Trilling's essay, a group of Americanists took its rather disapproving description of American novelists and found in this nonrealism or romanticism the essentially American quality they had been seeking. The idea of essential Americanness then developed in such influential works of criticism as *Virgin Land* by Henry Nash Smith (1950), *Symbolism and American Literature* by Charles Feidelson (1953), *The American Adam* by R. W. B. Lewis (1955), *The American Novel and its Tradition* by Richard Chase (1957), and *Form and Fable in American Fiction* by Daniel G. Hoffman (1961). These works, and others like them, were of sufficiently high critical quality, and sufficiently like each other, to compel assent to the picture of American literature that they presented. They used sophisticated New Critical close-reading techniques to identify a myth of America which had nothing to do with the classical fictionist's task of chronicling probable people in recognizable social situations.

The myth narrates a confrontation of the American individual, the pure American self divorced from specific social circumstances, with the promise offered by the idea of America. This promise is the deeply romantic one that in this new land, untrammeled by history and social accident, a

[14] *The Liberal Imagination,* 206.

person will be able to achieve complete self-definition. Behind this promise is the assurance that individuals come before society, that they exist in some meaningful sense prior to, and apart from, societies in which they happen to find themselves. The myth also holds that, as something artificial and secondary to human nature, society exerts an unmitigatedly destructive pressure on individuality. To depict it at any length would be a waste of artistic time; and there is only one way to relate it to the individual—as an adversary.

One may believe all this and yet look in vain for a way to tell a believable story that could free the protagonist from society or offer the promise of such freedom, because nowhere on earth do individuals live apart from social groups. But in America, given the original reality of large tracts of wilderness, the idea seems less a fantasy, more possible in reality or at least more believable in literary treatment. Thus it is that the essential quality of America comes to reside in its unsettled wilderness and the opportunities that such a wilderness offers to the individual as the medium on which he may inscribe, unhindered, his own destiny and his own nature.

As the nineteenth century wore on, and settlements spread across the wilderness, the struggle of the individual against society became more and more central to the myth; where, let's say, Thoreau could leave in Chapter I of *Walden*, Huckleberry Finn has still not made his break by the end of Chapter XLII (the conclusion) of the book that bears his name. Yet, one finds a struggle against society as early as the earliest Leatherstocking tale (*The Pioneers*, 1823). In a sense, this supposed promise of America has always been known to be delusory. Certainly by the twentieth century the myth has been transmuted into an avowedly hopeless quest for unencumbered space (*On the Road*), or the evocation of flight for its own sake (*Rabbit, Run* and *Henderson the Rain King*), or as pathetic acknowledgment of loss—e.g., the close of *The Great Gatsby* where the narrator Nick Carraway summons up "the old island here that flowered once for Dutch sailors' eyes—a fresh, green breast of the new world . . . the last and greatest of all human dreams" where man is "face to face for the last time in history with something commensurate to his capacity for wonder."

We are all very familiar with this myth of America in its various fashionings and owing to the selective vision that has presented this myth to us as the whole story, many of us are unaware of how much besides it has been created by literary Americans. Keeping our eyes on this myth, we need to ask whether anything about it puts it outside women's reach. In one sense, and on one level, the answer is no. The subject of this myth is supposed to stand for human nature, and if men and women alike share a common human nature, then all can respond to its values, its promises, and its frustrations. And in fact as a teacher I find women students responsive to the myth insofar as its protagonist is concerned. It is true, of course, that in order to represent some kind of believable flight into the wilderness, one must select a protagonist with a certain believable mobility, and mobility has until recently been a male prerogative in our society. Nevertheless, relatively few men are actually mobile to the extent demanded by the story, and hence the story is really not much more vicarious, in this regard, for women than for men. The problem is thus not to be located in the protagonist or his gender per se; the problem is with the other participants in his story—the entrammelling society and the promising landscape. For both of these are depicted in unmistakably feminine terms, and this gives a sexual character to the protagonist's story which does, indeed, limit its applicability to women. And this sexual definition has melodramatic, misogynist implications.

In these stories, the encroaching, constricting, destroying society is represented with particular urgency in the figure of one or more women. There are several possible reasons why this might be so. It seems to be a fact of life that we all—women and men alike—experience social conventions and responsibilities and obligations first in the persons of women, since women are entrusted by society with the task of rearing young children. Not until he reaches mid-adolescence does the male connect up with other males whose primary task is socialization; but at about this time—if he is heterosexual—his lovers and spouses become the agents of a permanent socialization and domestication. Thus, although women are not the source of social power, they are experienced as such. And although not all women are engaged in socializing the young, the young do not encounter women who are not. So from the point of view of the young man, the only kind of women who exist are entrappers and domesticators.

For heterosexual man, these socializing women are also the locus of powerful attraction. First, because everybody has social and conventional instincts; second, because his deepest emotional attachments are to women. This attraction gives urgency and depth to the protagonist's rejection of society. To do it, he must project onto the woman those attractions that he feels, and cast her in the melodramatic role of temptress, antagonist, obstacle—a character whose mission in life seems to be to ensnare him and deflect him from life's important purposes of self-discovery and self-assertion. (A Puritan would have said: from communion with Divinity.) As Richard Chase writes in *The American Novel and its Tradition,* "The myth requires celibacy." It is partly against his own sexual urges that the male must struggle, and so he perceives the socializing and domesticating woman as a doubly powerful threat; for this reason, Chase goes on to state, neither Cooper nor "any other American novelist until the age of James and Edith Wharton'' could imagine ''a fully developed woman of sexual age.''[15] Yet in making this statement, Chase is talking about his myth rather than Cooper's. (One should add that, for a homosexual male, the demands of society that he link himself for life to a woman make for a particularly misogynist version of this aspect of the American myth, for the hero is propelled not by a rejected attraction, but by true revulsion.) Both heterosexual and homosexual versions of the myth cooperate with the hero's perceptions and validate the notion of woman as threat.

Such a portrayal of women is likely to be uncongenial, if not basically incomprehensible, to a woman. It is not likely that women will write books in which women play this part; and it is by no means the case that most novels by American men reproduce such a scheme. Even major male authors prominent in the canon have other ways of depicting women; e.g., Cooper's *Pathfinder* and *The Pioneers,* Hemingway's *For Whom the Bell Tolls,* Fitzgerald's *The Beautiful and The Damned.* The novels of Henry James and William Dean Howells pose a continual challenge to the masculinist bias of American critical theory. And in one work—*The Scarlet Letter*—a ''fully developed woman of sexual age'' who is the novel's protagonist has been admitted into the canon, but only by virtue of strenuous critical revisions of the text that remove Hester Prynne from the center of the novel and make her subordinate to Arthur Dimmesdale.

So Leslie Fiedler, in *Love and Death in the American Novel,* writes this of *The Scarlet Letter:*

> It is certainly true, in terms of the plot, that Chillingworth drives the minister toward confession and penance, while Hester would have lured him to evasion and flight. But this means, for all of Hawthorne's equivocations, that the eternal feminine does not draw us on toward grace, rather that the woman promises only madness and damnation. . . . [Hester] is the female temptress of Puritan mythology, but also, though sullied, the secular madonna of sentimental Protestantism (236).

In the rhetorical ''us'' Fiedler presumes that all readers are men, that the novel is an act of communication among and about males. His characterization of Hester as one or another myth or image makes it impossible for the novel to be in any way about Hester as a human being. Giving the novel so highly specific a gender reference, Fiedler makes it inaccessible to women and limits its reference to men in comparison to the issues that Hawthorne was treating in the story. Not the least of these issues was, precisely, the human reference of a woman's tale.

Amusingly, then, since he has produced this warped reading, Fiedler goes on to condemn the novel for its sexual immaturity. *The Scarlet*

[15] Richard Chase, *The American Novel and its Tradition* (New York: Anchor, 1957), 55, 64.

Letter is integrated into Fiedler's general exposure of the inadequacies of the American male—inadequacies which, as his treatment of Hester shows, he holds women responsible for. The melodrama here is not Hawthorne's, but Fiedler's—the American critic's melodrama of beset manhood. Of course, women authors as major writers are notably and inevitably absent from Fiedler's chronicle.

In fact many books by women—including such major authors as Edith Wharton, Ellen Glasgow, and Willa Cather—project a version of the particular myth we are speaking of but cast the main character as a woman. When a woman takes the central role, it follows naturally that the socializer and domesticator will be a man. This is the situation in *The Scarlet Letter*. Hester is beset by the male reigning oligarchy and by Dimmesdale, who passively tempts her and is responsible for fathering her child. Thereafter, Hester (as the myth requires) elects celibacy, as do many heroines in versions of this myth by women: Thea in Cather's *The Song of the Lark,* Dorinda in Glasgow's *Barren Ground,* Anna Leath in Wharton's *The Reef.* But what is written in the criticism about these celibate women? They are said to be untrue to the imperatives of their gender, which require marriage, childbearing, domesticity. Instead of being read as a woman's version of the myth, such novels are read as stories of the frustration of female nature. Stories of female frustration are not perceived as commenting on, or containing, the essence of our culture, and so we don't find them in the canon.

So the role of entrapper and impediment in the melodrama of beset manhood is reserved for women. Also, the role of the beckoning wilderness, the attractive landscape, is given a deeply feminine quality. Landscape is deeply imbued with female qualities, as society is; but where society is menacing and destructive, landscape is compliant and supportive. It has the attributes simultaneously of a virginal bride and a nonthreatening mother; its female qualities are articulated with respect to a male angle of vision: what can nature do for me, asks the hero, what can it give me?

Of course, nature has been feminine and maternal from time immemorial, and Henry Nash Smith's *Virgin Land* picks up a timeless archetype in its title. The basic nature of the image leads one to forget about its potential for imbuing any story in which it is used with sexual meanings, and the gender implications of a female landscape have only recently begun to be studied. Recently, Annette Kolodny has studied the traditional canon from this approach.[16] She theorizes that the hero, fleeing a society that has been imagined as feminine, then imposes on nature some

[16] Annette Kolodny, *The Lay of the Land* (Chapel Hill: Univ. of North Carolina Press, 1975).

ideas of women which, no longer subject to the correcting influence of real-life experience, become more and more fantastic. The fantasies are infantile, concerned with power, mastery, and total gratification: the all-nurturing mother, the all-passive bride. Whether one accepts all the Freudian or Jungian implications of her argument, one cannot deny the way in which heroes of American myth turn to nature as sweetheart and nurture, anticipating the satisfaction of all desires through her and including among these the desires for mastery and power. A familiar passage that captures these ideas is one already quoted: Carraway's evocation of the "fresh green breast" of the new world. The fresh greenness is the virginity that offers itself to the sailors, but the breast promises maternal solace and delight. *The Great Gatsby* contains our two images of women: while Carraway evokes the impossible dream of a maternal landscape, he blames a nonmaternal woman, the socialite Daisy, for her failure to satisfy Gatsby's desires. The true adversary, of course, is Tom Buchanan, but he is hidden, as it were, behind Daisy's skirts.

I have said that women are not likely to cast themselves as antagonists in a man's story; they are even less likely, I suggest, to cast themselves as virgin land. The lack of fit between their own experience and the fictional role assigned to them is even greater in the second instance than in the first. If women portray themselves as brides or mothers it will not be in terms of the mythic landscape. If a woman puts a female construction on nature—as she certainly must from time to time, given the archetypal female resonance of the image—she is likely to write of it as more active, or to stress its destruction or violation. On the other hand, she might adjust the heroic myth to her own psyche by making nature out to be male—as, for example, Willa Cather seems to do in *O Pioneers!* But a violated landscape or a male nature does not fit the essential American pattern as critics have defined it, and hence these literary images occur in an obscurity that criticism cannot see. Thus, one has an almost classic example of the "double bind." When the woman writer creates a story that conforms to the expected myth, it is not recognized for what it is because of a superfluous sexual specialization in the myth as it is entertained in the critics' minds. (Needless to say, many male novelists also entertain this version of the myth, and do not find the masculinist bias with which they imbue it to be superfluous. It is possible that some of these novelists, especially those who write in an era in which literary criticism is a powerful influence, have formed their ideas from their reading in criticism.) But if she does not conform to the myth, she is understood to be writing minor or trivial literature.

Two remaining points can be treated much more briefly. The description of the artist and of the act of writing which emerges when the critic uses the basic American story as his starting point contains many attributes of the basic story itself. This description raises the exclusion of women to a more abstract, theoretical—and perhaps more pernicious—level. Fundamentally, the idea is that the artist writing a story of this essential American kind is engaging in a task very much like the one performed by his mythic hero. In effect, the artist writing his narrative is imitating the mythic encounter of hero and possibility in the safe confines of his study; or, reversing the temporal order, one might see that mythic encounter of hero and possibility as a projection of the artist's situation.

Although this idea is greatly in vogue at the moment, it has a history. Here, for example, is Richard Chase representing the activity of writing in metaphors of discovery and exploration, as though the writer were a hero in the landscape: "The American novel has usually seemed content to explore . . . the remarkable and in some ways unexampled territories of life in the New World and to reflect its anomalies and dilemmas. It has . . . wanted . . . to discover a new place and a new state of mind."[17] Richard Poirier takes the idea further:

> The most interesting American books are an image of the creation of America itself. . . . They carry the metaphoric burden of a great dream of freedom—of the expansion of national consciousness into the vast spaces of a continent and the absorption of those spaces into ourselves. . . . The classic American writers try through style temporarily to free the hero (and the reader) from systems, to free them from the pressures of time, biology, economics, and from the social forces which are ultimately the undoing of American heroes and quite often of their creators. . . . The strangeness of American fiction has . . . to do . . . with the environment [the novelist] tries to create for his hero, usually his surrogate.[18]

The implicit union of creator and protagonist is made specific and overt at the end of Poirier's passage here. The ideas of Poirier and Chase, and others like them, are summed up in an anthology called *Theories of American Literature,* edited by Donald M. Kartiganer and Malcolm A. Griffith.[19] The editors write, "It is as if with each new work our writers feel they must invent again the complete world of a literary form." (Yet, the true subject is not what the writers feel, but what the critics think they feel.) "Such a condition of nearly absolute freedom to create has appeared to our authors both as possibility and liability, an utter openness suggesting limitless opportunity for the imagination, or an enormous vacancy in which they create from nothing. For some it has meant an oppor-

[17] Chase, *American Novel,* 5.
[18] Poirier, *A World Elsewhere,* 3, 5, 9.
[19] Donald M. Kartiganer and Malcolm A. Griffith, eds., *Theories of American Literature* (New York: Macmillan, 1962).

tunity to play Adam, to assume the role of an original namer of experience'' (4–5). One can see in this passage the transference of the American myth from the Adamic hero *in* the story, to the Adamic creator *of* the story, and the reinterpretation of the American myth as a metaphor for the American artist's situation.

This myth of artistic creation, assimilating the act of writing novels to the Adamic myth, imposes on artistic creation all the gender-based restrictions that we have already examined in that myth. The key to identifying an ''Adamic writer'' is the formal appearance, or, more precisely the *informal* appearance, of his novel. The unconventionality is interpreted as a direct representation of the open-ended experience of exploring and taming the wilderness, as well as a rejection of ''society'' as it is incorporated in conventional literary forms. There is no place for a woman author in this scheme. Her roles in the drama of creation are those allotted to her in a male melodrama: either she is to be silent, like nature; or she is the creator of conventional works, the spokesperson of society. What she might do as an innovator in her own right is not to be perceived.

In recent years, some refinements of critical theory coming from the Yale and Johns Hopkins and Columbia schools have added a new variant to the idea of creation as a male province. I quote from a 1979 book entitled *Home as Found* by Eric Sundquist. The author takes the idea that in writing a novel the artist is really writing a narrative about himself and proposes this addition:

> Writing a narrative about oneself may represent an extremity of Oedipal usurpation or identification, a bizarre act of self fathering. . . .American authors have been particularly obsessed with *fathering* a tradition of their own, with becoming their ''own sires.'' . . . The struggle . . . is central to the crisis of representation, and hence of style, that allows American authors to find in their own fantasies those of a nation and to make of those fantasies a compelling and instructive literature.[20]

These remarks derive clearly from the work of such critics as Harold Bloom, as any reader of recent critical theory will note. The point for our purpose is the facile translation of the verb ''to author'' into the verb ''to father,'' with the profound gender-restrictions of that translation unacknowledged. According to this formulation, insofar as the author writes about a character who is his surrogate—which, apparently, he always does—he is trying to become his own father.

We can scarcely deny that men think a good deal about, and are profoundly affected by, relations with their fathers. The theme of fathers and

[20] Eric Sundquist, *Home as Found* (Baltimore: Johns Hopkins Univ. Press, 1979), xviii-xix.

sons is perennial in world literature. Somewhat more spaciously, we recognize that intergenerational conflict, usually perceived from the point of view of the young, is a recurrent literary theme, especially in egalitarian cultures. Certainly, this idea involves the question of authority, and "authority" is a notion related to that of "the author." And there is some gender-specific significance involved since authority in most cultures that we know tends to be invested in adult males. But the theory has built from these useful and true observations to a restriction of literary creation to a sort of therapeutic act that can only be performed by men. If literature is the attempt to *father* oneself by the author, then every act of writing by a woman is both perverse and absurd. And, of course, it is bound to fail.

Since this particular theory of the act of writing is drawn from psychological assumptions that are not specific to American literature, it may be argued that there is no need to confine it to American authors. In fact, Harold Bloom's *Anxiety of Influence*, defining literature as a struggle between fathers and sons, or the struggle of sons to escape from their fathers, is about British literature. And so is Edward Said's book *Beginnings*, which chronicles the history of the nineteenth-century British novel as exemplification of what he calls "filiation." His discussion omits Jane Austen, George Eliot, all three Brontë sisters, Mrs. Gaskell, Mrs. Humphrey Ward—not a sign of a woman author is found in his treatment of Victorian fiction. The result is a revisionist approach to British fiction that recasts it in the accepted image of the American myth. Ironically, just at the time that feminist critics are discovering more and more important women, the critical theorists have seized upon a theory that allows the women less and less presence. This observation points up just how significantly the critic is engaged in the act of *creating* literature.

Ironically, then, one concludes that in pushing the theory of American fiction to this extreme, critics have "deconstructed" it by creating a tool with no particular American reference. In pursuit of the uniquely American, they have arrived at a place where Americanness has vanished into the depths of what is alleged to be the universal male psyche. The theory of American fiction has boiled down to the phrase in my title: a melodrama of beset manhood. What a reduction this is of the enormous variety of fiction written in this country, by both women and men! And, ironically, nothing could be further removed from Trilling's idea of the artist as embodiment of a culture. As in the working out of all theories, its weakest link has found it out and broken the chain.

Margaret McFadden

In preparation for writing this response to Nina Baym's 1981 article, "Melodramas of Beset Manhood: How Theories of American Fiction Exclude Women Authors," I went to the library to see who had cited the article in the years after it was published. A reference librarian agreed to search the database in which this information is stored. She typed in the author's name, and screen after screen of data scrolled by. "Hmmmph, prolific," she muttered. Prolific indeed. We narrowed down the hundreds of references to Baym's numerous books and articles to those pertaining to the 1981 article. "Do you want them all?" inquired the librarian. "Sure," I said cheerily and unwarily. Whoops.

Warning: do not try this at home; these services charge by the item. The cost of these citations was staggering, because there were just *so many* of them. But the expensive printout turned out to be very instructive. How could I have known that "Melodramas" had been cited in articles in many different journals, in many different languages even, on subjects ranging from American literary history to masculinity in postmodern rock music? Clearly, this article has helped to enable a quite wide range of scholarship in feminist literary criticism and in American studies more generally.

In her important 1978 study, *Woman's Fiction: A Guide to Novels by and about Women in America, 1820–1870*, Baym suggested, "It is time, perhaps . . . to re-examine the grounds upon which certain hallowed American classics have been called great."[1] In "Melodramas," Baym accepts her own challenge. She argues that male literary critics' theories about what constitutes the best of American literature—and thus what characterizes the writing worthy of inclusion in the American literary canon—have been hopelessly gender-biased. Influential critics have defined the central myth of American culture as the struggle of an (implicitly male) individual against the natural world of the wilderness and the constraints of society, both of which are coded as female. The "best" American literature, according to these critics, exemplifies this myth. Baym concludes that these theories about which stories constitute the "essence" of American culture, and the reading strategies that support these theories, combine to make it virtually impossible for fiction written by or about women to measure up. The canon thus consists of a collection of what Baym calls "melodramas of beset manhood," a national literature from which women's writing has been systematically excluded.

"Melodramas" seems to me to have been an important intervention in two intersecting scholarly developments of the 1970s and early 1980s. First, it participates in the feminist literary critical project of analyzing the hidden assumptions and the politics that have profoundly shaped the literary canon. Baym's work is in dialogue, if not always in agreement, with many other liberal feminist critics interested in the relationship between women writers and the dominant male literary tradition, as well as with those who seek to reevaluate canonical works for their gendered assumptions.[2] This article raised crucial questions that many other scholars have pursued in fruitful directions.

Second, "Melodramas" takes part in a larger 1970s critique of early works of the American studies movement, taking to task scholars like Henry Nash Smith, R. W. B. Lewis, and others who came to be lumped together by their critics as practitioners of a "myth and symbol" approach to American literature. Many scholars had come to regard these founding works as undertheorized and as offering accounts of American culture that universalized the experience of white males into "the" American experience.[3] Critics of myth and symbol scholarship called for an American studies practice which could encompass the great diversity of American experience and cultural production that their research was uncovering. For example, Baym's *Woman's Fiction* recuperates the vast literary production of antebellum white American women and takes it seriously as important in its own time and thus useful to study in ours.

Both these scholarly trends were logical outgrowths of the expansion of higher education in the 1960s, an expansion that coincided with the emergence of powerful demands for social change from the women's liberation, civil rights, labor, and antiwar movements, among others. As white women, people of color, workers, and other heretofore marginalized groups began to explore their own histories and cultures, the inadequacies and biases of disciplines structured by the concerns and values of a largely white male elite were exposed. "Melodramas" is part of this ongoing rethinking of what would constitute a more inclusive and arguably more honest American cultural history.

I suspect "Melodramas" is not read all that often these days. While it made an extremely important contribution when it was first published, its claims have come to seem limited by the white, liberal feminist assumptions implicit within it. For better or worse, feminist literary theory has gone in quite different directions from the ones Baym and her colleagues outlined in the 1970s and early 1980s. But I would argue that their work crucially enabled the remarkable growth of feminist literary criticism that continues today.[4] At the same time, work like this also helped to make a space for the exciting recent expansion of American studies, a field growing to include the concerns of ever-larger and more diverse constituencies. And that matters.

NOTES

1. Nina Baym, *Woman's Fiction: A Guide to Novels by and about Women in America, 1820–1870* (Ithaca: Cornell University Press, 1978), 15. Baym also pursued some of the questions she raised in this article in her *Novels, Readers, and Reviewers: Responses to Fiction in Antebellum America* (Ithaca: Cornell University Press, 1984). In this book, she explores what contemporary critics thought about the work of various antebellum writers, many of whom subsequently entered the canon.

2. See, e.g., the essays collected in Elaine Showalter, ed., *The New Feminist Criticism: Essays on Women, Literature, and Theory* (New York, 1985). The canon has, of course, also been extensively analyzed for the assumptions about race and class on which it is based.

3. See, e.g., Bruce Kuklick, "Myth and Symbol in American Studies," *American Quarterly* 24 (fall 1972): 435–50 (reprinted in this volume); Robert Sklar, "The Problem of an American Studies 'Philosophy': A Bibliography of New Directions," *American Quarterly* 27 (summer 1975): 245–62; Gene Wise, " 'Paradigm Dramas' in American Studies: A Cultural and Institutional History of the Movement," *American Quarterly* (bib. issue, 1979): 293–337 (reprinted in this volume); Alan Trachtenberg, "Myth and Symbol," *Massachusetts Review* 25 (winter 1984): 667–73.

4. Baym has been critical of the directions taken by feminist literary criticism in the 1980s and 1990s, arguing that a pluralist, liberal feminist approach is still the most appropriate. See "The Madwoman and Her Languages: Why I Don't Do Feminist Literary Theory," in her *Feminism and American Literary History* (New Brunswick, N.J.: Rutgers University Press, 1992), 199–213. The essay was originally published in 1984.

JANICE RADWAY

The Utopian Impulse in Popular Literature:
Gothic Romances and "Feminist" Protest

ALTHOUGH HISTORICAL STUDIES OF AMERICAN POPULAR LITERARY forms have proliferated in recent years, theories about the connection between mass-produced art and culture have not. In fact, studies characterized by considerable variety in subject matter and method are united by their common assumption that popular literature tends *only* to reconfirm cultural convention.[1] In the face of this critical consensus, however, several theorists have elaborated a qualified version of the traditional approach, suggesting that the power of popular literature's conservatism rests with its ability to disarm, even if only temporarily, actual dissatisfaction with the social institutions and forms legitimated by those conventions.

Fredric Jameson and Umberto Eco agree with the early theorists of mass culture who defined its function as the expression of the ideological status quo.[2] Their agreement is tempered nonetheless by their additional

---

[1] For a historical review of the debate over the functions and value of popular culture, see Leo Lowenthal, *Popular Culture and Society* (Englewood Cliffs, N. J.: Prentice Hall, 1961). Two useful collections of essays representing the varied ways in which popular culture's conservatism can be analyzed and assessed have been compiled by Bernard Rosenberg and David Manning White, eds., *Mass Culture: The Popular Arts in America* (Glencoe, Ill.: Free Press, 1957) and Norman Jacobs, ed., *Culture for the Millions? Mass Media in Modern Society* (Princeton: Van Nostrand, 1961). For a more recent evaluation of the vagaries of popular culture criticism, see John G. Cawelti, *Adventure, Mystery and Romance* (Chicago: Univ. of Chicago Press, 1976), especially 5–36. Cawelti also includes an excellent bibliographic essay on popular culture theory and criticism, 319–24.

[2] In two recent articles, Jameson specifically attends to the interaction between the capitalist mode of production, ideology, and the formal structures of art forms. See his "Reification and Utopia in Mass Culture," *Social Text*, 1 (Winter 1979), 94–109 and "Ideology, Narrative Analysis and Popular Culture," *Theory and Society*, 4 (Winter 1977), 135–63. I find Jameson's work on mass culture more rigorous than most, exciting, and highly suggestive. The present essay will demonstrate the extent of his influence on my work and I would gratefully like to acknowledge that debt here. I have also found Umberto Eco's work very useful, especially his essays on popular narrative forms in *The Role of the Reader: Explorations in the Semiotics of Texts* (Bloomington: Indiana Univ. Press, 1980).

argument that a social group's desire for repetitive reassurance can be traced to the particular failure of social and economic institutions to address basic psychological needs of individuals within the group. The primary function of mass culture, as Jameson points out, is the "legitimation of the existing order."[3] That legitimation is possible, however, only because imaginative forms engage individuals in a dynamic process of meaning-production through which potentially subversive dissatisfactions are initially expressed, and then managed, recontained, and temporarily explained away by subsequent constructions.

For example, no matter how simple popular novels appear on the surface, they are always composed of a linear narrative whose temporal stages and ultimate meaning must be actively constructed by individuals from material encountered only sequentially and in piecemeal form. Because of the unavoidable temporality of this reading process, popular novels can freely prompt their readers to construct situations which will arouse in them, through identification and response, latent discontent and a previously suppressed desire for change, precisely because the ordered narrative will later prompt the same readers to demonstrate through new constructions the needlessness of their earlier reaction. The narrative resolutions reconcile them, then, to the social order which originally gave rise to the disaffection expressed through their construction of the early stages of the narrative. Popular literature can be said to legitimate the social order only because it also embodies the materials of a historical protest. Detection of this complex process of expression and eventual recontainment of dissatisfaction is dependent on the adoption of an analytical method which will take as its subject the developing response of a reader to constructions which he or she elaborates gradually in collaboration with the ordered language of the text.[4]

Although it may yet be too early to adopt Jameson's hypothesis as a major theoretical statement about the social function of all contemporary mass-produced literature, significant evidence corroborating it is fast accumulating. One of the most interesting cases is that of the modern "gothic" romance, a genre that enjoyed enormous popularity throughout the 1960s and into the early 1970s. Careful examination of the works of such authors as Victoria Holt (Eleanor Hibbert), Mary Stewart, Dorothy

---

[3] Jameson, "Reification and Utopia," 144.

[4] Throughout this essay, I have tried to adhere to Stanley Fish's dictum that literary analysis should not ask what a given text "means" but rather what it "does" to the reader. I have not, however, posited an ideal, "informed" reader as Fish does in his early essay, "Literature in the Reader: Affective Stylistics," *New Literary History,* 2 (Autumn 1970), 123–62, but have worked instead with a composite reader based on the comments of gothic authors and editors about their own understanding of modern gothic novels. I have assumed that their reading of the gothic text is probably very similar to the readings produced by typical readers. This is necessary since very little is known about romance readers. For a complete list of the authors' comments and the editors interviewed, see note 15.

Eden, and Phyllis Whitney demonstrates convincingly that while the popular gothic is essentially conservative in its recommendation of conventional gender behavior, its conservatism is triumphant because the narrative permits the reader first to give form to unrealized disaffection before it reassures her that such discontent is unwarranted.[5]

The popularity of romances, of course, is not a new phenomenon. In fact, the sentimental romance has been a staple in the American public's reading diet since Benjamin Franklin first printed *Pamela* in 1744.[6] Although most popular romances have never achieved the specificity of Samuel Richardson's analysis of women's possibilities in bourgeois society, the genre does share its prototype's concern with "the woman question." It is interesting to note that despite widespread agreement that popular romances possess little aesthetic merit, a critical debate has arisen nonetheless over the precise nature of the ideological bias of the stories. Whether their subject is the domestic romance of the nineteenth century or the gothics and Harlequins of the twentieth, scholars cannot agree about whether the stories are conservative reaffirmations of "the cult of domesticity" and "the feminine mystique" or covert feminist protests at the subjugation of women.

The disagreement can be explained, I think, by noting that those who argue for the romance's essentially conservative nature tend to focus on the resolution of the *narrative* itself which invariably establishes its heroine's happiness by throwing her into the arms of a traditionally protective male.[7] Those who disagree note instead that a good portion of the

---

[5] The interpretation offered in the following pages will refer only to a few "token" texts representative of the generic "type." The type-text has been developed from a much larger sample including most of the novels published by Victoria Holt, Phyllis Whitney, and Mary Stewart in the years 1960 to 1979. In addition, certain selected texts by Dorothy Eden, Norah Lofts, and Andre Norton have been considered as well. For a full listing of the novels consulted for this study, see the Appendix.

[6] James Hart, *The Popular Book: A History of America's Literary Taste* (Berkeley: Univ. of California Press, 1963), 47. For additional material on the importance of the sentimental novel in America's literary development, see Herbert Ross Brown, *The Sentimental Novel in America: 1789–1860* (Durham, N.C.: Duke Univ. Press, 1940) and Leslie Fiedler, *Love and Death in the American Novel*, rev. ed. (New York: Stein and Day, 1966).

[7] Although many monographs and books have advanced this argument about the conservative nature of the fiction produced by the "scribbling women," four perhaps can be cited as seminal. See Alexander Cowie, "The Vogue of the Domestic Novel, 1850–1870," *South Atlantic Quarterly*, 41 (Oct. 1942), 416–25; Barbara Welter, "The Cult of True Womanhood: 1820–1860," *American Quarterly*, 18 (Summer 1966), 151–74; Ellen Moers, *Literary Women* (Garden City: Doubleday, 1976); and Ann Douglas, *The Feminization of American Culture* (New York: Knopf, 1977). For a more extensive bibliographic review of conservative interpretations, see Mary Kelley, "The Sentimentalists: Promise and Betrayal in the Home," *Signs*, 4 (Spring 1979), esp. 434–35. On the conservative nature of modern gothics, see Joanna Russ, "Somebody's Trying to Kill Me and I Think It's My Husband," *Journal of Popular Culture*, 6 (Spring 1973), 666–91; and Kay Mussell, "Beautiful and Damned: The Sexual Woman in Gothic Fiction," *Journal of Popular Culture*, 9 (Summer 1974), 84–89.

romantic narrative permits the *reader* to identify with a heroine who is either wrongly abused by men or who remains unusually independent.[8] The story must be termed at least mildly feminist, they reason, because it provides the reader with the opportunity to express anger at patriarchal domination and to identify with a woman who does not fully adhere to conventional sex-role stereotypes.

Although the first group is certainly justified in maintaining that endings are significant, their opponents are also correct in noticing the importance of the experience the narrative discourse promotes in the reader. The contradictory hypotheses arise because neither group combines an analysis of the entire narrative structure with an assessment of the manner in which the developing story engages and manages real readers' responses. A full accounting of the meaning of the popular romance depends on the ability to indicate how the narrative develops for the reader, to speculate on her likely response to that evolving account, and finally, to explain the social function performed by eliciting and controlling her reactions in that particular manner.[9]

Specification of a single date as the definitive beginning of the most recent "rebirth" of the gothic novel is virtually impossible, not least because the formal limits of the genre are difficult to identify. As Kay Mussell points out in her bibliographic essay about the genre, the "true" gothic novel enjoyed its greatest popularity during the late eighteenth and early nineteenth centuries, although a small but consistent demand for this form combining romantic fantasy with a mystery and an apparent upsurge of supernatural evil continued well into the twentieth.[10] Paperback publishers, however, like to point out that the popularity of a

[8] The two most important interpretations focusing on the domestic text's effect on its reader can be found in Helen Waite Papashvily, *All the Happy Endings: A Study of the Domestic Novel in America, The Women Who Wrote It, The Women Who Read It, in the Nineteenth Century* (New York: Harper and Row, 1956) and Nina Baym, *Woman's Fiction: A Guide to Novels By and About Women in America, 1820–1870* (Ithaca: Cornell Univ. Press, 1978). See also Kelley's comments on this interpretation in "Sentimentalists." For a similar interpretation of modern gothics, see Josephine A. Ruggiero and Louise C. Weston, "Sex-Role Characterization of Women in 'Modern Gothic' Novels," *Pacific Sociological Review*, 20 (Apr. 1977), 292–300.

[9] In addition to Mary Kelley, three other analysts have recently attempted to assess both the structure of romantic fiction and its developing impact on the reader. On nineteenth-century romances, see William Veeder, *Henry James—The Lessons of the Master: Popular Fiction and Personal Style in the Nineteenth Century* (Chicago: Univ. of Chicago Press, 1975). Although the approach has not been previously attempted with gothics, it has been applied to the Harlequin romance by Ann Barr Snitow, "Mass Market Romance: Pornography for Women Is Different," *Radical History Review*, 20 (Spring/Summer 1979), 141–61; and Tania Modleski, "The Disappearing Act: A Study of Harlequin Romances," *Signs*, 5 (Spring 1980), 435–48.

[10] Kay J. Mussell, "Gothic Novels," in M. Thomas Inge, ed., *Handbook of American Popular Culture* (Westport, Conn.: Greenwood Press, 1978), 153–69.

distinct narrative form, which they also call the "gothic," increased dramatically around 1960 after Ace Books editor Gerald Gross reprinted Phyllis Whitney's *Thunder Heights* in the hope of appealing to the same readers who were responsible for the unusually long reprint life of Daphne DuMaurier's 1938 novel, *Rebecca*.[11] Both Gross and his counterparts at Doubleday, who simultaneously issued Victoria Holt's *Mistress of Mellyn* (1960), were searching for a new form capable of counteracting declining paperback sales in the mystery category. Reasoning that the recent turn to the hard-boiled stories of Mickey Spillane had alienated the female paperback audience, these editors deliberately sought novels that retained the mystery but combined it with a typical love story. This particular combination they dubbed "the modern gothic." It differs substantially from the original gothic in that its explorations of evil and terror are more fully subordinated to the details of the primary romantic plot.

Although the swift success of the Whitney and Holt novels soon prompted paperback publishers to issue other kinds of romances, the modern gothic, retaining its special status both as a narrative form and a publishers' category, continued to dominate paperback sales for close to ten years. During the peak period of 1969 to 1974, gothics by top authors like Holt and Whitney outsold their equivalents in all other categories including straight mysteries, historicals, westerns, and science fiction.[12] Acknowledging that their readers preferred the gothics to other forms of the romance, the publishers facilitated ready identification of the genre by adopting a stock cover. Nearly every modern gothic issued before 1974 sported a predominantly green and blue drawing exhibiting a terrified woman, clad in a long, swirling robe, who was fleeing from a darkened mansion lit only by a glow in an upper window. The cover proved so effective that gothic popularity developed into a cultural "phenomenon" worthy of comment and analysis in innumerable news magazines, daily papers, and general interest monthlies.[13]

The popularity of the form dropped off only when Avon Books published Kathleen Woodiwiss's four-hundred-page historical novel, *The*

---

[11] Pam Proctor, "Phyllis Whitney: She Writes Best-Sellers the Old-Fashioned Way," *Parade* (Nov. 2, 1975), 20; see also Martha Duffy, "On the Road to Manderley," *Time* (Apr. 12, 1971), 95–96.

[12] Proctor, 20.

[13] In addition to the Proctor and Duffy articles noted above, see also the following: F. W. J. Hemmings, "Mary, Queen of Hearts," *The New Statesman* (Nov. 5, 1965), 698–99; Mopsy Strange Kennedy, "How to Write a Gothic Novel," *New England–Boston Sunday Globe* (Oct. 8, 1979), 11, 14–15; Regina Minudri, "From Jane to Germaine With Love," *Library Journal*, 98 (Feb. 15, 1973), 658–59; Eric Pace, "Gothic Novels Prove Bonanza for Publishers," *New York Times* (June 18, 1973), 31–34; "Pulp Feminists: Gothic Liberation," *Human Behavior*, 7 (Feb. 1978), 50; and H. Rogan, "How To Write a Gothic Novel," *Harper's*, 250 (May 1975), 45–47.

Flame and the Flower (1972), which not only eliminated the mystery from the romantic plot, but also substituted long descriptions of erotic encounters between hero and heroine. The publication of her novel, in fact, marked the beginning of a decline in the modern gothic's popularity. Although occasional examples are still published, very few contemporary romances combine a love story with a mystery plot. In focusing analysis on the function of the detection story within the larger romantic structure, I think it will be possible to explain why, after roughly ten years of devotion to the form, romance readers no longer found the experience prompted by the modern gothic enjoyable, useful, or necessary.

The interpretation set forth in the following pages is based on an analytical procedure characterized by two distinct stages. In the first, I have attempted to determine how the essential characters are "coded" in the text.[14] This involved the isolation and specification of those characteristics, personality traits, and features commonly correlated with characters at the outset of the story. However, the list of traits discussed here does not include *all* distinctive features appended to the various characters. Rather, this limited set of traits has been determined "significant" because it conceptually differentiates those characters who are structurally articulated by their opposition to each other in the course of the narrative.[15]

[14] For a more detailed discussion of codes and coding procedures see Umberto Eco, *A Theory of Semiotics* (Bloomington: Indiana Univ. Press, 1976). For further material on popular culture's ability to function as "a series of models of relevant social action," see Will Wright, *Sixguns and Society, A Structural Study of the Western* (Berkeley: Univ. of California Press, 1975).

[15] Although I find it difficult to agree with certain structuralists like Claude Lévi-Strauss who maintain that all meaning is not only diacritically determined but structured in binary and antonymous pairs, I have discovered that the character traits employed by romantic novelists are not only few in number but generally organized in just this binary fashion. This is made clear not only in the novels themselves, but also in several articles on "how to write a gothic" where the authors insist on contrasting their characters across certain very basic categories. I have also discovered in personal interviews with editors at several publishing houses that they too differentiate essential characters using very similar categories. Accordingly, I have found it useful to employ a diagramming procedure common in structural analysis in order better to demonstrate the manner in which conceptually opposed terms are distributed among the major characters in the genre. The opposed pairs have been derived from the texts and checked against the comments of authors found in the following articles: Phyllis Whitney, "The Satisfying Element," *The Writer,* 78 (Feb. 1965), 11–14, 42; Phyllis Whitney, "Writing the Gothic Novel," *The Writer,* 80 (Feb. 1967), 11; Elsie Lee, "When You Write a Gothic," *The Writer,* 86 (May 1973), 17–19, 35; Elizabeth Peters, "Modern Gothics . . . The Willing Suspension of Disbelief," *The Writer,* 87 (Feb. 1974), 15–17; Susan Howatch, "Realism in Modern Gothics," *The Writer,* 87 (May 1974), 11–13; Willo David Roberts, "The Heroine Doesn't Have to Be an Idiot," *The Writer,* 88 (Jan. 1975), 12–14.

My knowledge of editors' approaches to gothic novels comes from a series of personal interviews with the following editors: Sally Arteseros, Senior Editor, Doubleday and Co., April 12, 1979 and Nov. 30, 1980; Vivien Stephens, Editor, Dell Books, April 12, 1979; Kate Duffy, Editor, Dell Books, April 12, 1979; Sheila Levine, Editor, Fawcett Popular Library, April 13, 1979; Patrick O'Connor, Editor-in-Chief, Fawcett Popular Library, April 13, 1979; and Maureen Baron, Executive Editor, Gold Medal Books, Nov. 30, 1980.

The second stage of analysis details the narrative structure of the gothic tale. Although I have done this by specifying a set of necessary functions that constitutes the genre, I have also deliberately ordered those functions in an effort to duplicate the precise way in which events are temporally disclosed, transformed, and then explained in the actual process of reading.[16] I have assumed throughout that the meaning of the genre cannot simply be found in the final disposition of the characters, nor in the way they are newly coded by readers at the conclusion of the tale, but in the way both situational transformations and coding changes are explained for them by the *developing* action.

Modern gothics all possess extraneous characters, but five, including the heroine, the hero, male and female foils, and an evil force, are essential to the narrative form. Of course, the principal figure is the heroine, that individual who tells the tale (most of Holt's and Whitney's are first-person narratives) or the one whose point of view is consistently adhered to in an omniscient narration that reports thoughts indirectly. The consistency of the single point of view narration seems clearly designed to guarantee the reader's identification with the heroine alone.

When the gothic novel opens, this heroine is typically identified by subordinate characters as physically pleasing although she herself is obsessed with her unexceptional appearance. The author very early establishes therefore that, like the reader who is undoubtedly plagued by feelings of inadequacy, even fictional heroines worry about whether they measure up to the feminine ideal. Sexually innocent and highly romantic, this heroine also dreams only vaguely about the future because her innate modesty prevents her from envisioning an assignation with a handsome Prince Charming. Although marked by this self-deprecatory tendency, she is nonetheless proud, indeed, almost haughty about her resourcefulness and courage, or "pluck," as she often terms it. In addition, when first presented to the reader, the gothic heroine has almost always been recently orphaned. Frightened by her consequent loss of social position and identity, she vows in spite of her fear to take care of herself rather than to subsist on the pity and generosity of friends. She seeks neither money nor status, she claims, only the opportunity to survive.

---

[16] A narrative function is "the act of a character, defined from the point of view of its significance for the course of the action." See Vladimir Propp, *Morphology of the Folktale*, trans. Alan Sheridan (Austin: Univ. of Texas Press, 1968), 21. The particular analytical procedures I have used here to identify and order functions and narrative sequences in the modern gothic have been based on Will Wright's critique of Propp in *Sixguns and Society*, 25–28 and 124–29.

Because Victoria Holt's initial presentation of Martha Leigh in *Mistress of Mellyn* has been endlessly duplicated by Holt herself, Mary Stewart, Phyllis Whitney, and others, her description serves adequately as a "type" presentation of the heroine at the beginning of the gothic tale.

> I pictured myself as I must appear to my fellow travelers if they bothered to glance my way, which was not very likely; a young woman of medium height, already past her first youth, being twenty-four years old, in a brown merino dress with cream lace collar and little tufts of lace at the cuffs. (Cream being so much more serviceable than white, as Aunt Adelaide told me.) My black cape was unbuttoned at the throat because it was hot in the carriage, and my brown velvet bonnet, tied with brown velvet ribbons under my chin, was of the sort which was so becoming to feminine people like my sister Phillida but, I always felt, sat a little incongruously on heads like mine. My hair was thick with a coppery tinge, parted in the center, brought down at the side of my too-long face, and made into a cumbersome knot to project behind the bonnet. My eyes were large, in some lights the color of amber, and were my best feature; but they were too bold—so said Aunt Adelaide; which meant that they had learned none of the feminine graces which were so becoming to a woman. My nose was too short, my mouth too wide. In fact, I thought, nothing seemed to fit; and I must resign myself to journeys such as this when I travel to and from the various posts which I shall occupy for the rest of my life, since it is necessary for me to earn a living, and I shall never achieve the first of those alternatives; a husband.[17]

Although the paragraph establishes Martha's awareness that others believe her inadequately feminine, the mildly ironic tone creates distance between their pity and her own rebellious acceptance of her "destiny." The reader is later assured that this resignation is in fact born of her refusal to conform to ordinary standards of femininity when she admits that there is good reason for her sister to believe that she "scares off" her male admirers because she, Marty, is too "gruff."[18] Although troubled by her sister's disapproval, Marty strategically confesses that she finds such femininity boring and that she just cannot help responding "pertly" when confronted by obviously overbearing men.

Holt expands on her heroine's unique difference from the mass of women throughout the novel's early pages, but saves her account of Marty's most egregious departure from the ideal of feminine passivity for her first interaction with the hero. The resulting verbal altercation, included below, serves the triple purpose of designating this male character

[17] Victoria Holt, *The Mistress of Mellyn* (New York: Fawcett Crest, 1960), 5.
[18] Ibid., 8.

as the hero, further delineating Marty's combativeness, and establishing their fundamental conflict.

> "So Miss Leigh, at last we meet." He did not advance to greet me, and his manner seemed insolent as though he were reminding me that I was only a governess. "It does not seem a long time," I answered, "for I have only been in your house a few days." "Well, let us not dwell on the time it has taken for us to get together. Now you are here, let that suffice." His light eyes surveyed me mockingly, so that I felt awkward and unattractive, and was aware that I stood before a connoisseur of women when even to the uninitiated I was not a very desirable specimen. "Mrs. Polgrey gives me good reports of you." "That is kind of her." "Why should it be kind of her to tell me the truth: I expect that from my employees." "I meant that she has been kind to me and that has helped me to make this good report possible." "I see that you are a woman who does not use the ordinary clichés of conversation but means what she says." "I hope so." "Good. I have a feeling that we shall get on well together." His eyes were taking in each detail of my appearance, I knew. He probably was aware that I had been given a London season and what Aunt Adelaide would call "every opportunity" and had failed to acquire a husband. As a connoisseur of women he would know why. I thought: At least I shall be safe from the attentions which I feel sure he tries to bestow on all attractive women with whom he comes in contact.[19]

The opposition begun here between the two major characters gradually develops as the heart of the gothic plot. Although the heroine always feels inexplicably drawn to the hero, she is also outraged by his strength and smug self-assurance, which are of course necessarily detailed from her point of view. It seems entirely likely that the gothic author's repeated return to confrontations between a hero who is carefully established as unreasonable and a heroine who refuses to be "dominated" by him grants the reader license to give free reign to any pent-up resentment she may feel toward men and to identify with and support a woman who at least initially refuses to be cowed.

Interestingly enough, there is some evidence that the text does function in this manner for at least some of its consumers. Not only do gothic authors themselves frame or type such behavior as "independent," "defiant," and "spunky" in commentaries on the form, but when asked to describe a "good" gothic heroine (one likely to be popular with readers), the editors also inevitably turn to the word "independent." They believe very strongly that although gothic readers demand the traditional

---

[19] Ibid., 36–37.

romantic ending, they also enjoy identifying with a strong woman who can occasionally best a man in verbal repartée.[20]

It is nonetheless important to point out here that the gothic heroine's courage and defiant demeanor are always carefully softened by her kindness and "becoming reserve." While her feistiness thus establishes her deviation from the feminine ideal, it usually fails to secure her what she wants. Despite her protestations to the contrary, the gothic heroine is nearly always dominated by events and set scurrying about by the unexpected. She prides herself on her characteristically "unfeminine" strength and intelligence, but circumstances inevitably develop in such a way that her actual ability to act is severely circumscribed.

The typical first encounter between hero and heroine further clarifies their conflict because the two are coded as opposites. Where she is romantic and poor, he is merely practical, usually highly prosaic, and always wealthy. Filled with scorn for the idea of love, he is also ambitious, ruthless, and reserved to the point of indifference. His desire for wealth, social success, and/or revenge are always emphasized, as are his courage and determination to pursue these goals. Like Conan TreMellyn, gothic heroes are invariably described as "strong," "arrogant," "gaunt," "careless," "elegant," "sensual," "insolent," and "cruel."[21] Furthermore, they are always portrayed as sexually experienced, aloof from emotional attachments, and accustomed to dominating the women in their households. The gothic aristocrat does not differ substantially from the typical male stereotype of twentieth-century America; as such, he is the perfect antagonist for the uncommon heroine.

That these two are not really so different from each other, however, is later made abundantly clear as other minor characters wander in and out of the narrative. The special qualities shared by the heroine and her aristocratic antagonist soon stand out as valuable because most other individuals reveal themselves to be fearful or weak, remarkably stupid, or devoid of their competitive instinct and assertive ability. The female foil, for instance, emphasizes the heroine's innocence and reserve because her passionate sexuality is always linked by juxtaposition with her distasteful ambition, greed, ruthlessness, and vanity. Holt's presentation of Isa Bannock in *The Pride of the Peacock* deviates little from innumerable other descriptions of this siren figure. It serves well as a token example of a standard presentation:

She was obviously several years younger than her husband, I thought, as she

[20] For instance, Vivien Stephens remarked that favorite heroines are "brave" and have "resources of their own." Sally Arteseros characterized them as "plucky ladies" and Maureen Baron commented that "they mustn't appear too silly or ignorant."
[21] Holt, *Mellyn*, 38.

turned her lovely topaz-colored eyes upon me and scrutinized me with probing interest. She reminded me of a tigress. There were tawny lights in her hair to match her eyes; and there was something about her that reminded me of the jungle, for she moved like a cat with immense grace. "I can see I'll have to start saving up," commented Ezra. Joss turned to me again. "Isa has one of the finest collections of opals. She doesn't necessarily want to deck herself out in them. She takes them out and gloats over them."

Isa laughed, her tigress face animated by an expression I could not fathom. There was triumph in it and a certain greed.[22]

It is easy to see here that in the modern gothic, the female foil is used as a contrast for the heroine's virginity, romanticism and desire for love. Her function is not unrelated to that performed by earlier references to passive and overly "feminine" women like Martha Leigh's sister. Where the siren emphasizes the heroine's essential innocence and goodness, thus differentiating her from the stereotype of the "loose woman," the passive women serve to point out her strength of character, thereby setting her apart from the stereotyped image of woman as a "clinging vine." The heroine is consequently established for the reader as a "unique" individual. The discursive structure which creates this "uniqueness," however, also covertly informs the reader that female sexuality may be combined with active independence only if that independence expresses itself in something other than a woman's sexual behavior.

The male foil performs a similar function with respect to his counterpart. Where the hero dominates everyone about him, the male foil is usually overwhelmed by events. He tends to be as romantic as the heroine and as fearful as the servants and extraneous females. Although he usually extends friendship and sometimes love to the heroine, his passivity, gentleness, and kindness fail to excite her. She much prefers the challenge posed by the aggressive virility of the gothic aristocrat. As the heroine of *The Shadow of the Lynx* puts it, she "loves" the male foil but she is "in love" with the hero.[23]

Because the evil force is not coded until the end of the narrative, it seems best to stop at this point to summarize the set of conceptual oppositions that distinguishes characters for the reader as the story develops in its initial stages. Table 1 suggests that the principal conflicts of the novel involve the heroine and the hero, the heroine and the female foil, and the hero and the male foil. These couples are distinguished by the largest number of meaningful oppositions. In effect, their conflicts define the conceptual concerns of the modern gothic.

---

[22] Victoria Holt, *The Pride of the Peacock* (New York: Fawcett Crest, 1976), 198, 303.
[23] Victoria Holt, *The Shadow of the Lynx* (New York: Fawcett Crest, 1971), 123.

Table 1. CONCEPTUAL OPPOSITIONS AT THE
OPENING OF THE GOTHIC NOVEL

	Heroine	Hero	Male Foil	Female Foil
romantic	+	−	+	−
practical	−	+	−	+
love	+	−	varies	−
money	−	+		+
virginal	+	−	varies	−
experienced	−	+		+
reserved	+	+	varies	−
passionate	−	−		+
kind	+	−	+	−
cruel	−	+	−	+
proud	+	+	−	+
modest	−	−	+	−
isolated	+	+	varies	varies
secure	−	−		
courageous	+	+	−	varies
fearful	−	−	+	
dominated	+	−	+	−
dominator	−	+	−	+
vain	−	+	−	+
self-deprecatory	+	−	+	−
rich	−	+	−	+
poor	+	−	+	−

The above correlations between characters and identifying features are established and then transformed through the course of a story whose basic structure is represented by the following list of narrative functions. It is worth noting again that the meaning of the genre rests not in the list alone but in the internal organization of the structure as an explanatory device capable of instructing the reader about the likely consequences of adopting the personality traits and particular behaviors characterizing the principal actors. The narrative sequences include the following:

1) The heroine's identity is destroyed.
2) The heroine seeks to rediscover herself through attachment to a disordered family.
3) The heroine confronts an unsolved mystery alone.
4) An aristocratic male (the hero) challenges the heroine's right to solve the mystery.

5) The heroine responds ambivalently to the hero.
6) The heroine develops a friendship with a secondary male (the male foil).
7) The heroine is jealous of a flirtatious female foil.
8) The heroine recognizes she is not in love with the male foil.
9) The heroine accepts the fact of her sexual attraction to the hero.
10) The heroine is brought close to death when she refuses to be stopped by the hero's objections.
11) The hero admires the heroine's combined independence and vulnerability.
12) The hero rescues the heroine.
13) The hero recognizes his need of the heroine and his conversion to the principles of love.
14) The heroine solves the mystery with the aid of the hero.
15) The heroine agrees to establish a new family with the aristocratic male.
16) The heroine achieves fulfillment and secures a new identity.

This sequence of functions operates as a comprehensive "explanation" because it is composed of several interlocking "narratives," each of which contains at least three stages organized in such a way that the transformation of the first into the third is accounted for by the action occurring in the second. For example, the modern gothic begins with its heroine's loss of identity and sense of self (no. 1). This initial situation is then transformed by the entire narrative development of the story into a final situation where she achieves self-fulfillment as an "individual" (no. 16). The change is "explained" by the fact that she discovers that her proper place is at the side of her true love. This explanatory function (no. 15) is itself a transformation of her previous attempts to rediscover and redefine her self within a disordered and alien family (no. 2). This transformation, embedded within the first, is itself produced because she learns to accept the assistance of a man who is physically stronger than she (no. 14) but who has also been previously established as someone who loves and "needs" her (no. 13). The logic of the genre as a "theory" about proper human behavior can therefore be fully comprehended only when all essential narrative functions are displayed analytically and exhibited as the ordered or determined transformations of previous functions. A schematic diagram representing the internal organization of the modern gothic's narrative functions will do away with the need to rehearse the plot step by step. Keep in mind, however, that the structure displayed here in spatial form is always experienced temporally by the constructing reader (see Figure 1).

Figure 1.

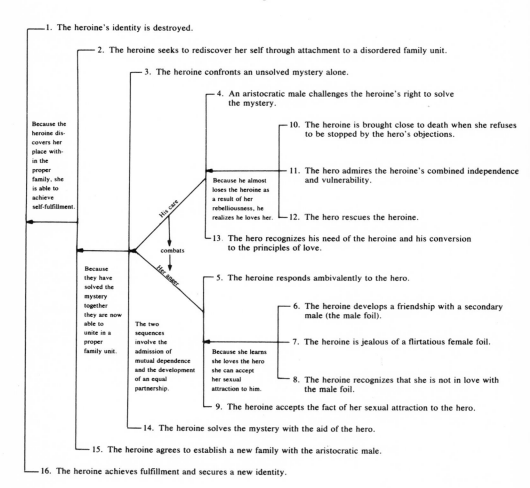

When considered in conjunction with the conceptual oppositions previously established, this narrative structure demonstrates that the gothic's central concern is its preoccupation with the proper way to realize female identity. In providing its particular solution, the gothic also exhibits a secondary interest in changing standards or models of gender behavior as well as in developing threats to the stability of the family. Since the "aggressive" and "sexual" female foil is discarded because the hero expresses a preference for the heroine's more balanced demeanor, it seems obvious that the novel intends to suggest that sexual aggression by women cannot lead to love and indeed may destroy it. Their contrasting fates also imply that women who subordinate their capacity to care for others to an extreme individualism associated with vanity and desire for material things will never realize their truest selves. Later developments in the plot additionally suggest that, like the heroine, a woman may use her intelligence and demonstrate her courage if she thereby insists on her independence only to a certain point. When her ultimate survival is at stake, she must inevitably rely on a stronger male by accepting his protection.

By the same token, while a man may exhibit strength, courage, experience, and interest in worldly affairs, those traits, the gothic plot explains, must finally be subordinated to an expression of love for another. The hero protects the woman he cares for but this assertion of power is subsequently qualified by his admitted conversion to her ideal of love. Explicit domination of one partner by the other is purged in the gothic plot by a symmetrical internal development that establishes the mutual dependency of hero and heroine and witnesses their parallel expressions of affection. In effect, the desire for love triumphs over self-interest in the modern gothic just as human greed is exposed as the principal threat to stable gender arrangements. The exposé is achieved by the narrative's discrediting of the female foil and by its final unmasking of the evil force— a character, it always turns out, who has been motivated by extravagant ambition and simple greed.

The resolution of the modern gothic is a utopian vision representing an ideal companionate marriage through which, its heroine characteristically informs us, female identity and fulfillment are naturally achieved. For example, in concluding her narrative, Phyllis Whitney's heroine in *The Golden Unicorn* remarks that "his tenderness was healing and I knew that all my searching was over." [24] The search refers not to a quest for a husband but to her attempts to find her real parents and to establish her true identity. Nearly identical sentiments are echoed by Holt's only slightly more assertive heroine in *The Pride of the Peacock*. When her son is born, she tells the reader, "this was the culmination of my happiness." Her further description and, significantly, the final passage in the book, given the last line, leaves no doubt about her sense of her own power.

> Joss came and looked at the baby, marvelling at the tiny creature as though he couldn't believe he was real. Then he turned to me. "It's good, eh?" he said.
> "What?" I asked.
> "Life," he answered. "Just life."

[24] Phyllis Whitney, *The Golden Unicorn* (New York: Fawcett Crest, 1976), 315.

"It's good," I agreed, "and going to be better."

"Who can be sure of that?" he asked.

"*I* can," I retorted, "And I will." [25]

Although such verbal claims about the compatibility of marriage and female self-realization typically conclude the gothic, it is important to note that the heroine achieves the security that makes her self-discovery possible only by relinquishing some of her independence and self-control to the hero who saves her from almost certain death. Once she accepts his protection, she is free to acknowledge her sexual feelings and occasionally to give passionate expression to them precisely because she has implicitly admitted her willingness to be ruled by this man.

The final shift in the balance of power between hero and heroine is assured by the fact that they are coded differently at the end of the tale. Where the heroine has begun as a lonely but proud, ostensibly courageous adolescent, personally assured of her ability to demand what she wants, she is transformed into a secure, modest, and strong woman who is now sometimes fearful and thus in need of loving protection and care by another. While the gothic superficially asserts the validity of a feminist goal, self-realization for women, its narrative structure demonstrates that achievement of it comes only with submission to traditional gender arrangements and assumption of a typically female personality structure. In representing character coding at the end of the novel, Table 2 demonstrates that despite the many transformations of his personality, all of which are the consequence of his conversion to the heroine's principles of love, the hero is yet more courageous than she and therefore qualifies as her rightful protector.

As might be expected in a still patriarchal society, the popular romance clearly recommends adherence to traditional standards of gender behavior just as it counsels against substantial challenges to accepted sexual arrangements. Yet the particular manner in which that social order is established within the fictional world provides a lengthy interlude during which the heroine repetitively, consistently, and successfully refuses to be ruled by an aggressive, domineering man. Equally significant, the ending of the tale demonstrates that despite the heroine's final acceptance of his protection, this hero is made over by her influence into an individual who is not only more affable, but more openly nurturant as well. It is now time to consider the effects of developments like these on the reader, for it seems entirely likely that they activate reactions and responses that could

[25] Holt, *Peacock*, 301–02.

Table 2. CONCEPTUAL OPPOSITIONS AT THE CLOSE
OF THE GOTHIC NOVEL

	Heroine	Hero	Evil Force
romantic	+	+	−
practical	−	−	+
love	+	+	−
money	−	−	+
virginal	−	−	varies
experienced	+	+	
reserved	−	−	varies
passionate	+	+	
kind	+	+	−
cruel	−	−	+
proud	−	−	+
modest	+	+	−
isolated	−	−	+
secure	+	+	−
courageous	±	+	+
fearful	±	−	−
dominated	±	±	varies
dominator	±	±	
vain	−	−	varies
self-deprecatory	+	+	
rich	+	+	−
poor	−	−	+

conceivably thwart her acceptance of the final, conservative restoration of the patriarchal status quo.

Although the modern gothic ends, as do all romances, with the happy union of the two principals, nearly two-thirds of the typical narrative chronicles the heroine's attempts to resist the control of a hero who is always "seen" by the reader through her eyes. Assuming that the narrative point of view prompts the reader to identify with this heroine, it seems inevitable that the deliberate enumeration of her conflicts with a man who is patronizing, overbearing, and antagonistic would cause that reader to feel the same intense anger and indignation which his behavior prompts in the heroine. If such discontent is indeed the initial effect of the act of reading a gothic, it behooves us to explain why, in the late sixties and early seventies, so many women found enjoyable an activity, termed by all involved "escapist," that nonetheless activated feelings of resentment at social relations which most still would have characterized, if asked, as natural and necessary.

It is not possible to recount here the social history of women in post-World War II America. It should be noted, however, that despite their early return to the home from wartime assembly lines and the subsequent, well-publicized "baby boom," American women were beginning to work in increasing numbers outside the home during the following two decades.[26] Although William Chafe and Carl Degler have both documented the fact that female entry into the work force was *not* accomplished at the expense of marriage and motherhood, they have also noted that despite women's conscious justification of their work as necessary to the family welfare, many of them apparently grew to like their jobs because of the benefits employment gave them as individuals. Chafe cites two studies, for instance, that indicate that although women believed themselves to be working for the family, they also often mentioned "the ancillary benefits of social companionship and the sense of independence represented by a paycheck" when asked to comment about their jobs.[27] Although Degler resolutely insists that postwar female employment was virtually always justified by reference to familial needs, he also admits that the move into the work force may have interacted with developing feminism inadvertently to change middle-class women's beliefs about their own possibilities.[28] He adds, however, that such a change in attitude could not have been effected easily or without conflict since any "realization of female individuality in work" must be based on a set of beliefs fundamentally at odds with "the central values of the modern family," to which most women still declared their primary allegiance.[29]

If Degler is correct about this value conflict, as I believe he is, it is highly likely that growing awareness of alternate possibilities, when confronted with this persistent tendency to insist on the primacy of woman's duty to family as selfless wife and mother, may have fostered in many an unconscious ambivalence about the worth of the traditional female role. If so, it then seems plausible that the twin phenomena of gothic reading and feminism were differing but parallel responses to growing uneasiness and uncertainty about model female behavior as well as dialectically related

---

[26] On the movement of American women into the labor market throughout the fifties and sixties, see William H. Chafe, *The American Woman: Her Changing Social, Economic and Political Roles, 1920–1970* (New York: Oxford Univ. Press, 1972), 217–25; Carl Degler, *At Odds: Women and the Family in America from the Revolution to the Present* (New York: Oxford Univ. Press, 1980), 418–35.

[27] Chafe, 219–20.

[28] Degler, 448.

[29] Ibid., 436–73 passim.

efforts to satisfy a slowly growing desire for individual self-realization. Where feminism consciously admitted the validity of female resentment and anger about the traditional destruction of the female self and attempted to secure every woman's right to self-determination by provoking widespread social change, gothic reading undercut that anger by providing an entirely safe arena for its expression, displacement, and defusion. At the same time, the gothic cagily adopted the language of feminism by endorsing its heroine's quest for her "identity" only to demonstrate that even this new demand could adequately be accommodated by traditional sexual arrangements.

To explain precisely how the gothic successfully disarms the anger it induces, it is necessary to examine the function of the internal mystery plot and the exaggerated fear it seems to trigger in the heroine and thus in the reader. If, as suggested here, the gothic narrative provides its typical reader with an occasion for the expression of previously repressed resentment at male domination and the opportunity to enjoy an "independent" woman's defiance of social expectations, it undoubtedly also activates a deeply unconscious fear that if permitted to surface unchecked, such feelings of resentment and rebellion could seriously undermine the stability of gender relations which, though not entirely desirable, are at least familiar, predictable, and the only apparent way to insure female survival. Should the narrative lead the reader to locate the source of her fear in her vicarious enjoyment of the heroine's rebelliousness and independence, it is likely that these related and dangerous impulses would be denied and perhaps even more forcefully submerged as unconscious but still active urges. Although such a process would lead the reader to an assertion of satisfaction with the status quo, it would do nothing to dissipate those potentially subversive feelings that could continue to grow within her. The mystery plot performs the important function of providing a convincing and *different* explanation for the fears already activated by her early identification with the heroine and thus thwarts the reader's impulse to connect them with her own vicariously experienced anger and appreciation of the heroine's atypical behavior. By dovetailing the story of the heroine's quest for identity with the tale of her effort to unmask external forces that are threatening her, the gothic manages to provide an alternative focus for the reader's efforts to locate the source of her own uneasiness which she is, in fact, encouraged to feel even more intensely by subsequent peculiar disturbances and "gothic" devices. In holding out the guarantee of a suitable external explanation for her fear, the narrative therefore enables the reader to indulge that much longer in feelings of resentment and longing for new goals.

Once the essential conflict between the heroine and the hero has been established and extended through the mystery plot's suggestion that the hero may be the villain, the narrative escalates the tension by intensifying the threats to the heroine's life. Although she doesn't want to believe it possible, she does suspect the hero of this inexplicable aggression. At this point, her dislike and her fear of the hero seem entirely justified to the reader. The narrative comes perilously close to suggesting that men are themselves the real threat to harmonious male-female relations and the cause of women's unhappiness. Having posed the suggestion, however, it then deftly retreats from the precipice. The heroine's stubborn refusal to be cautioned or aided by others places her in extreme danger. When she can no longer resist the villain and is about to succumb, the hero conveniently arrives, to her surprise and the reader's delight, proclaiming that all along he found her unorthodox behavior beguiling. Female independence, it would seem, does not threaten men or cause them to retaliate; rather it seduces and transforms them.

The "sudden" revelation of the hero's ultimate benignity is made palatable (though not, perhaps, entirely convincing to the analytical reader) by the fact that his vindication occurs simultaneously with another's exposure. The anger and fear originally thought to have been caused by the hero when the mystery subplot was first set in motion are thus neatly attributed to another source. Men are not inherently antagonistic to women, the narrative assures its reader, nor are they intolerant of a woman's desire to assert her own individual identity. There is no real reason to be angry with men as a group, just as there is no reason to assume that female independence is incompatible with marriage. The gothic announces, in effect, that the true threat to harmonious and balanced male-female relations comes from outside, in the form of selected others who are motivated by greed and exaggerated self-interest or narcissism. The resolution of the gothic finally instructs the reader that she need not search within herself or examine her own situation for the causes of her anger and disaffection, because her feelings, like the heroine's, are inevitably caused by other individuals. In displacing the blame for women's discontent, the narrative ingeniously deflects any move toward critical analysis of the structure of gender arrangements which is, in actuality, the cause of the incipient unrest.

It is important to recall, however, that the villain's exposure is always accompanied by the final defeat of a woman whose unchecked sexuality and aggressive pursuit of individual aggrandizement are extreme versions of the heroine's pert independence. The narrative resolution also cautions therefore that even though a modicum of independence and self-possession can help a woman to instruct her man to take account of her needs as an individual, those traits can never be fully expressed in the sexual domain. The gothic carefully reestablishes the basic structure of patriarchy in this crucial area of gender relations by demonstrating to the reader that in the heroine's world, sexual submission wins a woman both the protective care of another *and* an opportunity to realize her truest self.

The modern gothic can afford to provoke attitudes and feelings which implicitly challenge fundamental cultural beliefs because those attitudes are qualified or rendered unnecessary by the plot's resolution. The fairy-tale fantasy concluding the narrative excuses the other two-thirds of the novel devoted to the explicit reversal of common cultural assumptions about gender behavior because it demonstrates that the implied dissatis-factions motivating those reversals are adequately addressed by the very social institutions and roles originally overturned. Therefore, while gothic novels might be termed "feminist" novels because they portray heroines who exhibit characteristics usually precluded by the "feminine" sex-role stereotype and because they provide the reader with at least a temporary opportunity to experience both anger and unfulfilled desire, they are also reactionary in their assertion that the feminist goals of individual fulfill-ment and independence can be achieved through the maintenance of tradi-tional male-female relations. We simply cannot overlook the fact that the feminist protest is not sustained. The novel may temporarily express a subconscious desire for a reordering of relations between men and women, but that subversive desire is always turned aside in the end in a way that shows it to have been unnecessary at the outset.

The peculiar popularity of the gothic tale in the 1960s and 1970s can be traced to the highly specific way in which it "works" the social context for its readers. Although the novels are certainly not mimetic portraits of their actual behavior in the arena of sexual politics, they are nonetheless useful guides to the emotional and intellectual turmoil probably experi-enced by those readers as a consequence of social changes. The gothic's fantasy resolution represents, finally, an imaginative compromise be-tween slowly developing psychological needs generated by changing so-cial possibilities for women and its readers' still more powerful desire to keep gender relations as they were.

It seems possible that as romance readers accepted, if only on a sub-conscious level, the validity of this new interest in themselves as indi-viduals, the act of identifying with a "strong," "intelligent" woman cap-able of defying a man may have inspired considerably less fear, thus obviating the need for the detection subplot. If, in addition, the increased attention to female sexuality which developed as a consequence of feminism and "the sexual revolution" of the sixties made these same readers more conversant with the equally disturbing idea that women might legitimately seek sexual fulfillment, it is not hard to understand why they found Woodiwiss's novel preferable to the gothics. *The Flame and the Flower,* like the gothic, traces the fortunes of a spunky and independent heroine as she battles with her aristocratic antagonist. Unlike the gothic, however, it explicitly concerns itself with the heroine's sexual awakening which it details with great specificity and even more exaggerated ardor. Of course, the novel demonstrates at the end that even though women have sexual needs and feelings like men's, theirs can only be adequately addressed in romantic love relationships with single, "right" individuals. As the gothic version of the romance had dealt with the challenge posed by a yearning to develop the female self, Woodiwiss's "bodice-ripper" admitted the legitimacy of its readers' growing interest in sexual fulfillment only to demonstrate through narrative explanation that true satisfaction could in fact be achieved within the familiar institution of patriarchal marriage.

If the contemporary romance is any indication, popular literature does indeed function as a conservator of social values. However, each form's particular conservatism also appears to be a response to specific material changes posing a threat to the social structure's legitimating belief system. Textual analysis capable of isolating the particular needs and desires that any given narrative attempts to fulfill by demonstrating their strict compatibility with conventional social relations can therefore apparently serve as evidence of germinating change in cultural attitudes and beliefs.

APPENDIX: NOVELS CONSULTED FOR STUDY

Holt, Victoria (Eleanor Burford Hibbert)

Mistress of Mellyn	1960
Kirkland Revels	1962
Bride of Pendorric	1963
Menfreya in the Morning	1966
The Shivering Sands	1969
The Shadow of the Lynx	1971
On the Night of the Seventh Moon	1972
Lord of the Far Island	1975
The Pride of the Peacock	1976
The Devil on Horseback	1977

Stewart, Mary

Nine Coaches Waiting	1959
My Brother Michael	1960
The Ivy Tree	1961
Airs Above Ground	1965
The Gabriel Hounds	1966

Whitney, Phyllis

Thunder Heights	1960
Window on the Square	1962
Black Amber	1964
Sea Jade	1965
Columbella	1966
Listen for the Whisperer	1971
Snowfire	1972
The Turquoise Mask	1973
Spindrift	1975
The Golden Unicorn	1976
The Stone Bull	1977
The Glass Flame	1978
Domino	1979

Eden, Dorothy

Ravenscroft	1964
Melbury Square	1970
Speak to Me of Love	1972

Lofts, Norah

Lost Queen	1969
Lovers All Untrue	1970

Norton, Andre

The White Jade Fox	1975
Velvet Shadows	1977

Christopher P. Wilson

As an early foray into the complex interpretive negotiations of the mass cultural book market, popular reader-response, and the contested terms of patriarchal authority—all further explored three years later in her influential *Reading the Romance* (Chapel Hill: University of North Carolina Press, 1984)—Janice Radway's "Gothic Romances and 'Feminist' Protest" still seems, in many ways, an uncanny essay. In retrospect, the essay seems both to have established Radway's fundamental ground and yet also to have propelled the continual self-questioning that would, so usefully, characterize her future work. With equal dexterity, she both elucidated the containing powers of patriarchal authority, yet also empathized with—even expressed—the restlessness those powers elicited in the lengthy interlude of reading. The essay was thus itself what Radway terms a "dynamic process of meaning production," in no small part because it seemed to project multiple trajectories for future argument.

Reading the Romance, of course, would be reviewed or cited in journals in political science, communications, sociology, women's studies, semiotics, anthropology, art history, film—and "literature," the category Radway's work most obviously challenged. As well as providing a meeting ground between structuralism and Jamesonian theory, on the one hand, and feminist American cultural history on the other, Radway's scholarship also propelled an accelerating interest in the now-thriving field of the "history of the book." It provoked new questions by giving aesthetic forms, cultural gatekeepers, and audiences (rather than merely authors) a presence in remaking those fields of inquiry. And yet, few scholars proved more ready to question the terms of their own canonization. Over time, Radway herself would offer some of the best commentaries on interpretive rubs still evident here: the scare quotes in this essay's title around "feminist"; the assumptions made about a reader not long to be a composite fiction; the ideological seams and disjunctures between the interpretations of mass readers and those of the critic as the essay con-

Janice Radway, "The Utopian Impulse in Popular Literature: Gothic Romances and 'Feminist' Protest," originally appeared in *American Quarterly* 33, no. 2 (summer 1981), Copyright © 1981 Trustees of the University of Pennsylvania.

structs her. That self-construction seems dynamic itself, restless, sometimes more apparent in candid parentheses than its otherwise deliberate, occasionally deadpan voice. In the book version, Fredric Jameson and Umberto Eco and Vladimir Propp would be joined by Nancy Chodorow, the pseudonymous Dot, and of course those "Smithton" readers; inevitably, we are all readers of those readers now.

In looking back at this earlier foray, however, it may be helpful to seek out what one had forgotten about it—as it were, if only to reconnect the dots differently. For example, this essay more explicitly reminded me of connections of Radway's emerging hypothesis about modern romance to eighteenth- and nineteenth-century sentimental fiction, the object of a concurrent recovery project in American studies in the 1970s and 1980s (and still ongoing). Indeed, connections to a tradition Radway still called "domestic"—as if to underscore the patriarchal construction, or even orchestration, of a space that combined, even in the now-familiar denomination, confinement and luxury, subordination and class-inflected safety. As in Cathy Davidson's work, reading is seen not only as a textual act, but as a byproduct of something like Raymond Williams's long revolution: a paradoxical process in which gender roles are both scripted and yet also reenacted.

Radway's examination of a modern Gothic, however, also disallowed any comfort of long historical retrospect. As the book would, this early project brilliantly extracted not only the social contract still enacted by modern domesticity, but—in its vexatious portrait of male aggressions only apparently "tamed" (domesticated)—the psychic labor involved as well. In more ways than one, this struck close to home. Looking back from the 1990s, in fact, the essay also seems prescient, rigorously intent—in a way that surely *still* challenges disciplinary norms across the board—upon capturing the affective and (in Renato Rosaldo's term) "processual" dimensions of reading. Radway's challenge to attend to the first dimension (the affective), it might be argued, is still something that American studies neglects, perhaps because of its continuing attachment to delineating "playbook" norms of culture. Yet if Radway's readers read schematically, they also read temporally, while the Gothic transforms its only-apparent cultural oppositions into new and more disarming ones. It is also easy to overlook the weight borne by the simple word "change" in the essay's closing, subtly reminding us that any undue emphasis on ideological containment (and those playbook norms) threatens to result in a flat and static historicism. Indeed, the illusory irony produced by such monochromatic historicism might isolate the critic from the very audience she or he means to address.

It is also intriguing to rediscover what happened to the term "the Gothic" here—and I don't mean only as a genre term from which *Reading the Romance* partly tracks away. In genre terms, the Gothic is dealt with dutifully: pegged to critical classifications and to editors' market savvy; periodized (given a peak period from 1969 to 1974); and then contextualized, positioned dialectically (through the work of Carl Degler and William Chafe) with a reemergent feminist movement. In turn, the Gothic is then described as a form soon eclipsed by rivals more explicitly erotic—a transformation, as the familiar lament goes, which takes all the mystery out. Of course, the essay takes it out too: with the mystery plot described as only providing a spurious unmasking of power, the Gothic might seem emptied of the mysterious, the supernatural, the scary. But in Radway's account we discover something far better: an intricately coded structure of restless foiling between, across, and within gender identities. Leading couples are "distinguished," we are told with perhaps unintended wit, "by the largest number of meaningful oppositions" the text generates within and around them. The uncanny thing is that with such precise aesthetic rendering, the Gothic thus becomes something more than literary: in Radway's telling phrases, the "logic of the genre" becomes a "theory" of human behavior itself.

For this reason, it is not simply that one hears a critical voice here, pushing the questions much as, say, Barbara Ehrenreich would in *The Hearts of Men* (Garden City, N.Y.: Anchor Press/Doubleday, 1983), about male and female autonomy in the postwar era and who liberated whom to do what. Rather, it is through its relentless byplay of foils that this essay best illuminates the seductions of patriarchy, so devious in its seemingly rational definition of the female reader's best interest. Perhaps most importantly, the form is portrayed here as "cagily" adopting the language of feminism itself. Radway's scare quotes around "feminist" therefore are not, as I misremembered them, meant to signal inauthenticity, or the supposed failure of readers to achieve a political standard the critic would prefer. Rather, in this pretext to Radway's own still-developing argument, they expose the Gothic's own ventriloquism of dissent. And that's something *really* scary.

HOUSTON A. BAKER, JR.

Modernism and the Harlem Renaissance

Harlem is vicious
modernism. Bangclash.
Vicious the way its made.
Can you stand such Beauty?
So violent and transforming.
—Amiri Baraka, "Return of the Native"

THE TERM "MODERNISM" HAS SOMETHING OF THE CHARACTER OF KEAT'S COLD pastoral. Promising a wealth of meaning, it locks observers into a questing indecision that can end in unctious chiasmus. Teased out of thought by the term's promise, essayists often conclude with frustratingly vague specifications. Harry Levin's essay "What Was Modernism?", for example, after providing lists, catalogues, and thought problems, concludes with the claim that modernism's distinguishing feature is its attempt to create "a conscience for a scientific age" (630).[1] Modernism's definitive act, according to Levin, traces its ancestry to "Rabelais, at the very dawn of modernity."

Such an analysis can only be characterized as a terribly general claim about scientific mastery and the emergence of the modern. It shifts the burden of definition from "modernism" to "science," without defining either enterprise.

Robert Martin Adams, in an essay bearing the same title as Levin's offers a key to modernism's teasing semantics.[2] Adams writes:

> Of all the empty and meaningless categories, hardly any is inherently as empty as "the modern." Like "youth," it is a self-destroying concept; unlike "youth," it has a million and one potential meanings. Nothing is so dated as yesterday's modern, and nothing, however dated in itself, fails to qualify as "modern" so long as it enjoys the exquisite privilege of having been created yesterday. (31-32)

This essay is, in part, a direct excerpt from a book-length study of the same title that will be issued by the University of Chicago Press in the fall of 1987, and, in part, an abbreviated summary of claims argued at some length in that book. The principal aim of both the essay and the book is to suggest a problematic, or an analytical model, that will enable a useful reassessment of the Harlem Renaissance. Such an analysis would escape the pitfalls of a period analysis of Afro-American expressivity and take Harlem as a moment not in a developing and exclusive literary enterprise, but as a moment in a general and distinctive Afro-American discursive history comprised of a definable array of strategies. The presentation that follows will, hopefully, give impetus to such a reassessment. Versions of this essay were prepared and delivered as lectures for the English Institute (August 1985) and the Afro-American Studies Department at Yale University (November 1985). At Yale, I had the privilege of delivering the Richard Wright Lecture.

Adams implies that bare chronology makes modernists of us all. The latest moment's production—by definition—instantiates "the modern." And unless we arbitrarily terminate modernism's allowable tomorrows, the movement is unending. Moreover, the temporal indeterminacy of the term allows us to select (quite randomly) structural features that we will call distinctively "modern" on the basis of their chronological proximity to us. We can then read these features over past millennia. Like Matthew Arnold in his Oxford inaugural lecture entitled "On the Modern Element in Literature," we can discover what is most distinctively modern in works a thousand years old.

As one reads essay after essay, one becomes convinced that Ihab Hassan's set of provocative questions in a work entitled "POSTmodernISM A Paracritical Bibliography" are apt and suggestive for understanding the frustrating persistence of "modernism" as a critical sign. Hassan queries:

> When will the Modern Period end?
> Has ever a period waited so long? Renaissance? Baroque? Neo-Classical? Romantic? Victorian?
> When will Modernism cease and what comes thereafter?
> What will the twenty-first century call us? and will its voice come from the same side of our graves?
> Does Modernism stretch merely to stretch out our lives? Or, ductile, does it give a new sense of time? The end of periodization? the slow arrival of simultaneity?
> If change changes ever more rapidly, and the future jolts us now, do men, paradoxically, resist both endings and beginnings?[3](7)

Certainly it is the case that scholars resist consensus on everything—beginnings, dominant trends, and endings—where *modernism* is concerned.

Yet, for Anglo-American and British traditions of literary and artistic scholarship there is a tenuous agreement that some names and works *must* be included in any putatively comprehensive account of modern writing and art. Further, there seems to be an identifiable pleasure in listing features of art and writing that begin to predominate (by Virginia Woolf's time line) on or about December, 1910.

The names and techniques of the "modern" that are generally set forth constitute a descriptive catalogue resembling a natural philosopher's curiosity cabinet. In such cabinets disparate and seemingly discontinuous objects share space because that is the very function of the cabinet—to house or give order to varied things in what appears a rational, scientific manner. Picasso and Pound, Joyce and Kandinsky, Stravinsky and Klee, Brancusi and H. D. are made to form a series. Collage, primitivism, montage, allusion, "dehumanization," and leitmotifs are forced into the same field. Nietzsche and Marx, Freud and Frazier, Jung and Bergson become dissimilar bedfellows. Such naming rituals have the force of creative works like *Ulysses* and *The Waste Land*. They substitute a myth of unified purpose and intention for definitional certainty. Before succumbing to the myth, however, perhaps we should examine the "change" that according to Woolf's calendar occurred on or about December, 1910.

Surely that change is most accurately defined as an acknowledgment of radical uncertainty. Where precisely anyone or anything was located could no longer be charted on old maps of "civilization," nor could even the most microscopic observation tell the exact time and space of day. The very conceptual possibilities of both time and space had been dramatically refigured in the mathematics of Einstein and the physics of Heisenberg. A war of barbaric immensity combined with imperialism, capitalism and totalitarianism's subordination or extermination of tens of millions to produce a reaction to human possibilities quite different from Walt Whitman's joyous welcoming of the modern. Whitman in the nineteenth century exalted: "Years of the modern! years of the unperform'd!"

For T. S. Eliot, the completed and expected performance of mankind scarcely warranted joy. There was, instead, the "Murmur of maternal lamentation" presaging:

> Cracks . . . and bursts in the violet air
> Falling towers
> Jerusalem Athens Alexandria
> Vienna London
> Unreal.[4]

Eliot's speaker, however, is comforted by the certainty that there are millennia of "fragments" (artistic shrapnel) constituting a *civilization* to be mined, a cultured repertoire to act as a shore against ruins. That is to say, Fitzgerald's Tom Buchanan in *The Great Gatsby* seems to be a more honestly self-conscious representation of the threat that some artists whom we call "modern" felt in the face of a new world of science, war, technology, and imperialism. "Civilization's going to pieces," Tom confides to an assembled dinner party at his lavish Long Island estate while drinking a corky (but rather impressive) claret. "I've gotten to be a terrible pessimist about things," he continues.[5]

Now, I don't mean to suggest that Anglo-American, British, and Irish moderns did not address themselves with seriousness and sincerity to a changed condition of humankind. Certainly they did. But they also mightily restricted the province of what constituted the tumbling of the towers, and they remained eternally self-conscious of their own pessimistic "becomings." Tom's pessimism turns out to be entirely bookish. It is predicated upon Stoddard's (which Tom remembers as "Goddard's") racialistic murmurings. What really seems under threat are not the towers of civilization, but rather an assumed supremacy of boorishly racist, indisputably sexist, and unbelievably wealthy Anglo-Saxon males. One means of shoring up one's self under perceived threats of "democratization" and a "rising tide" of color is to resort to elitism—to adopt a style that refuses to represent any *thing* other than the stylist's refusal to represent (what Susan Sontag refers to as an "aesthetics of silence").

Another strategy is to claim that one's artistic presentations and performances are quintessential renderings of the unrepresentable—human subconsciousness, for example, or primitive structural underpinnings of a putatively civilized mankind, or the simultaneity of a space-time continuum. Yet another strategy—a somewhat tawdry and dangerous one—is advocacy and allegiance to authoritarian movements or institutions that promise law and order. Regardless of their strategies for confronting it, though, it was *change*—a profound shift in what could be taken as unquestionable assumptions about the meaning of human life—that moved those artists whom we call "moderns." And it was only a rare one among them who did not have some formula—some "ism"—for checking a precipitous toppling of man and his towers. Futurism, imagism, impressionism, vorticism, expressionism, cubism—all offered explicit programs for the arts *and* the salvation of humanity. Each in its turn yields to other formulations of the role of the writer and the task of the artist in a changed and always, ever more rapidly changing world.

Today, we are "postmodern." Rather than *civilization*'s having gone to pieces, it has extended its sway in the form of a narrow and concentrated group of power brokers scarcely more charming, humane or informed than Tom Buchanan. To connect the magnificent achievements, breakthroughs and experiments of an entire panoply of modern intellectuals with fictive attitudes of a fictive modern man (Fitzgerald's Tom) may seem less than charitable. For even though Tom evades the law, shirks moral responsibility, and still ends up rich and in possession of the fairest Daisy of them all (though he ends, that is to say, as the capitalist triumphant, if not the triumphant romantic hero of the novel), there are still other modes of approach to the works of the moderns.

Lionel Trilling, for example, provides one of the most charitable scholarly excursions to date.[6] He describes modern literature as "shockingly personal," posing "every question that is forbidden in polite society" and involving readers in intimate interactions that leave them uneasily aware of their personal beings in the world. One scholarly reaction to Trilling's formulations, I'm afraid, is probably like that of the undergraduates whom he churlishly suggests would be "rejected" by the efforts of Yeats and Eliot, Pound and Proust. It is difficult, for example, for an Afro-American student of literature like me—one unconceived in the philosophies of Anglo-American, British, and Irish moderns—to find intimacy in either the moderns' hostility to *civilization* or in their fawning reliance on an array of images and assumptions bequeathed by a *civilization* that, in its prototypical form, is exclusively Western, preeminently bourgeoisie, and optically white.

Alas, Fitzgerald's priggishly astute Nick has only a limited vocabulary when it comes to a domain of experience that I, as an Afro-American, know well: "As we crossed Blackwell's Island a limousine passed us, driven by a white chauffeur, in which sat three modish negroes, two bucks and a girl. I laughed aloud as the yolks of their eyeballs rolled toward us in haughty rivalry" (69). If only Fitgerald had placed his "pale well-dressed negro" in the limousine or if Joseph Conrad[7] had allowed his Africans to actually be articulate or if D. H. Lawrence[8] had not suggested through Birkin's reflection on African culture that:

Thousands of years ago, that which was imminent in himself must have taken place in these Africans: the goodness, the holiness, the desire for creation and productive happiness must have lapsed, leaving the single impulse for knowledge through the senses, knowledge arrested and ending in the senses, mystic knowledge in disintegration and dissolution, knowledge such as the beetles have, which live purely within the world of corruption and cold dissolution. (245-46)

Or if O'Neill[9] had only bracketed the psycho-surreal final trappings of his Emperor's world and given us the stunning account of colonialism that remains implicit in his quip at the close of his list of dramatis personae: "The action of the play takes place on an island in the West Indians, as yet un-self-determined by white marines." If any of these moves had been accomplished, then perhaps I might feel, at least, some of the intimacy and reverence Trilling suggests.

But even as I recall a pleasurable spring in New Haven when I enjoyed cracking Joycean codes in order to teach *Ulysses*, I realize that the Irish writer's grand monument is not a work to which I shall return with reverence and charitably discover the type of inquisition that Trilling finds so engaging: "[Modern literature] asks us if we are content with our marriages, with our family lives, with our professional lives, with our friends"(7-8). I am certain that I shall never place *Ulysses* in a group of texts that I describe, to use Trilling's words, as "spiritual" if not "actually religious." Perhaps, the reason I shall not is because the questions Trilling finds—correctly or incorrectly—intimately relevant to his life are descriptive only of a bourgeois, characteristically twentieth-century, white Western mentality. As an Afro-American, a person of African descent in the United States today, I spend a great deal of time reflecting that in the world's largest geographies the question "Where will I find water, wood, or food for today?" is (and has been for the entirety of this century) the most pressing and urgently posed inquiry.

In "diasporic," "developing," "Third World," "emerging"—or whatever adjective one chooses to signify the non-Western side of Chenweizu's title "The West and the Rest of Us"—nations or territories there is no need to pose, in ironical Audenesque ways, questions such as: Are we happy? Are we content? Are we free?[10] Such questions presuppose, at least, an adequate level of sustenance and a faith in human behavioral alternatives sufficient to enable a self-directed questioning. In other words, without food for thought, all modernist bets are off. Rather than reducing the present essay to a discourse on underdevelopment, however, or invoking a different kind of human being, what I want to evoke by emphasizing concerns other than those of "civilization" and its discontents is a discursive constellation that marks a change in Afro-American nature that occurred on or about September 18, 1895. The constellation that I have in mind includes Afro-American literature, music, art, graphic design, and intellectual history. It is *not* confined to a traditionally defined belles lettres, or, to Literature with a capital and capitalist "L".

In fact, it is precisely the confinement (in a very Foucaultian sense discovered in *Madness and Civilization*) of such bourgeois categories (derivatives of Kantian aesthetics) that the present essay seeks to subvert.[11] Hence, there will be few sweeps over familiar geographies of a familiar Harlem Renaissance conceived as an enterprise of limited accomplishment and limited liability—"Harlem Renaissance, Ltd." Instead, I shall attempt to offer an account of discursive conditions of possibility for what I define as "renaissancism" in Afro-American expressive culture as a whole. I am, thus, interested less in *individual* "artists" than in areas of expressive production. It is my engagement with these areas of Afro-American production (intellectual history, music, graphic design, stage presence, oratory, etc.) that provides intimacy and that leads me, through a specifically Afro-American modernism, to blues geographies that are still in search of substantial analysis—and liberation.

* * *

The affinity that I feel for Afro-American modernism is not altogether characteristic. Scholars have been far from enthusiastic in their evaluation of the "Harlem Renaissance" of the 1920s—an outpouring of Afro-American writing, music, and social criticism that includes some of the earliest attempts by Afro-American artists and intellectuals to define themselves in "modern" terms. Few scholars would disagree that the Harlem Renaissance marks a readily identifiable "modern" movement in Afro-American intellectual history, and most would concede that the principal question surrounding the Harlem Renaissance has been: "Why did the renaissance fail?"

Scarcely four years after "Black Tuesday," that awful moment which plummeted American into depression, a prominent intellectual and contemporary of the renaissance wrote:

> It is a good thing that [the editor] Dorothy West is doing in instituting a magazine [*Challenge*] through which the voices of younger Negro writers can be heard. The term "younger Negro writers" connotes a degree of disillusionment and disappointment for those who a decade ago hailed with loud huzzas the dawn of the Negro literary millennium. We expected much; perhaps, too much. I now judge that we ought to be thankful for the half-dozen younger writers who did emerge and make a place for themselves.[12]

James Weldon Johnson's disillusionment that the Harlem Renaissance "failed" finds its counterparts and echoes in the scholarship, polemics, and popular rhetoric of the past half-century. An avatar of Johnson's disillusionment, for example, is the scholarly disapprobation of Nathan Huggins' provocative study *Harlem Renaissance* (1971).[13]

Huggins charges that the *Harlem Renaissance* failed because it remained provincial. Its spokespersons unfortunately accepted the province of "race" as a domain in which to forge a New Negro identity. Mired in this ethnic provincialism, writers like Countee Cullen, Claude McKay, Langston Hughes, Alain Locke and others failed to realized that they did not have to battle for a defining identity in America. They needed only, in Huggins' view, to claim "their *patria*, their nativity" as American citizens (309). The Harvard historian believes that Afro-Americans are—and have always been—inescapably implicated in the warp and woof of the American fabric. In fact, he holds that they are nothing other than "Americans" whose darker pigmentation has been appropriated as a liberating mask by their lighter complexioned fellow citizens. Hence, Afro-Americans are fundamentally bone of the bone—if not flesh of the flesh—of the American people, and the intricacies of minstrelsy and the aberrations of the Harlem Renaissance are both misguided, but deeply revelatory, products of the way race relations have stumbled and faltered on the boards of progressive optimism in the United States.

While Huggins adduces provinciality and narrowness as causes for a failed Harlem Renaissance, his contemporary and fellow Afro-American historian David Levering Lewis takes a contrary view.[14] Lewis ascribes Harlem's failings to a tragically wide, ambitious, and delusional striving on the part of renaissance intellectuals. Writing ten years after Huggins, Lewis describes the appearance of Alain Locke's compendium of creative, critical, and scholarly utterances *The New Negro* (1925) as follows:

> its thirty-four Afro-American contributors (four were white) included almost all the future Harlem Renaissance regulars—an incredibly small band of artists, poets, and writers upon which to base Locke's conviction that the race's "more immediate hope rests in the revaluation by white and black alike of the Negro in terms of his artistic endowments and cultural contributions, past and prospective." To suppose that a few superior people, who would not have filled a Liberty Hall quorum or Ernestine Rose's 135th Street library, were to lead ten million Afro-Americans into an era of opportunity and justice seemed irresponsibly delusional. (117)

Lewis suggests that this delusional vision was a direct function of a rigidly segregated United States. Unlike Huggins, who assumes *patria* as a given, Lewis claims that Afro-Americans turned to art during the twenties precisely because there was no conceivable chance of their assuming *patria*—or anything else in white America. Art seemed to offer the only means of advancement because it was the *only* area in America—from an Afro-American perspective—where the color line had not been rigidly drawn. Excluded from politics and education, from profitable and challenging areas of the professions, and brutalized by all American economic arrangements, Afro-Americans adopted the arts as a domain of hope and an area of possible progress.

Lewis' stunningly full research reveals the merits of his thesis. He provides a grim look at dire economic and social restrictions that hedged blacks round everywhere in the United States during the 1920s. Exceptional art—like effective and liberating social strategies—was, perhaps, a quite illusory Afro-American goal. In the end, all of Harlem's sound and flair could not alter the indubitably American fact that black men and women, regardless of their educational or artistic accomplishments, would always be poorer, more brutally treated, and held in lower esteem than their white American counterparts. The renaissance, thus, reveals itself in retrospect, according to Lewis, as the product of middle-class black "architects [who] believed in ultimate victory through the maximizing of the exceptional. They [members of the 'talented tenth'] deceived themselves into thinking that race relations in the United States were amenable to the assimilationist patterns of a Latin country" (305-06).

The gap between the Afro-American masses and the talented tenth could not have been manifested more profoundly than in the latter's quixotic assimilationist assumptions. For, ironically, the most acute symbol of Harlem's surge at the wall of segregation is not poems nor interracial dinner parties, according to Lewis, but rather the Harlem riot of 1935, in which thousands took to the streets and unleashed their profound frustrations by destroying millions of dollars' worth of white property. The riot, for Lewis, offers the conclusive signal that the strivings of the twenties were delusional and that the renaissance was fated to end with a bang of enraged failure.

Johnson, Huggins, and Lewis are all scholars who merit respect for their willingness to assess an enormously complex array of interactions spanning more than a decade of Afro-American artistic, social, and intellectual history. Thanks to their efforts, we have far more than a bare scholarly beginning when we attempt to define one of the seminal moments of Afro-American "modernism." Yet, the scholarly reflections that we possess are, unfortunately, governed by a problematic—a set of questions and issues—that makes certain conclusions and evaluations inevitable. For if one begins with the query that motivates Johnson and others, then one is destined to provide a derogatory account of the twenties. "Why did the Harlem Renaissance fail?" is the question, and the query is tantamount to the unexpected question sprung by a stranger as one walks a crowded street: "When, Sir, did you stop beating your wife?" Both questions are, of course, conditioned by presuppositions that restrict the field of possible responses. To ask "why" the renaissance failed is to agree, at the very outset, that the twenties did not have profoundly beneficial effects for areas of Afro-American discourse that we have only recently begun to explore in depth. Willing compliance in a problematic of "failure" is equivalent, I believe, to efforts of historians—black and otherwise— who seek causal explanations for the "failure" of the Civil Rights Movement.

It seems paradoxical that a probing scholar of Lewis' caliber—an investigator who implies strongly that he clearly understands the low esteem in which Afro-Americans will *always* be held—devotes three hundred pages to proving the "failure" of a movement that in the eyes of white America could never have been a success—precisely because it was "Afro-American." The scholarly double bind that forces Afro-Americanists to begin with *given* assessments of black intellectual history and thus laboriously work their way to dire conclusions is, quite simply, an unfortunate result of disciplinary control and power politics. The purely hypothetical injunction to an Afro-Americanist from the mainstream might be stated as follows:

Show me, by the best scholarly procedures of the discipline, why the Harlem Renaissance was a failure, and I will reward you. By explaining this *failure*, you will have rendered an "honest" intellectual service to the discipline, to yourself, and to your race.

The primary evaluation where such an injunction is concerned remains, of course, that of the dominating society whose axiological validity and aptitude are guaranteed by its dictation of the governing problematic.

If, for the moment, we return to Anglo-American and British modernism, it is difficult to conceive of scholars devoting enormous energy to explicating the "failure" of modernism. Surely it is the case that the various "isms" of the first decades of British and American modernism did not forestall wars, feed the poor, cure the sick, empower coal miners in Wales (or West Virginia), or arrest the spread of bureaucratic technology. Furthermore—though apologists will not thank me for saying so—the artistic rebels and rebellions of British and American modernism were often decidedly puerile and undeniably transient. The type of mind-set that has governed a Harlem Renaissance problematic would be in force vis-à-vis British and American modernism, I think, if a scholar took Ranier Marie Rilke's evaluation in a letter to a friend as the indisputable truth of modernism's total effect on the world. Writing at the outbreak of World War I, Rilke laments:

> that such confusion, not-knowing-which-way-to-turn, the whole sad man-made complication of this provoked fate, that exactly this incurably bad condition of things was necessary to force out evidence of whole-hearted courage, devotion and bigness? While we, the arts, the theater, called nothing forth in these very same people, brought nothing to rise and flower, were unable to change anyone.[15]

A too optimistic faith in the potential of art may, in fact, be as signal a mark of British and American modernism's "failure" as of the Harlem Renaissance. I suspect, however, that no group of British or white American scholars would take *failure* as their watchword and governing sign for an entire generation and its products. The predictable corollary of my suspicion is my belief that a new problematic is in order for the Harlem Renaissance. What is needed, I believe, is a reconceptualization of the questions we will ask in order to locate the efforts of the 1920s.

* * *

The new problematic that I am attempting to formulate begins with turn-of-the-century Afro-American discursive strategies and their motivation. My claim is that Afro-American spokespersons in late nineteenth-century America were primarily interested in a form of discourse—of public address and delivery—that would effectively articulate the needs, virtues, and strengths of a mass of Afro-Americans stranded by Jim Crow discrimination and violent lynch law in the "country districts" of the South. Both Booker T. Washington and W. E. B. DuBois set forth statements that define strategies of discourse—a black "discursive field," as it were—that are southern in focus and revolutionary in implication. For in *Up From Slavery* (1901) and *The Souls of Black Folk* (1903) alike, we find that the "subject" is the black masses of southern country districts; the goal of both works is the effective liberation of this mass group from feudal subsistence economies and legally reinforced conditions of ignorance and illiteracy. In order to be recognized and heard as Afro-American spokespersons, however, both Washington and DuBois had to assume a discursive stance in relationship to the signal white American *form* for representing blacks—the minstrel mask.

Briefly, minstrelsy is a perduring legacy and strategy of representation when blacks appear in white discourse. It offers a form of appropriation, a domestic space for taking, hearing, and containing the black OTHER. Only by assuming a posture relative to this space could turn-of-the-century, Afro-American spokespersons become effectively articulate.

While the options of such spokespersons were not as clear-cut as a simple duality would suggest, I claim that Washington and DuBois, in their deployment of a "mastery of form" and a "deformation of mastery," respectively, set the contours of a field of Afro-American phonics that marks the birth of Afro-American modernism.

"Mastery" is such a common term in colleges and universities with the MA and MPhil degrees that the first strategy—"mastery of form"—is easily understood. But "deformation" is a more difficult concept.

What I intend by the term is akin to what the deconstructionist Jacques Derrida calls the "trace." The deformative sounds of Afro-America are the group phonics and common language of the masses, sounds that are traditionally labelled "substandard," "nonsensical," or "unlearned" by white speakers. But such commonly understood sounds, under a linguist's scrutiny, reveal themselves as normal, standard, literate components of one dialect. The provisional and dialectical character of Black English infects, as it were, assumptions by all speakers in the United States that their language variety is anything other than a quite provisional dialect. It is impossible to sustain a master, standard, or absolute position in the face of the radically demonstrated provisionality of one's position. When Caliban knows himself as a usurped king, it is time for Prospero to depart the island.

Deformation, then, is the putative bondsperson's assured song of his or her own exalted, expressive status in an always coequal world of sounds and soundings. Anecdotally, one can image Paul Whiteman trying to sustain the title "King of Jazz" in the presence of Louis Armstrong. In the context of the present discussion, it is very difficult to imagine ninety-nine percent of the Anglo-American population of the years between 1899 and 1920 attempting to convince itself that it sounded in any way as brilliant as W. E. B. DuBois, who takes apart—or de-forms—illusions of such equality through the lyrical brilliance of his prose and his deliberately ironical and satirical mockeries of such illusion.

Washington intersperses *Up From Slavery* with outrageous darky jokes, caricatures of elderly black southern men and women, aspersions against overly ambitious northern blacks, and insulting stereotypes of the race, including a portrait of his own mother as a CHICKEN THIEF. But he also devotes a quarter of his autobiography to the art of public speaking, and his outlandish portrayals of the folk of the "country districts" reveal themselves, finally, as means of holding the attention of an audience that knows but one sound—minstrelsy—of the Negro. In effect, Washington employs sounds of the minstrel mask, or form, to create a space and audience for black public speaking. That public speaking, in turn, is employed to secure philanthropic funds for a black vocational educational institution that constitutes a moral skills center for the black folks of the country districts. Tuskegee Institute is the ultimate result of Washington's sounding on, and mastery of, the minstrel form. His mastery of form is, in fact, signified by the transcendence of minstrel *non-sense* represented by Tuskegee.

In contrast to Washington's mastery of form is DuBois' deformation of mastery. Refusing the sounds of minstrelsy, DuBois instituted black song, specifically the Afro-American spiritual, as the carrier of a black folk energy from southern country districts. Fisk University, built, in part, by monies obtained from concerts of spirituals presented by the Fisk Jubilee Singers, becomes a symbol of the type of educational centers that are needed to move Afro-Americans into the first ranks of twentieth-century life. For DuBois, the black university is the site where black folk energies and Western high culture merge, producing a sound that surpasses all traditional American music, or minstrelsy. In its emphasis on the symbolic weight of black folk spirituality and spiritual singing, *The Souls of Black Folk* stands as a singing book.

The defining discursive models of mastery and deformation provided by Washington and DuBois produce not a binary opposition, but, rather, a type of Cartesian plane—a system of coordinates in which any point on, say, a horizontal axis of mastery implies a coexistent point on a vertical axis of deformation. Hence, the notion of a discursive field.

Alain Locke, a key Afro-American spokesperson of the 1920s, seems to have possessed a brilliant comprehension of this field. For his anthology *The New Negro* (1925) represents Afro-American discourse in its myriad stops and resonances. Locke's collection is a blend of business-like mastery and lyrical and intrepid deformation. It is a public document geared toward specifically in-group and distinctively racial ends. Its purpose is to sound a comprehensive Afro-American voice, one capable of singing in the manner of spirituals (Locke himself wrote the very centerpiece essay on the Afro-American spirituals), yet adept in the ways of southern education and vocation. There are essays devoted both to Hampton-Tuskegee vocationalism and to black business enterprise in the South. Moreover, *The New Negro* employs a rich array of African and Afro-American graphics in order to frame its claims for the emergence of a "New Negro" with venerable visuals drawn from centuries-old traditions. The result is a landmark in Afro-American discourse: a collection that sounds a resonantly new note as both a public speaking manual and a deeply racial (and vernacular) singing book.

High cultural and vernacular expressivity merge in the office of moving Afro-America from subservience, low esteem, and dependency to the status of respected and boldly outspoken nation. What is signal in Locke's venture is the unabashed coalescence of mass and class, "standard" dialect and black vernacular, aesthetic and political concerns. A long and probing essay addressed to the cause of African decolonization and written by DuBois is the concluding section of Locke's work.

If *The New Negro* is representative of efforts of Harlem Renaissance spokespersons (and I believe it is), then the discursive results of Harlem in black intellectual history can scarcely be deemed failures. For Locke's work both enjoins and represents a successful expressive moment in the field constituted by a mastery of form and a deformation of mastery. *The New Negro* is a kind of manual of maroonage, a voice of a northern, urban black population that has radically absented itself from the erstwhile plantations and devastated country districts of the South. Combining a panoply of folk sounds with traditional artistic forms and entrepreneurial and practical concerns of black liberation, *The New Negro* projects an articulate, nationalistic, and independent black voice. That voice—if at times too sanguine, overly self-conscious and self-confident—constitutes a high point for energies set in motion at the turn of the century.

Further, the voice of the New Negro comprised a model for subsequent generations. When Sterling Brown, who is preeminently a poet and critic of the 1930s, assumed the mantle of "folk poet" as a natural wrap, he demonstrated the efficacy and effects of a successful Afro-American modernism. For what the Harlem Renaissance, as a masterfully achieved space within a black discursive field, enabled was a speaking or sounding place where a middle-class, Phi Beta Kappa, college-bred poet like Brown could responsibly play a distinctive note. DuBois' black, country folk as university pupils find their voice and representation in the Jubilee Singers of Nashville. The urbane Sterling Brown met the blues singer Gertrude "Ma" Rainey in Nashville (home of Fisk University). He was in the company of the famous black musicologist and Fisk faculty member John Work when they encountered Rainey at a Nashville club. What the two men drew from the tradition of folk sound represented by Rainey is now a matter of black discursive history.

Brown's *Southern Road* (1932) is one of the most outstanding collections of modern, black verse in existence. Work's collections and analyses of black song (*Folk Song of the American Negro, Jubilee, Ten Spirituals*) are unsurpassed. The productions of the two men not only guaranteed their own recognition, reward, and employment, but also brought new perspective to the group portrait of the Afro-American that had been in formation since the turn of the century. This perspective was a usable construction for writers like Richard Wright and Zora Neale Hurston who had their maturation in the thirties.

* * *

The success of the Harlem Renaissance as Afro-American modernism's defining moment is signalled by *The New Negro*'s confidently voiced plays within a field marked by the mastery of form and the deformation of mastery. Only by reconstructing or re-membering a discursive history of Afro-America and its socioeconomic and sociopolitical motivations and objectives can one see Harlem and its successors as articulations that carry a population not away from querulous literary ancestors, but rather *up from slavery*. Modernism for Afro-America finds impetus, empowerment, and inspiration in the black city (Harlem). No cracks and bursts in the violet air here, only soundings designed to secure the highest available social, economic, and artistic rewards for a generation that moved decisively beyond the horrors of old country districts.

A blues sound rolled forth, producing the sense of a moment's speaking, an augury of possibilities for finance and even fusion (jazz) that surely became orchestrated during the 1960s and 1970s, the period of a Black Arts Movement that referred to itself in energetically self-conscious ways as "Renaissance II."

Perhaps the eternally modern in Afro-American discursive and intellectual history is not so much signalled by the single "Harlem Renaissance" as by a more inclusive "renaissancism" defined as an ever-present, folk or vernacular drive that moves always up, beyond, and away from whatever forms of oppression a surrounding culture next devises. "Renaissancism" is, finally, the sign of the modern that joins Harlem and the *Indigene* movement of Haiti and African Negritude. One might say that the success of Afro-American renaissancism consists in its heralding of a countermodernism, as it were, a drive unlike the exquisite disillusionment and despair of Britain and Jazz Age U.S.A. I use "counter" just as advisedly as I earlier employed "modernism" alone, for now I believe the complexities—a very peculiar set of expressive manifestations and critical and theoretical issues—of Afro-American twentieth-century expression should be comprehensible. Recognition of such complexities leads to the recognitions of a trace, a something not accounted for in traditional, Anglo-American definitions of modernism. One definition of what can be recognized is a "countermodernism."

This countertradition found its socioeconomic and sociopolitical groundings in what the sagacious Franz Fanon called "dying colonialism." *The New Negro*, as stated earlier, concludes with an essay by DuBois that sings, figuratively, this death of colonialism and sounds a note of liberation to which hundreds of millions of formerly colonized, darker peoples of the world can march. This note from Harlem, as any scan of the global scene today will reveal, is, perhaps, the most thoroughly modern sound the United States has yet produced.

NOTES

[1]Harry Levin, "What Was Modernism?", *Massachusetts Review* 1 (1960): 609-30. All citations are marked by page numbers in parentheses.

[2]Robert Martin Adams, "What Was Modernism?", *Hudson Review* 31 (1978): 19-33. Hereafter in my notes, I will list the full reference. Subsequent cites will be marked by page numbers in parentheses.

[3]Ihab Hassan, "POSTmodernISM A Paracritical Bibliography," *New Literary History* 3 (1971): 5-30.

[4]T. S. Eliot, "The Waste Land," in *Modern Poetry*, ed. Maynard Mack et al., 2nd ed. (Englewood Cliffs, N.J.: 1961), 157-58.

[5]F. Scott Fitzgerald, *The Great Gatsby* (New York, 1953), 13.

[6]Lionel Trilling, "On the Teaching of Modern Literature," in *Beyond Culture* (New York, 1965), 327.

[7]I refer, of course, to Conrad's "Heart of Darkness."

[8]D. H. Lawrence, *Women in Love* (New York, 1974).

[9]The reference is to Eugene O'Neill's *The Emperor Jones*.

[10]Wystan Hugh Auden's ordinary citizen as "Modern Man" is coldly described by the speaker of "The Citizen (To JS/07/M/378 This marble Monument Is Erected by the State)," a 1940 poem, as "in the modern sense of an old-fashioned word, he was a saint." Quoted from Mack, *Modern Poetry*, 206. The speaker is not undone when his/her report is broken by someone's question about such exemplary conduct: "Was he free? Was he happy?" The speaker answers: "... The Question is absurd:/Had anything been wrong, we should certainly have heard."

[11]In *Madness and Civilization*, Michel Foucault argues that it is *de rigueur* for a rational, bourgeois, capitalist state to "confine" the poor, the criminal, and the insane in order to know the boundaries of affluence, sanity, and innocence. It is, however, *confinement* in itself that enforces the categories; if you are an inmate of a "total institution" (like a prison, or, American Slavery as the "Prisonhouse of Bondage"), then you are automatically classified according to the defining standards of that institution. The Kantian reference is, of course, to the *Critique of Judgement* (1790). Once "ART" and "AESTHETICS" are distinguished from "popular culture" and "low taste," then one has effected a confinement that can be enforced merely by mentioning a word. Such distinctions—resting on Western metaphysics—can be used to defend and preserve canons of literature and to protect "artistic" masterpieces from all criticism. Only "*men* of Taste" are held to possess the developed "aesthetic sense" and sensibility requisite to identification and judgment of genuine works of "art." If such men declare that a product is *not* ART but a product of some other category, there is no escape from their authority of confinement—except subversion.

[12]"Foreword," *Challenge* 1 (1934):1.

[13]Nathan Huggins, *Harlem Renaissance* (New York, 1971). Subsequent citations appear in text.

[14]David Levering Lewis, *When Harlem Was in Vogue* (New York, 1981). Subsequent citations appear in text. The phrase "when Harlem was in vogue" is drawn from the section of Langston Hughes' autobiography *The Big Sea* (1940) devoted to the Harlem Renaissance. Hughes writes of the renaissance as a mere "vogue" set in motion and largely financed by white downtowners while Negroes played minstrel and trickster roles in it all. A time of low-seriousness and charming highjinks is what Highes (one hopes ironically) portrays. In fact, I think Hughes' characterization is as much a product of the dreadful disappointment he suffered when his patron (Mrs. R. Osgood Mason) dumped him because he decided to write an "engaged" poem, a "socialist" response to the opening of a luxury hotel in New York when so many were starving. He reads treacherous patronage over the entire Harlem Renaissance. Further, to say, as Hughes does, that you were "only funning" is to dampen the pain that results if *you* were really serious and your patron was "funning" all along. In any case, I believe Hughes' account (partially because he lived and produced wonderful work through subsequent generations) has had an enormous effect on subsequent accounts of the renaissance. In many ways, this effect has been unfortunate.

[15]Quotes from Miklos Szabolcsi, "Avant-garde, Neo-avant-garde, Modernism: Questions and Suggestions," *New Literary History* 3 (1971): 75.

COMMENTARY

Robert B. Stepto

Houston Baker's thought-provoking 1987 essay, "Modernism and the Harlem Renaissance," needs to be read in the context of three discussions that were engaging scholars at that time: the discussion of modernism as many modernisms, not one; the reconsideration of traditional American literary movements or periods in light of the inclusion of African American authors (how does including Frederick Douglass or Harriet Jacobs change our views of the American Renaissance?); and the reassessment of traditional African American literary movements or periods, most obviously as a result of fresh attention to the women writers, but perhaps, too, because by 1987 African American literature had been taught widely for twenty years, and the field was in sore need of new approaches and fresh conceptualizations.

In this essay, Baker joins those scholars of the day (see, for example, the contributors to Amritjit Singh et al., eds., *The Harlem Renaissance: Revaluations* [New York: Garland, 1989]) who were reassessing the most revered African American literary movement, the Harlem Renaissance. He announces that he seeks both new approaches and fresh concepts, and that what he desires in particular is an analytical model enabling a reassessment of the Harlem Renaissance that skirts the quagmire of period analysis, and that situates it in a contour of African American "discursive history"—as opposed to literary history alone. One may say, then, that since Baker here sees the Harlem Renaissance not as a body of literature, but rather as a "constellation" of literature, art, and intellectual history, what he seeks is an American studies—or African American studies—model for reassessing the Harlem Renaissance.

While not employing terms such as "cultural studies," it is clear that Baker here is moving toward some sort of cultural studies approach to the Harlem Renaissance of his own devising. Pertinent in this regard is his deployment of phrases like "expressive culture" and "expressive production." What he means by "expressive production," for example, is usually no different from what the cultural studies scholars mean when

Houston Baker, "Modernism and the Harlem Renaissance," originally appeared in *American Quarterly* 39, no. 1 (spring 1987), © 1987 American Studies Association.

they employ "cultural production." Yet his term situates him at the periphery, not the heart, of the Marxist arguments encoded in "cultural production," and certainly closer to the work of the intellectual predecessor Baker lauds most in this essay, the scholar-poet Sterling Brown.

Although it is curiously not cited here, Brown's groundbreaking anthology, *Negro Caravan* (New York: Dryden Press, 1941), edited with Arthur P. Davis and Ulysses Lee, is clearly a model for Baker, for until quite recently no anthology of African American materials did a better job of collecting both vernacular and written texts and insisting that its readers absorb both. Brown et al. were, in Baker's terms, assembling an African American "discursive history," and in the more personal moments of this essay one senses Baker's lament that he will probably attend yet another English department meeting, and again be exposed to the "disciplinary control and power politics" of that portion of the academy, long before he gets to do something equivalent to joining Sterling Brown and John Work while they chat with Ma Rainey.

It is here, then, that we find a suggestion that writing this essay signaled a turning point in Baker's career. While Baker here neither leaves the literature profession nor eschews its trendiest argot, he does work to free himself from the projects and methods of traditional literary analysis. The scholar Baker is becoming here wants to take on the whole of African American discourse, and soon write about just about anything in the expressive culture, including, as we have come to see, rap music.

Like all good provocative essays, Baker's has its strengths and its curiosities, sometimes in equal measure. Early on, he writes passionately about his own sense of alienation, as an African American scholar of literature, from the prevailing definitions of modernism, adding Ellisonian flourishes (e.g., the world from which these definitions arise is "optically white") while borrowing Chenweizu's phrase, "The West and the Rest of Us," to drive home the point that in Africa and the rest of the "Third World," where the basic issues of subsistence are paramount, "there is no need to pose, in ironical Audenesque ways, questions such as : Are we happy? Are we content? Are we free?" This is a powerful, unassailable argument, yet like most arguments of the "what about the Third World" variety, it does not speak to the issue at hand: Baker and the rest of us Americans (of any race) "unconceived in the philosophies of Anglo-American, British, and Irish moderns" are not denizens of the Third World scratching out a life. What's needed here is some direct acknowledgment of the complexity of the situation; at very least, a nod in the direction of Du Bois's concept of the "double-consciousness" of the black American.

In a most provocative section, Baker inveighs against the strictures of disciplinary methodologies and against the questions the traditional disciplines tend to ask about African Americans in particular, citing as examples the widely read histories of the Harlem Renaissance written by two African American historians, Nathan Huggins and David Levering Lewis. Baker's claim is that both scholars, in emphasizing the shortcomings of the Renaissance, are guilty of "willing compliance in a problematic of failure." This, Baker adds, has been to their benefit since the academy tends to reward scholars whose work confirms the failures of black America in general. This is angry stuff, but curious stuff, too, since the premise of this essay is to rescue the study of the Harlem Renaissance not from the clutches of the historians but from those of the literature scholars—those who would see the Renaissance as an "exclusive literary enterprise." Why are Huggins and Lewis alone the "straw dogs" here? Are there no literary critics to be taken to task? Are Huggins and Lewis alone excoriated because their histories are the most influential, or is it because they are most easily criticized, leaving aside that in fact neither scholar is an English professor?

A strength of the essay's third section is that it outlines the kind of discursive history Baker is calling for, and offers in the process a positioning of Booker T. Washington and W. E. B. Du Bois in that history that comprehends their mutuality, instead of sustaining the tired idea that the two spokesmen must be seen as binary opposites. This is the discussion most useful in teaching: students will profit from Baker's depiction of how Washington and Du Bois each assume a "discursive stance" in relationship to the minstrel mask, and of how the various combinations of these stances, no matter whether found in texts such as Alain Locke's *The New Negro* (New York: Boni, 1925) or in the careers of writers like Sterling Brown, point to a history of African American discourse which is *the* history of African American modernism. In teaching, the instructor would want to bring Paul Laurence Dunbar into the discussion, since it is unimaginable to teach turn-of-the-century African American stances regarding the minstrel mask without including the author of "We Wear the Mask" and other highly pertinent poems. The instructor would also want to point out that when Baker finds proof of success, not failure, in *The New Negro* and in Brown, he is actually supporting Brown's claim that the New Negro movement in all of its venues (including Brown and

Locke's Washington, D.C.) was more important and lasting than any-thing construed as a renaissance in Harlem.

This essay deserves continued reading, though I am sure Baker would prefer that readers seek out the more developed versions of these argu-ments in his book of the same title. Baker's work proves that nothing intrigues African Americanists more than seeing African America's dis-course whole; it also reminds us of how difficult that task is.

ROBERT F. BERKHOFER, JR.

A New Context for a
New American Studies?

A PRIMARY IMPETUS TO THE AMERICAN STUDIES MOVEMENT AFTER WORLD
War II was the effort to escape the narrow focus of the New Criticism in
favor of a broader interpretation based upon contextual study. Context seemed
to be found in a vague but polysemic definition of culture. Under the rubric
of "culture," scholars of America in disciplines as diverse as music, art,
literature, and intellectual history believed that they were all studying and
thereby constituting a common context in order to move beyond the special
interests and methods of their separate fields. By exploring the myths, symbols,
and images embedded in texts, tales, and artifacts, those scholars thought
they exposed the "masked" and other deep patterns underlying American
culture. Those covert foundations revealed the ambivalences, ironies, and
paradoxes of the American mind whether found in the dream of the self-made
man, classic and later individualism, industrialism and agrarianism, the Brooklyn Bridge and the American Adam.[1]

Today's American Studies scholarship repudiates most of the cultural and
political premises of the myth-symbol-image school; less clear is how far
current approaches to context supersede past practices. New subject matter
and new terminology would seem to indicate at first reading a new approach
to American Studies, if not a new American Studies. The concern with myths,

An earlier version of this article was presented as a paper at the 1988 American Studies
meeting in Miami. I would like to thank my three commentators, Giles Gunn, Carroll
Smith-Rosenberg, and Werner Sollors for their help in improving this version. Valuable
comments and references also came from Martin Burke, Joan Burbick, Michael Geyer,
James Henretta, Linda Kerber, and Lisa McFarlane. Three "institutions" also helped: the
anonymous reviewers and editorial board of the *American Quarterly,* my colleagues at the
Friday lunch group of the Program in American Culture at the University of Michigan,
and my fellow fellows at the Stanford Humanities Center, where I spent the academic year
1987–88.

symbols, and images, which marked the classical period of American Studies, has given way to an overwhelming interest in class, ethnicity, race, and gender.[2] Such once popular terms as *paradox, ambiguity,* and *irony* have been replaced by *domination, hegemony,* and *empowerment.* The definition of culture has changed from one stressing eclecticism but unity to one emphasizing division and opposition. The exemplary works have moved from stressing the basic homogeneity of the American mind and uniformity of the American character to noting the diversity of the American population and divisiveness of the American experience.[3] As a result, the idea of society as a system of structured inequality receives priority over the concept of culture as the basis for understanding American life.[4]

Do new vocabularies and new subject matter also betoken new ways of conceiving of context in American Studies? Or, does what appears like a new phase of American Studies continue to rely upon old ways of contextualization? Have the larger intellectual trends of the last few decades significantly altered how scholars in American Studies conceive of context and how they go about contextualizing their subject matter in their own texts? Should we speak in the end, therefore, of a New American Studies or only of a new phase of American Studies?

If the disparate interests that comprise American Studies are united about anything, it is the necessity of contextual knowledge. There are many ways of providing context and therefore many meanings of that much used, and abused, word.[5] At one pole are the presuppositions of a basic, or "simple" contextualism, or what we might call "contextual fundamentalism" in analogy to religious faith. Two clusters of basic postulates characterize such an approach.

At the heart of contextual fundamentalism is the premise that documents, artifacts, or texts are basically self-interpreting without recourse to any explicit framework. As practice, such an approach acts as if the text's words or the artifact's existence were determinative, that is conceptually coercive, of the "reading" they are to receive—regardless of the reader's values, politics, interpretive paradigm, or interpretive community. Thus "facts" are discovered, not created or constituted by the frameworks that enable their existence. While such an approach seems most obvious in some earlier material culture studies where the presence of the artifact was presumed to determine its interpretation,[6] an analogous approach to the uses of literary texts, especially by historians, "guts" the texts for propositions about ideas and behaviors, past and present.[7] Its parallel is also found in the naive premise of those accepting documents at their face value as proving, that is, telling, a story to which they are already committed.[8] In practice such contextual fundamentalism frequently comes down to the quest for one meaning—usually read as authorial intention in text, document, or even artifact—as a way of curtailing a multiplicity of interpretations being read as multiple realities.[9]

The documentary or artifactual analysis so fundamental to a simple contextualism assumes a second premise about history as the ultimate context. Normal historical practice rests upon a matrix of assumptions about the essential narratability of the past. Such an approach to contextualism postulates at bottom that a historical narrative is verified in its essential structure by its parallel in past reality. In the end the variant versions or interpretations could—and should—be reconciled as constituting a single (hi)story from a single viewpoint of presentation told by a single voice. This understanding of the past as the "Great Story"[10] presumes that all the various documents and artifacts can—and should—be "woven" into some sort of overall story.

Classic American Studies questioned the simple link between texts and social reality; now a second major thrust in this direction is being mounted by contemporary American Studies. Classic American Studies challenged the first cluster of premises of contextual fundamentalism by transmuting what historians and other scholars had considered past reality into myths and images. What had been described as the history, and therefore the "reality" of the frontier or self-made man, for example, became myth or image—or ideology in modern parlance,[11] and therefore a different kind of "reality." As Henry Nash Smith first explained his use of "myth" and "symbol,"

> I use the words to designate larger or smaller units of the same kind of thing, namely an intellectual construction that fuses concept and emotion into an image . . . . I do not mean to raise the question whether such products of the imagination accurately reflect empirical fact. They exist on a different plane. But as I have tried to show, they sometimes exert a decided influence on practical affairs.[12]

The transition from Progressive to Consensus or counter-Progressive historiography mirrored not only the cold war era[13] but also the questioning of a simple link between language and texts and the construction of reality, and so it also challenged any simple understanding of context.[14]

Now a second, more fundamental challenge to the understanding of context as social reality is apparent in the call for a new approach to American Studies. This challenge arises from efforts to incorporate the new continental scholarship in the human sciences, especially as absorbed through literary theory in the past few decades. It not only denies all documentary and artifactual fundamentalism but also rejects the second premise of the Great Story as nothing but another social and cultural construction.

Some indication of what premises such a new approach entails can be found in the summary by Sacvan Bercovitch of the "similar convictions about the problematics of literary history" shared by his collaborators in *Reconstructing American Literary History*:

that race, class, and gender are formal principles of art, and therefore integral to
textual analysis; that language has the capacity to break free of social restrictions and
through its own dynamics to undermine the power structures it seems to reflect; that
political norms are inscribed in aesthetic judgment and therefore inherent in the process
of interpretation; that aesthetic structures shape the way we understand history, so
that tropes and narrative devices may be said to use historians to enforce certain views
of the past; that the task of literary historians is not just to show how art transcends
culture, but also to identify and explore the ideological limits of their time, and then
to bring these to bear upon literary analysis in such a way as to make use of the
categories of culture, rather than being used by them.[15]

He proposes this set of propositions as resolving old and new problems alike.
First, the problematic avoids the older shortcomings of both "the narrow
textuality of the New Criticism" and the "naiveté of the old historicism as
'background' or 'context.' " Second, the problematic attempts to steer a middle
course among the conflicting implications of the several new currents in literary
theory and the incompatible basic premises underlying the varieties of new
scholarship.[16] Third, the problematic seeks a reflexive understanding and
fusion—some would say confusion—of text and context as applied to scholars'
own textualization of context and, perhaps, to the scholarly context as well.

Whether and why this proposed set of propositions might resolve new and
old problems alike for a new American Studies depends upon how one looks
at the new scholarship and theory. Even where the middle of the road lies
depends upon how the width of the road is conceived, and the issue of the
width is at the center of the contest over problematics. To show the possible
pathways such a middle course hopes to follow, we must therefore consider
the edges, so-to-speak, of the conceptual highway. If simple contextualism
lies at one edge of the road, then what is popularly referred to as deconstruction
or the linguistic turn lies at the opposite edge.

Without tracing—some would say creating—the history of recent scholarship
or disciplinary politics in the human sciences, I hope to show that some of
the major implications—others might argue achievements—of this scholarship
subvert not only the basic premises of contextual fundamentalism but also
challenge new theories of representation and social production associated with
the new cultural studies. The attempt to find a single methodology for the
new cultural studies founders upon the diversity of approaches to contextualism.[17]

The implications of so-called grand theory in the human sciences revolve
about and culminate in the current tendencies to denaturalization, demystification, deconstruction and, if I may coin some words to continue the allit-
eration and rhyme, dehierarchicalization and dereferentialization so evident
in so much humanistic scholarship today. Some of these trends focus on, and
result from, contemporary concerns with race, ethnicity, class, and gender.
But the implications spread far beyond these categories to the foundations
assumed fundamental to all fields of human study because these implications

challenge our ways of understanding what we are about as scholars and people and how we represent our understandings.[18] In the end, these trends question any easy separation of texts from contexts and vice versa, any easy division of politics from methodology.

The clearest, and perhaps most widely accepted, trend is the denaturalization of race, ethnicity, and sex. Much of what previous generations of scholars ascribed to the effects of biology in the understanding of racial and ethnic differences among peoples, and the sexual differences between men and women, recent scholars attribute to social and cultural arrangements. Thus so much of what was once explained by inevitable natural distinctions is now explained by theories of social construction.[19] The biology of race, ethnicity, and sex, in short, has become the culture or ideology of racism, ethnocentrism, and sexism. Even the conception of human nature as a uniform biological grounding for all human behavior has been denied in favor of a highly change-able, plastic conception of human conception.[20] What distinguishes recent denaturalization from the anti-racism and the rise of the culture concept after World War II is how thorough the penetration of culture has been into areas hitherto considered natural; so thorough that the priority of the nature/culture dichotomy has been reversed in the human sciences, and culture has become the privileged explanation of human behavior more than ever before.[21]

Accompanying and reinforcing this trend is one we might call demystification which traced human behavior, texts, and artifacts to their social production or class origins. At its core such an approach postulates social relationships as systems of structured inequality. Presumption of such structured inequalities in a society transforms groups into class(es), sexes into gender systems and peoples into racial systems. To tie literature, the arts, and nonfiction to class and political power turns ideas into ideologies and texts into discourses.[22] The revival of class analysis in literary, historical, and other scholarships results in the renewed emphasis on ideology and the prevalence of such terms as *hegemony* and *domination* in academic texts and discourse. Even the con-ception of human nature as the universal biological foundation of all human behavior is portrayed as nothing more than a rationale for bourgeois hegemony and a liberal economy. As Roland Barthes argued long ago: "The status of the bourgeoisie is particular, historical: man as represented by it is universal, eternal."[23]

The difference between the problematics of earlier and recent American Studies in regard to denaturalization and demystification is illustrated dra-matically by the explicit themes as well as the underlying presuppositions of Henry Nash Smith's *Virgin Land* as opposed to Alan Trachtenberg's *Incor-poration of America*. Race and gender play almost no role in Smith's exposition of western imagery, while they receive much more attention in Trachtenberg's interpretation of the relationship between late nineteenth-century culture and social relations. Although Smith implies some class divisions among those who held differing images of the frontier, he rarely mentions them explicitly. Such division seems repressed in his analysis in favor of a generalized or unified model of cultural imagery held in common by all, or at least most, Americans. Trachtenberg, on the other hand, separates the official culture from the oppositional culture generated by those who were subordinated during the emergence of the new "incorporated" society. Trachtenberg argues in the end that the official culture of Americans was hegemonic because it divided production from consumption and presented spectacle and mere appearance as reality in order to hide the genuine conflicting interests among American citizens, who were increasingly being absorbed into a corporate society. Such official culture confused, and thereby repressed, opposition to the emerging way of life. In the end, no matter how the two authors might differ on uses of denaturalization of race and gender or the demystification of social origins in their books, they seem equally sure of how to textualize the differing realities they presume at the base of American culture.[24]

Still another clear tendency in recent theory is one I shall label dehierarchicalization. Such a trend is most evident in the erosion, even dissolution, of the scholarly and aesthetic boundaries dividing elite from popular cultures. Although it may be difficult to pinpoint when the Beatles became as legitimate to study as Beethoven, or *The Virginian* as *Moby-Dick,* or everyday objects as high art ones, American Studies was in its classic period already a leader in the trend.[25] With the erosion of the boundaries between popular and elite cultures, the criteria sustaining the canons in literature, art, and music were also called into question. If Russian formalism made folktales a model for all narrative, then semiotic, structuralist, and poststructuralist methodologies further homogenized the distinction between the study of elite and popular forms.[26]

Culture with a capital *C* became just another part of culture with a small *c,* but that "reduction" — some would say degradation — rested upon certain ways of understanding texts as context and contexts as texts and had political as well as cognitive and aesthetic implications. Repudiation of the criteria distinguishing elite from popular, folk, and other cultures rested upon a denial of transcendental or universal principles or values in the evaluation of literature, art, and music and the relativization of aesthetic standards in general. When judgments of taste, form, and pleasure are demystified, they are connected to the specific social location of an observer, to a specific interpretive community in a society. Once again cultural and social arrangements circum(in)scribed what had been previously presumed transcultural.

Much of the new historicization in the humanities, particularly in the new cultural studies, seems devoted to the demystification of abstract terms, subjects, or categories long considered basic to our culture, hence universal to culture and therefore fundamental to the humanities themselves. As Richard Johnson says:

> I would describe the evolving agenda [of cultural studies] as a series of critiques of innocent-sounding categories or innocent-sounding practices . . . obviously culture and art and literature, but also communication, and consumption, entertainment, education, leisure, style, the family, femininity, and masculinity, and sexuality and pleasure, and, of course, the most objective sounding categories of all, knowledge and science.[27]

The study of how such concepts or categories emerged reveals how they became reified as abstract concepts and mystified as essential and universal categories and thus exposes their political uses. In the end, such demystification creates a story of how a presumably shared culture, eclectic in both its contents and the class of its audiences, was transformed into categories of culture segregated by class. This is the history summarized in the title of Lawrence Levine's new book: *Highbrow/Lowbrow: The Emergence of Cultural Hierarchy in America.*[28]

The new cultural studies seek to fuse cultural and political critique in practice through contextualization.[29] The aim of combining cultural and political critique is not new but its current vitality represents a new phase in American Studies. If to demystify the class origins of ideas transmutes them into ideologies, however, then do cultural and social arrangements also determine or circumscribe their own theorization? Such is the reflexive dilemma of the sociology of knowledge as Karl Mannheim noted long ago.[30] Should the study of how ideas arose in the past also reveal the scholar's own political uses of denaturalization, demystification, and de-essentializing in the present? Does — must — the reflexive critique of culture lead to the questioning of its own premises of contextualization as ideology and politics? Must—should?—the social construction of cultural reality give way to the cultural or textual construction of social reality?

Dehierarchicalization culminates in challenging the whole idea of privileging some foundational assumptions over others for the grounding of judgments, be they conceptual or aesthetic. In the realm of ideas, it is anti-essentialist, hence anti-foundationalist.[31] In aesthetics, it is anti-universalist, anti-elitist, even anti-aestheticist in a sense. It denies the traditional distinction between literary and other forms of languages and impugns theories as metalanguages serving as mediation.[32] The questioning of all essentialism as a form of unwarranted privileging implies that conceptual and aesthetic judgments are as much politics as philosophy. As Barthes said, "The disease of thinking in essences . . . is at the bottom of every bourgeois mythology of man."[33]

The dehierarchicalization of language eventuates in what I shall call dereferentialization and ultimately in deconstruction. My use of a coined term dereferentialization (or perhaps dereferentialism) is only meant to suggest that among the recent trends in the human sciences is one questioning the extra-linguistic "reality" as well as essentialism of abstract concepts. The denial of representation as realism challenges referentialism not only in literature and the arts but especially in history and the social sciences.[34] Not only are such categories as race, ethnicity, and gender thereby transformed into cultural constructions, but even such other conceptions as class and the state are categorized as essentialist and foundational if they are not construed as culturally arbitrary because they are historically specific.[35]

In the end, transforming the social construction of concepts into culturally construed categories reduces all modes of human communication to forms of representation. When dereferentialization questions what is the real status of the subject or object, it also questions the nature of the entities that go into constructing a context. Such obscuring, if not denying, of the referentiality of the subject therefore undermines the legitimacy and authority of all con-textualism, particularly that traditional to history.[36]

Deconstruction—whether defined in the European or American manner—is the ultimate de-hierarchicalization of language, for it treats texts and discourses as nondeterminative of their ostensible meaning. Ultimately the suspicion of language as subversive of its own meaning allows the de(con)struction of a text through freewheeling critical interpretation in which the critic supplements the voids and pursues the duplicities of the text's language far beyond its apparent significations.[37] While deconstruction subverts attempts at totalization, it also undermines efforts at mediation between texts and "reality," especially if that reality is presumed socially rather than textually constructed. Men and women may make their worlds, their world views, and their words, but can they make the connections among them in ways that can be comprehended according to their own theories of language?[38]

Given the difficulties of uniting a signifier with its signified, let alone any referent in post-Saussurian theorizing, many commentators see the larger implications of deconstruction as ending in conceptual relativism, intellectual if not social anarchy, and philosophical and political nihilism. In other words, this other side of the conceptual road is too far out for many scholars supporting contextualism. As one historian reviewing the implications of the "linguistic turn" for all understanding warns:

> If we take them [those of a strong linguistic turn] seriously, we must recognize that we have no access, even potentially, to the unmediated world of objective things and processes that might serve to ground and limit claims to knowledge of nature or to any transhistorical or transcendent subjectivity that might ground our interpretation of meaning. Knowledge and meaning are not discoveries but constructions. The world and the subject that confronts it are "always already" present to us as culturally

constructed. This perspective (and one may call it "grand" in its sweeping reformulation of the way we live ourselves and our worlds) has a number of significant
implications. It is radically historicist in the sense that all knowledge is time-bound
and culture-bound, but it also undermines the traditional historians' quest for unity,
continuity, and purpose by robbing them of any standpoint from which a relationship
between past, present, and future could be objectively reconstructed. By conceiving
of knowledge as a form of action, as creation, domination, or communicative engagement, moreover, this perspective implicates all forms of knowing in the social
and political practices of a specific sociocultural formation. Finally, the new grand
theory tends to dissolve the analytical distinctions between, and hierarchical ordering
of, different modes of knowing and the disciplines connected to them.[39]

Scholars trying to bound the free play of interpretations, forestall the collapse
of cultural pluralism into conceptual relativism, and legitimate traditional
historical practices must rest their case on denying the more radical conceptual
implications of the "linguistic turn" for a form of realism that allows a mild
pluralism without various sceptical relativisms. Such a realism must predicate
not only the existence of a past as actuality independent of the would-be
interpreter but also assume that accounts of the past represent it as it was.
The validity of these accounts, moreover, must be measured by correspondence
with that presumed actuality. Such an approach to realism seems to keep the
conceptual road both narrower and safer than language theorists would advocate or allow.[40]

At the heart of the controversy over realism in contextual practice is the
relation between a traditional construction of the past grounded mainly on
referentiality as opposed to a construction seen primarily as another form of
representation. If contextualists, even of the new sort, do not hold to their
traditional claims to the primacy of experience over meaning, to context over
text, to reference over representation, then how can they assert the "truth"
in both their social ontology and their politics? Thus the "linguistic turn"
with its reversal of what was traditionally privileged in the relations between
meaning/experience, representation/reference, text/context seems as political
as it is conceptual. The politics of contextualism, like its epistemology, are
framed in terms of a philosophy postulating realism, because the very foundations—the "common sense"—of the disciplines relied on privileging the
"real" world over (that is, as grounding) the assertions about it.[41]

In the end, incompatible premises and methodologies in the human sciences
pose major problems of mediation between text and context, between textualism and contextualism as ways of understanding the past. As a consequence
of this conceptual conflict there are also contests within and between disciplines. The dilemmas of the underlying and opposing problematics can be
focused if we examine three different definitions of context which resemble
older arguments over text and context but rest upon recent intellectual trends
and theories from abroad.

1) context$_1$. In the first definition, context reduces to the verbal fabric itself

in a text and therefore contextual understanding is derived solely from the text by the reader, whether inscribed there by an author according to some intentional model of communications or constructed by the reader in some reader-response model.[42] Such an approach to context represents the "linguistic turn" in its strong version. In an approach modeled upon Saussurian linguistics, meaning derives from its linguistic context. Critics charge such an approach to meaning resembles tautology because, in the end, the signified is reduced to the signifier. As one scholar phrases this critique: "The system of linguistic signs becomes a self-contained, endless, internal self-referential system of signifiers, whose meanings are generated by their own network."[43] Such seeming (linguistic) solipsism appears to lead only to a useless scepticism or an unacceptable idealism in the eyes of its critics. This definition of context contradicts the traditional understanding of context because it depends upon evidence or analysis internal rather than external to the text. In consequence its opponents might label this textual fundamentalism in contrast to its contextual opposite.[44]

Many scholars see the New Criticism as preparing the way for later textualist approaches in the United States. Thus they often accuse deconstructive criticism, like its predecessor, of focusing exclusively on the text to derive its meaning and denying the value of context in interpreting a text.[45] Unlike the earlier New Critics, however, many of the strong textualists extended the premises of their approach to the very understanding of life as a text. Not only does human behavior and social interaction from this view produce texts, but humans and their societies can only be understood as textualizations they produce about themselves. All behavior is interpreted like texts because it is only interpreted through texts.[46]

2) context$_2$. In the second definition, the context of a text comes from, or is constructed from, other texts. This approach may be called "intertextuality" in one sense of that word.[47] Once again, this definition is considered a product of structuralist and poststructuralist theories of language and textuality. Thus its critics see context$_2$ as only slightly less self-referential and solipsistic than context$_1$, for the interpretation of context$_2$ is still within the closed conceptual realm postulated by the "linguistic turn." For that reason, we could call both contexts$_1$ and $_2$ textualist in their problematics and their methodologies. The basic methodology rests upon some version of narrative theory or other form of poetic, discursive, rhetorical, or stylistic analysis. Social reality appears both to be constituted and understood through forms of signifying practices broadly conceived. Such an approach to context leads to understanding the human sciences as poetics or rhetoric.

The earlier formalist analyses by Henry Glassie of folkhousing in eighteenth-century middle Virginia and Will Wright of the western movie both juxtapose precise formalist analysis of their "texts" with vaguer attributions of historical social structure derived according to a more traditional contextualism.[48] In other words, like so many cultural studies, the authors use a meticulous formal analysis on the cultural texts they explore but not on the social "texts" they accept as givens. They, in the terminology of this argument, present their main analyses in terms of contexts$_1$ and $_2$ but embed them in a presumably transparent history constructed as context$_3$. Werner Sollors's recent book, *Beyond Ethnicity: Consent and Descent in American Culture,*[49] presents a more complete example of contexts$_1$ and $_2$ than these earlier works, because it treats the history of ethnicity like the understanding of ethnicity itself as subject to, and derivative of, rhetorical and other textualist forms of analysis. Contexts$_1$ and $_2$ result in understanding the past as *a* history, because it is always a textualization, that is, always *a* construction, never a reconstruction as such.

3) context$_3$. In this third definition, the context of a text is found in the extra-textual(ist) world. This approach breaks out of the circularity of the textualist definition of context, whether linguistic or even hermeneutic, in the opinion of its proponents. We might label this approach as properly contextualist, for this is the usual definition of context as employed in the normal contextualist practice of literature, music, and art scholars as well as historians and social scientists. In practice, context$_3$ receives a variety of definitions depending upon methods of contextualization, but the fundamental premise of each rests upon a form of realism that posits the conceptually coercive structure of the extratextualized world. Today this contextualization is usually some version of the social construction of reality. The stronger the version of social construction, the more likely the past is interpreted as traditional history and the more it is considered a *re*construction of past reality according to the ideal of the "Great Story."

If we take Cathy N. Davidson, *Revolution and the Word: The Rise of the Novel in America,*[50] and Michael Denning, *Mechanic Accents: Dime Novels and Working-Class Culture in America,*[51] as examples of a new generation of cultural studies, then their formal analysis of textual structure rests upon a contextualist$_3$ approach to the social system said to generate the novels and their reception. Both authors divide their books into a first third expositing a history of the larger social context of the publication of novels and their readers and the remaining two-thirds examining the themes and formulas of the novels as understood and used by their readers. Although both authors are well aware of textualist challenges to traditional contextualizing of past realities, they, like those they accuse of fostering a hegemonic canon and history, resort to a transparently unambiguous social and cultural history as the matrix of their own versions of past context.[52] If Davidson in her afterword, "Texts as Histories," argues against universalism as a basis for textualizing the past, she also assures her reader she is against relativism as a way of coding history.

Opponents of context$_3$ as an approach ask how the world can be described in light of the challenges raised to any textualization by the "linguistic turn." How can contextualists$_3$ resolve the dilemmas of representation without masking (mystifying) what they do through reification in—and of—their constructions? Do not all contexts$_3$ reduce in actual practice as well as in theory into contexts$_1$ or $_2$? Cannot the methodologies of context$_3$ be studied as rhetoric or poetics or narrative, so that the *practice*, if not the presumptions, of context$_3$ is just like that of contexts$_1$ and $_2$?

Contested, even contradictory, definitions of key vocabulary reveal opposing problematics for they postulate—and therefore constitute?—relationships among language, behavior, and social reality and even the nature of the state with its relations of power and domination.[53] Contested methods result from opposing methodologies which in turn depend upon contradictory frameworks about texts and their relation to contexts. In turn contested methodologies and contradictory problematics provide the focus and the medium for the political contests over, and for, the control of meaning in a discipline, between disciplines, and beyond them.

Therefore defining text and context in a discipline is intertwined with contentions within the disciplines itself considered as context. The basic issue for those supporting the strong contextualist position seems to revolve around the relation postulated between power and knowledge, while for those advocating the strong textualist approach the issue at bottom seems to depend upon the relation between language and the world. Hence the opposing sides taken by the two camps on the possibility of distinguishing between signified and referent, text and discourse, meaning and experience, cultural constitution and social construction of reality. The perspectivalism of the textualists leads in the eyes of their opponents to self-defeating relativisms which vitiate any secure foundations for either political critique or explanatory and interpretive security. The theory and the politics of the contextualists appear to produce naught but more texts or ideology to the textualists. Strong textualists tend to treat contextual reality and the politics of power as poetics or rhetoric, since all such approaches must be produced as another text. Strong contextualists question the politics of a textualism that denies the effects of power and the social construction of the world in which we feel we experience our lives as real beyond mere language. So methodological stands upon the use of poetics or politics in explicating texts and contexts in the human sciences leads inevitably to a reflexive poetics and politics of the human sciences themselves as texts and contexts.[54]

From the viewpoint of a strong textualism, contextualization demands some kind of poetic analysis, so let the phrase "poetics of context" remind us of the basic premise. How is the nature and unity of the subject/object constructed? What narrative, rhetorical, and other devices or structures enable descriptions of context to have the forms they do? Once the conception of an overall poetics of context is generated, then it is easy to conceive of a poetics of ethnicity,[55] a poetics of race,[56] a poetics of gender,[57] or a poetics of class[58] or even of a poetics of society,[59] a poetics of culture,[60] and a poetics of history.[61] In all cases the seeming arbitrariness of texts as constructions might lead to a politics of will and desire.[62]

On the other hand, the politicization of texts and contexts results from a strong social constructionist position applied to texts and contexts and to the human sciences themselves. The politics of texts embraces such questions as: Why look at contexts as poetics rather than politics? Whose poetics and whose ideology is employed and why? As one scholarly wit summarizes the basic issue: the politics of texts asks not "is there a text in this class?" but rather "is there class in this text?"[63] What are the politics of communications theory?[64] Why, in short, mystify the "power" of language as determinant or constitutive of social reality, and whose collective interests does such a mystification serve?

The politics of texts and contexts results in the definition of politics itself being contested. If politics might be defined as contests for control of the structures of meaning whether in a discipline, in a society, or in the world,[65] then textualists and contextualists can argue over the ambiguity of both of the major words in the phrase "structures of meaning." A textualist asks: how is meaning structured in a poststructuralist, post-Marxist world? A contextualist inquires: who controls the social structure determining meaning? Even this definition of politics, therefore, takes a stance on the issues, for it too revolves around the power/knowledge dilemma. Any understanding of context necessitates contested canons, contested histories as part of the political contests over both the nature of social reality and the ways of understanding it in American Studies. To treat the human sciences only as ways of understanding, however, subverts both them and politics in the view of most strong social constructionists. If, as Louis Althusser remarked, "philosophy is, in the last instance, class struggle in the field of theory,"[66] only a philosophy of realism justifies ideals as politics and the human sciences as praxis.[67] But is modern realism part of bourgeois ideology, when the mystified universal essentialist definition is traced to its class origins?[68]

The problem of synthesizing American history reveals the politics *of* and *in* our field. The very search for a new synthesis in United States history results from the success of revisionist efforts to incorporate the implications of new presumptions and their "facts" about race, ethnicity, gender, and class for constructing the American past. The result of such re-envisioning of the American past fragmented, or pluralized, its comprehension as a unified subject told as single story from a single voice or viewpoint. For political as much as for conceptual reasons demands arose for a synthetic key or "master interpretive code"[69] that would offer a new, more comprehensive unity beyond the plurality of partial histories of particular groups hidden by a previously unified but hegemonic history.

A recent debate over synthesis in the *Journal of American History* focused on the evolution of a public realm in United States history as a synthetic key to bring conceptual unity to the field and therefore to the story. Thomas Bender suggested that the making of an American public culture, or the changing formations of a public arena resulting from the clash of classes and the interaction of groups, provided the basis in past social reality for a new synthesis.[70] Although Bender allowed for contending groups and ideologies, his critics still accused him of subscribing to an image of society and power based upon the theory and politics of liberal pluralism. As a result one critic complained that Bender's model was just another history told from the top down which would continue to marginalize the victims of hegemonic history.[71] All suggested by inference the replacement of Bender's competitive but still pluralistic model of politics by a more thorough conflict model of society and politics that not only created central and peripheral groupings in the past but also their history in the present.[72] Thus this proposed synthesis was as political as its focus. (All the scholars presumed context$_3$ as the foundation of their historical and political practices.)[73]

This call for synthesis therefore did not resolve the crisis of history because it too became yet another contest over methodology and politics. What or whose form is the synthesis to take? Whose voice and viewpoint should prevail in the Great Story and partial stories, including what political message and how to code it?[74] Who, in short, should be the Great Storyteller and what should be the message? The plea for a synthesis must therefore be seen as both a political act and a judgment on contextualism versus textualism. Is any history as overall context naught but an ideology therefore from both a strong contextualist and a strong textualist viewpoint?

The clash of interpretive principles and therefore communities—or vice versa—in the opposing approaches to context shows the lack of agreement among the players and their problematics on the very nature of what constitutes the game, so-to-speak, let alone what are the rules of the game, which games are to be played, by whose or what rules, and what or whose plays count.[75] If the answers come from how to decide or who or what decides, then the answers must be sought in the politics within and of a profession. At least that would seem to account for the recent popularity of the histories of professional discourse, especially in literary criticism and literary theory.[76] But how these histories should be constructed or plotted raises the very specter they were meant to dispel: what or whose definition of context should prevail in these histories of context?

If politics within and of a discipline like those in the larger world equals the contest for control of the structures of meaning, then how resolve the ambiguities of the words "meaning" and "structure" when they are at the heart of the controversy between the textualists and the contextualists? The questions that identify the camps and their loyalties seem patent. (1) Why do things take the form they do? marks a textualist. (2) Why do the forms arise when they do? distinguishes a contextualist. Of course, both camps answer both questions in their own way. One can answer, mediate, reduce these questions by conceptual and/or political choices but the answers like the questions remain grounded by textualist or contextualist postulates about words, world views, and worlds.

Has the New American Studies found a methodology that will ground both its intellectual and political practices and still avoid the dilemmas of contemporary contextualism and textualism, especially the "narrow textuality" and the "old historicism as 'background' or 'context' "? At the same time as old ways of construing the past as history are challenged by the new intellectual and political trends as a way of providing overall context, there is a call for a new historicism or historicization to mediate the differing approaches to context and thereby steer a middle course among the pitfalls opened by modern theory.

The energetic role proposed for a new kind of history is part of an effort to escape from the dilemmas of the human sciences, particularly as inscribed in literary theory.[77] In order to escape the scepticism produced by the free play of interpretations and also the privileging of reified concepts and categories through essentialism, scholars look to the history of the cultural construction of these categories and their signifieds.[78] In this way many of these scholars hope to secure a foundation for their epistemologies as well as their politics. Such new historicization seeks to avoid the problems of poststructuralist, post-Marxist, posthistoricist textualist criticism of contextualism at the same time as it uses its results to provide a new, more reflexive context for contextualization without the problems of the old.

The new trend to historicization in American Studies seeks a construction of the United States past that would provide a firm foundation to constrain the free play of interpretations while at the same time being sensitive to the problems of representation and textualization that form so important a part of the new trends. If simple contextualism presumed that the construction of history is transparent to its supposed referent, universal or omniscient in viewpoint, and self-evidently "realistic" in narrative construction, the new trend to historicization tries to reconcile the dilemmas introduced by the incompatible premises of demystification through social production and deconstruction through dereferentialization.

But what can Fredric Jameson's advice to "always historicize," that is, to always contextualize, mean in this postmodern period? His own dilemmas of interpretation reveal all too well the problems for one who would be a contextualist but who sees the claims of textualism in a post-Marxist, poststruc-turalist, posthistoricist world.[79] Surely the effort must advance beyond the recent flood of new but normal histories of methodologies, disciplines, and schools of criticism, if it is to serve as the new contextualism. It must at least mediate between—if not proceed beyond—textualism and contextualism as versions of context, between poetics and politics as textual versions of social reality. It cannot accept and base its narrative upon a transparent social history as normally written for grounding its own analysis of the social production and consumption of texts through demystification. It cannot rehierarchicalize or re-essentialize some basic social and cultural categories as it poeticizes the contextualization of other concepts and categories. It cannot move the marginal peoples to the center of the story in the guise of the other but still resort to the traditional paradigm of the past as the Great Story. Lastly, it ought not pretend to a middle way, if it narrows the road to achieve that path.

These many problems bring us back to Bercovitch's proposed resolution through a new problematics for the historicization of cultural studies. To repeat his statement:

> [T]hat race, class, and gender are formal principles of art, and therefore integral to textual analysis; that language has the capacity to break free of social restrictions and through its own dynamics to undermine the power structures it seems to reflect; that political norms are inscribed in aesthetic judgment and therefore inherent in the process of interpretation; that aesthetic structures shape the way we understand history, so that tropes and narrative devices may be said to use historians to enforce certain views of the past; that the task of literary historians is not just to show how art transcends culture, but also to identify and explore the ideological limits of their time, and then to bring these to bear upon literary analysis in such a way as to make use of the categories of culture, rather than be used by them.

With the change of a few words specific to literary history could this statement constitute the methodological call, if not program, for a new American Studies?

Using this problematic as a basis, can American Studies now abandon at long last the *methodenschmerz* expressed so poignantly in that old, plaintive question about whether the field has a method? I believe that American Studies students are trying like other scholars today to achieve a new intellectual security in the face of the scepticism bequeathed to us by grand theory in the human sciences. This quest for a postscepticism in a postmodern world can only be understood as a hope for a new realism based upon cultural pluralism without lapsing into any extreme conceptual relativisms. The move from the seeming consensus of liberal politics in and of the myth-and-symbol-image school[80] to the conflict model underlying as well as justifying so much of the would-be, new contextualism still rests upon a social construction view of reality. A conflict model of society and politics grounds the mediation of the three versions of context in most of new cultural studies methodology. Thus many of the new would-be contextualists favor a normal historicization in a world they consider deconstructed or decentered rather than a new kind of deconstructed historicism as a contextualization of that world.[81]

While a consensus appears to exist in the new cultural studies on the advantages of using a conflict model in the field, disagreement still prevails over the new contextualism itself, on applying a conflict model to texts and the textualization of their contexts. Both Jean-Christophe Agnew in his *Worlds Apart: The Market and the Theater in Anglo-American Thought, 1550–1750,*[82] and Walter Benn Michaels in *The Gold Standard and the Logic of Naturalism: American Literature at the Turn of the Century,*[83] would seem to be contributing to the same larger narrative of the parallel rise of capitalism and the transformation of people's self-conscious understanding of themselves and the world they make. Their own texts, however, disagree on how to represent these representations in their relation to their contexts. The issue dividing their own texts is their position on the relations between textualism and contextualism in the present and therefore in the construction of the past.

Historian Agnew takes as his chief theme "the complex and mutually illuminating relation between the two ideas [of play(s) and market]—between the practical liquidity of the commodity form and the imaginative liquidity of the theatrical form" (xiii). He argues that "commerciality and theatricality are inescapably dialectical ideas—labile, reflexive, deconstructive—and like the practices of which they are abstracted properties" (xiii). In spite of this seeming espousal of reflexive deconstruction, Agnew, in his own representation of the spectacles of the market and the theater, assumes the pose of the grand spectator, that is, the Great Storyteller, with one voice, viewpoint, and story that counteracts the reflexivity, let alone the deconstruction of the supposed dialectic between work and play(s), capitalism and culture. In other words, he seems to construe contexts$_1$ and $_2$ almost solely as context$_3$ without worrying about the textualizing of his own account of texts and contexts.

Literary critic Michaels seems to agree with Agnew's approach when he argues about the relation between texts and their context in relation to naturalism:

> . . . the only relation literature as such has to culture as such is that it is part of it. If I speak of the logic of naturalism, it is not to identify a specific ideological function of literature and the real. I want instead to map out the reality in which a certain literature finds its place and to identify a set of interests and activities that might be said to have as their common denominator a concern with double identities that seem, in naturalism, to be required if they are to be identities at all. (27)

But Michaels brings more of a textualist sensitivity to his own essays as well as to past texts and therefore gives them a more problematical relationship to the contexts he constructs for them. For example, some sense of this difference can be seen in his explication of the logic of naturalism:

> Why does the miser save? He saves to escape the money economy; he saves to reenact for himself the origin of the economy. How can metal become money? How can paint become a picture? One set of answers to these questions repeats the escape from money: metals never did become money; they always were; hence they never are; a picture is just paper pretending to be something else. The logic of these answers is the logic of the goldbugs and Bryanites, *trompe l'oeil,* and a certain strand of modernism. The attraction of writing is that it escapes this logic. Neither a formal entity in itself nor an illusionistic image of something else, it marks the potential discrepancy between material and identity, the discrepancy that makes money, painting, and, ultimately, persons possible. But how are persons possible? Or, to put the question in its most general form, how is representation possible? (169–70)

In Michaels's essay the three versions of context combine to produce a more ambiguous stance on the underlying issues.[84] The issue dividing the two authors appears to be less politics than problematics, less disciplinary affiliation than commitment to realism as the basis for contextual construction.

Given my reading of these two books, then, the new problematic proposed by Bercovitch still leaves major options for one trying to mediate the incompatible premises underlying the new historicization and the search for a new kind of realism through contextualism. Thus if the old question "Does American Studies have a method?" appears superseded by "Does American Studies have a problematic?", the answer to the new question still leads all too often to the old answers even as the field tries to cope with the implications of the new trends in the human sciences. From a strong contextualist position, the answers arise all too often from the relation of power to changing times and to professional concerns ascribed according to unproblematized contextualist premises. From the textualist position the forms of these answers seem as familiar as the form of the question. In brief, to paraphrase an old adage, the more the times change (a contextualist view), the more the forms remain the same (a textualist view) so that all sides feel justified in their methodologies. Must all who would mediate between the divergent positions reify social structure as they demystify social production and reconstruct their own Great Story as they deconstruct our hegemonic heritage? Or must all textualize as they contextualize, poeticize as they politicize? Must any new American Studies like its forebears issue forth in not one methodology but many like the diverse, conflictual America of which it is said to be producer and product, according to so many cultural studies? What issues forth seems to be the very issue dividing what I have termed the textualist and contextualist problematics. Not only where the road leads but also its width, to use my well-worn metaphor one last time, seems fundamental to the contest.

Proponents of both a textualist poetics and contextualist politics seek to constitute the conceptual framework of a new American Studies, but they basically oppose, even deconstruct, each other. At bottom, poetics and politics rest on contradictory approaches to that classic concern of American Studies:

context. Just as their proponents in the larger intellectual world engage in mutual deconstruction without convincing their opponents, so too the efforts to transcend the conceptual problems only reinforce the dilemmas of philosophical and political choice necessary in American Studies at this moment. Thus we must look not only at poetics and politics in American Studies discourse and texts but also at the politics and poetics of American Studies itself as text and discourse. We must look at current American Studies scholarship as text and its context with all the problems of reflexivity this perspective suggests. From this viewpoint problems become matters of problematics.

Even how we should plot the narrative of the story about the quest for a new American Studies rests upon, as it takes positions upon, the problematics. Should we assume that the changing vocabularies during the past four decades represent progress in refining our terminology in the light of increasing conceptual sophistication, or merely altered intellectual and political preferences? Should we tell the story as one of changing climates of opinion (old vocabulary) or struggles for intellectual and political hegemony (new vocabulary)? Should it be emplotted according to the trope of irony—or of romance?[85] Has the American Studies movement entered its own postmodern phase because of its engagement(s) with poststructuralist, post-Marxist, postfeminist, and even posthistoricist theory and practice?[86] Does this answer depend upon one's choices of narrative plotting and viewpoint or perspective on discourse and politics? Should we postulate rupture or continuity, and what difference does each plotting make for what and for whom? Will the return to a neo-Progressive version of American history as overall context bring back a simpler link between text and context, between language and social reality that denies the more sceptical implications of the linguistic turn for interpretive security and political certainty? Only the future can reveal the answers to these questions, but will the construction of that history be plotted any differently in form than what now converts the past into present use?[87]

NOTES

1. We today probably portray the era of classic American Studies as more unified than it was in practice, but see Gene Wise's delineation of the essential assumptions of classic American Studies in his " 'Paradigm Dramas' in American Studies: A Cultural and Institutional History of the Movement," *American Quarterly* 31 (bibliography issue, 1979): 306–07. Compare "masked patterns" and "metapatterns" as covert foundations in Richard Sykes, "American Studies and the Concept of Culture: A Theory and a Method," *American Quarterly* 15 (Summer 1963): 259–60.

2. Note, for instance, the overall theme, the session titles, and the paper topics of the 1988 American Studies Association meeting.

3. Contrast as exemplars of consensus and division respectively Henry Nash Smith, *Virgin Land: The American West as Symbol and Myth* (Cambridge, Mass., 1950), with Alan Trachtenberg, *Incorporation of America: Culture and Society in the Gilded Age* (New York, 1982).

4. I argue this in spite of the renewed popularity of cultural studies. Compare, for example, the presuppositions of the first extended discussion of the culture concept in the *American Quarterly* by Richard Sykes, cited in note 1, or Cecil Tate, *The Search for a Method in American Studies*

(Minneapolis, 1973) with those of Lawrence W. Levine, *Highbrow/Lowbrow: The Emergence of Cultural Hierarchy in America* (Cambridge, 1988) or John Fiske, "British Cultural Studies and Television," in *Channels of Discourse: Television and Contemporary Criticism*, ed. Robert C. Allen (Chapel Hill, 1987), 254–89. For a brief overview of the transition in anthropology, see Sherry Ortner, "Theory in Anthropology Since the Sixties," *Comparative Studies in Society and History* 26 (1984): 126–66. Following the transition from cultural unity to social division as the clue to interpreting culture has been the passing of the patron sainthood of cultural studies from Clifford Geertz to Raymond Williams.

5. A convenient list of six ways of contextualizing is provided by Dominick LaCapra, *Rethinking Intellectual History: Texts, Contexts, Language* (Ithaca, 1983), 35–59. Hayden White, *Metahistory: The Historical Imagination in Nineteenth-Century Europe* (Baltimore, 1973), provides a definition of contextualization, 17–19. David Boucher, *Texts in Context: Revisionist Methods for Studying the History of Ideas* (Dordrecht, the Netherlands, 1985), discusses the issues as argued recently but traditionally by intellectual historians.

6. The authors collected in Thomas J. Schlereth, ed., *Material Culture Studies in America* (Nashville, 1982), and *Material Culture: A Research Guide* (Lawrence, Kansas, 1985), seek a better methodology for the field.

7. Compare Gordon R. Kelly, "Literature and the Historian," *American Quarterly* 26 (May 1974): 141–59, with Dominick LaCapra, "History and the Novel," in his *History and Criticism* (Ithaca, 1985), 115–34.

8. As seen in many of the interviews summarized by Walter Rundell, Jr., *In Pursuit of American History: Research and Training in the United States* (Norman, Okla., 1970).

9. As argued about the meaning of a literary work, for instance: compare P. D. Juhl, *Interpretation: An Essay in the Philosophy of Literary Criticism* (Princeton, 1980), and Steven Mailloux, *Interpretive Conventions: The Reader in the Study of American Fiction* (Ithaca, 1982), 93–125. Compare my notion of simple contextualism with the premises of what Peter Novick terms "objectivism" in *That Noble Dream: The "Objectivity Question" and the American Historical Profession* (Cambridge, 1988), 1–2.

10. As I christen it in "The Challenge of Poetics to (Normal) Historical Practice," *Poetics Today* 9 (1988): 435–52. My thoughts on this matter were inspired by Louis Mink, "Narrative Form as a Cognitive Instrument," in *The Writing of History: Literary Form and Historical Understanding*, ed. Robert H. Canary and Henry Kozicki (Madison, 1978), 129–49. The premise of the "Great Story" holds true even if the explicit form of the history is not narrative but quantitative or other form of argument.

11. Henry Nash Smith discusses these three terms in his "Symbol and Idea in *Virgin Land*," in *Ideology and Classic American Literature*, ed. Sacvan Bercovitch and Myra Jehlen (Cambridge, 1986), 21–35.

12. Compare this quotation from the first paragraph of the preface to the first edition of *Virgin Land* with his reconsideration of the matter in the preface to its twentieth anniversary republication (Cambridge, Mass., 1970), and his article cited in preceding note. To what extent did the early debate about whether American Studies had a method revolve about how to achieve this peculiar fusion of text and context?

13. As argued by, for example, Marian J. Morton, *The Terrors of Ideological Politics: Liberal Historians in a Conservative Mood* (Cleveland, 1972), and Jesse Lemisch, *On Active Service in War and Peace: Politics and Ideology in the American Historical Profession* (Toronto, 1975). See on the transition Bernard Sternsher, *Consensus, Conflict, and American Historians* (Bloomington, 1975), and Gene Wise, *American Historical Explanations* (Homewood, Ill., 1973).

14. Was this primarily a contribution of American Studies? See Gene Wise, "Political 'Reality' in Recent American Scholarship: Progressives Versus Symbolists," *American Quarterly* 19 (Summer supplement 1967): 303–28; Robert F. Berkhofer, Jr., "Clio and the Culture Concept: Some Impressions of a Changing Relationship in American Historiography," in *The Idea of Culture in the Social Sciences*, ed. Louis Schneider and Charles Bonjean (Cambridge, 1973), 77–100.

15. Sacvan Bercovitch, *Reconstructing American Literary History* (Cambridge, Mass., 1986), viii. Has the increasing use of the term *problematic* in American Studies broadened its meaning so as to become synonymous with one sense of *paradigm* as defined earlier?

16. Introductions to these theories and their implications may be found conveniently in such recent anthologies as Allen, ed., *Channels of Discourse*; Ann Jefferson and David Robey, eds.,

Modern Literary Theory: A Comparative Introduction (2d ed., London, 1986); Joseph Natoli, ed., *Tracing Literary Theory* (Urbana, Ill., 1987). For interpretive introductions to these implications, see, among many others, Terry Eagleton, *Literary Theory: An Introduction* (Minneapolis, 1983); and Howard Felperin, *Beyond Deconstruction: The Uses and Abuses of Literary Theory* (Oxford, 1985).

17. Compare, for example, Fiske, "British Cultural Studies and Television," with the introduction to Lynn Hunt, ed., *The New Cultural History* (Berkeley, 1989), and Ortner, "Theory in Anthropology Since the Sixties."

18. Myra Jehlen argues, for example, that the two chief contemporary developments inspiring *Ideology and Classic American Literature* are the "political categories of race, gender, and class" entering into the very realm of language itself and the "education of American critics in European theories of culture" (1).

19. The connection between the social construction of reality and the cultural construction of reality is an ambiguous one depending upon the relationship presumed between texts and reality. Although both the social and cultural construction of reality presume that concepts, categories, and other ideation are culturally persistent (but still politically arbitrary), the causes of such ideation may be ascribed differently according to the interpreter's views of the role of language, ideation, social class, and material circumstances in the creation of "reality."

20. Compare the usage of "plastic" and "autonomous" in Martin Hollis, *Models of Man: Philosophical Thoughts on Social Action* (Cambridge, 1977). This argument is allied to, but not the same as, the one over human agency versus structural explanation in interpreting social behavior.

21. Or so argued Richard Harlan, *Superstructuralism: The Philosophy of Structuralism and Post-Structuralism* (London, 1987), 67–68. Of these trends to denaturalization, those of feminist theory are most advanced in conceptualization but even in this field not all problems are resolved to everyone's satisfaction. Compare in literature, for example, Toril Moi, *Sexual/Textual Politics: Feminist Literary Theory* (New York and London, 1985); and Janet Todd, *Feminist Literary Theory* (New York, 1988). In history, see for example, Joan W. Scott, "Gender: A Useful Category of Historical Analysis," *American Historical Review* 91 (Dec. 1986): 1053–75; and Carroll Smith-Rosenberg, *Disorderly Conduct: Visions of Gender in Victorian America* (New York, 1985), 11–52.

22. I distinguish between text and discourse in this article because the two terms follow from the differing premises of textualism and contextualism respectively. As Gunther Kress, "Ideological Structures in Discourse," in *Handbook of Discourse Analysis,* ed. Teun A. van Dijk (London, 1985), vol. 4: 27, states: "Discourse is a category that belongs to and derives from the social domain, and text is a category that belongs to and derives from the linguistic domain." Or, as Giles Gunn, *The Culture of Criticism and the Criticism of Culture* (New York, 1987), 74, argues succinctly ". . . that discourse is rhetorical, that rhetoric is a form of persuasion, and that persuasion is a form of power, an instrument of social manipulation and control." Diane Macdonell, *Theories of Discourse: An Introduction* (London, 1986), consonant with her title, stresses that speech and writing are shaped by social conflict and the struggle for power.

23. Roland Barthes, *Mythologies,* trans. Annette Lavers (New York, 1972), 141. The denial of a biological basis to human nature and the invention of a universal self-interestedness in the eighteenth century is fundamental to the historical and political argument of Joyce Appleby, *Capitalism and the New Social Order: The Republican Vision of the 1790s* (New York, 1984), 26–27, 34–35, 101. Denaturalization of race combined with demystification of its class origins can lead to a rematerialization of class as the social reality of race and ethnicity, as, for example, in Barbara J. Fields, "Ideology and Race in American History," in *Region, Race, and Reconstruction: Essays in Honor of C. Vann Woodward,* ed. J. Morgan Kousser and James M. McPherson (New York, 1982), 143–77.

24. The scholarly repudiation of a general American mind and an overall national character in favor of a divided America began with New Left, Bottom-up, and working-class scholarship. See the interviews from *Radical History Review* reprinted in Henry Abelove, *et al.* eds., *Visions of History* (New York, 1984).

25. Wanda Corn, "Coming of Age: Historical Scholarship in American Art," *The Art Bulletin* 70 (June 1988): 199–200, but compare her entire narrative with my version of the changes in

American Studies. Tom Kando, "Popular Culture and Its Sociology: Two Controversies," *Journal of Popular Culture* 9 (Fall 1975): 439–55, dehierarchicalized while he discussed the various "kinds" of culture(s). How the cultures became hierarchicalized in the first place is the story of Levine, *Highbrow/Lowbrow*.

26. For two early examples of formalist/structuralist analysis of popular culture in American Studies, see Will Wright, *Six Guns and Society: A Structural Study of the Western* (Berkeley, 1975); and Henry Glassie, *Folk Housing in Middle Virginia: A Structural Analysis of Historic Artifacts* (Knoxville, 1975).

27. As quoted in an article on a session devoted to cultural studies at the 1988 Modern Language Association convention in *The Chronicle of Higher Education* (Jan. 18, 1989): A4.

28. Cited in note 4 above.

29. The theme of the article in the *Chronicle of Higher Education* cited in note 27. The combination of cultural and political criticism is not new: see Giles Gunn, *The Culture of Criticism and the Criticism of Culture* (New York, 1987).

30. And noted again more recently by Anthony Giddens in *Central Problems in Social Theory: Action, Structure and Contradiction in Social Analysis* (Berkeley, 1979), 168–74, but see whole chapter on the reflexive problems of ideological analysis.

31. Richard Rorty, *Philosophy and the Mirror of Nature* (Princeton, 1979), was important for this movement in the United States.

32. Hayden White, "Structuralism and Popular Culture," *Journal of Popular Culture* 7 (1974): 759–75, was a significant early statement on the implications of structuralism for denying essentialism as well as hierarchy in understanding culture(s) and language use.

33. *Mythologiques*, 75. Do demystification of social origins and dehierarchalization of cultures also deny reification of the abstract concepts used to describe themselves or might they have no effect on the textualization of their own description?

34. See the fears expressed by John Toews, "Intellectual History after the Linguistic Turn: The Autonomy of Meaning and the Irreducibility of Experience," *American Historical Review* 92 (Oct. 1987): 879–907. No social scientist in the United States has argued more persistently for a transformation of his discipline's orientation than Richard H. Brown, whose most recent book's title conveys the general idea: *Society as Text: Essays on Rhetoric, Reason, and Reality* (Chicago, 1987), as does his earlier *A Poetic for Sociology: Toward a Logic of Discovery for the Human Sciences* (Cambridge, 1977). In history the seminal American thinker is Hayden White, *Metahistory: The Historical Imagination in Nineteenth-Century Europe* (Baltimore, 1973); *Tropics of Discourse: Essays in Cultural Criticism* (Baltimore, 1978), and *The Content of the Form: Narrative Discourse and Historical Representation* (Baltimore, 1987).

35. Cultural construction as opposed to social construction of "reality" seems more "textually arbitrary" to me.

36. Transforms "history" into ideology and/or text. See my "The Challenge of Poetics to (Normal) Historical Practice" for argument and references.

37. The difference between the nature of deconstruction in France and the United States is the major theme of Art Berman, *From the New Criticism to Deconstruction: The Reception of Structuralism and Post-Structuralism* (Urbana, 1988). Compare, among many, on deconstruction Vincent B. Leitch, *Deconstructive Criticism: An Advanced Introduction* (New York, 1983); and Christopher Norris, *Contested Faculties: Philosophy and Theory after Deconstruction* (New York, 1985).

38. White, *The Content of the Form*, 189–90, provides a very brief summary of what some basic theories of language postulate about their own understanding of and place in the world.

39. Toews, "Intellectual History after the Linguistic Turn," 901–02.

40. See, for example, the essays on "Realism," "Relativism," and "Skepticism" in Harry Ritter, *Dictionary of Concepts in History* (Westport, 1986), 366–72, 376–83, 402–08. Lionel Gossman, "History and Literature: Reproduction or Signification" in Canary and Kozicki, eds., *The Writing of History*, 3–39, treats realism among other topics in his brief historical survey.

41. For arguments on the importance of realism to historical practice in general and in Marxism specifically, Christopher Lloyd, *Explanation in Social History* (Oxford, 1986), esp. 96–177; and Gregor McLennan, *Marxism and the Methodologies of History* (London, 1981), 24–44, 66–91. Compare the classic Marxian doctrine that social existence determines, influences, etc., social

consciousness. The debate over structure/superstructure and difficulties of text/context in regard to this matter for some modern Marxists can be seen in Raymond Williams, *Marxism and Literature* (Oxford, 1977); Fredric Jameson, *The Political Unconscious: Narrative as a Socially Symbolic Act* (Ithaca, 1981).

42. For contrasting reader-response models in American Studies see Mailloux, cited in note 9 above, and Janice Radway, *Reading the Romance: Women, Patriarchy, and Popular Literature* (Chapel Hill, 1984); Elizabeth Long, "Women, Reading, and Cultural Authority: Some Implications of the Audience Perspective in Cultural Studies," *American Quarterly* 38 (Fall 1986): 591–612.

43. Berman, *From the New Criticism to Deconstruction,* 169.

44. Compare Richard Rorty, *Consequences of Pragmatism* (Minneapolis, 1982), 151, who distinguishes between strong and weak textualists.

45. That the narrow textualism of the New Criticism is presumed to have prepared the way for structuralism and poststructuralism in the United States can be found in the very titles of Berman, *From the New Criticism to Deconstruction,* and the earlier book by Frank Lentricchia, *After the New Criticism* (Chicago, 1980). The differing reception of structuralism and poststructuralism in the United States as opposed to in France, as Berman argues, constitutes an interesting topic for American Studies itself through a study of contextualization. Do different ways of textualizing the story produce *the* differing views of context, or do differing views of *the* context produce different histories?

46. For an early statement in this vein, see Paul Ricouer, "The Model of the Text: Meaningful Action Considered as Text," in *Interpretive Social Science: A Reader,* ed. Paul Rabinow and William M. Sullivan (Berkeley, 1979), 73–101. Compare Brown, *Society as Text,* cited in note 36 above, esp. chap. 6: "Social Reality as Narrative Text: Interactions, Institutions, and Polities as Language."

47. Definitions of intertextuality differ according to the relationship presumed between texts and their contexts and how to go about understanding that relationship. Compare, for example, "Intertextuality" in *Semiotics and Language: An Analytical Dictionary,* ed. A. J. Greimas and J. Courtés, trans. Larry Crist, Daniel Patte, *et al.* (Bloomington, 1982), 160–61; with Julia Kristeva, *Revolution in Poetic Language,* trans. Margaret Waller (New York, 1984), 59–60.

48. Wright much more so, in my opinion, than Glassie, both works cited in note 28 above.

49. Werner Sollors, *Beyond Ethnicity: Consent and Descent in American Culture* (New York, 1986).

50. Cathy N. Davidson, *Revolution and the Word: The Rise of the Novel in America* (New York, 1986).

51. Michael Denning, *Mechanic Accents: Dime Novels and Working-Class Culture in America* (London, 1987).

52. Similarly, even though Trachtenberg in *The Incorporation of America* hopes to convince his reader that what most Americans in the past, and therefore present, see as reality in contrast to appearance is just the opposite when considered as hegemonic and authentic cultures, he too presents no doubt about how easy it is for him to understand the past and present as context in his own textualization.

53. The trend started by Raymond Williams, *Key Words: A Vocabulary of Culture and Society* (New York, 1976), in portraying contending definitions as stances in ideological battles eventuates in such works as Robert Alford and Roger Friedland, *Powers of Theory: Capitalism, The State, and Democracy* (Cambridge, 1985), esp. the glossary, 444–51, or Daniel T. Rodgers, *Contested Truths: Keywords in American Politics Since Independence* (New York, 1987).

54. No one contributed more to this end than Michel Foucault. For a collection of recent essays on both the achievement(s) and the so-called "problem" of Foucault, see *Foucault: A Critical Reader,* ed. David C. Hoy (Oxford, 1986). Is the role of power in a society as tautologically omnipresent for the contemporary contextualist position as the role of language is tautologically self-referential for today's textualist stance?

55. In addition to reading Sollors, *Beyond Ethnicity,* as a contribution to the poetics of ethnicity, could one view Dale T. Knobel, *Paddy and the Republic: Ethnicity and Nationality in Antebellum America* (Middletown, Conn., 1986), as pointing in a similar direction?

56. To what extent could the image studies of race be read in this way? For example, see the light-handed approach of Raymond W. Stedman, *Shadows of the American Indian: Stereotypes in American Culture* (Norman, Okla., 1982), or Robert F. Berkhofer, Jr., *The White Man's Indian: Images of the Indian from Columbus to the Present* (New York, 1978).

57. Does Nancy Miller, ed., *The Poetics of Gender* (New York, 1986) live up to its title? Teresa de Laurentis, *Technologies of Gender: Essays on Theory, Film, and Fiction* (Bloomington, Ind., 1987), 1–50, offers many interesting suggestions along these lines. See also Linda Kerber, "Separate Spheres, Female Worlds, Woman's Place: The Rhetoric of Women's History," *Journal of American History* 75 (June 1988): 9–39.

58. Gareth Stedman Jones, *Languages of Class: Studies of English Working Class History, 1832–1982* (Cambridge, 1983), and Zygmunt Bauman, *Memories of Class: The Pre-History and After-Life of Class* (London, 1982), suggest some possibilities in this direction.

59. In addition to Brown, *Society as Text* and *Poetics of Sociology,* could some histories of sociological theory be reconstrued as guides to a poetics of society? For example, Robert A. Nisbet, *Social Change and History: Aspects of the Western Theory of Development* (New York, 1969), on the metaphor of growth, and Werner Stark, *The Fundamental Forms of Social Thought* (London, 1962), on society as an organism or mechanism.

60. Anthropologists seem farther along toward a reconsideration of their basic working concept than sociologists: James A. Boon, *Other Tribes, Other Scribes: Symbolic Anthropology in the Comparative Study of Cultures, Histories, Religions, and Texts* (Cambridge, 1982); *Writing Culture: The Poetics and Politics of Ethnography,* ed. James Clifford and George E. Marcus (Berkeley, 1986); George E. Marcus and Michael M. J. Fischer, *Anthropology as Cultural Critique: An Experimental Moment in the Human Sciences* (Chicago, 1986); Clifford Geertz, *Works and Lives: The Anthropologist as Author* (Stanford, 1988).

61. In addition to White's books cited in note 36 above, see *History and Theory,* Beiheft 26 (1987): "The Representation of Historical Events," and Hans Kellner, *Language and Historical Representation: Getting the Story Crooked* (Madison, 1989).

62. Should one draw this conclusion from White, *Metahistory?*

63. Martin Burke, personal communication, September 5, 1988, playing on the now classic title of Stanley Fish, *Is There a Text in This Class?* (Cambridge, Mass., 1980). Richard Terdiman has also queried: "Is there class in this class?"

64. See, for example, Mary Pratt, "Interpretive Strategies/Strategic Interpretations: On Anglo-American Reader-Response Criticism," in *Postmodernism and Politics,* ed. Jonathan Arac (Minneapolis, 1986), and "Ideology and Speech Act Theory," *Poetics Today* 7 (no. 1, 1986): 59–72. Frederick J. Newmeyer, *The Politics of Linguistics* (Chicago, 1986), provides a brief history of its topic until recent times.

65. This is my modification of a definition by Peter C. Sederberg, *Politics of Meaning: Power and Explanation in the Construction of Social Reality* (Tucson, 1984), 9: "politics . . . [is] the deliberate effort to control shared meaning," but see chs. 1–3 in general.

66. Quoted in Macdonnell, *Theories of Discourse,* 76.

67. On the importance of realism to Marxism, McLennan, *Marxism and the Methodologies of History,* 24–44, 66–91.

68. Can the critique of the realistic novel as bourgeois in origin be extended to other forms of realism? See for a provocative interpretation, Donald M. Lowe, *History of Bourgeois Perception* (Chicago, 1982).

69. To borrow Jameson's term for a meta-narrative, "Marxism and Historicism," *New Literary History* 11 (Autumn 1979): 46.

70. Thomas Bender, "Wholes and Parts: The Need for Synthesis in American History," *Journal of American History* 73 (June 1986): 120–36.

71. Nell Irvin Painter, "Bias and Synthesis in History," Ibid. 74 (June 1987): 109–12.

72. Richard Wightman Fox, "Public Culture and The Problem of Synthesis," Ibid., 113–16; Roy Rosenzweig, "What *Is* the Matter with History?" Ibid., 117–22.

73. The political contentions and assumptions underlying American historiography and methodology in the last two decades are the subject of Robert F. Berkhofer, Jr., "The Two New

Histories: Competing Paradigms for Interpreting the American Past," *Organization of American Historians Newsletter* 2 (May 1983): 9–12; Fred Matthews, "Hobbesian Populism: Interpretive Paradigms and Moral Vision in American Historiography," *Journal of American History* 47 (June 1985): 92–115; John D. Diggins, "Comrades and Citizens: New Mythologies in American Historiography," *American Historical Review* 90 (June 1985): 614–38.

74. The difficulty of changing voice and viewpoint in the presentation of history, let alone in finding a new key to synthesis, is illustrated in the efforts of the D'Arcy McNickle Center for the History of the American Indian at the Newberry Library to integrate the history of American Indians into the teaching of United States history. See, for example, the topics and voices in *Indians in American History: An Introduction*, ed. Frederick E. Hoxie (Arlington Heights, Ill., 1988). See also the essays in *The American Indian and the Problem of History*, ed. Calvin Martin (New York, 1987), on adopting an "Indian" viewpoint in history.

75. Alford and Friedland, *Powers of Theory*, 411, liken the contending theories of the state with their assumptions about power to disputes about what constitutes proper plays in a game, rules of the game, and the very game itself.

76. On the methodological conflict in literature over the theory of literature versus current literary theory and the historicization of critical practices and schools: Gerald Graff, *Professing Literature: An Institutional History* (Chicago, 1987); Vincent B. Leitch, *American Literary Criticism from the Thirties to the Eighties* (New York, 1988); Russell Reising, *The Unusable Past: Theory and the Study of American Literature* (New York, 1986). Does Novick, *That Noble Dream*, serve a similar function for the historical profession?

77. Murray Krieger in his introduction to *The Aims of Representation: Subject/Text/History* (New York, 1987), plots the history of changing critical concerns in the United States, as the subtitle suggests, from first a focus on the author then to writing itself and now to the social and political context producing the text. This is also the message of Bercovitch and Jehlen in *Reconstructing American Literary History*. In the move from grand theory to historicization, the literary critics seem to be following the earlier cycle of the social sciences. Among many arguing for a historical sociology as antidote to the grand theorizing of Talcott Parsons and others, see Philip Abrams, *Historical Sociology* (Ithaca, 1982); Theda Skocpol, *Visions and Method in Historical Sociology* (Cambridge, 1984). Naturally the approaches to textualization and context differ among social scientists as well as between the literary and the sociological approaches to historicization, but few espouse a very strong textualist stand. See, for example, Anthony Giddens coping with recent trends in the human sciences in his exposition on "Structuralism, Post-structuralism and the Production of Culture," in *Social Theory Today*, ed. Anthony Giddens and Jonathan H. Turner (Stanford, Calif., 1987), 195–223.

78. Whether this sentence should also read "the history of the *social* construction of these categories and their *referents*" depends once again upon the positions taken on textualism and contextualization.

79. On Jameson's dilemmas, see among others William C. Dowling, *Jameson, Althusser, Marx: An Introduction to The Political Unconscious* (Ithaca, 1984), and Cornel West, "Ethics and Action in Fredric Jameson's Marxist hermeneutics," in Arac, ed., *Postmodernism and Politics*, 123–44.

80. But see the usable revision of history offered by Guenter Lenz, "American Studies and the Radical Tradition: From the 1930s to the 1960s," *Prospects* 12 (1987): 21–58. Compare Gunn, *The Culture of Criticism and the Criticism of Culture*, ch. 7.

81. As Wendy Steiner, "Collage or Miracle: Historicism in a Deconstructed World," in Berkovitch and Jehlen, *Reconstruction of American Literary History*, 323–51, seems to do in the end. Whether such an era of postscepticism should be achieved in that way I leave to my readers. Will future historians of American intellectual life interpret this search for explanatory and interpretive security in so many disciplines through contextualization by normal historical practice as a return to methodological conservatism after a period of interpretive free play and disciplinary scepticism? Is the search for a new realism the conceptual analogue to Reaganism in the ways of academic understanding, even though the explicit political messages may be liberal or even radical? Do radical political messages code more convincingly using conservative or traditional forms of representation?

82. Jean-Christophe Agnew, *Worlds Apart: The Market and the Theater in Anglo-American Thought, 1550–1750* (Cambridge, 1986).

83. Walter Benn Michaels, *The Gold Standard and the Logic of Naturalism: American Literature at the Turn of the Century* (Berkeley, 1987). This is listed as the second volume in "The New Historicism: Studies in Cultural Poetics."

84. As he writes, "the deconstructive interest in materiality in signification is not intrinsically ahistorical" in spite of conventional wisdom to the contrary (28). For a good introduction to recent thinking on this point, see *Post-Structuralism and the Question of History*, ed. Derek Attridge, Geoff Bennington, and Robert Young (Cambridge, 1987).

85. Or, more precisely, comedy, to employ the approach of White, *Metahistory*, to the tropological nature of historical representation. See also James M. Mellard, *Doing Tropology: Analysis of Narrative Discourse* (Urbana, 1987), for an introduction to the topic.

86. To what extent does the prefix *post* mean more than to speak of recent intellectual movements in the past tense as so many recent discussions do? For a brief guide to the issues and bibliography of postmodernism, consult Arac, ed., *Postmodernism and Politics*, ix–xliii. If postmodernism is defined as the end of grand or meta-narrative, following Jean Lyotard in *The Postmodern Condition*, trans. Geoff Bennington and Brian Masumi (Minneapolis, 1984), should we liken it to the earlier end of ideology debate, for which see Job. L. Dittberner, *The End of Ideology and American Social Thought, 1930–1960* (Ann Arbor, 1979)?

87. Is this the lament of Sande Cohen, *Historical Culture: On the Recoding of an Academic Discipline* (Berkeley, 1986), on the problems of narrativizing the past as history?

COMMENTARY

Barry Shank

In the late 1990s, American studies finds itself questioning not only whether it is a discipline or a set of interdisciplinary perspectives, and whether or not it has a method; American studies is also interrogating the very stability of the founding term, "America." In many ways, the "new" American studies recognizes a fundamental absence at the heart of its venture. The most exciting new scholarship is briskly dismantling the traditional reliance on political-geographic borders to mark the appropriate contexts for tracing and analyzing the flows of cultural history. Obviously, "America" is not geographically coincident with the United States. Equally obviously, America does not exist in isolation from the rest of the world and never has (as the very names of the continents demonstrate). These simple observations, which have been curiously de-emphasized throughout most of the history of American studies, open immense areas for new research. Not only does recent "American culture" seem to be an unstable and uncontainable subset of global cultural flows, but also the history of American culture now appears as a conflicted yet continual crossbreeding, a surfeit of miscegenating forms, images, technologies, styles and identities with no founding and continuous grand national tradition.

Yet American studies ought not to relinquish its claim to this troublesome and indeterminate signifier. For the vitality of the field has never been stronger. In many ways, the current strength in American studies is the result of efforts to move "beyond the great story," to abandon the project of panning a more or less pure ore of American identity from the many streams of historical experience. Grand historical narratives have often served to legitimate specific nation-states by linking the identity of the nation to the culture of its people. Grand cultural narratives — the traditional work of traditional American studies — have been used as part of an effort to establish an "American way of life" out of the historical mix of cultures and to legitimate governments that have based their

Robert F. Berkhofer, Jr., "A New Context for a New American Studies?," originally appeared in *American Quarterly* 41, no. 4 (December 1989), © The American Studies Association.

claim to authority on the imperative of advancing this way of life. In moving beyond grand cultural narratives, the new American studies denaturalizes societal divisions along lines of race, ethnicity, gender, and sexuality even as it repudiates the concept of a single American culture; it not only demystifies the amorphous American middle class, it strives to specify the interactive relationships between cultural production and material conditions; and it not only deconstructs monolithic interpretations of American myths, but interrogates the need for such myths for the structuring of an American polity.

As it pursues these projects, the new American studies has rethought the relationships between text and context. In "A New Context for a New American Studies?," which first appeared in 1989, Robert Berkhofer outlined a range of positions on these relationships, arguing that the stance one took on this key set of issues determined much of one's approach to the subject matter of American studies. In *The White Man's Indian* (New York: Knopf, 1978), Berkhofer's own work had already illustrated the importance of developing a complex understanding of the relationships between text and context. One of the closing questions of the book asks, "Can the 'reality' of Native American life ever be penetrated behind the screen of White ideology and imagination no matter how benevolent those conceptions?" In this formulation, however, "reality," even if in quotation marks, stands in the background, while the screen of ideology and imagination figures as the text. Akin to the Cartesianism that Bruce Kuklick critiqued in "Myth and Symbol," this separation of ideas from reality must have troubled Berkhofer, for in "A New Context," he redefines the reality/ideology problem by refiguring it as the issue of text and context.

Once realigned in this way, some of the classic positions on the philosophical problems of representation can be seen as alternative methodological strategies for unlocking the meanings of documents and artifacts. Contextual fundamentalism is Berkhofer's term for the belief that the meaning of a text is simply locatable within the text by virtue of its use of traditional means of referring to a stable and consistent context. In this way of understanding context, an historical document tells us something solid and reliable about the world through constant gestures outside of itself which establish this world as both the founding context for the production of the document and as its ultimate referent. In effect, the document can only tell us specifics about a world we already know by other means. The language within the document merely reflects this reality. Berkhofer's term for the opposite of contextual fundamentalism is deconstruction. In the version of deconstruction that was most familiar to American literary critics and historians of the mid-1980s, reality seems to have disappeared as a viable methodological concept: no attempt to ground meaning outside of the textualized document could be considered valid. This textual fundamentalism denies the capacity of documents to tell us anything at all about the world and, therefore, bears an astonishing similarity to the New Criticism that dominated literary interpretations of the 1950s and early 1960s.

Berkhofer goes on to argue that in between these two described extremes lies the possibility of incorporating the linguistic turn—that is, some recognition of the determining power of language—while retaining a meaningful connection to a shared social world, the understanding of which remains ostensibly the object of American studies. In this article, Berkhofer negotiates the controversy over the referential function of language (with its philosophical opposition of realism versus relativism) by establishing three different understandings of context after the linguistic turn. Context is the textual fundamentalism described above with the additional axiom that textual metaphors and means of analysis represent the best means of understanding life itself. $Context_2$ derives from a concept labeled intertextuality. In an intertextual framework, the production of meaning derives from the gestures that the text makes outside of itself (as in contextual fundamentalism), yet these gestures do not point directly at a social world, but at other texts. While no claims about a social real can be warranted on this basis, intertextuality —the grounding of the meanings of one text in the meanings of others— can provide the basis for an argument about shared understandings of this world. $Context_3$ depends upon the concept of the "social construction of reality." In this paradigm, there is an extratextual real which is the product of human endeavors, but $context_3$ asserts that distinctive qualities of this social real cannot be captured by textual metaphors. The greater the theoretical distinction between social construction and cultural construction, the more likely that practitioners of $context_3$ will approach contextual fundamentalism. The lesser the distinction—that is, the greater the agency that cultural forms in themselves are granted in the construction of reality—the closer $context_3$ approaches textual fundamentalism.

In "A New Context," Berkhofer argues that much American studies scholarship in the 1980s—including highly praised works such as Cathy

Davidson's *Revolution and the Word* (New York: Oxford University Press, 1986) and Michael Denning's *Mechanic Accents* (New York: Verso, 1987)—continued to rely on a version of context₃ that emphasized the extratextual world. To that extent, these works had not advanced the theorizing of context much further than had the myth and symbol scholarship before them. They depended on a more or less traditionally historicized context to ground their textual analyses. Berkhofer contrasts the contextual strategies deployed in these works to that of Walter Benn Michaels's *The Gold Standard and the Logic of Naturalism* (Berkeley: University of California Press, 1987), a book which seems to deny the possibility of political action in its very emphasis on poetics and linguistic determinism. This prompts two questions: does the scholarly emphasis on poetics require an understanding of context that limits political agency? and conversely, does the scholarly emphasis on political agency require an understanding of context that limits the agency of linguistic and cultural forms? These questions add a necessary layer of self-reflection to the scholar's approach to contextual matters. To what extent do the professional and extra-professional goals of scholarship determine the theoretical framework within which the scholarship appears? As Berkhofer put it, "Any understanding of context necessitates contested canons, contested histories as part of the political contests over both the nature of social reality and the ways of understanding it in American Studies."

Near the closing of the article, Berkhofer points towards a reflexive conceptualization of context that he will further elaborate in his book-length treatment of these issues, *Beyond the Great Story* (Cambridge: Harvard University Press, 1995). He suggests that "we must look not only at poetics and politics in American Studies discourse and texts but also at the politics and poetics of American Studies itself as text and discourse. We must look at current American Studies scholarship as text and its context with all the problems of reflexivity this perspective suggests." This reflexive concern with our own practice is one of the forces that is driving the new American studies in the late 1990s. This new work must consider not only the most appropriate means for contextualizing its work on the past, but it must also strive to contextualize the motivations for and the effects of its work in the present. In a time of growing economic and cultural globalization, intensifying restrictions on immigration, increasing attempts to turn back affirmative action, and the disturbing reappearance of racialist justifications for these transformations, the destabilizing of "America" as the founding context for American studies derives from a blending of both poetical and political motivations and strategies, from a textualizing of context along with a contextualizing of texts, and a move to realize the most significant implications of Berkhofer's influential article. The increase in the possible meanings for that central term, America, is an acknowledgment that there is no longer an a priori context that establishes the boundaries and legitimates the interpretations of the textual analyses and historiographical arguments produced within the new American studies. If the ultimate context for American studies is to remain America, then that context must be redefined and reimagined in and for each work of scholarship.

GEORGE LIPSITZ

Listening to Learn and Learning to Listen: Popular Culture, Cultural Theory, and American Studies

ACCORDING TO A STORY OFTEN TOLD AMONG JAZZ MUSICIANS, WHEN trumpet player Clark Terry first joined the Duke Ellington Orchestra in 1951, he rehearsed in his mind every complicated technical maneuver that might be expected of him. The young musician waited anxiously for instructions from the legendary band leader, but all his new boss asked him to do was "to listen." When Terry complained that anyone could just sit and listen, the ever enigmatic Ellington informed him that "there's listening, and then there's listening, but what I want from you is to *listen*."

Eventually, Terry came to understand what Ellington wanted. Terry had been so preoccupied with what he might contribute to the orchestra as an individual, that he had not taken time to hear what the other musicians needed. He had not yet learned to hear the voices around him nor to understand the spaces and silences surrounding them. Ellington knew that his young trumpeter had talent as a virtuoso, but he felt that Terry had to learn how to bring his virtuosity in harmony (literally and figuratively) with the rest of the orchestra.

Ellington's admonition might serve as a useful way of conceptualizing the present moment for scholarly research in American Studies. In this period of creative ferment and critical fragmentation, virtuosity entails

American Quarterly, Vol. 42, No. 4 (December 1990) © 1990 American Studies Association listening as well as speaking; it requires patient exploration into spaces and silences as much as it demands bold and forthright articulation. As a field, American Studies always has been at its best when engaged in dialogue with the complex and conflicted realities of American life and culture. Yet too often its dominant paradigms have suffered from an over-emphasis on what has been articulated from within the profession, and a consequent underemphasis on the voices, power struggles, and ideological conflicts outside it. The complicated relationship between scholarly methods and the popular cultures, political economies, and ideologies of America demand a scholarship capable of adopting Duke Ellington's advice and learning how to do careful and comprehensive listening.

It is my view that we are facing a crisis in American Studies scholarship as we enter the 1990s. Now that Henry Luce's "American Century" has turned into something like the "American half-century," analyses of "American Exceptionalism" are less credible than ever.[1] The ever-increasing reach and scope of commercialized leisure has eclipsed both "high culture" art and "folk culture" artifacts, replacing them with cultural products resistant to traditional methods of criticism. In addition, the cultural politics of neo-conservatism and the political economy of higher education in this age of deindustrialization undermine the constituencies historically associated with critical examination of the myths and realities of American culture—women, ethnic minorities, and the working class. To say that the field faces a crisis is not necessarily to say something negative or pessimistic. American Studies as a field emerged out of the historical crises of the 1930s and 1940s, and its most creative turning points have come in response to subsequent social, cultural, and political problems. We are not facing the "end of American Studies," but rather only the latest in a long series of cultural problems and possibilities.

Cultural Theory and American Studies

A specter is haunting American Studies, the specter of European cultural theory. During the past two decades, European critics from a variety of perspectives have theorized a "crisis of representation" that has called into question basic assumptions within the disciplines central to the American Studies project—literary studies, art history, anthropology, geography, history, and legal studies.[2] From the structuralist-Marxism of Louis Althusser to the psychoanalytic interventions of Jacques Lacan, from Foucauldian post-structuralism to the French feminism of Luce Irigiray and

Hélène Cixous, from Derridean deconstruction to the dialogic criticism of Mikhail Bakhtin, European theory has revolutionized the study of culture.

The frequently confusing and often acrimonious debates engendered by the rise of European cultural theory within academic disciplines have important ramifications for all scholars of culture, but they are especially important for those in American Studies because they challenge so many of the theoretical assumptions and methodological practices of this field. Their challenges to the project of the Enlightenment involve a radical skepticism about the utility and wisdom of reason, language, and history as tools for understanding the world. At their best, they offer radical interrogation of concepts too often undertheorized within American Studies: the utility of national boundaries as fitting limits for the study of culture, the reliability of categories that establish canons of great works or that divide "high" and "low" culture, the ability of art and literature to mirror a unified culture uniting the intentions and subjectivities of artists and audiences. As Michael Ryan explains with elegant precision, much of contemporary European cultural criticism revolves around one central dialectical premise—that cultural texts are inescapably part of social processes and that social processes are themselves always textualized in some form.[3] The current "crisis of representation" stems from the inevitability of representation and from an attendant recognition of the necessity for understanding how the mechanisms of representation contain covert as well as overt ideological messages.[4]

Like most specters, the threat posed to American Studies by contemporary European cultural theory is more apparent than real, more a product of our own fears than of any concrete social reality. Indeed, far from representing the end of American Studies, European cultural theory offers an opportunity to reconnect with some of the important aims and intentions of our field in new and exciting ways. Here I want to describe some of the central premises and preoccupations of contemporary European cultural theory and then locate them within the traditions of American Studies scholarship. In addition, I want to explore the relationship between the rise of contemporary European cultural theory and the crisis of deindustrialization in the United States.

Contemporary European Cultural Theory: Its Aims and Intentions

When confronted with radically new information, the women in Toni Morrison's wonderful novel *Beloved* "fell into three groups: those that believed the worst; those that believed none of it; and those, like Ella, who thought it through."[5] American Studies scholars have confronted European cultural theory in much the same way. The translation of European cultural theory into an American Studies context poses some serious problems, but whatever the past practice in the discipline has been, it seems most desirable for us neither to accept nor to reject theory out of hand but, like Morrison's Ella, to think it through.

Over the past twenty years, European cultural theory has reproblematized and reframed essential categories about communication and culture. For example, Lacanian psychoanalysis and Althusserian structuralist-Marxism enabled British film critics in the 1970s to begin challenging the "naturalness" of film narrative conventions and cinematic subject positions, identifying them as social and historical constructs, rather than as essential and inevitable properties of storytelling or filmmaking. The sophisticated work of Laura Mulvey and Stephen Heath drew upon Althusser for theories of the subject as socially constructed by "ideological state apparatuses" and upon Lacan for explanations about how individual subjects are "hailed" by visual, verbal, and social forms of address.[6] British Cultural Studies theorist Stuart Hall tempered the structuralist and essentialist implications of Lacanian and Althusserian criticism by blending them with the concept of hegemony advanced by the Italian Marxist Antonio Gramsci.[7] This combination enabled Dick Hebdige, Angela McRobbie, and Iain Chambers (among others) to produce studies of British subcultural practices that treat popular culture as a crucial site for the construction of social identity, but also as a key terrain for ideological conflict.

These inquiries into the nature of subjectivity and the relationship between culture and power helped prepare many American readers for French deconstruction, post-structuralism, and post-modernism. Deconstruction, as articulated by Jacques Derrida, has challenged the very fiber of criticism and interpretation by revealing the metaphysical priority given to language within Western thought. This "logocentrism" presumes that careful naming can uncover fixed meanings about the world, but deconstruction's interrogation of language reveals the provisional, contingent, and unstable nature of naming. Derrida finds Western thinkers to be uncritical about their "standpoint," about their insistence on unifocal and univocal investigations outward from a privileged center that deny opportunities for reciprocal perspectives and multivocal dialogues. Uncritical acceptance of language as an unmediated vehicle for understanding experience underlies much of the arrogance of Western thought for Derrida—its privileging of written texts over other forms of discourse, its dangerous instrumentality, its crude dismissal of competing systems of thought as "primitive" and "barbaric." In short, the logocentrism of Western culture undergirds the "humanism" which presents the experiences of modern Europeans and North Americans as "human," while dismissing much of the rest of the world as some kind of undifferentiated "other." Logocentrism establishes a symbolic order which naturalizes oppression and injustice.[8] Deconstruction has helped cultural critics to break with logocentrism, to be self-reflexive about the tools they wield, and to investigate the ways in which language positions the subjects and objects of knowledge.

Similarly, the post-structuralism advanced in the work of Michel Foucault has challenged radically the traditional premises of cultural investigation and interpretation. Foucault has demonstrated how discursive categories constitute sites of oppression—for example, how the medicalization of sexuality or the criminalization of "antisocial" behavior has constructed the body as a locus of domination and power. Thus for Foucault, centralized economic and political power rest not so much on direct authority, force, or manipulation, but more on the capacity to disperse power to localized sites where the symbolic order constrains, contains, silences, and suppresses potential opposition. This approach calls attention to marginal social positions, to diffuse sites of oppression and resistance, and to practices capable of resisting or at least interrupting domination.[9]

The concept of post-modernism as developed in the work of Jean-François Lyotard helps locate the work of Derrida and Foucault within the contemporary cultural crisis of representation. Although Lyotard insists that post-modernism is more of a sensibility than a time period, he does acknowledge that the delight in difference, self-reflexivity, detached irony, and "incredulity toward metanarratives" that define the post-modern "condition" stem from the modern sense of living in a "post" period characterized by the exhaustion of modernism and Marxism as ways of understanding and interpreting experience.[10] Thus the rejection among deconstructionists and post-structuralists of the "grand master narratives" emanating from the Enlightenment represents more than methodological or theoretical novelty in culture studies. Rather, the fragmented, decentered, and divided world uncovered by cultural theory reflects a recognition of contemporary social and economic crises including deindustrialization in the West, de-Stalinization in the East, and imperatives imposed on the Third World by First and Second World imperialisms—austerity, hunger, debt, and dependency.

Lacanian psychoanalysis, Althusserian structuralist-Marxism, British Cultural Studies, deconstruction, post-structuralism, and post-modernism represent the most important strains of European cultural theory influencing cultural studies in America, but this list is hardly an exhaustive one. Explorations into taste cultures by the French sociologist Pierre Bourdieu, the rediscovery of the body and the insistence on gender as an independent frame of inquiry by Luce Irigiray and other French feminists, the theories of communicative rationality advanced by the German sociologist Jürgen Habermas, and the scholarly exhumation of Russian literary critic Mikhail Bakhtin's "dialogic criticism" have each played an important role in redefining cultural studies in America.[11]

Yet scholars should not regard European cultural theory uncritically, as if it were a panacea. Gayatri Chakravorty Spivak has demonstrated how post-structuralists, in their ignorance of the Third World and their unwillingness to search out other voices, often share the Eurocentric biases they presume to challenge.[12] Those who privilege "marginality" as an abstraction may forget that what is marginal from one perspective may be central to another. In a wickedly clever and perceptive article, Michelle Lamont has shown how the emergence of Jacques Derrida as a "dominant" philosopher owes a great deal to his ability to benefit from the "cultural capital" institutionalized in the power structures of academic discourse.[13]

Similarly, Judith Lowder Newton notes the disturbing unwillingness among many European cultural theorists to acknowledge their debt to feminism and to the women's movement which initially raised the issues of subjectivity and representation that now serve as the basis for the more generalized critique of power raised within cultural theory.[14] Indeed, feminists have legitimate reasons to be suspicious of theories that proclaim the "death of the subject" at a time when women are finally beginning to emerge within cultural discourse as speaking subjects that celebrate the "end of history" at the precise moment when cultural criticism is beginning to deal more fully with the consequences of historically grounded oppressions. Beyond the problem of internal contradictions within European cultural theory lie larger questions about its reification as a method and its application to the American context.

Few scholars engaged in any form of cultural studies over the past decade have been able to avoid the acrimonious debates provoked by the rise of European cultural theory. At one extreme, they have seen a resistance to theory, an anti-intellectual dismissal of new methods and approaches (especially of deconstruction and post-structuralism). At the other extreme, they have seen a reification of theory into a "magic bullet" that can by itself position scholars outside the oppressions and exploitations of history.[15] The tragedy of this debate—as is often the case in such moments of antagonism—is that each side often misses what the other has to offer. Sometimes what seems like anti-intellectualism on the part of critics of theory is really a justifiable critique of theorists who become (in the words of one of my colleagues) "spiritless automatons designing ever more elaborate theoretical machines."[16] On the other hand, what sometimes seems like self-serving jargon and "intellectual-speak" to non-theorists is in reality an important effort to create a language capable of interrupting and opposing the dominant ideologies of the past. In my view, American Studies would be served best by a theory that refuses hypostatization into a method, that grounds itself in the study of concrete cultural practices, that extends the definition of culture to the broadest possible contexts of cultural production and reception, that recognizes the role played by national histories and traditions in cultural contestation, and that understands that struggles over meaning are inevitably struggles over resources.

One of cultural theory's great contributions has been to challenge the division between texts and experience. Literary critic Terry Eagleton especially has taken pains to affirm that the construction of texts is a social process, while at the same time insisting that no social experience exists outside of ideology and textualization. However, Eagleton's healthy warning sometimes has led to an unhealthy result—the fetishizing of texts through the interpretation of reality as simply one more text. It is one thing to say that discourse, ideology, and textualization are inevitable and necessary parts of social experience, but it is quite another thing to say that they are the totality of social experience. As a quip reported by Jon Wiener phrases it, "Tell that to the veterans of foreign texts."[17] Stuart Hall describes the goal of cultural criticism as the reproduction of the concrete in thought—"not to generate another good theory, but to give a better theorized account of concrete historical reality."[18] Hall's formulation combines "high" theory and "low" common sense and is an essential corrective to uses of theory that lose touch with particular historical and social experiences. It prevents the self-reflexivity of contemporary theory from degenerating into solipsism, seeing theoretical work itself as a part of larger social processes. Finally, it enables cultural critiques to evolve into cultural interventions by engaging dominant ideology at the specific sites where it may be articulated and disarticulated.[19]

Innovations within European cultural theory over the past twenty years have raised issues and concerns that seem to threaten the traditional practices of American Studies. They bring a specialized language to bear on key questions about the creation and reception of culture in modern societies, and their methodological sophistication seems to render obsolete traditional American Studies questions about "what is American?" On closer inspection, however, contemporary European cultural theory resonates with the categories and questions of American Studies traditions; indeed, it is fair to say that the development of American Studies itself anticipated many of the cross-disciplinary epistemological and hermeneutic concerns at the heart of contemporary European cultural theory.

As Michael Denning has argued, "American Studies emerged as both a continuation of and a response to the popular 'discovery' and 'invention' of 'American culture' in the 1930s."[20] Ethnography and folklore studies by New Deal–supported scholars, the "cult of the common man" pushed by Popular Front Marxism, and the use of "American Exceptionalism" to stem the country's drift toward involvement in World War II, all combined to focus scholarly attention upon the contours and dimensions of American culture. Anti-communism and uncritical nationalism during the early years of the Cold War transformed the study of American culture in significant ways, imposing a mythical cultural "consensus" on what previously had been recognized as a history of struggle between insiders and outsiders.[21] While the hegemony of the consensus myth in the 1950s and 1960s served conservative political ends, it did not prevent American Studies scholars from asking critical questions about the relationship between the social construction of cultural categories and power relations in American society. As Giles Gunn so convincingly demonstrates, scholars of the myth-and-symbol school consciously sought to "overcome the split between fact and value" by explaining how value-laden images influence social life. He points out that the principal project of these scholars revolved around increasing "comprehension of the historical potentialities and liabilities of different ways of construing the relationship between consciousness and society."[22] Most important, Gunn reminds us that their project was both diagnostic and corrective because they recognized the interpenetration of symbolism and semiotics with power and privilege.[23]

In their sensitivity to language as a metaphorical construct with ideological implications, the myth-and-symbol scholars anticipated many of the concerns of contemporary cultural theory. In his introduction to the 1970 edition of *Virgin Land,* Henry Nash Smith claimed that "our perceptions of objects and events are no less a part of consciousness than are

our fantasies," and he described myths and symbols as "collective representations rather than the work of a single mind."[24] Similarly, in his 1965
study of the Brooklyn Bridge, Alan Trachtenberg insisted that "surely the
conventions of language themselves suggest predispositions among Americans to react in certain ways at certain times."[25] Yet for all their attention
to the role of language in shaping and reflecting social practice, the myth-
and-symbol scholars still tended to make sweeping generalizations about
society based upon images in relatively few elite literary texts, and they
never adequately theorized the relationship between cultural texts and social
action.

Bruce Kuklick's devastating 1972 critique of the myth-and-symbol
school provided the focal point for an emerging anthropological approach
within American Studies which advanced the field's reach and sophistication in significant ways. Yet without an adequate interrogation of the
ways in which all communication is metaphorical and by which all language
inscribes a sedimented subjectivity in researchers, these efforts did not do
enough to show how Americans made meaning for themselves out of
cultural practices. Moreover, they tended to stress the uses and effects of
cultural artifacts at the expense of their ideological and historical meanings.[26] Reviewing the field in 1979, Gene Wise argued for a new American
Studies, one that would be self-reflexive, pluralistic, and focused on the
particular and concrete practices of American everyday life, while at the
same time remaining comparative and cross-cultural.[27]

Contemporary European cultural theory goes a long way toward meeting
Wise's goals. While most directly relevant to the "new historicism" within
literary criticism, contemporary cultural theory's location of language
within larger social and discursive contexts inevitably leads it toward
cultural practices beyond literature, especially to popular culture. In recent
years, many of the most effective applications of European cultural theory
within American Studies have been presented within analyses of popular
culture. This affinity between "high" theory and "low" culture may seem
surprising at first, but each category contains elements of great importance
to the other. Cultural theorists trained to see literary texts as "multivocal"
and "dialogic" find rich objects of study within the vernacular forms and
generic recombinations collectively authored within commercial culture.
The fragmented consciousness, decentered perspective, and resistance to
narrative closure that post-modernists labor so diligently to produce within
"high" cultural forms are routine and everyday practices within popular
music and television. On the other hand, investigators of popular culture

find their objects of study so implicated in commercial and practical activities, that it is sometimes difficult to distinguish the text from its conditions of creation, distribution, and reception. For those engaged in research about commercialized leisure and electronic mass media, the approaches advanced within European cultural theory may provide the only adequate frameworks for exploring and theorizing the full implications of their objects of study.

For scholars working in the American Studies tradition, the affinity between European cultural theory and American popular culture offers an opportunity to do the kind of listening that Duke Ellington recommended to Clark Terry, a listening that promises to reconnect American Studies to its original purpose and potential. Writing in *The Negro Quarterly* in 1943, Ralph Ellison suggested that "perhaps the zoot suit conceals profound political meaning; perhaps the symmetrical frenzy of the Lindy-hop conceals clues to great political power."[28] Two years later, Chester Himes incorporated Ellison's sense of the specific in his novel *If He Hollers Let Him Go*. In that book, Himes's characters negotiate identities of race, gender, and class in dialogue with the icons and images of popular music, film, folklore, and fashion.[29] Less than a decade after Ellison's article, the great jazz musician Charlie Parker argued for a necessary connection between his art and his experience, explaining "if you don't live it, it won't come out of your horn."[30]

In the decade that proved crucial to the development of scholarly research in American Studies, Ellison, Himes, and Parker all understood something important about their historical moment—the way that popular culture, political economy, and cultural theory defined new possibilities for studying and understanding American culture. Provoked by the social and cultural changes of the 1940s, Ellison, Himes, and Parker fashioned works of art and criticism that pointed to the obsolescence of old boundaries dividing popular culture from "high" culture. By focusing on the contexts and processes of cultural creation, rather than just on validated texts, they recognized that the generation and circulation of ideas and images pervades all forms of social life. They conceived of art and culture as a part of everyone's everyday life, not just as the domain of artists and critics. The zoot suit, the Lindy-hop, and bop music constituted commodities within commercial culture, but they also served as cultural practices, as critiques of dominant values. They disclosed what Albert Murray, rebuking white supremacist assumptions, later would call "the inescapably mulatto nature of American culture."[31] These African-Americans revealed the importance of popular cultural texts and practices in the construction of individual and group identity, challenging a reductionism that concentrated solely on social and economic categories as crucibles of interests and ideas. They exposed an interaction between art and life that refuted formalist assumptions about the autonomy of art.

Perhaps most important, in their understanding of the ways in which the zoot suit, bop music, and the Lindy-hop manifested a new kind of "prestige from below" made possible by the migrations and shop floor interactions of the war years, these artists illustrated the ways in which changes in political economy necessitated new forms of cultural practice and new theories of cultural studies. The immediate, emotional, and participatory aspects of this new popular culture privileged coded, indirect, and allegorical propensities deeply embedded within the art, music, dance, and speech of aggrieved populations. The expanded reach and scope of electronic mass media called into being a fundamentally new audience, one that was unified and diverse at the same time. Describing the postwar world and its culture, Ellison wrote prophetically:

> there is not stability anywhere and there will not be for many years to come, and progress now insistently asserts its tragic side; the evil now stares out of the bright sunlight. New groups will ceaselessly emerge, class lines will continue to waver and break and re-form.[32]

Some of the best early work in American Studies addressed topics of cultural production in broad-minded and sophisticated fashion. The first issues of the *American Quarterly* featured important discussions by David Riesman and Charles Seeger on popular music, by Parker Tyler about film, and by Gene Balsley on subcultural practice.[33] Yet despite this early impetus within American Studies to investigate popular culture, the field — like the rest of the scholarly community — became isolated from the social bases and oppositional ideologies necessary for a break with the past. Consequently, despite significant accomplishments over the years, American Studies scholars too often have been accomplices in an unjust representation of American culture, depicting it as more monolithic and less plural than the realities of American life and history warrant.

The positions advanced by Ellison, Himes, and Parker during the decade that gave birth to the discipline of American Studies call attention to a lost opportunity for scholarship and criticism. Had they been fully understood by American Studies scholars, these provocations by Afro-American artists and critics might have helped to shape the field along radically different lines. They might have led to an American cultural criticism that did more to resist the idea of a unified and static American identity, one that more thoroughly explored the complicated relationship between social processes and cultural texts, one that inquired more effectively into the sedimented subjectivities of language and thought that lay beneath the surface appearances of texts or social processes. What might have been a watershed for scholarship and criticism turned out to be merely a detour — one of those many "turning points" in history that failed to turn.

For many years, American Studies has needed more explorations into popular culture grounded in political economy and guided by theoretical critique. Despite the field's recurrent preoccupations with myths and symbols (even with the eclipse of the myth-and-symbol school), as well as with the sociology of cultural production and reception, most scholarly work still focuses on validated literary and historical texts, and one can understand why. How, for example, can we begin to fathom Rupert Murdoch's directive as the new publisher of *TV Guide* that he wanted the editors to make that publication "less cerebral and more popular"?[34] Exactly what can scholars add toward understanding a popular song such as the Angry Samoans' "My Father is a Fatso"? Yet our inquiries into literary and historical texts take place within a society where people like Rupert Murdoch and the Angry Samoans have extraordinary influence, and we neglect them only at our peril.

Even if popular culture contained only debased and banal images it would be necessary for us to understand and explain them; but we know that popular culture also reflects the extraordinary creativity and ingenuity of grass roots artists and intellectuals. American Studies scholars read Ralph Ellison's *Invisible Man* but still know too little about the Lindy-hop. We identify Chester Himes as the author of popular detective novels, but not as the important theorist of race and culture that he was. The 1988 motion picture *Bird* (directed by Clint Eastwood) revived the importance of Charlie Parker, but it did so in a manner so oblivious to the specific historical and social contexts essential to the development of bop music that the film just as well might have been titled *Amadeus and Andy* or *Every Which Way But Black*.

Recent trends make the present moment seem similar to the 1940s: once again the work of artists from seemingly marginal communities calls attention to unprecedented opportunities for serious study of popular culture, for explorations into politics and economics, and for renewed theoretical inquiry. Fourteen-year-olds with digital samplers may not know Jacques

Lacan from Chaka Khan, but they can access the entire inventory of recorded world music with the flick of a switch. The musics of Laurie Anderson and David Byrne presume that artifacts of popular culture circulate within the same universe as artifacts of "high" culture, and they build their dramatic force from the juxtaposition of these seemingly incompatible discourses. Motion pictures such as David Lynch's *Blue Velvet* anticipate viewer competence in the codes of popular culture as well as in the concerns of contemporary cultural criticism.

As Horace Newcomb observes, the industrial mode of television production in the United States favors serial narratives, resisting ideological closures in a manner that has profound influence on the nature of narrative itself in our culture.[35] At the same time, post-modernism in literature and the visual arts follows some of the sensibilities of electronic mass media, especially through forms of inter-textuality and inter-referentiality that call attention to the entire field of cultural practices surrounding any given cultural utterance. Indeed, one might argue that the most sophisticated cultural theorists in America are neither critics nor scholars, but rather artists — writers Toni Morrison, Leslie Marmon Silko, Rudolfo Anaya, and Maxine Hong Kingston or musicians Laurie Anderson, Prince, David Byrne, and Tracy Chapman. Their work revolves around the multiple perspectives, surprising juxtapositions, subversions of language, and self-reflexivities explored within cultural theory. It comes from and speaks to contemporary cultural crises about subjectivity and nationality. Issues that critics discuss abstractly and idealistically seem to flow effortlessly and relentlessly from the texts of popular literature and popular culture.

For example, Toni Morrison's radical interrogation of commodities and collective memory along with her relentless critique of the role of language and textuality in maintaining social hierarchies in *Beloved* provides readers with a work of art that fundamentally resists traditional methods of criticism. Morrison's book provides a particularly vivid illustration of the necessary connection between the basic categories of European cultural theory and the basic concerns of American cultural discourse. The entire novel revolves around the core issues evident in European cultural theory — desire, fragmentation, subjectivity, power, and language. One of Morrison's villains is a schoolteacher who beats a slave "to show him that definition belonged to the definers—not the defined" (190). The schoolteacher also silences those whom he oppresses— "the information they offered he called backtalk and developed a variety of corrections (which he recorded in his notebook) to reeducate them" (220).

This "power to define" that Morrison reflects on constructs subjectivity from the white perspective, leaving Afro-Americans as the objects of the white gaze. Whites possess "the righteous Look every Negro learned to recognize along with his ma'am's tit," while blacks know that when their pictures appear in the newspaper it means trouble because those pictures are always constructed from within white subjectivity (157). Consequently, black subjectivity is problematized and fragmented. In a Derridean moment, one character ruminates on his identity—"When he looks at himself through Garner's eyes, he sees one thing. Through Sixo's another. One makes him feel righteous. One makes him feel ashamed" (267). At times in the novel, desire and selfishness define individual subjectivity, but in the end it is recognition of a collective subjectivity and a collective project that resolves the dilemmas posed by power and language. Perhaps most significantly, the resolution of *Beloved* comes through song and sound— "the sound that broke the back of words" (261).

The issues that inform Morrison's *Beloved* pervade European cultural theory. They focus on diversity, difference, and fragmentation but find that centralized and localized sources of oppressive power also have created an extraordinary oppositional unity in diversity. Her work, like so much else in contemporary culture, underscores the necessity of theoretically informed criticism capable of examining the processes and contexts of cultural creation as well as its products.

The dynamism of contemporary popular culture has been especially important in sparking an attendant sensitivity among scholars to the importance of cultural studies. Six significant anthologies about American popular culture have appeared since 1987, and these anthologies ride the crest of a wave of fine monographs and articles about popular literature by Janice Radway, Michael Denning, and Elizabeth Long; on television by Lynn Spigel, John Fiske, and David Marc; about film by Dana Polan, Michael Ryan, and Rosa Linda Fregoso; on music by Lisa Lewis, Herman Gray, and Leslie Roman; and about sports by Jeff Sammons, Steve Hardy, and Elliott Gorn.[36] In addition, investigations presently underway by graduate students in programs all across the country promise to open up new and exciting areas of research, such as Brenda Bright's study of Chicano low-riders, Barry Shank's exploration into local music communities, Joe Austin's work on graffiti artists, Tricia Rose's explorations into rap music, and Henry Jenkins's examination of commercial network television.[37] This work is not confined solely to cultural criticism; it also takes the form of cultural intervention. Reebee Garofalo's involvement with "Rock Against

Racism" in Boston, Doug Kellner's activism with "Alternative Views" on public access television, and Ed Hugetz's efforts on behalf of independent filmmakers with the Southwest Alternate Media Project in Houston all combine important cultural criticism with creative cultural practice.

Cultural Studies and the Crises of Representation

Much of what is new in contemporary cultural criticism comes from self-conscious recognition of the "crisis of representation."[38] The inevitable gap between cultural accounts and cultural experiences has honed an extraordinary sensitivity among researchers to the ways in which scholarly conventions of representation are not complete, objective, or impartial, but rather partial, perspectival, and interested. Problematizing representation has been especially important to scholars in feminist and ethnic studies as they challenge the unconscious sexism and racism sedimented within presumably neutral scholarly methods and perspectives. Indeed, one can argue that the friendly reception accorded European cultural theory in the United States largely stems from the political and cultural struggles waged by women and ethnic minorities inside and outside of universities over the past two decades.

These struggles call attention to a crisis of representation in a different sense of the word, not as artistic representation through characters and symbols, but rather as political representation through action and speech on behalf of particular groups. Scholarly commitments to the agenda raised by European cultural theory often are belittled as "trendy," "careerist," and "arcane," but their emergence in America is tied directly to real crises confronting key constituencies, including women, people of color, blue-collar workers, state employees, and scholars themselves. The emergence of European cultural criticism on this continent has been less the product of internal debates within American Studies and related disciplines than of a recognition of changing conditions in American society brought on by the crises of deindustrialization and the rise of neo-conservatism.

Just as the African-American art and criticism of the 1940s both reflected and shaped a concrete historical moment, contemporary cultural creation and criticism take place within a cultural and social matrix made possible by social change. In the 1980s, the transition to a "high tech" service and sales economy has deindustrialized America, fundamentally disrupting the social arrangements fashioned in the 1950s. Structural unemployment, migration to the Sunbelt, and the radical reconstitution of the family all have worked to detach individuals from the traditional authority of work, community, and family, while the individualistic ethic of upward mobility encourages a concomitant sense of fragmentation and isolation. As the economy focuses less on production and more on consumption, cable television, video recorders, digital samplers, and compact discs expand both the reach and scope of media images. Popular culture intervenes in the construction of individual and group identity more than ever before as Presidents win popularity by quoting from Hollywood films ("make my day," "read my lips"), while serious political issues such as homelessness and hunger seem to enter public consciousness most fully when acknowledged by popular musicians or in made-for-television movies.

It should not be surprising then that radical changes in society and culture in the 1980s once again have provoked an emphasis on popular culture within American Studies. However, the current moment of academic cultural studies differs sharply from that of the 1950s. Part of the revived interest in popular culture stems from victories by women and racial minorities in winning access to university positions and their consequent interest in those voices silenced in "high" culture but predominant within some realms of popular culture.

Defeats for the democratization of society also have played a major role in shaping contemporary scholarly concerns. In the decades after World War II, the university could be seen as part of an ascendent social formation. As educators of a new class of technicians and administrators, scholars in the 1950s could see themselves as a plausible part of an expanding elite and as beneficiaries of dominant ideology. Six times as many students attended college in 1970 than had done so in 1930, and the numbers of faculty rose from 48,000 in 1920 to 600,000 by 1972. Between 1965 and 1970 alone, the numbers of college faculty grew by 138,000.[39] These years also witnessed a dramatic growth in student enrollments, especially among women and ethnic minorities. Yet the economic recessions of the 1970s and the attendant fiscal crisis of the state curtailed this growth. Neo-conservative ideologues launched an attack on public sector employment, arguing that such jobs drained capital from the private sector and functioned to subsidize what neo-conservatives described as the "adversary culture" (a phrase borrowed from Lionel Trilling and F. O. Matthiessen in the early days of American Studies).[40] Budget cuts served to undermine the economic base of public education, while reversals of hard-won commitments to equal opportunity for women and ethnic minorities undermined some of the constituencies bringing new voices and concerns to academic life. In addition, while raising payroll and sales taxes, neo-conservative policies for the cutting of income and capital gains taxes have left the United States with the most regressive tax structure of any western nation. This economic situation pits educators against low- and middle-income taxpayers and allows wealthy individuals and large corporations to reap most of the benefits of higher education, while paying ever smaller proportions of its costs.[41]

In the 1980s, it has become clear that most academics are tied to a declining social formation, to the residues of commitments to equal opportunity and to increased access to education that characterized some aspects of the politics of the 1960s and 1970s. Despite lavish salaries paid to a few scholars with international reputations and despite increasing total budgets for higher education, the social power of most scholars involved in cultural studies has declined drastically over the past twenty years. Since the economic crises of the 1970s, a radical reallocation of capital has voided unilaterally the social bargain made in the post-war years, marginalizing almost all but the most technical and vocational forms of education. Between 1975 and 1986 the percentage of current-fund revenue for higher education coming from federal, state, and local governments dropped from 51.3 percent to 44.9 percent. This decline led to serious increases in student tuition which further skewed the class base of student populations. As shown in a recent survey by the American Council on Education, there have been severe declines in the numbers of minority and poor students enrolled in college since 1976, and there seems to be little concrete action being taken to reverse that trend.[42]

Of course, private sector donations to education increased during the 1980s but in such a way as to put the resources of the university at the disposal of the highest bidders. Distinguished universities have eliminated entire geography, linguistics, and sociology departments, not because of declining enrollments, but to finance the ever-increasing costs of scientific research which might lead to lucrative licensing and selling of patent rights.[43] Military and business research thrives, while other areas face severe budget shortages. This is not just a problem for the humanities; funding for social science research from the National Science Foundation fell 75 percent in the early 1980s; and between 1975 and 1982 the number of social science graduate students receiving federal support at leading research universities fell 53 percent, while federal support for students in other scientific fields rose by 15 percent.[44] Like industrial workers and inner city dwellers, scholars in cultural fields not only confront a power structure hostile to their ideological interests, they face as well a political and economic apparatus determined to undermine public education, cultural diversity, and mechanisms for equal opportunity—in short the entire social base necessary for their survival.

Neo-conservatives know full well that academics suffering from the transformations in culture and economics during the 1970s and 1980s pose a threat to the emerging hegemony of neo-conservatism. From the attacks on critical scholarship by William Bennett and Lynne Cheney at their posts as heads of the National Endowment for the Humanities to corporate funding for neo-conservative scholarship (The Olin Foundation's backing of Allan Bloom and the Exxon Foundation's support for E. D. Hirsch) to Senator Jesse Helms's disgraceful efforts to cut off federal funding for controversial works of art, neo-conservatives have demonstrated their understanding of how struggles over meaning are also struggles over resources.[45] As Michael Denning observes, "The post–World War Two university is a part of 'mass culture,' of the 'culture industry,' a central economic and ideological apparatus of American capitalism."[46] As such, its battles resonate with the struggles over resources operative in society at large.

Under these conditions, struggles over meaning are also struggles over resources. They arbitrate what is permitted and what is forbidden; they help determine who will be included and who will be excluded; they influence who gets to speak and who gets silenced. Investigations into popular culture are not merely good-hearted efforts to expand the knowledge base of our field, they are also inevitably a part of the political process by which groups—including scholars—seek to reposition themselves in the present by reconstituting knowledge about culture and society in the past.

Traditional American Studies inquiries about "What is an American?" have insufficiently problematized the ways in which scholars perceive culture being produced and received in any given circumstance. These questions have imposed premature closures on open questions and have presumed a more unified American experience than the evidence can support. Yet questions of national identity are crucial to culture, and American Studies has an important role to play by applying the categories raised within European cultural theory to the American context, as well as by raising new questions that emerge from the particular complexities and contradictions within American culture.[47]

Most important, a theoretically informed American Studies would begin by listening for the sounds that Toni Morrison describes, the sounds capable of "breaking the back of words." These sounds cannot be summoned up by theoretical expertise alone. They cannot be constructed out of idealized subject positions emanating from reforms in discursive practices. They are to be found within the concrete contests of everyday life. Accessible by listening to what is already being said (and sung and shouted) by ordinary Americans, these sounds hold the key toward understanding the zoot suit and the Lindy-hop, and so much more. To paraphrase Ellison's narrator in *The Invisible Man*: who knows; perhaps they speak for you.

NOTES

1. See Thomas J. McCormick, *America's Half Century* (Baltimore, 1989).
2. See esp. the challenges raised within geography by Edward Soja's *Postmodern Geographies* (London, 1988); and in legal studies by Kimberle Crenshaw, "Race, Reform, and Retrenchment: Transformation and Legitimation in Antidiscrimination Law," *Harvard Law Review* 101 (May 1988): 1331–87; and Mari Matsuda, "Affirmative Action and Legal Knowledge: Planting Seeds in Plowed-Up Ground," *Harvard Women's Law Journal* 11 (Spring 1988): 1–17.
3. Michael Ryan, "The Politics of Film: Discourse, Psychoanalysis, Ideology," in *Marxism and the Interpretation of Culture*, ed. Lawrence Grossberg and Cary Nelson (Chicago, 1988), 478.
4. George Marcus and Michael M. J. Fischer, *Anthropology as Cultural Critique* (Chicago, 1986).
5. Toni Morrison, *Beloved* (New York, 1987), 255; hereafter, cited in the text.
6. Laura Mulvey, "Visual Pleasure and Narrative Cinema," *Screen* 16 (1975): 6–18. Stephen Heath, *Questions of Cinema* (London, 1981).
7. See Stuart Hall, "The Toad in the Garden: Thatcherism Among the Theorists," in Grossberg and Nelson, *Marxism and the Interpretation of Culture*, 35–73; as well as George Lipsitz, "The Struggle for Hegemony," *Journal of American History* 75 (June 1988): 146–50.
8. Jacques Derrida, *Of Grammatology* (Baltimore, 1976).
9. Michel Foucault, *The History of Sexuality* (Harmondsworth, England, 1976); Foucault, *Language, Counter-memory, Practice* (Ithaca, 1980). For an extraordinary application of Foucault's work to American culture, see Thomas L. Dumm, *Democracy and Punishment* (Madison, Wis., 1987).
10. Jean-François Lyotard, *The Postmodern Condition* (Minneapolis, 1984), 71–82.
11. Pierre Bourdieu, "The Aristocracy of Culture," *Media, Culture, and Society* 2 (1980): 225–54; Toril Moi, *Sexual/Textual Politics: Feminist Literary Theory* (London, 1985); Luce Irigiray, *Speculum de l'autre Femme* (Paris, 1974); Jürgen Habermas, *Legitimation Crisis* (Boston, 1975); Mikhail M. Bakhtin, *Rabelais and His World*

(Bloomington, Ind., 1984). Bourdieu's great contributions have been in bringing a convincing sociological frame to aesthetic questions, as well as his discovery that cultural categories bear a fundamental relationship to the circulation and distribution of capital. Lawrence Levine's fine work in *Highbrow/Lowbrow* (Cambridge, Mass., 1989) on the changing reputation of Shakespeare in America reflects one manifestation of Bourdieu's influence. Irigiray and Hélène Cixous have been most important in raising questions about the body and subjectivity in feminist psychoanalytic film criticism. See Teresa de Lauretis, *Alice Doesn't: Feminism, Semiotics, Cinema* (Bloomington, Ind., 1984); and Tania Modleski, *The Women Who Knew Too Much* (New York, 1988) for important discussions of their methods in relation to film criticism. Also see de Lauretis's *Technologies of Gender* (Bloomington, Ind., 1987) for a critique of post-structuralists' neglect of feminist theory. Habermas's *Legitimation Crisis* provides an important perspective on ideological legitimation and historical change that has exerted great influence on Fredric Jameson's exemplary essay "Reification and Utopia in Mass Culture," *Social Text* 1 (1979): 130–48; as well as on my own *Time Passages* (Minneapolis, 1990). Bakhtin is perhaps the European cultural theorist most influential on American scholars today; see Horace Newcomb's "Dialogic Aspects of Mass Communication," in *Critical Studies in Mass Communication* 1 (1984): 34–50; and Dana Polan's *Power and Paranoia* (New York, 1986).

12. Gayatri Chakravorty Spivak, "Can the Subaltern Speak?" in Grossberg and Nelson, *Marxism and the Interpretation of Culture,* 271–313; Gayatri Chakravorty Spivak, *In Other Worlds: Essays in Cultural Politics* (New York, 1987).

13. Michelle Lamont, "How to Become a Dominant French Philosopher: The Case of Jacques Derrida," *American Journal of Sociology* 93 (1987): 584–622. I cite Lamont's critique because it effectively explains Derrida's reception within scholarly communities in Europe and America, but I do not intend to use it to belittle Derrida's contributions or to call into question his own historical knowledge of marginality as an Algerian in France.

14. Judith Lowder Newton, "History as Usual? Feminism and the 'New Historicism' " in *The New Historicism,* ed. H. Aram Veeser (New York, 1989), 153–54.

15. See Lynne Cheney's incoherent references to post-structuralism in "Report to the President, the Congress, and the American People," *Chronicle of Higher Education* 35 (21 Sept. 1988): 18–23, esp. 18, 19, for an example of anti-intellectualism; and Sande Cohen's *Historical Culture* (Berkeley, 1986) for an example of the reification of theory. The exchange among members of the Syracuse University English Department in the *Syracuse Scholar* (Spring, 1987) demonstrates just how acrimonious this debate can become.

16. I thank Reda Bensmaia for this turn of phrase although he should bear no responsibility for its meaning here.

17. Jon Wiener, "The De Man Affair," *The Nation* 246 (9 Jan. 1988): 22.

18. Hall, "The Toad in the Garden," 69–70.

19. In British Cultural Studies, "articulation" has two meanings. One sense of the word refers to speech acts of enunciation. The other refers to a state of connection or jointedness. Thus ideology can be seen as the product of utterances, as well as a device for connecting individuals and groups.

20. Michael Denning, "The Special American Conditions: Marxism and American Studies," *American Quarterly* 38, Bibliography Issue (1986): 357; Giles Gunn, *The Culture of Criticism and the Criticism of Culture* (New York, 1987), 147–72.

21. See David W. Noble, *The End of American History* (Minneapolis, 1985).

22. Gunn, *The Culture of Criticism,* 161.

23. Ibid., 160, 172.

24. Henry Nash Smith, *Virgin Land* (Cambridge, Mass., 1970), ix, ii.

25. Alan Trachtenberg, *Brooklyn Bridge* (New York, 1965), 117.

26. Bruce Kuklick, "Myth and Symbol in American Studies," *American Quarterly* 24 (Oct. 1972): 435–50.

27. Gene Wise, " 'Paradigm Dramas' in American Studies: A Cultural and Institutional History of the Movement," *American Quarterly* 31, Bibliography Issue (1979): 293–337.

28. Ralph Ellison, "Editorial Comment," *The Negro Quarterly* (Winter-Spring 1943): 301.

29. Chester Himes, *If He Hollers Let Him Go* (New York, 1945).

30. Ben Sidran, *Black Talk* (New York, 1971), 18.

31. Albert Murray, *The Omni Americans* (New York, 1983), 22.

32. Ellison, "Society, Morality, and the Novel," in *The Living Novel: A Symposium,* ed. Granville Hicks (New York, 1962), 66. I am indebted to John S. Wright for calling this quote to my attention.

33. See especially David Riesman, "Listening to Popular Music," *American Quarterly* 2 (Winter 1950): 359–71; Russell Roth, "The Ragtime Revival: A Critique," *American Quarterly* 2 (Winter 1950): 329–39; Charles Seeger, "Music and Class Structure in the United States," *American Quarterly* 9 (Fall 1957): 281–94; Parker Tyler, "Hollywood as a Universal Church," *American Quarterly* 2 (Summer 1950): 165–76; Gene Balsley, "Hot Rod Culture," *American Quarterly* 2 (Winter 1950): 353–58.

34. Mark Schwed, "Don't Mind Murdoch," *Los Angeles Herald Examiner,* 21 Dec. 1988, A2.

35. Horace Newcomb, "Untold Stories," presentation at the University of Southern California, Los Angeles, 30 Nov. 1989. Quoted from author's notes.

36. Ian Angus and Sut Jhally, eds., *Cultural Politics in Contemporary America* (New York, 1988); Paul Buhle, ed., *Popular Culture in America* (Minneapolis, 1987); Richard Butsch, ed., *For Fun and Profit* (Philadelphia, 1990); Donald Lazere, ed., *American Media and Mass Culture* (Los Angeles, 1987); Lary May, ed., *Recasting Postwar America* (Chicago, 1989); Tania Modleski, ed., *Studies in Entertainment* (Bloomington, Ind., 1987). See Michael Denning, *Mechanic Accents* (London, 1988); Janice Radway, *Reading the Romance* (Chapel Hill, 1984); Elizabeth Long, *The American Dream and the Popular Novel* (London, 1985); Lynn Spigel, "Television and the Home Theater," *Camera Obscura* 16 (1988): 11–46; John Fiske, *Television Culture* (London, 1987); David Marc, *Comic Visions* (Boston, 1989); Dana Polan, *Power and Paranoia* (New York, 1986); Michael Ryan and Doug Kellner, *Camera Politica* (Bloomington, Ind., 1988); Rosa Linda Fregoso, "Born in East L.A. and the Politics of Representation," *Cultural Studies* 4 (Oct. 1990); Lisa Lewis, "Form and Female Authorship in Music Videos," *Communication* 9 (1987): 355–77; Herman Gray, *Producing Jazz* (Philadelphia, 1989); Jeff Sammons, *Outside the Ring* (Urbana, 1987); Elliott Gorn, *Boxing in America* (Chicago, 1986).

37. Bright, Rice Univ.; Shank, Univ. of Pennsylvania; Austin, Univ. of Minnesota: Rose, Brown Univ.; and Jenkins, Univ. of Wisconsin.

38. Marcus and Fischer, *Anthropology as Cultural Critique,* 7.

39. Peter Steinfels, *The Neo-Conservatives* (New York, 1979), 51.

40. Ibid., 56.
41. See Jodie T. Allen, "Moynihan Pushes Administration to 'Fess Up' to Social Security Tax Scam," *Washington Post,* 10 Jan. 1990, B3.
42. The study by the American Council on Education revealed that the percentage of low-income black high school graduates going to college fell from 40% to 30% and that the percentage of low-income Latinos fell from 50% to 35%. In addition, the study showed that even among middle-income blacks the rate of college participation fell from 53% to 36% in 1988 and for middle-income Latinos the rate of college participation fell from 53% to 46%.
43. See Leonard Minsky and David Noble, "Corporate Takeover on Campus," *The Nation* 249 (30 Oct. 1989): 494–96.
44. National Center for Education Statistics, *1988 Digest of Educational Statistics* (Washington, D.C.: Department of Education, 1988), 258; Chris Raymond, "Social Scientists, Used To Drastic Reagan-Era Fund Cuts, Hope Worst Is Over," *The Chronicle of Higher Education,* 17 May 1989, A20. I am grateful to Charles Betz for calling these statistics to my attention in his undergraduate honors thesis "Reconstructing the Academy: The Political Economy of Higher Education" (University of Minnesota, 1989).
45. I do not wish to assert that all of these people have exactly the same agenda, but Bennett's attacks on student loans, Cheney's condemnations of critical theory and non-traditional curricula, and Helms's fulminations against decisions by the National Endowment for the Arts all have functioned to limit access to already scarce public resources by what they view as the "adversary culture." On the other hand, intervention by tax-exempt, neo-conservative foundations has been important in funneling private funds (no doubt, tax deductible) to ideologically acceptable academics. The John M. Olin Foundation has channeled $3.6 million to Allan Bloom to run the John M. Olin Center for Inquiry into the Theory and Practice of Democracy at the Univ. of Chicago, $1.4 million to Samuel Huntington for the Olin Institute for Strategic Studies at Harvard Univ. (and a $100,000 research fellowship for Huntington himself), $1 million to J. Clayburn LaForce and James Wilson to set up the Olin Center for Policy at U.C.L.A.'s Graduate School of Management, $376,000 to Irving Kristol, $200,000 to Walter Williams, and $5.8 million for law schools to establish programs in "Law and Economics" that apply "free market principles" to legal studies, according to Jon Wiener, "Dollars for Neocon Scholars," *The Nation* 250 (1 Jan. 1990): 12–13.
46. Denning, "The Special American Conditions," 356–80.
47. The structuralist and post-structuralist emphases of European cultural theory might seem to eclipse the nation as a unit of study. Yet while cultural practices like the social construction of gendered subjects, the medicalization of sexuality, and the tyranny of univocal narratives transcend national boundaries, they are inflected differently in each national context. Part of the attraction of European cultural theory in the U.S. stems from its bold skepticism about the cherished American ideal of "progress." Conversely, America's complex social and cultural formations often seem "postmodern" to Europeans unaccustomed to the ethnic diversity and physical mobility common in the United States. As Todd Gitlin quips, "Postmodernism is born in the USA because juxtaposition is one of the things that we do best" (Gitlin, "Postmodernism: Roots and Politics," in Angus and Jhally, *Cultural Politics,* 355).

COMMENTARY

Amy Kaplan

Duke Ellington's injunction to Clark Terry to "listen" best describes the character of George Lipsitz's groundbreaking work in American studies. Lipsitz has been our virtuoso listener, attentive to a myriad—at times a cacophony—of voices, many of which had not previously been heard within the academy: both voices of ordinary people engaged in the concrete struggles of everyday life and voices of extraordinary artists, musicians, and cultural producers previously excluded from the "high culture" definition of art. This act of creative listening informs all of his recent work, from *A Life in the Struggle: Ivory Perry and the Culture of Opposition* (Philadelphia: Temple University Press, 1988), a collaborative work based on oral history; to *Time Passages: Collective Memory and American Popular Culture* (Minneapolis: University of Minnesota Press, 1990), which attends to both the producers and consumers of popular culture as creators of historical memory; to his most recent book, *Dangerous Crossroads: Popular Music, Postmodernism, and the Poetics of Place* (New York: Verso, 1994), which locates dispersed communities of artists and listeners in global circuits. Lipsitz also listens afresh to theoretical clamors within the academy, to set in dialogue interlocutors who would otherwise not cross paths, or whose views would remain too polarized even to debate one another. Throughout his work, Lipsitz, in addition, pays heed to the historical silences and ruptures that both undergird and challenge social and political structures of power and injustice.

"Listening to Learn and Learning to Listen: Popular Culture, Cultural Theory, and American Studies" played a key role in reimagining the field of American studies by facilitating a dialogue between students of European theory and American popular culture, at a time when theory seemed to some threateningly elitist, trendy, and mechanical, and the attack on theory seemed to others stifling, simplistic, and anti-intellectual. In this essay, Lipsitz innovatively turns the hierarchy of theory and practice on its head, ultimately to dismantle the dichotomy between them. He does not simply advocate that we apply theoretical insights to decode and deconstruct cultural practices, but instead that we *listen* to the producers of culture themselves for the theories that spring from their practices. Here specifically he calls attention to the work of African American artists in the 1940s—Ralph Ellison, Chester Himes, and Charlie Parker—not as objects of theoretical analysis, but as theorists of American culture, who posed compelling questions about art's engagement with everyday life, the limits and potentials of commodification, the centrality of race to national culture, and the ways in which changes in political economy necessitated new cultural formations. Later in the essay he relates the 1940s to the present, by similarly drawing on the writing of Toni Morrison to reformulate the pressing questions which theory raises about the relationship between representation and social reality. In a recent essay review on the new historicism and the study of race, Lipsitz characteristically starts not by asking how literary critics can theorize race, but instead by asking them to "listen" to the metaphors of Himes and Malcolm X, who offer "epistemological insights for scholars trying to understand the role of white supremacy and anti-black racism in the American literary imagination."[1] Lipsitz listens to the metaphors of artists and political figures not to deconstruct them, but to learn new ways of thinking about the connections among language, knowledge, and political change.

As always for Lipsitz, questions of cultural theory and practice are inseparable from questions of history. In this essay, the works of Ellison, Himes, and Parker offer not only alternative theories and practices, but also an alternative historical narrative for the creation of American studies as a field grounded in the study of popular culture. Lipsitz argues that their theories of culture embodied a "missed opportunity" for the foundation of the discipline, missed because of an array of forces inside and outside the academy. This understanding of history implicitly claims that dominant historical narratives are shaped not only by the victors but by the contest with narratives that might have been, with what Lipsitz calls "detours," the "turning points in history that failed to turn." His approach does not simply express nostalgia for lost struggles, but instead explores a complex sense of history writing as the interweaving of both victorious narratives and compelling detours that wrestle with and inform one another. He shows that the representations of historical identity do not solely belong to the definers—the schoolteachers of the world, in Morrison's terms—but to those who struggle against the grain to redefine their collective lives, memories and aspirations. Thus Lipsitz treats the writing of history itself as a vibrant form of listening, not only of the present listening to the past, but of the past listening to the needs, concerns and crises of the present. This is less an imposition of contemporary categories on the past than a dialogue in which urgent questions posed to the past elicit new historical responses. Such a dialogue makes it possible for Lipsitz to see the historical affinities and convergences between the moments of the 1940s and 1980s, for example, by raising questions about the contemporary crisis of representation in a way that reopens the field of inquiry to earlier voices that had been forced underground.

Finally, this essay exemplifies Lipsitz's acute attention to the historically contingent nature of the present and of our own intellectual inquiries, to the ways debates within the academy are both enabled and truncated by broader social and economic changes and political struggles of which the university is a part. This essay links the crisis of representation articulated by theory to the crisis of political representation and the struggle over resources provoked by the conservative assaults on the gains made by women and minorities in the 1980s, as part of profound institutional changes in the role of higher education in a narrowing democracy. In later essays, Lipsitz similarly insists on connecting the academic discourses on race to broad institutional and legal challenges in society at large, or on connecting the analysis of popular music across national boundaries to documenting the vast international movements of migration and global capital. This firm grasp of sweeping institutional and transnational changes does not dwarf but rather enriches the way Lipsitz listens to the sounds of people engaged in the "concrete contests of everyday life."

Thinking about the importance of listening to George Lipsitz's theory and practice of American studies, I was reminded of a scene from Toni Morrison's *Beloved*, in which the narrative of Sethe's escape from slavery emerges from her daughters' storytelling. Beloved is starving to hear Denver speak about the past, as she grows equally hungry to tell her stories. In response to Beloved's eager listening, "Denver's monologue became in fact, a duet." To reconstruct their mother's history, as well as their own, "Denver spoke, Beloved listened and the two did the best they could to create what really happened."[2]

NOTES

1. George Lipsitz, " 'Swing Low, Sweet Cadillac': White Supremacy, Antiblack Racism, and the New Historicism," *American Literary History* 7 (1995): 700–725.

2. Toni Morrison, *Beloved* (New York: Knopf, 1987).

ALICE KESSLER-HARRIS

Cultural Locations: Positioning American Studies in the Great Debate

SINCE WE LAST MET, THE WORLD HAS SEEN MOMENTOUS CHANGES. The United States organized an international coalition to fight and win a war in the Persian Gulf. Apartheid in South Africa is in the process of crumbling. General Noriega has become an American prisoner. Communism is shattered; the evil empire of the Soviet Union has disintegrated. The cold war is no longer. At this speaking, Arabs are sitting down with Israelis. And we are engaged in a bitter debate over multiculturalism.

I could go on. Unemployment insurance, sexual harassment, national health care, abortion rights, family leave, civil rights, and a newly virulent conservatism are all burning issues of the moment. None of them has occupied our daily thoughts more than issues of multiculturalism. Now I confess to more than a bit of puzzlement over all this. We seem to have won the war against communism. American free enterprise is a clear victor in the struggle for what we once called the minds and hearts of the people. Yet somehow we have become enmeshed in a battle over the idea of America. What is at stake in this

This paper is a slightly revised version of my presidential address to the American Studies Association Meetings, Baltimore, MD, October 31, 1991. My deepest appreciation to Martha Banta, Arthur Dudden, Dee Garrison, and Robert Zangrando for feeding me helpful material. And thanks to Doris Friedensohn and Bert Silverman for help in framing the issues.

American Quarterly, Vol. 44, No. 3 (September 1992) © 1992 American Studies Association battle? How are we, as students of American Studies, to think about it?

The absence of a common enemy, you might say, makes room for internal dissent. So it seems no more than reasonable that the same year that witnessed the demise of what appeared to be a major threat to the United States should witness the escalation of a fiery internal controversy that has left none of us untouched. Who has not participated in debates over revising the curriculum to meet the changing needs of students with new demographic profiles? Who has not written and read reviews of the several books that indict campuses as hotbeds of political correctness? Who has not watched as "Firing Line," "Nightline," "McNeil-Lehrer" and other television programs have each in turn provided a forum for debate? And who has not noted with pain or pleasure the emergence of an oppositional group in the form of Teachers for a Democratic Culture?

How should we respond as academics and particularly as students of the United States? How should we position ourselves? Let us look a little more closely at the debate and then see if we can't forge an American Studies position.

In its simplest form, multiculturalism acknowledges and attempts to incorporate into the curriculum and campus environment "the wide range of cultures that cohabit the U.S." It represents, as even its detractors acknowledge, "the discovery on the part of minority groups that they can play a part in molding the larger culture even as they are molded by it."[1] The trouble, according to its critics, is that multiculturalism is rarely benign. Rather, critics fear that multicultural courses will displace traditional subjects, depriving students of what they call the heritage of western culture.

For the purposes of this argument, I want to separate that central issue from arguments about political correctness. Opponents of multiculturalism often argue that codes of conduct and attempts at curricular reform designed to promote tolerance, in practice, inhibit our capacity to speak our minds. They accuse advocates of diversity of imposing particular standards of behavior. But what is often called political correctness detracts from the issues surrounding multiculturalism. Lest we substitute one myth for another, we can and should decry excesses perpetrated in the name of that endeavor. We need only recall some of our earlier experiences as Marxists, feminists, and activists in the 1960s to remember how important it was to be allowed to speak our piece and to despair when we hear reports that in the name of multi-culturalism, students try to restrict classroom speech or attempt to bar some speakers from campus, or resort to intimidating criticism.

Still most efforts to achieve a multicultural curriculum can hardly be defined as excessive behavior. Though no one would deny the existence of occasional harassment or alarming insinuations, the degree to which intimidation and coercion of the kind that can be defined as politically correct behavior actually exists on American campuses remains an open question. The American Council on Education, the American Civil Liberties Union, and the Carnegie Foundation for the Advancement of Teaching all agree that the problem of coercion from the politically correct is far less prevalent than the rising numbers of incidents of racial intolerance, homophobia, and sexism.[2] So we puzzle about how the issue of multiculturalism got turned into "Left-wing McCarthyism" or "Fascism of the Left."

But the issue of political correctness may be something of a red herring. At the heart of the attack on multiculturalism lies a concern not for rights but for community. To its opponents the idea of what constitutes America seems to be at stake; the meaning conjured up when we think of our nation is threatened. That meaning is intimately tied to ideas about the nature of Western civilization and the particular humanistic values it is said to represent. Those values are constructed in opposition to a feared and unnamed enemy.[3] Thus, what is at stake has two levels: one, a set of Western ideas on which the concept of America as it is defined in these United States is said to rest, and the other, the material set of relations that we see around us and that is in danger of disintegration. They emerge clearly in the language in which the discussion is formulated.

In the spring of 1991, Lee M. Bass gave 20 million dollars to Yale to fund a course of study in Western civilization. The *New York Times* article that announced the gift commented that this was "a field that for more than a decade has been under attack while many colleges and universities increased their emphasis on the study of people and cultures outside the Western tradition."[4] A month later, George Will used the pages of *Newsweek* to rise in defense of Western civilization. The curriculum wars, he declared, were "related battles in a single war, a war of aggression against the Western political tradition and the ideas that animate it."[5]

The themes of aggression and war permeate the rhetoric. Speaking of the resistance to Carol Iannone's nomination to the national board of the National Endowment for the Humanities, Will wrote, "In this low-visibility, high intensity war, Lynne Cheney is secretary of domestic defense. The foreign adversaries her husband, Dick must keep at bay are less dangerous, in the long run, than the domestic forces with which she must deal."[6]

Conceiving of the battle of ideas as neither more nor less than war, those who protest multiculturalism construct powerful enemies against whom they urge resistance. A. M. Rosenthal, in an essay revealingly titled "Suicide on the Fourth" conflated Communists and Fascists with America's racial bigots and "their emotional cousins" who were members of the Left.[7] Others have suggested that those who support a "common cultural ground" are at war against "tribalism" and that claims to ethnicity are at war with efforts to forge a common identity.[8] Calling those in favor of multiculturalism "new segregationists," Rosenthal argued that they "were undermining the great act of political genius upon which this country rests. That is, of course, the concept that this nation was to be based on a variety of identities from which one new identity would spring."[9]

The war is defensive. It aims to prevent fragmentation and disintegration of something variously called identity or common cultural ground or cultural unity. As Rosenthal put it, the question is "whether this country is to be etched indelibly in the minds of young Americans simply as a strange collection of races and ethnic groups without real identity or purpose in common, or as a great creative action of nationhood in which the building of one became the purpose of many."[10] And in the words of George Will, the forces of multiculturalism "are fighting against the conservation of the common culture that is the nation's social cement."[11]

At the core of protest, then, is the central importance of cultural unity. When a specially appointed committee of New York State educators recommended a dramatic revision of the social studies curriculum in the state's schools last year, the ensuing disagreements echoed arguments all over the nation. The *New York Times* devoted several pages to the controversy. The committee, it reported, had concluded "that the teaching of social studies as a single officially sanctioned story was inaccurate as to the facts of conflict in American history, and further that it was limiting for white students and students of color alike." This led critics to suggest that "the old orthodoxies glorifying developments like the Pilgrims' journey to Plymouth Rock or the westward migration might be replaced by a new orthodoxy that would be critical of them." A dissenting committee member commented dolefully that a focus on ethnicity "opens the way for the kind of ethnic strife that has divided . . . nations where there is no consent on a common culture. The people of the United States will recognize," he added, "even if this committee does not, that every viable nation has to have a common culture to survive in peace." Under these circumstances, it was hardly hyperbole for the *Times* to note that "the battle over the New York State social studies curriculum is fundamentally a battle over the idea of America."[12]

A battle over the idea of America? Yes, and one in which the issue is what constitutes "American" and in which fears of fragmentation and loss of identity have replaced the fears of secret enemies conjured up by the old FBI. Those who attack what they call a politically correct stance seem to be supporting the idea of America as something fixed and given, deriving from Western civilization, while those who resist attach themselves to an idea of America that is more fluid and susceptible to change. One side constructs democratic culture as a tradition to be defended, a flag to be protected; the other as an ongoing process whose meanings are diffuse and changing. One side fears fragmentation of cultural unity; the other derides unity as a myth and protests loss of identity. The issue is joined: how do we preserve cultural unity and still do justice to the multiplicity of American cultures? To accomplish this, we must redefine what we mean by identity.

These are not new issues for American Studies, but their entry into so broad a public sphere pushes us, as scholars (once again) into a posture of self-examination. The political debate calls on myths about a past that we, in the field of American Studies have helped to create and interpret, and then popularize among an unsuspecting public. The political battle that rages around us is partly of our making. We, as historians, as cultural critics, as intellectuals who shape image and self-image have (if you will forgive the metaphor) built the bombs being used in the battle we now seek to avoid.

And so, perhaps reluctantly, we must take on the task of asking how we construct ourselves as a nation. In the past, we have accessed this question through a variety of methods so versatile that Marshall Fishwick once argued that to ask for method in American Studies was to descend into rigidity and restriction.[13] Norman Holmes Pearson put it another way. "American Studies," he said, "is what you make of it . . . it has to do with your eyes and what you see and what you do with America."[14] The eyes with which we have seen have desperately wanted to see unity. Our great heroes have been scholars such as David Riesman, David Potter, Frederick Jackson Turner, and Henry Nash Smith who have chosen to present images of a shared and stable identity. Our eagerness to see through their eyes has shaped not only our field, but also the conception of America now in dispute.

In the late 1940s and 1950s, Lionel Trilling noted, "even the most disaffected intellectual must respond . . . to the growing isolation of his country amid the hostility which is directed against it."[15] The desire for unity inhibited any public critique of institutions that accepted the tempting funds offered by foundations like Carnegie and Rockefeller to develop American Studies programs with the explicit aim of shoring up national identity in the face of a perceived totalitarian threat. Institutions like Yale, Barnard, Brown, and the University of Wyoming benefited from grants—grants that only became controversial in the sixties and after.[16] Then, the impact of funding sources on the shape of intellectual life generated a controversy that brought to consciousness an ongoing debate about the relationship between culture and politics. That debate is perhaps responsible for the relatively hospitable response of the American Studies Association to demands for political voice from those seeking cultural representation in that period.

For American Studies has another tradition that parallels the search for unity. In a much discussed presentation at the 1990 meetings of the association, Leo Marx argued that American Studies had a long heritage of efforts to deal with the complexity of cultural differences— a heritage that extended back to the 1930s when distinguished scholars such as F. O. Mathiessen challenged then-accepted universalisms. Past presidents Allen Davis and Linda Kerber, among others, have pointed to the recent efforts of the discipline of American Studies to pay attention to calls for opening the doors of intellectual inquiry. In her 1988 presidential address, Kerber traced the efforts of the American Studies Association to integrate diversity into its organizational structure and scholarly enterprise.[17] I came into the association on the wings of that change. Just out of graduate school, I was invited to give a paper at the Washington convention in 1971. It took only a day to realize that my connections in the association would be with the radical caucus—the group actively seeking to reconcile the style, form, and content of American Studies with new understandings of the world around them. With the women's movement in full throttle, I joined the efforts of women for greater representation on the council. Arguably the search for diversity has constituted the creative dynamic of American Studies for many years.

But in recent years efforts to look at the lives of people of color, of members of various ethnic groups, and of women have lost some of their legitimacy—some of the impetus they provided for a continuing dialogue over the meaning of culture. The difficulties are rooted in the efforts of scholars to reconcile our rich new knowledge about previously neglected groups with the challenges they offer to cherished notions (myths if you will) about the American past. In an earlier moment, we simply insisted on the importance of certain myths and defended them as legitimate efforts to construct a persuasive narrative around which to develop an estimable national identity. These myths were for many years taken for granted, either as real or as markers on the road to a democratic utopia. If the effort to describe the United States as homogeneous was unavailing, our predecessors could and did succeed in defining what they called the American Character. They constructed images of national identity with such concepts as individualism, pragmatism, optimism, ambition, idealism, and progress and attributed them variously to the influence of the frontier, affluence, and a classless and nonhierarchical society. The effort to put these together into a manageable whole resulted by the early twentieth century in a celebration of liberalism as the apotheosis of the democratic ideal. As Americans, we celebrated an aggressive individualism, nurtured by political democracy and producing economic prosperity as its much desired offspring.

But this interpretation of our past was built on silences—silences that were rudely shattered when in the 1960s the search for identity exacerbated differences among us and destroyed our faith in the union of individualism and democracy. The events of that decade (the civil rights movement, feminism, Vietnam, the search for authenticity, and the cry for participatory democracy) called the parameters of cultural homogeneity into question, pushing many American Studies practitioners into a critical stance and encouraging the development of new social and cultural theory that relied heavily on a revisionist history, women's studies, and a new consciousness of racial and ethnic divisions. By themselves, these concerns might have been temporary phenomena—we had, after all, absorbed immigrant groups for many years. But the shift to a new pluralism was accompanied by a simultaneous disavowal of notions of common identity, a fragmentation of any unified meaning to the word "American." The result was a search for the sources of individual and group identity in the lives of ethnics, blacks, women, and poor and working-class people, as well as of elite businessmen and socially prominent reformers. The 1970s and 1980s witnessed the simultaneous discovery of the nonpowerful and a refusal among many historians to fit the newly discovered into old myths about the past. The new narrative, they insisted, could not simply suggest that those who were different were "other." It had to incorporate some understanding of the dynamic effect of how differences among individuals and groups moved the historical process forward.

The twin rebellion against conceptions of common identity and the new pluralism proved to be crucial in the development of a relational stance. Black history, for example, which had not proved especially troublesome when it evoked the moral possibilities of Frederick Douglass, Harriet Tubman, or Martin Luther King, became contentious when historians started to ask how it had shaped the white mind and the dominant economy. In that guise, it raised questions not only about a common vision, but about the role of domination in constructing economic and political democracy as well. It also called into question the plausibility of the liberal ideal of inevitable progress. The study of women, hardly a threat when it spoke to the accomplishments of great women like Jane Addams, Eleanor Roosevelt, or even Elizabeth Cady Stanton, created a backlash when it asked about how a gender system sustained racial and class divisions. From that standpoint, the study of women constituted an attack on the very definition of "American," identifying as masculine (rather than universal) metaphors that derived from such stalwarts as Whitman and Melville, and raising questions about the gendered content of individualism, self-reliance, pragmatism, and optimism. Conceptions of community, interdependence, piety, and nature changed their form and exerted greater influence as female concerns entered into definitions of American character. In this new environment, writing women and people of color into our understandings of culture required redefining "American" to incorporate multiple definitions of identity. One result, as Werner Sollors notes, is the disbelief with which conceptions of universalism are greeted when they enter into the discourse of cultural criticism—the scorn with which members of the American Studies community now see efforts at social generalization as merely a thin camouflage of power relations.[18]

The result, by the 1980s, was methodological ferment. The search for the particular yielded a fragmentation of subject that made a mockery of a single synthesis or interpretation of the American past. By the early 1980s, criticism of what later became known as multiculturalism had already begun, and calls for "synthesis" could be heard everywhere. Even social critics longed for the old history—a clear narrative line with a little literature or anthropology thrown in to help define culture. Alas, an easy synthesis was no longer possible. The search for the particular that had underlined and identified a fully pluralist America had repudiated old certainties of consensus, centrality, and truth without creating anything to replace them.

If some of us in American Studies have incorporated the disturbing results of this new knowledge, we have not yet conveyed it to the world. Somehow we need to argue that to construct a new identity does not mean to abandon the concept of American identity. Rather it should spur us to think about democratic culture as a continuing and unending process. The easiest way to illustrate this is with a personal example.

If you ask me where I come from, I'll tell you that I was born in England during World War II of refugee parents who were Hungarian-speaking, Czech citizens. We (my brothers and I) grew up speaking first Hungarian, then German—the language of the refugee community. Finally, we were sent to school to learn English—an event that happened shortly before we all moved to Wales where I lived until we emigrated to the United States. By then I was a teenager. How do I construct myself? It depends on the circumstance. Neither Hungarian nor Czech, neither English nor Welsh, I claim identities as my sense of otherness requires. I suppose that makes me a certain kind of American. For I fully understand the advantages of my other persona—after all, the transformation from an immigrant outsider in Britain to a British émigré in America brought with it instant privilege and insider status that transcended and covered up other disadvantages.[19]

That story is filled with silences. Listen to how loudly they scream a contradictory tale that undermines the urbane and cosmopolitan image I want to construct for you. My father, whom I like to imagine was no ordinary worker, nevertheless worked with his hands all his life.

My mother, who died when she was barely forty, left three children to be defended from the good intentions of the British state authorities. Imagine now the refugee father with his tattered English trying to hang on to what was left of his family. I reconstruct myself as orphan child, desperately shamed by a parental heritage from which I could not wait to distance myself; I am revealed as a grammar school product who bore the weight of many exceptionalisms in a country unified by a language and culture I thought I would never fully possess. The saga of emigration becomes an escape that parallels those of my immigrant forebears. It is the transformation from undifferentiated alien to ethnic identity, from state protection to visible poverty, ultimately from unwanted outsider to the constructed self you see before you.

Like the process of construction on a personal level, creating a national image requires us to make conscious and unconscious decisions about what to include and exclude. It asks of us a negotiation between our efforts to retain the particular sense of self that links us to a special tradition and the efforts of such cultural forces as schools and the mass media to impose a sense of commonality that threatens to reduce each of us to what we share. Guenter Lenz puts it this way:

> Obviously, any culture in some political sense is 'unified' from the top down, and in any culture a utopian desire toward unity and wholeness . . . is at work, but it is only through processes of self-reflection, self-differentiation, alternative visions and expressive forms, discontinuity and displacements that a culture continually reconstitutes 'itself' as always contested and emergent.[20]

When we construct ourselves, we do so out of a sense of what makes us distinctive. Those of us who are immigrants, African American, Latin, gay or lesbian, or any combination of these and a dozen other identities have no difficulty seeing in ourselves the otherness out of which we construct the persona that faces the world and limits or expands our vision. As powerful as these perspectives are in shaping a sense of well-being or grievance, they provide us with only partial visions — visions that each of us daily reconciles with the larger culture.

Our insistence on a multicultural curriculum, on a multicultural view of American experience, grows out of the clarity with which we see the pitfalls of adopting an image of anything as complex as America as a unified enterprise. "Who cuts the border?" asks Hortense Spillers in the introduction to a new collection of essays. "Who has the right to claim America?" she asks angrily. America has been constructed out of

> a dizzying concoction of writing and reportage, lying and 'signifying,' jokes, 'tall tales,' and transgenerational nightmare, all conflated under the banner of Our Lord . . . [it exemplifies] for all intents and purposes the oldest game of trompe de l'oeil, the perhaps-mistaken-glance-of-the-eye, that certain European 'powers' carried out regarding indigenous Americans.

America, she suggests was " 'made up' in the gaze of Europe . . . as much a 'discovery' on the retinal surface as it was the appropriation of land and historical subjects."[21]

Nearly thirty years ago, John Kouwenhoven asked us to think about how common our common culture was, as he put it, to "determine the limits of our community of experienced particulars."[22] When we have heeded his warning, we have been able to separate the need for synthesis that shapes ideas to tell a story in a particular way and is therefore inherently political from the realities of everyday belief and aspiration that rely on lived experience and are therefore cultural. We have been able to see the differences between essentially political patterns within which we reside and daily experiences that we continually create. The result is less fragmentation than it is a richer view of culture as the double effect of the given and the self-generated. The perspective draws on the deeply rooted ambiguity that has allowed American Studies practitioners to see the relational ways in which a culture operates—to observe the frictions and tensions that serve both to name particular experiences and to trace the products of social consensus in ways that continually reformulate the mechanism by which a unified culture is constituted.

The questioning of universalism has led to an exciting search for a common vocabulary. It encourages us to enter into a conversation about whether there is still a "we" at the heart of American culture and to wonder how that "we" is constituted. It requires us to reconstruct the disembodied voice—sometimes known as "the American people"—under whose rubric we are all subsumed in a way that will simultaneously provide a more inclusive framework and take a standpoint that distinguishes our perspective from that of an earlier and narrower notion of the American persona. It creates the possibility that "we" can unify around the search for a democratic culture, instead of finding ourselves incorporated into a set of tropes such as individualism and equality from which many feel excluded. Tom Bender illustrated how that had been done by Lionel Trilling who moved from a radical "we" to one that represented an intellectual middle class and in the process extended the reach of his audience by thousands of people.[23] Though Trilling remained caught in a narrow world of narrow definitions, the process enables us to see how he reconstructed himself.

But if the old universalisms have gone, can we find a "we" that experiences culture in shared ways, that encompasses some sense of common identity? Surely that is our task. We can be helped to it by drawing some lessons from postmodernism and particularly from feminist theory. Sandra Harding reminds us that knowledge is socially situated and that claims to knowledge of dominant groups are conditioned by their desire to preserve power.[24] In turn, these claims produce the institutional support systems that validate them. Asking whose claim to knowledge we are validating reminds us of what we lose when we are exclusive—reminds us that the answer depends on a fuller vision that incorporates all of our lives, and urges us to operate from an intellectual position that takes such a stand.

Speaking of the uses of theory for black feminist academics, Patricia Hill Collins has noted that while black women possess a unique standpoint that produces "certain commonalities of perception," individual differences result in diverse experiences of common themes.[25] The outsider/within status produces a creative tension that enables women of color to see the limits of the insider's knowledge and attempt to redefine it. Barbara Johnson warns us of the fragility of such identities: the insider, she suggests, becomes an outsider the minute she steps out of the inside.[26] To some extent, every student of American Studies participates in the profoundly political process of determining a stance from which to see. Collins's advice is not dissimilar from that of John Fairbank, who, in his presidential address to the American Historical Association, asked historians to look at America from the outside and see how it changed our conception of ourselves. "What image have we of our self-image?" Fairbank asked. "What do we think we are doing in the world?"[27]

If the fight for multiculturalism is a request for inclusion, if the heart of American Studies is the pursuit of what constitutes democratic culture, then we need to see the struggle over multiculturalism as a tug of war over who gets to create the public culture. For too long that culture has been the province of a narrow sector of society—its universals shaped our sense of the world, turning each of us into a problematic other. But the effort to alter a static and unitary notion of America has persisted for too long to be denied. Just as I construct myself in relation to my audience, just as American Studies constructs itself in relation to the politics of time and place, so America will reconstruct itself both in response to our multiple identities and in response to our efforts as scholars to describe it.

In that sense, we are all "other." The particular standpoints from which we operate may be differently revealing, but they all participate in the construction of the self (collective and individual) that will become the "other" of the next generation. Our project can be neither a false universalism, nor the reification of pieces of the culture at the expense of the whole. Rather we need to explore how people become part of, not separate from, that unified whole called America. As students and scholars of American Studies, we are called on to engage in, to facilitate, the conversation that occurs in the public marketplace by ensuring the perpetuation of a processual notion of America.

Far from undermining the search for unity, identity, and purpose, the multicultural enterprise has the potential to strengthen it. It provides a way of seeing relationally that is consistent with the early founders of American Studies as well as with its more recent protagonists. If it redefines identity from a fixed category to a search for a democratic culture, if it refuses to acknowledge a stable meaning or precise unchanging definition of America, multiculturalism nevertheless opens the possibility of conceiving democratic culture as a process in whose transformation we are all invited to participate.

NOTES

1. Fred Siegel, "The Cult of Multiculturalism," *The New Republic,* 18 Feb. 1991, 35.

2. Huntly Collins, "Study: Few 'Politically Correct' Disputes," *Philadelphia Inquirer,* 29 July 1991, 3A.

3. Arthur M. Schlesinger, Jr., for example, describes the ideas at the core of the Western traditions as "not Asian, nor African, nor Middle-Eastern ideas, except by adoption." See *The Disuniting of America: Reflections on a Multicultural Society* (New York, 1992), 127.

4. Anthony dePalma, "Another Bass Gives Yale $20 Million," *New York Times,* 18 Apr. 1991, A20.

5. George F. Will, "Curdled Politics on Campus," *Newsweek*, 6 May 1991, 72.

6. George F. Will, "Literary Politics," *Newsweek*, 22 Apr. 1991, 72.

7. A. M. Rosenthal, "Suicide on the Fourth," *New York Times*, 5 July 1991, A21.

8. William A. Henry III, "Upside Down in the Groves of Academe," *Time*, 1 Apr. 1991, 69, offers some examples. See also Paul Berman, ed., *Debating P.C.: The Controversy over Political Correctness on College Campuses* (New York, 1992).

9. Rosenthal, "Suicide on the Fourth," A21. This is an argument with which Arthur Schlesinger concurs. See *The Disuniting of America*, ch.5.

10. Rosenthal, "Suicide on the Fourth," A21.

11. Will, "Literary Politics," 72.

12. Joseph Berger, "Arguing About America," *New York Times*, 21 June 1991, A1, B4.

13. Marshall Fishwick, "American Studies: Bird in Hand," *International Educational and Cultural Exchange* (Winter 1968): 7.

14. In Josephine Martin Ober, "History of the American Studies Association," Master's thesis, Bryn Mawr College, 1971, 23. Thanks to Arthur Dudden for obtaining a copy of this for me.

15. Lionel Trilling, "Our Country and our Culture," *Partisan Review* 3 (Autumn 1952): 319.

16. Ibid., 31.

17. Allen F. Davis, "The Politics of American Studies," *American Quarterly* 42 (Sept. 1990): 353–74; Linda K. Kerber, "Diversity and the Transformation of American Studies," *American Quarterly* 41 (Sept. 1989): 415–31.

18. Werner Sollors, "Of Mules and Mares in a Land of Difference; or Quadrupeds All?" *American Quarterly* 42 (June 1990): 181.

19. Several people asked me after the talk why I had omitted Jewishness as one of my identities. Perhaps the answer is that my parents' strong secular beliefs left little room for religious identity. Mine emerged, as a child, in powerful but sporadic moments, and was not developed until after we emigrated. I have been struck in reading Susan Groag Bell's *Between Worlds: In Czechoslovakia, England, and America* (New York, 1991), by her similar stance with regard to assuming identities.

20. Guenter H. Lenz, " 'Ethnographies': American Culture Studies and Postmodern Anthropology," *Prospects* 16 (1991): 22.

21. Hortense J. Spillers, "Who Cuts the Border?: Some Readings on 'American,' " in *Comparative American Identities: Race, Sex, and Nationality in the Modern Text*, ed. Spillers (New York and London, 1991), 4–5.

22. John Kouwenhoven, "American Studies: Words or Things?" in *American Studies in Transition*, ed. Marshall W. Fishwick (Boston, 1964), 23.

23. Thomas Bender, "Lionel Trilling and American Culture," *American Quarterly* 42 (June 1990): 324–47.

24. Sandra Harding, *Whose Science? Whose Knowledge?: Thinking From Women's Lives* (Ithaca, 1991), 119.

25. Patricia Hill Collins, "Learning from the Outsider Within: The Sociological Significance of Black Feminist Thought," *Social Problems* 33 (Oct./Dec. 1986): 16.

26. Barbara Johnson, *A World of Difference* (Baltimore 1987), 173.

27. John K. Fairbank, "Assignment for the '70's," *The American Historical Review* 74 (Feb. 1969): 863.

Cathy Davidson

Alice Kessler-Harris's 1991 presidential address speaks to one of the most significant crises facing academics during the 1990s: the attack on multiculturalism by a virulent and articulate right wing. Indeed, since Kessler-Harris gave her address, the weapons in the attack on multiculturalism have become more powerful and the successes of the right more apparent.

On 20 June 1996, for example, the board of regents approved a resolution forbidding the University of California from using "race, religion, gender, color, ethnicity or national origin" in its admissions, hiring, and contracting. In November of the same year, California voters passed the California Civil Rights Initiative (Proposition 209) extending the anti-affirmative action ruling to all government agencies, including state universities. Emboldened by California's Proposition 209, other states began to work on passing similar initiatives and many universities across the country began either abolishing or simply ignoring their own affirmative action guidelines.

Thus, Kessler-Harris's address is more urgent than ever. Its main thrust is to require that American studies intellectuals think about our work and our history as a discipline within the context of multiculturalism and the forces that threaten its existence. I like the way Kessler-Harris holds *us* responsible and accountable for the implications of our work, especially for work characterized by an "exceptionalism" that passes for "universalism," work that, implicitly or explicitly, promulgates an "idea of America" in a singular sense. As she implies, the American studies impetus to find some underlying principle that binds "us all" — whether it be individualism, progress, optimism, or Puritanism — is too readily turned into a weapon of discrimination. It creates bad history by minimizing or even erasing that which does not conform to the line drawing of the nation. And, in Kessler-Harris's memorable phrase, it "impose[s] a sense of commonality that threatens to reduce each of us to what we share."

That phrase brilliantly captures the most damaging aspect of the universalist strain of American studies. That is, because we may share certain characteristics, the rest are to be discarded, ignored, or rendered insignificant. More to the point, this high nationalist mode of American studies frequently echoes and influences more popular (and, again, typically reactionary) visions of what the country is and must be. Why do pundits from Lionel Trilling in the 1940s to George Will in the 1990s demand such a rigid definition for the nation? Why must the national self be so rigorously policed? Why such watchfulness and fear?

I would like to posit a few ideas about what might be called the paranoid aspects of American studies prevalent in the popular press but also among conservative intellectuals. This model is based on a paradoxical definition of America, both triumphal and inherently fragile. On the one hand, America's present, powerful place in the world makes us triumphant; on the other, America is fragile, as testified by our past as a relatively new country and our historical lack of unity given the national, ethnic, religious, and class diversity of our immigrant origins. We have been the country that has taken in the "tired, the poor, the hungry" of other nations (especially European) to which, culturally, we have often deemed ourselves inferior. Most accounts of the "idea of America" thus work mightily to cover the insecurities of the latter (our migrant history) by glorifying the former (our powerful present). Or they do just the opposite, using our virtuous history (as an asylum for the poor and the persecuted) to mitigate present imperialist tendencies. In either case, the result is intellectual bad faith. There is something distorted about a nation as powerful, vast, wealthy, and globally acquisitive as the United States harboring any illusions of itself as a powerless, emerging nation.

A multicultural perspective exposes that illusion, and thus threatens the unitary "idea of America." Kessler-Harris notes that the various kinds of oppositional studies—feminist, multiculturalist, gay and lesbian, or even Marxist—were not seen as dangerous so long as they celebrated the contributions of minorities or the working class to the great American ideal. Every American kid learns in fifth grade that it was an African American who discovered hundreds of uses for the peanut. The threat comes when multiculturalist scholars expose a history of American violence, genocide, slavery, or discrimination. As Ronald Takaki, Lisa Lowe, and others have shown, at the same time that Europe's tired and hungry immigrants were finding a foothold in American society, discriminatory laws—such as the Chinese Exclusion Act—made it impossible for immigrants from Asia even to achieve citizenship.[1] Similarly, Jim Crow laws instituted a legalized form of segregation and discrimination in the South that ended barely a generation ago. In the unitary version of American studies, we cling to a notion of ourselves as the virtuous persecuted. But a multiculturalist perspective exposes the ways that the "we" (as in that past sentence) erases rhetorically those instances where some of "us" do injury to others of "us." If the American "we" really is to be inclusive, then we must all admit that, in the course of our history, we have done some heinous things to ourselves.

I have used a number of psychological terms to describe a certain exceptionalist and universalizing strain in American studies—distorted, paranoid, insecure, fearful. What would a fearless pedagogy look like? A fearless pedagogy must be, at its base, multicultural or it is not radical and fearless enough. And, I am arguing, because of *our* heinous history, *we* need affirmative action—and now I mean, precisely, all of us. Affirmative action is the institutional and legal manifestation of multiculturalism. Affirmative action has, as its underlying principle, the idea that America is not a fair place, that discrimination—not equality—has been one of its ongoing historical and present practices. It asserts that, unless there are legal and institutional supports for antidiscriminatory behaviors, the institutional default will be not fairness and equality but prejudice and discrimination. In America, on a "level playing field," all the participants will be white.

Ending affirmative action hurts American society as a whole, not just people of color. Right now, of all the industrialized nations of the world, the United States has the widest gap between its richest and its poorest citizens. People of color make up a disproportionate percentage of the poor. I don't know anyone who wants to live in this version of America. It is not even good for business to permanently impoverish one segment of our population, which is one reason that corporate America, ironically, has recently become one of the most ardent supporters of affirmative action even as academics are more and more allowing affirmative action to disappear. This is appalling. Affirmative action has been our most successful tool for reversing the economics of discrimination in America and for ensuring that our classrooms and our curriculum will be diverse, challenging, and vital. We cannot allow this powerful tool to be taken away from us.

Affirmative action specifically and multiculturalism more generally disrupt the unitary America. For this reason, and for many others, intellectuals practicing American studies need to fight to preserve affirmative action in the academy today. Without affirmative action, I fear that we truly will be, to again paraphrase Alice Kessler-Harris, "reduced to what we share."

NOTE

1. See, e.g., Ronald Takaki, *Strangers from a Different Shore* (Boston: Little Brown, 1989), and Lisa Lowe, *Immigrant Acts: On Asian American Cultural Politics* (Durham: Duke University Press, 1996).

RAMÓN GUTIÉRREZ

Community, Patriarchy and Individualism: The Politics of Chicano History and the Dream of Equality

THIS ESSAY IS AN ATTEMPT TO MAP IN BROAD GENERAL TERMS THE origins and development of the Chicano movement in the United States from approximately 1965 to the present. As a prolegomenon to a larger research project on this topic, what is sketched below is but a thematic blueprint, devoid of all the baroque embellishments that greater space and time would permit. As a person who was weaned politically on the rhetorical claims of the movement, and as a university professor who has taught courses on Chicano history for well over ten years, the account presented here mixes insider and outsider knowledge drawn primarily from the fields of anthropology, history, literature, and sociology.

* * *

Mexican Americans fought in World War II to make the world safe for democracy. Fighting beside other assimilated immigrants, they believed the national promise that when they returned home, the American Dream of social mobility and middle-class status would be theirs. The troops returned to what became a period of unprecedented economic growth in the United States. It was in this period, between 1945 and 1960, that America's global economic hegemony was truly consolidated. For white American men the dream was indeed realized.

American Quarterly, Vol. 45, No. 1 (March 1993) © 1993 American Studies Association

The G.I. Bill of Rights helped educate many of them. The consumer goods, the cars, the stocked refrigerators, money to spare, and government loans to educate their children soon followed. But the benefits, the dreams, and the cash were not equitably distributed. Blacks, Mexicans, and persons of Asian ancestry, all legitimately Americans, had been left out. The 1960 census of the United States graphically showed how far the minority populations lagged behind white America.

These realizations were made potent by the peaceful activism of Cesar Chavez, who was trying to win better wages and work conditions for farmworkers; by Reies López Tijerina's attempts to regain lands fraudulently stolen from New Mexico's *hispanos*; and by the worldwide crumbling of imperialism and the rise of new nationalisms. This complex conjuncture of structural forces was what sparked the Chicano movement. What differentiated the Chicano movement from the civil rights activities of such groups as the League of United Latin American Citizens (LULAC), the American G.I. Forum, or the numerous mutual aid societies that *Mexicanos* had created to better their socioeconomic situation, was the *Movimiento's* radical political stance. The civil rights movement of the 1940s and 1950s had sought slow, peaceful change through assimilation, through petitions for governmental beneficence, and through appeals to white liberal guilt. The Chicanos, largely a contingent of educated students, in a revolution sparked by rising expectations, demanded equality with white America; demanded an end to racism, and asserted their right to cultural autonomy and national self-determination.

Since so much of the ethnic militancy that Chicanos articulated was profoundly influenced by black nationalism, it is important to recall one of the truly poignant insights in the *Autobiography of Malcolm X*. Reciting the psychic violence that racism and discrimination had wrecked on African Americans, Malcolm X noted that the most profound had been the emasculation of black men. In the eyes of white America blacks were not deemed men. Thus whatever else the Black Power movement was, it was also about the cultural assertion of masculinity by young radical men.

Chicanos faced what was undoubtedly a rather similar experience— social emasculation and cultural negation—by seeking strength and inspiration in a heroic Aztec past. The Aztec past they chose emphasized the virility of warriors and the exercise of brute force. Young Chicano men, a largely powerless group, invested themselves with images of power—a symbolic inversion commonly found in the fantasies of powerless men worldwide, a gendered vision that rarely extends to women.

Equally important to the young Chicano radicals was the construction of a moral community that was largely imagined as spatial and territorial. Aztlán, the legendary homeland of the Aztecs, was advanced as the territory Chicanos hoped to repossess someday. Despite the fuzziness of the concept, its imprecise geographic limits, and the previous claims to the territory that American Indians could justly claim, the dream of Aztlán sank deep roots.

The idea and theory of internal colonialism flowed quite logically from this spatial concept of community. Chicanos were an internally colonized population within the United States. They were socially, culturally, and economically subordinated and territorially segregated by white Anglo-Saxon America. These concepts receive definition in the works of Rudy Acuña and myself in history, Tomás Almaguer in sociology, Mario Barrera and Carlos Muñoz in political science, and in numerous cultural productions and artistic works.[1]

When this analysis was taken from the global to the local, the *barrio* became its focus. We see this very clearly in the scholarly works that provide the foundation for Chicano history: Albert Camarillo's *Chicanos in a Changing Society: From Mexican Pueblos to American Barrios in Santa Barbara and Southern California, 1848–1930,* Richard Griswold del Castillo's *The Los Angeles Barrio, 1850–1890,* and Ricardo Romo's *East Los Angeles: A History of a Barrio.*[2]

If anything defined the ethics of this moral community, it was the belief in collectivism and an explicit rejection of individualism.[3] *Chicanismo* meant identifying with *la raza* (the race or people), and collectively promoting the interests of *carnales* (or brothers) with whom they shared a common language, culture, religion, and Aztec heritage.

Examining any of the Chicano scholarly or artistic productions between 1965 and 1975 clearly indicates one point. The history of Chicanos was thought to have begun in 1848, at the end of the U.S.-Mexican War. This date heightened the legacy of Anglo racism toward Chicanos. For as Armando Navarro would write, "Chicano politics [and history have] always been imbued with a spirit of resistance toward Anglo-American oppression and domination." The relationship between Anglos and Chicanos was conceived out of a master-servant relationship between the Anglo conqueror and the Chicano conquered. The Chicano reacted politically in two ways to the master-servant relationship. Some Chicanos collaborated and accommodated the Anglo invader and engaged in "ballot box politics." Other Chicanos, however, rejected the conquest and resorted to violence, guerrilla warfare and banditry.[4]

The years 1965 to 1969 were heydays of Chicano activism, largely, though not exclusively, on college and university campuses. Coming from working class backgrounds and feeling privileged by their college draft exemptions, Chicanos identified with workers and peasants, and indeed, wrote a heroic past of worker struggles and strikes, resistance to Anglo oppression, and indigenous cultural pride.

But all was not well in Eden. By 1969, at the very moment Corky Gonzales was trying to weld a fractured Chicano student movement into a national force, the more radical Chicanas were beginning to see themselves as triply oppressed—by their race, their gender, and their class. "Women students were expected by their male peers to involve themselves actively but in subordination," recalled Adelaida del Castillo. It was not uncommon in those days for the movement's men "to request sexual cooperation as proof of commitment to the struggle, by gratifying the men who fought it."[5] Although the movement persistently had advocated the self-actualization of all Chicanos, Chicanos still actually meant only males.

Within the Chicano student movement, women were denied leadership roles and were asked to perform only the most traditional stereotypic roles—cleaning up, making coffee, executing the orders men gave, and servicing their needs. Women who did manage to assume leadership positions were ridiculed as unfeminine, sexually perverse, promiscuous, and all too often, taunted as lesbians. "When a woman leader had a compañero, he was frequently taunted or chided by the other men for failure to keep her under his control," recalled one woman.[6]

A 1970 incident at San Diego State University was particularly telling of the tenor of those days. There women had managed to assume leadership over the campus Chicano student group. When it was announced that Corky Gonzalez was going to visit the campus, an intense debate ensued. "It was considered improper and embarrassing for a national leader to come on campus and see that the organization's leadership was female," recalled one of the campus leaders.

"Consequently, the organization decided that only males would be the visible representatives for the occasion. The female chairperson willingly conceded."[7]

The sexism rampant in the Chicano movement was increasingly critiqued in various forms. Marcela Christine Lucero-Trujillo made the point powerfully in her poem, "Machismo Is Part of Our Culture."

Hey Chicano bossman
don't tell me that machismo is part of our culture
if you sleep
and marry W.A.S.P.
You constantly remind me,
me, your Chicana employee
that machi-machi-machismo
is part of our culture.
I'm conditioned, you say,
to bearing machismo
which you only learned
day before yesterday.
At home you're no patrón
your liberated gabacha
has gotcha where
she wants ya,
y a mi me ves cara
de steppin' stone.
Your culture emanates
from Raza posters on your walls
from bulletin boards in the halls
and from the batos who hang out at the barrio bar.
Chicanismo through osmosis
acquired in good doses
remind you
to remind me
that machi-machi-machismo
is part of our culture.[8]

In the poem "You Cramp My Style, Baby," Lorna Dee Cervantes took the rhetorical language of the Chicano movement, mixed it with elements from Mexican culture, and drew the appropriate sexual lesson:

You cramp my style, baby
when you roll on top of me
shouting, "Viva La Raza"
at the top of your prick.

You want me como un taco
dripping grease,
or squeezing masa through my legs,
making tamales for you out of my daughters.[9]

Articles were also beginning to appear in the movement press highlighting the contradiction between racial and sexual oppression in the Chicano movement. Irene Rodarte posed the question: "*Machismo* or revolution?"[10]; a question Guadalupe Valdes Fallis reformulated as tradition or liberation.[11] Others such as Anna Nieto-Gómez, Velia García [then Hancock], and Mirta Vidal spoke out about the sexism in the *movimiento* and militated for the liberation of women.[12]

Chicano men initially regarded the feminist critique as an assault on their Mexican cultural past, on their power, and by implication, on their virility. If Chicanos were going to triumph in their anticapitalist, anticolonial revolt, divisiveness could not be tolerated. Bernice Zamora in "Notes from a Chicana COED," captured the tenor of the tug of war that would characterize this period.

To cry that the *gabacho*
is our oppressor is to shout
in abstraction, *carnal.*
He no more oppresses us
than you do now as you tell me
"It's the gringo who oppresses you, Babe."
You cry "The gringo is our oppressor!"
to the tune of $20,000 to $30,000
a year, brother, and I wake up
alone each morning and ask,
"Can I feed my children today?" . . .

And when I mention
your G.I. Bill, your
Ford Fellowship, your
working wife, your
three *gabacha guisas*
then you ask me to
write your thesis
you're quick to shout,
"Don't give that
Women's Lib trip, mujer
that only divides us, and we have to work
together for the *movimiento*
the *gabacho* is oppressing us!

Oye carnal, you may as well
tell me that moon water
cures constipation, that
penguin soup prevents *crudas,*
or that the Arctic Ocean is *menudo* . . .[13]

Men responded to the assault on their privileges by resorting to crass name calling, labeling Chicana feminists as "malinchistas," traitors who were influenced by ideas foreign to their community—namely bourgeois feminist ideology. One Chicana complained in 1971 that Chicanos viewed the Chicana feminist as "a white, thick calved, lesbian-oriented, eye-glassed gal."[14] Be "Chicana Primero" the men exhorted, asking the women to take pride in their cultural heritage and to reject women's liberation.[15] Adelaida del Castillo, among others, retorted that women were not seeking to dominate the movement. They only sought full equality:

> true freedom for our people can come about only if prefaced by the equality of individuals within La Raza. Chicanos must be convinced that Chicanas do not wish to dominate, which would be a negation of equality. Their concern is with the liberation of La Raza; the Chicano movement would be enhanced (and perhaps rejuvenated) if men and women were free to be mutually supportive.[16]

Theresa Aragón was but one of the many women who would clearly and unequivocally state that Chicanas, by incorporating feminist demands in their anticolonial revolution, were not dupes of white bourgeois feminists. "The white women's movement at present is not generally aware of or sensitive to the needs of the Chicana," Aragón wrote, and as such, "Chicanas would have to define their own goals and objectives in relationship to their culture, and their own feminist ideology in relation to those goals."[17] Consuelo Nieto argued that while Anglo feminists operated as individuals with individual goals, Chicanas belonged to a community of interest with whom they intended to cast their lot.[18] Class and racial oppression could not be overlooked only to privilege caste oppression. While in some circles "sisterhood was powerful," for the Chicana, perhaps, it was not.

*   *   *

Just as Chicano scholars who were interested in interpreting the history of the Southwest as a history of racial conflict between Anglos and Mexicans explicitly chose 1848 as the beginning of Chicano history, Chicana feminists began re-envisioning a history ordered by a different sense of time. For women it was not the U.S.-Mexican War that was most important. Instead, it was the first major act of conquest in the Americas, Spain's defeat of the Aztec empire.

As far as I can ascertain, Judith Sweeney, in her 1977 historiographic review of literature on Chicanas, was the first person to propose a new chronology for Chicano history. That history, she stated, began in 1519 and could "be divided into three major periods: the colonial period (1519–1821); the nineteenth century (1821–1910); and the contemporary period (1910–1976)."[19] Others writing on Chicanas quickly took up Sweeney's lead. Alfredo Mirandé and Evangelina Enríquez wrote in their 1979 book, *La Chicana: The Mexican-American Woman,* that the "roots of the Chicana . . . in the United States, date back to the conquest of Mexico in 1519."[20]

A chronology for Chicana history that began in 1519 — not 1848 — was not an arbitrary act. Rather, it placed the issues of gender and power at the very center of the political debate about the future and the past. By choosing 1519 women focused attention on one of Mexico's most famous women, Doña Marina. Doña Marina was a Maya woman of noble ancestry who befriended Hernán Cortés in 1517. Cortés availed himself of Doña Marina's considerable knowledge of the local political geography and of her knowledge of various indigenous languages. Acting as his mistress, translator and confidant, Marina helped Cortés to forge local antipathies toward the Aztecs into a fighting force that Cortés successfully unleashed on Tenochtitlán.

In Mexican history Doña Marina, or la Malinche, had always been seen as a villain, as the supreme betrayer of her race.[21] Luis Valdez in his 1971 play, "The Conquest of Mexico," depicted Malinche as a traitor because: "not only did she turn her back on her own people, she joined the white men and became assimilated."[22] In expressing this sentiment, Valdez, the playwright who generated so much of the popular culture that became identified as Chicano in the 1970s, was simply reiterating what was well-established dogma among Mexican intellectuals. Octavio Paz in his book *The Labyrinth of Solitude* referred to Mexicans as the Sons of Malinche, *hijos de la chingada.*[23] In a long disquisition on the word *chingar,* Paz argued that it meant to do violence to another. The verb is masculine, active, cruel: it stings, wounds, gashes, stains. And it provokes a bitter, resentful satisfaction. The person who suffers this action is passive, inert and open, in contrast to the active, aggressive and closed person who inflicts it. The *chingón* is the *macho,* the male; he rips open the *chingada,* the female, who is pure passivity, defenseless against the exterior world. The relationship between them is violent and it is determined by the cynical power of the first and the impotence of the second. The idea of violence rules darkly over all the meanings of the word.[24]

Paz asserted that just as the power and violence of the *macho* or the *gran chingón* was similar to that of the Spanish conquistador, so too the passivity of the violated mother, or *la chingada,* found an analog in Malinche. "It is true," Paz writes,

that she gave herself voluntarily to the conquistador, but he forgot her as soon as her usefulness was over. Doña Marina becomes a figure representing the Indian women who were fascinated, violated or seduced by the Spaniards. And as a small boy will not forgive his mother if she abandons him to search for his father, the Mexican people have not forgiven La Malinche for her betrayal.[25]

For activist Chicanas, the historical representations of Malinche as a treacherous whore who betrayed her own people were but profound reflections of the deep-seated misogynist beliefs in Mexican and Mexican-American culture. The only public models open to Mexican women were those of the virgin and the whore.[26] If women were going to go beyond them, then they had to begin by rehabilitating Malinche.

The literary vindication of Malinche began with Sylvia Gonzales's poem, "I Am Chicana":

I am Chicana
Waiting for the return
of la Malinche,
to negate her guilt,
and cleanse her flesh
of a confused Mexican wrath
which seeks reason
to the displaced power of Indian deities.
I am Chicana
Waiting for the coming of a Malinche
to sacrifice herself
on an Aztec altar
and Catholic cross
in redemption of all her forsaken daughters.[27]

Adelaida R. del Castillo took up the crusade in historical writing, stating in 1977 that "Doña Marina should not be portrayed as negative, insignificant or foolish, but instead be perceived as a woman who was able to act beyond her prescribed societal function, namely, that of being a mere concubine and servant, and perform as one who was willing to make great sacrifices for what she believed to be a philanthropic conviction."[28] Never mind the fine details; what was important to Chicanas was that Malinche was the primordial source of the two concepts that were at the core of the Chicana movement—*mexicanidad* and *mestizaje*. Malinche, noted del Castillo:

> is the beginning of the mestizo nation, she is the mother of its birth, she initiates it with the birth of her mestizo children. Even her baptism is significant. She is, in fact, the first Indian to be christianized (catechized and baptized to Catholicism) in her native land, that land which metamorphizes into our mundo mestizo—again she is the starting point! Thus any denigration made against her indirectly defames the character of the . . . chicana female. If there is shame for her, there is shame for us; we suffer the effects of those implications."[29]

Following del Castillo's lead, other women joined the fray. Cordelia Candelaria in 1980 saw in Malinche "the prototypical Chicana feminist." Malinche, claimed Candelaria, embodied "those personal characteristics—such as intelligence, initiative, adaptability, and leadership—which are most often associated with Mexican-American women unfettered by traditional restraints against activist public achievement. By adapting to the historical circumstances thrust upon her, she defied traditional social expectations of a woman's role."[30]

Whatever the facts—in the case of Malinche there are dreadfully few—the crafting of a her-story and feminist chronology had shifted the debate away from racism to sexism, away from the male ethos of *carnalismo,* or brotherhood, and *chicanismo,* to *mexicanidad y mestizaje*. Equally important, by examining the life of Malinche the "first" Mexican convert to Christianity, attention was given to the role of religion in maintaining female subordination, with its patriarchal God and its phallocentric clergy.[31]

*　　*　　*

If the aim of the Chicano movement had been to decolonize the mind, as the novelist Tomás Rivera proposed, the Chicana movement decolonized the body. Male concerns over job discrimination, access to political power, entry into educational institutions, and community autonomy and self-determination, gave way to female demands for birth control[32] and against forced sterilizations,[33] for welfare rights,[34] for prison rights for *pintas*,[35] for protection against male violence, and most importantly, for sexual pleasure both in marriage and outside of it. "La Nueva Chicana," the new woman, shattered the cultural stereotypes and defined herself.[36]

Of course, this is not to imply that what had traditionally been the "meat and potatoes" of the Chicano movement, that is, an interest in working class struggles, ceased with the rise of Chicana feminist writing. It did not. The literature on the condition of Mexican-American working women remained prolific, dating all the way back to the 1930s.[37] What did change in feminist-inspired Chicana cultural production, even when it examined traditional topics, was the centrality that the intersection of race, gender, and class assumed. The example of the case of Mexican immigration to the United States illustrates the point well. A whole generation of Chicano scholars earned tenure at universities by describing the nature and dimensions of the immigration process. More than half of all of the Mexican immigrants entering the United States since 1945 have been women, but this fact eluded most earlier authors—Mario García being the exception. The works of Vicki L. Ruiz and Susan Tiano, Margarita B. Melville, Rosalinda Gonzalez, Gilbert Cardenas and Esteban Flores, and Rita Simon and Caroline Brettell, were important correctives to this oversight.[38]

But even more exciting were the works by women that linked race, class, and gender domination at the work place with gender domination within the home. Patricia Zavella's splendid work, *Women's Work and Chicano Families,* studied women cannery workers in the Santa Clara Valley of northern California, and showed how mechanization had contributed to female labor segregation and how the labor market reinforced traditional family roles within the household. Vicki L. Ruiz covered very similar terrain in her masterful *Cannery Women, Cannery Lives,* a study of Mexican women's unionization attempts in the California food processing industry.[39]

In addition to these very traditional topics, what was perhaps most revolutionary was that Chicanas began to write and to express a complex inner emotional life. Reflecting in 1970 on the participation of Chicanas in the liberation movement, Enriqueta Longauex y Vasquez stated that

while the role of the Chicana previously "has been a very strong one—
[it has been] . . . a silent one."[40] That silence was shattered.

> I am here. (do
> you hear me?) hear
>   me. hear me
> I am here. birthing
>   (yourself) is
>   no easy task.
> I am here. (pleading)
> I am here. (teasing)
> I am here. (taunting)
> I am here. (simply)
>   I am here.[41]

So wrote Alma Villanueva in her poem "Inside," crafting a female
literary voice, and birthing a Chicana poetic consciousness.

Unlike Chicanos who took their sex/gender privileges for granted,
Chicanas, as victims of those privileges, realized that an essential part
of their literary birthing had to include an exploration of their sexuality.
"Our sexuality has been hidden, subverted, distorted within the 'sacred'
walls of the 'familia'—be it myth or reality—and within the even more
privatized walls of the bedrooms. . . . In the journey to the love of
female self and each other we are ultimately forced to confront father,
brother, and god (and mother as his agent)," wrote Norma Alarcón,
Ana Castillo, and Cherríe Moraga.[42]

Things that formerly were taboo now appeared in print. Arcelia
Ponce, in her short story "La preferida," described how a young girl
named Julia had been sexually abused by her father from the age of
six to fourteen. Victoria Alegría Rosales vividly recounted the brutal
beatings she had received in marriage. Lesbianism, the love that dare
not speak its name, was brought out of the closet by Veronica Cunningham in the poem "When all the yous":

> when all the yous
> of my poetry
> were really
> she or her
> and i could never
> no
> i would never write them
> because

of some fears
i never even wanted
to see.
how could i have been frightened
of sharing
the being
and me.

In "The Love Making," Cenen writes:

When the swell of your clitoris came bulging into the roll of my sucking
tongue, I knew tonight's sweetness would be long. My excited body moved
closer into the swelling folds of your labia, rubbing my teeth, my lips, my
whole face into your wetness. Your body jumped and turned spasmodically
pressing my head between your legs. As I tried to release my head from
your grip, my mouth lost your swollen clitoris.

Ana Castillo shattered all Catholic conventions by describing her sexual
desire and fulfillment. Here is her poem "Coffee Break":

15 minutes
        They take
        their morning papers
        monogrammed mugs
        to the lounge
        moaning and groaning
        of monday monotony
        & self boredom—
she
        does a 2 step down
        the narrow hall
        to the small room
        where toilet paper
        plugs the keyhole
        whitewashed windows
        graffiti wallpaper
        designed by unknown
        heroes and scholars—
A tiny streak
        of sun leaks
        through a space
        of unpainted glass
        makes as a spotlight
        for 2 talented fingers
        creating fast—

ART IN MOTION!
A STAR IS BORN!
SUCH STYLE!
WHAT GRACE![43]

Given the importance that sexuality had in the Chicana feminist movement, it is not coincidental that so much of the writing would dwell on the mother-daughter relationship. The confrontation between two cultures and between two ways of life was often played out as a generational struggle between mothers and daughters. Alma Villanueva expresses this sentiment well in her poem "Blood Root":

I vowed
    to never
        grow up
to be a woman
and helpless
like my mother.[44]

In "Aztec Princess," Pat Mora casts mothers as the persons who were holding back the liberation of women.

Her mother would say, "Look in
the home for happiness. Why do you stare out
often with such longing?" One day,
almost in desperation, her mother said,
"Here. See here. We buried your umbilical
cord here, in the house. A sign that you,
our girl-child, would nest inside."

That night the young woman quietly dug
for some trace of the shriveled woman-to-woman
skin, but all she found was earth, rich earth,
which she carefully scooped into an earthen jar
whispering, "Breathe."[45]

For Tina Bénitez, the love/hate relationship that existed between Chicanas and their mothers was the result of the mother's desire to reproduce in her daughter the values of a patriarchal culture. "The mother blocks her desires by telling her what 'good girls' should and should not do," asserted Bénitez, "thereby, condemning her to emulate a role of powerlessness."[46] Rina Rocha captured the essence of this sentiment when she wrote in her poem "Baby Doll":

Mothers can be
jealous gods
Just like
husbands
Unforgiving and demanding.

Saying
naughty girl,
naught ought
to have done that.
Naught, ought
to have said that . . .

And I . . .
am amazed still—
at me!
That I should wait for these
candied coated loving
words of approval
from
jealous gods.[47]

Mothers came to be despised by their Chicana daughters in large part because of their subordination/accommodation to patriarchal power. As mothers who often favored assimilation, they urged their daughters to learn English, to get educated, to marry well (to wealthy Anglo men all the better), and, if necessary, to abandon their cultural past.

The generational conflict took its most confrontational and accusatory tones when daughters, be they lesbian or heterosexual, started to assert their sexuality. To an older generation, sex was not a topic for public discussion, and even in private it was not a topic broached comfortably. To daughters, many as participants in the sexual revolution of the 1960s, female sexuality was something to celebrate openly, to talk about, to write about, and to represent in a myriad of open ways. For mothers such behavior was tantamount to the abandonment of *mexicano* cultural values and the acceptance of the Anglo ways.[48] Mothers thus accused their daughters of assimilationism; daughters accused their mothers of accommodationism—and here was the problem.

Perhaps the most intense discussion of the mother/daughter relationship yet written was Cherríe Moraga's *Loving in the War Years: lo que nunca pasó por sus labios*—the subtitle translates as "what never crossed her lips."[49] Here Moraga returns to a re-evaluation of

Malinche as the traitor and *chingada,* seeing in her historical dilemmas a way to confront her own (that is, Moraga's) dilemmas in life. Moraga felt betrayed by her mother because she loved her sons much more devotedly than her daughters. This was complicated further by two additional levels of betrayal. As a lesbian, Moraga felt accused of betraying her race by choosing the sex of her mother as the object of sexual desire. As a *coyota,* the half-breed daughter of an Anglo father and Chicana mother, Moraga saw herself as the daughter of Malinche, suffering her mother's betrayal of her people.

Moraga is wrenched by the multiple levels of contradiction these betrayals create. On the one hand she loves her mother deeply, treasures the closeness family provides, and realizes that the mother/daughter relationship is "paramount and essential in our lives [in which the daughter always] . . . remains faithful a la madre."[50] And on the other hand, she realizes that while the daughter is taught to be faithful to her mother, mothers do not always reciprocate.

Most Chicanas who explored issues of gender and sexuality through reflections on Malinche often cast themselves as the victimized daughters of Malinche. Moraga is unique in that she focuses not on Malinche, but on Malinche's mother, comparing her to her own mother. Thus, in the expository parallels, Moraga and Malinche are identical.

Moraga clearly believes that her mother betrayed her by loving her sons much more than her daughters. We see this resentment when Moraga writes:

> If somebody would have asked me when I was a teenager what it means to be Chicana, I would probably have listed the grievances done me. When my sister and I were fifteen and fourteen, respectively, and my brother a few years older, we were all still waiting on him. I write "were" as if now, nearly two decades later, it were over. But that would be a lie. To this day in my mother's home, my brother and father are waited on, including by me. I do this now out of respect for my mother and her wishes. In those early days, however, it was mainly in relation to my brother that I resented providing such service. For unlike my father, who sometimes worked as much as seventy hours a week to feed my face every day, the only thing that earned my brother my servitude was his maleness.[51]

Moraga continues to describe how her mother treated her own father, conforming to Mexican cultural norms that expected feminine subservience to men. When her mother became a wife, the act of treachery was again repeated; favoring her sons, revering her husband, and taking her daughters for granted. "Traitor begets traitor," Moraga writes, like mother, like daughter. Malinche's mother was the first traitor (mother) who begot the second one (daughter).[52]

To assert her Chicana identity and to reclaim "the race of my mother," Moraga breaks free from Malinche and Malinche's mother by choosing to "embrace no white man."[53] She is finally united with the race of her mother through Chicana lesbianism, by loving other women. By refusing to give her sexual loyalty to Chicano men, by refusing to live as a heterosexual, Moraga realizes that, in the eyes of the *movimiento* men, she has become a *"malinchista,"* a traitor. This she proudly accepts, stating at the end of her book that she comes from a long line of *vendidas* (traitors).

If the generational tension in Chicana expression is between mothers and daughters, the generational refuge is between grandmothers and granddaughters. In various essays Tina Bénitez, Norma Alarcón, and Diana Fey Rebollero have explored the ways in which "the grand-mother/granddaughter relationship gives the Chicana an escape from her gender role expectations enforced by the mother."[54]

To achieve what Tina Bénitez believed was a necessary reconciliation with the mother, she proposed that the mother/daughter relationship had to be conceived as evolutionary.

> As a young girl the mother is portrayed as nurturing and loving. However, as the Chicana matures she becomes more critical of her mother and the role she succumbs to. When the mother tries to impose this self-sacrificing role upon her daughter, what emerges from the literature is the daughter/ writer's repulsion and rejection of the mother and veneration of the grand-mother. As the Chicana strives for a new vision of transformation she turns to the mother for reconciliation and thereby draws strength for the rebirth and empowerment of herself and all Chicana women."[55]

Early explorations of the relationships between mothers and daughters were hostile, but gradually some women came to realize that they could not blame their mothers for what their mothers themselves had not been able to control. Guadalupe Valdes-Fallis reconciled herself with her mother when she acknowledged that her mother had not had any other options open to her. In an autobiographical essay titled "Re-cuerdo," Valdes stated:

> My story . . . might well be entitled "Mother's Advice." It is a bitter story, written at a time in which I was angry about my own life and about having

followed my own mother's counsel. I was trying to make sense of the world, trying to understand why one could follow all of the (cultural) rules and yet end up unhappy. I felt betrayed, trapped and all alone. Until recently, it had not occurred to me that my mother has also been betrayed and trapped . . . like so many women, she had also tried to follow rules; to make sense of so many things that seemed unfair; and to hope that somehow, for her daughters, things would be different. Clearly, my anger was misdirected. My mother gave me what she could. She said, 'Marry a man who doesn't drink.' Amazingly that, like the mother in "Recuerdo," her formula for happiness was so simple. She focused on the one thing that had made her life unhappy, and she wanted more for me. It seems sad now, that I blamed her for so many years, blamed her because I believed her, blamed her because the formula was not complete and did not bring happiness.[56]

The ultimate solution to this relationship was, according to one Chicana feminist, for mothers to give their love and approval to their daughters freely, and for daughters to relieve their mothers of all the psychic burdens they too had endured. "The choice is to either passively sit and watch our sisters and mother be beaten into the ground, or to help them rise above by giving them the love and support they so often seek from men."[57]

*   *   *

The theme of the individual in our capitalist, postmodern society forms the last section of this historiographic survey. Postmodernism is one of those much bantered but illusive terms. It usually refers "to a certain constellation of styles and tones in cultural works: pastiche; blankness; a sense of exhaustion; a mixture of levels, forms, styles; a relish for copies and repetition; a knowingness that dissolves commitment into irony; acute self-consciousness about the formal, constructed nature of work; pleasure in the place of surfaces; a rejection of history." A postmodern culture is one in which a formerly unified subject is split into his or her constituent parts; in which a single homogeneous style is superseded by a number of heterogeneous fashions. We see this tendency toward fragmentation, eclecticism and reflexivity in television advertising and on MTV. But in addition to being a general cultural style, postmodernism is, says Raymond Williams, a general orientation. It is a "structure of feeling" for apprehending and experiencing the world and our place, or placelessness, in it.[58]

In the past five years some Mexican-American intellectuals have embraced the subversive experimentation of postmodernism to describe the fragmentation of Chicano culture, showing how there never was, nor currently is, one "Chicano movement," with a capital "C." Instead, they view the Chicano movement as an eclectic composition of peoples and traditions. In recent years the names of those whose works could be considered postmodern are Gloria Anzaldúa, Guillermo Gómez-Peña, Richard Rodriguez, Renato Rosaldo, and Tomás Almaguer. I will return to them shortly, but before I do, I want to focus first on John Rechy. In 1963, when the thought of a Chicano movement hardly existed, John Rechy exploded onto the American scene with the publication of *City of Night,* an autobiographical novel that described vividly, through the eyes of a male prostitute, the sexual underworld that pulsated in the very heart of Los Angeles, New York City, Chicago, El Paso, and San Francisco. In *The Sexual Outlaw* and *Rushes,* Rechy further elaborated on "the narcissistic pattern of my life," a life that was governed by the narcotic of "sexmoney." From room to room, from bed to bed, from face to face, at a dizzying pace, Rechy showed us his tricks. In bar rooms and back rooms, in restrooms and parks, and behind bushes that barely concealed, men of every sort played out their own fantasies with him. Men fellated him, they furtively groped and caressed his body, they licked his legs and boots and drank his urine; a scenario that always ended with him mounting his partners and "play[ing] the male role with [these] men."[59]

At the 1989 meeting of the National Association for Chicano Studies, Rechy was finally honored with a panel on his work. But in the 1960s, Chicanos refused to acknowledge Rechy as a Chicano or even to accept his novels as Chicano literature. Though his mother was a *mexicana* and had raised him the barrios of El Paso, it was his Scottish father who had given him a name and abandoned him and his mother. It was his name, his homosexuality, and the themes he explored in print that excluded him from the community young men defined as Chicano. Ironically, at the very time that he was being rejected by Chicanos, the Texas Hall of Fame inducted him into its ranks as a Chicano author, an identity Rechy has always proudly claimed.

Rechy's novels were intellectual forerunners to postmodernism among Mexican Americans. The themes of marginality, of fractured identities, of suspension betwixt and between worlds, were themes he first articulated, but which would not emerge again until 1987. In that year Gloria Anzaldúa's book, *Borderlands/La Frontera: The New Mes-*

tiza appeared. The book defies easy classification. It is a combination of history (much of it wrong), poetry, essays, and philosophical gems, in which Anzaldúa describes her fractured identity—an identity fractured by not only the reality of the border between the United States and Mexico, but also the numerous borders in personal life. Anzaldúa claims to be a *mestiza* or mixed-blood lesbian, and we can see the meaning of that in her poem "Del otro lado":

> She looks at the Border Park fence
> posts are stuck into her throat, her navel,
> barbwire is shoved up her cunt.
> Her body torn in two, half a woman on the other side
> half a woman on this side, the right side
> And she went to the North American university,
> excelled in the Gringo's tongue
> learned to file in folders.
> But she remembered the other half
> strangled in Aztec villages, in Mayan villages, in Incan village . . .
>
> She remembers
> The horror in her sister's voice,
> "Eres una de las otras,"
> The look in her mother's face as she says,
> "I am so ashamed, I will never
> be able to raise my head in this pueblo."
> The mother's words are barbs digging into her flesh.
> *De las otras*. Cast out. Untouchable.
> "But I'm me," she cries, "I've always been me."
> "Don't bring your queer friends into my house,
> my land, the planet. Get away.
> Don't contaminate us, get away."
>
> Away, she went away.
> But every place she went
> they pushed her to the other side
> and that other side pushed her to the other side
> of the other side of the other side
> Kept in the shadows of other.
> No right to sing, to rage, to explode . . .
> Always pushed toward the other side.
> In all lands alien, nowhere citizen.
> Away, she went away
> but each place she went
> pushed her to the other side, al otro lado.[60]

In "To live in the Borderlands," she writes,

> means you are neither *hispana india negra española*
> *ni gabacha, eres mestiza, mulata,* half-breed
> caught in the crossfire between camps
> while carrying all five races on your back
> now knowing which side to turn to, to run from; . . .

> *Cuando vives en la frontera*
> people walk through you, the wind steals your voice,
> you're a *burra, buey,* scapegoat,
> forerunner of a new race,
> half and half—both woman and man, neither—
> a new gender;

> To live on the Borderlands means to
> put *chile* in the borscht
> eat whole wheat *tortillas,*
> speak Tex-Mex with a Brooklyn accent;
> be stopped by *la migra* at the border checkpoints; . . .

> To survive the Borderlands
> you must live *sin fronteras*
> be a crossroads.[61]

In her essay "How to Tame a Wild Tongue," Anzaldúa vividly shows, through the example of language, the complexity of Mexican-American cultures. She begins by identifying eight forms of Spanish:

> My "home" tongues are the languages I speak with my sister and brothers, with my friends. They are [*Pachuco* (called *caló*), Tex-Mex, Chicano Spanish, North Mexican Spanish dialect, and Standard Mexican Spanish, with Chicano Spanish] being the closest to my heart. From school, the media and job situations, I've picked up standard and working class English. From Mamagrande Locha and from reading Spanish and Mexican literature, I've picked up Standard Spanish and Standard Mexican Spanish. From *los recién llegados,* Mexican immigrants and *braceros,* I learned Northern Mexican dialect . . .[62]

She then goes on to describe how and when she uses each type, proving the point that the relationship between language and identity is not a neat and easy one, and that Mexican Americans are a complexly stratified group.

Another person who had been extremely influential in the Chicano postmodernist movement is Guillermo Gómez-Peña, a performance artist in San Diego. He identifies himself as "a child of crisis and cultural syncretism, half hippie and half punk. . . . In my fractured reality, but a reality nonetheless, there cohabit two histories, two languages, cosmologies, artistic traditions, and political systems which are drastically counterposed."[63] His ecleticism poignantly emerges in a poem "Good Morning, This Radio Latino Spoiling Your Breakfast as Always":

> Alien-ation
> alien action
> alien-ated
> alguién ate it
> alien hatred
> aliens out there
> hay alguién out there
> "aliens" the album
> "aliens" the movie
> cowboys vs. aliens
> bikers vs. aliens
> the wet-back from Mars
> the Mexican transformer & his radioactive torta
> the conquest of Tenochtitlán by Spielberg
> the reconquest of Aztlán by Monty Python
> the brown wave vs. the microwave
> invaders from the South
> vs. the San Diego Police reinforced by
> the Border Crime Prevention Unit reinforced by
> your ignorance, dear San Diego . . .[64]

The Pompidou Center in Paris is often given as a splendid example of postmodern architecture, because instead of concealing its wiring, its vents, its plumbing, and its foundations, everything is exposed. In social science writings on Chicanos, Tomás Almaguer's recent essay "Ideological Distortions in Recent Chicano Historiography" lays open the historiography on Chicanos, exposing the false epistemological closures and the simplistic ideas that he, as well as other Chicano radicals and intellectuals, claimed as their credo in the 1960s. Almaguer argues that, motivated primarily by the desire to challenge the dominant assimilationist model of the 1950s, Chicano radicals embraced a colonial analysis that depicted the history of Chicanos as that of a colonized minority. In this internal colony, racism and economic exploitation were the dominant themes—themes that had been born as a result of the U.S.-Mexican War. Almaguer shows how in the scholarly works of political scientists Mario Barrera and Carlos Muñoz; historians Ricardo Griswold del Castillo, Albert Camarillo, Ricardo Romo, Juan Gómez-Quiñones, Guillermo Flores, and Rudy Acuña; and sociologists such as Joan Moore, Charles Orneales, and Almaguer, colonialism and racism became the dominant themes of their analytic frameworks. These themes cast the present and the past as a conflict between Anglos and Chicanos that politically called for a cultural nationalist movement to crush imperialism.[65]

However strongly these sentiments were felt in the 1960s, Almaguer argues that the analysis was wrong. A cursory examination showed that Native Americans had been ignored. Mexican Americans historically straddled several classes, and in the racial hierarchy Mexicans occupied an intermediate position between Anglos and Indians. In short, much of what had been written was an ideological distortion of the past, fashioned to fit the political tenor of the day.

Alex Saragoza recently made a similar point.[66] The Chicano radicals of the 1960s chose 1848 as the beginning of Chicano history because that date more conveniently highlighted Anglo-Mexican conflicts. "Why did Chicano history not begin in 1836?" Saragoza asks. The answer is simple. During the Texas War for Independence, *Tejanos* and Anglos fought alongside each other as allies. This date complicated the dichotomous "Them/Us" racial vision too much and just did not meet their political needs.

Let me conclude by bringing together the various strands that I have tried to weave together here. I began by outlining the shape and dimensions of that political community Chicano radicals forged in the 1960s, turning next to the feminist assault on that vision and the construction of her/story; a story that was rooted in the politicization of the body. Postmodernism fractured all of this into bits, exploded the categories, and left a disordered and disordering vision of the past and the future. Chicano cultural nationalism had a clear vision. However misdirected and obtuse, by defining Anglos and colonialism as the enemies, a plausible strategy for revolutionary change was close at hand. With Chicana feminism, too, the political vision and strategy were clear. Women unite against your fathers, brothers and sons, to overthrow patriarchy. But what is the political vision of postmodernism with its emphasis on alienation, despair, confusion, and the layer upon layer of splinterings and fractures?

Twenty years ago Enriqueta Longauex y Vasquez, an early Chicana feminist, uttered the following words:

> The Raza movement is based on brother- and sisterhood. We must look at each other as one large family. We must look at all of the children as belonging to all of us. We must strive for the fulfillment of all as equals, with the full capability and right to develop as humans.[67]

At this time, the majority of the persons living in poverty in this country are Chicana single-mothers and their children. Chicanas over the age of twenty-five, on the average, complete only 8.4 years of schooling, in comparison to the 13.5 of their white counterparts. And when the average income of a Chicana-headed household is still only $4,930, the burning issues that sparked the Chicano movement have only intensified and taken a clearer class form.[68] Indeed, if one takes a long view when analyzing what the ultimate impact of the Chicano movement was on the daily lives of ethnic Mexicans in the United States, it was to obscure the class character of the racial order. No matter whether one subscribed to the masculine Chicano vision of the nation with its emphasis on *la raza* (the race) and *carnalismo* (brotherhood) or the Chicana nationalism of feminists who turned to *mestizaje* (race mixture) and *mexicanidad* for inspiration, the imagined community was stratified by region, by class, by generation, by color, and by political persuasions. The various strands of Mexican-American activism that did manage to extract social and political concessions from the state and regional capitalists were those segments of the movement that never lost sight of their class character and class aims. Cesar Chavez organized agricultural workers throughout the Southwest through his United Farmworkers of America, militating for better wages and work conditions—concessions his union was able to extract, if only for a short period of time. Reies López Tijerina created the Alianza Federal de Mercedes in northern New Mexico and southern Colorado, and through this organization was able to get Hispano land claims favorably settled. The impact of the struggles that both of these men led are still felt in labor relations and land rights litigation. As for the student component of the movement, perhaps the most significant and enduring legacy were the curricular changes and the creation of Chicano Studies programs and departments.

NOTES

1. Rodolfo Acuña, *Occupied America: The Chicano's Struggle Toward Liberation* (San Francisco, 1972); Ramón A. Gutiérrez, "Mexican Migration to the United States, 1880–1930: The Chicano and Internal Colonialism" (M.A. thesis, University of Wisconsin, 1976); Tomás Almaguer, "Toward the Study of Chicano Colonialism," *Aztlán* 2 (Spring 1971): 7–21, and "Historical Notes on Chicano Oppression: The Dialectics of Racial and Class Domination in North America," *Aztlán* 5 (Spring-Fall 1974): 27–56. Mario Barrera, "Colonial Labor and Theories of Inequality: The Case of International Harvester," *Review of Radical Political Economics* 8 (Summer 1967): 7–27, and *Race and Class in the Southwest: A Theory of Racial Inequality* (Notre Dame, Ind., 1979); Mario Barrera, Carlos Muñoz, Charles Ornelas, "The Barrio as Internal Colony," *Urban Affairs Annual Reviews* 6 (1972): 465–98.

2. Albert Camarillo, *Chicanos in a Changing Society: From Mexican Pueblos to American Barrios in Santa Barbara and Southern California, 1848–1930* (Cambridge, Mass., 1979); Richard Griswold del Castillo, *The Los Angeles Barrio, 1850–1890* (Berkeley, Calif., 1979); Ricardo Romo, *East Los Angeles: A History of a Barrio* (Austin, Tex., 1983).

3. Acuña, 230.

4. Armando Navarro, "The Evolution of Chicano Politics," *Aztlán* 5 (Spring and Fall 1974): 57–84, quotation from 57–58.

5. Adelaida R. del Castillo, "Mexican Women in Organization," in *Mexican Women in the United States,* eds. Magdalena Mora and Adelaida R. del Castillo (Los Angeles, 1980), 7–16, quotation from 10.

6. Ibid, 7–16, quotation from 9.

7. Ibid, 7–16, quotation from 8.

8. Marcela Christine Lucero-Trujillo, "Machismo Is Part of Our Culture," in *The Third Woman,* 401–02.

9. Lorna Dee Cervantes, "You Cramp My Style, Baby," quoted in Yvonne Yarbro-Berjarano, "The Female Subject in Chicano Theatre: Sexuality, 'Race,' and Class," *Theatre Journal* 38 (Dec. 1986): 402.

10. Irene Rodarte, "Machismo vs. Revolution," in *La mujer en pie de lucha,* ed. Dorinda Moreno (Mexico City, 1973).

11. Guadalupe Valdes Fallis, "The Liberated Chicana: A Struggle Against Tradition," *Women: A Journal of Liberation* 3 (1974): 20–21.

12. Anna Nieto-Gómez, "Sexism in the Movimiento," *La Gente* 6 (Mar. 1976): 10. Velia Hancock, "La Chicana: Chicana Movement and Women's Lib," *Chicano Studies Newsletter* (Feb.–Mar. 1971): 1; Mirta Vidal, *Chicanas Speak Out* (New York, 1971).

13. Bernice Zamora, "Notes from a Chicana COED," *Caracol* 3 (1977): 19, as quoted in M. Sanchez, *Contemporary Chicana Poetry* (Berkeley, Calif., 1985), 231–32.

14. Una Chicana, "Abajo con los Machos," *La Raza* 1 (1971): 3–4.

15. Enriqueta Longauex y Vásquez, "Soy Chicano Primero," *El Cuaderno* 1 (1972): 17–22 and "The Mexican-American Woman," in *Sisterhood is Powerful,* ed. Robin Morgan (New York, 1970), 379–84.

16. Theresa Aragón de Valdez, "Organizing as a Political Tool for the Chicana," *Frontiers: A Journal of Women's Studies* 5 (1980): 11.

17. Ibid., 10.

18. Consuelo Nieto, "Interaction of Culture and Sex Roles in the Schools: Chicana Identity and its Educational Implications," (unpublished paper), quoted by Theresa Aragón de Valdez, "Organizing as a Political Tool for the Chicana," *Frontiers: A Journal of Women's Studies* 5 (1980): 10.

19. Judith Sweeney, "Chicana History: A Review of the Literature," in *Essays on la Mujer,* ed. Rosaura Sánchez (Los Angeles, 1977), 99–123, quotation from 100.

20. Alfredo Mirandé and Evangelina Enríquez, *La Chicana: The Mexican-American Woman* (Chicago, 1979), 2.

21. T. R. Fehrenbach, *Fire and Blood: A History of Mexico* (New York, 1973), 131.

22. Luis Valdez, "La Conquista de Méjico," *Actos y el Teatro Campesino* (Fresno, Calif., 1971), 131.

23. Octavio Paz, *The Labyrinth of Solitude: Life and Thought in Mexico* (New York, 1961).

24. Ibid., 77.

25. Ibid., 86.

26. Sylvia A. Gonzales, "La Chicana: Guadalupe or Malinche," in *Comparative Perspectives of Third World Women: The Impact of Race, Sex, and Class,* ed. Beverly Lindsay (New York, 1980), 229–50. For a more succinct theoretical statement of the problem see Evelyn P. Stevens, "Marianismo: The Other Face of Machismo in Latin America," in *Female and Male in Latin America,* ed. Ann Pescatello (Pittsburgh, 1973), 89–102.

27. Sylvia Gonzales, "I Am Chicana," in *Third Woman,* 442.

28. Adelaida R. del Castillo, "Malintzin Tenépal: A Preliminary Look into a New Perspective," in *Essays on la mujer,* ed. Rosaura Sánchez (Los Angeles, 1977), 124–49, quotation from 126.

29. Ibid., 141. Adelaida del Castillo's essay was also a profound critique of Octavio Paz's work on Malinche. See for example 413–32.

30. Cordelia Candelaria, "La Malinche, Feminist Prototype," *Frontiers: A Journal of Women's Studies* 5 (1980): 1–6, quotation from 6.

31. Norma Alarcón, "Chicana's Feminist Literature: A Re-Vision through Malintzín/ or Malinche: Putting Flesh Back on the Object," in *This Bridge Called My Back: Writings by Radical Women of Color,* eds. Cherríe Moraga and Gloria Anzaldúa (New York, 1983), 182–90; Rachel Phillips, "Marina/Malinche: Masks and Shadows," in *Women in Hispanic Literature: Icons and Fallen Idols,* ed. Beth Miller (Berkeley, Calif., 1983), 97–114; Shirlene Soto, "Tres modelos culturales: La Virgen Guadalupe, La Malinche y la Llorona," *fem* 10 (Oct.–Nov. 1986): 13–16.

32. Sylvia Delgado, "Young Chicana Speaks Up on Problems Faced by Young Girls," *Regeneración* 1 (1978): 5–7; Kathy Flores, "Chicano Attitudes Toward Birth Control," *Imagenes de la Chicana* (1st issue): 19–21; Melanie Orendian, "Sexual Taboo y la Cultura?" *Imagenes de la Chicana* (1st issue): 30. Theresa Aragon de Valdez chronicles a 1971 San Antonio case in which Mexican-American women were used as guinea pigs for a birth control experiment without being informed. See "Organizing as a Political Tool for the Chicana," *Frontiers: A Journal of Women's Studies* 5 (1980): 9.

33. Carlos G. Velez-I, "Se me Acabó la Canción: An Ethnography of Non-Consenting Sterilizations among Mexican Women in Los Angeles," in *Mexican Women in the United States,* eds. Magdalena Mora and Adelaida del Castillo (Los Angeles, 1980), 71–94.

34. Clemencia Martinez, "Welfare Families Face Forced Labor," *La Raza* 1 (Jan. 1972): 41; Mary Tullos and Dolores Hernandez, "Talmadge Amendment: Welfare

Continues to Exploit the Poor," *La Raza* 1 (Jan. 1972): 10–11; Anna Nieto-Gómez, "Madres Por la Justicia," *Encuentro Femenil* 1 (Spring 1973): 12–19; Alicia Escalante, "A Letter from the Chicana Welfare Rights Organization," *Encuentro Femenil* 1 (1974): 15–19.

35. Renne Mares, "La Pinta: The Myth of Rehabilitation," *Encuentro Femenil* 1 (1974): 27–29; Josie Madrid, Chata Mercado, Priscilla Pardo and Anita Ramirez, "Chicanas in Prison," *Regeneración* 2 (1973): 53–54.

36. Viola Correa, "La Nueva Chicana," in *La Mujer en Pie de Lucha*, ed. Dorinda Moreno (Mexico City, 1973); Maxime Baca Zinn, "Gender and Ethnic Identity among Chicanos," *Frontiers: A Journal of Women's Studies* 5 (1980): 18–24.

37. Ruth Allen, *The Labor of Women in the Production of Cotton* (1933; reprint, New York, 1975) and "Mexican Peon Women in Texas," *Sociology and Social Research* 16 (Nov.–Dec. 1931): 131–42. See also Mary Loretta Sullivan and Bertha Blair, "Women in Texas Industries, Hours, Working Conditions, and Home Work," *Bulletin of the Women's Bureau* 126 (1936). Selden C. Menefee and Orin C. Cassmore, *The Pecan Shellers of San Antonio: The Problem of Underpaid and Unemployed Mexican Labor* (Washington, D.C., 1940). Melissa Hield, "Union-Minded: Women in the Texas ILGWU, 1933–1950," *Frontiers* 4 (Summer 1979): 59–70. See also George N. Green, "ILGWU in Texas, 1930–1970," *Journal of Mexican-American History* 1 (1971): 144–69; Mario F. Vásquez, "The Election Day Immigration Raid at Lillie Diamond Originals and the Response of the ILGWU," *Mexican Women in the United States*, eds. Magdalena Mora and Adelaida del Castillo (Los Angeles, 1980), pp. 145–48; Douglas Monroy, "La Costura en Los Angeles, 1933–1939: The ILGWU and the Politics of Domination," in *Mexican Women in the United States*, eds. Magdalena Mora and Adelaida del Castillo (Los Angeles, 1980), 171–78. Jane Dysart, "Mexican Women in San Antonio, 1830–60: The Assimilation Process," *Western Historical Quarterly* 7 (Oct. 1976): 365–75. Ester Gallegos y Chavez, "The Northern New Mexican Woman: A Changing Silhouette," in *The Chicanos: As We See Ourselves*, ed. Arnulfo D. Trejo (Tucson, Ariz., 1979): 67–80. Mario García, *Desert Immigrants: The Mexicans of El Paso, 1880–1920* (New Haven, Conn., 1981).

38. Vicki L. Ruiz and Susan Tiano, eds., *Women on the U.S.-Mexico Border: Responses to Change* (Boston, 1987); Margarita B. Melville, "Mexican Women Adapt to Migration," in *Mexican Immigrant Workers in the United States*, ed. Antonio Rios-Bustamante (Los Angeles, 1981), 119–26; Gilbert Cardenas and Estevan T. Flores, *The Migration and Settlement of Undocumented Women* (Austin, Tex., 1986); Rita J. Simon and Caroline B. Brettell, eds., *International Migration: The Female Experience* (Totowa, N.J., 1987).

39. Patricia Zavella, *Women's Work and Chicano Families: Cannery Workers of the Santa Clara Valley* (Ithaca, N.Y., 1987); Vicki L. Ruiz, *Cannery Women, Cannery Lives: Mexican Women, Unionization, and the California Food Processing Industry, 1930–1950* (Albuquerque, N. Mex., 1987).

40. Enriqueta Longauex y Vasquez, "The Mexican-American Woman," in *Sisterhood is Powerful*, ed. Robin Morgan (New York, 1970), 379–84, quotation from 380.

41. Alma Villanueva, "Inside," in *Mother May I?* (San Francisco, 1972), 54.

42. Norma Alarcón, Ana Castillo, Cherríe Moraga, eds., *Third Woman: The Sexuality of Latinas* (Berkeley, Calif., 1989), 9.

43. Arcelia Ponce, "La preferida," in *Third Woman: The Sexuality of Latinas*, eds. Norma Alarcón, Ana Castillo, Cherríe Moraga (Berkeley, Calif., 1989), 85–89; Victoria Alegría Rosales, "To All Women Who Have Followed the Same Road as I," in *Third Woman: The Sexuality of Latinas*, eds. Norma Alarcón, Ana Castillo, Cherríe Moraga (Berkeley, Calif., 1989), 99–100; Veronica Cunningham, "When all the yous,"

quoted in Yvonne Yarbro-Berjarano, "The Female Subject in Chicano Theatre: Sexuality, 'Race,' and Class," *Theatre Journal* 38 (Dec. 1986): 402; Cenen, "The Love Making," in *Compañeras: Latina Lesbians (An Anthology)*, ed. Juanita Ramos (New York, 1987), 141–43; Ana Castillo, "Coffee Break," *The Invitation* (Berkeley, Calif., 1979), 19.

44. Alma Villanueva quote in Tina Benítez, "The Mother Daughter Relationship," in *Palabras Chicanas* (Berkeley, Calif., 1988), 28.

45. Pat Mora, "Aztec Princess," *Chants* (Houston, Tex., 1984), 28.

46. Tina Bénitez, "The Mother Daughter Relationship," in *Palabras Chicanas,* eds. Lisa Hernández and Lisa Bénitez (Berkeley, Calif., 1988), 23–29, quotation from 24.

47. Rina Rocha, "Baby Doll," *Eluder* (Chicago, 1980).

48. Eliana Ortega and Nancy Saporta Sternbach, "At the Threshold of the Unnamed: Latina Literary Discourse in the Eighties," in *Breaking Boundaries: Latina Writings and Critical Readings,* eds. Asunción Horno-Delgado, et al. (Amherst, Mass., 1989), 2–26.

49. Cherríe Moraga, *Loving in the War Years: lo que nunca pasó por sus labios* (Boston, 1983).

50. Ibid., 139.

51. Ibid., 90.

52. Ibid., 103.

53. Ibid., 94.

54. Tina Bénitez, "The Mother Daughter Relationship," in *Palabras Chicanas* (Berkeley, Calif., 1988), 25. On the mother/daughter relationship see also Lucy Guerrero, "Tu Eres Mujer: The Chicana Mother-Daughter Relationship," in *Palabras Chicanas* (Berkeley, Calif., 1988), 37–46. On the grandmother/granddaughter relationship see: Barbara Brinson-Pineda, " 'Donde Estas Grandma' Chicana Writers and the Rejection of Silence," *Intercambios Femeniles: The National Network of Hispanic Women* 2 (1984); Diana Rebolledo, "Abuelitas: Mythology and Integration in Chicana Literature," *Revista Chicano-Riqueña* 11 (1983): 149–60; Nan Elsasser, Kyle MacKenzie and Yvonne Tixier y Vigil, eds., *La Mujeres: Conversations from a Hispanic Community* (Old Westbury, N.Y., 1980), esp. 8–42; Adeny Schmidt and Amado N. Padilla, "Grandparent-Grandchild Interaction in a Mexican-American Group," *Hispanic Journal of Behavioral Sciences* 5 (1983): 195; Lisa Hernández, "Canas," in *Palabras Chicanas* (Berkeley, Calif., 1988), 47–50; Norma Alarcón, "What Kind of Lover Have You Made Me Mother?: Theory of Chicanas' Feminism and Cultural Identity Through Poetry," in *Women of Color: Perspectives on Feminism and Identity* (Bloomington, Ind., 1985), 75.

55. Tina Bénitez, "The Mother Daughter Relationship," 29.

56. Guadalupe Valdes-Fallis, "Recuerdo," *De Colores* (1975): 60–65. For a very similar statement see Claudia Colindres, "A Letter to My Mother," in *Third Woman: The Sexuality of Latinas,* eds. Norma Alarcón, Ana Castillo, Cherríe Moraga (Berkeley, Calif., 1989), 73–79.

57. Francesca S. Burroughs, "Joining the Future and the Past," in *Palabras Chicanas,* eds. Lisa Hernández and Tina Bénitez (Berkeley, Calif., 1988), 55–57.

58. Todd Gitlin, "Postmodernism: Roots and Politics," in *Cultural Politics in Contemporary America,* ed. Ian Angus (New York, 1988), 347–85, quotation from 347.

59. John Rechy, *City of Night* (New York, 1984), 18, 23, 40.

60. Gloria E. Anzaldúa, "Del otro lado," in *Compañeras: Latina Lesbians (An Anthology)*, ed. Juanita Ramos (New York, 1987), 3–4.

61. Gloria Anzaldúa, *Borderlands/La Frontera: The New Mestiza* (San Francisco, 1987), 194.

62. Ibid., 55–56.

63. Guillermo Gómez-Peña, "Documented/Undocumented," *The Graywolf Annual Five: Multi-cultural Literacy* (St. Paul, Minn., 1989), 127–29.

64. Guillermo Gómez-Peña, "Good Morning, This is Radio Latino Spoiling your Breakfast as Always," *La Linea Quebrada/The Broken Line* (San Diego, 1989), 12.

65. Tomas Almaguer, "Ideological Distortions in Recent Chicano Historiography," *Aztlán* 18 (1989): 7–27.

66. Alex M. Saragoza, "The Significance of Recent Chicano-Related Historical Writings: An Appraisal," *Ethnic Affairs* 1 (Fall 1987): 24–62.

67. Enriqueta Longauex y Vasquez, "The Mexican-American Woman," in *Sisterhood is Powerful*, ed. Robin Morgan (New York, 1970), 379–84, quotation from 384.

68. Elizabeth Waldman, "Profile of The Chicana: A Statistical Fact Sheet," in *Mexican Women in the United States*, eds. Magdalena Mora and Adelaida R. del Castillo (Los Angeles, 1980), 195–204.

COMMENTARY

Vicki L. Ruiz

Ramón A. Gutiérrez persuasively argues that one legacy of the Chicano student movement has been the creation of Chicano studies, both as intellectual praxis and as academic department. Blending literature, history, feminist discourse, cultural studies, and the social sciences, Gutiérrez assumes the role of theoretical cartographer, mapping out the contours of Chicano/Chicana intellectual thought from the internal colonialism of the 1970s to postmodern criticism and performance of the 1990s. Through the prisms of gender and sexuality, he goes beneath the superficial celebrations of an imagined Chicano community united in vision, brotherhood, and *familia* to bring out (in the words of writer Rubén Martínez) the "swirls of cultural contradictions" within Aztlán's intellectual Eden.

Chicana struggles to be heard, to be taken seriously, to assume leadership, and to reclaim their histories sparked the articulation of a contemporary Chicana feminist consciousness. Gutiérrez suggests that men "initially regarded the feminist critique as an assault on their Mexican cultural past, on their power, and by implication, on their virility." But Chicana feminism was never monolithic, with representations encompassing "straight" political economy to lesbian postmodern theorizing. With an historian's eye and a poet's pen, the author finds within Chicana feminist discourses a common thread, "a story rooted in the politicization of the body."

Eschewing jargon-laden categories or answers, Gutiérrez offers his readers an ideological map of Chicana/Chicano intellectual thought from the late 1960s to the present. When teaching this essay, I challenge students to reassess essentialized notions of Chicanismo, to problematize notions of insider/outsider. The question of whose voices count and who decides reverberates throughout the text. The article elicits ranges of responses from undergraduates, particularly among Chicanas and Latinas. What starts out as "I'm a feminist (and/but) I love my mother" ends up being a thoughtful discussion of the politics of familialism. Gutiérrez not only allows students an intellectual space to create their own interpretations but gives them permission to do so.

The themes of community, patriarchy, and individualism are not dusty relics resuscitated by the author. In a 1996 Chicano studies anthology, historian Ignacio García warns of "gender nationalists" who "find the lurking 'macho' in every Chicano scholarly work." He continues: "Postmodern sectarianism—lesbian-feminism, neo-Marxism and a militant form of Latinoism—is another challenge to the field since the 1980s."[1] Such an interpretation seems curiously out of sync but articulates the sentiments held by some who consider themselves "veteranos" of the Movement. Cultural studies, queer theory, and feminist and critical race dialogics contribute to a postmodern *mestizaje* of Chicana/Chicano intellectual thought and, by extension, American studies.

In sharing research with community groups and college students and in conducting oral history interviews over the past two decades, I am still struck by questions of nomenclature which invariably arise. Why do you call yourself a Chicana? Who are Latinos? Or as cannery activist Carmen Bernal Escobar informed me early on in our 1979 interview, "You may be a Chicana, but I'm *Mexicana*." Illuminating the shading of identities among women of Mexican birth or descent speaks volumes about regional, generational, and even political orientations. The term Mexicana typically refers to immigrant women, with Mexican American signifying U.S. birth. Chicana reflects a political consciousness born of the Chicano student movement, often a generational marker for those of us who came of age during the 1960s and 1970s. Chicana/o has also been embraced by our elders and children who share in the political ideals of the movement. Some prefer regional identification such as Tejana (Texan) or Hispana (New Mexican). Spanish American is also popular in New Mexico and Colorado. Latina emphasizes a common bond with all women of Latin American origin in the United States, a politicized Pan American identity. Even racial location can be discerned by whether one favors an Iberian connection (Hispanic) or an indigenous past (Mestiza or Xicana).

Using humor as a "tool of reconstructing ways of understanding the self," lesbian comic and writer Monica Palacios articulates her multiple identities as follows:

> When I was born
> I was of Mexican-American persuasion
> Then I became Chicana
> Then I was Latina
> Then I was Hispanic

Then I was a Third World member
(my mom loved that)
Then I was a woman of color
Now I'm just an Amway dealer
And my life is happening.[2]

NOTES

1. David R. Maciel and Isidro D. Ortiz, eds., *Chicanas/Chicanos at the Crossroads: Social, Economic, and Political Change* (Tucson: University of Arizona Press, 1966).

2. Alicia Arrizón, "Monica Palacios: 'Latin Lezbo Comic,' " in *Crossroads* 31 (May 1993): 25.

KEVIN J. MUMFORD

Homosex Changes:
Race, Cultural Geography, and
the Emergence of the Gay

IN THE 1931 HOMOSEXUAL NOVEL, *STRANGE BROTHER*, WHITE AUTHOR
Blair Niles explores the world of Greenwich Village bohemians and
urban speakeasies. In many ways, Niles is critical of these sophisticated
bohemians who, in search of pleasure and excitement, go "slumming"
to the teeming underworld of Harlem. Indeed, the novel's central
character, June Westbrook, represents the stereotypical slummer: one
who admires but also objectifies the black entertainers and patrons of
the Harlem speakeasy scene. Another white character in *Strange
Brother,* Mark Thornton, receives a more sympathetic portrayal because
he is a homosexual. Raised in a small Midwestern town, Mark reads an
article in *Survey Graphic*, a leading social reform journal that featured
the burgeoning culture of Harlem. Of course, that issue of the journal
eventually was reprinted as *The New Negro*, edited by Alain Locke; it
would deeply influence a generation of African American writers and
artists. Significantly, the volume also influences Mark, who, allured by
the prospects of urban excitement, leaves rural America and sets out for
New York. After arriving, Mark discovers the homosexual scene and
the slumming areas on the periphery of Harlem. Like June, Mark
travels to Harlem to patronize the speakeasy scene. Eventually, through
sexual contacts in the Harlem library, Mark is introduced to the
underground world of black/white homosexual speakeasies. In search

American Quarterly, Vol. 48, No. 3 (September 1996) © 1996 American Studies Association of freedom, like many African Americans of the era, Mark too has made a journey to Harlem.[1]

The cultural history of the novel *Strange Brother* tells us another important story about the place of homosexuality in the urban north, providing a precedent for Mark's claim that he felt a kind of affinity with African American culture and institutions. In the early 1930s, the sociologist Ernest Burgess and his students at the University of Chicago conducted a survey of the city's rental libraries and drug stores in order to document the circulation of novels with homosexual themes. Their reports indicated that, in general, retailers "can't keep up with public demand for risque and sex books." Homosexual men, the reports indicated, read these texts as a way to escape isolation, resist prejudice, and reconstruct their sexual subjectivities. In a sociological interview, for example, one homosexual subject recalled that he had read "'Weel of Lonlieness' [*sic*] as well as 'Strange Brother.'" The young man valued these books because he "would like to live their lives."[2] Many retailers reported that *Strange Brother* was among the most widely read books that they carried. Significantly, in several rental libraries, proprietors placed *Strange Brother* and other homosexual novels in the "colored section." Thus, while Mark, a white homosexual, found affirmation and tolerance by traveling to black Harlem, urban retailers displayed novels with homosexual themes in black sections, suggesting the extent to which the borders between black and homosexual geographical spaces were blurred by clandestine crossings.[3] At the same time, these proprietors distinguished *Strange Brother* from mainstream novels not by stigmatizing it as homosexual (many did not even have a "homosexual section"), but rather by locating it within another, readily available system of social and spatial hierarchy—race. In other words, searching for a way to classify *Strange Brother*, the proprietors "racialized" the homosexual text.

The definitional power of texts versus that of subculture, the significance of urban borders, the racialization of sexuality: these issues are addressed in the following attempt to enter the long-standing historical debate on the emergence of homosexuality in the early twentieth century. Through the creative use of medical texts, official investigation documents, and personal interviews, historians have identified the decades between 1890 and 1930 as a kind of turning point in the formation of homosexuality.[4] In his influential 1983 article, "Capitalism and Gay Identity," John D'Emilio argued that in the twentieth century, the emergence of capitalism opened up new spaces for same-sex desire by accelerating the process of urbanization.[5] Freed from the constraints of small-town family life, homosexuals could socialize, make sexual contacts, and form social communities. The endurance of "Capitalism and Gay Identity" as a seminal piece speaks for itself. D'Emilio's history of the modern homosexual is based upon the experience of white men under capitalism. My essay centers the structural transformation of the Great Migration.[6]

In addition to the social structural arguments of the new social history, scholars also have researched the medical or scientific "construction" of homosexuality. Two conceptions of homosexuality competed for authority during the 1920s. According to one theory, male/male sexual desire was defined through a model of gender inversion. In this conception, male inverts—men who desired other men—appropriated the female gender cultural mode, reflecting the dominant belief that sexual being and gender role were inextricably linked. The invert's partner performed the masculine role and did not necessarily distinguish his relations with men from his relations with women.[7] George Chauncey locates the origins of the invert in working-class neighborhoods and institutions. The available evidence suggests that, at least within the medical discourse, another model of homosexuality developed. In this model, drawing on Freud's theory of perversion, the key signifier of homosexuality was not gender reversal but the object to which sexual desire was directed. The historical problem is measuring dispersal: To what extent was the emergence of the object-relations model in medical science actually dispersed and accepted among the men who desired other men? In an essay on the social history of homosexuality, Chauncey sought to qualify his earlier discursive thesis and shift interpretive emphasis to subculture, and argued for the centrality of subcultural definitions of inverts. Currently, a generation of historians are studying the sexual dimension of everyday life, through the methods of ethnographical historiography. While not ignoring discourse—by which I mean texts and rituals—the most important recent studies privilege subculture over all else. In this method, the early twentieth century represented an era of continuity, in which gender inversion, originating in working-class culture, defined homosexual desire, while emergent theories of "object choice" may have interested and influenced doctors but not sexual life on the streets of New York.[8]

My reading of Chauncey's *Gay New York,* combined with my own research, nevertheless suggests, first, that the early twentieth century was an era of sexual change and, more importantly, that the social and textual remain interrelated and reciprocal. The issue can be most clearly stated as a collegial question to the ethnographic approach: If discourse actually followed social historical developments, then what precisely causes and shapes sexual change? The point is that one can go too far in centering subcultural experience, or memory, to the detriment of discourse—to the detriment, that is, of an individuality constituted through the idiosyncratic absorption of material culture, novels, music, and films. In searching for the moments of historical transformation of homosexuality in the 1920s, then, I would not dismiss discursive events, but I would not end my historical analysis there. One answer to the question of historical causation is to suggest that both discourse (a novel like *Strange Brother*) and urban social developments (the events described in *Strange Brother*) caused the diversification of models or modes of homosexuality. The purpose of this article is to understand the ways in which "race" and African American cultural discourse figured in this transformation.

Through re-reading some documents from 1930s sociology of deviance, it is possible to provide preliminary theoretical answers to these questions of group relations and cultural interaction. In one such essay written for a seminar on "social deviance," a University of Chicago graduate student argued that the homosexual, like other social outcasts psychically injured by modern anomie, suffered from social ostracism.[9] The student's comparison was more accurate than he realized: African American urban culture, specifically black/white vice districts and institutions, directly influenced white homosexual men.

Historians have located male invert communities in several northern cities as early as the 1890s. According to sexologist Havelock Ellis, "the world of sexual inverts is, indeed, a large one in any American city." Further, "every city has its numerous meeting places: certain churches where inverts congregate; certain cafes well known for the inverted character of their patrons." Inverts gathered in clubs that, according to one observer, "were really dance-halls attached to saloons, which were presided over by [invert] waiters and musicians . . ."[10] In Chicago, reformers reported on "men who impersonate females [and] are among the vaudeville entertainers, in the saloons. Unless these men are known, it is difficult to detect their sex." A similar report stated that the clubs included "men who dress in women's clothing and women who dress in men's clothing."[11] The central distinguishing feature of invert institutions, at least to outside observers, was the creative reversal of gender roles—men behaved like women and women like men.

Some of the invert dance halls and social rituals included interracial association. According to one report, for example, invert meeting places included "certain cafes patronized by both Negroes and whites, and were [considered to be] the seat of male solicitation."[12] In 1893, Charles H. Hughes reported "that there is, in the city of Washington, D.C., an annual convocation of Negro men called the drag dance, which is an orgy of lascivious debauchery." According to Hughes, a "similar organization was lately suppressed by the police of New York city."[13] One authority on sexual disorders, after witnessing such a dance, believed that the participants were "Homosexual complexion perverts"—men who suffered from a kind of "social reverse complexion" syndrome, in which color or racial difference substituted for the gender difference in the sexual relationship. In discussing the prevalence of this disorder, the observer compared homosexual with heterosexual relations, noting that "even white women sometimes prefer colored men to white men and vice versa." In 1913, prison reformer Margaret Otis observed intense personal relations between black and white female inmates; in her nascent theory of "situational lesbianism," she argued that the difference in color substituted for gender difference. Otis refers to the white women involved with black women as "nigger lovers," suggesting the extent to which reformers understood black/white homosexual relations through reference to the taboo against black/white heterosexual relations. Likewise, one observer termed a social gathering of black and white homosexual men a "*miscegenation* dance."[14] These references to race reveal the extent to which social outsiders relied on racial difference—specifically the ideology of "miscegenation"—to conceptualize sexual attraction between people of the same gender.

Racialization was more than a matter of reformers relying on race to understand inversion. Ideologies of racial difference also shaped the subculture from within.[15] In an interview between a University of Chicago sociologist and a black homosexual, the young man recounted his earliest experiences socializing with other male inverts. Leo reported that at age 16, he had read about same-sex desire and learned that men who desired men were effeminate—a lesson that made a deep impression on him. At age 18, Leo was introduced to the sexual underworld of inverts "through a friend from Milwaukee," who invited Leo to a party: "I saw boys dance together, calling each other husband and wife, and several of them were arguing about men." Indeed, Leo's choice of terms that denoted homosexuality—words like "sissy" and "nelly"—ultimately described a kind of gender reversal.[16] One can read this evidence from both black and white participants in the invert clubs to reveal a shared language, a common set of social practices, and similar constructions of sexuality. At the same time, fragments of evidence describing black/white male homosexuality before 1900 almost always indicate that black men adopted the female role The opposite was true of black female inverts, who were seen as more manly.[17]

I want to suggest that the invert's performance of polarized gender roles—the exaggeration of the difference between the highly feminine female roles and the masculine male roles—paralleled the constructed opposition between blackness and whiteness. Miscegenation dances were, first and foremost, racial events, and yet when inverts formed black/white dances, the fundamental opposition between "races" historically central to "miscegenation" rituals probably enhanced the pleasurable opposition between gender roles within the invert culture. After 1900, many inverts gathered in "Black and Tans," which were saloons that catered primarily to black men and white women. Established in New York in the early-nineteenth century, and in Chicago in the 1870s, the Black and Tans were considered outlaw institutions because they fostered a sexual world turned upside down—with black men dancing the lead and, symbolically, on the top. Given the marginal position of the Black and Tan, it was possible for inside-out, upside-down inverts, and their potential partners, to enter some Black and Tan-style clubs and enjoy the pleasures of forbidden nightlife.

By the beginning of the 1910s, another formation of same-sex desire, distinguishable from inversion, filtered through the sexual subcultures in Chicago and New York. As the traditional historiography suggests, beginning in the 1890s, scientists and physicians reconceptualized the theory of same-sex desire from one based on a model of gender inversion to a theory that we would recognize as modern homosexuality. In the theory of inversion, the man who desired other men adopted the gender identity of a woman. This was the only way to make sense of same-sex desire. By the 1920s, physicians were likely to formulate theories of individual deviance, attributing more power to sexuality as a singular force shaping human personalities. Freudian theories of polymorphous perversity reinforced the new conception of homosexuality. With this historical separation of gender from sexuality, it was now possible for a small minority of physicians, psychologists, and sexologists to conceive of a man who desired men and who still behaved like a man. But within the subculture, as recent ethnohistories demonstrate, the older cultural tradition of gender inversion did not disappear.[18]

Whether through flamboyant bohemianism or, as I emphasize, the entrance of more black people into the city, it is possible to map the transformation of definitions of homosexuality emerging in the 1920s. The Chicago School sociologist Harvey Zorbaugh's study indicated that the bohemian section of Chicago, Towertown, included homosexual men and women. Also known as the "Village," this enclave was inhabited primarily by white homosexuals. Noting the events of a Sunday tea party, Zorbaugh observed that "there was a good deal of taking one another's arms, sitting on the arms of one another's chairs, and of throwing arms about one another's shoulders. Soon the men were fondling each other, as were the women." These were "fairies" and "lesbians." Like bohemianism in New York, Towertown bohemians constructed homosexuality as a mode of cultural rebellion in the tradition of Free Love. For the most part, these were white men and women. Indeed, as an example of racial prejudice, Zorbaugh noted that a man named "Alonzo," who claimed to be a Spaniard, was shunned by "Village" homosexuals because he was reputed to be an "octoroon." The more renowned homosexual restaurants were also predominately white. Public sex institutions—bathhouses "frequented by queers" or public toilets "notorious" for same-sex activity—were located on the predominately white North Side. But these institutions were not all-white, since African American men had occasion to travel to the North Side and to use the toilets. In addition to the bohemians, there were also the "hobos" who formed homosexual attachments, often involving age difference; while their ranks may have been interracial, the manuscripts dealing with homosexual hobos do not indicate racial background.[19] Zorbaugh did overhear a conversation between two men in a tearoom change suddenly, when "a group of 'homos' from the [predominately African American] South Side also came in." That homosexual men resided near a black neighborhood suggests the possibility of cultural interchange.[20]

Sociological interviews are more suggestive of cultural interaction within specific areas located in black neighborhoods. In his interview entitled, "My Story of Fags, Freaks, and Women Impersonators," a young black man, Walt Lewis, recalled in explicit detail his experiences with both men and women. One incident of public sex with a woman occurred in Washington Park, near Cottage Grove, deep in the heart of Chicago's Black Belt. Washington Park was also known as an area where white and black homosexual men found sexual partners.[21] In Chicago, then, homosexual men, but not lesbians, explored African American neighborhoods for public sex encounters. The few available fragments of evidence suggest that lesbians and homosexual men were more likely to socialize separately. In one Chicago report, the investigator pointed out that "there are very few lesbians and those that do come do not seem to mingle with the others."[22] Although Clark Street or Hobohemia were areas of not only black/white but also male/female interaction, the leisure institutions remained sex segregated.[23]

In New York, homosexuals congregated in several areas, including Times Square and Greenwich Village, but some also participated in the black/white vice districts in Harlem. The black gay artist, Richard Nugent, recalled his numerous visits to the Village; the black dancer, Mabel Hampton, remembered the Village as the "place where other lesbians hung out."[24] In the 1920s, the Village became a kind of urban homosexual satellite (and remains central in gay American culture) but another New York neighborhood—Harlem—should also be understood as sexually historic, even if today few gay New Yorkers socialize there. In 1927, in its special investigation, the New York vice commission known as the Committee of Fourteen revealed the existence of black/white homosexual institutions in Harlem. In their published report, the Committee made only a veiled reference to the establishments, referring to "dives" that catered to "specialized types of degeneracy and perversion," but the investigators filed detailed, sometimes sexually explicit, reports. In one, an investigator described the typical underground club: "there were the usual trappings—a large speakeasy room and four rooms for prostitution," with "liquor being served from a five gallon jug." "Couples committed acts of sexual intercourse, unashamed, in view of others." Indeed, on "one visit the investigator saw three couples in the act at the same time." However, the investigator then noted, almost as an afterthought, that in addition to black and white prostitutes and customers, there were "some fairies." It would be too much to say that the multisexual institutions were ubiquitous in the underground, or even that they were common, but it is worth noting that the investigator was not particularly shocked or surprised by the presence of homosexuals, making only a brief statement buried underneath a descriptive paragraph.[25]

In whatever matter they were described, the speakeasies were almost always portrayed as the most immoral and degenerate of leisure institutions. I argue that it was largely because of their location within African American neighborhoods—and because of the presence of black/white mixing—that the speakeasies were stigmatized. To that extent, homosexuality anointed rather than fundamentally constituted the status of the speakeasies as outlaw institutions. For the most part, the colored clubs were located in Harlem, in the area from 126th Street to 152nd Street between Fifth and St. Nicholas Avenues, with a few in Brooklyn.[26] In Chicago, they were located in the "Bright Lights" district, a black neighborhood located between 33rd and 35th Streets, along State Street. Some were black/white clubs, catering to black and white, heterosexual and homosexual, patrons. The investigator also classified some clubs as colored, though white homosexuals also patronized these establishments. One Committee of Fourteen file contained reports of approximately 400 investigations, of which approximately eighty were classified "white and colored" and an additional sixty were considered "colored." The remainder were exclusively white clubs. Reports of homosexuality occurred most often in the colored clubs, and then in the colored and white establishments, while none of the reports within this folder indicated the presence of homosexuality in the "white" speakeasies.[27] To draw a non-systematic, tentative conclusion regarding the investigations into New York sex districts: where African Americans socialized, New York investigators most often identified explicit homosexuality.

From the perspective of the investigators, all black/white mixing was immoral, but some investigators seemed especially disturbed by the presence of same-sex commingling or intimacy. Investigators characterized the homosexual clubs as the "worst." In the margins of one report, the New York investigator noted in pencil: "Very Bad." Another report opened with the familiar statement: "This place is very disreputable." Like the clubs that included black homosexual men, the lesbian clubs were also viewed as immoral. For instance, one investigator wrote that he was introduced to a "Pussy Party," located in a basement where "various forms of sex perversion [were] committed." Near the top of the entry, his penciled notation reads: "Very Bad."[28]

Unlike in Chicago, where the admittedly small body of evidence indicates sex segregation, New York speakeasies frequently welcomed both men and women.[29] While there were the all-male clubs, in which women were not permitted to enter, most New York speakeasies included women and men.[30] Even at a so-called "women's party," in which lesbians performed various sexual acts on each other, there were some men in attendance. Outside the speakeasies, as well, black lesbians socialized with men, at rent parties and buffet flats. Mabel Hampton remembered a series of parties given by A'Leila Walker; she attended one party with a white friend, and witnessed homosexual men and women conversing, dancing, and sometimes engaging in sexual activity. The major exception to the rule that lesbians mixed with homosexuals seems to have been the "sex circuses," in which lesbians often engaged in sexual relations.[31] In general, there were fewer separate lesbian institutions than separate male homosexual institutions, probably because women had less access to the resources necessary both to own and to patronize clubs.

If one were to make a kind of speculative historical thesis about the changing nature of marginal, or underground, sexual institutions, then it would be that the 1890s invert institutions were predominately male but that, in Prohibition-era speakeasies, lesbians were active participants in clubs located in African American geographical spaces. My reading of the sources, as well as my historical interests, point to a central characteristic of the underground speakeasy: the diversity of patrons. A rare but telling observation of a nightclub makes the point: "Every night we find the place crowded with both races, the black and the white, both types of lovers, the homo and heterosexual."[32] Some of these underground speakeasies included Chinese and Filipino men (who, according to the evidence, were heterosexual). This multitude of differences—racial, gender, sexual, ethnic—helped to create a speakeasy culture of fluidity that sharply contrasted with the ritualized rigidity of gender or racial dichotomy characteristic of the old-style Black and Tan and invert drag dance. The earlier invert rituals persisted into the 1920s—Langston Hughes termed them the "Spectacles in Color"—but, in this instance, gender reversal and cross-dressing were

less the direct expression of a thriving subculture and more a performance for white tourists in search of the exciting and exotic. In the "new"
clubs, inversion was only part of the story—one among several options
of erotic pleasure.[33]

Drag dances, cross-dressing, sex inversion did not, of course,
disappear from the 1920s speakeasy. Rather, in the clubs, on the
margins, "sexual inverts" were joined by homosexual men and women
who did not necessarily privilege gender—specifically the cultural
accoutrements of manhood and womanhood—as the mode through
which to express sexual desire. The point I am making is far outside
current theorizing, and cannot be supported with extensive evidence,
but the available sources, combined with my critical position, prompt
me to argue for a discursive rupture in the definitional structure of
sexual desire that originated in the urban matrix of georgraphical
transformation, border crossings, and cultural interchange.

One indication of the softening of the rigid inversion model and the
diversification of modes of sexual expression is found in the reports
written by virtual insiders, the vice investigators. From the perspective
of the investigators, cross-dressing itself did not serve as the privileged
signifier of homosexuality. In classifying a given patron's sexuality, an
investigator surely would label as homosexual any man dressed as a
woman; but the investigator classified a man as homosexual, however
he dressed, whatever his comportment, when he exhibited sexual
attraction toward another man. If there was cross-dressing—and there
probably was—in sharp contrast to the witnesses of turn-of-the-century
invert rituals, 1920s vice investigators did not find the practice especially notable. The underground speakeasies most often investigated
were not apparently popular among sex inverts, and "sexual behavior"
rather than gender performance was an increasingly popular way to
express intimate desire.

Urban sociologists in the field reported examples of homosexual
men who actually behaved like "men." These scholars were now more
likely to employ a popularized version of Freud to describe the same-
sex phenomena. Certainly the tradition of inversion persisted—at least
to the extent that some social scientists believed that the homosexual
personality was "effeminate"—but now gender inversion was but one
among several theories of same-sex desire. In a discussion of homosexuals and speakeasies, a University of Chicago graduate student
pointed to a club "located in the Negro district of the south side where

a cabaret of the black and tan variety operates mainly for their [homosexuals'] benefit." In his view, in such clubs "the social taboos of a conventional society have been raised and the repressed individual can find full expression for those smoldering desires burning within."[34] Rather than gendered artifice, homosexuality is an overwhelming sexual instinct. Throughout his essay, the student draws on concepts like "polymorphous perversity," "instinctive craving," and "neurotic state" to make sense of his observations of black and white homosexual men dancing at a Black and Tan. The student's relatively novel conception of Freudianism—the opposition between society and individual desire, the language of "repression" and "expression"—mark this description of homosexuality as decidedly more modern than the racialized discourse of miscegenation employed by the authorities who studied inversion. But the significance of race did not decline with the rise of Freudianism. For the point of the graduate student's Freudian description was to suggest that a black context—a "black and tan" cabaret in a "Negro district"—was critical to releasing the "internalized inhibitions of civilization." Because they were the most marginalized of dance clubs, the Black and Tans tolerated stigmatized behavior, providing a context in which homosexual men and women could experience and perform their desires. Rather than a world turned upside-down, I want to suggest, the Black and Tan speakeasy attempted to offer a place in which there were no prohibitions or inhibitions. Indeed, the above description ultimately reveals the extent to which Freudianism in America relied on a particular racialized conception of the id. Some black men probably accepted the Freudian theories. In his correspondence, gay black social worker Glen Carrington sometimes invoked Freudianism, particularly the drive theory of homosexual desire.[35] Nevertheless, psychological concepts like internal drives and sex instinct were associated with the primitive. By the 1920s, as Ann Douglas demonstrates, the primitive in turn had become closely linked to the construction of black sexuality.[36] By absorbing black sexuality in the vice districts, the figure of the feminized (sexually impotent) invert was, in effect, sexualized—transformed into the modern homosexual, with a powerful, if pathological, erotic instinct.

The contacts between African Americans and homosexuals in speakeasies constituted direct cultural exchange through the creation of sexualized social practices. The reports can be read to suggest that in the diverse, fluid context of the speakeasy the single unifying theme was explicit sexuality. In one speakeasy, for instance, the investigator reported that "two men were dancing with each other kissing and sucking tongues." In another club, an investigator observed, the "women were dancing with each other, imitating the motions of sexual intercourse and the men were dancing with each other, all indecently." Another report on an all-black speakeasy indicated that "the women were dancing with one another and going through the motions of copulation, and the men were dancing with one another."[37] Patrons probably danced the "Black Bottom" or the "Turkey Trot"—dances brought by African Americans from the south that circulated in a variety of northern urban venues—but the underground homosexual speakeasy versions were sexualized. These reports support the thesis that African American cultural practices, especially dance, shaped homosexuality not in some abstract, indistinct way, but directly through the communal molding of dance forms that were often indistinguishable from sexual intercourse.[38] It does not require a huge leap of faith to believe that this public, interactive construction of sexualized dance extended its influence off the dance floor, choreographing the supposedly "private" performance of sexual intercourse.[39]

The music of the speakeasy reinforced the sexualized dancing. As the historian Eric Garber has demonstrated, black blues singers, including Gladys Bentley, Alberta Hunter, George Hanna, and Ma Rainey, performed songs with sexually explicit lyrics, featuring terms like "sissy" and "bulldagger." Some of the lyrics hinted at the fluidity of sexual desire: "if you can't bring me a woman, bring me a sissy man."[40] Lyrics dealing with women suggested the superiority of lesbian sexual practices, entreating men, for example, to perform oral sex. Lillian Faderman interprets several of the blues songs as nascent radical lesbian texts, which proclaim the superiority of lesbianism. In a sense, homosexual themes were common among certain blues lyrics, but it would be wrong to deduce from their frankness that the blues reflected a broad acceptance of homosexuality in African American neighborhoods. Faderman relies on evidence of Harlem lesbians who received marriage licenses and lived as married couples, but the countervailing evidence of antivice rhetoric among black reformers and religious leaders suggests that genuine tolerance was rare. Moreover, as indicated, the majority of Harlem clubs that catered to homosexuals were deeply marginalized, frequently located in tenement apartments. The more visible and accessible a Harlem club became, it seems, the more heterosexual its patrons. The homosexual speakeasies were hypervigilant for good reason: they feared exposure and expulsion. Nevertheless, the clubs were located in Harlem, and not in white neighborhoods. This could represent the relative inability of black Harlemites to evict the institutions they viewed as harmful; or the presence of clubs in Harlem could suggest a greater acceptance of the marginalized.[41]

Still, with titles such as "Boy in the Boat," the songs left little to the imagination. But, of course, that was the point: like speakeasy dances, African American songs helped to create the performance and experience of same-gender sexual relations. So central was the institutional culture of the speakeasy to the "practices" of homosexuality that it shaped white homosexual life outside of the clubs. For example, in the 1930s, Earl Bruce, a University of Chicago graduate student, studied the patterns of behavior among white homosexual men at a private party, at which the men attempted to recreate the speakeasy scene. According to Bruce, "When we arrived at the apartment, one of the homosexuals sent out for a gallon of beer and a few pints of whiskey." The ages of the members ranged from twenty-six to thirty-seven. According to Bruce "the owner of the apartment, a homosexual about 25 years of age, runs a small dancing school downtown. Many of his pupils are homosexual." At the party a "Mr J. [the host] played a number of pornographic records sung by some Negro entertainers; a homosexual theme ran through the lyrics." These homosexual men could be found "swaying to the music of a colored jazz orchestra," providing the "unconventional sight" of "two young men in street clothes dancing together, cheek to cheek."[42] During interviews, white homosexual men revealed not only that they liked to dance, but also that they "like music, singers, especially negro singers."[43] Mabel Hampton also noted the significance of private parties, particularly because the gatherings were interracial. Of course, in the background of the typical gathering one could hear "jazz"—a word that not only denoted black music, but also, in the parlance of some African Americans, prostitutes, and homosexuals, jazz meant sexual intercourse.[44]

The common usage of jazz among inhabitants of the urban sexual margins suggests the historical significance of the circulation and exchange of cultural forms. Because of the racial segregation of vice, African Americans represented the primary group influencing the fundamental culture of the vice districts. Because of social repression, some stigmatized white groups temporarily inhabited these districts. Sharing space in the speakeasies resulted in shared music, dance, and language. In my work, I have chosen African American spaces as sites for historical exploration, so my findings tend to emphasize the ways in which black culture influenced, indeed constituted, groups who socialized within these marginal zones. Clearly, however, white homosexual culture also constituted black homosexuality and, perhaps, influenced African American heterosexuality in general. Thus, sociological interviews with African American men often indicate that their earliest homosexual experiences were with white men, who were already initiated into a world of same-sex desire.[45]

In any case, as several scholars have argued, Freudian theories of homosexuality detached gender from sexuality and privileged sexuality as a discrete, fundamentally determinative aspect of the human psyche.[46] Freud supplied the formal modern theory of homosexuality. Yet, within African American neighborhoods, and within the outlaw tenement clubs, the carefully constructed languages, dances, and music interacted with discourses of "perversion" circulating in the mainstream. Text and context, performance and practice, combined to create a fledgling version of modern homosexuality.

To return to the story of black homosexuals: it would be wrong to leave the impression that these homosexual men and women lived in some sort of urban utopia. A brief, concluding analysis of Wallace Thurman, probably the most gifted writer of the Harlem Renaissance, makes the point. Wallace Thurman grew up in Salt Lake City, Utah, attended the University of Southern California, and after reading about the city, moved to Harlem in 1925. Soon after arriving, Thurman found himself virtually alone, with few resources, and unemployed. Writing about himself in the third person, Thurman recounted his initial hardship to William Rapp, a close friend: "he [Thurman] had a little stake which has soon gone. He found no job. He had no room rent and was hungry." Thurman secured a job as an elevator man, but then lost the position. That day "he returned homeward." According to Thurman's recollection, "At 135th St. he got off the subway, and feeling nature's call went into the toilet. There was a man loitering in there. The man spoke." At this point in the letter, at precisely the moment when the homosexual act surfaces, Thurman switches from the third to the first person. Thurman wrote: "He did more than speak, making me know what his game was. I laughed. He offered me two dollars. I accepted." At some point during the sexual exchange, police men burst out of a porter's mop closet, and arrested the two men. Thurman found himself in night court. He was fined twenty-five dollars. At this point, in recounting the story, Thurman draws a sharp distinction between himself and the man who propositioned him. According to Thurman, the man was a "Fifth Avenue hair dresser," who had been previously arrested for approaching men in bathrooms.[47]

Over and again, throughout his correspondence, Thurman denies his allegations. His personal papers and literary inclinations suggest that Thurman was a pioneer of the black gay imagination. As Thurman proclaimed, "there was certainly no evidence therein that I was homosexual." His strident denials were not sufficient to save his reputation. "You can also imagine with what relish a certain group of Negroes in Harlem received and relayed the news that I was a homo."[48]

Seven years after his arrest for the homosexual incident, Wallace Thurman published a roman à clef of the Harlem Renaissance, entitled *Infants of the Spring*.[49] The novel, more than any other of the several works about Harlem in the 1920s, centered on black/white sexual relations. Indeed, the central black character, Raymond, becomes enamored with the central white character, Stephen (a Swedish man visiting Harlem for the first time). Raymond believes that their relationship can transcend race: "There was something delightfully naive, and childlike, about their frankly acknowledged affection for one another. Like children, they seemed to be totally unconscious of their racial difference." Ultimately, however, Stephen begins dating two black women, then abandons Raymond, and eventually his admiration for Harlem devolves into a crude racism.[50] Thurman's *Infants of the Spring* is the first published novel by an African American writer that portrays black/white homosexual relations, and perhaps more significantly, the depths and expression of sexual racism.

In the marginal geographies of black/white vice districts, the fictional character whom I discussed in the opening of the essay, Mark Thornton, would have read and appreciated Wallace Thurman's novels about Harlem nightlife and homosexuality. And, certainly, Thurman could have had a brief liason with an urban explorer like Mark in a Harlem speakeasy or subway toilet. The story of their liasons suggest the complex phenomenon—social structural, ethnographic, discursive, intersubjective—that variously intersect to create American culture.

NOTES

The author wishes to thank Herman Gray, Michael Cowan, Scott Bravmann, the audiences of the history department at the University of California at Berkeley, the cultural studies reading group at the University of California at Santa Cruz, and the American studies department at the University of Minnesota.

1. Blair Niles, *Strange Brother* (1931; London, 1990).

2. "Homosexual Interview," Ernest Burgess Collection, Regenstein Library, University of Chicago, box 127, folder 8. Ernest Burgess headed the study of the social deviance at the University of Chicago throughout the 1920s and 1930s. An obsessive researcher, Burgess saved thousands of documents, ranging from his research notes to essays he assigned graduate students. Included in his collection are boxes of material regarding homosexuality, which, interestingly, he did not use in a published work, probably because of the stigma associated with the study of same sex desire.

3. Although the *New York Times* reviewed fourteen of Niles's previous novels, they refused to review *Strange Brother*, probably because of its sympathetic treatment of homosexuality. See Jonathan Ned Katz, *Gay/Lesbian Almanac: A New Documentary* (New York, 1983), 468; on survey of rental libraries, see Burgess Collection, mss., box 89, folder 11.

4. An excellent summary and conceptualization of the medical literature is Katz, *Gay/Lesbian Almanac*, 137–74; Kenneth Plummer, ed., *Making of the Modern Homosexual* (London, 1981).

5. D'Emilio's essay was first published in Ann Snitow, Christine Stansell, and Sharon Thompson, eds., *Powers of Desire: The Politics of Sexuality* (New York, 1983), 100–113; it has been reprinted in numerous anthologies, but never revised. See introductory note in John D'Emilio, *Making Trouble: Essays on Gay History, Politics, and the University* (New York, 1992), 3; this theory forms the theoretical structure for John D'Emilio and Estelle B. Freedman, *Intimate. Matters: A History of Sexuality in America* (New York, 1988).

6. For a critique of D'Emilio's racial exclusion, see Scott Bravmann, "Telling Histories: Rethinking the Lesbian and Gay historical Imagination," *Out/Look* 8 (spring 1990): 68–74; D'Emilio, "Capitalism and Gay Identity," 9.

7. Michel Foucault, *The History of Sexuality, Volume I, An Introduction*, trans. Robert Hurley (New York, 1978); George Chauncey Jr., "From Sexual Inversion to Homosexuality: Medicine and the Changing Conceptualization of Female Deviance," in Kathy Peiss and Christina Simmons, eds., *Passion and Power*, 87–117; Jeffrey Weeks, *Coming Out: Homosexual Politics in Britain From the Nineteenth Century* (London, 1978).

8. Chauncey, "From Sexual Inversion to Homosexuality," 93–98; Foucault, *History of Sexuality, Volume I*; on inverts, George Chauncey, Jr., "Christian Brotherhood or Sexual Perversion? Homosexual Identities and the Construction of Sexual Boundaries in the World War I Era," in *Hidden from History: Reclaiming the Gay and Lesbian Past*, ed. Martin Duberman, Martha Vicinus, and George Chauncey, Jr. (New York, 1991), 294–317. The finest study of the discourse/community issue is Lisa Duggan's analysis of narratives and lesbian subjectivity, which combines a discussion of a lesbian murder trial and the popular press with a discussion of sexology. See Lisa Duggan, "The Trials of Alice Mitchell: Sensationalism, Sexology, and the Lesbian Subject in Turn-of-the-Century America," *Signs* 18 (summer 1993): 791–815.

9. The pioneering theoretical essay that questions the hegemony of gender analysis

is Gayle Rubin's "Thinking Sex: Notes for a Radical Theory of the Politics of Sexuality," in *The Lesbian and Gay Studies Reader,* ed. Henry Abelove, Michele Aina Barale, and David M. Halperin (New York, 1993), 3–44; Burgess Papers, ca. 1930s, box 145, file 10.

10. Greg Sprague, "On the 'Gay Side' of Town: The Nature and Structure of Male Homosexuality in Chicago, 1890–1935," 7; Katz, *Gay American History,* 80–81.

11. The Vice Commission of Chicago, *The Social Evil in Chicago* (Chicago, 1911), 127; Havelock Ellis quoted in Katz, *Gay American History* (New York, 1976), 80–81.

12. Katz, *Gay/Lesbian Almanac,* 307.

13. Quoted in Katz, *Gay American History,* 66–67.

14. Greg Sprague, "On the Gay Side of Town," 13–15; Margaret Otis, "A Perversion Not Commonly Noted," *Journal of Abnormal Psychology* 8 (1913): 113–17; Katz, *Gay American History,* 75.

15. Thus in a discussion of public sexual activity, one Washington D.C. authority reported that "under the very shadow on the White House," one could find inverts searching for partners. "Both white and black were represented among these moral hermaphrodites, but the majority of them were negroes." See Katz, *Gay/Lesbian Almanac,* 234. William Jones argues that in Washington D.C., commercial amusements and, presumably, sexual relations were strictly segregated. This was not the case for same-sex relations, as much of the evidence of Washington D.C. indicates extensive racial mixing. See William H. Jones, *Commercial Amusements Among Negroes in Washington D.C.* (Washington D.C., 1927).

16. "Leo," Burgess Collection, box 98, folder 11, 1, 12–15.

17. Again see Katz, *Gay American History,* 66–67, 75; Sprague, "On the Gay Side of Town," 13–15; Katz, *Gay American History,* 101–2; also see George Henry, *Sex Variants: A Study of Homosexual Patterns,* vol. 1 (New York, 1941), 350–51, 425–26, 438–45.

18. George Chauncey, Jr., "From Sexual Inversion to Homosexuality: Medicine and the Changing Conceptualization of Female Deviance," in *Passion and Power: Sexuality and History,* ed. Kathy Peiss and Christina Simmons (Philadelphia, 1989), 93–98.

19. On the unique sexual practices of the hobo subculture, see interview with J. P. Smith, 13 Oct., 1934, Burgess Collection, box 134, folder 2, 9 pp.; also see Sprague, "On the Gay Side of Town," 15–16.

20. Harvey Warren Zorbaugh, *The Gold Coast and the Slum* (1929; Chicago, 1976), 96, 102, 100; quoted in Sprague, "On the Gay Side of Town," 19; The corner of Randolph and State Streets, near the Navy base, was another site of public sex activity, particularly among sailors who solicited "fairies" for money. See Burgess Collection, 29 Jun. 1933, location unknown.

21. "My Story of Fags, Freaks and Women Impersonators by Walt Lewis," Burgess Collection, mss., box 98, file 11, 2; quoted in Sprague, "On the Gay Side of Town," 20; "Mr. K.," Burgess Collection, mss., box 98, file 11.

22. Burgess Collection, mss., 21 June 1928, box 145, folder 10; virtually all of the literature on lesbianism supports the thesis of separate socialization, which, therefore, makes my findings on Harlem cross-gender social institutions all the more significant. See Lillian Faderman, *Odd Girls and Twilight Lovers: A History of Lesbian Life in Twentieth-Century America* (New York, 1992).

23. Katz, *Gay American History,* 76–77; Katz, *Gay/Lesbian Almanac,* 307.

24. Mabel Hampton, interview five, with the kind permission of Joan Nestle.

25. Committee of Fourteen, Investigator Report, 21 June 1928, box 85.

26. Committee of Fourteen, mss., 8 Jun. 1928, box 37; Committee of Fourteen, mss., 16 May 1928, box 37; *Annual Report of the Committee of Fourteen* (1928), 31–34.

27. Committee of Fourteen, Investigator Report, 1928, box 37.

28. Committee of Fourteen, Investigator Report, 8 June 1928, box 37.

29. An investigator reported that "in thirteen night clubs and speakeasies, there were fourteen homo-sexual of both sexes observed." Committee of Fourteen, mss., Investigator Report, box 37.

30. Committee of Fourteen, mss., 1928, box 85.

31. Faderman, *Odd Girls and Twilight Lovers*, 76; "Sex Circuses" were often discussed in connection with homosexuals and lesbians, but an interview with a young black men about the sexual underground of Chicago reveals that there were also heterosexual "sex circuses." See "My Story of Fags, Freaks and Women Impersonators by Walt Lewis," Burgess Collection, box 98, file 11; on lesbian circuses, see Eric Garber, "A Spectacle in Color: The Lesbian and Gay Subculture of Jazz Age Harlem," in *Hidden from History*, 322–23.

32. Burgess Collection, box 121, folder 6. The black gay artist, Richard Nugent, pointed out that not only ethnic difference, but also class diversity was a feature of some establishments. He recalled a certain club where men could find "rough trade." See Garber, "Spectacle in Color," 323.

33. Langston Hughes, *The Big Sea: An Autobiography* (1940; New York, 1986), 273.

34. Burgess Collection, box 127, folder 8; The German Freudian psychoanalyst, Wilhelm Stekel, was influential in American discussions of sexuality. See, for instance, Wilhelm Stekel, *Impotence in the Male*, 2 vols. (New York, 1927), including his detailed discussion of homosexuality, in Ibid., vol. 2, chaps. 18, 20.

35. Glen Carrington Papers, correspondence from Glen Carrington, to David, 8 Feb. 1926, box 5.

36. For an important discussion of Freud, race, and urban culture, see Ann Douglas, *Terrible Honesty: Mongrel Manhattan in the 1920s* (New York, 1995), 95–97.

37. Committee of Fourteen, Investigator Report, box 36 (25 May 1928); Committee of Fourteen, Investigator Report, n.d., box 37; also "pervert practices" in majority heterosexual black/white speakeasy, Committee of Fourteen, mss., Investigator Report, box 36, "Lenox Avenue Club," investigated in February, March, June, 1928.

38. Committee of Fourteen, Investigator Report, 28 May 1928; box 36; Committee of Fourteen, Investigator Report, 8 June 1928, box 37; investigators reported sexualized dance in heterosexual speakeasies as well, Committee of Fourteen, Old Kid Morris Dance Hall, 22 June 1928. There are limitations of the evidence here: we do not know the precise movements of each dance.

39. Lynne Fauley Emery, *Black Dance in the United States From 1619 to 1970* (Palo Alto, Calif., 1972); Katrina Hazzard-Gordon, *Jookin': The Rise of Social Dance Formations in African-American Culture* (Philadelphia, 1990).

40. See Eric Garber, "T'Ain't Nobody's Business: Homosexuality in 1920s Harlem," in *Black Men, White Men, A Gay Anthology*, ed. Michael J. Smith (San Francisco, 1983), 7–16; Garber, "A Spectacle in Color," 320.

41. Faderman, *Odd Girls and Twilight Lovers*, 76–78; Garber, "T'Ain't Nobody's Business," 7–16; Garber, "A Spectacle in Color," 320.

42. "Observations by Earle Bruce," Burgess Collection, box 127, file 8.

43. "Harold, age twenty-one," Burgess Collection, box 127, folder 8, 5.

44. M. Hampton, Joan Nestle's possession, interview 5; for use by a black man in a

homosexual context, see "My Story of Fags, Freaks and Women Impersonators by Walt Lewis," Burgess Collection, box 98, file 11, 1; for use by white prostitutes, see Chicago Committee of Fifteen, Investigator Manuscripts, 12:340–41.

45. "My Story of Fags," Burgess Collection, box 98, file 11; "Lester," Burgess Collection, box 98, file 11; "Leo," ca. 1930s, Burgess Collection, box 98, file 11.

46. Chauncey, "From Sexual Inversion to Homosexuality," 93–98; Foucault, *History of Sexuality, Volume I*; on inverts, George Chauncey, Jr., "Christian Brotherhood or Sexual Perversion? Homosexual Identities and the Construction of Sexual Boundaries in the World War I Era," in Duberman, *Hidden From History*, 294–317.

47. Wallace Thurman to William Rapp, ca. 1926, James Weldon Johnson Collection, Beineke Library, Yale University, box 1, file 7.

48. Wallace Thurman to William Rapp, 1 June 1929, James Weldon Johnson Collection, box 1, file 7; Wallace Thurman to William Rapp, ca. 1926, James Weldon Johnson Collection, box 1, file 7; on his divorce and marriage, Wallace Thurman to Claude McKay, 4 Oct. 1928, James Weldon Johnson Collection, box 5.

49. Wallace Thurman, *Infants of the Spring* (1932; Boston, 1992).

50. Ibid., 34.

Robert K. Martin

Although it remains convenient to think of the 1969 Stonewall riots as a turning point, as a moment of resistance that created community, focus on the riots as a trope for the "new" homosexuality can in turn lead to unfortunate simplifications. Part of the convenience of the "Stonewall" trope, apart from the name itself and its echoes, comes from the way it identifies homosexuality as a construct of homosexuals, and not of doctors and sociologists. At the same time "Stonewall" assumes American hegemony, it also assumes that what happened in New York is what happened in Amsterdam or Stockholm (or even Boston) and thus erases local history in the name of what one might have thought of as a *grand récit*. History does not begin at Stonewall, and any portrait one can draw of Stonewall, no matter how inclusive, will remain partial.

The book that made the Stonewall narrative impossible is George Chauncey's *Gay New York* (New York: Basic Books, 1994). Chauncey's masterly work, a tribute to scholarship and cultural investigation, begins by asserting that "the gay world that flourished before World War II has been almost entirely forgotten" (1) and then proceeds to document the magnitude of that act of collective forgetting. Precisely why the 1890s should mark the beginning of a new subculture is still a matter of dispute; many critics, including myself, remain skeptical about any view that begins so late and seems to portray a narrative so different from that in Europe (the Wilde trial in 1895 may help constitute the homosexual but it also responds to what was seen as the threat of a new taxonomy). Understanding the prehistories of homosexuality, from the Molly houses of the eighteenth century to Stonewall, makes possible a more complex and multiple history, one that is careful in its assertion of a gay culture when there may indeed be many, overlapping cultures.

Early accounts of a homosexual culture were most often blind to the role of race. One of the merits of Kevin Mumford's challenging and intelligent essay is its attention to the ways in which Harlem of the 1920s not only provided a space for homosexual life but also charted a connection between the racial and the sexual. Mumford argues for a direct relation between African American culture and gay life—for instance suggesting that African American dance "shaped homosexuality . . . directly." Mumford enters into the debate over the role of discourse in sexual (or other) practices. Where Chauncey makes very little use of literary sources, deriving much of his evidence from interviews and court records, Mumford's essay is framed by literary texts. His position mediates between the extremes of the debate: for him, "the social and textual remain interrelated and reciprocal."

Current work in the histories of sexuality concentrates on public space, on the visibility of sexual minorities in spaces they create or have assigned to them. This leads to important work in local history at the same time that it interestingly confirms Foucault's notion of a counter-discourse: the "gay ghetto" both liberates and forms identity *and* controls deviance. Unless one adopts a flexible notion of public space, however, there may be a built-in but neglected factor of class. That is, the public space of the bars or of cruising may not be central to the lives of middle and upper middle class gays in the same way that it is to the working class. *La vie Bohème* may be a performance for some; it is home for others. A recent eccentric and brilliant study, Douglass Shand-Tucci's *Boston Bohemia* (vol. 1 of *Ralph Adams Cram: Life and Architecture* [Amherst: University of Massachusetts Press, 1995]), traces a homosexual culture that is focused both on a Beacon Hill street (Pinckney) and a church (The Advent). Boston may indeed be a very different site from New York, but it seems fair to assume that a study of the mosaic of homosexual lives and ideologies would need to incorporate, as Shand-Tucci does, the role played by Anglo-Catholicism. There was a time when, if one did not know the location of a gay bar in a strange city, one could always make the right connections at coffee after High Mass at the local High Church parish. That such evidence is often neglected is due, in part, to an assumption of current social patterns and thus a failure to historicize adequately.

Mumford obliges us to come to terms with the fact that most histories of gay culture have been histories of gay white male culture posing as universal history. His account of *Strange Brother* suggests that it was possible for the white American to be transformed by reading *The New Negro* and hence "make [his] journey to Harlem." This is a fascinating scene of reading that may recall Stephen Gordon in her father's library in Radclyffe Hall's *The Well of Loneliness* (New York: Covici Friede, 1928). Harlem no doubt did exert a siren call, offering an entrée into a more open life in Prohibition era America. But what Mark discovers in *Strange Brother* is "the homosexual scene and the slumming areas." How can we tell the story of gay Harlem without the wealthy white slummers, especially in a text by a white and presumably heterosexual woman? How can one avoid a voyeurism that reconstitutes, if in different terms, the objectification of the other? Our accounts of gay Harlem come as an important challenge to received notions of gay history, complicating, even contradicting, them. They need to be situated in a larger context of social history and Orientalism. Works such as *Strange Brother* or Carl Van Vechten's *Nigger Heaven* (New York: Knopf, 1926) are travel narratives and part of a tradition of sexual ethnography. To say this is not to condemn them, merely to remind us of the need for a complex model of social interaction and of the permeable boundaries of desire and identity in the constitution of selves. Mumford's essay asks us to look more carefully.

K. SCOTT WONG

The Transformation of Culture:
Three Chinese Views of America

FOR THE PAST FIFTY YEARS, AMERICAN HISTORICAL SCHOLARSHIP documenting the Chinese presence in the United States has focused largely on various aspects of the anti-Chinese movement, often paying more attention to the "excluders" than the "excluded." This obvious trend in the historiographical record prompted Roger Daniels in 1966 to write, "Other immigrant groups were celebrated for what they had accomplished; Orientals were important for what was done to them."[1] Currently, despite a growing body of literature on Chinese American labor and legal history and Asian American literary criticism, little scholarship has appeared that gives voice to the Chinese in America, thus impeding the development of a Chinese American intellectual or cultural history.[2]

Ironically, the politics surrounding the development of Asian American studies has contributed to this trend. Asian Americans, long considered perpetual foreigners, rightfully sought to claim themselves as Americans, full participants in American democratic society, unquestionably deserving of the respect and privileges that accompany membership in the American polity. For Asian American scholars and activists, however, the cost of this strategy often meant distancing themselves from their historical ties to Asia. By focusing primarily on the American perspective of the Asian American experience, the Asian voice has often been neglected. In an article published in 1991, Sucheta

Mazumdar challenged Asian American scholars to recontextualize their work so that it included a broader, more international perspective. She wrote, "Asian American Studies has been located within the context of American Studies and stripped of its international links. . . . To isolate Asian American history from its international underpinnings, to abstract it from the global context of capital and labor migration, is to distort this history."[3] This essay, using both Chinese- and English-language sources, attempts to respond to this challenge. Although not rooted in the capital and labor migration context of which Mazumdar spoke, it seeks to widen the range of Chinese American studies by exploring the links between Chinese and Chinese American intellectual and cultural history. More to the point, a study of this kind can contribute to the ongoing internationalization of Asian American and American studies.

This essay examines three Chinese perceptions of American culture during a time of social transformation in China, when many Chinese intellectuals looked to the United States as a model for modernization and an ally against European imperialism. Specifically, it utilizes Chinese representations of George Washington, the travel diary of Liang Qichao (1873–1929) published in 1904, and the personal memoirs of Yung Wing (1828–1912). These three views of America reflect a developing understanding of American society on the part of the Chinese as each one comes closer to America spatially, in the amount of time spent in this country, and in their appreciation and appropriation of American culture. These examples also disclose a growing sense of how Chinese intellectuals and political reformers were influenced by what they found in the United States and its attendant culture, thus revealing that the Chinese presence in America had a mutually transformative effect on both Chinese and Americans. Not only was the American landscape transformed through Chinese labor while American immigration policy became increasingly racialized and class biased through the passage of exclusionary legislation enacted against Chinese immigrants, the Chinese experience in America also had an important cultural impact on the Chinese, similar to what Mary Louise Pratt terms *transculturation*. She defines this term as the process whereby "subordinated or marginal groups select and invent from materials transmitted to them by a dominant or metropolitan culture."[4] The examples of Chinese perceptions of George Washington, Liang Qichao's views of the Chinese in San Francisco, and Yung Wing's vision of the salvational qualities of an American education speak eloquently of the process of cultural borrowing, adaptation, and transformation. By encountering a variety of "Others," in the United States, these Chinese intellectuals, political reformers, and diplomats came to reevaluate their Sinocentrism and thereby laid the foundations for an early Chinese American cultural outlook, which, during this period, was a blend of Chinese and Western social and political values.

Research approaches that can give voice to the Chinese immigrant experience in America are often determined by the availability of sources. Social historians in the field have had to rely mainly on records kept by government agencies (federal, state, and local archives), federal and state hearings on Chinese immigration, and journalistic impressions of the Chinese community, almost always written by authors hostile to the Chinese or, at best, those written from an Orientalist perspective. When using sources written by the Chinese, in either the Chinese or English language, there is yet another set of problems to confront. Because only a small segment of the Chinese population received a formal education, those who learned to read and write well were in a minority, and those fluent in both Chinese and English were even fewer. Most important, those who wrote well enough, had the leisure time to write essays and keep journals, and had the connections to publish them were a select few. Therefore, the vast majority of textual sources surviving from this period come from a small, scholarly elite. It was through their hands that the received textual tradition passed, thus shaping the body of documents available to modern scholars and reflecting the values and sensibilities of this privileged segment of Chinese society. Until contemporary scholars uncover a sizable cache of reliable documents (letters, journals, pamphlets) that reflect the views of Chinese peasants in Guangdong (the region of China from which most pre-1965 Chinese immigrants came), early Chinese laborers, and the various residents of Chinatown, historians of Chinese America are largely restricted to writings from this Chinese elite. Even the extant writings that supposedly speak for the merchant class in Chinatown during this period should be considered elite, as they represent the literate class of the community and usually reflect the traditional elite Chinese values embedded in Confucianism.[5] Therefore, the available sources have limited this essay. Not reflected here are the views of working- or merchant-class immigrants, nor are those of the small number of Chinese born in the United States by this time.

However, the texts used here do reflect the perceptions of a group of educated Chinese who consciously sought to incorporate American culture into their worldview, offering us an opportunity to explore the early development of a Chinese American intellectual and cultural history. This study, therefore, aims to contribute to an understanding of that development and offer avenues for future consideration.

This essay also attempts to broaden the discourse of the Other, to expand its usual binary construct to one that can include multiple perspectives and competing elements. It is often the case that when self/Other relationships are examined, especially in American ethnic or racial studies, the focus is on the misconceptions or prejudices one race or ethnic group holds of another and how these perceptions contribute to unequal relationships of power. This article offers a different approach to this line of inquiry by presenting examples of an evolving Chinese use of the American Other in order to critique Chinese, American, and Chinese American culture. As will be seen, the Other was not solely American society or immigration policies, but Chinese culture and the Chinese in America as well. Therefore, by crafting their arguments in a manner that used one group to achieve the agenda of criticizing another, the elite Chinese addressed in this essay manipulated self/Other relationships in a novel fashion.

Rather than situate the self/Other relationship in a construct that would simply place Chinese and Americans at odds with each other, I will present these three clusters of images whereby the Other is not always of the opposite race, nor necessarily regarded as inferior. By casting George Washington as the familiar Other, Chinese immigrants as third-party Others, and Yung Wing as a doubly excludable Other, I suggest new ways in which to view cross-cultural contact and comparisons, contributing to the process of disentangling the complex web of Chinese, American, and Chinese American cultural encounters and the transformation of cultural sensibilities that took place among the Chinese and Chinese American immigrant elite.

China and the United States: A Special Relationship

The Chinese had long considered themselves the center of the civilized world. This Sinocentric worldview colored their relations with other countries and cultures and would inform their initial response when confronted with a technologically superior West. At the core of the traditional Chinese world order was the concept of *tianxia* ("all under Heaven"), which designated the Chinese empire and provided the Chinese with a "sense of all-embracing unity and cultural entity."[6] The concept evolved as Chinese civilization, which began in the fifth millenium B.C., expanded from the Yellow River in the north to the Yangtze River in the south. Although vaguely aware of other cultural centers to the west, the Chinese viewed the kingdoms that fell early under their influence as the center of their known world. These kingdoms or states were regarded as the central states (*Zhongguo*, which later became the term for China), and those who lived outside of the Chinese cultural purview or beyond the political borders of these states were seen as marginal peoples of underdeveloped cultures that were "wanting" (in both senses of the term) of the benefits of Chinese civilization.

Chinese authors articulated the dichotomy between the Chinese and those beyond the pale of Chinese civilization very early in Chinese history. The *Shan Hai Jing* (Classic of Mountains and Oceans) is an anonymous, illustrated compilation that appeared sometime during the Zhou or Han periods (sixth century B.C. to first century A.D.) and has been termed the "oldest traveller's guide in the world."[7] The text purports to describe the lands and peoples well beyond the borders of China: the "hairy white people" (possibly the Ainu of northern Japan) and "malodorous barbarians" (perhaps of the Siberian coast). A large proportion of the beings described and illustrated are fabulous: "heads that fly about alone, winged men, dog-faced men, bodies with no heads, and the like."[8] Those images were often contrasted in the text with images of the Chinese as paragons of the true human social being. These representations distinctly differentiated the inhabitants of the central states, depicted wearing identifiable Chinese apparel, from the peoples and cultures outside of China's physical and cultural borders.

The Chinese made very clear distinctions between themselves and their neighbors in terms of cultural attainment, and descriptions of the Other became prescription, as is readily apparent in the following passage from the *Lunyu* (Confucian Analects, ca. 150 B.C.):

> Confucius expressed his desire to live among the nine tribes of Yi. One of his followers said, "The Yi are ignorant. How can you think of such a thing?" Confucius replied, "Should a Gentleman live among them, how could they remain ignorant?"[9]

This passage represents two important facets of the Chinese attitude toward the Other. While the Chinese distinguished themselves from the ignorant tribes of the Yi (non-Chinese living in the north and east of ancient China) and expressed contempt for their uncivilized state, Confucians also expressed a belief in the capacity of the superior Chinese culture to transform and uplift the barbarian Yi. This belief granted the Yi the capacity to be transformed, a malleability of character that actually denoted their humanness. The presence of a "gentleman," a man of virtue imbued with the Chinese cultural tradition, would serve as a model for the benighted Yi (and for Others) to emulate, thereby enabling them to cross the boundary of Chinese civilization.

This image of Chinese superiority and its transforming power vis-à-vis Others remained an integral component of the Chinese worldview and determined for centuries how Chinese dealt with foreigners. Nearly always acting from a position of perceived cultural superiority, the Chinese virtually never entered into relations with non-Chinese on the basis of equality, but rather with a hierarchical sense of measurable superiority.

Western imperialism in Asia, however, challenged this worldview. When the British won the first Opium War in 1842, it became obvious that the Chinese could no longer maintain the fiction of cultural superiority. The British victory opened Chinese ports to a greater number of foreign ships and, subsequently, increased contact with Western nations, including the United States. For the most part, the Chinese viewed Americans as less aggressive than the British and French in their efforts to "open" China, and American merchants had achieved the reputation of being "properly deferential" in their dealings with the Chinese in Canton.[10] To counteract the power of Britain, the Chinese attempted to fall back on an age-old practice of compensating "for weakness by drawing the least threatening power(s) to her side."[11] For much of the nineteenth century, that ally was the United States. This policy, as proposed by the great statesman Zeng Guofan (1811–1872) and his protege "self-strengthener" Li Hongzhang (1823–1901), was another version of the Chinese method of "using barbarians to check barbarians."[12] For this purpose, Zeng put forth a view of Americans as "pure-minded and honest" and "long recognized as respectful and compliant toward China."[13]

The choice of the United States as an ally was not entirely a free one.

Compared to the other major powers of the time, the United States did not appear to be much of a threat to China's territory. In other words, the United States seemed to the Chinese to be the least offensive barbarian with which to ally. The Americans, for their part, saw advantage in a benign international image of the United States. In the course of diplomatic correspondence, the U.S. Department of State frequently referred to the record of peaceful negotiations between the United States and China, the absence of American colonial ambitions, and Americans' reluctance to use force in China.[14]

China's attraction to the United States was, of course, not only ideological and for reasons of diplomacy, but for financial gain as well. Drawn to California after the discovery of gold there in 1848, some 400,000 Chinese emigrated to the United States between 1849 and 1882, at which time Congress passed the first Chinese Exclusion Act.[15] Although Chinese immigrants initially ventured to the United States in search of gold, calling the United States "Old Gold Mountain," Chinese eventually filled a variety of occupational niches in the American economy. They worked in the fishing industry, built railroads, found employment at all levels of the agricultural business, engaged in light manufacturing and cigar making, opened restuarants and laundries, and hired themselves out as domestic servants and common laborers. A smaller number also entered the country as merchants, students, and religious figures.[16]

As the Chinese turned their gaze to the American shore, their Chinese cultural perceptions and historical experience framed their impressions of the United States. Just as there was no single China for Americans, there was likewise no single, static Chinese understanding of America. Rather, the Chinese viewed the United States during this period from three primary intersecting angles: (1) China's faltering yet persistent Sinocentric worldview, challenged by (2) a growing perception of China's material and political weakness vis-à-vis the foreign powers, and (3) the immigration experience itself, made worse by the stigma of American exclusion legislation. These three elements, interacting with coeval political events and with each other, reflect a persistent and shifting ambivalence in Chinese views of America and in their perceptions of themselves as well. As the context changed in which Chinese and Americans interacted with each other, their views of each other were naturally affected. For a segment of the elite and other Chinese who were in contact with Euro-Americans, the instability of the Chinese national identity, coupled with the sociopolitical changes of the time and the humiliating immigration experience, revealed cracks in the once solidly Sinocentric worldview.

Other writers have argued that the ambivalence in Chinese impressions of the United States was rooted in their "unwarranted expectations and ethnocentric attitudes."[17] In addition, however, elite Chinese images of the United States and of their own culture were determined by their interaction with Euro-Americans and with Chinese immigrants living in the United States. The process of analyzing the formation of cultural images and expectations is more complex than simply privileging the observer's point of view; one must also acknowledge the reciprocal influence of whom or what they are observing, the sociocultural environment in which this process takes place, and the history of the relationship between the observer and the observed. Images are not formed through one-sided observations, but through the process of interaction. Following are three cases in which American culture can be seen as a "contact zone" in which Chinese and American culture and expectations collided, revealing the degree to which American values influenced a changing Chinese worldview.[18]

George Washington and the Chinese

One of the strongest images of the United States held by members of the Chinese elite during the late nineteenth century was that of George Washington. A number of Chinese intellectuals, rooted in the Confucian tradition of rule by virtuous example rather than by force, revered Washington, placing him on a level with the mythical kings and great generals of China's glorious imperial past, even though their knowledge of the first president was extremely limited. The most influential "biography" of Washington to appear in Chinese during the nineteenth century was written by Xu Jiyu (1795–1873) in his geographical treatise *Yinghuan zhilue* (A Short Account of the Oceans Around Us) written in 1848. Xu, the governor of Fujian province, never traveled abroad, but constructed this work through extensive reading of translated Western works and contact with foreigners. The province of Fujian, in southeastern China, had a long history of foreign contact, and after the Opium War, it was open to an increase in foreign trade, affording Xu more opportunities to avail himself of foreign texts, ideas, and personal contacts. His treatise became the main source of geographical knowledge of the Western world in China and an indispensible tool for China's diplomats in the latter part of the nineteenth century.[19] And, his near apotheosis of George Washington would influence the views of the Chinese elite for years to come, as Washington came to symbolize the power and virture of the United States.

Rooted in a Confucian prescription of moral example as proper government, Xu placed Washington within a well-developed Chinese paradigm of good government that, in fact, very few Chinese rulers could even attain. His biography of Washington is worth quoting at length:

> There was one named Washington *(Huashengdun)* from another part of the United States, who was born in 1731 [actually, 1732]. When he was ten years old his father died, and his mother raised him. In his youth he had great ambitions, and he was naturally gifted in both civil and military affairs, and his bravery and virtue surpassed all others.
>
> When Washington had settled the country, he handed over his military authority and desired to return to his fields. The people were unwilling to part with him and chose him to be the country's ruler. Washington then said to the people that it was selfish to take a country and pass it on to one's descendants; he said it was better to choose a person of virtue for the responsibility of governing people.
>
> As for Washington, he was an extraordinary man. In raising a revolt, he was more courageous than Sheng or Guang. In carrying out an occupation, he was braver than Cao or Liu. When he took up the three-foot double-edged sword and opened up the boundaries for ten thousand *li,* he did not assume the throne and was unwilling to begin a line of succession. Moreover he invented a method of election. He established a "world for everyone" *(tianxia weigong),* and he swiftly carried out the traditions of the Three Dynasties *(sandai).* He governed his country with reverence and respected good customs. He did not esteem military achievements, and he was very different from [the rulers] of other countries. I have seen his portrait; his bearing is imposing and excellent. Ah! Can he not be called a hero? . . . Of all the famous Westerners of ancient and modern times, can Washington be placed in any position but the first? [20]

Obviously, Xu's description of Washington was meant to serve a political purpose. As the Chinese confronted a militarily superior West, they sought to lessen the sting of their humiliation at the hands of the West by transforming Washington into a Chinese statesman, thereby making the Other as familiar as possible. This account of Washington's early childhood is in fact a form of Confucian hagiography. The death of Washington's father while he was young and his upbringing by his mother match exactly the childhood circumstances of Mencius, the next major philosopher after Confucius and one of the early shapers of the Chinese concept of proper behavior in the public sphere. Washington's desire to return to his farm corresponds both to the Chinese reverence for agriculture and the pastoral life and to the tradition of eremitism for officials. And yet, when called upon by the people, Washington served the country, which was also in the spirit of Chinese recluses who gave up personal desires and comfort to aid the people and the government.[21]

This biographical sketch declares that Washington was a man of great military prowess, comparing favorably to heroes of China's past. More importantly, Washington did not emphasize the martial aspect of ruling but instead focused on justice, again conforming to Confucian ideas about good government. Finally, Washington did not attempt to pass the presidency on to his descendants, but "abdicated" to a man of virtue.[22] Here, he is compared to the Sage Kings Yao, Xun, and Yu of the ancient Three Dynasties period who were said to have established the idea of ruling through merit rather than descent. In short, Washington was the perfect example of a ruler who practiced the proper way of a king *(wangdao)*.[23]

Used in a contrasting manner, later intellectuals invoked the image of Washington for other political reasons. Addressing the poor treatment of Chinese immigrants in America, Huang Zunxian (1848–1905) used the appeal of Washington to express his indignation over the subjugated status of Chinese in America. While serving as consul general in San Francisco, he wrote a long poem entitled "Zhuke pian" (Expelling the Visitor) in 1882, the year Congress passed the original Chinese Exclusion Act. In one section of the poem Huang Zunxian writes:

> I sadly think back to George Washington,
> Who certainly had the talent to be a forceful ruler.*
> He proclaimed that in America
> There is a broad expanse of land in the western desert.
> There, the "nine tribes and eight barbarians"**
> Are all allowed to go and settle in the frontier.***
> The yellow, white, red and black races
> Are all equal to our native people.
> Not even a hundred years till today,
> They are able to eat his words without shame.[24]

And, in a poem about the presidential election of 1884, Huang wrote:

> Alas! George Washington!
> It is nearly a hundred years now
> Since the flag of independence was raised
> And oppressive rule was overthrown.
> Red and yellow and black and white
> Were all to be treated as one.[25]

The source of Huang's image of Washington's views on racial equality is uncertain but it is clear that Huang felt betrayed by the land that had given birth to a man whom he and many other learned Chinese admired greatly. Viewing Washington as the embodiment of all that was good in America and all that China could become, Xu, Huang, and other Chinese intellectuals looked to the United States for salvation and used the imagery of George Washington to praise and criticize both Chinese and American societies.[26] Other scholars have interpreted the Chinese appreciation for George Washington as an indication of the decline of Sinocentricism.[27] I suggest, however, that the Chinese reverence for Washington points to a much more complex stage in the transculturation process that took place among these Chinese elites in the American "contact zone." By equating Washington with the mythical progenitors of Chinese culture, members of China's elite revealed the constraints of their discourse and their inability or unwillingness to transcend their own cultural frame of reference. Washington was not a man of virtue merely because of his own deeds, but because he resembled what the Chinese valued in a Chinese gentleman. In effect, Washington is a later example of the *hua-hu* (conversion of the barbarians) theory, a Han Dynasty argument claiming that the Buddha was actually Laozi and thus Chinese.[28] The image of Washington as a familiar Other in the likeness of the Chinese Sage Kings, satisfied the Chinese belief in the superiority of their own standards of good government and affirmed their confidence in Chinese institutions. However, by 1882, no longer comfortable claiming Chinese cultural superiority in the shadow of American exclusion policy, Huang Zunxian drew on a thoroughly egalitarian and democratic image of Washington to legitimize the anger and frustration felt by Chinese in response to their degraded status in the United States. This use of the images of Washington fits well with Gary Okihiro's position that Asian Americans have long exhibited an appreciation for American civic values and have sought inclusion in

American society. He writes, "In their struggles for equality [Asian Americans and other minorities], these groups have helped preserve and advance the principles and ideals of democracy and have thereby made America a freer place for all."[29] However, another Chinese intellectual, Liang Qichao, spent time in the United States and expressed doubts whether the Chinese in America fully appreciated American concepts of freedom and democracy. He used the Chinese immigrant community as a means to critique Chinese society.

Liang Qichao and the Chinese of America

Despite the appreciation of American values by some Chinese, many Americans did not hold reciprocal feelings toward Chinese immigrants in the United States. Soon after Chinese immigrants arrived in the gold fields of California, they encountered hostilty in the form of legislation such as the Foreign Miners Tax (1850), which demanded that all noncitizens pay an extra tax for permission to engage in mining, and in the form of constant threats of physical violence. In addition, the American government politically disenfranchised Chinese immigrants by forbidding them to testify for or against a white person in a court of law, and most importantly, by denying them the right of naturalization. Based in racial antipathy and class antagonisms, the anti-Chinese movement severely restricted Chinese immigrants' civil rights, stunted the normal development of families since very few women were allowed to immigrate, tilted the class composition toward merchants at the expense of workers, and drove the Chinese into segregated residential and business enclaves generally referred to as Chinatowns.[30]

And yet, in the face of such adversity and hostility, Chinese immigrants continued to seek new lives in America, either temporarily or permanently. By the turn of the century, Chinese immigrant communities could be found in all of the Western states and in the larger cities of the Midwest and the East Coast. The Chinatown in San Francisco, however, became the cultural heartland of Chinese America, serving as the gateway through which most Chinese immigrants entered the country. Therefore, when Liang Qichao toured North America in 1903, it was natural that he would spend a substantial amount of time with the Chinese of San Francisco.

In order to place Liang's writings on Chinese immigrants within the contexts of his career and of Chinese American history, one must have an understanding of the intellectual and political priorities that mediated Liang's field of vision. Liang was, first and foremost, a Confucian scholar and a political activist. Considered by some to be "China's first true modern intellectual,"[31] Liang was devoted to the transformation of Chinese society. He came of age during a time of grave political turmoil in China and became politically active due to the crisis of China's relations with the Western powers and Japan. Trained and influenced by his mentor Kang Youwei (1858–1927), Liang's Confucian outlook was grounded in the *jingshi* (practical statesmanship) tradition of the late Qing.

Adherence to this tradition was not merely a commitment to political activism or a general sense of social responsibility; it meant a dedication to institutional reform. For example, while in the capital in 1895 to take the triennial metropolitan civil service examinations, Kang and Liang used the occasion to rally the patriotic fervor of the assembled literati by organizing them to protest the humiliating terms of the Treaty of Shimonoseki, which the Chinese court had signed earlier that spring to end the 1894–1895 Sino-Japanese War. In what Liang would later describe as "waking China from its 4,000 year-long dream,"[32] Kang and Liang persuaded the 1,300 examination candidates to join them in protesting the treaty and petitioning for institutional and political reform.

For the next several years, Liang Qichao and Kang Youwei led a growing movement for political reform in China. However, conservative elements at court crushed what came to be known as the 1898 Reform Movement, forcing Kang and Liang into exile in Japan, where they remained influential in Chinese political reform and intellectual circles both in China and Japan. Throughout his life, Liang Qichao would be drawn to various schools of thought, Chinese and Western, but he would never abandon his dedication to the traditional Confucian emphasis on the duty of intellectuals to serve the state by demanding the best from it and its citizens.

The fourteen years in exile, almost all of which were spent in Japan, proved to be critical to Liang's intellectual and political development. Japan in 1900 was already a modern nation-state and the only one with which Liang had direct contact. This first-hand exposure to a nation of power would affect how he came to view international relations and concepts of human progress. Already exposed to Social Darwinism in China through his relationship with Yen Fu (1854–1921), a leading translator and promoter of Western ideas, Liang found kindred souls in Japan who espoused similar theories.[33]

Thus Liang Qichao came to the United States ideologically rooted in Confucian ideals of political reform and social hierarchy, but also influenced by Social Darwinist notions of race and power that privileged Anglo-Saxon supremacy. Dismayed by the turn of events in China and inspired by the example of growing Japanese power, Liang believed that the nature of the "Chinese character" had to be transformed in order for political and social reform even to be possible. That transformation, however, would call for national self-examination, generated by and resulting in a restructuring of the Chinese worldview. This complex agenda for political reformation and social transformation would influence Liang's perspective of Chinese America.

Liang toured North America at the invitation of the Baohuang hui (Protect the Emperor Society), a political reform association founded in Canada by Kang Youwei in 1899, to raise funds and gather support for reform ideas. The Baohuang hui, also known as the Weixin hui (Reform Association), was one of the first political parties in Chinese history. It favored preserving the power of the emperor through a constitutional monarchy. Over the next ten years, this party would compete for followers with Sun Yat-sen's revolutionary parties, the Xingzhong hui (Revive China Society) and the Tongmeng hui, the forerunner of the Guomindang or Nationalist Party. Most Chinese immigrants in America supported one of these parties as they believed that political reform in China would bring about a stronger government with international respect, resulting in improved conditions for overseas Chinese.[34]

Liang left Yokohama in February 1903 and landed in Vancouver in early March. For the next seven months, he crossed the continent twice by rail, visiting three Canadian cities and twenty-eight American cities and towns. Throughout his stay in the United States and Canada, Liang took copious notes on the people he met, what he observed, and what the Chinese could gain from American culture. When he returned to Japan, he assembled these notes into his now-famous *Xin dalu youji jielu* (Selected Memoir of Travels in the New World), which he published in 1904.[35]

Aside from being one of the first texts written in Chinese that describes Chinese life in the United States, this travel diary presents a unique opportunity to examine a new perspective in self/Other relations. Most other well-known travel accounts reflect a dichotomous relationship between the observer and the observed (such as Marco Polo and the Chinese or Tocqueville and the Americans), who are usually separated in terms of discrete cultural and ethnic spheres. These writers tended to set themselves quite apart from the cultures they observed and reveal little of how they may have affected the "host" culture by their presence or whether these "foreign" societies had much of a lasting influence on their own cultural values and worldviews. Liang's text, however, is unique in that it offers an elite Chinese evaluation of people like himself—at least racially alike if not also in terms of class—who lived and labored in a foreign environment and his explicit reactions to their lives in America.

A great deal of Liang's text describes his travels in various cities, including his visit to the site of the Boston Tea Party and to Independence Hall to see the Liberty Bell, revealing that he too held the American Revolution in high esteem. However, it is his appraisal of the Chinese in America that is most important to the study of the transculturation process that occured for the Chinese visiting or living in the United States.[36] Liang met with the resident Chinese population in nearly all of the towns and cities he visited, and he launched a scathing attack on the Chinese in America in response to his month-long stay in San Francisco's Chinatown. At the root of Liang's criticism of the overseas Chinese was his belief that they did not possess the qualities required of citizens in a democracy. Often ignoring the pernicious effects of American racism that kept the Chinese immigrant community confined to Chinatown, Liang pointed to Chinese provincialism as the primary reason the Chinese could not rise above regional and surname loyalties to see themselves as members of a larger, more important, political entity. Of this problem Liang wrote:

> Chinese can be clansmen but not citizens. I believe this all the more since my travels in America. There you have those who have left villages and taken on the character of individuals and come and go in the most free of the great cities and [enjoy] all that they have to offer, and still they cling to the family and clan systems to the exception of other things. . . . When I look at all the societies in the world, none is so chaotic [divided] as the Chinese community in San Francisco.[37]

This chaotic and divided state, according to Liang, left the Chinese ill prepared to assert themselves in American society and, on a larger scale, to participate as equals in world politics. Athough Liang goes to great lengths to enumerate the various provincial, surname, and occupations associations found throughout Chinese American communities, he does not adequately acknowledge the social functions of these fraternal organizations. Acting as surrogate families, these associations offered shelter from a society from which Chinese immigrants found themselves alienated. As Sucheng Chan points out, the associations "provided mutual aid to their members and served as settings where coethnics could partake of warmth and conviviality. At the same time, they functioned as instruments of social control over the masses of immigrants and as legitimizers of the status accorded particular immigrant leaders. The latter exercised power and acquired prestige not only by virture of being officers of commmunity organizations but also by serving as communication links—and consequently, as power brokers—between their compatriots and the external world."[38] Although sensitive to the problems that emerged because of this system and the Chinese identification with regional and surname loyalties, Liang chose, in this text, to ignore the power of racial discrimination and political disenfranchisement that placed Chinese immigrants in a subordinate position.[39]

The provincialism that Liang criticized, however, was only one manifestation of the "cultural deficiencies" that he found in the Chinese of San Francisco. He went to great lengths to enumerate these shortcomings, stating that

> Westerners work eight hours each day and then rest on Sunday. Chinese open their shops each morning at seven o'clock and work until eleven or twelve and only then begin to shut down. They stay in their shops all day long and still do not rest on Sunday. And yet, they cannot compete with Westerners, because they are too tired. And being too tired, they do not have high goals. This carries over to education as well. American students only study five to six hours a day, for 140 days a year, but their educational level is much higher than the Chinese.

> The Chinese operate small shops and hire up to ten or more people. Americans also run small stores but only employ one or two workers. Thus one [American] can do the work of three Chinese. It is not that the Chinese are not industrious, but that they are less intelligent.

> At public gatherings of more than several hundred Chinese, no matter how serious the occasion, one will hear four kinds of noises: coughing, yawning, sneezing, and the blowing of noses. However, I have been in Western theaters with several thousands in the audience and did not hear a sound.

> Spitting is forbidden in the streets of San Francisco as is littering. Offenders are fined five dollars. Spitting on the streetcar in New York is a five hundred dollar fine. They value cleanliness to the point that they are willing to interfere and restrict freedom. Chinese (in breaking these regulations) are seen as disorderly and dirty citizens. It is any wonder that they are so hated?[40]

Liang continues by even discussing the manner in which Chinese walk, "with their heads bowed in a servile pose while Americans walk erect. . . . Americans, when walking in a group, are orderly like geese, but the Chinese are scattered like ducks."[41] Finally, Liang ends his vehement assault on these so-called character flaws by writing,

> Confucius taught, "Without studying the *Odes,* you are unfit to converse. Without studying the *Rites,* you cannot establish your character." A friend has said, "The Chinese have not yet learned to walk, speak, nor read." This is no exaggeration. These may seem like small issues, but they reflect larger ones.[42]

The larger issues to which Liang refers here are those that he believed prevented the Chinese from becoming citizens of a modern nation-state. By ending his critique of the Chinese in America by referring to the Confucian canon in relation to the inability of the Chinese to act like citizens of a democracy (which, for the most part, they were legally barred from becoming), it is evident that Liang was caught in an intellectual and cultural dilemma. Wishing to save the Chinese from being dominated by the Western powers but finding little desirable in the Chinese "national character," Liang's experience in the "contact zone" of the United States left him with little faith in the readiness of the Chinese to participate in an American democratic society. Although there are no written records that indicate how the people of San Francisco Chinatown reacted to Liang's views, after publication of his travel memoir, the *Chung Sai Yat Po,* one of the leading Chinese-language newspapers in the community, never again printed an editorial in praise of Liang's political reform efforts.[43]

Liang's embrace of Western political and social standards and his view that the Chinese were unable to meet those standards led him to temper his quest for democratic reform in China. Upon his return to Japan, he was increasingly attracted to the authoritarian models of the Meiji oligarchy in Japan and nineteenth-century German statism.[44] As Stefan Tanaka has argued, Japanese intellectuals were in similar straits during this period as well. They too reacted to the intrusion of the West while trying to preserve a Japanese state. Rather than accepting one or the other, the Japanese grappled with the issues of how to "regenerate society by adapting from the alien West while still retaining its own distinctiveness."[45] In Japan's case, Japanese intellectuals turned to the study of Asia to find common historical roots that would link Europe and Japan. Tanaka points out that "in this way, Japanese were using the West and Asia as other(s) to construct their own sense of a Japanese nation as modern and oriental."[46] Likewise for Liang, the Other, as expressed in his travel account, was not the racially and culturally different Euro-American population of the United States but rather the Chinese immigrant community which he used as a third-party Other in order to address a broader political agenda, the cultural critique of Chinese tradition and society.

Yung Wing: Becoming Chinese American?

Ironically, while Liang Qichao was touring the east coast of the United States, he stopped in Hartford, Connecticut, to visit Yung Wing, an American-educated Chinese who had embraced much of the Western political values and social habits that Liang found wanting in the majority of his countrymen.

Yung Wing was born in 1828 near Macao and was enrolled in a missionary school at the age of seven. After four years there, he spent five years in another missionary school in Hong Kong run by Rev. Samuel Brown, an 1832 graduate of Yale University. This association would begin Yung's life-long relationship with Yale. More importantly, Yung, unlike most Chinese children who were fortunate enough to go to school, would receive an American education, becoming fluent in English at an early age. Although unique at the time, Yung's experience established a pattern that would become more prevalent in the next generation of Chinese students, a generation on which Yung would have a major influence. In 1846, Brown announced that he was returning to New England and offered to take a number of students with him to study in the United States. Yung and two other students made the journey to America with Morrison and enrolled in the Monson Academy in Monson, Massachusetts. From there, Yung Wing went on to become the first Chinese to graduate from an American university (Yale in 1854).[47]

During these early years in the United States, Yung Wing became increasingly attracted to American social and political mores. His reevaluation and rejection of a Sinocentric worldview is evident in his decision to remain in the United States after his graduation from the Monson Academy. While deciding the direction of his future education, Yung Wing corresponded with Samuel Wells Williams, the American charge d'affaires to China and a Morrison Education Society trustee, a life-long friend with whom Yung had become acquainted while a student in Hong Kong. Yung wrote to Williams explaining his desire to remain in the United States rather than return to China:

> Of course you are aware that my feelings would not allow me to leave my mother and brothers and sisters, since I promised them all when I left China to return in two or three years and you know ful [sic] well the prejudice of the Chinese, how they misrepresent things, and that they are not able to see as you or any enlightened mind do, the object, the advantage, and value of being educated. Ignorance and superstition have sealed the noble faculties of their minds, how can they appreciate things of such worth?[48]

Clearly, Yung had already distanced himself from a strictly Chinese worldview and had begun privileging Western learning. He rejected what he saw as Chinese "prejudice" and "ignorance and superstition" and favored the "enlightened mind" produced by an American educa-tion. Chinese "misrepresented things" and were unable to see the "value of being educated." Of course, a Confucian education was highly valued in China, but Yung, not thoroughly grounded in the classical Confucian tradition, did not consider it in the same category as a Western education. Yung believed there were stark differences in the manner in which Chinese and Americans viewed the world, and the American approach was certainly the better of the two.

Yung robustly embraced American culture during his years at Yale. The most striking example of this embrace was his naturalization as an American citizen on 30 October 1852 in New Haven.[49] Curiously, he does not mention this important event either in his autobiography or in his surviving unpublished papers. Nonetheless, it is a telling indication of Yung's commitment to a life in the United States. His attainment of citizenship revealed his evolving cultural identity: a Chinese student in America officially staking his claim as a Chinese American.

Although Yung rejected certain aspects of Chinese culture and embraced America as his adopted country, he never abandoned his desire to see China modernize so that it could fully participate as a nation-state in the geopolitical arena. His lengthy exposure to American educational practices and values, and his own transformation thereby, led him to believe that China's rejuvenation depended on the training of China's youth in Western learning. He later wrote:

> Before the close of my last year in college I had already sketched out what I should do. I was determined that the rising generation of China should enjoy the same educational advantages that I had enjoyed; that through Western education China might be regenerated, become enlightened and powerful. To accomplish that object became the guiding star of my ambition.[50]

After his graduation from Yale, Yung returned to China and worked at various occupations, always hoping that he would find a way to promote his idea of sending Chinese youths to America for an education. Finally in 1870 in the wake of the Tianjin Massacre, Yung presented his ideas to Zeng Guofan and other members of the Zongli Yamen.[51] Over the next few months, officials within the Zongli Yamen hammered out the details and the project now known as the Chinese Educational Mission came to fruition.

The mission was to send thirty students between the ages of twelve and sixteen to the United States each year for four years. These 120 students would study in America for fifteen years and would be allowed to travel for another two years before returning to China. They would then report to the Zongli Yamen for assignment to useful occupations in service of the country. Chen Lanbin (fl. 1853–1884), an official with the Board of Punishment, was to be in charge of their Chinese education while abroad, and Yung was responsible for their Western curriculum. It was also decreed that the students read the *Sacred Book of Imperial Edicts* at specified times and that students must consult Chinese almanacs in order to observe the proper rituals at their designated times, ensuring that they maintain their sense of Chinese propriety and reverence for Chinese tradition.[52]

Soon after the mission was established in Hartford, Connecticut, Yung and Chen clashed over the direction, operation, and goals of the mission as well as over the behavior of the students.[53] From early on, Chen was disturbed that the students wanted to shed their traditional scholar's gowns and cut off their queues. Eventually, Yung and Chen reached a compromise wherein the students wore their gowns when they were with their Chinese teachers.[54] Their hair, however, was another issue. Given that the mission existed under the auspices of the

Imperial Court, Chen would not permit the students to cut off their queues, which were symbols of Chinese obedience to Manchu rule. Offenders were to be sent back to China. The great majority of the students retained their queues, but they learned to conceal them with hats and pins or inside the back of their coats.[55]

More important than their outward appearance were the perceived changes in the behavior and values of the mission students. Conservative officials complained that the students had become spoiled by the luxurious accommodations at the mission, had lost their Chinese language skills, and most important, had become deracinated and denationalized.[56]

Yung's perception of the differences between Chinese and American approaches to education and the conduct of students is best captured in his evaluation of the reasons for Chen Lanpin's dissatisfaction with the mission:

> The only standard by which he measured things and men (especially students) was purely Chinese. The gradual but marked transformation of the students might well be strange and repugnant to the ideas and senses of a man like Chin Lan Pin [sic], who all his life had been accustomed to see the springs of life, energy and independence, candor, ingenuity and open-heartedness all covered up and concealed, and in a great measure smothered and never allowed their full play.[57]

As in his earlier correspondance with Samuel Wells Williams, Yung here reveals the extent to which he disdained and rejected what he perceived as certain Chinese cultural traits. Contrasting American "energy and independence, candor, ingenuity and open-heartedness" with a Chinese tendency to "cover up, conceal, and smother," Yung decidedly turned his back on what he viewed as the stultifying character of Chinese society and chose instead the "springs of life" that he found in America.

Eventually, Yung would take much of the blame for the students' behavior, as a number of them like Yung Wing himself did cut off their queues, convert to Christianity, and later, marry white American women.[58] The Chinese Government recalled the mission in 1881. The reasons often cited include the expense, not many of the students had learned enough technical skills, and conflicts occurred between the principal figures. But the underlying reasons were much more fundamental. Those officials who did not share Yung's attraction to American culture worried that the mission students would adopt Western ideas and practices that contradicted fundamental aspects of the Sinocentric worldview and thereby reject their original culture. This rejection might, in turn, result in the loss of their nationalistic sense of purpose to serve China. This loss would represent not only a failure of the mission's goals, but would also indicate a loss of control by officials of their overseas subjects. The closing of the mission signified a crisis for Chinese intellectuals who had attempted to create a new role for China in the modern family of nations while still retaining a Sinocentric worldview. This proved to be impossible in the case of sending young students to live in the United States. These students, like Yung Wing, represented a new era in Chinese history and in Chinese American history as well. Charged with the mission of transforming China into a modern nation, they had turned their attention to America in search of a modernizing vision that a Sinocentric worldview could not accommodate.

Because Yung Wing spent most of his official career in the service of the Chinese government, and for some, because he converted to Christianity, Yung Wing is often marginalized in the study of the Chinese American experience.[59] He was, however, an important figure in the development of late-nineteenth and early-twentieth century Chinese American history, representing for that generation and class of Chinese immigrants, the transition from a primarily China-oriented life to an American-oriented life. The fact that he was devoted to China's modernization in no way decreased his commitment to a life in America. In fact, he based his model for China's modernization on what he loved about American society. Yung Wing spent nearly half of his life in the United States and was profoundly affected by what he experienced here. He was one of the first of the Chinese elite to recognize the confines of Sinocentrism on the world historical stage, and he sought to liberate modern China, or at least a few score of the younger generation, from its grip. In this undertaking, however, Yung adopted the sociopolitical hegemony of Western thought. Although he was not as disdainful of the Chinese immigrant population in America nor as critical of Chinese social habits as Liang Qichao, Yung Wing clearly accepted a Western-centered world order.

Contrary to the racialist thinking prevalent during the anti-Chinese movement that deemed Chinese unassimilable, Yung Wing's life in America can be seen as one of assimilation in progress. His American education, religious background, family, friends, and career were all part of and products of a worldview that was becoming fundamentally American and less rooted in Chinese tradition. Indeed, by rejecting much of his traditional Chinese cultural ties, Yung sought to become American. He thus continued the process of transculturation initiated earlier by Xu Jiyu and Liang Qichao by reinventing himself in the American province by using what he found desirable here and shaping these cultural practices to suit his needs.

In the end, however, Yung's legal status did not match his cultural and intellectual embrace of America. While doing business in China in 1898, the American government stripped Yung of his American citizenship due to the enforcement of the 1878 *In re Ah Yup* decision, which declared Chinese immigrants ineligible for American citizenship.[60] Ironically, Yung's American leanings cost him the favor of those in power in China as well. During this trip to China, Yung played a minor role in the same reform movement that exiled Liang Qichao to Japan. Yung, too, had to flee China, finding refuge in the British colony of Hong Kong. Fortunately, in spite of his loss of American citizenship, Yung managed to return to the United States where he lived until his death in 1912.[61] He had, however, lost his legal status in both countries. Education, religion, family concerns, and cultural affinities notwithstanding, in the eyes of American law, Yung was still an excludable Other in America. And in China, he was also viewed as an Other, dangerous to the Sinocentric governmental structure that once placed him in power. Legally excluded from two conflicting social and political systems, Yung attempted to act as a cultural bridge between his country of origin and his adopted home. Although stigmatized as an Other in both countries, he seems to have felt most comfortable in the United States; perhaps the poles of self and Other found a synthesis in this early Chinese American patriot and reformer.

Conclusion

Since the publication of Harold Isaacs' *Scratches on Our Minds* in 1958, there has been considerable scholarship on American images and perceptions of China and other Asian countries, but the study of Asian views and representations of the United States and American society has been slower to develop.[62] There have been even fewer studies that address how these images and expectations of the United States influenced how the Chinese came to view themselves and their culture. By analyzing a number of these images and impressions, I have argued that members of the Chinese elite, both those in China and those who either visited or lived in America, were transformed by their encounter with the United States, and that these shifts in Chinese perceptions of the West and of themselves were part of a transculturation process that took place because of this collision of cultures.

The three Chinese views of America presented here disclose shifting and ambivalent perceptions of American, Chinese, and Chinese American society and culture. Xu Jiyu's icon of George Washington represents an image of America held by many Chinese elites during the preexclusion era of Chinese immigration to the United States. However, the poor treatment experienced by Chinese immigrants in America prompted later writers to implore the American people to "return" to the moral example set forth by George Washington. Thus Xu used the George Washington icon as a familiar Other to praise American society while Huang Zunxian later used Washington to criticize it. By using Chinese images of Washington as a focal point, one can explore the influence of a traditional worldview on immigrant perceptions and expectations of the country of their destination and how the uses of the image shift when their expectations are not met. Although handled in contrasting ways, the image of George Washington illustrates how the Chinese used an American icon as a vehicle to express their perceptions of both themselves and American society.

In contrast, Liang Qichao used the Chinese immigrant community in San Francisco as a third-party Other to address his concerns about Chinese society and culture. The Chinese in San Francisco, because of their continued emphasis on regional and surname loyalties, led Liang to believe that the Chinese national character was unfit for democratic reform. Once drawn to democratic liberalism, Liang's time with the overseas Chinese caused him to reevaluate that option for reform. In this manner, Chinese self-images were transformed through the encounter with the lived experiences of the Chinese in America.

Still another set of images and examples of cultural transformation can be apprehended in the life and career of Yung Wing. Educated primarily in American institutions, Yung wholeheartedly embraced American culture and sought to rejuvenate China along American lines, in ways similar to his own cultural transformation. In doing so, however, he was eventually driven from China and yet simultaneously stripped of his American citizenship. Although a doubly excludable Other, Yung Wing is a clear example of the process of transculturation as he sought to shed his ties to certain facets of Chinese culture and become American.

Chinese intellectuals, some encountering the Western presence in China and a number of them arriving in the United States themselves, thus attempted to reformulate Chinese culture in order to ensure China's national survival. Addressing mounting internal disorder and foreign encroachment in China as well as the poor treatment of Chinese immigrants in America, intellectuals and reformers often saw these two situations as intertwined. Some blamed the weak Chinese government and the Chinese national character for the plight of overseas Chinese. At the same time, however, these intellectuals remained rooted in the very tradition, Confucianism, that informed the policies of the Chinese government and the behavior of many Chinese abroad. Caught in this conflict of tradition and modernity, Chinese elites sought to maintain an allegiance to China while grappling with its weaknesses, especially as it was reflected in the poor treatment Chinese received in the United States. This developing elite culture of the late nineteenth and early twentieth century, therefore, tried to encompass both worldviews, that of traditional China and a modernizing America, in an attempt to forge a new and distinctively Chinese American cultural sensibility, one that would allow for the blending and embrace of both sets of conflicting cultural practices and values.[63] As seen in these three cases, however, the process was not an easy one, as it necessitated the rejection of fundamental aspects of Chinese culture in favor of American values and practices. Seen in this light, the Chinese response to the West took place not only in China, but in the "contact zone" of America as well, where a Chinese American identity evolved during this cultural transformation.

NOTES

This essay, in its present form, has benefitted from helpful comments and suggestions from several colleagues. I would like to thank Sarah Deutsch for being so generous with her time to offer advice on revisions, Gary Kulik and Lucy Maddox for their patience and encouragement, and the anonymous readers for making me clarify my arguments.

1. Roger Daniels, "Westerners from the East: Oriental Immigrants Reappraised," *Pacific Historical Review* 35 (Nov. 1966): 375.

2. Notable exceptions are Him Mark Lai, Genny Lim, and Judy Yung, *Island: Poetry and History of Chinese Immigrants on Angel Island, 1910–1940* (San Francisco, 1981); and Marlon Hom, *Songs of Gold Mountain: Cantonese Rhymes From San Francisco Chinatown* (Berkeley, Calif., 1987). For a recent publication in Chinese American cultural studies that is framed as a study of anti-Chinese imagery, see James S. Moy, *Marginal Sights: Staging the Chinese in America* (Iowa City, Iowa, 1993).

3. Sucheta Mazumdar, "Asian American Studies and Asian Studies: Rethinking Roots," *Asian Americans: Comparative and Global Perspectives* (Pullman, Wash., 1991), 29–30, 41.

4. Mary Louise Pratt, *Imperial Eyes: Travel Writing and Transculturation* (London, 1992), 6.

5. For example, see Lai Chun-chuen, *Remarks of the Chinese Merchants of San Francisco, upon Governor Bigler's Message and Some Common Objections: With Some Explorations of the Character of the Chinese Companies, and the Laboring Class in California* (San Francisco, 1855); Chinese Consolidated Benevolent Association, *A Memorial to His Excellency U. S. Grant, President of the United States from Representative Chinamen in America* (n.p., 1876); and Chinese Consolidated Benevolent Association, *Memorial of the Six Companies: An Address to the Senate and House of Representatives of the United States* (San Francisco, 1877). The best study that links the merchant class in Chinatown to the scholarly elite culture of China is Kim Man Chan, "Mandarins in America: The Early Chinese Ministers to the United States, 1878–1907" (Ph.D. diss., University of Hawaii, 1981). A major source of documents from Chinatowns are the newspapers published in these communities. These, too, were controlled by the elites as the editors were usually better educated than their readers, often in Western missionary schools, and often with ties to the Chinese government or other political groups in China. For two studies that make extensive use of these newspapers, see Judy Yung, "Unbinding the Feet, Unbinding Their Lives: Social Change for Chinese Women in San Francisco, 1902–1945" (Ph.D. diss., University of California, Berkeley, 1990); and L. Eve Armentrout Ma, *Revolutionaries, Monarchists, and Chinatowns: Chinese Politics in the Americas and the 1911 Revolution* (Honolulu, 1990).

6.. John K. Fairbank, "A Preliminary Framework," in *The Chinese World View*, ed. John K. Fairbank (Cambridge, Mass., 1968), 5.

7. Joseph Needham, et al., *Science and Civilisation in China* (Cambridge, England, 1959), 3:504.

8. Ibid., 505. Needham offers a facinating discussion of these images in comparison to similar images found in Greek and Roman texts of this period, but such a discussion is well beyond the scope of this study.

9. *Lunyu* (Confucian Analects), 9: 13: 1–2. Translation by the author. For another English translation, see Arthur Waley, trans. *The Analects of Confucius* (New York, 1938), 141.

10. Chang-fang Chen, "Barbarian Paradise: Chinese Views of the United States, 1784–1911" (Ph.D. diss., Indiana University, 1985), 17. From a different perspective, however, Stuart C. Miller points out that American traders in Canton had very negative images of the Chinese by this time. See Stuart Creighton Miller, *The Unwelcome Immigrant: The American Image of the Chinese, 1785–1882,* 2d ed. (Berkeley, Calif, 1974), 16–37.

11. Michael Hunt, *The Making of a Special Relationship: The United States and China to 1914* (New York, 1983), 115.

12. Zeng Guofan and Li Hongzhang were statesmen and officials who were both prominent in the self-strengthening movement of the late nineteenth century. This movement was based on the belief that China had to modernize in order to compete in the Western world and that this was only possible by learning from the West and by acquiring Western technology. For a brief survey of how the Chinese traditionally attempted to keep foreigners and border peoples under control, see Lien-sheng Yang, "Historical Notes on the Chinese World Order," in *The Chinese World Order,* ed. John K. Fairbank (Cambridge, Mass., 1968), 20–33.

13. Quoted in Hunt, *Making of a Special Relationship*, 59.

14. Merle Curti and John Stalker, "'The Flowery Flag Devils'—The American Image in China 1840–1900," *Proceedings of the American Philosophical Society* 96 (20 Dec., 1952), 680.

15. The original Chinese Exclusion Act prohibited the immigration of Chinese laborers into the United States for a period of ten years. It was revised and renewed in 1888, 1892, 1894, 1898, 1902, and 1904. The evolution of these acts can be traced in *U.S. Statutes at Large* 22 (1881–1883): 58–61; *U.S. Statutes at Large* 25 (1887–1889): 476–79; *U.S. Statutes at Large* 27 (1891–1893): 25–26; *U.S. Statutes at Large* 28 (1893–1895): 1210–12; *U.S. Statutes at Large* 32 (1901–1903): 176–77; *U.S. Statutes at Large* 33 (1903–1905): 428; and *U.S. Statutes at Large* 43 (1923–1925): 153–69. For studies that analyze the effects of exclusion on the Chinese immigrant community, see Sucheng Chan, ed., *Entry Denied: Exclusion and the Chinese Community in America, 1882–1943* (Philadelphia, 1991). The two main works that document the Chinese American challenges to exclusion through the American legal system are Hudson N. Janisch, "The Chinese, the Courts, and the Constitution: A Study of the Legal Issues Raised by Chinese Immigration to the United States, 1850–1902" (J.D. diss., University of Chicago, School of Law, 1971); and Charles J. McClain, *In Search of Equality: The Chinese Struggle against Discrimination in Nineteenth-Century America* (Berkeley, Calif., 1994).

16. For general overviews of this period of Chinese immigration to the United States, see Sucheng Chan, *This Bittersweet Soil: The Chinese in California Agriculture, 1860–1910* (Berkeley, Calif., 1986), 1–78; Roger Daniels, *Asian America: Chinese and Japanese in the United States since 1850* (Seattle, Wash., 1988), 9–99; and Ronald Takaki, *Strangers From a Different Shore: A History of Asian Americans* (New York, 1989), 79–131.

17. Chang-fang Chen, "Barbarian Paradise," 21.

18. I am borrowing the term *contact zone* from Pratt who uses it to denote "the space in which peoples geographicaly and historically separated come into contact with each other and establish ongoing relations, usually involving conditions of coercion, radical inequality, and intractable conflict. . . . [It] is an attempt to invoke the spatial and temporal copresence of subjects separated by geographic and historical disjunctures, and whose trajectories now intersect." Pratt, *Imperial Eyes*, 6–7.

19. Fred W. Drake, *China Charts the World: Hsu Chi-yu and His Geography of 1848* (Cambridge, Mass., 1975), 5. Conservatives within the Imperial Court perceived Xu's positive portrayal of the West as a threat to the notion of Chinese cultural superiority. Xu was dismissed from office in 1851 and did not return to official duty until thirteen years later.

20. Xu Jiyu, *Yinghuan zhilue* (Short Account of the Oceans Around Us) in *Zhonghua wenshi congshu* (Collection of Chinese Literature and History) (Taibei, 1968), 6:732–36. The historical personages refered to in this section are Chen Sheng and Wu Guang, leaders of peasant revolts in the third century b.c. and Cao Cao and Liu Pei, rivals for the throne during the Three Kingdoms period (220–265). The Three Dynasties period

(2357–2198 B.C.) is generally seen as the earliest golden age in Chinese history when Chinese cultural values were first formulated.

21. The most famous example of this kind of service to the country in Chinese history is that of Zhuge Liang (181–234). During the Three Kingdoms period (222–265), Zhuge Liang agreed to leave his reclusion in order to assist the remaining descendants of the fallen Han Dynasty in their attempts to regain the empire. As a military strategist, Zhuge Liang was said to be incomparable. His exploits are celebrated in the famous novel *Sanguo Zhi Yenyi* (Romance of the Three Kingdoms) attributed to Luo Guancheng (twelfth century). This novel became one of the major sources for Chinese theater and opera, popular in both China and Chinese American communities. The standard translation in English is Lo Kuan-chung, *Romance of the Three Kingdoms* 2 vols., trans. C. H. Brewitt-Taylor (Rutland, Vt., 1959).

22. Xu was apparently unaware of, or chose not to mention, the fact that Washington left no direct descendants.

23. The legends of the Sage Kings of the Three Dynasties period are first found in the *Book of History,* one of the Confucian classics normally attributed to the early Zhou period (ca. 800 B.C.). The first textual discussion of the way of the king *(wangdao)* is also found in this text. Washington has, of course, been the object of myth-making in this country as well. Some important works that address this process are Marcus Cunliffe, *George Washington: Man and Monument* (Boston, 1958); Paul K. Longmore, *The Invention of George Washington* (Berkeley, Calif., 1988); Barry Schwartz, *George Washington: The Making of an American Symbol* (Ithaca, N.Y., 1987); Garry Wills, *Cincinnatus: George Washington and the Enlightenment* (Garden City and New York, 1984); and W. E. Woodward, *George Washington: The Image and the Man* (New York, 1926). I am grateful to Robert Dalzell and Patricia Tracy for discussions about the American imagery of George Washington.

24. Huang Zunxian, "Zhuke pian" (Expelling the Visitor), reprinted in *Fan Mei Huagong jinyue wenxue ji* (A Collection of Literature Written in Opposition to American Restriction of Chinese Laborers), ed. A Ying (Beijing, 1962), 3. My translation of these sections of the poem differs from those of J. D. Schmidt's found in Irving Yucheng Lo and William Schultz, eds., *Waiting for the Unicorn: Poems and Lyrics of China's Last Dynasty, 1644–1911* (Bloomington, Ind., 1986), 333–36 and R. David Arkush and Leo O. Lee, eds., *Land Without Ghosts: Chinese Impressions of America from the Mid-Nineteenth Century to the Present* (Berkeley, Calif., 1989), 61–65, as well as Chang-fang Chen's translation in "Barbarian Paradise," 229. These differences, though minor in regard to the overall meaning of the poem, are intriguing in light the image of George Washington as a sage hero and Chinese conceptions of the Other. In the first example (*), the Chinese written characters used are *bawang*, meaning one who rules by force rather than righteousness (Schmidt and Chen offer "great ruler"). The items marked by double asterisk (**) refer to *jiu Yi, ba Man*, phrases used since early times to denote various barbarian tribes on the borders of China (Schmidt: "All kinds of foreigners and immigrants"; Chen: "A variety of ethnic groups notwithstanding"). These peoples are described in the poem as settling in (***) *qiongzuo,* an ancient name for one of the barbarian kingdoms in southwest China (Schmidt: "new lands"; Chen: "this nation"). Although it is difficult to ascertain Huang's original intentions, I believe that they are revealing in their denotion of Otherness, thus delineating the separate spheres of those settling in America by comparing them to similar patterns in Chinese history. I have tried to retain this sense in my rendering of the poem.

25. Quoted in Arkush and Lee, eds., *Land Without Ghosts,* 70.

26. At least two other Chinese intellectuals and writers of this period visited Mount Vernon and wrote poems commemorating their visits. Zhigang (mid-nineteenth century) came to the United States as part of the Burlingame Commission in 1868 and wrote of his visit to Mount Vernon as did the famous reformer Kang Youwei. See Zhigang, *Chushi taixi ji* (First Mission to the Far West) in *Qingmo minchu shiliao congshu* (Collection of Historical Sources from the Late Qing and Early Republican Period) (Taipei, 1969), 38:59; and Robert L. Worden, "A Chinese Reformer in Exile: The North American Phase of the Travels of K'ang Yu-wei, 1899–1909" (Ph.D. diss., Georgetown University, 1972), 158.

27. Chen, "Barbarian Paradise," 68.

28. The *hua-hu* theory is centered around the Daoist (Taoist) assertion that Laozi (Lao Tzu), the spiritual progenitor of the Daoist religion and philosphical system, left China in the fourth century B.C. and departed to the west, going on to Central Asia and India to instruct the barbarians and became the Buddha. For a general account of this controversy, see Erik Zucher, *The Buddhist Conquest of China* (Leiden, Netherlands, 1959), 291–94.

29. Gary Okihiro, *Margins and Mainstreams: Asians in American History and Culture* (Seattle, Wash., 1994), ix. See esp. chap. 6, "Margins and Mainstreams," 148–75.

30. The body of literature on the anti-Chinese movement is quite large and impossible to summarize in an endnote. Aside from the texts already mentioned, other useful studies include Mary Roberts Coolidge, *Chinese Immigration* (New York, 1909); Elmer C. Sandmeyer, *The Anti-Chinese Movement in California,* 2d ed. (Urbana, Ill., 1973); Alexander Saxton, *The Indispensable Enemy: Labor and the Anti-Chinese Movement in California* (Berkeley, Calif., 1971); Cheng-Tsu Wu, ed., *"Chink!": A Documentary History of Anti-Chinese Prejudice in America* (New York, 1972); and Roger Daniels, ed., *Anti-Chinese Violence in North America* (New York, 1978).

31. *Land Without Ghosts*, Arkush and Lee, eds., 81. The major works on Liang Qichao include Joseph R. Levenson, *Liang Ch'i-ch'ao and the Mind of Modern China* (Cambridge, Mass., 1953); Hao Chang, *Liang Ch'i-ch'ao and Intellectual Transition in China, 1890–1907* (Cambridge, Mass., 1971); Philip C. Huang, *Liang Ch'i-ch'ao and Modern Chinese Liberalism* (Seattle, Wash., 1972); and Ma, *Revolutionaries, Monarchists, and Chinatowns.* One of the most useful collections of documents by and about Liang in Chinese is Ding Wenjiang, *Liang Rengong xiansheng nianpu changpian chugao* (Chronological Biography and Letters of Liang Qichao), vols. 1–2 (Taipei, 1962); also published as *Liang Qichao nianpu changpian* (Shanghai, 1983).

32. Ding Wenjiang, *Liang Rengong xiansheng nianpu changpian chugao,* 1:24.

33. For the definitive study of Yen Fu's intellectual impact on China, see Benjamin Schwartz, *In Search of Wealth and Power: Yen Fu and and the West* (Cambridge, Mass., 1964); and for Yen's influence on Liang, see also Y. C. Wang, *Chinese Intellectuals and the West, 1878–1940* (Chapel Hill, N.C., 1966), 218–21.

34. For the best study that documents the relationship between these political parties and the Chinese in the United States, see Ma, *Revolutionaries, Monarchists, Chinatowns.*

35. Liang Qichao, *Xin dalu youji jielu* (Selected Memoir of Travels in the New World) in *Yinbingshi heji* (Collected Writings From an Ice-drinker's Studio) zhuanji 22 (Shanghai, 1936). For an analysis of this text as a source for Chinese American history, see K. Scott Wong, "Liang Qichao and the Chinese of America: A Re-evaluation of his *Selected Memoir of Travels in the New World,*" *Journal of American Ethnic History* 11 (summer 1992): 3–24.

36. For Liang's account of his visits to Boston and Philadelphia, see Liang Qichao, *Xin dalu youji jielu*, 48–54, 71–77.

37. Ibid., 122.

38. Sucheng Chan, *Asian Americans: An Interpretive History* (Boston, 1991), 63.

39. In another text, usually ignored by scholars of Liang's political thought, Liang condemned American immigration very forcefully. See *Ji Huagong jinyue* (Notes on the Exclusion of Chinese Laborers) in *Yinbingshi heji* zhuanji 22, 149–84.

40. Liang Qichao, *Xin dalu youji jielu*, 125–26.

41. Ibid., 126.

42. Ibid. The reference to the *Odes* and the *Rites* is a paraphrase of a longer passage in the *Lunyu*,16: 13: 1–3. See also Waley, trans. *The Analects*, 207–8.

43. Ma, *Revolutionaries, Monarchists, and Chinatowns*, 94.

44. Chang, *Liang Ch'i-ch'ao and Intellectual Transition*, 243.

45. Stefan Tanaka, *Japan's Orient: Rendering Pasts into History* (Berkeley, Calif., 1993), 31.

46. Ibid., 18.

47. The most useful sources which focus on Yung Wing and his life in the United States are Yung Wing, *My Life in China and America* (New York, 1909); Thomas E. LaFargue, *China's First Hundred* (Pullman, Wash., 1942); William Hung, "Huang Tsun-hsien's Poem, 'The Closing of the Educational Mission in America,'" *Harvard Journal of Asiatic Studies* 18 (1955): 50–73; Edmund Worthy, "Yung Wing in America," *Pacific Historical Review* 34 (Aug. 1965): 265–87; Ruthanne Lum McCunn, *Chinese American Portraits: Personal Histories, 1828–1988* (San Francisco, 1988); and Charles Desnoyers, "'The Thin Edge of the Wedge': The Chinese Educational Mission and Diplomatic Representation in the Americas, 1872–1875," *Pacific Historical Review* 61 (May 1992): 241–63. An important collection of Yung's own writings can be found in the "Yung Wing Papers," Manuscripts and Archives, Yale University Library (microfilm), New Haven, Conn.

48. Yung to Williams, 15 Apr. 1849, Yung Wing Papers.

49. Worthy, "Yung Wing in America," 270. Yung was one of a small number of Chinese who managed to attain American citizenship before the 1882 Exclusion Act. For an important study of the early Chinese American communities on the East Coast in which some of the Chinese attained citizenship, see John Kuo Wei Tchen, "New York Chinese: The Nineteenth-Century Pre-Chinatown Settlement," *Chinese America: History and Perspectives, 1990* (San Francisco, 1990), 157–92.

50. Yung, *My Life in China and America*, 41.

51. The Zongli Yamen was the office in charge of foreign affairs from 1861 to 1901. It handled treaty negotiations with foreign countries, established language schools with Western curricula, and sponsored research of Western forms of government and international law. For a study of its creation, see Masataka Banno, *China and the West, 1858–1861: The Origins of the Tsungli Yamen* (Cambridge, Mass., 1964).

52. Y. C. Wang, *Chinese Intellectuals and the West, 1872–1949* (Chapel Hill, N.C., 1966), 43.

53. Despite their differences over how the Chinese Educational Mission should be run, Yung's and Chen's experience in dealing with the West led the imperial court to assign them to diplomatic duties. In 1874, Chen was sent to Cuba to investigate the conditions of Chinese laborers there and Yung was sent to Peru to do the same. In large part, because of their efforts, the infamous "coolie trade" came to an end. After completing this mission, Chen and Yung were appointed ministers to the United States, Spain, and Peru, posts they held until the Chinese Educational Mission was recalled in 1881.

54. Charles A. Desnoyers, "Chinese Foreign Policy in Transition: Ch'en Lan-pin in the New World, 1872–1882" (Ph.D. diss., Temple University, 1988), 96.

55. LaFargue, *China's First Hundred,* 39. During his years at Yale, Yung apparently sometimes wore his queque pinned up under a hat. Once, while participating in a ball game, "His hat went off; his queue burst from the pins and streamed out behind him like a pump-handle." *Hartford Daily Times,* 17 Nov. 1922. Quoted in Worthy, "Yung Wing in America," 272.

56. These concerns are conveyed quite strongly in Huang Zunxian's poem (The Closing of the Educational Mission in America).

57. Yung, *My Life in China and America,* 202–3.

58. Yung Wing married Mary Louise Kellog in 1875, and they remained married until her death in 1886. They raised two sons. His nephew, Yung Kwai, who was among the second group of students to attend the mission, also married an American woman, Mary Burnham, in 1894. During his 1903 tour of North America, Liang Qichao met with Yung and about ten former mission students who had remained in the United States. Liang mentioned that they had married American women and thus their sense of Chinese patriotism had faded. Liang Qichao, *Xin dalu youji jielu,* 47. Brief biographical sketches of a few of them are found in LaFargue, *China's First Hundred,* 140–44, Wang, 96–98, and Yung Shang-him, "The Chinese Educational Mission and its Influence," *T'ien Hsia Monthly* 9 (Oct. 1939): 241–56.

59. The writer Frank Chin takes a very critical approach to Yung Wing and his life in America, attacking his conversion to Christianity and his use of autobiography as examples of Yung's "white-washing." Chin characterizes Yung's autobiography as "mission-schoolboy-makes-good Gunga Din licking up white fantasy." While Chin is correct in pointing out that Yung and many of his generation did seek China's salvation in the ideologies of the West, he does not take the Chinese political situation or relevant trends in Chinese intellectual history well enough into account to provide for a solid contextualization of these intellectuals' attraction to the West. Nor does he take into account the long history of Christianity in China. For Chin's searing critique of Yung Wing and other Chinese American writers who use autobiography, a literary form he considers to be solely rooted in the Western literary tradition and now used as an expression of Chinese American desire for white acceptance, see his essay "Come All Ye Asian American Writers," in *The Big Aiiieeeee! An Anthology of Chinese American and Japanese American Literature,* eds., Jeffery Paul Chan, Frank Chin, Lawson Fusao Inada, and Shawn Wong (New York, 1991), 1–92. For a recent study that firmly places autobiography in the Chinese literary tradition, independent of Western influence, see Pei-yi Wu, *The Confucian's Progress: Autobiographical Writings in Traditional China* (Princeton, N.J., 1990).

60. *In re Ah Yup* (C.C.D. Cal. 1878). In this case, the federal circuit court denied Chinese immigrants the right to naturalization because they were neither "a free white person nor a person of African nativity or descent," as required by the existing naturalization laws. See Janisch, "The Chinese, the Courts, and the Constitution," 201. This ruling was reiterated in the 1882 Chinese Exclusion Act, *U.S. Statutes at Large* 22 (1881–1883): 61.

61. For details about Yung losing his citizenship and his reentry into the United States, see Worthy, "Yung Wing in America," 283–85.

62. Major works examining American images of China and the Chinese (and the Chinese in America) include Jules Becker, "The Course of Exclusion, 1882–1924: San Francisco Newspaper Coverage of the Chinese and Japanese in the United States" (Ph.D. diss., University of California, Berkeley, 1986); Limin Chu, "The Images of China and the Chinese in the *Overland Monthly,* 1868–1875, 1883–1935" (Ph.D. diss.,

Duke University, 1965); Warren I. Cohen, "American Perceptions of China" in *Dragon and Eagle: United States-China Relations: Past and Future,* eds., Michel Oksenberg and Robert B. Oxnam (New York, 1978), 54–86; Harold Isaacs, *Images of Asia: American Images of China and India* (New York, 1962; originally published as *Scratches on Our Minds,* 1958); Robert McClellan, *The Heathen Chinee: A Study of American Attitudes Toward China, 1890–1905* (Columbus, Ohio, 1971); Colin Mackerras, *Western Images of China* (New York, 1989); Miller, *The Unwelcome Immigrant*; and William Wu, *The Yellow Peril: Chinese Americans in American Fiction, 1850–1940* (Hamden, Conn., 1982). Studies that explore Chinese images of the United States are fewer in number. The most useful are Chang-fang Chen, "Barbarian Paradise: Chinese Views of the United States, 1784–1911"; Curti and Stalker, "'The Flowery Flag Devils'—The American Image in China, 1840–1900"; David Shambaugh, *Beautiful Imperialist: China Perceives America, 1972–1990* (Princeton, N.J., 1991); Tu Wei-ming, "Chinese Perceptions of America," in *Dragon and Eagle,* eds., Oksenberg and Oxnam, 87–106; and Kevin Scott Wong "Encountering the Other: Chinese Immigration and its Impact on Chinese and American Worldviews, 1875–1905" (Ph.D. diss., University of Michigan, 1992). A useful collection of translations of Chinese views of the United States is Arkush and Lee, eds., *Land Without Ghosts.* An indepth study of these two groups of imagery found in the visual arts is greatly needed.

63. This attempt to reconcile Chinese and American cultural values is still an issue for the Chinese American community today. As immigration continues and the children of immigrants become more involved with American society, there are tensions between parents who want their children to follow traditional practices and the children who want American lives. A recent example of this conflict can be seen in the film *The Wedding Banquet* (1993), directed by Ang Lee, who was born and raised in Taiwan and now lives in the United States.

Gary Y. Okihiro

On the evening of 13 November 1856, the Chinese merchants of Honolulu and Lahaina, Maui organized a "grand ball" in honor of the recently married King Kamehameha IV and Queen Emma. The Chinese hosts, in preparation for the occasion, practiced quadrilles so they could join in the dancing, and they hired four white men to dress in Mandarin clothing to assist them at the ball. The cross-dressed men were Edward "Weong Chong" Hoffman, Barnum "Chong Fong" Field, Gustav "Ming Ching" Reiners, and C. C. "Weong Kong" Waterman. In the opening quadrille, the king danced with Mrs. Gregg, the queen with Mr. Yung Sheong, Mr. Afong with Mrs. W. C. Parke, and Mr. Ahee with Mrs. Cody. The hosts were lavish with their expenditures, and the party was pronounced "the most splendid affair of the kind ever seen in Honolulu" by one account. Indeed, the Chinese ball "was the talk of the town for a month after" (Tin-Yuke Char, ed., *The Sandalwood Mountains* [Honolulu: University Press of Hawaii, 1975], 90–91).

K. Scott Wong's wonderfully conceived "The Transformation of Culture: Three Chinese Views of America" is notable for its resemblance to that "splendid affair" of 1856. I am thinking thereby to the several crossings and convergences occasioned by that grand ball, indeed its ambiguities—"Sinocized" white men, Hawaiians marked as royalty by their European garb and accouterment, Chinese men dancing the quadrille, inter-raced, gendered, and perhaps sexed couples, the site's location in the midst of the Pacific Ocean. The borders of race, gender, sexuality, culture, and space were possibly breached, and surely tested and secured, by that "talk of the town."

I suppose what most impresses me about Wong's marvelous essay is its pedigree and contexts. Time was that the Asian experience in the United States barely registered as American studies. And I am not referring to geologic time. I recall how, about two decades ago, a leading historian of the American West and the editor of a respected journal explained to me that he failed to see how my account of the detention of the West Coast's Japanese Americans during World War II qualified as "Western history." I wonder what he might have meant by that. Could he have thought that the event fell under the rubric of diplomatic history or perchance Asian studies? Would my explanation have mattered, that two-thirds of the detainees were U.S. citizens and that they had lived and labored in the American West for over fifty years? Although that historian's opinion of Asian American studies has persisted in academe and the American imagination, Wong's article in the organ of the American Studies Association in 1996 hardly requires explanation.

"Transformation of Culture," accordingly, rightly scores Asian Americanists for their brand of American exceptionalism in grounding their field of study as emphatically and exclusively within the geopolitical confines of the United States, but that extravagance was won only after decades of protest and hard labor. The point was not easily conceded; it was struggled over. Asians in America, historically and within our time, have been and are rendered perpetual aliens, strangers in the land of their birth and adoption. Simultaneously, Orientalism has conflated the diverse ethnicities that constitute Asian America and therewith has exacted similar treatment of and tribute from those dissimilar groups. Those commonalities—the ties that bind—arose within the context of the United States. Little wonder that activists and intellectuals seized upon the United States as the site for contestation, to claim as a politicized, pan-Asian peoples its spaces and its ideals.

While some Asian Americanists worked their version of American exceptionalism, others sought authenticity in Asia. "Go to the source" was their mantra. America's war in Vietnam was raging during the early years of Asian American studies' founding, and America's streets and campuses buzzed with talk of decolonization, self-determination, liberation. Enraptured with the gleam of Third World solidarity, I somehow missed the shadow of Japan's complicity in global capitalism and colonialism when first I made my pilgrimage to my "roots" in 1970. Much to my dismay, I quickly discovered that I was not wholly "Japanese" and was a stranger in the land of my grandparents' birth. And I learned too that Asian studies was not the "natural" home of Asian American studies when I presented papers at their conferences. Why were my panels invariably scheduled on the morning of the last day? I wondered. And why were there more members on the panel than in the audience?

The publication of Wong's essay coincides with intellectual ferment along the borders of Asian, American, and Asian American studies. No longer assumed as given or impervious are the social constructs "Asia," "America," and "Asian America," along with the binaries they impose of homeland and diaspora, West and East, alien and citizen. Those categories no longer delineate boundaries and boundedness, and fluidity and interstitial formations are the privileged sites of inquiry because of their perceived capacities for interventions in hegemonic structures and discourses. Further, multiplicities, as opposed to binaries, complicate not only the units of analyses and their articulations but also the centers and relations of power implicit within dualisms such as the self and other. "Transformation of Culture" sits at the confluence of those surging currents.

Peering through the lenses of Chinese elites, Wong brings into sharp focus aspects of Chinese and American cultures and the processes of hegemony and transculturation that defy Sinocentric and Eurocentric pretenses at primacy, insularity, and univocality. I find it unremarkable, nonetheless, that Wong should select and read texts that mirror his intellectual lineages and contexts. I do not mean to diminish, by so stating, Wong's considerable achievement, and I find neither unqualified virtue in studies deemed universal and timeless nor value in the immediate. I am simply arguing for a self-consciousness of claims and purposes. Authors and their texts, we know, are situated in time and place. In truth, the acumen of "Transformation of Culture" derives from its inheritances and coeval engagements.

Both American and Asian studies have met on the dance floor of transnationalism, and scholars on both sides of the Pacific have cross-dressed and learned the quadrille. Asians in America have earned the right to claim multiple identities as Americans, but also as Asians as well as gendered, sexualized, and classed peoples. Needless to say, all is not well in multicultural America, however, and those transgressions of naturalized boundaries have stirred vehement and sometimes violent responses. Armed soldiers now patrol the U.S.-Mexican border, and impregnable fences are a favorite topic of U.S. politicians (and contractors). And yet, as in the past, there is this reality that people will resist the cages that were designed to contain them, and that others will assuredly work to restore them to preserve their nests of privilege. That dialectic, in truth, is complicated by a multitude of competing interests. The "most splendid affair" of 1856 involved foreigners, both whites and Asians, and indigenous peoples, all of whom clashed over power but shared a class interest and perhaps consciousness that barred workers, who might have pronounced the "grand ball" a conspiracy of the ruling class and a colossal waste of resources. The dance floor accommodated both inclusions and exclusions.

More than a meeting point or bridge for East and West, Hawaii is a place of its own. Not a destination but a home, the volcanoes that create it, the waters that embrace it, the vegetation and animal life that fill it are the embodiments of the people, the Hawaiians, who were entrusted with their care and upkeep. Similarly, Asians in America are more than cultural brokers between discrete and clashing bodies. They are in process, but they are also complete. Displacement is not a permanent state of affairs. Strangers eventually make themselves indigenous. But for the moment and foreseeable future, indigenization must defer to the interstitial location of Asians in America as raced, gendered, sexualized, and classed peoples, and Asian American studies, in the academic universe, as neither wholly American nor Asian studies. Discomfort, however, goes both ways. Asian Americans and Asian American studies are situated in the midst of binaries, but they also create anxieties over the categories and their validities. Those ambiguities, it appears, are at once quieting and disquieting of the social and intellectual order, and therein rests the potential and power for conservation or transformation.

Library of Congress
Cataloging-in-Publication Data
Locating American studies : the evolution of
a discipline / edited by Lucy Maddox.
     p.   cm.
"Each of the essays first appeared in
American quarterly, the journal of the
American Studies Association" — Pref.
Includes bibliographical references.
ISBN 0-8018-6056-3
1. United States — Civilization — Study and
teaching.   I. Maddox, Lucy.
E175.8.L78   1998
973 — dc21   98-18959